INVESTMENTS
ANALYSIS AND MANAGEMENT

McGRAW-HILL SERIES IN FINANCE
PROFESSOR CHARLES A. D'AMBROSIO
University of Washington
CONSULTING EDITOR

INVESTMENTS
ANALYSIS AND MANAGEMENT

Jack Clark Francis

Bernard M. Baruch College
City University of New York

Second Edition

McGRAW-HILL BOOK COMPANY

New York　St. Louis　San Francisco
Auckland　Düsseldorf　Johannesburg
Kuala Lumpur　London　Mexico
Montreal　New Delhi　Panama
Paris　São Paulo　Singapore
Sydney　Tokyo　Toronto

INVESTMENTS: ANALYSIS AND MANAGEMENT

1234567890DODO79876

This book was set in Palatino by Progressive Typographers. The editor was J. S. Dietrich; the designer was Joseph Gillians; the production supervisor was Joe Campanella. New drawings were done by J & R Services, Inc.
R. R. Donnelley & Sons Company was printer and binder.

Library of Congress Cataloging in Publication Data

Francis, Jack Clark.
    Investments.

    (McGraw-Hill series in finance)
    Includes bibliographies and index.
    1. Investments.   2. Securities.
HG4521.F685   1976   332.6   75-30826
ISBN 0-07-021787-4

To my wife, Debbie,
and our sons, Jim and Steve

CONTENTS

PREFACE

This second edition of *Investments: Analysis and Management* has the same purpose as the first edition — to facilitate the teaching and learning of traditional as well as newer investments ideas. Accomplishing this objective can be a challenge because of the increasing use of quantitative tools in financial economics. The movement toward quantitative analysis probably started gaining momentum in 1952, with the publication of Harry Markowitz's classic article, "Portfolio Selection." Since then the march of events has accelerated the use of mathematics and statistics in finance.

Of course, there are different opinions about these changes in investments. I receive a steady trickle of comments from investments people informing me that "the pendulum is now swinging away from quantitative analysis in investments." I find that difficult to believe in view of the millions of dollars that institutional investors are spending annually for quantitative investments analysis, the rising level of mathematics taught to most business students, and the continued growing use of computers in business. So, this second edition was prepared to help bridge the gap between the old and the new. It begins with the traditional investments topics and progresses to modern abstract models.

Readers with no background in business finance (for example, foreign-born students and new MBA students with bachelor degrees in liberal arts or engineering) will typically find the first 14 chapters of this book difficult. However, it is essential to understand the organizations and methods discussed in the first half of the book in order to apply the theories explained in the latter half. In contrast, men and women in business, as well as veteran students of finance, typically find the second half of the book more difficult because of its heavier use of mathematical conventions. The eleven mathematical appendixes in Part 7 can be of invaluable aid in filling any gaps in the reader's mathematical background. In fact, many professors, myself included, assign the mathematical appendixes to be read with the chapters (for example, Chapters 7 and 8 presume a knowledge of Appendixes A and K) and teach mathematics along with investments concepts.

Most investments professors will probably prefer to pick and choose among the chapters and appendixes as they structure their courses. To facilitate such flexibility, the book is organized so that each of its six text sections can be read alone. The eleven mathematical appendixes were included so that other books need not be consulted to answer questions about the quantitative tools.

Potential readers should not be intimidated by the fact that this book is on a higher level than the more traditional investments textbooks. The only prerequisite for mastery of *Investments: Analysis and Management* is an interest in the topic. Courses in freshman college algebra, statistics, economics, and accounting would doubtlessly yield more rapid learning progress, but the book can be read from cover to cover without them.

The comprehensive coverage of this book touches upon many areas, and I am grateful to the people, too numerous to name, who graciously assisted me in the formulation of each discussion. First and foremost I owe thanks to my wife, Debbie, who wrote Chapters 2 and 6 as well as doing editing and some typing. While taking leave of absence from teaching accounting and economics at Gloucester County College in Sewell, New Jersey, to raise our sons, she made many constructive contributions to this book. Valuable guidance was also provided by faculty colleagues Peter Gutmann and Jerry Pogue at Baruch College; Jim Morris, Hans Stoll, and Jim Walter at the Wharton School; Professor Larry Schall from the University of Washington; Marty Liebowitz, partner at Solomon Brothers in New York City; Don Farrar at UCLA; J. K. Dietrick at University of Arizona; and George Racette at University of Oregon. All these people and others have assisted in the preparation of this book. But any errors or shortcomings remaining are undeniably and inexcusably my own.

Let me close by noting that any and all comments, criticisms, and suggestions will be considered carefully in the preparation of future printings, and perhaps editions, of this book. I find them invaluable and will be grateful to those who share their thoughts with me.

Jack Clark Francis

INVESTMENTS
ANALYSIS AND MANAGEMENT

One

Introduction

This book is about marketable financial papers, such as common stocks, preferred stocks, bonds, puts, calls, and commodity future contracts—to name a few of the more popular ones. These assets, the markets in which they are traded, the laws governing the trading, valuation of the assets, construction of a portfolio of different investments, and the important economic factors affecting investments management will be analyzed in the chapters which follow.

Evolution of Investments Teaching

The development of investments management can be traced chronologically through three different phases. First, investments management was a *skill* or an *art*. To make millions in the market, the traders of yesteryear needed to be ruthless, emotionless, courageous gamblers who possessed an animal-like cunning about markets, were quick to exploit any opportunity, were pathologically greedy, had the connections to raise large sums of capital, and had the deadpan poker faces to carry out all these activities without tipping their hands. The names of the few men who possessed very many of these skills—names such as Vanderbilt, Drew, Fisk, Gould—are still familiar today. However, the tyrannical speculations they and others engineered were essentially ended in the United States by the passage of the Securities Act of 1933 and the Securities Exchange Act of 1934. These laws outlawed price and market manipulation schemes.

The unscrupulous skills used to make large investment trading profit around the turn of the century are best learned by observation and experience; hence no investment textbooks have been written to teach them. The spine-tingling stories of how millions were made and lost by ruthlessly manipulating the markets are to be found only in the records of congressional hearings and reports and newspapers from the 1800s and early 1900s.

During the 1930s investments management entered its second phase: a phase of *professionalism.* After the regulations governing investment trading were passed around 1934, the whole investments industry followed the lead previously taken by the New York Stock Exchange and seriously set about the task of upgrading its ethics, establishing standard practices, and cultivating a good public image. As a result, security and commodity exchanges tightened their entrance requirements; fair practice codes and self-policing bodies were set up to oversee investment activity; and investors busied themselves studying the fine print on their financial contracts, calculating financial ratios, and investigating the professional reputations of those with whom they dealt.

Since the professionalism of investments management began, investment textbook writers have been busy. As the body of investments law has expanded—and investment markets became safer places, so that the man in the street began investing—numerous books have been written describing the laws and procedures to be followed by investors.

Most recently, investments management has begun to undergo *scientific analysis;* this is the third phase in its development. It is impossible to specify the date when one stage ended and the next began, but some people tend to point to a paper published by Dr. Harry Markowitz[1] in 1952 as the beginning of a scientific approach—although scientific analysis of investments can be found as far back as 1900.[2] In fact, the last two phases, professionalism and scientific analysis, are currently advancing simultaneously.

One of the most recent developments in the professionalization of investments management is the designation of Chartered Financial Analyst for investment analysts who have passed a series of examinations to demonstrate their proficiency. Interestingly, these exams have contained questions about economic theory and mathematical statistics—tools of the scientist. Thus, the professionalization of investments management is continuing, but assuming a more scientific bent. This book reflects that trend.

Burgeoning Literature Dichotomized Investments Students

During the 1960s the literature published about investments grew rapidly. As had been true in the preceding decades, excellent books and articles appeared, explaining and rationalizing securities and other investments, the markets in which they were traded, and the relevant laws, procedures, and vocabulary. In addition, a whole new set of scientific research findings was

---

[1] "Portfolio Selection," *Journal of Finance,* vol. VII, no. 1, pp. 77–91, March 1952.

[2] L. Bachelier, "Theory Speculation," *Ann. Sci. École Norm. Sup.* (3), no. 1018 (Paris: Gauthier-Villars, 1900). Reprinted in Paul Cootner, *The Random Character of Stock Market Prices* (Cambridge, Mass.: M.I.T., 1964), pp. 17–78.

published. Finance professors, security analysts, portfolio managers, economists, and others interested in investments management were partially dichotomized by the rapid publication of both traditional investments lit-erature and the new esoteric scientific studies. Many people teaching investments seemed either to ignore the traditional institutional material and concentrate on the new scientific literature, or vice versa. The two groups were almost mutually exclusive. One of the aims of this book is to reverse the dichotomization by combining the most important elements from both the traditional camp and the new analytical group into one publication which suits the needs of both. The material is presented in such a fashion that those who want only the traditional material can find it—mostly in Chaps. 2 through 6, but elsewhere too. And those who want to confine their attention to analysis and exclude material about the investment institutions can achieve this by selecting relevant material from Chaps. 7 through 22 and the appendixes.

Organization

This text is written so that a beginning student can start at the front and move directly toward the back of the book. After Chap. 6 reference to the Mathematical Appendixes (Part 7) may be required to sustain progress. But the material does flow logically and increases in difficulty as the chapters pass, so that a front-to-back reading plan makes good sense. However, too much material is included to be covered in most one-quarter or one-semester courses, and so some chapters must be omitted. Which chapters are read is a matter of the professor's tastes. The book is laid out so that by picking and choosing among the chapters, the teacher can construct many different courses. Essentially, it is organized into seven main parts:

Part 1, The Setting, explains the investment institutions found in the United States.

Part 2, Bond Valuation and Present Value Theory, shows how the time value of money affects security prices.

Part 3, Common Stock Valuation, analyzes the procedures used by fundamental stock analysts.

Part 4, Other Investments, describes the characteristics of the long and short positions, options, and commodities.

Part 5, Portfolio Theory, explains the techniques of portfolio management.

Part 6, Behavior of Stock Prices, reviews the debate between technical analysts and the random-walk theorists about the manner in which security prices fluctuate.

Part 7, Mathematical Appendixes, explains various mathematical and statistical tools used in some later chapters and chapter appendixes.

These parts are fairly independent of one another. That is, they can be read without reference to the preceding parts; this is particularly true of Parts 1, 2, 5, 6, and 7. Part 3 does assume a knowledge of Part 2, but those readers already familiar with the present value concept developed in Part 2 can read Part 3 independently. Part 4 presumes the reader has mastered Chap. 2.

All the parts are organized into related chapters which should usually be read in the order presented. But there is no reason why some of the later chapters in any part cannot be omitted; and the end-of-chapter appendixes can certainly be skipped. Most of these appendixes delve into a more detailed treatment of the material in the chapter, and the majority of classes will read only those few which the teacher feels are particularly appropriate for the class within the time allotted.

The end-of-chapter appendixes are provided mainly for those students whose intellectual curiosity is not satiated by the chapter. The tiny bit of calculus which has crept into this book is confined to the appendixes. It is not essential for a basic grasp of the concepts under discussion. Instead, it is provided for those few readers who may want to see proof of some of the assertions made or to see how to use the tools under discussion to solve real problems. The mathematical appendixes in Part 7 are provided to help the student refresh his or her memory of mathematical procedures which are quickly forgotten if not used regularly.

The Objective of Investment

This book is written to develop investment managers who are interested in investing their funds in assets which have the maximum expected rate of return at any selected level of risk or, conversely, the minimum risk of all assets with a given expected rate of return. An example involving the six hypothetical assets listed below should make this clearer.

Asset	Expected rate of return	Risk	Dominated?
M	.1 = 10%	.1	No
B	.05 = 5%	.1	Yes, by T and M
C	.1 = 10%	.2	Yes, by M and A
A	.15 = 15%	.2	No
E	.15 = 15%	.3	Yes, by A
T	.05 = 5%	.05	No

Figure 1-1 represents these six assets in risk-return space. That is, the six assets are graphed on the two-dimensional graph with their expected rate of return, denoted $E(r)$, on the vertical axis and their risk measured numerically on the horizontal axis.[3]

According to the investment objective assumed, assets T, M, and A

[3] The quantitative risk measure used in Fig. 1-1 is explained in detail in Chap. 12.

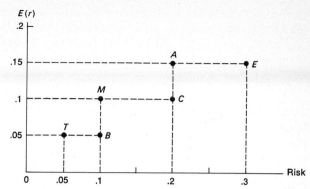

FIG. 1-1 Assets graphed in risk-return space.

dominate assets *B*, *C*, and *E*, respectively, because they have less risk for their given levels of expected return. Similarly, assets *M* and *A* dominate assets *B* and *C*, respectively, because they have the largest expected rates of return in their risk-classes. Thus, the type of investor addressed by this book will prefer investing in assets *T*, *M*, or *A* rather than in assets *B*, *C*, or *E*.

Which of the dominant assets the investor prefers depends on his or her own personal investment preferences. A timid investor will prefer dominant investment *T*, whereas an aggressive investor will prefer dominant investment *A*. A "medium investor," halfway between timidity and aggressiveness, will prefer asset *M*; but the investment objective assumes that no investor would prefer assets *B*, *C*, or *E*.

Stating that the investment objective is to select assets which have the maximum expected rate of return in their risk-class is like saying the objective is to maximize the investor's expected wealth at some preferred level of risk, since the larger the rate of return, the larger the terminal wealth.[4] It should be noted that this objective does not assume the investor to be greedy. Other objectives, such as accumulation of power, social reform, or attainment of prestigious position, may often be obtained through manipulation of wealth if the manipulator has a sufficient amount of it. The skills used in wealth maximization can also be useful in attaining these other objectives. Therefore, we shall confine our attention to the wealth maximization objective within whatever risk-class the investor prefers.

It is an oversimplification to assume that the objective of financial investing is pure and simple wealth maximization. There are constraints imposed by the investor's physical, intellectual, and emotional resources which frequently cause investors to prefer investments expected to yield

[4] For a one-period time horizon the sentence is true. But for a multiperiod time horizon, the statement refers only to the geometric mean rate of return if the rates of return vary from period to period. The geometric mean return is explained in Mathematical Appendix J in Part 7.

only mediocre returns. Risk aversion is the main constraint on wealth maximization. The assumption of large financial risk can cause the investor to lose sleep, become irritable, develop ulcers, or even commit suicide. Time is another constraint which limits wealth accumulation. Many investors are only amateurs who "play the stock market" after work. These investors simply cannot find enough hours in the day to pursue every opportunity which may increase their wealth. Inadequate managerial skill can also limit people's achievements—many either cannot or do not want to manage a portfolio. Most investors try to overcome the constraints imposed by limitations on their time, management skill, wealth, or other factors by confining their investments to a preferred risk level. By limiting the riskiness of their investments, these investors are usually able to limit the amount of time, managerial skill, and other factors which they must devote to investment management. For example, U.S. Treasury bonds are an investment which involves little risk or management effort if the investor is willing to earn low returns. Thus, the objective of wealth maximization at some preferred risk level may mean simply buying the U.S. government bonds with the highest yield.

The investment objective assumed here is maintained throughout the book; it furnishes a continuous thread of logic which ties the various discussions of portfolio management together. This objective is covered in detail in Chap. 17, which explains the rationale behind this investment objective. Appendix D to Chap. 15 and Chap. 18 defend the objective against other investment objectives which have been suggested.

Despite the fact that investors are assumed to prefer dominant assets throughout the book, this becomes an issue only in a few places in Part 5. The other chapters are concerned with other phases of investment analysis, and they are appropriate for any investment objective which involves some dislike for taking risks and some preference for more wealth over less wealth.

PART ONE

THE SETTING

CHAPTER 2 SECURITIES defines bonds and shares of stock and explains their owners' legal rights.

CHAPTER 3 SECURITIES MARKETS explains how the various security markets operate.

CHAPTER 4 REGULATION OF THE SECURITIES MARKETS discusses some economically harmful securities transactions and the laws that have been passed to curtail such activities.

CHAPTER 5 TAXES tells how tax laws and transaction costs can affect investment decisions.

CHAPTER 6 SOURCES OF INVESTMENT INFORMATION gives sources of information the investor needs to manage a portfolio.

These chapters explain in some detail the places, people, transactions, and laws which make up the securities markets in the United States. This material is presented first so that the reader will be able to relate it to the concepts developed in the later chapters.

Two

Securities

Investors face a staggering array of investment possibilities: stocks, bonds, warrants, mortgages, commodities, education, works of art, automobiles, ad infinitum. Of these numerous investment alternatives, stocks and bonds are among the most widely purchased. This chapter defines and discusses various features of common stock, preferred stock, and bonds. Table 2-1 suggests a method of classifying the main types of securities. The table furnishes a very compact summary of some of the salient points of this chapter. It should not be taken too literally, however. For example, the common stock issued by American Telephone and Telegraph is less risky than bonds of many corporations. Table 2-1 refers only to the main general types of securities; it is not applicable to every individual security.

This chapter's discussion of securities begins with private debt instruments, namely, corporate bonds. Next, the discussion focuses on equity instruments, that is, common stock. Then preferred stock, a hybrid security possessing characteristics of both the equity and the debt securities, is explained. U.S. government bonds are taken up; it will be seen that these pieces of the national debt assume several interesting forms. Finally, mutual fund shares and other portfolios are explained.

2-1 CORPORATE BONDS

Bonds are a promise to pay a stated rate of interest for a defined period and then to repay the principal at the specific date of maturity. Bonds differ according to their terms concerning provisions for repayment, security pledged, and other technical aspects. They represent the formal legal evidence of debt and are the senior securities of the firm. The indenture, or

TABLE 2-1 CLASSIFICATION OF SECURITY TYPES
BY RISK, RETURN, AND DEGREE OF OWNER
CONTROL OVER MANAGEMENT

Security type	Control	Return	Risk
Common stock	1, most	1, most	1, most
Preferred stock	2	2	2
Corporate bonds	3	3	3
Government bonds	4, least	4, least	4, least

deed of trust, is the legal agreement between the corporation and the bond-holders. Each bond is part of a group of bonds issued under one indenture. Thus, they all have the same rights and protection from the issuing company. Sometimes, however, bonds of the same issue may mature at different dates and have correspondingly different interest rates.

General Features of Corporate Bonds

Bond interest is usually paid semiannually, though annual payments are also popular. The method of payment depends upon whether the bond is a registered or coupon bond. *Coupon bonds* have a series of attached coupons that are clipped out at the appropriate time and sent to a bank for collection of the interest. Because interest is paid to the bearer of the coupon, the ownership of these bonds may be transferred simply by endorsement over to the new owner; however, this ease of transfer increases the danger of loss to the careless owner. The interest on *registered bonds* is paid to the holder by check. Therefore, the holders must be registered with the trustee to ensure proper payment. Registered bonds can be transferred only by registering the name of the new owner with the trustee and canceling the name of the previous owner.

The *trustee* is the third party with whom the bond contract is made. It is the trustee's job to make sure that the issuer lives up to the provisions contained in the indenture.

The *indenture* is a long, complicated legal instrument made up of carefully worded phrases containing the restrictions, pledges, and promises of the contract. The trustee, usually a bank, ensures that the firm keeps its promises and obeys the restrictions of the contract; the trustee also takes any appropriate legal action to see that the terms of the contract are kept and that the rights of the bondholders are upheld. Because the individual bondholders are usually not in a position to make sure that the company does not violate its agreements and because the bondholders cannot take substantial legal action if the firm does violate them, the trustee assumes these responsibilities. The trustee does this "watchdog" job for all the bondholders.

The *coupon rate* is the interest paid on the face value of a bond. It is one fixed dollar amount that is always paid as long as the debtor company is solvent. (Income or adjustment bonds are the only exceptions.) The coupon rate is decided upon after the investment banker and/or the financial analysts of the firm have taken into account risk of default, the credit standing of the company, the convertible options, the investment position of the industry, the security backing of the bond, and the market rate of interest for the firm's industry, size, and risk-class. After all these factors have been taken into account, a coupon rate is set with the objective that it will be just high enough to attract investors to pay the face value of the bond. Later, the market price of the bond may change from its face value as market interest rates change, while the contractual coupon rate remains fixed.

Generally, the higher the *yield* or rate of return, the riskier the security.[1] Yield rather than coupon rate is more significant in buying bonds. If the bond is selling at a *discount,* its market price is below its face value. In this case, the yield is higher than the coupon rate. If it is selling at a *premium,* the market price of the bond is above its face value. In this case, the coupon rate is higher than the yield. In buying bonds, the investor should be aware of possible capital gains or losses due to changes in the market price of a bond, since this is as important as the interest income in calculating yield. Chapter 7 explains how to calculate bond yields.

Maturities vary widely. The actual term to maturity of a new bond issue does not really matter in this discussion because as long-term bonds come closer and closer to their maturity dates, they become medium-term and then short-term bonds. Bonds are usually grouped by their maturity classes. *Short-term bonds* are any bonds maturing within 5 years. They are common in industrial financing and may be secured or unsecured. *Medium-term bonds* mature in 5 to about 10 years. If a bond is originally issued as a medium-term bond, it is usually secured by a real estate or equipment mortgage, or it may be backed by other security. Railroads and utilities are common users of this type of financing. *Long-term bonds* may run 20 years or more. Capital heavy industries with long expectations of equipment life, such as railroads and utilities, are the greatest users of this form of bond financing; it is rarely used in industrial financing.

A *call provision* may be included in the indenture. This provision allows the debtor to call or redeem the bonds at a specified amount (above par) before maturity date. The difference between the par value of the bond and the higher call price is called the *call premium.* The call provision is advantageous to the issuing firm but potentially harmful to the investor. If interest rates should decline, it may be wise for the firm to call in its bonds and issue new ones at the lower market interest rate. This action, however, leaves investors with funds they can invest only at the lower interest rate. To compensate for the undesirable callable feature, a new issue

---

[1] The term *yield* is used synonymously with *yield to maturity* or *average rate of return compounded annually to maturity.* These terms refer to the effective rate of return to the owner if the bond is held to maturity. Bonds' yields to maturity are discussed in detail in Chap. 7.

of callable bonds will sell at a higher interest rate than a comparable issue of noncallable bonds.

Sinking fund and *serial bonds* are not special types of bonds but just names given to describe the method of repayment; thus, any bond can be such by merely specifying it in the indenture.

Sinking fund bonds arise when the company decides to retire its bond issue systematically by setting aside a certain amount each year for that purpose. The payment, usually a fixed annual dollar amount or a percentage installment, is made to the sinking fund agent who is usually the trustee. This person then uses the money to call the bonds annually at some call premium or to purchase them on the open market if they are selling at a discount.

Sinking fund bonds have been common in industrial financing that involved some risk because risky debt issues are more attractive to investors with a promise of faster repayment. Where risk is lower (for example, in utilities), sinking fund bonds are less frequently used. Perhaps half the industrial issues and one-third of the utilities' issues have such a provision.

Serial bonds are appropriate for firms that wish to divide their bond issues into a series, each part of the series maturing at a different time. Ordinarily the bonds are not callable, and the company pays each part of the series as it matures.

Secured Bonds

The most important classifying criterion of corporate bonds is whether they are secured or unsecured. That is, what security, if any, has been pledged to help pay investors if the company should be unable to live up to its obligations, or should default?

If the indenture provides for a lien on a certain designated property, the bond is a secured bond. A lien is a legal right given to the bondholders, through the trustee, to sell the pledged property to obtain the amount of money necessary to satisfy the unpaid portion of interest or principal. Pledged security is naturally used to make the bonds more attractive to investors by making them safer investments. The reasoning is that if investors see the bonds as safer than similar nonsecured bonds, they will pay a higher price or accept a lower interest rate for them. In reality, the security is seldom sold in the case of default. The company is usually reorganized with new securities issued for the defaulted bonds. The presence of a lien on the property has a very favorable influence on the treatment of the bondholders' interests in the reorganization, however.

Mortgage bonds.   A bond issue secured with a lien on real property or buildings is a mortgage bond. If all the assets of the firm are collateral under the terms of the indenture, it is called a *blanket mortgage.* The total assets need not be pledged, however; only some of the land or buildings of the company may be mortgaged for the issue. These can be first, second, or subsequent mortgages, each with its respective claim to the assets of the firm in case of default. A first mortgage is the most secure because it enjoys first claim to assets. A mortgage bond may be *open-end, limited open-end*, or *closed-end*, or it may contain an *after acquired property* clause.

An *open-end mortgage* means that more bonds can be issued on the same mortgage contract. The creditors are usually protected by restrictions limiting such additional borrowing. The open-end mortgage will normally also contain an *after acquired property* clause which provides that all property acquired after the first mortgage was issued be added to the property already pledged as security by the contract. A *limited open-end mortgage* allows the firm to issue additional bonds up to a specified maximum (for example, up to 50 percent of the original cost of the pledged property). A *closed-end mortgage* means no additional borrowing can be done on that mortgage. This, with an after acquired property clause, guarantees an increasing security base for the creditors. Investors should know the kind of mortgage they have and the provisions that are behind their mortgage bonds, since they determine the risk and return.

Collateral trust bonds. When the security deposited with the trustee of a bond issue consists of the stocks and bonds of other companies, these newly issued secured bonds are called *collateral trust* bonds. Since the assets of holding companies are usually largely in the form of stocks and bonds of their subsidiaries, holding companies are the main issuers of such bonds.

Collateral must, as a rule, be 25 to 33 percent greater than the value of the bonds in order to ensure adequate protection if liquidation is necessary. The borrower may remove this collateral and substitute other assets for it as long as the required margin of coverage is maintained. Such bonds are issued when this method is easier than issuing mortgage bonds or when the holding company wants to consolidate a number of smaller issues at a better market price.

Unsecured Bonds

Debenture bonds or simply *debentures* are unsecured bonds. They are issued with no lien against specific property provided in the indenture. They may be seen as a claim on earnings and not assets. This is not to say that the bondholders are not protected in case of default but, rather, that they are general creditors. All assets not specifically pledged or any balance remaining after payment of secured debts from previously pledged assets are available to pay the legal claims of general creditors. The debenture indentures usually take this added riskiness into account and contain specific protecting provisions. They may restrict any further issuing of debentures unless earnings over a certain number of years are two or three times what is needed to cover the original debenture interest. Another common clause says that if any secured debt is issued, the debentures will be secured by an equal amount. Sometimes working capital (that is, current assets minus current liabilities) must be maintained at a certain ratio to the principal amount of the debenture or the debtor is not allowed to pay dividends on its common stock.

Subordinate debentures are simply debentures that are specifically made subordinate to all other general creditors holding claims on assets. These other creditors are usually suppliers or financial institutions that have granted credit and loans to the firm.

Many debentures, because they are unsecured, have in recent years been issued as convertible debentures. They then have all the characteristics of bonds, but under certain conditions they may be converted into a specified number of shares of common stock. This conversion privilege is a "sweetener" to make the unsecured debt more attractive. It will be covered more thoroughly later in this chapter and elsewhere.

Bonds with Special Characteristics

Several types of bonds have the general characteristics of bonds, but, because they have some special distinguishing characteristic, they are given special names. For example, if a mortgage bond is secured so that it covers only part of the property of the firm or only a specific section of a railroad, it is called a *divisional bond*. It is the first mortgage on that operating division of the railroad or industrial firm. If the division is highly productive, the bonds will be strong; weak divisions will mean correspondingly weak bonds.

Direct lien bonds. These are special bonds secured by one piece of property such as a railroad terminal, dock, or bridge. Such a bond might then be referred to as a *terminal bond* or a *bridge bond.* If two or more companies own the property that is securing the bond, such as a railroad bridge, it is called a *joint bond.*

Prior lien bonds. These are bonds that have been placed ahead of the first mortgage, usually during the reorganization of a bankrupt firm. Only with the permission of the first mortgage bondholders can prior lien bonds be issued, taking over the first mortgage's first claim on assets.

Junior mortgage bonds. These bonds have a secondary claim to assets and earnings behind senior mortgage bonds. Because it is poor public relations for an issue to bear the title *second mortgage,* these issues typically have names such as *refunding mortgage* or *consolidated mortgage.*

Assumed and guaranteed bonds. When a large firm (usually a railroad) takes over a small one in a merger or consolidation, the bonds of the small company must be recognized. If the small company is dissolved by the merger, the new entity assumes the liability represented by the bonds. These bonds are then covered not only by the specific property pledged in the indentures but also by the large firm's promise-to-pay clause.

If the merged company continues to operate as a unique division within the large company, its bonds will be guaranteed by the larger firm. Depending upon the willingness of the parent company to continue the guarantee through endorsement of the bonds, rental of its property, or some other legal agreement between the two companies, these bonds may be solid or very weak.

Participating bonds. These bonds share in the earnings of the firm. They have a guaranteed rate of interest but may also participate in earnings up to an additional specified percentage. Because they have this characteristic of increased dividends with increased earnings, they are unpopular bonds with the common stockholders of the company, who prefer to keep all earnings for themselves. For this reason, participating bonds are issued only by companies with poor credit positions. The most common users of such bonds have been bridge companies.

Bonds' One-Period Returns

Since the most important outcome from an investment is the investor's rate of income, the bond investor's one-period rate of return is explicitly defined. Regardless of whether the period over which a bond's rate of return is calculated is a day, a week, a month, a quarter, a year, or a 5-year period, the definition of its one-period rate of return is given in Eq. (2-1):

$$r_t = \frac{p_{t+1} - p_t + i_t}{p_t} \qquad (2\text{-}1)$$

The symbol r_t denotes the one-period rate of return in the tth period. The tth period can be whatever period you are interested in—this year, next week, or last quarter. The p_{t+1} and p_t terms are dollar quantities defined as the market price of the bond at the beginning of period $t + 1$ and period t, respectively. And i_t is the dollar amount of coupon interest paid on the bond in period t. A numerical example should clarify all this.

If a bond sells at $995 on January 1 of some year and it sold at $950 on January 1 of the preceding year, then $p_{t+1} = \$995$ and $p_t = \$950$. If this hypothetical bond paid $50 coupon interest per year, then its 1-year rate of return is 10 percent, as shown in Eq. (2-1a).

$$10.0\% = .1 = \frac{\$95}{\$950} = \frac{\$995 - \$950 + \$50}{\$950} \qquad (2\text{-}1a)$$

If the bond's market price had fallen to $852.50 instead of rising to $995, the year's return would have been a negative 5 percent.

$$-5.0\% = -.05 = \frac{-47.50}{\$950} = \frac{\$852.50 - \$950 + \$50}{\$950} \tag{2-1b}$$

If it were a participating bond, some earnings paid to bondholders should be added into the numerator of Eq. (2-1) to increase the bond's return. But, aside from this one possible addition, Eq. (2-1) is the one-period rate-of-return definition for secured and unsecured bonds alike.

Some people refer to a bond's one-period rate of return as its one-period yield. However, this language seems inadvisable because it could get confused with a bond's yield to maturity—a different concept which will be discussed later in Chap. 7 on bond valuation.

2-2 COMMON STOCK

By definition, all corporations issue common stock. It is the first security of a corporation to be issued and the last to be retired. Common stock represents a share in the ownership of the firm. It has the last claim on earnings and assets of all other securities issued, but it also has an unlimited potential for dividend payment and capital gain through rising prices. All other corporate securities (that is, corporate bonds and preferred stock) have a contract for interest or dividend payout that common stock does not have. If the firm should fail, common stockholders get what is left after everyone else has been completely repaid. The chance of getting anything back is highly unlikely. Risk is highest with common stock and so must be its expected return.

When investors buy common stock, they receive certificates of ownership as proof of their part as owners of the firm. The certificate states the number of shares purchased, their par value, if any, and usually the transfer agent. When stock is purchased on the market (that is, when it is not a new issue which is purchased from the company), the new owner and the number of shares bought are noted in the stock record book of the transfer agent. The former shareholder's certificate is canceled, and the new certificate sent to the registrar, which is usually another bank or trust company. The registrar checks to verify that no errors were made, and when all checks are completed, the certificate is sent to the new shareholder.

Voting

Common stock is voting stock. The power to vote for the board of directors and for or against major issues belongs to common stockholders because they are the owners of the corporation. Most stockholders are not very much interested in the voting power they possess and will sign and return the proxies that are mailed to them by the company. A *proxy* allows a named person, usually part of the management, to vote the shares of the proxy signer at the stockholders meeting. The use of proxies usually allows management, which normally by itself does not control enough votes to run the company, to be able to vote its decisions into effect.

Many corporate charters allow for *cumulative voting.* This permits a stockholder to have as many votes as he or she has shares of stock times the number of directors being elected. The stock owner may cast all these cumulative votes for only one director or divide them among several. This provision allows for stockholders with a significant minority of shares to gain representation on the board of directors. As mentioned before, small and large institutional stockholders are usually not interested in voting or will vote with management. However, in some unusual instances stockholders have banded together to oppose management. In 1970, for example, several groups of General Motors stockholders, including large institutions, chose to vote against management on its air pollution proposal in favor of stronger measures.

Preemptive Right

The *preemptive right* allows existing stockholders the right to subscribe to any new issue of stock so that they can maintain their previous fraction of total outstanding shares. Some states automatically make the preemptive right a part of every corporate charter; in others, its inclusion as part of the charter is optional. The reasoning behind the preemptive right is the recognition that stockholders are part owners of corporations and as such should have an interest in earnings and assets and a voice in management proportionate to the fraction of voting shares they own. The preemptive right, if exercised, prevents the dilution of ownership control inherent in additional stock issues. For example, if Ms. Stockholder owns 25 percent of Corporation Z, and Z floats a stock issue that doubles the number of shares outstanding, Ms. Stockholder's share of ownership and control diminishes to 12.5 percent unless she has the preemptive right which allows her to buy 25 percent of the new issue. The preemptive right, then, if exercised, guarantees the undiluted maintenance of voting control, share in earnings, and share in assets.

Par Value

Par value is the face value of a share of stock. It was originally used to guarantee that the corporation receive a fair price for the value of the firm represented by a share of stock. The idea was to guarantee that the creditors' principal would be protected; however, in practice the concept did not work well. Many times "watered" stock was issued; that is, stock was sold for less than its par value. For example, when United States Steel was formed in 1901, much of its stock was watered—sold at less than par. In 1912 New York became the first state to allow stock to be issued with no par value. Such stock can be issued at any price because it has no par to dictate

TABLE 2-2 COMPARISON OF 1973 PAR, BOOK, AND MARKET VALUES
FOR SHARES OF RANDOMLY SELECTED CORPORATIONS

Corporation	Par value	Book value, $	Range of market price per share, $
Firestone Tire & Rubber	No par	35.25	13–27
General Motors Corp.	1⅔	42.96	44–84
Liggett & Myers, Inc.	1	42.06	24–45
RCA Corporation	No par	14.79	16–39
Shell Oil Company	1	45.94	45–67

Source: Moody's Handbook of Common Stocks, 1974.

a minimum value. However, since no-par stock's peak of popularity in the 1920s, corporations have largely given it up in favor of low-par shares. Today most companies set a low minimum par value on their stock at the level they feel sure is below the actual price the shares will command on the market. Railroad stocks still have high par values, with $100, $50, and $25 being common. Utilities most frequently use $5 or $10 limits, while industrial firms most often choose a $1 par value.

Investors must realize that the par value of the stock has very little to do with the value of their shares. They should be interested in the value of their stock as determined by earnings and capital gains and not by any value set as the par value of the stock.

The same misplaced concern is placed on *book value.* Book value can be calculated by adding the common stock and surplus accounts of the balance sheet and then dividing by the number of shares of common stock. Book value does give an indication of the assets of the corporation, but it has no real effect on stock prices. In the Depression, many companies had high book values but found their stock was selling far below book value. Book and market values will probably be equal when the stock is issued, but after that, it appears that only coincidence will keep them equal at any given moment. Table 2-2 shows how book value and par value compare with the actual market price of the stock for a few randomly selected corporations. The variations in the three values for each corporation are wide.

Classified Common Stock

Occasionally an investor will come across *classified* common stock. Traditionally the stock referred to as class A was nonvoting, dividend-paying stock issued to the public. Class B stock was voting stock and was held by management, which therefore had control of the firm. It paid no dividends, however, although the owners did enjoy the residual benefits of a growing company.

In the 1920s, classified common stock became very popular with managers and investment bankers because it allowed them to maintain complete control of a company with a minimal investment while still being able to sell stock to the public to finance expenditures. Investors, not much interested in voting rights, saw it as an attractive issue. It offered the speculative advantages of common stock and the protected stability and return of preferred stock. However, much criticism of classified stock arose, and in 1924 the New York Stock Exchange stopped listing any more issues of non-voting, classified stock. More recently, however, small new companies have found the issuing of voting, classified stock advantageous. They sell class A stock, which pays regular dividends and carries full voting rights, to the public. Class B common is purchased by the organizers of the corporation, but it does not pay dividends until the firm's earnings have grown to respectable levels.

Cash Dividends

According to their investment goals, some stockholders may be very much concerned about dividends. There is no general rule regarding the size or regularity of dividends. Generally, however, rapidly growing corporations pay little or no dividends in order to retain as much capital as possible for internal financing. Established firms tend to pay out a larger portion of their earnings in dividends.

Some companies, such as American Telephone and Telegraph, take pride in their regular, substantial dividend policies, while others, such as Litton Industries have no cash dividend payouts. At one time it was thought desirable to pay dividends and maintain some kind of stable policy toward them. Today most companies determine dividends according to the need of financing and investor expectation about growth. Dividends may or may not be important to the investor. If investors prefer regular income from large cash dividends, they will buy dividend-paying stock. If they are more concerned about making a capital gain (a higher selling price than purchase price), the investor will look at the growth prospects of the company and prefer a firm which retains its earnings rather than pay cash dividends.

Common Stocks' One-Period Rate of Return

Continuing the convention that p_t refers to the market price per security at the beginning[2] of period t, the one-period rate of return from an equity share is defined in Eq. (2-2).

---

[2] If p_t were used to denote *end*-of-period prices, Eq. (2-2) must be modified as shown in Eq. (2-2a).

$$r_t = \frac{p_t - p_{t-1} + d_t}{p_{t-1}} \tag{2-2a}$$

Equations (2-2) and (2-2a) produce identical results; they differ only by whether p_t denotes beginning or end-of-period price.

$$r_t = \frac{p_{t+1} - p_t + d_t}{p_t} \tag{2-2}$$

The d_t term in Eq. (2-2) represents the cash dividends per share paid to shareholders of record during period t. Conceptually, p_t is the stock's purchase price if it had been bought at the beginning of the tth period, and the quantity $(p_{t+1} - p_t)$ is called the capital gain or loss, depending on whether the stock appreciated or depreciated during the "period." Calculating a stock's returns is more difficult if the corporation has split its shares or paid stock dividends.

Stock Dividends

Stock dividends are paid in shares of the issuing company's stock. When a stock dividend is paid, the stock account is increased and the capital surplus account is decreased. Except for the accounting procedures, stock dividends and stock splits are identical. For this reason, the New York Stock Exchange has adopted a rule calling all distributions of stock under 25 percent per share *dividends* and distributions over 25 percent *splits* even if the corporation involved calls its action something different.

Stock Splits

When a company divides it shares, it is said to have "split its stock." If a corporation had 2 million shares outstanding and splits them 2 for 1, it would end up with 4 million shares outstanding. In a stock split, the firm must correspondingly reduce the par value of the common stock, but it does not change its capital stock and paid-in surplus accounts. If the firm's stock had a par of $1 before the split, then the 2 for 1 split would give it a par of 50 cents.

A corporation's major reason for splitting its stock is to reduce its market value. The split divides the market price per share in proportion to the split. For example, a $100 per share stock will sell at $50 after a 2 for 1 split, just as a $100 per share stock will sell at $50 after a 100 percent stock dividend. In both cases there will be twice as many shares outstanding so that the total market value of the firm is unchanged by such paper shuffling. In essence, stock splits and stock dividends do not affect the value of the firm or the shareholder's returns (contrary to what many people think). In any event, most companies do not like the prices of their stock to rise too high because the high cost may decrease its marketability. The $30 to $60 range seems to be most popular among investors. Thus, a stock split may be used to restore a popular market price.

Calculating Returns after Splits

Equation (2-2) can be rewritten as (2-2b). To calculate a common stock's single-period return after a stock split or stock dividend, Eq. (2-2b) may be useful.

$$r_t = \frac{\text{capital gain or loss} + \text{cash dividends}}{\text{purchase price}} \qquad (2\text{-}2b)$$

Each share's price must be adjusted for stock splits and dividends before rates of return can be calculated. These price adjustments are needed to ensure that only actual changes in the investor's wealth will be measured, rather than the meaningless price changes which are associated with a stock dividend or split. For example, if a 2 for 1 split or a 100 percent stock dividend occurred, the share prices would be halved before the stock dividend or split (or doubled afterward) so that no changes in the investor's wealth would be attributed to it in calculating rates of return.

The following numerical example shows how a share or stock, originally selling for $100 per share, can fall to $50 per share owing to a 2 for 1 split or 100 percent stock dividend without changing the owner's 5 percent rate of return. The change in the unit of account (that is, the stock dividend or stock split) occurred between periods 2 and 3. Since the investor owns twice as many shares after the stock split but since each has half the previous market price, the investor's wealth is unchanged. And the investor's income in this simple example is $5 of cash dividends per period per $100 of investment both before and after the change in the unit of account, that is, a constant 5 percent rate of return per period.[3]

Time period (t)	$t = 1$	$t = 2$	$t = 3$	$t = 4$
Market price per share	$100	$100	$50	$50
Cash dividend per share	$ 5	$ 5	$ 2.50	$ 2.50
Earnings per share	$ 10	$ 10	$ 5	$ 5
Number of shares held per $100 original investment	1	1	2	2
Rate of return per period	5%	5%	5%	5%
Shares outstanding	100,000	100,000	200,000	200,000

2-3 PREFERRED STOCK

Preferred stock is just that: preferred stockholders have preference over common stockholders (but not bondholders) as to after-tax earnings in the form of dividends and assets in the event of liquidation. Therefore, in terms of risk, the preferred stockholder is in a less risky position than the common stockholder but in a more risky position than the corporate bondholder. Preferred stockholders generally receive a greater rate of return on their investment than bondholders in compensation for the slightly greater risk they assume. However, they generally receive a lesser rate of return than the common stockholder because they assume less risk. In fact, unlike common, preferred is limited (except with participating preferred) in the

[3] The true economic effect of stock dividends and splits is analyzed later in Chap. 22 along the lines of E. Fama, L. Fisher, M. Jensen, and R. Roll, "The Adjustment of Stock Prices to New Information," *International Economic Review*, vol. 20, no. 2, pp. 1–21, February 1969.

amount of dividends it can receive. If the firm is prosperous, the preferred receives only its stipulated dividend and all the residual earnings go to common stockholders. In terms of control, the preferred stockholder, as part owner, is in a better position than the bondholder, since the preferred stockholder is frequently given voting rights. Of course, common stockholders today are always given voting rights.

Voting

Prior to 1930, preferred stockholders had few, if any, voting rights. The theory was that as long as holders of this class of stock received their dividends, they should have no voice in the company. Currently, however, there is a pronounced trend to give preferred shares full voting rights. Moreover, nonvoting preferred may become voting stock if preferred dividend payments are missed for a stated length of time. This is consistent with the idea that as long as dividends are paid, preferred stock should have no voice in management. Also, nonvoting preferred may be given voting rights for special circumstances, such as authorization of a new bond or stock issue or the merger of the company.

Preemptive Right

Common law statute gives share owners, common or preferred, the right to subscribe to additional issues to maintain their proportionate share of ownership. However, as was explained in the section on common stock, the existence of the preemptive right depends on the law in the state where the corporation was chartered and the provisions of the company's articles of incorporation. The right is a bit more likely to be waived (unless the state law forbids it) for preferred stock than for common, particularly if preferred is nonvoting.

Par Value

Most preferred stock has a par value. When it does, the dividend rights and call prices are usually stated in terms of the par value. However, these rights would be specified even if there were no par value. It seems, therefore, as with common stock, that preferred that has a par value has no real advantage over preferred that has no par value.

Dividends

Dividends are the most significant aspect of preferred stock, since preferred stockholders invest more for gain from dividends than for gain from capital appreciation. The dividend paid is usually a stipulated percentage of par value, or for a stock with no par, a stated dollar amount.

Most of the preferred issues outstanding today have a *cumulative dividend* clause. This means that the preferred stockholder is entitled to a dividend whether the firm earns it or not. If the corporation "misses" a preferred dividend, or any part of it, it is not lost but must be made up in a later year before any dividend can be paid to the common stock. For example, if a firm is unable to meet its $6 preferred dividend this year, but next year has $8 to disperse as dividends, all $8 will go to the preferred stock rather than $6 to preferred and $2 to common. After this payment, the firm will still owe $4 per share to its cumulative preferred stockholders.

Not all preferred stock is cumulative. Noncumulative stock is entitled to its dividends if they are earned. If they are not, the dividend is completely lost to the preferred stockholders. Of course, the corporation cannot legally pay dividends to its common stock if it has missed a preferred dividend during that dividend period (typically 1 year).

It should be noted that even with a cumulative provision, preferred stock carries no obligation to pay if the dividends are not earned. This provision may lead to difficulty if there is a question as to whether a dividend has been earned. If the directors decide to apply profits to a capital improvement (and who is to say what this is?) and not to pay a dividend, the preferred stockholders have no legal recourse, as do the bondholders; they are stuck with the directors' decision.

Call Feature

With many guarantees and "sweeteners" needed to make a preferred stock issue attractive, and with the preference and restrictions for dividend payments it demands, companies want to be in a position to call in these preferred shares if they become financially able. A redemption clause gives the company the right to redeem or call in the issues. As in a bond redemption, a preferred stock redemption is made at some time after the announcement of such action, and a call premium is paid above the par value of the stock and its regular dividend. Though railroads seldom have this privilege industrials and utilities almost all carry it. The premium above par for utilities runs from 5 to 10 percent and from 10 to 20 for industrials. For both types of issuers, 10 percent is most common.

As with the bondholder, the call feature is seldom advantageous to a preferred stockholder. However, it is a desirable provision for the firm since it allows a prospering corporation to bring an end to relatively high fixed charges, namely, preferred dividends. The call price has the effect of setting a ceiling price on preferred stock, since it is reasonable that an investor would be reluctant to pay a market price for a preferred share in excess of the amount for which the corporation could redeem it.

Sinking Funds

If a preferred stock issue is not convertible, it may include provisions for a *sinking fund*. This sinking fund may take the form of a simple accounting manipulation (debiting earned surplus and crediting a sinking fund for the preferred stock account), or it may entail an orderly annual retirement of the issue. If it is the latter, the shares will probably be redeemed at the call price unless the market price is significantly below the call price, in which case it might be less costly (even after brokerage commissions) for the firm to buy the preferred shares on the market.

A corporation's sinking fund for preferred stock has a much different legal status from that of a similar fund for bonds. A firm's inability to meet payments for a bond sinking fund may precipitate bankruptcy. Default on payments into a preferred stock sinking fund, though, has minor, if any, consequences. Occasionally, if the preferred stock is normally nonvoting, the preferred stockholders are given voting rights after a certain number of payments have been missed.

Participating Preferred Stock

Participating preferred stock, like a participating bond, is uncommon. Both are entitled to a stated rate of dividends (interest) and then a share of the earnings available to be paid to the common stock. Since participating preferred stock is not very popular with the common shareholders, only weak firms will use such a provision as a "sweetener" to help sell this type of stock. Because preferred stock is basically a fixed-income investment like a bond but has few, if any, of the legal guarantees and recourses as to payment of interest that are inherent in a bond, the issuer may add protective clauses to the contract in order to make the stock safer and more salable.

In sum, preferred stock is a curious hybrid between debt and equity. Although it is technically a form of equity investment, it has many of the characteristics of debt, such as fixed-income return, sinking fund provisions, and call provisions. Its one-period rate of return is calculated with Eq. (2-2) like common stock returns (see page 20).

2-4 CONVERTIBLE SECURITIES

A convertible security is usually preferred stock or a bond that can be converted into common stock. Once converted into stock, it cannot be changed back. If it is a bond, the convertible security provides the investor with a fixed interest payment; if preferred stock, with a stipulated dividend. The investor also receives the option to convert the instrument into common stock, and thus has the speculative aspects of equity ownership. The conversion option allows investors to participate in the residual earnings of the firm that are reflected in rises in the stock prices. They can earn their guaranteed fixed return until they are assured of a capital gain, convert, and make a profit. The convertible may also be an inflation hedge. If inflation significantly reduces the real value of the fixed interest payment, chances are that the common stock price may also be inflated, and convertible holders can convert their security.

Many convertibles have a specific period in which the issue may be converted. They may stipulate that conversion cannot take place until 2 or 3 years after the issue. This stipulation allows the money obtained through such financing to be utilized by the corporation for investment and growth that will show up in higher common stock prices only after a period of time. A limited issue will place a time limit as to when the conversion can take place, typically 10 to 15 years. Convertible preferred stocks are usually unlimited as to time horizon for conversion. An unlimited bond is eligible for conversion for the entire time the bond is outstanding.

As a rule, convertible securities are callable. The call privilege allows the company to call in the security for redemption just as it permits the company to call in preferred stock or a straight bond. The purpose of the call provision is not to redeem the bonds or preferred stock but to force conversion of the issue when the conversion value of the security is well above the call price. In practice, few convertibles are ever redeemed.

Conversion Ratio

The *conversion ratio* is the ratio of exchange between the common stock and the convertible security. For example, a $1,000 convertible bond may provide for a conversion to 10 shares of common stock. The conversion price is then simply the $1,000 face value divided by the conversion ratio ($1,000 ÷ 10 = $100 per share conversion price). This ratio may be stated as 10 shares of stock for each bond.

There are instances when the conversion price is not constant over time. The conversion price might change simply with the length of time outstanding or with the proportion of the issue converted. A bond might have a conversion price of $100 per share the first 5 years, $105 per share for the next 5 years, $110 for the third 5 years, and so on. Under a provision stipulating increasing price with amount redeemed, a bond might have a conversion price of $100 per share for the first 25 percent of the shares converted, $105 for the second 25 percent, $110 for the third, and $115 per share for the final 25 percent converted. Such provisions for increasing conversion prices give the issuer some power to force investors to convert their issues as fast as possible when the market price has substantially exceeded the conversion price.

Conversion value is the market price per share of common stock times the conversion ratio. In the foregoing example, if the stock were selling at $105 per share, the conversion value of the bond would be 10 × $105 = $1,050. If the price were $95 per share, the conversion value would be $950 for the $1,000 face value bond.

The market price of a convertible security will be higher than the conversion value at time of issue. The difference between the two is the *conversion premium*. For example, the TWA convertible subordinated debentures issued in March 1967 were sold at about par, $1,000 per bond. At that time the market price of the stock was $88 per share. The conversion ratio was

$1,000 ÷ $100 = $10; thus, the conversion value was 10 × $88 = $880. Subtracting this from the bond price ($1,000) gives a conversion permium of $120. Frequently the conversion premium is expressed as a percentage (for example, $120 ÷ $880 = 13.6 percent conversion premium).

Dilution

Dilution of an investor's position is possible on both sides of a convertible issue. If the firm splits its stock or declares a stock dividend, the conversion value of the convertible instrument is lowered appropriately. For example, if the conversion price of a bond were $100 per share and the conversion ratio were 10 shares per bond, a 2 for 1 stock split would change the conversion ratio from 10 to 20 (just as the number of shares would be doubled) and the conversion price from $100 to $50 (just as the market price of the common stock would be halved).

The existing investors in a company's stock also run the risk of dilution of their position. They usually recognize this well before conversion takes place, and on the announcement of a convertible issue the market price of the stock often declines. To keep the current stockholders' position stable, the convertible security can be covered by the provision for preemptive rights in the corporate charter. Under this provision, the convertible must be offered to the existing stockholders before it can be sold to the general public. However, over half the states allow corporations to deny preemptive rights in their corporate charters.

An example will illustrate the diluting effect of a convertible. We assume that a corporation issues $50 million of 7 percent convertible debentures at a conversion price of $25 per share. Upon conversion the total number of additional shares would be ($50 million ÷ $25 =) 2 million new shares. Suppose that the company has 4 million shares outstanding originally and, for simplicity, no other debt. It expects earnings of $20 million in 3 years; the income tax rate is 50 percent. Table 2-3 shows what earnings per share would be before conversion and after conversion.

Table 2-3 shows that, with conversion, the earnings per share are diluted. The impact of such dilution upon the market share price must be carefully considered by the investors. However, when the debentures are

TABLE 2-3 DILUTION EFFECT OF CONVERSION

	Debentures outstanding, $	Converted, $
Earnings before interest & taxes	20,000,000	20,000,000
Interest on 7% debenture	3,500,000	0
Profit before taxes	16,500,000	20,000,000
Taxes at 50%	8,250,000	10,000,000
Profit after taxes	8,250,000	10,000,000
Shares outstanding	4,000,000	6,000,000
Earnings per share	2.06	1.67

converted, the corporation is relieved of the interest burden of debentures or the dividends to preferred stock. Conversion has the effect of issuing equity to pay off debt.

Reasons for Convertible Financing

This method of delayed equity financing gives several advantages to the corporation. One is a delayed dilution of common stock and earnings per share as shown in Table 2-3. Another advantage is that the firm is able to offer the bond at a lower coupon rate, or preferred stock at a lower dividend rate, than it would have to pay on a straight bond or preferred stock. The rule usually is that the more valuable the conversion feature, the lower the yield that must be offered to sell the issue—the convertible feature is a "sweetener."

Companies with poor credit ratings often issue convertibles in order to lower the yield necessary to sell their debt securities. The investor should be aware that some financially weak companies will issue convertibles just to reduce their costs of financing, with no intention of the issue's ever being converted. There are also corporations whose credit rating is weak but who have great potential for growth. Such a firm will be able to sell a convertible debt issue at a near-normal cost, not because of the quality of the bond but because of the attractiveness of the conversion feature for this "growth" stock. Times of tight money and growing stock prices will find even very credit-worthy companies issuing convertible securities in an effort to reduce their cost of obtaining scarce capital.

A definite disadvantage to the firm that is financing with convertible securities is that it runs the risk of diluting not only the earnings per share of its common stock but also the control of the company. If a large part of the issue is purchased by one buyer, typically an investment banker or insurance company, conversion may shift the voting control of the firm away from its original owners and toward the converters. This is not a significant problem for large companies with millions of stockholders, but it is a very real consideration for the small firm or one just going public.

Overhanging Issue

When a company is unable to force the conversion of an issue because the market price has not risen to a point that will induce investors to convert, the issue is said to be an *overhanging issue*. Ordinarily a company will plan for the issue to be converted within a certain period of time. A growth company may expect conversion within 18 months. The failure of the market price of the stock to rise sufficiently for conversion to occur might indicate a failure of the company to perform as expected. Such an overhanging issue can cause serious problems, since the company would find it difficult to gain market acceptance for another convertible issue or even for nonconvertible financing. While Control Data's 1965 convertible preferred stock was overhanging, the company did not make any attempt at additional financing. At time of issue the price of common stock was $57 per share, but it fell to a low of 23⅝ in 1966, making conversion unprofitable for investors.

The possibility of an overhanging issue and the associated limitations on financial flexibility will definitely reduce the advantages of a convertible over an equity issue. A common stock issue brings in equity capital at the moment, whereas a convertible entails the uncertainty of whether it will ever be converted into common stock.

Reasons for Investment in Convertible Securities

The investor should be aware that the conversion option is not free. Convertible securities sell above the price of comparable nonconvertible securities. This additional cost may be worthwhile, however, for a convertible security has value in two forms rather than in just one. First, it has value as a bond or preferred stock. (Since convertible preferred stock and convertible bonds are so similar, the discussion will pertain also to convertible bonds.) Second, it allows the investor to hedge against the future. If the price of the stock rises, the convertible is valued at or near its conversion value. But if the market price should decline, the convertible value will fall only to its value as a straight bond.

To illustrate, assume a 20-year, 7 percent convertible debenture has been issued by the XYZ Corporation. A straight 20-year debenture for the same firm would require an 8 percent yield to maturity. The 7 percent bond must sell at a discount if it is to yield 8 percent to maturity. Consequently, a $1,000 face value debenture must sell for about $902. Therefore, $902 is the value floor for XYZ's debenture. This means that if the market price of the stock should deteriorate to a point that makes the conversion value negligible, the bond price could not fall below $902. At the price, given that there is no significant change in the corporation's financial condition since the date of issue, the convertible will sell as if it were a straight bond. This bond "floor" is, of course, subject to the changes in interest rates and risk conditions of the firm, as are all bond prices. Bond valuation is covered in detail in Chaps. 7 and 8.

It is interesting to note that the popularity of convertibles with institutional investors has to some extent meant higher premiums over bond value. Many institutions are legally restricted from speculating in common stock. The convertible bond helps them enjoy the benefits of rising prices in the stock market without violating the law. The institution can buy the convertible as a bond and either sell it as its value rises with the climbing stock prices or wait to convert the bond and immediately sell the stock without penalty. Indeed, convertible securities are attractive to all classes of investors, offering protection against falling stock prices and the speculative advantage of capital gains.

2-5 GOVERNMENT SECURITIES

Since World War II, government securities have played an increasing role in the decisions of investors. By 1970, the total debt of the federal government was over $381 billion; of that total, nearly $370 billion was interest-bearing public debt. Most of it was in the form of U.S. Treasury bonds, notes, bills, certificates of indebtedness, and U.S. savings bonds. Demand for increased government services has also expanded the debt issues of government agencies and state and local governments. These debt issues have been increasing not only in absolute amounts but also on a per capita basis.

Government securities represent the amount of indebtedness of our governmental bodies. The owners of the securities are creditors; the governmental bodies are debtors. A clear distinction should be drawn between the debt of the federal government and the debt of state and local governments. In particular, the investor should be aware of different levels of risk involved and the different tax treatment for each. Therefore, they are discussed under separate headings.

U.S. Government Securities

United States government securities are of such high quality that their yield is often used as an example of a risk-free interest rate. Indeed, they are very safe, since the United States government has unlimited power to tax whenever such action becomes necessary.

Nonmarketable issues. Approximately 16 percent of the public debt consists of nonmarketable issues. These cannot be traded in the securities market; they are not transferable or negotiable; they cannot be used as collateral for a loan; they can be purchased only from the Treasury and they can be redeemed only by the Treasury. By far the major portion of nonmarketable securities are U.S. saving bonds, Series E and H.

The shrewd investor looking at government bonds will realize that savings bonds, with their low interest rates, yield poor returns. Indeed, in recent years, the rate of inflation has exceeded the rate of return on these bonds, meaning that they are granting the owner a negative *real* rate of return. There is no point in discussing the one-period rate of return for nonmarketable bonds because they have no market prices to observe. The redemption prices and yields of these bonds, if held to any point in time, are printed on the bond.

Marketable issues. These issues make up about two-thirds of the federal debt. They are usually purchased from outstanding supplies through a dealer or broker. However, the purchaser may subscribe for new issues through a Federal Reserve Bank. The holder of marketable government securities stands to gain not only from the interest paid on these bonds, like the owner of nonmarketable bonds, but also from price appreciation (higher selling price than purchase price), unlike the owner of nonmarketable bonds. Bid and ask prices for these marketable issues are published daily in such newspapers as *The New York Times* and *The Wall Street Journal.* Their prices are quoted in thirty-seconds of 1 percent of par; fractions are written as though they were decimals. For example, 70.16 means $70\frac{16}{32}$ percent of par. Chapter 7 explains in detail how the yield on these marketable issues is calculated. For now, however, the potential investor should become aware of the types and maturities of the various issues that are available.

Treasury bills are extremely liquid, short-term notes that mature in 13, 26, or 52 weeks from date of issue. The Treasury usually offers new bills every week, selling them on a discount basis. The discount to investors is the difference between the price they have paid and the face amount they receive at maturity. For example, a \$10,000 Treasury bill maturing in 13 weeks (that is, "a 90-day T-bill" to bond traders) could be purchased for \$9,750 if it were to yield 10.6 percent at an annual rate (or 2.56 percent = .0256 = \$250/\$9,750 on a quarterly basis). Then at the end of the 90 days the buyer would be repaid \$10,000 by the U.S. Treasury. The \$250 capital gain is the interest income for the 13 weeks; it equals the discount from the bond's face value when the bond was first sold.

Certificates of indebtedness are similar to bills but are issued at par (later being traded in the market) and bear fixed interest rates. They mature about a year from the date of issue, but the Treasury can set the period of time in order to adjust the stipulated interest rate to the current market credit conditions. They have been issued only sparingly in recent years.

Treasury notes are similar to certificates except with regard to time of maturity. Notes typically have a maturity of 1 to 7 years.

Treasury bonds make up by far the largest segment of the federal debt. Bonds differ in form from notes and certificates only as to maturity; they generally run from 7 to 40 years from date of issue. One significant difference is that some issues are callable at times prior to maturity. For example, the May 1985, 4.5 percent bonds are callable any time after 1975; thus, they are usually listed as $4\frac{1}{2}$'s 75–85, May. If the bonds are selling in the market above par, yield to maturity is calculated to the nearest call date. If they are selling at a discount, yield is calculated on the basis of their maturity date.

Approximately 17 percent of the government debt consists of *special issues.* These federal obligations cannot be purchased by the public and are sold by the Treasury to the special government funds with cash to invest. The Government Employees' Retirement Fund, the Federal Old-Age and Survivors Insurance Fund, and the National Service Life Insurance Fund are examples of such funds. The one-period rate of return from marketable government bonds is calculated with Eq. (2-1) on page 20.

Securities of Federal Agencies

The Federal Land Banks, the Federal Home Loan Banks, the Central Bank for Cooperatives, the Federal National Mortgage Association (called Fannie Mae),[4] Government National Mortgage Association (called Ginnie Mae), the Postal Service, and the Federal Intermediate Credit Bank are all U.S. government agencies allowed to issue their own debt obligations. Such bonds are similar in substance to other government bonds. The federal government makes no guarantee that the interest and principal of these "independent" bonds will be paid; therefore, their yield is higher than federal bonds. However, it would be poor political and economic policy for the government to allow any of its own agencies to default. There have been instances in which the Treasury has provided the funds needed to prevent any such financial embarrassment. The debt of two agencies is *officially* guaranteed by the Treasury: the outstanding debt of the District of Columbia Armory Board and some of the Federal Housing Administration (FHA) bonds.

The income from federal agency bonds, as other federal government bonds, is taxable. See Fig. A2-1 on page 43 for examples of market prices for U.S. government and agency bonds.

Municipal Securities

The bonds of states, counties, parishes, cities, towns, townships, boroughs, villages, and any special tax districts or municipal corporations are all referred to by security traders as *municipals*. They include the obligations of state and local commissions, agencies, and authorities as well as state and community colleges and universities. With such a wide assortment of issuing entities, there is naturally just as wide a variety of agreements with the bondholders.

The traditions of a federal political system have provided that the income derived from the obligation of a political subdivision be exempt from federal income taxes. This tax exemption makes municipal securities highly attractive to people in high income tax brackets. They are widely held by wealthy individuals, trusts, and partnerships (whose income may be taxed at the high personal tax rates).

This tax advantage works to the benefit of the issuers. The bonds are attractive because they are generally regarded by the holders as high in quality and lucrative in their exemption from taxes. This makes them easier for the issuer to market. These popular bonds therefore command a premium in the form of higher prices or lower interest rates in the market.

There are exceptions to the high-quality rating of municipal bonds. Some local governments are already too burdened with debt or have a tax base so limited that experts refuse to consider the bonds as top rate. Other

---

[4] For a monetary economist's view of Fannie Mae, Ginnie Mae, Maggie Mae (or Magic), and Freddie Mac, see J. C. Francis, "Helping Americans Get Homes," *Business Review,* Philadelphia Federal Reserve Bank, January 1974. Free copies available from the Bank on request.

issues are supported only by limited revenue-producing property and are not considered able to guarantee payment. For example, New York City offered a bond issue in 1975 with a coupon rate of over 9 percent and was still unable to sell the issue.

Municipal bonds, regardless of their exact contract provisions, fall into one of two categories, general or limited obligation bonds.

General obligations. Often referred to as *full faith and credit bonds* because of the unlimited nature of their pledge, *general obligation* securities originate from government units that have unlimited power to tax property to meet their obligations and that promise to pay without any kind of limitation. About two-thirds of the bonds issued by actual governments such as states, counties, and cities are of this type because these entities have the revenue-generating (that is, taxing) power to go to the politically feasible limit to pay their debts.

Limited obligations. This term is applied when the issuer is in some way restricted in raising revenues used to pay its debts. *Revenue bonds* are the most significant form of limited obligation. The distinguishing aspect of such bonds is that they are entitled to only the revenue generated from the specific property that is providing service for which rates or fees are paid. These bonds are widely used to finance municipally owned utilities, such as water works, electricity, gas, sewage disposal systems, and even public swimming pools.

2-6 INVESTMENT COMPANY SHARES

Many people with less than $30,000 to invest may not be well advised to buy securities, if for no other reason than that they have insufficient funds to buy a diversified portfolio. Since investors should buy stock in lots of 100 shares or more to incur lower stockbroker round-lot commissions, and since the average New York Stock Exchange (NYSE) stock costs about $30 per share, it takes, on average, $3,000 per issue (100 shares times an average price of $30 per share) to buy one round lot of stock. Multiplication of $3,000 per stock issue by 10 different stock issues needed to obtain diversification gives $30,000 (10 issues times $3,000 per issue) as the minimum needed to begin investing in individual securities in a diversified manner. Diversification is, of course, valuable as a means of reducing investment risks.[5]

Since millions of aspiring investors lack (1) sufficient capital to buy a diversified portfolio, (2) the expertise to manage a portfolio, and/or (3) the

[5] Selection of the number 10 as the minimum number of stock issues needed to obtain diversification is discussed analytically in Chap. 15. The discussion is based on the work by John H. Evans and S. H. Archer, "Diversification and the Reduction of Dispersion: An Empirical Analysis," *Journal of Finance,* December 1968, pp. 761–67.

time to manage a portfolio, enterprising portfolio managers have created public portfolios of diversified securities in which investors can buy a small or large number of shares. These public portfolios are called investment companies and typically assume one of two basic forms: (1) the open-end investment company, usually called a mutual fund, and (2) the closed-end investment fund.

Mutual Funds

More than 10 million persons, companies, and other organizations own shares in over 500 different open-end investment companies in the United States.[6] The size of these individual accounts ranges from a child's single share, valued at only a few dollars, to a multimillion-dollar pension fund's numerous shares in several different mutual funds. Likewise, the total asset holdings of individual mutual funds range from only a few million dollars to hundreds of millions.

Mutual funds are conduits from savings to investment. The funds pool the savings of many people by commingling them into one large, diversified investment portfolio. Many mutual funds own over 100 different issues of stocks and/or bonds. But no single investor owns any particular asset. Instead, an investor who has purchased a certain percentage of the mutual fund's total shares outstanding owns that percentage of every asset and every liability the fund obtains. Investors can cash in their shares in the fund whenever they wish, at the net asset value per share on that day. The *net asset value per share* equals the value of the fund's total net assets after liabilities divided by the total number of shares outstanding on that day. Thus, the net asset value per share fluctuates every time any asset experiences a change in its market price.

According to Subchapter M of the Internal Revenue Code, all income earned by a mutual fund is tax-exempt if the fund (1) distributes at least 90 percent of its cash dividend and interest income as it is received; (2) diversifies by placing no more than 5 percent of its total assets in any one security issue; and (3) is registered with the Securities Exchange Commission under the provisions of the Investment Company Act of 1940. Since practically every mutual fund meets these provisions, there is no double taxation (that is, taxation paid by both the company and the shareholder on the company's earnings).

By law, open-end investment companies are required to publish and adhere to a statement of the fund's investment objective. These statements are typically one or two paragraphs long and can be grouped into five main categories:

1 *Growth or "go-go" funds.* These funds tend to invest only in common stock and plan to assume some risks to obtain stocks which are expected to yield higher returns.

[6] Investment Company Institute, *Mutual Fund Fact Book,* 1973.

2 *Income funds.* Investment in stocks that pay high and consistent cash dividends is the objective of income funds. Risky stocks offering higher potential capital gains tend to be avoided in favor of "blue-chip" stocks (that is, those of large, old, stable companies).

3 *Balanced funds.* These funds divide their holdings between fixed-income securities and low-risk common stocks in order to avoid the risk of loss. These conservative funds usually have the lowest rates of return.

4 *Liquid asset funds.* These mutual funds invest in money market instruments such as Treasury bills. One of the main assets of some liquid asset funds is bank deposits (called certificates of deposit or CDs) of over $100,000 which are left with the bank for a specified number of days. The 90-day or 180-day CDs sometimes pay one of the highest rates of interest available on practically riskless bank deposits. The liquid asset funds started in the 1970s when interest rates rose above 10 percent. Their objective is to earn high rates of interest from liquid, low-risk, short-term bonds, bank deposits, and other money market instruments.

5 *Municipal bond funds.* These funds buy only municipal bonds to obtain their tax-exempt income. Only substantial individuals (a stockbroker's euphemism for rich people) who are in high income tax brackets usually buy shares in municipal bond mutual funds.

Investors obtain three types of income from owning mutual fund shares: (1) cash dividend or interest disbursements, denoted d; (2) capital gains disbursements, denoted c; and (3) change in the fund's net asset value (nav) per share from capital gains and cash dividends which were not distributed to the owners, denoted by $(\text{nav}_{t+1} - \text{nav}_t)$ for the tth period. Thus, the one-period rate of return for a mutual fund share is defined in Eq. (2-3).

$$r_t = \frac{c_t + d_t + (\text{nav}_{t+1} - \text{nav}_t)}{\text{nav}_t} \tag{2-3}$$

Mutual fund investors do not receive the entire rate of return defined in Eq. (2-3) because of two deductions. First, the fund's management fee of from .5 percent to 1.5 percent per year of the net asset value is deducted to pay the portfolio's management expenses. And second, some mutual funds, called *load funds,* deduct from 1 percent to 8.5 percent (usually the latter) of the mutual fund owner's original investment to pay a commission to the mutual fund salesperson. *No-load funds* are mutual funds that sell their shares by mail without sales representatives and charge their investors no sales commission.

All mutual funds are called open-end because they can keep selling more shares and thus keep growing larger as long as investors will buy more shares. Fund managers want their funds to grow larger so that they can charge their management-fee percentage on a larger amount of total

assets and thus pay themselves higher salaries. The investment performance of actual mutual funds is analyzed in Chap. 19, where the rates of return, risk, and overall performance of funds are evaluated and ranked.

Closed-End Funds

Closed-end investment companies are like mutual funds to the extent that
they are both publicly owned investment portfolios. But closed-end funds
differ in several important respects. First, as their name implies, a closed-
end fund cannot sell more shares after its initial offering—thus, its growth
is limited. Second, the shares of closed-end funds are not redeemable at
their net asset value, as are the shares in a mutual fund. Instead, the shares
of closed-end funds trade on stock exchanges at market prices which may be
above or below their net asset values.[7] These two distinctions between
closed-end and open-end funds are essentially the best way to define the
closed-end funds. Closed-end funds have diversification and investment
objectives that differ over a much wider range than the open-end funds,
making them very difficult to describe.

Over the years, the two distinguishing features of closed-end funds
have fallen into enough disfavor to limit their growth and importance.
Thus, there are fewer closed-end funds than open-end funds, and, they
have not grown significantly in recent years.

Since closed-end funds are essentially marketable shares of common
stock, their one-period rates of return are calculated using Eq. (2-2), just
like common stock returns.

2-7 EMPIRICAL EVIDENCE[8]

Table 2-1 at the beginning of this chapter suggests that U.S. government
bonds are the least risky investment and have the lowest rate of income of
the various types of securities, on average. And common stocks tend to
have the highest risk and rate of return, on average. Some explicit numerical analysis of empirical evidence is offered to substantiate these
suggestions.

A share of IBM common stock and a marketable U.S. Treasury bond
are compared. These two securities were selected for comparison because
they are so different. One is a residual-income security involving ownership risks; the other is a fixed-interest debt security involving no risk of
bankruptcy or missed payments.

[7] For a discussion of the prices of closed-end shares, see Ken J. Boudreaux, "The Pricing of
Mutual Fund Shares," *Financial Analysts Journal,* January–February 1974, pp. 26–32.
[8] For a risk-return analysis of preferred stock see John Bildersee, "Some Aspects of the Performance of Non-Convertible Preferred Stocks," *Journal of Finance,* December 1973, pp.
1187–1201.

Time Periods Analyzed

For purposes of this inquiry, the stock and the bond are observed from 1964 until 1974—one decade. A decade is long enough for temporary market disequilibriums to pass so that the long-run equilibrium tendencies of these two securities should emerge.

Rather than observe the securities only at the beginning and the end of the decade, they will be observed every 6 months during the decade.

TABLE 2-4 DATA FOR U.S. TREASURY BOND

Name of issuer: U.S. Treasury   Researcher: Mark Lewis
Type of security: Marketable bond   Face value: $1,000
Fixed income: 3 percent of face value per annum
Maturity date (if any): February 15, 1995
Source of data: Bank and Quotation Record

Half years	Beginning market price, $	Semi-annual interest, $	Semiannual rate of income, %†	Annualized rate of return, %‡
1974-I	742.50	15	n.a.§	n.a.§
1973-II	740.00	15	2.36	4.72
1973-I	782.50	15	−3.61	−7.21
1972-II	762.50	15	4.59	9.18
1972-I	789.38	15	−1.50	3.01
1971-II	726.25	15	12.13	24.26
1971-I	685.63	15	8.11	16.22
1970-II	653.75	15	7.17	14.34
1970-I	642.50	15	4.09	8.17
1969-II	703.75	15	−6.57	−13.14
1969-I	983.44	15	−16.75	−33.50 Lowest return
1968-II	786.88	15	26.89	53.77 High return
1968-I	758.13	15	5.77	11.54
1967-II	795.63	15	−2.77	−5.54
1967-I	840.00	15	−3.5	−7.0
1966-II	805.00	15	6.21	12.42
1966-I	831.88	15	−1.43	−2.86
1965-II	863.13	15	−1.88	−3.76
1965-I	887.81	15	−1.09	−2.18
1964-II	864.38	15	4.44	8.88
1964-I	845.63	15	4.0	8.0

Mean: 4.49 percent
Variance: 309.32
Standard deviation: 17.59 percent

† The semiannual rate of income is calculated with Eq. (2-1).
‡ The *annualized* rate of return is twice the semiannual rate of return, that is, the annualized rate of return equals

$$r_t = \frac{2[(p_{t+1} - p_t) + i_t]}{p_t}$$

§ n.a. means not available because 1974-II price is not shown.

This will produce 20 observations instead of only 2. In essence, it is assumed that the securities are purchased, held 6 months, sold, and then repurchased and held for another 6-month period, repetitively. This is a good framework in which to analyze a security's risk and return characteristics.

Raw Data for the Bond

The raw data for the marketable Treasury bond are shown in Table 2-4. The bond pays a 3 percent coupon rate on its face value of $1,000; that is, the owner of the bond receives $30 interest each year, or, actually, $15 every 6 months. When the bond matures on February 15, 1995, its owner will receive the $1,000 face value. In the meantime, the market price fluctuates freely. The *income* to the owner of the bond is $15 interest every 6 months plus or minus whatever capital gain or loss has occurred during the period. Thus, the owner's rate of income per period is calculated with Eq. (2-1) on page 15.

Raw Data for the Common Stock

The raw data for the IBM common stock are shown in Table 2-5. The data sheet is more complicated for the common stock than for the bond because of stock splits and stock dividends, that is, changes in the unit of account. Columns 1 and 2 in Table 2-5 show the reported prices and dividends. Column 3 indicates what changes in the unit of account occurred. For example, a 2 for 1 stock split or 100 percent stock dividend occurred in May 1968. Columns 4 and 5 show the price and dividend data after they have been adjusted for the changes in the unit of account. For example, all reported prices and dividends prior to the 2 for 1 split in May 1968 are halved before being entered in the columns for adjusted data. If these adjustments for changes in the unit of account had not been made, it would appear as if a $677 investment in IBM in January 1968 would have fallen to a market value of $355 in July 1968. In fact, what happened is that the $677 share grew in value to two shares at $355 each during the 6 months, with a total value of $2 \times \$355 = \$710$. The owner's rate of income is calculated with the adjusted data using Eq. (2-2) on pages 20 and 21.

Table 2-6 compares the IBM stock and the Treasury bond with reference to several points. The IBM stock earned much more income per dollar invested than the Treasury bond and its rate of income was more erratic than the income from the bond. Thus, the stock was a riskier investment.

Figure 2-1 is a smoothed approximation of the relative-frequency distribution of returns from the two assets. This graph shows that the stock has considerably more *variability in its rate of income* — that is, risk — than the bond because its probability distribution is wider. The purpose of this numerical example is to add realism to the abstract assertion in Table 2-1 that common stock is riskier and has higher average returns than bonds.

TABLE 2-5 DATA FOR IBM COMMON STOCK

Name of firm researched: IBM   Researcher: Peggy Cava
Type of security: Common stock
Industry: Electronics
Source of data: Bank and Quotation Record

		Reported data		Adjusted data			
		Beginning market price, $	Semi-annual div., $	Change in unit of account	Beginning market price, $	Semi-annual div., $	Annualized rate of return†
Date	Half years						
		(1)	(2)	(3)	(4)	(5)	(6)
1/2	1974-I	246.75	2.80		246.75	2.80	n.a.‡
7/2	1973-II	314	2.80		314	2.80	−41.05
1/1	1973-I	404.5	2.70	5-4 5/10/66	323.625	2.16	−4.61
7/3	1972-II	393.75	2.70		315	2.16	6.85
1/3	1972-I	338.5	2.60		270.75	2.08	34.2
7/1	1971-II	317	2.60		253.625	2.08	15.2
1/4	1971-I	364.75	2.40		291.75	1.92	−24.9
7/1	1970-II	250	2.40		200	1.92	93.7§
1/2	1970-I	364.75	2.00		291.75	1.60	−61.8¶
7/1	1969-II	337.75	1.60		270.25	1.28	16.9
7/2	1969-I	315	1.30		252	1.04	15.3
7/1	1968-II	355	1.30	2-1 5/9/68	284	1.04	−21.8
7/2	1968-I	677	2.60		266.75	1.04	27.4
7/1	1967-II	499	2.20		199.625	.88	52.2
1/3	1967-I	370	2.20	2.5% 5/4/67	144.125	.86	77.0
7/1	1966-II	352.25	2.20		137.375	.86	11.2
1/3	1966-I	497.5	2.60	3-2 5/3/66	128.75	.816	14.0
7/1	1965-II	458	3.00		119.25	.78	17.4
1/4	1965-I	410.5	3.00		106.75	.78	24.6
7/1	1964-II	478.75	2.50		124.375	.57	−27.2
1/2	1964-I	510	2.50	5-4 5/5/64	106	.59	35.8

Mean: 11.82 percent
Variance: 1449.27
Standard deviation: 38.05

† The annualized rate of return is twice the 6-month return; that is, the annualized return equals

$$r_t = \frac{[(p_{t+1} - p_t) + d_t]^2}{p_t}$$

‡ n.a. means not available because 1974-II price is not shown.
§ Highest return.
¶ Lowest return.

TABLE 2-6 COMPARISON OF IBM COMMON STOCK AND U.S. TREASURY BOND OVER DECADE 1964 TO 1974

	Treasury bond	IBM stock
Arithmetic average return per year	4.49%	11.82%
Range of returns	20 points	32 percentage points
Standard deviation of returns	17.59%	38.05%

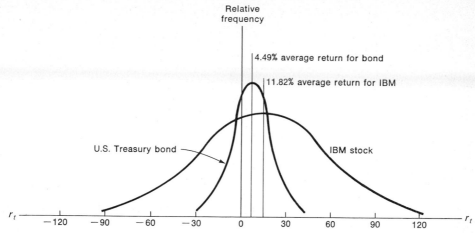

Relative
frequency

4.49% average return for bond

11.82% average return for IBM

U.S. Treasury bond

IBM stock

r_t

−120   −90   −60   −30   0   30   60   90   120

r_t

FIG. 2-1 Smoothed relative-frequency distributions comparing rates of return for IBM common stock and U.S. Treasury bonds.

QUESTIONS

1 Differentiate between the coupon rate of a bond and its yield. Which should be more important to the potential investor?

2 Why can a call provision be potentially detrimental to a bondholder or preferred stockholder?

3 In the event of bankruptcy and liquidation, in what order (from first to last) will the contributors of capital be repaid?

4 Why is an issue of participating bonds or participating preferred stock rather infrequent?

5 "Stock dividend and stock splits have no effect on the value of a company." True, false, or uncertain? Discuss.

6 How much importance should be attached to book value and par value in evaluating the investment qualities of a corporation's common stock?

7 Why may a firm wish to raise capital through a convertible securities issue? Why may a firm prefer not to issue convertible securities?

8 From the point of view of the investor, what factors should be considered before investing in a convertible security rather than a straight bond or preferred stock?

9 What are the differences between U.S. government marketable and nonmarketable securities? Give examples of each.

10 What characteristics of municipal bonds are important to the potential investor?

11 Calculate five annual rates of return for Dreyfus and T. Rowe Price mutual funds, using Eq. (2-3). The raw data needed may be obtained from the reference book *Investment Companies* (published annually by Arthur Wiesenberger Company). Which fund did better before load fees? Which did better after the appropriate load fees are deducted at the start of the five-year period?

SELECTED REFERENCES

Clendenin, J. C., and George A. Christy, *Introduction to Investments,* 5th ed. (New York: McGraw-Hill, 1969).
    Chapters 3–7 provide a nonmathematical explanation of the various types of securities.

Sauvain, H., *Investments Management,* 4th ed. (Englewood Cliffs, N.J.: Prentice-Hall).
    Chapters 2 and 3 provide a nonmathematical discussion of securities.

Scott, I. O., Jr., *Government Securities Markets* (New York: McGraw-Hill, 1965).
    A nonmathematical discussion of U.S. government bonds and their markets may be found in chaps. 1–3.

Weston, J. F., and E. Brigham, *Managerial Finance,* 4th ed. (New York: Holt, 1972).
    Chapters 13–15 present a nonmathematical description of securities and a review of some relevant literature.

Wiesenberger Services, Inc., *Investment Companies* (New York), published annually.
    This large reference book explains investment companies, summarizes the relevant laws, and gives raw financial data for many open-end and closed-end funds.

APPENDIX TO CHAPTER 2
Mortgage Securities

Mortgages are debt instruments whose collateral is residential or business properties. They are analogous to a corporate bond which has some specific asset for collateral. Mortgage contracts are marketable securities, and the market prices of even the highest-quality mortgage security, like those of corporate bonds, fluctuate minute by minute. However, mortgage securities differ from corporate bonds in several respects.

A2-1 MORTGAGE ORIGINATION

The average home buyer in the United States buys a $35,000 home, puts $9,000 down, and obtains a $26,000 mortgage to finance the balance. This average mortgage is scheduled to be paid off with monthly installment payments of about $200 per month for 25 years. However, many families sell their homes and buy new ones before their mortgages are fully paid off. Because of these prepayments, home mortgages are frequently paid off early — in about 12 years, on average.

Mortgages have long been favored investments for savings and loan associations (S&Ls), life insurance companies, and banks that originated mortgages themselves (by making mortgage loans to qualified applicants). Mortgage companies originate many mortgages, sell them to mortgage investors, collect the mortgage payments, and otherwise service the mortgage for a fee.

Some of the unique characteristics of mortgages kept them from becoming popular investment securities in years past. For example, the large denomination of most mortgage securities precluded small investors from being able to procure a diversified portfolio of mortgages. And the paperwork and administration involved in collecting monthly payments, paying property taxes, and occasionally foreclosing (less than 1 percent of all mortgages) deterred many investors, too. Furthermore, mortgages were not liquid. Secondary markets where mortgages could be bought and sold like other securities did not exist until recent years. However, a series of related events during the past few decades have made mortgage investing much easier.

FHA and VA Insurance

The federal government started making home buying easier for Americans long ago. The Federal Housing Authority (FHA) was established in 1934, and the Veterans Administration (VA) in 1944, to provide default insurance on home mortgages. The two insurance programs are similar. Essentially, they indemnify the lender against all or part of the losses realized on a guaranteed loan if the home buyer cannot meet the mortgage payments.

The FHA and the VA charge .5 percent of the value of the mortgage per year for their insurance service. As a result of FHA and VA insurance, savings and loans associations, banks, life insurance companies, and other groups that loan mortgage money are more willing to make loans to some risky home buyers who show promise of honoring their debts. But perhaps the most interesting thing about these insurance programs is that the charges add up to more than the FHA's total costs and losses on repossessions — that is, they pay their own way. Furthermore, the FHA and VA paved the way for the Federal National Mortgage Association (FNMA) and other government agencies which have made mortgage investing a viable alternative for small and large investors alike.

A2-2 NEW GOVERNMENT MORTGAGE AGENCIES

Fannie Mae

The Federal National Mortgage Association, nicknamed Fannie Mae, was created by an act of Congress in 1938. FNMA's job, as originally conceived, was to use the proceeds from selling U.S. government agency bonds—that is, her own FNMA bonds—to buy FHA- or VA-insured mortgages. Fannie did not interfere with the VA's and FHA's insurance programs in any way. She snared mortgage capital by selling her bonds—that is, bonds backed by a guarantee of the United States government—to investors who were unwilling to take the risk of investing in private business. Then this money was channeled into the mortgage markets. Investors who wish to buy FNMA bonds will find them listed in *The Wall Street Journal* every day, along with the other U.S. government and government agency bonds. (See Fig. A2-1.) Many stockbrokers are able to buy and sell FNMA bonds.

Fannie's goals. FNMA's purpose, as stated in the congressional charter which created her, is to help the housing business in several ways. First, by pouring the money from FNMA bonds (which are backed by the U.S. government) into the purchase of mortgages, Fannie was supposed to make more mortgage loans available to home buyers. Second, by increasing the supply of mortgage money available, Fannie Mae should put downward pressure on mortgage interest rates. Third, Fannie was charged with helping to smooth out any temporary restrictions in the availability of mortgage credit. Thus, families that must move during a period of "tight mortgage money" are more likely to be able to get a mortgage to buy another house.

Public to private. In an unusual move, Congress passed the 1968 Housing Act which transformed Fannie Mae from a government agency into a private corporation. She entered private corporate life with a flourish. During 1969 and 1970 there was a period of tight credit (called a credit crunch). As a result, many families that would ordinarily have no problem getting mortgages suddenly encountered difficulties in securing them. But, as her congressional charter stipulated, Fannie sold her FNMA bonds and bought FHA- and VA-insured mortgages from mortgage bankers and others who had been making mortgage loans. Thus she replenished the mortgage lenders' supply of funds and quietly helped would-be home buyers get mortgages that might not have been available to them otherwise.[1]

[1] Some of Fannie Mae's critics suggest that part of the money invested in FNMA's bonds may be savings deposits withdrawn from banks and S&Ls. This problem tends to be at its worst during periods when FNMA's bonds yield higher rates of interest than savings deposits. It is not possible to trace the flows of funds closely enough to measure this substitution of FNMA bonds for savings deposits. But, to the extent this substitution occurs, Fannie is not increasing the total supply of mortgage credit as much as her total borrowings would indicate.

Government, Agency and Miscellaneous Securities

Tuesday, September 23, 1975

Over-the-Counter Quotations: Source on request.
Decimals in bid-and-asked and bid changes represent 32nds (101.1 means 101 1-32). a-Plus 1-64. b-Yield to call date. d-Minus 1-64.

Treasury Bonds and Notes

Rate	Mat. date			Bid	Asked	Bid Chg.	Yld.
8⅜s,	1975	Sep	n	100.0	100.2	.....	3.64
7s,	1975	Nov	n	99.31	100.3	.....	6.16
7s,	1975	Dec	n	100.0	100.4	− .1	6.42
5⅞s,	1976	Feb	n	99.13	99.17	.....	7.07
6¼s,	1976	Feb	n	99.18	99.22	− .1	7.04
8s,	1976	Mar	n	100.11	100.15	.....	7.06
5¾s,	1976	May	n	99.1	99.5	.....	7.12
6½s,	1976	May	n	99.16	99.20	.....	7.11
6s,	1976	May	n	99.2	99.6	.....	7.24
8¾s,	1976	Jun	n	100.31	101.3	− .1	7.26
6½s,	1976	Aug	n	99.3	99.7	.....	7.42
7½s,	1976	Aug	n	100.1	100.5	.....	7.32
5⅞s,	1976	Aug	n	98.16	98.20	.....	7.42
8¼s,	1976	Sep	n	100.18	100.22	+ .10	7.53
6½s,	1976	Oct	n	98.25	98.29	.....	7.51
6¼s,	1976	Nov	n	98.17	98.21	.....	7.50
7⅛s,	1976	Nov	n	99.13	99.17	+ .2	7.55
7¼s,	1976	Dec	n	99.17	99.21	+ .2	7.54
8s,	1977	Feb	n	100.13	100.17	− .2	7.60
6s,	1977	Feb	n	97.17	97.21	+ .1	7.77
6½s,	1977	Mar	n	97.31	98.3	.....	7.86
7⅜s,	1977	Apr	n	99.3	99.7	− .1	7.91
6⅞s,	1977	May	n	98.11	98.15	− .1	7.89
9s,	1977	May	n	101.18	101.22	− .1	7.88
6¾s,	1977	May	n	98.1	98.5	− .1	7.94
6½s,	1977	Jun	n	97.16	97.20	− .2	7.97
7½s,	1977	July	n	99.3	99.5	− .1	8.00
7¼s,	1977	Aug	n	99.18	99.26	.....	7.86
8¼s,	1977	Aug	n	100.10	100.12	− .4	8.04
7¾s,	1977	Nov	n	99.14	99.22	− .1	7.91
6¼s,	1978	Feb	n	96.6	96.14	− .4	7.92
7⅛s,	1978	May	n	97.18	97.26	− .2	8.06
7⅞s,	1978	May	n	99.7	99.11	− .4	8.15
7⅝s,	1978	Aug	n	98.18	98.22	− .3	8.16
8¾s,	1978	Aug	n	101.14	101.22	− .4	8.10
6s,	1978	Nov	n	94.6	94.14	− .4	8.04
7⅞s,	1979	May	n	98.31	99.7	− .5	8.13
7¾s,	1979	Jun	n	98.18	98.22	− .2	8.16
6¼s,	1979	Aug	n	93.16	93.24	− .6	8.16
8½s,	1979	Sep	n	100.24	100.28	+ .1	8.24
6⅝s,	1979	Nov	n	94.22	94.30	− .6	8.09
7s,	1979	Nov	n	96.15	96.23	− .3	7.94
4s,	1980	Feb		84.26	85.26	.....	7.89
6⅞s,	1980	May	n	95.17	95.25	− .1	7.98
9s,	1980	Aug	n	103.1	103.9	− .5	8.18
3½s,	1980	Nov		81.28	82.28	− .2	7.59
7s,	1981	Feb	n	94.22	94.30	− .2	8.18
7⅜s,	1981	Feb	n	96.8	96.16	.....	8.20
7s,	1981	Aug		94.24	95.24	.....	7.92
7¾s,	1981	Nov	n	97.20	97.28	− .5	8.22
6⅜s,	1982	Feb		91.0	92.0	.....	8.00
8s,	1982	May	n	98.20	98.24	− .4	8.24
8⅛s,	1982	Aug	n	99.1	99.5	− .7	8.29
3¼s,	1978-83	Jun		78.0	79.0	− .28	6.79
6⅜s,	1984	Aug		90.24	91.24	− .8	7.67
3¼s,	1985	May		77.24	78.24	−1.2	6.21
4¼s,	1975-85	May		78.12	79.12	− .20	7.25
6⅛s,	1986	Nov		85.18	86.18	− .8	7.97
3½s,	1990	Feb		77.20	78.20	−1.2	5.70
8¼s,	1990	May		98.16	99.0	+ .24	8.37
4¼s,	1987-92	Aug		77.24	78.24	− .30	6.32
4s,	1988-93	Feb		77.28	78.28	− .30	5.97
6¾s,	1993	Feb		86.2	87.2	− .10	8.16
7½s,	1988-93	Aug		91.30	92.30	− .8	8.26
4⅛s,	1989-94	May		77.24	78.24	−1.2	6.04
3s,	1995	Feb		77.26	78.26	− .28	4.68
7s,	1993-98	May		86.4	87.4	− .12	8.27
3½s,	1998	Nov		77.24	78.24	−1.6	5.06
8½s,	1994-99	May		99.8	99.24	− .10	8.52
7⅞s,	1995-00	Feb		93.16	94.16	− .10	8.44
8⅜s,	1995-00	Aug		98.24	99.0	.....	8.47
8¼s,	2000-05	May		96.20	97.4	− .14	8.33

n— Treasury Notes.

U.S. Treas. Bills

Mat	Bid Discount	Ask Discount	Mat	Bid Discount	Ask Discount
9-25	6.39	5.95	1-15	6.64	6.48
10- 2	6.19	5.75	1-22	6.70	6.54
10- 9	6.15	5.79	1-29	6.75	6.61
10-16	6.18	5.76	1-31	6.87	6.73
10-21	6.26	5.80	2- 5	6.80	6.66
10-23	6.30	5.90	2-10	6.82	6.68
10-30	6.29	5.91	2-13	6.85	6.71
11- 6	6.34	6.10	2-19	6.88	6.74
11-13	6.36	6.14	2-26	6.90	6.76
11-18	6.39	6.17	3- 4	6.90	6.78
11-20	6.40	6.24	3- 9	6.90	6.76
11-28	6.35	6.21	3-11	6.90	6.78
12- 4	6.40	6.28	3-18	6.89	6.79
12-11	6.40	6.28	4- 6	6.96	6.80
12-16	6.40	6.24	5- 4	7.05	6.89
12-18	6.37	6.27	6- 1	7.11	6.95
12-26	6.36	6.30	6-29	7.13	6.97
1- 2	6.55	6.39	7-27	7.21	7.05
1- 8	6.59	6.43	8-24	7.20	7.08
1-13	6.65	6.49	9-21	7.19	7.17

Fed. Home Loan Bk.

Rate	Mat	Bid	Asked	Yld
6½	11-75	99.28	100.0	6.36
7.05	11-75	99.31	100.3	6.33
9.10	11-75	100.10	100.14	6.25
7⅜	2-76	99.28	100.4	7.02
8.70	2-76	100.14	100.22	6.95
8¼	2-76	100.14	100.22	7.00
9.20	2-76	100.20	100.28	6.98
7.20	5-76	99.24	100.0	7.18
7.45	5-76	99.30	100.6	7.13
7.80	8-76	99.28	100.12	7.36
9.55	8-76	101.12	101.28	7.38
8.60	11-76	100.20	101.4	7.56
9.55	11-76	101.24	102.8	7.49
7.20	2-77	98.20	99.4	7.86
8.05	2-77	99.28	100.12	7.76
6.95	5-77	97.28	98.12	8.00
8.70	5-77	100.20	101.4	7.95
7.15	8-77	97.24	98.8	8.15
8.80	8-77	100.20	101.4	8.15
6.75	11-77	96.28	97.12	8.09
7.45	11-77	98.8	98.24	8.08
9.15	11-77	101.12	101.28	8.18
9⅜	2-78	102.4	102.20	8.15
7.60	5-78	98.0	98.16	8.23
9.10	11-78	101.20	102.4	8.32
8.65	2-79	100.4	100.20	8.43
9.45	2-79	102.16	103.0	8.42
8.65	5-79	100.4	100.20	8.44
8¾	5-79	100.12	100.28	8.46
9½	8-79	103.0	103.1	8.43
7½	11-79	96.12	96.28	8.40
8.15	11-79	98.20	99.4	8.40
7.05	2-80	94.20	95.4	8.39
7¾	2-80	96.24	97.24	8.37
7.80	10-80	96.20	97.20	8.38
8.65	11-81	100.1	100.28	8.46
6.60	11-81	90.16	91.16	8.39
8⅝	2-82	100.10	100.18	8.51
7.30	5-83	93.8	94.8	8.33
7⅜	11-83	92.24	93.8	8.54
8¼	5-84	100.12	101.12	8.52
7⅛	11-93	87.8	88.8	8.67

World Bank Bonds

Rate	Mat	Bid	Asked	Yld
6½	1-76	99.16	99.28	6.84
3	3-76	98.8	99.0	5.43
6.90	3-76	99.8	99.24	7.44
9	9-76	100.24	101.8	7.75
4½	1-77	95.16	96.0	7.91
6⅜	1-77	97.12	97.24	8.24
6.40	3-77	96.28	97.12	8.35
4¼	5-78	90.16	91.0	8.18
4¼	1-79	88.0	88.16	8.31
8	1-80	97.12	97.28	8.60
8.30	7-80	98.16	98.28	8.59
4¾	11-80	84.16	85.8	8.37
3¼	10-81	84.0	85.0	6.29
4½	2-82	80.24	81.16	8.3[illegible]
8.15	1-85	93.8	93.24	8.83
5	2-85	76.12	77.4	8.53
8.60	7-85	98.4	98.16	8.83
4½	2-90	65.16	66.4	8.65
5⅜	7-91	70.0	71.0	8.81
5⅜	4-92	69.16	70.16	8.80
5⅞	9-93	72.16	73.16	8.85
6½	3-94	77.16	78.16	8.89
6⅜	10-94	76.8	77.8	8.87
8⅝	8-95	94.0	95.0	9.18
8⅛	8-96	89.24	90.24	9.12

FIC Bank Debs.

Rate	Mat	Bid	Asked	Yld
7.35	10-75	99.31	100.1	5.19
7.05	11-75	99.30	100.2	6.17
6.15	12-75	99.25	99.29	6.44
6.05	1-76	99.19	99.23	6.88
6.65	1-76	99.25	99.29	6.89
6.60	2-76	99.22	99.26	6.96
6.15	3-76	99.13	99.17	7.12
5.80	4-76	99.3	99.7	7.27
7	5-76	99.21	99.25	7.30
7.60	6-76	100.0	100.4	7.37
7.70	7-76	100.1	100.3	7.57
7.10	1-77	98.16	99.0	7.93
8.70	4-77	100.20	101.4	7.90
7.10	1-78	97.8	97.24	8.20
7.40	1-79	96.28	97.12	8.33
7.40	1-80	95.24	96.8	8.46

Inter-Amer. Devel. Bk.

Rate	Mat	Bid	Asked	Yld
4¼	12-82	80.16	81.16	7.63
4½	4-84	77.0	78.0	8.14
4½	11-84	76.0	77.0	8.13
8¼	1-85	95.24	96.0	8.85
8	3-85	94.8	94.20	8.85
5.20	1-92	68.0	69.0	8.82
6½	11-92	78.0	79.0	8.91
6⅝	11-93	78.24	79.24	8.90
8⅝	10-95	94.0	95.0	8.18

Postal Service

Rate	Mat	Bid	Asked	Yld
6⅞	2-97	79.04	80.04	8.98

FNMA Issues

Rate	Mat	Bid	Asked	Yld
5.70	12-75	99.21	99.25	6.66
8¼	12-75	100.7	100.11	6.42
5.65	3-76	99.2	99.10	7.18
7⅛	3-76	99.24	100.0	7.11
5.85	6-76	98.16	99.0	7.30
6.70	6-76	99.4	99.20	7.23
10	6-76	101.12	101.28	7.21
5.85	9-76	98.0	98.16	7.50
6⅛	9-76	98.8	98.24	7.50
7½	9-76	99.20	100.4	7.36
6¼	12-76	97.28	98.12	7.67
7.45	12-76	99.8	99.24	7.65
8.45	12-76	100.12	100.28	7.66
4½	2-77	95.0	95.24	7.81
6.30	3-77	97.12	97.28	7.87
7.05	3-77	98.8	98.24	7.97
8.30	3-77	100.11	100.15	7.95
6⅜	6-77	96.28	97.12	8.04
6½	6-77	97.4	97.20	8.00
7.20	6-77	98.8	98.24	7.99
6⅞	9-77	97.16	98.0	7.99
7.85	9-77	99.8	99.24	7.99
7¼	12-77	97.28	98.12	8.06
7.55	12-77	98.16	99.0	8.04
8.45	3-78	100.0	100.16	8.22
6.70	3-78	96.8	96.24	8.18
7.15	6-78	96.28	97.12	8.24
7.45	6-78	97.16	98.0	8.28
7.15	9-78	96.16	97.0	8.31
6¾	12-78	95.4	95.20	8.32
8.95	12-78	101.0	101.16	8.40
7¼	3-79	96.8	96.24	8.35
7.85	6-79	97.28	98.12	8.36
9.80	6-79	103.8	104.8	8.43
6.40	9-79	92.28	93.12	8.40
7.80	9-79	97.16	98.0	8.40
6.55	12-79	93.0	93.16	8.41
7¼	12-79	97.4	97.20	8.43
6⅞	3-80	93.12	94.12	8.41
7¼	3-80	95.4	95.20	8.45
8½	6-80	99.20	100.4	8.46
7½	9-80	95.16	96.16	8.38
8¼	9-80	100.16	100.20	8.59
6.60	12-80	91.12	92.12	8.44
7.05	3-81	93.4	94.4	8.41
7¼	6-81	93.24	94.24	8.42
7¼	9-81	93.20	94.20	8.41
9.70	9-81	104.12	105.12	8.53
7.30	12-81	93.20	94.20	8.43
8⅞	3-82	100.28	101.12	8.59
6.65	6-82	90.4	91.4	8.40
6.80	9-82	90.16	91.16	8.44
7.35	12-82	93.4	94.4	8.45
6¾	6-83	89.16	90.16	8.45
7.30	6-83	92.16	93.16	8.46
6¾	9-83	89.12	90.12	8.43
8	12-83	96.8	96.24	8.56
6¼	6-84	86.16	87.16	8.29
8.20	7-84	97.12	97.28	8.55
7.95	9-84	95.12	96.12	8.54
6.90	12-84	90.0	91.0	8.32
7.65	3-85	93.24	94.8	8.55
7	3-92	85.4	86.4	8.59
7.05	6-92	85.20	86.20	8.57
7.10	12-97	83.20	84.20	8.67

Federal Land Bank

Rate	Mat	Bid	Asked	Yld
7.20	10-75	100.0	100.3	5.77
7.40	10-75	100.0	100.3	5.95
6¼	1-76	99.18	99.26	6.77
9.20	1-76	100.14	100.22	6.88
5	2-76	98.20	99.4	7.14
6¼	4-76	99.0	99.16	7.15
8¼	4-76	100.4	100.20	7.10
5⅜	7-76	97.16	98.16	7.28
7.05	7-76	99.12	99.28	7.19
7.15	10-76	99.0	99.16	7.64
7.20	10-76	99.4	99.20	7.56
7.45	1-77	99.0	99.16	7.84
8¼	4-77	100.0	100.16	7.90
7½	7-77	98.16	99.0	8.09
6.35	10-77	96.4	96.20	8.15
8.70	1-78	100.16	101.0	8.21
4⅛	2-78-73	90.8	91.8	8.21
5⅛	4-78	92.0	93.0	8.20
7.60	4-78	98.0	98.16	8.26
6.40	7-78	94.16	95.16	8.21
9.15	7-78	101.12	101.28	8.38
7.35	10-78	96.28	97.12	8.33
5	1-79	89.16	90.16	8.33
7.10	1-79	95.28	96.12	8.37
6.85	4-79	94.12	95.12	8.37
7.15	7-79	95.16	96.0	8.39
6.80	10-79	93.20	94.20	8.38
6.70	1-80	93.0	94.0	8.38
7½	7-80	95.12	96.12	8.43
8.70	10-80	100.8	100.24	8.51
6.70	4-81	91.16	92.16	8.41
9.10	7-81	101.20	102.20	8.51
7.80	1-82	96.4	96.20	8.50
6.90	4-82	91.16	92.16	8.41
8.15	4-82	97.20	98.4	8.53
7.30	10-82	92.24	93.24	8.49
8.20	1-83	98.0	98.16	8.48
7.30	10-83	92.8	93.8	8.47
8.10	7-85	96.20	97.4	8.54

Bank for Co-ops

Rate	Mat	Bid	Asked	Yld
5.85	10-75	99.30	100.0	5.69
6.15	11-75	99.27	99.31	6.29
5.80	12-75	99.23	99.27	6.54
5.65	1-76	99.18	99.22	6.71
6.80	2-76	99.25	99.29	7.00
7.40	3-76	100.0	100.4	7.07
7½	4-76	100.1	100.3	7.31
7.70	4-77	99.0	99.16	8.05
8.55	10-78	100.8	100.12	8.41
8 [illegible]	10-79	98.8	98.24	8.37

GNMA Issues

Rate	Bid	Asked	Yld
6½	82.0	82.24	8.97
8	92.8	93.8	8.96
8½	95.8	96.0	9.02
9	99.8	100.0	8.95

FIG. A2-1 U.S. government and agency bond listings from *The Wall Street Journal.*

Conventional mortgages. In 1970 Congress passed the Emergency Home Finance Act which, among other things, allowed FNMA to buy uninsured mortgages — or conventional mortgages, as they are usually called. Since about two-thirds of all mortgages on single-family homes are conventional mortgages, this new power widened Fannie's scope of operations.

As a result of her powers to raise large quantities of cash at market interest rates by selling government-guaranteed FNMA bonds, and also because of her congressional instructions to steady the housing business by buying mortgages, Fannie's holding of mortgages grew from slightly over $1 billion in 1952 to more than $18 billion by 1972. But this growth does not mean that FNMA never sells mortgages.

Making a secondary market. To interest more investors in buying mortgages, Congress directed Fannie Mae to try maintaining a secondary mortgage market. Accordingly, Fannie buys mortgages during periods of tight credit and sells a few mortgages when credit is plentiful. Such countercyclical buying and selling not only tend to smooth the ups and downs in the mortgage and housing business, but also to provide a secondary market which encourages more investors to invest in home mortgages. These secondary mortgages increase the liquidity and flexibility of all mortgage investors.

Ginnie Mae

In 1970 when Congress allowed FNMA to buy conventional mortgages, it also created a new government home-financing agency to replace its departed daughter FNMA. The new agency is officially named the Government National Mortgage Association (GNMA), but it has a nickname — Ginnie Mae.

Ginnie and Fannie are sisterlike creations of the federal government. Both perform similar home-financing functions and both are accountable to the Secretary of Housing and Urban Development. However, they differ in two important aspects. First, Ginnie Mae is still a federal agency, while Fannie is a private corporation. And second, whereas Fannie sells her own bonds to raise money, Ginnie borrows temporarily from the U.S. Treasury to buy mortgages and then sells them.

GNMA finances mortgages by first buying FHA- or VA-insured mortgages from mortgage bankers or others who may have originally made mortgage loans to the home buyers. Ginnie buys mortgages with money she borrowed from the Treasury and sometimes "pools" them. These pools have a minimum value of $2 million and contain mortgages on similar types of housing at similar interest rates, which are all VA- or FHA-insured. Ginnie then sells either individual mortgages or "shares" in pools of mortgages she has formed to obtain funds to repay the Treasury.

Proceeds from selling "shares" in a pool of mortgages entitle each "shareholder" to a piece of every mortgage in the pool. But these "shares" are riskless because all mortgages in the pool must be insured by the FHA or VA or Ginnie will not put them in the pool. Since the assets behind the "shares" in the pool are mortgages, the "shares" are often called *mortgage-backed securities.* These securities are also frequently referred to as *GNMA pass-throughs* because all the monthly mortgage payments by home buyers to the pool are passed through it to the investors who bought "shares." Thus, the investors who bought pass-through securities backed by mortgages receive guaranteed monthly payments until their investment is repaid with interest. GNMA also offers special bond-type pools in which the principal is reinvested as the mortgages are paid off. Then, when the mortgages all mature, the principal is repaid in one lump sum. GNMA's pass-throughs and bonds make good investments for risk-averse investors. They may be purchased in denominations of $25,000 from stock brokerages.

Freddie Mac for the S&Ls

Savings and loan associations take in millions of dollars every year and invest most of this money in mortgages. In fact, S&Ls make more mortgage loans than any other group of investors in the United States.

The S&Ls wanted an organization like Fannie Mae to provide them with the liquidity offered by a secondary mortgage market. But they wanted an agency which specialized in dealing with S&Ls. So, in 1970, Congress empowered the Federal Home Loan Bank Board, the government agency which oversees S&Ls, to start the Federal Home Loan Mortgage Corporation (FHLMC), nicknamed Freddie Mac.

Freddie Mac, a government agency, sells its own government-insured bonds and uses the proceeds to buy either insured or conventional mortgages from federally insured savings institutions. Freddie cannot issue pass-through securities like his sister organization Ginnie Mae. And he is not a private corporation like Fannie Mae. But they are all federally chartered organizations which have similar basic purposes—the financing of homes. And they have changed mortgage markets in the United States.

Evaluating the Benefits from the Mortgage Agencies

Measuring mortgage returns. A mortgage investor's one-period rate of return is calculated like the return on a bond—using Eq. (2-1) on page 15—if the mortgage is bought and sold before it is paid off. But, if the mortgage is held until finally paid off by the home owner, its rate of return is calculated like the yield to maturity from a bond. That is, the mortgage's effective multiperiod yield is the discount rate which causes the present value of all the mortgage's cashflows (that is, monthly payments) to be equal to the cost of the mortgage to the mortgage investor. (See Fig. A2-1 for a sample yield on FNMA and GNMA bonds.)

The rates of return from mortgages are calculated like bond yields to maturity for corporate and government bonds. (See Mathematical Appendix D, at the end of the book, regarding present value calculations.)

Mortgage money's geographic mobility. When Fannie buys mortgages on West Coast homes, she may pay for them with money from FNMA bonds sold on the East Coast. And when Ginnie buys mortgages in the North, she may pay for them with GNMA pass-throughs sold in the South. Also, Freddie Mac may buy mortgages from S&Ls that need cash in one part of the country and sell FHLMC bonds to finance purchases in some other place where cash is plentiful. As a result of transactions like these, mortgage credit flows freely from state to state. The funds are raised where they are plentiful and invested where they are scarce. This means that the money is spent where it is needed most, no matter where it comes from.

Lower mortgage interest rates. The funds that FNMA, GNMA, and FHLMC pull in are obtained at government agency bond rates, which are low. As a result of these low-risk, and therefore low-return, sources of capital and other factors, financial analysts estimate that mortgage interest rates are at least .5 percent less than they used to be at any given level of interest rates.[2] This second benefit from Fannie, Ginnie, and Freddie helps everyone who gets a mortgage loan, not just those whose mortgages they finance. Unfortunately, it does put private business borrowers in a weaker position, however.

Tight credit periods eased. FNMA, GNMA, and FHLMC also help home buyers and construction companies by smoothing the big hills and valleys (namely, the credit crunches) in mortgage credit which can occur. Thus, Fannie, Ginnie, and Freddie tend to concentrate their mortgage purchases in periods when credit is tight and when it is impossible for some credit-worthy families to get mortgages. This helps new home sales during those temporary credit crunches and reduces the risks faced by the home-building industry.

Housing starts dropped considerably during the credit crunches of 1966 and 1969–1970 because potential home buyers could not get mortgages. New construction might have dropped even more if the mortgage agencies had not been on hand to pour out mortgage money.

Mortgage investing expedited. The federal home-financing agencies have achieved some successes. By creating a viable secondary market for home

[2] J. B. Cohen and E. Zinbarg, "Investments Analysis and Portfolio Management" (Homewood, Ill.: Irwin, 1967), pp. 469–471, 702–703; William Atteberry, *Modern Real Estate Finance* (Columbus, Ohio: GRID, Inc., 1972), p. 287; and J. L. Kochan, "Federal Agency Issues: Newcomers in the Capital Market," *Economic Review of the Federal Reserve Bank of Cleveland*, February 1972.

mortgages, Fannie, Ginnie, and Freddie have strengthened the lending institutions that make mortgage loans and have increased the attractiveness of all phases of mortgage investing. And further developments in secondary markets to make it easier to buy and sell mortgage securities are continuing.

Amminet

In 1974 a nonprofit private corporation named Automated Mortgage Market Information Network—called Amminet—went into operation making a secondary mortgage market. Amminet is a computerized listing service for buyers and sellers of mortgages—it is like NASDAQ in the stock markets (as explained in Chap. 3), except that Amminet makes a market only in mortgage securities. It is sponsored by the members of the American Bankers Association, National Association of Savings Banks, National Savings and Loan League, U.S. League of Savings Associations, and the U.S. Department of Housing and Urban Development. Amminet is just one more force to reduce the costs of trading mortgages: It connects mortgage dealers from coast to coast and allows them to trade mortgages directly, inexpensively, and more rapidly.

A2-3 CONCLUSIONS ABOUT MORTGAGE INVESTING

Today mortgage investing is easier than ever before. The mortgage investor need never become involved in mortgage origination, payment collection, property taxes, and foreclosures—these matters are all handled by some mortgage-servicing company which remains in the background and performs its service for a fee. Mortgages are still not tiny securities like common stocks, which can be purchased through weekly payroll deduction plans. But they are liquid securities which institutional investors and substantial individuals should consider. Using GNMA pass-through securities, the mortgage investor can have monthly repayments. Or, lump-sum repayments are available with GNMA, FNMA, and FHLMC bonds. These U.S. government-insured instruments are practically riskless and offer higher rates of returns than some U.S. Treasury issues.

QUESTIONS

1 Compare and contrast the risk and rate of return from U.S. Treasury bonds and FNMA or GNMA bonds of a similar term to maturity.

2 Assume you are managing a portfolio containing mortgages. Where would you seek to buy and sell mortgages if your employer was a commercial bank? A savings and loan association? If you owned the portfolio yourself

as a private individual? What would each of the secondary markets require of your mortgages before it would trade them?

3 If you owned a Ginnie Mae pass-through security and one of the mortgages in your pool had to be foreclosed, how would you be affected?

4 How could you liquidate an investment in FNMA bonds?

SELECTED REFERENCES

Atteberry, William, *Modern Real Estate Finance* (Columbus, Ohio: GRID, Inc., 1972).
> This nonmathematical book contains detailed descriptions of the institutions of today's mortgage markets.

Federal Reserve Staff Study, *Ways to Moderate Fluctuations in Housing Construction,* 1972.
> This large book is composed of readings from the works of various economists. It contains no advanced mathematics but uses econometrics in some of its investigations related to mortgage financing.

Three

Securities Markets

Chapter 2 introduced the most frequently traded securities. Logical follow-up questions might be: How do these securities materialize, and how are they subsequently bought and sold? The answer to both questions is two short words—securities markets. Securities markets are a multibillion dollar business—a far cry from the auctioneers and merchants who bought and sold securities under a buttonwood tree on Wall Street in 1790. The markets have become so numerous and complex that they defy description in a few brief, well-chosen words. It is the aim of this chapter to discuss the functions, operations, and trading arrangements available in securities markets in the United States and to evaluate briefly the efficiency of these markets. Indeed, the average college student has a vested interest in becoming knowledgeable on the subject: the New York Stock Exchange's 1970 census of share owners shows that almost two-thirds of adult college graduates are share owners.

3-1 ORGANIZED EXCHANGES

The individual who is interested in "playing the stock market" may either arrange for the purchase of stock through a bank or go directly to a broker. Most investors prefer to go directly to a local brokerage house and request the services of one of its brokers. Either way, after the initial paperwork has been completed, the investor's order will be relayed to one of the exchanges handling the securities in which the investor is interested and the purchase will be consummated.

Individual investors most frequently utilize (through their brokers) the services of either the organized exchanges or the over-the-counter markets.

TABLE 3-1 DOLLAR VOLUME AND NUMBER OF SHARES TRADED ON THE NYSE, AMEX, AND REGIONAL EXCHANGES

	Volume by shares		Volume by value	
	Shares, thousands	% of total	Value, millions	% of total
New York Stock Exchange (NYSE)	4,496,187	71.4	$160	78.3
American Stock Exchange (AMEX)	1,103,222	17.5	$ 20	10.0
Midwest Stock Exchange				
Pacific Coast Stock Exchange				
Philadelphia-Baltimore-Washington Stock Exchange (PBW)				
Boston Stock Exchange				
Detroit Stock Exchange	699,793	11.1	$ 24	11.7
Cincinnati Stock Exchange				
Pittsburgh Stock Exchange				
National Stock Exchange				
Salt Lake Stock Exchange				
Spokane Stock Exchange				
Totals:	6,299,202	100%	$204	100%

Source: New York Stock Exchange, *1973 Fact Book.*

The discussion begins with the organized exchanges, of which the largest and best known is the New York Stock Exchange (NYSE), also known as the Big Board. Table 3-1 shows that the NYSE handled over two-thirds of all securities traded on organized exchanges registered with the Securities and Exchange Commission (SEC) during 1972.[1] The only other national exchange, the American Stock Exchange (AMEX), followed far behind with only 17 percent of total volume. The 11 other exchanges listed in Table 3-1 are known as regional exchanges and make up the balance. These regional exchanges were particularly important in history when proximity to the trading market was vital because of the undeveloped communications media; today they still provide a valuable service for small, local businesses whose securities are known only within a small area and for the issuers of municipal bonds.

Functions

Probably the most essential function performed by any exchange is the creation of a continuous market—the opportunity to buy or sell securities immediately at a price that varies little from the previous selling price. Thus, a continuous market allows investors to be liquid. That is, they are not obligated to hold their securities until maturity, or if they have common stocks, indefinitely.

---

[1] The SEC is a federal agency which regulates securities markets in the United States. The SEC and securities markets regulation will be discussed in detail in Chap 4.

An exchange also helps determine securities prices. Price is determined by buy and sell orders (or demand and supply); the exchanges bring together buyers and sellers from all over the nation and even foreign countries; anonymity between buyers and sellers is preserved.

The stock exchanges also provide a service to industry by indirectly aiding new financing. The ease with which investors can trade issues makes them more willing to invest in new issues.

Organization

Since most of the other exchanges follow the organizational pattern of the New York Stock Exchange, the discussion will focus on the dominant features of the NYSE.

The New York Stock Exchange has been described as a *voluntary association*. More specifically, it is a corporation that endeavors to maintain a smoothly operating marketplace.

The New York Stock Exchange, like others, is directed by a Board of Governors elected by its members. The NYSE board is composed of governors representing member firms and the public. The board is the chief policy-making body of the exchange. It approves or rejects applications of new members; it accepts or rejects budget proposals; it disciplines members through fines, suspension, or expulsion; it accepts or rejects proposals for new security listings; it submits requests to the SEC for changes; and, among other duties, it assigns securities to the various posts on the trading floor.

The main trading floor of the NYSE is about the size of a football field. There is an annex in which bonds and less actively traded stocks are bought and sold. Around the edge of both rooms are telephone booths, used primarily to transmit orders from the broker's office to the exchange floor and back again to the broker's office after execution of the order. On the floor are 18 U-shaped counters; each counter has many windows known as *trading posts*. A few of the 1,550 or so (it changes constantly) domestic corporations listed on the NYSE are assigned to be traded at each of the posts on the trading floor.

Membership

There are 1,366 members of the NYSE. This number has remained constant since 1953. Memberships are frequently referred to as *seats,* although trading is conducted without the benefit of chairs. In 1969, seats sold at a record high of $515,000, but by 1975 they were down to $65,000. In most years there are over 100 transfers of exchange memberships. The composition of the membership varies as to function, but certainly the majority are partners or directors of brokerage houses. Many of the large houses own more than one seat. For example, Merrill Lynch, Pierce, Fenner & Smith, the largest brokerage house, owns seven seats (and also uses several floor brokers). The exchange members act as brokers for the buying and selling of securities for customers, as dealers for their firm's own position, and sometimes as underwriters of new security issues. Members whose functions differ include floor brokers, floor traders, specialists, and odd-lot dealers.

Floor brokers. Floor brokers may be described as broker's brokers. They are ordinarily free-lance members of the exchange, not brokers for a member firm. At peak activity periods, they will accept orders from other brokers, execute them, and receive part of their commission in return. Floor brokers are useful in that they help prevent backlogs of orders, and they allow many firms to operate with fewer exchange memberships than would be needed without their services.

Floor traders. Floor traders differ from floor brokers in that they trade only for themselves. They buy neither for the public nor for other brokers. They are speculators, free to search the exchange floor for profitable buying and selling opportunities. Sometimes floor traders buy and sell the same stock on the same day, an activity occasionally referred to as *day-trading*. Over the years floor trading has declined probably as a result of higher costs (transfer taxes and clearing fees), unfavorable federal and state income taxes, and stricter regulations. However, floor traders trade free of commission since they own their own seats and trade for themselves.

Specialists. Approximately one out of every four seats on the New York Stock Exchange is owned by a specialist. The specialists are assigned to posts at which they specialize in the trading of one or more stocks. They may act as broker or dealer in a transaction. As a *broker,* the specialist executes orders for other brokers for a commission. As *dealers,* the specialists each buy and sell shares of the stock(s) in which they are specializing for their own accounts at their own risk. When there are more buy orders than sell orders, the specialist sells shares out of his or her inventory to meet the demand; when there are more sell orders than buy orders, the specialist buys to equalize supply and demand.[2] Thus, the specialist helps achieve an orderly, continuous market, ensuring only small incremental changes in price from trade to trade. To become a specialist requires experience, ability as a dealer, a seat on the exchange, selection by the Board of Governors, and a minimum capital requirement. All specialists are required to have adequate capital to assume a position of at least 4,000 shares of every stock in which they specialize. Each specialist on the floor of the exchange represents one of about 90 specialist firms which make the markets at the NYSE.

[2] For an analysis of specialists trading activities during periods of traumatic market change, see F. K. Reilly and E. F. Drzycimski, "Exchange Specialists and World Events," *Financial Analysts Journal,* July–August 1975, pp. 27–33.

Odd-lot dealers. The purchase or sale of less than 100 shares of a stock is referred to as an *odd-lot transaction.* Trades of 100 shares or multiples of 100 are referred to as *round-lot transactions.*[3] Odd-lot trades must be executed through odd-lot dealers who are members of the stock exchange. Brokers bring their customers' odd-lot orders to representatives of one of the odd-lot dealers on the trading floor; the odd-lot dealer executes the transaction and informs the broker of the trade; and the customer pays an odd-lot fee for the dealer's services in addition to the commission for the broker's services. Odd-lot trading costs exceed round-lot commissions to cover the expense of handling these small quantities. Round-lot and odd-lot commissions are discussed later in this chapter.

Listing Requirements

All firms whose stock is traded on an organized exchange must have at one time filed an application for listing. Some firms, such as American Telephone and Telegraph (AT&T), are listed on more than one exchange. The NYSE has the most stringent listing requirements of all the exchanges. For example, to be eligible the firm must have at least 1,800 stockholders who are holders of round lots; there must be a minimum of 1 million shares outstanding, of which 800,000 are publicly held; the company must demonstrate earning power of at least $2.5 million before taxes at the time of listing; and, among other obligations, the firm must be prepared to pay a listing fee.

Once a company has met all the requirements for listing and is allowed to have its securities traded on the NYSE, it must meet certain requirements established by the exchange and the SEC in order to maintain that privilege. For example, the listed firm must publish quarterly earnings reports; it must fully disclose financial information annually; it must obtain approval by the SEC of proxy forms before they can be sent to stockholders; and, among other things, insiders of the firm are prohibited from short selling.[4]

With the strict listing requirements and other requirements after membership, one wonders why firms seek listing on organized exchanges rather than settle for trading on the over-the-counter markets. Part of the answer lies in the fact that the listed firm benefits from a certain amount of "free" advertising and publicity, particularly if its stock is actively traded. This exposure probably has a favorable effect on the sale of its products to the extent that the company's name and its products are associated in the public's mind (for example, Ford Motor Company and its automobiles but not necessarily Ford Motor Company and its Philco products). Furthermore, listing may enhance the prestige of a firm, which may be helpful in reducing the firm's cost of raising equity capital. The investor benefits from

---

[3] There are a few stocks for which a round lot is considered a 10-share trade.
[4] Short selling is discussed in Sec. 13-1.

the large quantities of information published about the listed company (for example, the financial reports that the SEC requires the firms to distribute and news about dividends, new products, and new management) that are rapidly disseminated by the news media. Investors also can read in the financial pages the volume of trading that is being done in their companies and the daily high and low prices for shares traded. However, over half the total dollar volume of securities traded is done on the over-the-counter markets rather than on the 13 organized exchanges, and most of the securities traded over the counter are unlisted.

3-2 OVER-THE-COUNTER MARKETS

The term *over the counter* (OTC) is a bit anachronistic. It originated in the days when securities were traded over the counters of various dealers from their inventories, much as U.S. savings bonds are traded at banks today. Now, however, the over-the-counter market is more a way to do business than it is a place. It is a way of trading securities other than on a stock exchange. Many of the broker-dealers who engage in the trades of these securities are linked by a network of telephones, telegraphs, teletypewriters, and computer systems through which they deal directly with one another and with customers. Thus, prices are arrived at by a process which takes place over communication lines that span thousands of miles and allows investors to select between competing market-makers (instead of one monopolistic market-maker in each security, such as the NYSE specialists).

Securities Traded

The securities traded over the counter range from the most risk-free (that is, U.S. government) bonds to the most speculative common stocks. Historically, the OTC markets have been more important as bond markets than stock markets. Currently, virtually all U.S. government, state, and municipal obligations are traded over the counter, although U.S. government bonds are also traded at organized exchanges. More than 90 percent of corporate bonds are traded over the counter, although many of them are also listed on the NYSE. As a stock market, the OTC market is not quite so important, accounting for only about a third of stock trading in the United States. Many bank, insurance, and investment company stocks are traded over the counter because in the past the OTC markets required less financial disclosure. However, the 1964 Amendments to the Security Exchange Act of 1934 has changed this so that OTC securities must disclose essentially the same information as the exchange listed securities. For reasons that are not clear, many preferred stock issues are traded over the counter. And an increasing number of securities listed on the exchanges are being traded over the counter via the "third market," discussed later in this chapter.

Broker-Dealers

Of the registered broker-dealer houses (that is, those registered with the SEC), some are organized as sole proprietorships, some as partnerships, and many as corporations. Many of them have memberships in one or more stock exchanges. Some are wholesalers (that is, they buy from and sell to other dealers), some are retailers (selling only to the public), and some serve both functions. If the dealer buys and sells a particular security regularly, he or she is said to *make a market* in that security, serving much the same function as the specialist on the New York Stock Exchange. Dealer-broker firms can be categorized according to their specialties. For example, an OTC house specializes in OTC issues and rarely belongs to an exchange; an investment banking house that specializes in the underwriting of new security issues may diversify by acting as dealer in both listed and OTC securities; a commercial bank or a trust company may make a market in U.S. government, state, and local obligations; a stock exchange member house may have a separate department specifically formed to carry on trading in OTC markets; and there are houses that deal almost exclusively in municipal issues or federal government bond issues.

National Association of Security Dealers (NASD)

The National Association of Security Dealers (NASD) is a voluntary organization of security dealers which performs a self-regulating function for the OTC markets similar to what the NYSE does for its members. To qualify as a registered representative (that is, as a partner, officer, or employee of a broker-dealer firm which does business directly with the public), the candidate must pass a written qualifying examination prepared by the NASD and file an application with the NASD. The applicant must be recommended by a partner, owner, or voting stockholder of a member organization. Once a member, any individual who violates the rules of fair practice outlined by the NASD is subject to censure, fine, suspension, or expulsion, just as a member firm would be. The NASD is designed to protect the interests of its members by creating a favorable public relations image for the OTC dealers.

Over-the-Counter Quotations

As was mentioned previously, prices are determined by negotiation (bid and offer) on the OTC markets rather than by a specialist, as on the organized exchanges. Therefore, the prices of securities traded over the counter are published in daily newspapers as bid-and-ask prices. The interested investor thus sees a narrow range of prices within which the securities may be traded.

In 1971 a computerized communications network called NASDAQ

became operative in the OTC market. NASDAQ (pronounced Naz'dak) is an acronym for the initials NASD and *automated quotations*. It provides up-to-date bid-and-ask prices for thousands of securities in response to the simple pressing of appropriate keys on a console by subsequently flashing prices on a cathode-ray tube (like a TV screen) which is linked to NASDAQ's computer. Thus, the security sales representative knows immediately the bid-and-ask quotations of all dealers making a market in the stock he or she wishes to trade, and may then contact the dealer offering the *best* price and negotiate a trade. The primary advantage to investors is the assurance that they are receiving the best price. Prior to the inception of NASDAQ, the investor was dependent on the stockbroker's diligence in acquiring bid-and-ask prices from several different market-makers by contacting each individually. Thus, the investor could not be certain of receiving the best available price.

NASDAQ is designed to handle up to 20,000 stocks, but it currently lists less than half that many because most of the other stocks are not active enough to be included within the system. Thus, it has much unused capacity which may eventually be put to use by the inclusion of stocks listed on the exchanges. It is advantageous (for everyone except the NYSE specialists) to have all exchange listed and OTC securities reported through NASDAQ; this facilitates one composite ticker tape reporting the prices from competing market-makers. Closer competition should minimize the commission rates investors are charged to buy and sell securities.

Of the few thousand stocks quoted in NASDAQ, not all are published daily (that is, included in the national daily list). To make the national daily list (published in full by *The Wall Street Journal* and a few other newspapers), NASDAQ stocks must meet additional requirements, such as having at least three market-makers and a minimum of 1,500 stockholders distributed throughout the country.

For those OTC stocks not included in the national daily list, a more comprehensive quotation service is provided by the National Quotation Bureau, an organization whose subscribers are primarily security dealers. It quotes prices of over 8,000 securities on its daily "pink sheets." Its information is derived chiefly from wholesale OTC firms.

The commission rate at most of the security houses for OTC stocks is roughly equivalent to the commission charged for an equal number of shares at an equal price on the organized exchanges. However, the maximum commission rate that the NASD considers "normal" is 5 percent of the value of the transaction. Commissions over that must be justified in terms of excessive costs for arranging a trade, such as finding a buyer for the securities of small, unknown corporations. Sometimes commission rates are effectively reduced by charging the customer a commission rate but giving a price reduction on the security purchased.

3-3 TRADING ARRANGEMENTS

Before a buy or sell order can be executed, the stockbroker must have detailed information about trading arrangements desired by the customer. For example, if the customer desires an odd lot, the broker must deal with an odd-lot house. The broker must know whether the customer wants to specify a market, limit, or stop order, and also whether the customer prefers to buy on margin or pay cash. These arrangements are explained below.

Margin Trading

Technically, margin trading includes both margin buying and short selling. However, only a small portion of total trading on the margin is short selling. Short selling is discussed in detail in Chap. 13. For now, the concern is with buying on margin.

When investors buy stock on margin, they buy some shares with cash and borrow to pay for additional shares, using the paid shares as collateral. The Federal Reserve Board of Governors controls the amount that may be borrowed. For example, if the Federal Reserve Board stipulates a 55 percent margin requirement, the investor must pay cash equal to at least 55 percent of the value of the securities purchased. The buyer may borrow funds to pay for no more than 45 percent of the cost of the securities. The margin requirements have varied from a low of 40 percent to a high of 100 percent since the Federal Reserve Board was given authority to alter the percentage in 1934.

The investor who wishes to buy on margin is required to open a margin account with a stockbroker. Then the investor is required by the NYSE to make a minimum down payment of $2,000. Assume the margin requirement is 55 percent and Mr. Investor wishes to purchase 100 shares of a $100 stock. In other words, he wishes to make a total investment of $10,000, but assume he has only $5,500. Because of the Federal Reserve Board's 55 percent margin requirement, he can still buy 100 shares by paying for 55 of the shares and using them as collateral for a loan to pay for the other 45 shares. Assume Mr. Investor follows this procedure. Consider the position he will be in if his shares double in price to $200 each, and, conversely, his position if the price of his shares drop by one-half to $50 each.

If his shares double in value from $100 to $200, his total profit will be $100 profit per share, times 100 shares, or $10,000 before interest, commissions, and taxes, compared with $100 profit per share times 55 shares, or a $5,500 profit, if he has not bought on margin (that is, if he has invested only $5,500). In other words, his profit has increased because he bought on margin.

Suppose, now, that his shares decrease in price from $100 to $50 per share. The current market value of his investment has dropped from $10,000 to $5,000. Compare again his position as a margin buyer with that of a non-margin buyer. As a margin buyer, he has a $50 per share loss times 100 shares, or a $5,000 loss. If he had not bought on margin and had purchased only 55 shares, his loss would have been $50 loss per share times 55 shares, or $2,750. Therefore, by buying stock on 55 percent margin, Mr. Investor can increase his loss as well as he can his profit. However, this is not the end of his story. If the stock decreases in value sufficiently, Mr. Investor will receive a *margin call* from his broker. That is, the broker informs him he must put up more margin (increase his down payment). If Mr. Investor cannot come up with the additional margin, the broker must sell the stocks the investor owns in order to cover the value of the loan. Physically, this is no problem, since margin customers are required to deposit their stock with their brokers. If anything is left over after the sale and subsequent loan payment, the investor receives the balance. By how much must the stock decrease in value before there is a margin call? The New York Stock Exchange has answered this question by stipulating a *margin maintenance* requirement. According to this, a margin call must occur when the current market value of the stock is less than the amount of the loan plus 25 percent of that amount (that is, 125 percent of the loan). In the case of Mr. Investor, a margin call would have been required when his stocks decreased below a $5,625 value [$4,500, the amount of the loan, plus $1,125 (25 percent of the $4,500 loan), or $5,625]. In practice, however, most brokers have higher margin maintenance requirements than the minimum set by the NYSE.

The Federal Reserve Board's margin requirement is effective only on the initial margin purchase. After this, the Board is completely out of the picture. Even if the margin requirement is changed, the change affects only new margin purchases.

The primary benefit of buying on margin, then, is that it allows investors to magnify their profits by the reciprocal of the margin requirement (that is, 2 times if the margin requirement is $\frac{1}{2}$, 3 times if it is $\frac{1}{3}$, $\frac{4}{3}$ times if it is $\frac{3}{4}$, and so forth). The major disadvantage is that it forces losses of the same reciprocal if stock prices decline. There is the added disadvantage of fixed interest payments whether stock prices advance or decline. In sum, margin trading increases risk. Therefore, it should be used only by those financially sophisticated individuals who can gracefully assume such added risk.

When an investor buys on margin, the one-period rate of return is defined in Eq. (3-1).

$$r_t = \frac{p_{t+1} - p_t + d_t - i(1 - m)p_t}{mp_t} \qquad (3\text{-}1)$$

Equation (3-1) is different from Eq. (2-2) for the nonmargin buyer's return. The percentage down payment, or margin, is denoted *m* in Eq. (3-1). The denominator, mp_t, is the dollar amount of the margin buyer's equity invest-ment, ignoring commissions. The margin buyer borrowed $(1 - m)p_t$ dollars at an interest rate of i, so the dollar amount of the interest expense, $i(1 - m)p_t$, is deducted from the numerator to obtain the net income return on equity.

Types of Orders

Investors have several options when placing a buy or sell order. They may request that the broker place a market order, limit order, stop order, or open order.

Market orders. This type is the most common and most easily executed. With a market order, the customer is simply requesting that the securities be traded at the best possible price as soon as the order reaches the trading floor of the exchange. Market orders are usually traded very rapidly, some-times in minutes after the order is given the broker, since no price is specified.

Limit orders. These specify the maximum price at which the customer will buy or the minimum price at which he or she will sell. The customer must be willing to run the risk that the security will not reach the limit price, resulting in no trade. If the trade cannot be executed by the broker when the order reaches the trading floor, the broker will turn the order over to the specialist, who will execute the order if the limit price or better is reached.

Stop orders. Sometimes called stop-loss orders, these are usually designed either to protect a customer's existing profit or to reduce the amount of loss. For example, if Ms. Investor buys a stock for 50 and its current market price is 75, she has a *paper profit* of $25 per share. If the investor fears a drop in the current market price, she could request a stop order to sell at, say, 70. This stop order would in effect become a market order after the security reached 70, and it would be executed as soon after 70 was reached as pos-sible. The 70 price is not guaranteed. The stock might be down to 69 or 68 or even lower by the time it could be executed. However, the investor's profit position is protected to a large extent. Of course, she runs the risk of selling a security with a future of long-run price appreciation in a tempo-rary decline of the whole market.

To protect herself from excessive losses, our Ms. Investor may issue a stop order at a price less than purchase price. For example, if she buys a stock for 40 but feels that it is a speculative investment, she may wish to request a stop order to sell at, say, 39 in order to minimize her loss.

Specialists must keep a record of stop orders. They are executed in order of priority, as are limit orders. That is, the first stop order received at a given price is the first order executed. An accumulation of stop orders at a certain price can cause a sharp break in the market of the issue involved. In such an event, it is quite likely that the exchange would suspend the stop orders, just at the time the traders really needed their protection. Thus, the value of a stop order can be considerably diminished under such a contingency.

Open order or good-till-canceled (GTC) *order.* These terms refer to the time in which the order is to remain in effect. An *open order* or a *GTC order* remains in effect indefinitely, whereas a *day order* remains in effect only for the day that it is brought to the exchange floor. The vast majority of orders are day orders, probably because the customer feels that conditions are right for trading on that specific day. Market conditions may change the next day. However, customers may prefer a GTC order, particularly for limit orders, when they are willing to wait until the price is right for trading. GTC orders must be confirmed at various intervals to remain in effect.

Brokerage Services

The investor services provided by brokerage houses include the following:

1 *Free safe-deposit vaults for securities.* If investors leave their securities with the broker for safekeeping, they are relieved of the responsibility of renting a safe-deposit vault or finding some other means of storage, and they do not have to physically transfer their securities to and from the broker's office every time they wish to buy or sell. If the investor owns bonds and leaves them with the broker, the broker will clip the coupons, collect the interest due, and credit the customer's account.

2 *Free literature compiled and published by the research department.* This literature ranges from a booklet of essential information for the beginning investor to computer printouts of the most up-to-date information on securities compiled by the financial analysts of the firm's research staff. Some brokerage houses also provide free newsletters and brochures on commodity prices, foreign exchange, and various industries.

3 *A market for all types of trading.* The firm can arrange trades from the most speculative of commodities to the most risk-free investments.

4 *A credit agency.* When a customer is buying on margin, the broker will loan the funds. The rate of interest charged is usually at least 1 percent over the prime rate; it varies with the amount of margin provided.

5 *Services competition.* By law a broker is not allowed to give any client more than $25 worth of gifts per year — to make a more costly gift could be viewed as buying or bribing customers. However, some brokers "loan" cars to a favored customer for months at a time, "wine and dine" their best customers, and provide other questionable services (for example, pimping) in order to get lucrative customers. Such services were common before May 1, 1975, when fixed commissions precluded price competition between exchange brokerages.

3-4 THIRD AND FOURTH MARKETS

Security markets are sometimes classified into four divisions: exchanges, over-the-counter, third, and fourth markets. Third and fourth markets are newer markets but are sizable and are gaining in importance.

The Third Market

In the third market listed securities—primarily those listed on the NYSE—are traded over the counter. The third market is part of the over-the-counter market. It consists of securities broker-dealers, each making markets in anywhere from a few to over 300 securities. Each of these third-market dealers stands ready to buy or sell for its own account in sizes ranging from an odd lot to large blocks. In those listed securities in which it chooses to deal, each dealer owns an inventory (including short positions). Thus, the third-market broker-dealers are market-makers who are in direct competition with the specialists of the NYSE, AMEX, and other exchanges.

The third market developed as a response to the absence of volume commission-rate discounts on the NYSE. Prior to 1968 the NYSE's commission charge for, say, 20,000 shares was 200 times its round-lot charge for 100 shares. This system made large-volume trading very expensive. One way to achieve lower commission charges, then, was to seek a nonmember of the New York Stock Exchange who dealt in the OTC market but "made markets" in listed securities. The OTC dealers were not bound to the minimum commission rates which members of the NYSE set for themselves.[5]

The main participants in the third market are institutions such as bank trust accounts, mutual funds, and pension funds which believe that they can reduce their cost, obtain a better price, or effect a more rapid transaction there. Since the third-market makers deal almost exclusively with broker-dealers and institutions, the services offered (such as securities research, safe-deposit vaults, and sales representatives) are minimal. Therefore their overhead costs tend to be lower. These cost savings are frequently reflected in the lower net costs to the institutional investor. The gross profits taken out of a transaction by a third-market dealer are sometimes only a fraction as much as the gross profit taken out of a similar transaction conducted by a specialist on the NYSE. As might be expected, numerous large-block transactions are conducted in the third market.[6]

Because of the emergence of the third market, the United States now enjoys competitive multiple markets in some listed securities. While these

[5] In 1971 the SEC required that the portion of each order in excess of $500,000 be subject to a negotiated fee rather than a minimum commission rate on the organized exchanges. This ruling made the organized exchanges more competitive with the third market in large-block trades. But larger changes came later; they will be explained in this chapter.
[6] *New York Stock Exchange Fact Book, 1973.*

markets are organized separately, they do not operate independently of one another. The third-market makers and the specialists watch one another's prices and never differ very far.

NASDAQ, as it expands to include many listed stocks of the various organized exchanges, promises to foster further competition between the organized exchanges and the third market and to benefit investors by promoting more efficient securities pricing and lower commissions. As competition drives brokerage commissions down, securities research and other services provided free by NYSE brokers may be discontinued unless paid for separately from the commissions (sometimes called "unbundling" of the services).

The Fourth Market

The fourth market refers to those institutions and wealthy individuals who *directly* buy and sell securities among one another, completely bypassing brokerage services. Little is known about these direct trades since only the two parties to the trade and perhaps a person who helped arrange the transaction are involved, and registration is not required.

The *fourth markets* are essentially communication networks among block traders. The functions of inventory carrying, risk-bearing, credit provision, and dealers in other markets are lacking in the fourth market. The fourth-market maker is usually one individual or a few persons who communicate the buy-and-sell desires of their clientele to block traders and thus facilitate directly negotiated sales. The fourth-market organizer may collect a small commission or a flat annual retainer for helping to arrange these large transactions. Generally, the costs of trading large blocks are smaller in the fourth market than in other markets. Other reasons for operating in the fourth market include the expectation of obtaining a better price through direct negotiation, savings on commissions, rapid execution, and/or a desire to retain anonymity. These advantages suggest that use of the fourth market may become more widespread in the future, particularly as large institutions continue to grow. Fourth-market trading does not necessarily present a threat to the organized exchanges (although they may think it does). But its mere existence represents a competitive force in the marketplace and encourages the exchanges and the OTC market to handle large blocks efficiently at a lower cost (which tends to reduce the profits earned by the specialists on the NYSE and AMEX).

There are several privately owned fourth-market organizations. Each one operates slightly differently. Some use telephones to communicate with their institutional customers, whereas others keep their customers directly in touch with one another by using a teletype network. For example, consider a fourth-market firm which uses teletype machines. If Mr. Subscriber wants to buy or sell, he enters the name of the stock, its bid or asked price, and the number of shares into the network, plus a code number through which he can be contacted. If another subscriber is interested, he contacts the first firm and they actually dicker over the price via the teletype terminals in their offices. If they agree on the price and size of a trade, the market-maker's computer automatically closes the trade and prints out confirmation slips for both subscribers. The deal is completed without a middle party (such as a specialist) who charges a standard commission, carries inventories, or provides other services. And, the buying and selling subscribers never even need learn the other party's identity.

3-5 THE INVESTMENT BANKER

Literally billions of dollars worth of new securities are placed on the market each year. The agent responsible for finding buyers for these new securities is called the *investment banker*. This name is rather unfortunate, for these persons are neither investors nor bankers. That is, they do not permanently invest their own funds, nor do they provide a place for safekeeping of funds as a savings banker would. What, then, do they do? In short, they purchase new issues from corporations and state and local governments and then arrange for their sale to the public.

Who are investment bankers? Perhaps the names First Boston Corporation and Merrill Lynch, Pierce, Fenner & Smith sound familiar. These two large firms do the most underwriting of all the several thousand firms engaged in investment banking (there were over 4,000 firms doing some underwriting in 1962, but of these, 10 percent accounted for 75 percent of the capital and public new issue activity).[7] Almost all these firms did more than act as investment bankers. Today, most of them have diversified themselves into department stores of finance. Merrill Lynch, Pierce, Fenner & Smith is a case in point. To name just a few of its activities, this firm trades in the retail markets for government securities, commodities, and corporate stocks and bonds, and, through its subsidiaries, provides real estate financing and investment advisory services.

Underwriting refers to the guarantee by the investment banker that the issuer of the new securities will receive a certain minimum amount. Of course, inherent in this guarantee is some degree of risk for the investment banker. It is the underwriter's intention to buy the securities from the issuer at less than the expected selling price. This intention, however, can and has been foiled.

Not all new security issues are underwritten. If the investment banker finds one or more buyers for a new issue and arranges for a direct trade between issuer and investors, he or she is said to have made a *private placement*. Rather than perform the underwriting function, in a private placement the investment banker is compensated for acting as the middle link in bringing buyer and seller together and for his or her skill and speed in

[7] Sidney Robbins, *The Securities Markets* (New York: Free Press, 1966), pp. 166–167.

determination of a fair price and execution of the trade. Even in a *public* offering, the investment banker may not assume the role of underwriter, but may agree to use certain facilities and services in distributing new shares on a *best efforts* basis while assuming no financial responsibility if all the securities cannot be sold. More frequently, however, the investment banker is thought of as the underwriter for public offerings.

Functions of the Investment Banker

Advisory. In a corporation's first confrontation with an investment banker, the banker will serve in an advisory capacity. He will aid the firm in analyzing its financing needs and make suggestions about various means of financing. He may also function as an advisor in mergers, acquisitions, and refinancing operations. Occasionally, following a securities issue, the investment banker will be given a seat on the board of directors of the firm so that he may continue to give financial counsel to the firm and, in the process, help protect his reputation as the sponsor of profitable, financially sound firms.

Administrative. The investigations, paperwork, and "general red tape" are quite voluminous in a securities issue. The investment banker has the responsibility of seeing that they are all done and done correctly. Some of his specific administrative responsibilities will be discussed later.

Risk-bearing. The period elapsing between the time the investment banking houses purchase an issue from the issuer and the time they subsequently sell it to the public is *risky.* Because of an unforeseen change in market conditions, the underwriters face the possibility of either not being able to sell the entire issue or of selling it at less than the purchase price. Many examples of such an occurrence could be cited, but one may suffice. In 1970, Duke Power Company issued $100 million in bonds. Several investment banking firms purchased the bonds and offered them for sale at 99.733 percent of their face value to yield 8.65 percent. After trying to sell them at this price for 2 weeks, the investment bankers still held $70 million worth. Then they decided to disband and try selling the bonds on the open market. On the open market the bonds sold as low as 97, yielding 8.90 percent, and the investment banking syndicate stood to lose an estimated $800,000 on the financing.[8] Duke Power, though, had its needed cash and nothing to worry about. The investment bankers suffered losses because they misjudged the market.

Distribution. Distributing securities to investors is the central function of investment bankers. It is their primary concern to bring together buyer and

---

[8] "Interest Rates Climb on Bonds," *The New York Times,* Aug. 18, 1970, p. 47.

seller, whether they actually buy and then sell the securities themselves, or whether they simply act as intermediaries in bringing together issuer and investors in a private placement. To gain understanding of how a primary distribution of securities materializes, consider the issuance of a hypothetical $100 million debenture bond flotation by the XYZ Corp.

Public Distribution

Mr. X of XYZ Corp. and his associates have agreed that they need $100 million for expansion. They need advice about how to raise this much capital; therefore they go to a nearby investment banking house, say ABC & Co., and seek counsel.

Early conferences. The investment house that first reaches an agreement with the issuer is called the *originator;* the originator ultimately manages the flotation and coordinates the underwriting syndicate and selling group. At the outset, however, the originator and the issuer must determine how much capital should be raised, whether it should be raised by debt or equity, and whether XYZ Corp. is in a sound financial position. Investigations are conducted by accountants, engineers, and attorneys. The accountants assess the firm's financial condition. If the funds are to be used to acquire new assets, ABC's engineering staff will investigate the proposed acquisition. Attorneys will be asked to give interpretations and judgments about various documents involved in the flotation. And ABC & Co. will make an investigation of the firm's future prospects. Finally, the originator will draw up a tentative underwriting agreement between the issuer and investment banking house, specifying all terms of the issue except the specific price that will be set on the debenture.

The underwriting syndicate. With most large issues, such as the one under discussion, the investment banker will form a purchase syndicate made up of a group of investment banking houses, usually 10 to 60. There are at least three advantages to forming an underwriting syndicate. First, since it spreads around the purchase cost, ABC & Co. is not faced with an enormous cash drain while the securities are being sold. Second, it lessens the risk of loss, since several firms would bear the loss in case of failure instead of only ABC & Co. Third, the utilization of several underwriters and their selling groups encourages a wider participation of final ownership of the new securities. Figure 3-1 illustrates the relationship between issuer, originator, underwriting syndicate, selling group, and the ultimate investors.

The selling group. After the underwriters have purchased the issue from XYZ Corp., each uses its own selling group for distribution to the investing public. The selling group consists of other investment bankers, dealers, and brokers. Some firms, such as Merrill Lynch, Pierce, Fenner & Smith, per-

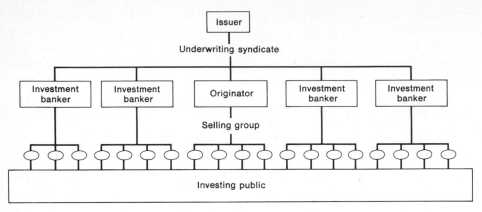

FIG. 3-1 Investment banking procedure flow chart.

form all these functions—from managing underwriter in some issues to brokers in others.

Disclosure requirements. The SEC requires that a registration statement be filed with the Commission. It must contain information for an investor to judge the investment quality of the new issue. After the filing of the statement, there is a 20-day waiting period during which the new issue may not be offered for sale. During this period the SEC analyzes the registration statement to determine if there have been any misrepresentations of fact or omissions. The SEC may act to delay approval or request amendment to the statement, in which case the waiting period will exceed 20 days. In practice, most delays are caused by the large number of statements filed that must be processed by the relatively small SEC staff.

A portion of the registration statement is the *prospectus.* After approval and after the price has been set, it is reproduced in quantity and delivered to potential investors. Investors must have a prospectus before they can invest. It contains information about XYZ's history, about those individuals who hold large blocks of XYZ stock, and other facts pertinent to the evaluation of the debentures offered. At the risk of overstatement, perhaps it should be emphasized that SEC approval of the registration statement and the prospectus within is not an endorsement by the SEC of the investment value of the securities offered. Its approval implies only that adequate information has been revealed for investors to make their own learned judgment about the value of the security offer.

Not all issues must be registered with the SEC. Included in this exempt classification are government issues and companies regulated by governmental agencies. The latter must apply for exemption, however. Other issues that are likely to be exempt include (1) intrastate offerings, (2) issues that are offered to only a few investors, and (3) issues of less than $300,000, the most frequently exempted group. Exemption does not make the issuer and underwriters immune from legal action if fraud is involved in the flotation, however.

Setting the price. Perhaps the most difficult decision in a flotation is setting the "right" price. The "right" price is one that is not too low; this would be unnecessarily costly to the issuer. It also cannot be too high; this might cause losses for the underwriters. Therefore, a very delicate balance is necessary.

The price is generally set at the end of the registration period. The syndicate prefers to wait to set the final price until the issue is ready for marketing so that it may have the latest, most up-to-date information on the market situation. As a rule, when the price is right, market conditions are good, and the issuer and underwriters are reputable, the flotation will "go out the window," that is, it will be sold in a few days or even hours. When one or more of these conditions is lacking, it may become a "sticky issue," taking a week, month, or even more to sell, and it may result in losses for the underwriting syndicate.

Market stabilization. During the distribution period, the manager of the underwriting firm endeavors to stabilize the price of the issue to prevent its drifting downward. To achieve this objective, he or she "pegs" the price by placing orders to buy at a specified price on the market. Although this procedure has been accused of being a monopolistic price-fixing agreement, the SEC has nodded approval as long as full, prior disclosure of intent to stabilize is made. It is defended on the grounds that if price-pegging were not allowed, the underwriting syndicate's risk would be greater; thus, the underwriting cost to the issuer would increase correspondingly. The price-pegging activity usually continues for about 30 days after the issue begins.

If the issue has been badly priced, even the pegging operation does not help substantially. In the most extreme occurrence, the managing underwriter would start buying back everything that had been sold in an effort to keep the price up. In such a case, all the underwriters would experience severe losses.

Flotation Costs

Investment bankers earn their income as would any other merchant; that is, their selling price is greater than their purchase price. The difference is called the *spread*. In the case of XYZ Corp., let us assume there is a 4-point spread (ABC & Co. bought the bonds for $960 each and they were ultimately sold to the investing public for $1,000 each). That 4 points, then, is compensation for various costs such as investigations, audits, printing, and registration fees; the discount given to the underwriting syndicate; and the additional discount given to the selling group members. The spread may very likely be divided as follows: ABC & Co., the managing underwriter, would keep $\frac{1}{2}$ point for originating and managing the syndicate; the entire underwriting group would earn about $1\frac{1}{2}$ points; and the members of the selling group would earn the remaining 2 points. If the managing underwriter should sell to an ultimate buyer, he would receive the full 4-point spread—$\frac{1}{2}$ point as originator, $1\frac{1}{2}$ points as part of the underwriting syndicate, and 2 points as a retailer. Likewise, if he sold part of the issue to his selling group, he would receive 2 points of the 4-point spread—$\frac{1}{2}$ as originator and $1\frac{1}{2}$ as part of the underwriting syndicate.

Of the various types of securities issued, the selling costs for bonds are much less than for either preferred or common stock. The selling costs for common stock range from 2 to 4 times more than for bonds and about 1.1 to 2 times more than for preferred stock, depending on the size of the issue. It seems reasonable that flotation costs of bonds would be less than for preferred or common stock since bonds are usually sold in large blocks to a few large institutional investors, whereas a stock issue may be sold to millions of stockholders. Thus, marketing costs and risk are significantly greater with stock issues.

Further, one need not look far to see why, as a percentage of gross proceeds, flotation costs for small issues are greater than for large issues. Fixed costs, such as registration fees and investigation expenses, account for about 85 percent of the cost of flotation. The greater the issue, then, the less the fixed cost per unit of new issue. Moreover, as a general rule, small issues are made by less well known companies, and the less well known the company, the more obligated is the managing firm to make an extremely intensive investigation of the issuing firm. Also, marketing the issue of an unknown firm is much more difficult and thus more costly than launching the issue of a well-known firm. Therefore, flotation costs for small issues are higher than for large issues on a per-unit basis.

3-6 EFFICIENT MARKETS

An *efficient capital market* will channel liquid capital quickly and accurately to where it will do the community (namely, the nation) the most good. For example, if a competent woman discovers and patents a "better mousetrap," forms a mousetrap corporation, and sells shares in it publicly, an efficient market will channel funds out of the stock of inferior mousetrap firms to the manufacturer of the "better mousetrap."

Essential Ingredients

Efficient markets will provide ready financing for worthwhile business ventures. It is essential that a country have efficient capital markets if that country is to enjoy the highest possible level of health, welfare, and education for its population. One of the main reasons that some still-developing countries do not advance is that they have inefficient capital markets. In efficient capital markets, prices may be fixed or manipulated rather than determined by supply and demand. Capital may be controlled by a few wealthy people, and not being fluid, it may not flow where it is needed; graft, corruption, and public distrust can cause money to be hoarded rather than invested in the capital market; or investors may be ignorant and unable to distinguish among worthwhile business ventures and bad investments.

For a securities market to be an efficient market, the following conditions must exist:

1 Prices must adjust efficiently so that new inventions and better products will cause a firm's securities prices to rise and induce investors to want to supply capital to the firm (that is, to buy its stock).

2 Information must be disseminated freely and quickly across the nation so that all investors can react to new information.

3 Transactions costs, such as sales commissions on securities, must be low enough so that investors can earn a net profit from wise investments after all transactions costs.

4 Investors must be rational and able to recognize efficient assets (that is, assets with relatively high returns in their risk-class) so that they will want to invest their money where it is needed most.

Efficient security markets are obviously very desirable. They provide capital when and where able business executives need it and reward the investors who provide this needed capital with capital gains. On the other hand, incompetent business managers and investors will be disciplined by failures in an efficient market since the value of the securities in an inefficiently managed firm will fall because of lack of demand. As a result, attention will be drawn to the firm's incompetent management and the incompetents will be forced to seek either tasks for which they are better suited or more training.

Imperfections

Many of the conditions for perfect capital markets are fulfilled in the United States today. As a result, its security markets are the most efficient in the world. However, imperfections do exist which allow capital to be misallocated. Some of the major imperfections in the capital market mechanism are listed below.

1 *Disinterested shareholders.* Shareholders frequently assign their voice in management to the corporation's executives by signing a proxy statement. Ineffective management may thus be perpetuated until such time as a majority of shareholders become dissatisfied with their returns, refuse to sign proxy statements, and vote in new managements.[9]

2 *Earnings retention used for financing.* Most corporations prefer to finance their expansion by retaining their earnings rather than by issuing new securities. Such internal financing is cheaper than the issuance of new securities, but it allows management to ignore the price of the firm's securities in the financial markets and to avoid the discipline of the market.

3 *Transactions costs.* Brokerage fees and transfer taxes on securities make investors reluctant to sell an asset which is only slightly inefficient and to reinvest their funds in more productive firms.[10]

4 *Investor ignorance.* Some investors buy securities on the basis of rumors, "hot tips," or the advice of a security broker without investigating to determine whether the investment has true value.

5 *Mob speculation.* Hysterical price speculation temporarily sets security prices when mob speculation (such as followed President Kennedy's assassination) occurs. This condition results in incorrectly priced securities and rates of return which misallocate capital to unproductive uses.[11]

In the final analysis, the more diligently investors investigate before they invest, the more efficient their capital markets will be. Furthermore, America's stock markets are currently undergoing a period of painful reorganization which should increase their efficiency.

3-7 ECONOMIC PRESSURES RESHAPE UNITED STATES STOCK MARKETS

Pressures for stock market reorganization have been building for years. However, a multivolume study published in 1971 by the Securities and Exchange Commission focused the attention of many business executives, investors, and government policymakers on the issues.[12] The pressures for reorganization come primarily from courts and from new stock market competition.

---

[9] One of the early classic studies documenting the phenomena of stockholder apathy was A. A. Berle and G. C. Means, *The Modern Corporation and Private Property* (New York: Macmillan, 1934).
[10] H. Demsetz, "The Cost of Transacting," *The Quarterly Journal of Economics,* vol. 82, 1968, pp. 33–53.
[11] For an analysis of NYSE specialists' effectiveness in protecting the market from mob hysteria and other destabilizing factors, see A. Barnea, "Performance Evaluation of NYSE Specialists," *Journal of Financial and Quantitative Analysis,* September 1974, pp. 511–536.
[12] Securities and Exchange Commission, *Institutional Investor Study Report* (Washington: Government Printing Office, 1971), vols. 1–8.

Court Pressures

In the past, investors have sued the NYSE to drop the minimum commission schedule which all member brokerages were required to charge their customers. In ruling on such a case in 1963, the United States Supreme Court said that the fixed minimum commission violated the spirit of the Sherman Antitrust Act, which outlaws monopolies and price fixing.[13] But the Court held that such problems were the responsibility of the SEC; therefore, it did not order the NYSE to abandon its minimum commissions because it did not want to infringe on the SEC's jurisdiction. The lawsuit and similar ones signaled the need for change. But some of the other pressures responsible for the current changes in securities markets are more subtle. New securities markets sprang up and gave the organized exchanges the first competition they had ever faced. These economic pressures moved faster and more effectively than the SEC did in reshaping America's stock markets.[14]

Third- and Fourth-Market Pressures

Some OTC brokerages were not satisfied with their traditional market role. Spotting a profit potential in trading the shares of major corporations, they started selling the stocks listed on the NYSE and the AMEX although they were not members of either exchange. As described earlier, these broker-dealers created the so-called third market. For over a decade, more aggressive OTC dealers have been making their own markets in stocks listed on the NYSE, the AMEX, and other organized exchanges. Recently the total volume of NYSE shares traded in these new markets has grown to nearly one-tenth of the Big Board's volume. Gone are the days when the NYSE held a monopoly on making markets for those selected stocks that were traded there.

To add to the NYSE's problems, the fourth market also competed away a portion of its business. The amount of business so diverted is unknown, since the fourth market operates in a confidential manner. As a result of all these competing market-makers, price competition forced down brokerage commission rates. But there were other pressures too.

Pressure from Institutional Investors

Pension funds, life insurance companies, mutual funds, trust departments of banks, and other business groups that routinely buy large blocks of

---

[13] Walter Bagehot, "The Only Game in Town," *Financial Analysts Journal*, March–April 1971, pp. 12–14.

[14] For several views on this reorganization of United States stock markets, see the Winter 1964 issue of *Journal of Contemporary Business*, vol. 3, no. 1, published by the University of Washington. The issue contains articles discussing the reorganization. Also, see the articles in Part I of *Readings and Issues in Investments*, edited by Frank K. Reilly, The Dryden Press, Hinsdale, Ill.

common stock are usually referred to as *institutional investors*. These investors wield a lot of clout in the securities industry because they are its biggest customers. They give the brokers who buy and sell their securities millions of dollars in commissions every year. Many of these investors push for changes in the securities industry because they are tired of paying high brokerage commissions and want to reduce their trading costs.

Institutional investors are barred from membership on the NYSE, the AMEX, and some other stock exchanges. Denial of institutional membership assures a big source of income for brokerages that specialize in selling to institutions. To avoid the exchange commissions, many institutional investors have turned to the third market and the fourth market where they can buy the same stocks but negotiate lower commissions on large trades. Loss of these profitable customers puts pressure on the organized stock exchanges either to admit the institutions as members or to further reduce commissions. In 1972, the NYSE responded to this competitive pressure and to suggestions from the SEC by lowering the minimum-sized trade on which member brokerages are allowed to negotiate commissions. Then congressional pressure for elimination of the fixed commission schedule prevailed, and pegged commissions were discontinued completely on May 1, 1975 (referred to by Wall Streeters as "May Day").

3-8 NEGOTIATING BROKERS' COMMISSIONS

Although the commissions paid to stockbrokers reach lower average rates when they are determined by competition rather than by the NYSE's fixed minimum commission schedule, these commissions are still an important cost in securities trading and they should be evaluated. There is an adage among stock traders that if an investor buys and sells securities too frequently, the only person that will get rich is the stockbroker who receives the commissions.

The stockbroker who recommends frequent buying and selling to a client is said to be *"churning* the customer for commissions," that is, turning over the account too fast for the customer's own good. Consider a classic case involving an aged widow. Aunt Jane (an old Wall Street nickname for elderly widows who invest) became a widow at the age of 80. Her husband's life insurance left her $100,000 cash. But Aunt Jane had never even balanced a checkbook and did not know how to manage her money. An unscrupulous stockbroker got Aunt Jane's name out of her husband's newspaper obituary and talked her into opening an account with his brokerage. Then the stockbroker called Aunt Jane every few days and recommended she buy or sell some stocks; she was putty in his hands and allowed him to manage her account pretty much as he wished.

During the two years after Aunt Jane put her $100,000 into the account at the brokerage, her broker talked her into hundreds of trades. The majority of the trades made at least a modest profit before commissions and Aunt Jane naively thought she was doing well — she ignored the broker's commission which was deducted from each buy and each sell transaction. As a result, Aunt Jane's $100,000 was churned away to zero in two years. She was unable to live on her social security and so she moved into the state's home for poor aged people. Luckily, in this particular case, Aunt Jane's nephew was an attorney who sued the stockbroker. The stockbroker worked for a reputable brokerage which fired the scoundrel and repaid Aunt Jane's $100,000. But such situations will occur again. And, on a smaller scale, churning goes on constantly.

To avoid being churned for commissions, investors should (1) manage their own portfolios rather than following their stockbrokers' advice, (2) negotiate to get their commission minimized, and (3) keep track of all transactions costs. To furnish a guideline against which investors can gauge their commission negotiations, the pre-1975 NYSE commission schedule may be useful.

Pre-1975 NYSE Commission Schedules

Tables 3-2 and 3-3 contain the fixed minimum commission schedules used by all NYSE member brokerages until they were discontinued in 1975.

Round lots represent 100-share groups or multiples of 100 shares. To illustrate the use of Table 3-2, assume 100 shares of a $10 stock are purchased for a total transaction value of $1,000. The pre-1975 commission would be:

$$1.3\% \times \$1,000 = \quad \$13$$
$$+ \underline{\quad 12}$$
$$\text{Commission:} \quad \$25$$

TABLE 3-2 PRE-1975 NYSE RATES FOR SINGLE 100-SHARE ORDERS

Amount involved	Minimum commission
Under $100	Negotiated
$100–799	2% + $ 6.40
$800–2,499	1.3% + $12.00
$2,500–4,780	.9% + $22.00
$4,780 and over	$.65 per share

TABLE 3-3 PRE-1975 NYSE RATES FOR MULTIPLE ROUND LOTS

Amount involved	Minimum commission
$100–2,499	1.3% + $12.00
$2,500–19,999	.9% + $22.00
$20,000–29,999	.6% + $82.00
$30,000–300,000	.4% + $142.00
Over $300,000	Negotiated

Plus for orders of 200 shares or more of the same security there is a $6 charge for each round lot up to 1,000 shares (including the first round lot at the 100-share level) and a $4 charge on each round lot starting at the 1,100-share level.

To illustrate the use of Table 3-3, assume the investor purchased 2,000 shares of a security for $30 per share for a total transaction value of $60,000. The commission for this purchase would then be:

$$.4\% \times \$60,000 = \$240.00$$
$$+ \quad 142.00$$
$$+ \$6 \text{ for each 100 shares up to 1,000} = \quad 60.00$$
$$+ \$4 \text{ for each 100 shares beginning at 1,100 shares} = \quad \underline{40.00}$$
$$\text{Commission} = \$482.00$$

Minimum Commission Rates for Odd Lots

Odd lots are purchases or sales of 1 to 99 shares of one security. The commission rate schedule is very similar to the round-lot schedule. Specifically, the odd-lot rate is $2 less than the rate for a round-lot trade involving the same amount of money. However, the "odd-lot differential" makes odd-lot trading more costly than round-lot trading.

Odd-lot orders are executed by odd-lot dealers who charge a fee for their services. This fee is in addition to the broker's commission. On the New York Stock Exchange, the odd-lot differential is $\frac{1}{8}$ point ($12\frac{1}{2}$ cents) per share on stock selling below $55. For stock selling at $55 or more, it amounts to $\frac{1}{4}$ point (25 cents) per share. The odd-lot differential is not specifically designated on the confirmation slip sent by the broker. Instead, it is included in the price per share. The odd-lot differential compensates the odd-lot dealer for the additional work involved in handling many small odd lots rather than the round lots most dealers handle. The effect of the extra fee is, of course, that it makes odd-lot buying relatively costly. Other noncommission transactions costs which cannot be negotiated are explained below.

Transfer Taxes

New York State transfer taxes are levied on security sales which occur in New York. In addition, a small fee is charged by the Securities and Exchange Commission for transfers.

The New York tax rate is $1\frac{1}{4}$ cents per share for stock selling at less than $5, $2\frac{1}{2}$ cents per share for stock selling between $5 and $10, $3\frac{3}{4}$ cents per share for stock selling between $10 and $15, and 5 cents per share for stock selling at $20 or more. Therefore, the New York State transfer tax on 100 shares of stock sold at $35 per share would be

$$5¢ \times 100 \text{ shares} = \$5$$

The SEC assesses the stock exchanges 1 cent per $500 of securities sold. The exchanges shift this fee onto its selling customers. In the example of 100 shares of stock sold at $35 per share for a total value of $3,500, the SEC fee would be

$$\$3,500 \div \$500 = 7$$
$$7 \times 1¢ = 7¢$$

To summarize, assume the investor both buys and sells 100 shares of stock X at $35 per share. The total transaction costs under the now-discontinued rate schedule would be:

Commission on purchase (.9% × $3,500) + $22 = $ 53.50⎱
Commission on sale (.9% × $3,500) + $22 =   53.50⎰negotiable
New York transfer on sale   5.00
SEC fee   .07
Total transaction costs $112.07

Investors with large portfolios should be able to negotiate commission rates below the old rates simply by threatening to take their business to another broker. But small investors have less bargaining power because brokers will not lose much commission if a small transaction is taken elsewhere. However, the transactions costs just outlined furnish inexperienced investors some rough guidelines with which to guard their own interests in their dealings with stockbrokers.

3-9 ONE CENTRALLY REPORTED MARKET FOR THE NATION?

Many knowledgeable economists who have studied the matter think that the United States public would benefit from having one big competitive national securities system that is centrally administered. This big central stock market made up of the NYSE, AMEX, the other 11 organized regional exchanges, and the OTC markets might all be channeled through one computer. The third market and the fourth market would be competitors in this centralized exchange.

In the new market, fully negotiated commission rates would be the rule. Dealers could vie among themselves to make markets in a given stock as long as the commission income seemed high enough to justify their involvement. And the commission rates would be negotiated between the investor and the broker because stockbrokers would compete with one another in the new market by price competition—that is, by reduced commissions. But all dealers in a given stock would tend to sell it at about the same price because their prices would compete in one nationwide computer hookup. Consequently, investors could buy the stock wherever it is offered at the lowest price or wherever they find the lowest brokerage commissions. For example, a Philadelphia investor could easily trade through a market-maker in Denver or in New York City.

Benefits of a New Central Market

Proponents of a new centralized stock market believe at least five basic improvements would result. Specifically, they contend that a new national system (or a good market of any kind) would (1) be conveniently located, (2) have minimum sales commissions, (3) offer competitive prices to all, (4) minimize transactions costs, and (5) reduce dishonest practices. The present stock markets perform these services. But a reorganized system could probably provide them better.

Convenient location. To assure its success, the new market should be convenient for all investors—ideally, it should blanket the nation. If the NYSE and AMEX in New York, the other 11 organized regional exchanges located around the United States, and the thousands of OTC market-makers across the country were connected by one centralized computer and public reporting system, they could all operate as one market. In fact, a communication system which meets most of these specifications is already in operation. It is called NASDAQ.

The National Association of Security Dealers' automated quotation system (NASDAQ) is a big computer connecting thousands of leased computer terminals located in the offices of most OTC brokers and dealers across the nation, as mentioned earlier. A securities dealer, when wanting to sell stocks, can then simply notify NASDAQ. NASDAQ makes the dealer's wishes public to any inquirer. So dealers wishing to sell stock may offer it at a slightly lower price than other dealers in an effort to attract customers. The buyers' brokers then contact the cheapest seller via NASDAQ and conduct the desired transaction. Thus, thanks to computer terminals, a geographically fragmented market becomes one central market.

Lower commissions. Third-market dealers have long been stealing customers from the NYSE by merely selling the same securities at a lower cost (stock price plus commission fee) than the best bid-and-offer price which might be obtained at the NYSE. If all dealers competed directly in one big market, all would have to adjust their prices in order to stay in the running. Thus the public would have a better chance of obtaining the best commission rate available—a *competitively* determined commission.[15]

Minimum transaction costs. Not only could a central computer bring many geographically separated brokers and dealers under one market reporting system, but, once established, it should be relatively inexpensive to operate. After a market-making computer like NASDAQ is purchased and operating, running a few thousand more transactions through it would cost relatively

[15] R. West and S. Tinic, *The Economics of the Stock Market* (New York: Praeger, 1971).

little. The costs of keeping the computer running must be paid whether or not it is busy. And the computerized market, once it is functioning, should minimize back-office paperwork delays and jam-ups and reduce costly administrative expenses.[16] These cost savings would be passed on to the participating stockbrokers in the form of lower charges for trading their customers' securities. Consequently, brokers who buy and sell securities through a computerized central market should incur lower transactions costs per trade. Competition between the different market-makers subscribing to the central computer system should force them to pass on most of these savings. Thus, reduced brokerage fees or improved services would await buyers and sellers of securities in the national market that economists hope to see emerge in the future.

Fewer dishonest practices. In the type of central market just outlined, competition between the various market-makers can be expected to discourage dishonest schemes. For example, suppose that an unethical market-maker acquired shares of some stock and then "pumped up" its price by circulating false rumors that its value would probably be increasing. Unsuspecting investors who responded to the rumors would bid the stock's price up. At that point, the price-manipulating dealer could sell his or her holdings at the inflated price for a profit. Such a scheme could be carried out on a small scale (in certain stocks which only had one market-maker) with small chance of detection by the authorities. But in a centrally reported market composed of various professional dealers who compete in making a market for this hypothetical stock, such price manipulation would probably fail.

Competing market-makers would watch one another's prices minute by minute through their computer terminals. To remain competitive, they would investigate any unusual price rise. If no reason for its occurrence surfaced, they would sell their holdings of the stock and recommend that their customers do likewise. These sales would help keep the stock's price from rising above its true value. Thus, increased competition in a national market tied together by a central computer could be expected to result in markets where dishonest traders would find it more difficult to ply their schemes. This additional insurance against dishonesty would be provided *free* to private investors by competition among market-makers.

A geographically separated but centrally reporting stock exchange provides a better securities market. But how well the benefits of a new market are realized will depend upon sound planning and skillful implementation — things which the SEC and other people who govern America's securities markets have lacked in the past.

---

[16] I. Friend and M. Blume, "Competitive Commissions on the NYSE," *Journal of Finance,* September 1973, pp. 795–819.

Unanswered Questions

Many questions regarding tomorrow's stock market remain unanswered. Conflicts must be resolved, and details must be hammered out before the new organization can become an operational reality.

Will the new exchange still need specialists who make markets in one or a few stocks, such as the NYSE and AMEX currently have? Or can the central market operate more efficiently if prices are continuously determined by the bids and offers of buyers and sellers who conduct business on the floor, just as commodity markets have done for years? The unique services of the specialist make this a difficult function to evaluate.

Uncertainties loom about the government of a new central market. Should the activities of whatever market emerges be supervised by the SEC? By a group of representatives from the NYSE, AMEX, and NASD? Or by some other groups?

Will institutional investors, such as pension funds and mutual funds, be granted memberships in the new market? If they are, they will siphon considerable commission income from the already-ailing brokerage industry. Policymakers for the new market must decide how far stock brokerages should be forced to undergo painful cost-cuttings and layoffs in order to make room for institutional investors.

Differences of opinion over participation and administration will no doubt delay implementing any new market. However, one thing is certain: Change is never-ending.[17]

QUESTIONS

1 What benefits do security exchanges provide for the country?

2 Name the types of securities most frequently traded over the counter.

3 How are selling prices determined over the counter and on the organized exchanges?

4 What are the advantages and disadvantages of trading on margin?

5 If the margin requirement is 65 percent and Mr. Investor intends to purchase 100 shares of $50 per share stock, what is the minimum down payment he would be required to make?

6 During the early 1970s, the NYSE endeavored to get the SEC to outlaw the third and fourth markets because they "fragmented" the stock market in the United States. Comment on this charge.

[17] Donald E. Farrar, "Wall Street's Proposed Great Leap Backward," *Financial Analysts Journal,* September–October 1971. Lawrence D. Jones, "Some Contributions of the Institutional Investor Study," *Journal of Finance,* May 1972. Also see D. E. Farrar, "The Coming Reform on Wall Street," *Harvard Business Review,* September–October 1972.

7 "Price-pegging assures the investment banking syndicate that no losses will be incurred." Discuss.

8 What are some of the benefits associated with efficient security markets?

9 In what ways are United States security markets inefficient?

10 In years past, the managers of large portfolios which spend thousands of dollars on brokerage commissions each year have been offered bribes (for example, free vacations, free research assistance, free prostitutes, gifts of various kinds, and other forms of illegal "payola," "under the table money," or "kickbacks") by unethical brokers in order to lure them into directing their portfolio transactions to the unethical broker. What effect do you think negotiated brokerage commissions will have on such practices? Explain.

11 List the pros and cons of having America's stock market policed by, first, the SEC or some other government agency, and second, competition in one big national securities market which is all reported through one computer system like NASDAQ and which has negotiated commission rates. Issues involved include: Would the SEC or competition be the least costly way for a nation to regulate its security markets? Or are both needed? Are there certain types of problems which the SEC or competition is not suited to regulate?

12 Do you see any conflict of interest between a stockbroker's roles as (*a*) a sales representative working to maximize commission income and (*b*) an investment advisor who is trying to give her or his clients advice to maximize their wealth? Explain.

SELECTED REFERENCES

Farrar, Donald E., "Toward a Central Market System: Wall Street's Slow Retreat into the Future," *Journal of Financial and Quantitative Analysis,* November 1974, pp. 815–827.
> An incisive nonmathematical discourse about changes in America's security market, written by the Director of the Institutional Investor Study.

Leffler, G. L., and L. C. Farwell, *The Stock Market,* 3d ed. (New York: Ronald, 1963).
> This book goes into detail explaining the institutions and practices making up securities markets in the United States. No mathematics used.

Robbins, Sidney, *The Securities Markets* (New York: Free Press, 1966).
> This book presents a picture of securities markets from the point of view of the Securities Exchange Commission. No mathematics used.

Securities and Exchange Commission, *Institutional Investor Study* (Washington: Government Printing Office, 1971), vols. 1–8.

> This voluminous report was prepared by a group of finance and economics professors under the direction of Professor Donald Farrar. The group spent several years in Washington investigating various aspects of investments. The report, mostly nonmathematical, is organized to discuss different problem areas separately.

Smidt, Seymour, "Which Road to an Efficient Stock Market: Free Competition or a Regulated Monopoly?" *Financial Analysts Journal*, September–October 1971.

> A nonmathematical discussion of the relative advantages of the NYSE dominated markets versus one new central securities market, written by the Associate Director of the Institutional Investor Study.

Four

Regulation of the Securities Markets

Millions of dollars change hands very rapidly in securities markets, providing opportunities for fraud and price manipulation. If these practices are common, investors will become reluctant to put their money in securities. Instead, they will tend to hoard their savings (by burying them in the backyard, for example). If these funds are not available to business to finance new and expanding activities, a nation's economy will tend to stagnate. In order to avoid this, the federal government has taken action to stop fraud and price manipulation in the nation's securities markets and to keep them safe, efficient allocators of investable funds. This chapter explains the government's measures. However, before examining these legislative programs, it will be helpful to consider the market disorders, fraudulent activities, and price manipulation schemes which led to federal regulation of securities markets.

4-1 REASONS FOR THE REGULATIONS

Most of the worst abuses in the securities markets occurred before any federal security regulations existed. A number of states had passed so-called blue-sky laws, but they were deficient in many respects. Often by the time a state got around to prosecuting for the sales of worthless or fraudulent securities, the promoters had long since left the state and were not, therefore, subject to its jurisdiction. Mainly because of a lack of effective federal legal controls, scandalous activities using "wash sales," "corners on the market," "pools," and excessive "pyramiding of debt" preceded the great crash of the stock market, which lasted from 1929 to 1933. In 1933 and 1934, legislation specifically designed to curb these activities was enacted. Since that time, more subtle problems involving "insider information" and fraud have occurred. Each of these disorders will be discussed briefly before we examine the regulations which have been enacted to stop them.

Wash Sales

A wash sale is, essentially, no sale at all. For example, if a man sells securities to his wife, this is a wash sale (assuming he can control his wife). Or a man may buy *and* sell a given quantity of some security in the same day; this, too, is a wash sale. The purpose of a wash sale is to establish a record of a sale. This may be done to establish a tax loss or to deceive someone into believing that the market price has changed.

For example, suppose a dishonest investor were trying to purchase shares in Company X at less than the current market price of $40 per share. If shares of X were inactively traded, wash sales could be used to create the illusion of a fallen price. The dishonest investor could buy and sell his or her own shares of X at prices below $40, using fictitious names and several different securities brokers. The prices of these sales would be a public record. This would create the illusion that shares in X had fallen in price. Then the dishonest investor might be able to purchase shares in X at less than $40 from an innocent party who owned shares but was unaware that the low prices from the wash sales were fraudulently generated.

Wash sales were made illegal by the Securities Exchange Act of 1934.

Corners

An investor who "corners the market" in some security or commodity buys all that item that is for sale. This person then owns the only source of supply and can raise the price. Price manipulators who obtain a corner on the market of some asset may then liquidate it at a high price for a capital gain, or a manipulating speculator will corner a market in hope of trapping or "squeezing" short sellers.

Short sellers are speculators who contract to sell an asset they do not own.[1] They expect the price of that asset to fall, enabling them to purchase the asset at the new lower price and then deliver at the higher price at which they had *previously* arranged to sell it. Thus, short sellers profit from price declines.

To see how a manipulating speculator who obtains a corner on the market can squeeze short sellers and profit from this action, consider an example. Suppose a price manipulator cornering the market in some asset drives its price up and up. Short sellers who notice the inflated price may sell the asset short in expectation of a price fall. When it comes time for the short sellers to deliver, they will find that prices have not fallen as they

---

[1] Short selling is defined and discussed in detail in Sec. 13-1.

expected: they must purchase the shares at whatever price the manipulator demands to cover their short sales.

One of the more spectacular market corners was obtained by Commodore Cornelius Vanderbilt in 1862. Vanderbilt started buying stock in the Harlem Railroad in New York City for $8 per share. He continued until the price was driven up to $100 per share and he had control of the railroad. Then Vanderbilt extended the railroad into Manhattan. Daniel Drew, a ruthless price manipulator, had also purchased shares in the railroad as the price rose. However, Drew wanted more profit, so he conspired to sell his shares to drive the price down and simultaneously to take a short position in the stock in order to profit from its decline in price. Drew influenced Boss Tweed and other dishonest New York City politicians to repeal the railroad's franchise. Then Drew sold all his holdings and also sold 137,000 shares short with the expectation that the price would fall rapidly from $100. The price fell to $72 but Vanderbilt used his great wealth to purchase every share which appeared for sale. Vanderbilt then raised the price of his shares to $179, and Drew was thrown for a loss on his short sales of 137,000 shares. There were only 27,000 shares of stock in the Harlem Railroad outstanding! So, Drew was forced to settle with the buyers of the 137,000 shares which he had contracted to deliver at prices below $100 while Vanderbilt held the price at $179. Since Vanderbilt had cornered the market, Drew's losses became Vanderbilt's gains.

The Securities Exchange Act of 1934 made such price manipulation in securities markets illegal.

Pools

A *pool* is a formal or informal association of two or more persons with the objective of manipulating prices and profiting therefrom. When this objective is completed, the pool is dissolved. A few manipulators may orally agree to operate as a pool, or a contract involving many members can be drawn up. Some of the pool members may provide capital, some may provide inside information, some may manage the pool's operations, or all members can participate in all these functions. Some pools have hired managers for a fee or a percentage of the profits. Some pools even have had specialists from securities exchanges in collusion as hired managers or members of the pool. In general, pools do not tend to conform to any particular organizational format.

During the early 1900s there were basically two kinds of pools — trading pools and option pools. A *trading pool* purchased the shares in which it was interested in the open market. The trading pools usually tried to acquire the securities quietly and discreetly in order to keep from driving up their price while they were buying. Sometimes they tried to depress the security's price while they were buying by disseminating unfavorable publicity about the firm.

An *option pool,* on the other hand, would arrange to acquire all or most of its securities at advantageous prices under option contracts. Many option pools had members who were on the board of directors of the firm whose securities were being manipulated. This board would vote to grant the pool options to buy blocks of new shares at a set price. When the market price rose above this option price, the pool would exercise its option to purchase the shares and then turn around and sell these shares at the higher market price. Although this maneuver diluted the profits accruing to the shareholders of the corporation who were not in the pool, the directors who were in the pool sometimes rationalized the income they derived from the pool by saying it was only compensation for their services as directors.

After a trading pool or an option pool had accumulated large quantities of the security at favorable prices, it would work to manipulate the price upward. Favorable information about the firm would often be disseminated in the form of rumors or "hot tips." Pool members who were brokers would recommend the security to their customers. Pool members within the firm whose securities were being manipulated would issue favorable publicity about the firm. Radio commentators and news reporters were paid by some pools to recommend securities. Pools also "churned" the market in their security by transacting numerous wash sales to call attention to the security and make it appear to have an active market at rising prices. The pool's tactics were often successful in manipulating naive investors into bidding up the price of the pool's security.

When the market price of the pool's securities reached a high figure and was supported there by strong demand, the pool would liquidate its holdings as quietly as possible. In liquidating, it was essential to be discreet so as not to break the wave of optimism supporting the price—a colluding specialist on an exchange could be very helpful at this. After liquidating their holdings at a profit, pool members often went on to sell short in anticipation of the fall in price which was likely to ensue. Any profits earned by pools were losses for investors who were not in the pool.

One of the most profitable pools was the Sinclair Consolidated Oil option pool of 1929. While Sinclair stock was selling in the $28 and $32 range, a contract was obtained from the Sinclair Company granting the pool an option to buy 1,130,000 shares at $30 per share. The pool then purchased 634,000 shares in the open market to bid up prices. The pool exercised its option, then liquidated all its holding while the stock was selling in the $40 range. The pool also sold 200,000 shares short as the price fell. The pool's total profit was approximately $12.5 million from the following sources: $10 million profit from optioned shares purchased at $30 per share; $500,000 profit from shares purchased in the market; $2 million profit from the short sales.[2]

Pool activities were outlawed by the Securities Exchange Act of 1934. The act made price manipulation illegal; required that all pools be reported;

[2] *Stock Exchange Practices,* Senate Report 1455, Seventy-third Congress, 2d session, p. 63.

forbade members of exchanges to participate in pools; forbade the churning and wash sales often used by pools; and required corporation executives, directors, and other insiders to report their transactions in the securities of their firm to the Securities and Exchange Commission.

The Great Crash

On September 3, 1929, the Dow Jones Industrial Average (DJIA) closed at 381. On October 2, 1929, the DJIA fell 49 points, only to be followed by a drop of 43 points the next day. On October 23, 1929, the DJIA had slipped to 306 — a decline of nearly 20 percent in less than 2 months — and it continued to drop. The worst bear market in the history of the United States had begun. The ensuing market decline continued for over 3 years. On July 8, 1932, the DJIA closed at 41 — less than 11 percent of its peak level in 1929! This was the era of the Great Crash and the Depression. Demand for goods and services decreased as pessimism set in and credit began to tighten. The Depression was a period of agonizing economic adjustment. Unemployment spread, reaching a peak of 24.9 percent in 1933 (see Table 4-1).

As unemployment rose, demand for goods continued to drop and prices fell. From 1929 to 1931 the price of a dozen eggs fell from 30 to 18 cents and corn sank from 80 to 32 cents per bushel in spot commodity markets.[3] Millions of unemployed consumers' purchases dropped to mere subsistence levels. As retail sales declined, inventories swelled, and production at many factories ceased. Numerous businesses shut down and eventually went bankrupt because of lack of sales.[4] Loan foreclosures occurred, and most creditors fell behind on their contractual repayments. As a result, commercial banks lacked liquid assets, and some defaulted when depositors demanded their money. When bank depositors could not obtain their funds, the news spread like wildfire. A banking panic began that caused even some of the most soundly managed banks to become temporarily insolvent. From 1930 through 1932 over 5,000 banks failed, causing a loss of $3 billion in deposit currency. President Roosevelt closed all banks on March 6,

[3] U.S. Dept. of Commerce, Bureau of the Census, *Historical Statistics of the U.S., Colonial Times to 1957* (Washington, 1960), pp. 294–304.
[4] J. K. Galbraith, *The Great Crash* (Boston: Houghton Mifflin, 1961).

TABLE 4-1 UNEMPLOYMENT IN THE UNITED STATES

Year	Unemployed	Percent	Year	Unemployed	Percent
1929	1,550,000	3.2	1935	10,610,000	20.1
1930	4,340,000	8.7	1936	9,030,000	16.9
1931	8,020,000	15.9	1937	7,700,000	14.3
1932	12,060,000	23.6	1938	10,390,000	19.0
1933	12,830.000	24.9	1939	9,480,000	17.2
1934	11,340,000	21.7	1940	8,120,000	14.6

Source: U.S. Dept. of Commerce, Bureau of the Census, *Historical Statistics of the U.S., Colonial Times to 1957* (Washington, 1960), p. 73.

1933—it was euphemistically called a "national banking holiday." A week later some of the banks were allowed to reopen on a restricted basis if they were solvent.

Due to the massive unemployment, widespread losses, deprivation, and anguish associated with the Depression, there was a great public demand for reform. Securities markets, which were partly to blame for creation of the economic bubble which burst in 1929, were dealt with swiftly. The Securities Act of 1933 and Securities Exchange Act of 1934 formed the basis for the regulations which still govern securities markets in this country. These and other regulations which were passed at about the same time forbid wash sales, corners on the market, pools, dissemination of fraudulent information, and use of insider information for speculative profits. Full disclosure of the financial conditions of firms issuing securities publicly was required, and the Federal Reserve Board was given control over margin requirements so it could limit speculative excesses resulting from borrowing too heavily and/or pyramiding debt. These changes and others have diminished the frequency of price manipulation schemes and other destabilizing forms of speculation and and have increased the robustness and stability of the security markets in the United States.

4-2 REGULATING THE SECURITIES INDUSTRY

In order to curb fraudulent practices, excessive debt pyramiding, dissemination of misleading or fraudulent information, and market breaks such as the Great Crash of 1929, and generally to increase the depth and stability of securities markets in the United States, the Congress enacted certain laws. The most important of these regulations governing the activity in securities markets are outlined below. The laws are explained in chronological order to show how legislative thinking evolved and to familiarize the reader with the individual acts.

Laws Existing Prior to the Great Crash

The United States government did little to regulate securities markets prior to 1933. Postal laws forbade using the mails to defraud; however, no noteworthy prosecutions were made for securities fraud under these statutes. Because two major stock exchanges, the New York Stock Exchange (NYSE) and the Curb Exchange, as the American Stock Exchange was called until 1953, were both located in the state of New York, New York State had statutes and legal precedents relating to securities markets. But these state laws were too localized to be very effective.

In 1912 the Sixty-second Congress instituted the Pujo Investigation of the "money trust." The investigation was aimed at breaking up the concentration of economic power attained by a group of men, called the money trust, who served as interlocking directors of many large banks and corporations. The investigation resulted in some drastic recommendations for strengthening securities markets but not in any legislation. It took the Great Crash of 1929 and the resulting public uprising to obtain the needed legislative programs. Thus, the securities laws which followed the Great Crash unfortunately resulted from the crisis rather than from foresight and planning.

The Securities Act of 1933

The Securities Act of 1933 (the Securities Act, hereafter) deals largely with primary issues of securities. This act, also known as the "truth in securities law," was supplemented by the Securities Exchange Act of 1934 (SEA). The SEA extends some of the disclosure requirements for primary issues to many secondary issues.[5] The primary purpose of these two laws is to require security issuers to fully disclose all information about themselves that affects the value of their securities. The Securities Act also prohibits certain types of fraud; let us consider it in some detail before discussing the SEA.

Registration of new issues. The main objective of the Securities Act is to provide the potential investor in *primary* issues with a full disclosure of the information needed to make a wise investment decision about new securities. To achieve this objective, the Securities Act specifies that the issuing firm and the investment banker must register the issue. Registration involves filing audited financial statements, other information about the firm, and information about the underwriting agreement with the Securities and Exchange Commission (SEC). Information required in the registration is listed below.

1 A statement as to the nature of the issuer's business, its organization, and its financial structure

2 A list of directors and officers of the issuer, their addresses, and their salaries

3 Details about the issuer's arrangements for bonuses, stock options, and profit-sharing

4 Contracts the issuer may have with subcontractors, consultants, and others

5 Audited balance sheets and income statements of the issuing firm for several preceding years

---

[5] A *primary* issue is a new issue of securities from the issuer to the investing public in which the issuing firm receives the cash proceeds. A *secondary* issue involves sales of previously outstanding shares between members of the investing public—the issuer receives no cash.

6 Copies of the issuer's articles of incorporation, bylaws, trust indentures, and agreement with the investment banker

7 A statement about other securities the issuer has outstanding and their rights

8 A statement about the terms on which the issuer offers its shares to the public

9 Any other statements the SEC may require and any other information that may materially affect the value of the securities

Registration statements may be obtained at the SEC by the general public.

Prospectus. The first part of the registration statement is prepared in the form of a booklet for public dissemination and is called a *prospectus*. It contains most of the information in the registration statement. According to the Securities Act, a prospectus must be given to every investor to whom the investment banker's syndicate sells the new securities. Thus, whether or not investors can comprehend the data in the prospectus, they are provided with one to ensure that they have information to make a decision.

Surprisingly, the Securities Act does not require that a prospectus be delivered before orders for the registered security may be solicited, received, or even accepted, but only that its delivery precede or accompany delivery of the security itself to the customer. This aspect of the act has been criticized by several commentators, who urge that the law require delivery of a prospectus before an order is taken for the issue.

After a firm registers the required information with the SEC, it must wait at least 20 days before issuing the securities. During this waiting period the SEC investigates the proposed prospectus to ensure that all the required information has been disclosed. The proposed prospectus may be circulated during this waiting period, but it must have a note in red ink on its front cover stating that it has not yet received SEC approval for issuance as a final prospectus. A prospectus so marked is sometimes called a "red herring."

If the issuer and the investment banker are not notified otherwise, they may issue their securities after the 20-day wait. By permitting securities to be issued, the SEC in no way implies its approval of them as a good investment. SEC approval merely indicates that the information has been disclosed for investors to analyze if they wish. An actual prospectus may be obtained from any stockbroker for the price of a phone call to request it.

The "small issues" exemption. According to Regulation A of the SEC, a firm issuing less than $300,000 per year of new securities need not comply with the full registration requirement. Such issuers are required only to furnish potential investors with an offering circular containing a limited amount of unaudited financial information.

Secondary sales are also exempt from registration under the Securities Act. Under this act, if more than 90 days have passed and the primary issue is completely distributed, the securities traded in the secondary market need not be accompanied by a prospectus, although it may have been required in the primary issue. However, the SEA requires issuers of securities traded in secondary markets to register and file information with the SEC. Thus, the SEA extends the full disclosure provisions of the Securities Act to cover secondary markets. This regulation will be discussed in more detail when the SEA is taken up later in this chapter.

Private offering exemption.   The Securities Act also exempts from the registration requirements stock issues which are offered to a small group of private subscribers who are sufficiently experienced or informed that the disclosure requirements are not necessary for their protection and who are purchasing the shares as an investment and not for resale to the public. Therefore, each purchaser is required to sign a letter stating that she or he is purchasing the shares for investment purposes. Hence, the shares issued under this exemption are often referred to as *letter stock*. The SEC has required that letter stock investors not sell their shares for at least 2 years after purchase as proof of their investment motives.

"No sale" exemption.   The Securities Act does not require the registration of securities issued in exchange for outstanding stock of the issuer as in a merger or consolidation. The rationale of the courts is that a merger acquisition is not ordinarily regarded as a sale because individual shareholders have little or no choice in the matter—they usually go along with whatever the directors or controlling officers have decided.

Antifraud provisions.   In addition to the requirements pertaining to full disclosure of information, the Securities Act contains some antifraud provisions. It provides court remedies against security salespersons or others who are disseminating untrue or misleading information about securities. Courts finding fraudulent statements being made about securities can issue injunctions to stop such action and require other civil law remedies, such as reimbursement for damages.

The Securities Act limits the techniques which can be used to sell securities. It provides the basis for a later SEC ruling that all public securities dealers imply, by offering their services to the public, that they will deal fairly. This ruling provides a basis for prosecuting security salespersons who issue misleading advice or act to perpetrate other frauds.

When the Securities Act was first passed, there was widespread concern that the legitimate needs of industry for funds would be hampered by the imposition of risks of legal liability or by the risk of harassment by shareholder suits. Nevertheless, the Securities Act provides for both civil and criminal liability when fraud occurs in connection with the issuance of securities or in the registration filed with the SEC; the test of time has shown that the fears were ungrounded.

A significant case under the Securities Act is *Escott vs. Bar Chris Construction Co.* In 1961 Bar Chris, which was in the business of constructing bowling alleys, filed a registration statement with the SEC for new debentures containing inaccuracies and misstatements. After the facts became known, a lawsuit was brought on behalf of individuals who had purchased these debentures. The court held the corporation and its underwriters liable for damages for the inaccuracies. All persons who signed the registration statement or who were officers, directors, or partners of the issuer at the time the registration statement was filed were held liable if it was shown that they failed to exercise *due diligence* in investigating the situation or in making the true facts known. The court also held that any accountant who certified portions of the registration statement which later turned out to be false could be held liable. The court stated that even if the accountants, underwriters, and the firm's lawyers did not know the true facts, they were under a duty to investigate the situation with "due diligence," and if they did not, they could be held liable.

The Bar Chris decision has produced consternation in the investment community. What has most distressed business executives is the possibility of being held liable when they had no intent to deceive as well as the lack of clear standards by which they can know if they have investigated with "due diligence."

The Securities Exchange Act of 1934 (SEA)

After the Securities Act of 1933 was passed, its limitations were quickly recognized, so the Congress immediately set about extending its provisions by enacting the Securities Exchange Act of 1934 (SEA). The primary objectives of the SEA are to (1) provide adequate information about securities being traded in secondary markets in order to facilitate their evaluation and discourage price manipulation, and (2) establish the Securities and Exchange Commission (SEC). The SEA also provides for the regulation of credit for security purchases and contains antifraud provisions.

SEC established. The SEA charged the SEC with the responsibility for regulating securities markets. The SEC is located in Washington, D.C., and is headed by five commissioners who are appointed by the President with the consent of the Congress. In recent years the SEC has had a staff varying in size from 1,000 to 1,500 people and has had an annual budget ranging from $8 million to over $15 million.

Disclosure for secondary securities. In order to ensure full disclosure of information for securities being traded in secondary markets, the SEA requires that an annual registration statement and other periodic reports be filed for public inspection with the SEC as a prerequisite for the listing of a security for trading. The Securities Acts Amendments of 1964 extended these registration requirements to securities traded in over-the-counter markets if the issuing firm has total consolidated assets in excess of $1 million and meets other requirements.

Registration of organized exchanges.   The SEA grants the SEC considerable authority over organized exchanges such as the NYSE. It requires that all exchanges register with the SEC and agree to (1) comply with the letter and spirit of the law; (2) adopt bylaws or rules for expelling and disciplining members of the exchange who do not conduct their activities in a legal and ethical manner; and (3) furnish the SEC with copies of its rules and bylaws and any amendments which are adopted. Within these guidelines the exchanges are free to regulate themselves. However, if an exchange fails to follow them, the SEC can intervene in the affairs of the exchange and alter penalties, expel members of the exchange, or even close the exchange. As a matter of practice, the SEC rarely has intervened.

Credit regulation.   Before the Great Crash in 1929, some speculators purchased securities by making small down payments in the neighborhood of 10 percent of the purchase price from their own funds and then borrowed the other 90 percent. As these securities rose in price, some lenders would count the capital gains as new equity. This interpretation entitled the borrower to borrow even more money. This pyramiding of debt on top of unrealized paper profits was disastrous when the crash came in 1929.

When securities prices began to fall in 1929, security price declines equal to speculators' 10 percent down payments were common. Thus, the first market decline bankrupted imprudent speculators who had overextended themselves by pyramiding debt. When lenders, many of them banks, tried to sell the securities they held as collateral, they often found the value was not sufficient to cover the debt. In order to avoid further capital losses, lenders who held securities as collateral hurriedly dumped the shares on the market for liquidation. This dumping probably accelerated the market's decline and further aggravated the financial crisis. The instability in the banking system and the money supply caused by pyramids of debt which came crashing down deepened the economic recession of the early 1930s.

The congressmen who wrote the SEA wanted to prohibit dangerous debt pyramids. Since the Federal Reserve Board is charged with controlling the money supply and credit conditions, it was given the authority to set margin requirements for credit purchases of securities.[6] The Federal Reserve

---

[6] The Board of Governors also controls banks' reserve requirements and Federal Reserve open-market operations, and sets the discount rate at which banks may borrow from the Federal Reserve System.

then wrote Federal Reserve Regulations T and U to cover initial margin requirements. The initial margin is the percentage of the purchase price which investors must be able to pay with their own funds. Regulations T and U allow the Board of Governors of the Federal Reserve to set the margin requirements for loans made by banks, security brokers, and dealers. In recent years the margin requirement has varied between 50 and 80 percent.[7] Thus, if the margin is 65 percent, an investor cannot initially borrow more than 35 percent of the market value of any security he or she purchases on credit. Maintenance margins (that is, margins which must be maintained as the prices of the securities vary after their purchase) may be set by the securities exchanges.

The SEA also limited security dealers' total indebtedness to 20 times their net capital. This provision is intended to keep securities firms from using excessive debt to carry inventories of securities which could bankrupt the firm in a market decline. Brokers and dealers hold the securities for many of their customers in the firm's name. As a result, the customers would suffer if the firm holding their assets went bankrupt. The SEA's limit on dealers' debt is therefore primarily intended to protect the investor rather than, as it may seem, the dealers and brokers.

In past market declines many brokerage houses came perilously close to collapse and several did go under. Thanks largely to behind-the-scenes efforts of the NYSE crisis committee, which arranged for the infusion of new sources of capital and acted as a merger broker between tottering firms and those in a solid financial position, a financial crisis was averted. It is hoped that the SEC will supervise brokerages more closely in the future to prevent the occurrence of such a dangerous situation again.

Proxy solicitation. The SEA requires that the SEC establish rules to govern solicitations by registered issuers to obtain their shareholders' votes (that is, proxies) on matters to come before the shareholders meeting (such as election of directors). In response to this statute, the SEC requires that all proxy solicitations contain (1) a reasonable amount of information about the issues to be voted upon; (2) an explanation of whether management or the stockholders proposed the issue; (3) a place for the shareholder to express approval or disapproval of each issue with the exception of election of directors; and (4) a complete list of candidates if the proxy solicitation is for election of directors. All proxy solicitations and consent forms must be submitted to the SEC for approval before they are sent to shareholders.

In this day of widespread share ownership and massive corporations,

---

[7] For a critical analysis of the effectiveness of margin requirements, see T. G. Moore, "Stock Market Margin Requirements," *Journal of Political Economy*, April 1966, pp. 158–167. For an analysis of the special margins imposed by the NYSE and AMEX, see James A. Largay, "100% Margins: Combating Speculation in Individual Security Issues," *Journal of Finance*, September 1973, pp. 973–86.

the SEC has sought to effect "shareholders democracy" by making proxy solicitation possible by insurgent groups without the incursion of huge costs. This objective is achieved by requiring that corporate management include a statement or proposal of up to 100 words by an insurgent group when management solicits proxies. This provision makes it less likely that an incompetent corporate management can perpetuate itself through proxy control.

Exemptions from the regulations. Securities of the federal, state, and local governments; securities which are not traded across state lines; and any other securities the SEC wishes to specify are exempt from registering with the SEC.[8] Certain organized exchanges may also be exempted from registering if the SEC chooses, As a matter of practice, certain small, local exchanges have been exempted from SEC registration (namely, the exchanges in Honolulu and in Wheeling, West Virginia). As a result, many of the provisions of the SEA do not apply to these exempted securities and exchanges.

Insider activities. Corporation directors, officers, and other executives and technicians who have access to inside information about the firm which employs them are forbidden by the SEA from earning speculative profits by trading in the firm's securities. To enforce this prohibition, the SEA requires that every officer, director, and owner of more than 10 percent of a listed firm must file a statement, called an *insider report,* of his or her holdings of that firm's securities in each month in which a change in those holdings occurs. These insider reports are made public. For example, *The Wall Street Journal* prints insider reports as they are released.

Section 16 of the SEA of 1934 forbids insiders from making short sales in the firm's shares and entitles stockholders to recover any speculative profits (that is, on holdings of less than 6 months' duration) which are earned by insiders. These provisions have greatly diminished the occurrence of option pools and other price manipulation schemes involving the complicity of insiders. However, insider information violations of a different variety do still occur. In fact, the SEC is still pressing new cases against insiders in an effort to prevent corporate officials and others from benefiting at the public's expense from the information available to them.

One of the most famous and significant cases dealing with the use of insider information is the *Texas Gulf Sulphur* case. In late 1963 Texas Gulf began drilling what turned out to be one of the richest mineral deposits discovered in the twentieth century. Although the initial drilling results of November 1963 were remarkable, announcement of the discovery was not made to the public until April 16, 1964. The firm indicated that this delay was necessary to complete a land acquisition program and to permit further

---

[8] See SEC Regulation A under the 1933 Act.

tests to be made to determine with certainty the magnitude of the discovery.

During the period from November until the announcement, various officers and employees of the corporation purchased shares and options on the corporation's stock, as did various private parties who were tipped off, at prices ranging from $18 to $30 per share. On the date of the announcement, the stock was selling at about $36, and subsequently the increase was even more dramatic, rising to as high as $160 per share 3 years later. In the suit that followed, a federal court of appeals found the officers and employees of Texas Gulf guilty of trading in the corporation's shares without disclosing all "material facts" to the public, an activity that, in effect, was fraudulent and deceitful.

Another landmark case pertaining to insider information was decided in 1966. Merrill Lynch, Pierce, Fenner & Smith (MLPFS) was the underwriter for a proposed issue of Douglas Aircraft Corporation's debentures. This relationship resulted in a case involving more subtle insider information problems. In preparing the financial reports and registration statements to precede the issue of debentures, MLPFS learned that Douglas's profits would be lower than generally anticipated. Before Douglas announced these earnings, MLPFS salesmen provided 12 institutional investors who were MLPFS customers with this information. The 12 recipients of this inside information sold their Douglas stock on the basis of this tip.

The SEC charged MLPFS *and* the 12 recipients of inside information with unlawful use of insider information. MLPFS accepted the penalties without admitting guilt. The 12 "tippees" were censured. In a public statement an SEC examiner said of the 12 institutions, "Blindness toward their obligations to the investing public must be attributed to undue self-interest."[9] Such actions seem to indicate that the SEC tends to give a strict interpretation to the law forbidding the use of insider information.[10] However, only time will reveal the list of legal precedents which will govern insiders' conduct in the future.

Down through the years, SEC rulings and court decisions have broadened the definition of an insider. The SEC's actions seem to be endeavoring to shift profit seekers' interest away from seeking "hot tips" and insider information and toward security analysis instead. As this will tend to decrease the possibility of price manipulation and increase the economic efficiency of securities markets, it is a desirable trend in public policy.

[9] *The Wall Street Journal,* Aug. 16, 1968, p. 1, col. 6, and July 1, 1970, p. 12.
[10] Section 10b of the SEA involves more subtle legal issues than the application of Sec. 16. Section 16 permits the stockholders to recover short-term profits earned by an insider regardless of whether or not the inside information was misused. On the other hand, Sec. 10b deals with fraudulent activities perpetrated by insiders or outsiders. The misuse of inside information is only one area covered by Sec. 10b.

Price manipulation. The SEA, as noted earlier, specifically forbids certain price manipulation schemes, such as wash sales, pools, circulation of manipulative information, and making false and misleading statements about securities. However, the SEA does allow investment bankers to manipulate prices to the extent that they temporarily stabilize a security's price during a primary offering.

The SEA also authorizes the SEC to supervise trading in the options (that is, puts and calls) markets.

The Maloney Act of 1936

Essentially an amendment to the SEA, the Maloney Act was adopted at the request of the over-the-counter (OTC) security dealers and provides for their self-regulation. The act stipulates that one or more associations of "qualified" OTC brokers and dealers may apply for registration with the SEC, the group may regulate itself within the guidelines laid down by the SEC, and the group may grant discounts on securities traded among its members. OTC dealers who are not members of an association deal with members of an association by paying full retail prices for any securities they purchase. This provides a strong incentive for all OTC dealers to belong to an association.

National Association of Securities Dealers (NASD). To date, only one association of OTC dealers has registered with the SEC under the provisions of the Maloney Act; the National Association of Securities Dealers (NASD). The NASD has about 6,000 member firms representing about 100,000 people selling securities in the OTC market. The NASD is headed by a board of governors which is assisted by 13 district business conduct committees. The association has established a testing procedure which must be passed by any individual wishing to join it; a set of rules forbidding fraud, manipulation, and excessive profit taking; a uniform practices code which standardizes and expedites routine transactions such as payments and deliveries; and a program to discipline its members for illegal or unethical conduct.

NASD discipline procedures. In addition to conducting themselves in an ethical manner, member firms of the NASD must submit their books for inspection at any time the association wishes. If any violation is discovered in these audits or if a violation is reported from any source, the NASD disciplines its own members. After hearing the charge against the member and the member's defense, one of the NASD's business conduct committees passes judgment. The charge may be dismissed, or penalties involving suspension and/or fines in the tens of thousands of dollars may be levied. Expulsion from the NASD is the severest penalty, since nonmembers cannot obtain the purchase discounts needed to survive as a dealer. All decisions may be appealed to the NASD's Board of Governors, the SEC, or the courts.

The SEC possesses direct power over the NASD. In particular, it must be given copies of all rules adopted by the NASD (or any other association of OTC dealers which may be formed). It may suspend or revoke the association's registration for failure to follow its guidelines. And the SEC may review and alter the verdict in any judicial proceedings convened by the association. However, the SEC does lack the power to write rules for an OTC association, a power it has for the organized exchanges.

The Trust Indenture Act of 1939

An indenture is a contract, written by a firm which issues bonds, stipulating certain promises the firm makes to its bondholders. A common provision of an indenture is that the issuing corporation can pay no dividends on common stock if the bond's interest payments are in arrears. A trustee (for example, a bank) is appointed to check the issuing corporation in behalf of the bondholders and to make certain that the provisions of the indenture are not violated. If a provision is violated, the trustee should bring a suit against the issuing corporation on behalf of the owners of the indentured securities. If this relationship is to function properly, the trustee must be independent of the issuing corporation so that it is not reluctant to bring suit.

Prior to 1939, corporations were sometimes able to violate the provisions of their indentures. These corporations might appoint their own banks as trustees, for example. Such a bank was dependent upon the indentured corporation for income and was therefore reluctant to sue it if it violated its indenture. To overcome such weakness, the Trust Indenture Act of 1939 requires that the indenture clearly specify the rights of the owners of the indentured securities, that the issuing corporation provide the trustee periodic financial reports, and that the trustee not impair its willingness or legal right to sue the issuing corporation.

Investment Company Act of 1940 (ICA)

The Investment Company Act of 1940 (ICA) is the main piece of legislation governing mutual funds and closed-end investment companies. The ICA extends the provisions of the Securities Act and the SEA. These earlier acts require that the investment companies (like other issuers of securities) avoid fraudulent practices, fully disclose their financial statements, and give their prospectuses to potential investors. The ICA also requires investment companies to publish statements outlining their investment goals (for example, growth, income, or safety); not to change their published goals without the consent of the shareholders; to obtain the stockholders' approval of contracts for management advice for the fund; to limit the issuance of debt; not to employ persons convicted of security frauds as officers; to have some outsiders on their boards of directors; to follow uniform accounting procedures; and to operate the fund for the benefit of its shareholders rather than for the benefit of its managers.

Investment Advisors Act of 1940 (IAA)

The Investment Advisors Act of 1940 (IAA) requires individuals or firms which *sell advice* about securities or investments to register with the SEC. These investment advisors are required to observe the legal guidelines pertaining to fraud, price manipulation, and other factors outlined earlier. The IAA requires that investment advisors' fees not be based on profits earned from the advice. A set fee or a percentage of the assets managed is a permissible compensation plan for advisors under this law. Although it has some good provisions, the IAA is largely ineffective. Practically anyone can qualify as an investment advisor. Although advisors must register with the SEC and disclose their age, experience, education, and other background information, the SEC cannot deny anyone the right to sell investment advice unless it can show that the customer would be cheated or defrauded.

The SEC has developed some policies which tend to limit the advertising practices of investment advisors. It forbids their using selected testimonials from customers, offering free advice unless it actually is free and without obligation, making "false and misleading" statements, and indicating that some graph, chart, or formula can be used by itself to make investment decisions.

Other Laws

In addition to the laws outlined above, there are a few laws which partly govern activity in securities markets. The Public Utility Holding Act of 1935 limits the integration of public utilities. The Bankruptcy Act of 1938 requires that the court supervising any bankruptcy involving listed liabilities of over $3 million ask the SEC for an advisory opinion about reorganization. The Bank Holding Company Act of 1970 forbids banks or their holding companies to own certain nonbanking assets. These laws and a few others which have not been mentioned have a minor effect on securities markets and the SEC at the present.

Enforcement Powers

Under these laws and several other statutes, private citizens are granted powers with which to enforce securities regulations. For example, one individual may charge another individual with fraud or other criminal offenses related to dishonest securities dealings which carry fines of up to $10,000 and imprisonment of up to 2 years. Or an individual may bring a civil suit against a securities firm or a securities exchange and be reimbursed for damages, cause the courts to discipline the offender, or both.

The SEC may also take action to require conformance with the securities laws. The SEC is granted the right to suspend trading in particular securities; to suspend the registration of a security exchange; to expel officers or members of an exchange who operate illegally; to suggest changes in an exchange's rules and bylaws and require their implementation; to collect financial statements and records; to conduct investigations and hearings as needed to enforce the law; to obtain injunctions requiring the cessation of activities violating the securities laws; and to obtain writs requiring violators to comply with the law.

4-3 CONCLUSION AND RECOMMENDATIONS

The regulatory system just outlined has greatly reduced the incidence of fraud and price manipulation, increased market stability, and fostered thoughtful investment analysis. For example, the Pecora hearings, conducted in 1933 and 1934, revealed that during 1927 and 1928 a group of highly respected investment houses had underwritten $90 million of Peruvian government bonds which, by the investment brokers' admission, would never have sold at all had adequate disclosure requirements been in effect at the time. Fortunately, in recent years the market seems to have been largely free of such flagrant abuses. Nevertheless, the regulator program has been far from perfect and bears constant evaluation and improvement. (See Appendixes A and B to this chapter for examples of flagrant law violation.)

SEC's Makeup

Enforcement of security laws and development of new regulatory programs for the United States are largely the responsibility of the SEC. Therefore, some background on this governmental agency will deepen one's insight.

The SEC's daily operations are governed by directors, associate directors, and assistant directors of its various divisions. These various directors are in turn overseen by the five commissioners who comprise the Securities and Exchange Commission. The vast majority of the Commissioners and directors who have managed the SEC since its inception have been attorneys. By and large, the SEC attorneys have been well educated and respectable. But, unfortunately, the homogeneity of their educational backgrounds has imparted a myopic outlook to the SEC's management. Strange as it may sound, the SEC's professional staff contains very few economists, financial analysts, and accountants. Indeed, many of the SEC's top management staff know virtually nothing about finance.

The SEC seems to have at least recognized the problem in recent years, as evidenced by its encouragement of its staff to take some economics and finance night courses at local universities. And the SEC created a position for a certified public accountant who is supposed to work with the accounting profession and the SEC's attorneys in developing better accounting statements. Although these changes represent improvement, the federal agency charged with overseeing the nation's securities markets, investment advisors, mutual funds, and other investment activities is still oversupplied with attorneys and under supplied with professional financial personnel.

Equity versus Resource Allocation

As a result of law school education, the SEC attorneys follow the usual legal procedure of (1) waiting until a law violation has occurred, (2) then gathering proof and assigning blame for wrongdoing, and finally (3) finding the wrongdoers and making them pay damages to the injured parties if possible. This procedure results in what is sometimes lightly referred to as "management by crisis" of America's security markets. That is, the SEC attorneys typically do not go into action until a law has been violated, and then they usually try only to punish the guilty. Unlike economists, attorneys are not trained to analyze resource allocation problems. And, because of its lack of accountants and professional people who are educated in finance, the SEC has difficulty perceiving problems. The fixed commission schedule of the NYSE which was in effect until 1975 is an example (previously discussed in Sec. 3-8).

Various courts, including the Supreme Court of the United States, handed down opinions suggesting that the NYSE's fixed minimum commission schedule was a form of price fixing which violated the Sherman Antitrust Act. This act makes monopolies and price-fixing arrangements illegal. However, the courts took no action and instead referred to the SEC's jurisdiction over the security exchange's rules for further action. Such court opinions, combined with the economic realities of the third and fourth markets, seem to have led to the demise of the fixed minimum commissions. The SEC itself appeared to support the fixed minimum commissions for the first 30 years of its existence because the legal precedent to permit them was set. The economic consequences of this price fixing apparently went unnoticed by the SEC attorneys, who were schooled in the importance of maintaining legal precedents. In the years ahead, it is hoped that the SEC will devote more of its resources to planning for programs to promote proper resource allocation in the nation's capital markets and fewer of its resources to seeing that equitable provisions are made for injured parties after the fact.

QUESTIONS

1 What harm can come to a national economy from corners on the market and pools?

2 Briefly outline the background which led to the development of a system in the United States for regulating the securities markets after 1933.

3 Compare and contrast the Securities Act of 1933 and the Securities Exchange Act of 1934 with respect to registration of securities.

4 What is a prospectus? What is its purpose? When should prospectuses be provided? When the SEC releases a prospectus, does it imply that it recommends the issue for investment?

5 What is the SEC? How did it develop? What functions does it perform? How could it be strengthened?

6 How is credit that is used to purchase securities regulated?

7 Is it illegal to trade securities on the basis of a "hot tip" from an employee of the firm which issues the securities? Explain.

8 What is the NASD? How did it develop? What are its functions? What powers can it use to enforce the law?

9 What is an indenture? What precautions discourage violation of an indenture?

10 What legislation governs the activities of mutual funds? What are the restrictions on the funds?

11 "The SEC's actions tend to ensure that investors will not lose their savings by investing them in securities." True, false, or uncertain? Explain.

SELECTED REFERENCES

Leffler, G., and L. Farwell, *The Stock Market,* 3d ed. (New York: Ronald, 1963).
> Chapters 24, 27, and 28 present a discussion of the history, laws, and administration of securities law. No mathematics.

Loss, Louis, *Securities Regulation* (Boston: Little, Brown 1961), vols. I–III.
> This set of legal volumes is written for persons specializing in securities law. No mathematics is used, but the volumes use technical legal terms.

Robbins, Sidney, *The Securities Markets* (New York: Free Press, 1961).
> This book describes the laws and administrative machinery governing securities markets and makes suggestions for needed reforms. No mathematics.

Securities and Exchange Commission, Securities Act of 1933, Release No. 4725; Securities Exchange Act of 1939, Release No. 7425.
> The SEC provides these and numerous other releases to document and explain its legal activity in the securities industry.

Wiesenberger Services, Inc., *Investment Companies* (New York), published annually.
> Chapter 4 presents a discussion of the law relating to investment companies with special emphasis on legal developments in the area. No mathematics.

APPENDIX A TO CHAPTER 4
The Westec Case[1]

On August 25, 1966, the common stock of Westec was suspended from trading on the American Stock Exchange (AMEX). The suspension followed a flood of sell orders from Ernest Hall, then president of Westec. These sell orders were undertaken to raise cash to cover Mr. Hall's purchases of 160,000 shares that could not be paid for. As the drama unfolded, it became apparent that the particular trades which led to the suspension of Westec stock were no isolated occurrence. Officers, relatives, and associates — abetted by numerous other parties — had (1) sold Westec stock by false and fraudulent representations; (2) unlawfully manipulated Westec stock on the AMEX; (3) embezzled and converted assets of Business Funds, Incorporated, a Houston investment company, to assist in financing these activities; and (4) conspired to create a false and misleading appearance of activity in Westec stock by buying and selling company shares on the open market and arranging loans to finance such trading.

The immediate aftermath of the suspension was the resignation of top Westec officials (James Williams and Ernest Hall) and the resort to chap. 10 of the Bankruptcy Act by Westec. Subsequently, some 93 individuals and firms, including 18 brokerage firms, were indicted or sued by private parties (see Table A4-5). Trading in Westec stock was not resumed until May 1969, almost 3 years later.

Company Background and Objectives

This story began in August 1963, when Messrs. Williams and Hall acquired secret control of approximately 310,000 shares of Western Equities common stock. This purchase from dissident stockholders of Western Equities (later named Westec) was designed to remove a major obstacle to merger activity. The purchase was partially financed by use of assets unlawfully obtained from Business Funds, Inc. At the time of the purchase, James Williams was senior vice president of Business Funds, Inc., while Ernest Hall was president of Geo Space Corporation. Business Funds had invested heavily in Geo Space. Western Equities acquired Geo Space in 1964, largely through the efforts of Business Funds. This brought Hall and Williams together.

Westec, with Hall as president and Williams as chairman of the board, decided to embark upon an ambitious growth program and to stress acquisitions as the principal means of achieving this growth. An avowed goal was to become a billion-dollar corporation by 1970. As outlined in an alleged memo (January 1966) from Ernest Hall to James Williams, "I would

---

[1] The author is indebted to Dr. James E. Walter, who prepared the cases, for permission to use them. Readers will note at several places that actions which a court might find illegal are described rather than merely labeled illegal. This was done so that professors may use the case method of teaching. There are also elements of sophistry to facilitate casework.

like to see us shatter all existing records when it comes to speed and frequency of new acquisitions. Litton has proved that high multiples (of stock price in relation to earnings) can be sustained indefinitely irrespective of what kind of businesses you acquire, providing you keep the growth noise high." The same memorandum further stated, "I think we should avoid a registration like a plague and also be very reluctant to give a breakdown of earnings such as is normally available from a long form audit report."

That Westec was initially successful in achieving its twin goals of sharply rising stock prices and rapid growth through acquisition is evident from the statistics. The price of Westec stock rose from $2 in 1964 and a low of $7.62½ in 1965 to a 1966 peak of $67.10½. Hall's stated objectives were for the stock to reach $12 a share in 1965, $24 in 1966, and $48 in 1967.[2]

In the merger area, some 11 companies were acquired within 18 months. At least four other mergers in process terminated as a result of the suspension of trading in Westec stock. With one exception (Table A4-4), these acquisitions tended to be financed largely by the exchange of stock

[2] Later amended to $305 a share by July 1967.

TABLE A4-1 WESTEC CORPORATION
CONSOLIDATED INCOME ACCOUNT,†
DECEMBER 31, 1965

Sales of:		
Manufacturing equipment		$31,691,154
Services		13,279,043
Other		8,987,390
Total		$53,957,587
Other income		927,180
Costs and expenses	$47,120,650	
Interest, etc.	1,093,572	
Income taxes	1,618,253	
Minority interest	83,371	
		−49,915,846
Net income		$ 4,768,921
Special credit		324,000
Total		$ 5,092,913
Previous retained earnings		513,440
Pooled companies' surplus		9,233,596
Pooled companies' dividends, etc.		3,099,848
Pooled companies' tax adjustment		(228,269)
Retained earnings (12/31/65)		12,068,378
Earnings per share		1.10‡

† Includes all companies acquired during period from March 1965 through April 1966 as "pooling of interest" for entire year.

‡ As reported, on average shares of 4,409,878.

(with the assets of the acquired firm frequently being used as the basis for obtaining additional cash). For example, Chemetron Corp. sold its interest in Pan Geo Atlas Corp. to Westec for 411,866 shares of Westec common stock and $3 million worth of 5 percent cumulative convertible stock. Seacat-Zapata Offshore S.A. was also acquired from Zapata Offshore through an exchange of shares. The exception, Camerina Petroleum Co., was acquired for $8.9 million borrowed from Chase Manhattan Bank.

Aided by the merger activity, Westec's sales grew from $2.3 million in 1963 to $14 million in 1964 and to $54.8 million in 1965. Reported profits, at $4.9 million, or $1.10 per share, in 1965, were some $3\frac{1}{2}$ times their level of the year prior (Table A4-1). Management's profit prediction for 1966 was $13 million, or $2.65 a share, with sales forcasted in excess of $100 million.

Manipulation

In their efforts to create a favorable atmosphere for merger activity, Westec principals (1) took substantial positions on their own account, (2) arranged for cross-trades to give the appearance of activity in Westec stock, (3) sought information about the depth of the AMEX specialist's book in Westec stock, (4) spread rumors, and (5) endeavored to manage earnings. Little was left to chance.

Position taken by the principals. Ernest Hall, together with family and friends, held more than 1,000,000 Westec shares throughout the 2 years prior to the company's collapse.[3] Notes and other obligations incurred to finance this position in Westec stock, when added together, amounted to almost $19 million. Interest payments on outstanding loans averaged on the order of $15,000 a month. Hall was periodically "desperate for cash."

James Williams, on the other hand, personally held less than 25,000 shares.[4] Williams was, however, subsequently accused of short-term trading in Westec common stock through a partnership arrangement with Mr. Evans, a Houston investor.

The mechanics of manipulation. In the case of Westec, the mechanics of creating an appearance of interest and activity were relatively straightforward. On the basis of recommendations by Hall or some other Westec officer, a brokerage house would open accounts for individuals who had no official connection with Westec. This was evidently done without the individuals' knowledge. For example, a Westec official would place an order for, say, 10,000 shares of Westec, to be credited to the account which had been opened in someone else's name for this purpose. Upon receipt of the stock

---

[3] The Haas brokerage firm alone handled purchase orders for about 250,000 shares of Westec (mostly placed by Hall and Williams) from May to August 1966.

[4] His holdings did, however, include an option to buy 50,000 Westec shares at $7.62\frac{1}{2}$ a share.

TABLE A4-2 WESTEC CORPORATION
CONSOLIDATED BALANCE SHEET
DECEMBER 31, 1965

Assets:

Cash	$ 4,969,913
Receivables (net)	16,014,697
Inventories†	7,356,572
Prepayments	310,934
Total current assets	$ 28,652,116
Net property, etc.‡	20,870,190
Real property for sale	2,552,724
Marketable securities	879,234
Installments receivable	1,185,856
Deferred charges	1,777,454
Total assets	$55,917,574

Liabilities and net worth:

Notes, etc. payable	$ 7,613,556
Accounts payable	4,797,597
Income taxes	957,888
Dividends payable	374,700
Accruals, etc.	1,726,751
Total current liabilities	$15,470,492
Long-term debt	13,510,305
Deferred liability and credit	550,430
Deferred federal income tax	253,688
Minority interest	698,088
5% Preferred A ($100)	280,500
5% Preferred C ($100)	160,000
5% Preferred D ($100)	3,000,000
Common stock ($0.10)	454,100
Capital surplus	9,503,454
Retained earnings	12,068,378
Reacquired stock	(31,861)
Net stockholders equity	$40,447,082
Total liability & net worth	$55,917,574

† First in/first out (FIFO).
‡ Depreciation, depletion, and amortization:
$15,102,616.

certificates from New York City, the brokerage firm would present the stock to an out-of-town bank which would pay for the securities and hold them as collateral. About a week later, the stock would be sold from the individual's account; such "wash sales" created the appearance of much interest and activity in Westec stock.

Specific illustrations of trades actually made can be cited. For example, in a hearing subsequent to the suspension in trading, Mr. Smyth, a former vice president of a Westec subsidiary, was shown 79 confirmation slips for orders of 54,000 shares placed through Moroney, Beissner, a brokerage house, in his name. Smyth said he had no knowledge of these orders. At the same hearing, a Westec engineer also professed ignorance of 12 confirmation slips of orders for 6,000 shares of Westec in an account bearing his name. Lester Lilley, a brother-in-law of Ernest Hall, traded 460,000 shares, or almost 10 percent of the outstanding shares, in the 5 months prior to suspension of trading. Much of this trading is believed to have been done by someone other than Lilley.[5]

Most large orders to purchase Westec came through R. W. Bull, a director of Westec and partner of Ross, Low, & Bull Co. Bull was alleged to have placed orders in Westec stock for over $6 million with G. C. Haas, a brokerage house, without ever doing a credit check on the individuals placing the orders, and, in many instances, without even seeking direct authorization from the individual himself. Arrangements made in the early summer of 1966 permitted Bull to transmit the orders directly to the Haas order room and to notify a Haas partner of the transaction later in the day rather than follow the usual safeguards and procedures.

Some well-known brokerage houses were included among those that permitted transactions of the kind just described. At Hall's request, for example, an account executive for Merrill Lynch, Pierce, Fenner & Smith accepted orders without written power of attorney in the name of Hall's secretary and for others as well. An official of A. G. Becker Co., in turn, was subsequently fired for dealings which involved arrangements for $8 million in loans to Westec officers and associates; finder's fees to A. G. Becker Co. for arranging those loans totaled some $95,000. In later indictments, some six brokerage houses were alleged to have knowledge of the manipulation scheme. An additional 12 houses were accused of negligently permitting transactions in Westec stock.

The specialist book.   Despite the fact that the specialists' trading book is not available to anyone but exchange officials, hearings conducted by the special counsel for the Westec trustee disclosed that information about the trading book had indeed been passed on to Hall. The intermediary between Joseph Petta, the specialist, and Hall was a public relations man named Alan Will Harris.[6]

Excerpts from the letters sent to Hall are most interesting. One letter from Harris, dated February 19, 1965, stated: "Our friend downtown tells me he has 10,400 shares on his book for sale at 10 and that it will probably take several days to absorb that amount if we are marching on higher levels. There's little stock offered at $10\frac{1}{2}$ to 12, so once the 10 mark is passed the

---

[5] From April to August 1966, the time of suspension, some 4,205,400 shares changed hands (a ratio to outstanding shares of .93); in the corresponding 1965 period, only 921,500 shares were bought and sold.

[6] Harris had been recommended by Petta in 1964 for his job as Westec's outside consultant. The two men had been acquainted for some 15 years.

going should be relatively easy and relatively fast." Another letter stated: "Petta tells us again there is considerable selling out of the Houston office of Merrill Lynch. . . . I don't know what you can find out or do but Petta takes it seriously." Harris testified that he received supposedly secret information from the specialist's (that is, Petta's) trading book perhaps a dozen times.

Rumors. As evidenced by quotations from other letters written by Harris to Hall, rumors and gossip contributed to the rapid price rise of Westec's stock. In one of Harris's letters the point was made that "the absence of . . . publicity, plus the pressure of those who went short in Westec, has created a tide of adverse activity. The word of mouth which has served us well for months is now hurting us to some extent." During the violent trading of Westec in 1966, Harris wrote, "Rumors are all over the place — you pay your money and you take your chances."

The amount of deliberate rumor activity is difficult to ascertain. Harris was, nonetheless, sued by a Westec shareholder who alleged that Harris engaged in deceptive practices by passing along a story that Westec had made a large mining strike in Ontario. Harris acknowledged efforts to firm up Westec's price through contacting customers' men in at least two dozen brokerage houses. Harris also passed along substantial information to Westec's public relations official in Houston. The latter, a Miss Betty Athanasiou, testified that Westec officials instructed her to "disseminate a rumor" about a copper strike just before Westec was suspended from trading on the AMEX (even though the discovery had little commercial value).

Managed earning. The long list of activities undertaken by Westec executives in an effort to generate favorable stock prices includes managed earnings.[7] In short, Westec officers predicted earnings levels in advance and then endeavored to see that these earnings levels were attained.

Profits were inflated by including transactions that had not occurred, as well as by the failure to stipulate that some income was not recurring. False reporting, initiated as early as 1964, involved both quarterly and annual reports. The 1964 report concealed the fact that net earnings included $115,364 in nonrecurrring income of Doliver Corporation resulting from real estate transactions. Quarterly reports for 1964 also included earnings attributable to purported sales of properties; these sales never occurred. The 1965 annual report, printed in May 1966, included net earnings of Engineers and Fabricators Co. ($896,178) on a pooling basis, even though the company had been acquired in April 1966. This inclusion was necessary

---

[7] In the opinion of Mr. Ince, director of Westec and president of G. C. Haas, the company's future prospects were so great that "whether the earnings were 50 cents a share of $1 a share really didn't make much difference. This company had a stamp of quality to which I attached a lot of weight."

to fulfill a previous forecast that Westec would earn more than $1 a share in 1965.

The Texas Securities Commission later concluded that all the 1965 profit of Westec, amounting to some $5.2 million, represented either nonrecurring income or *pro forma* income from five companies not actually acquired until 1966. Profits included (1) one-time production payments aggregating $1.2 million, (2) the pooled earnings of five companies acquired in early 1966 amounting to $2.1 million, (3) a special credit from a subsidiary totaling $300,000, (4) the sale of oil and gas properties to companies owned by Hall's brother in the amount of $1.7 million.

The figures for the first 6 months of 1966 were completely bogus. In subsequent testimony, it turned out that earnings for the first quarter were juggled to conform to earlier statements made by Williams and the second-quarter earnings figure of 63 cents a share included results of a $4.6 million sale of oil properties that was never completed.

Parties Involved

A truly amazing feature of the Westec story is the number of different parties who went along with the manipulation scheme. The list includes a major accounting firm, at least two commercial banks, some rather prominent financiers, a specialist on the AMEX, six brokerage houses that presumably knew of the scheme, and a dozen more that made little effort to check.

Two executives who were members of the AMEX and members of the Westec Board of Directors, together with the president of Haas Securities Corp., were subsequently disciplined by the exchange.[8] The exchange's governing board said that the two directors had both violated the exchange's rule 411, that is, the "know-your-customer rule." It alleged that both brokers "accepted accounts and G. C. Haas and Co. executed substantial orders in a listed security (Westec) for certain individuals and . . . through negligence, lack of investigation and lack of adequate supervision, they failed to conduct their business in a manner consistent with prudent and acceptable standards required of Exchange members and member organizations." They allegedly "failed to make inquiry of customers as to the circumstances surrounding these substantial purchases and the ability of these customers to pay for such purchases." The brokers also were alleged to have violated the Federal Reserve Board's regulation "by failing to obtain appropriate agreements from certain customers that they would

---

[8] The original firm, G. C. Haas and Co., ceased doing business with the public in October 1966. Haas's liabilities from unsettled Westec purchase orders and from unpaid loans collateralized with Westec stock were judged to exceed $5 million, or about one-half of Haas's capitalization prior to Westec. The successor firm, Haas Securities Corp., began operations with total assets of $1,495,000 and assumed no liabilities of the old partnership.

promptly make full cash payment for stock purchased in cash accounts and by failing to require such payment to be promptly made."

In June 1969, the governing board of the AMEX, in addition, suspended the two specialists formerly assigned to make a market in Westec stock.[9] The board stated that the senior specialist had violated AMEX rules and the SEA by disclosing to unauthorized persons information regarding orders which had been entrusted to him as a registered stock specialist. Both parties had broken AMEX rules by "disclosing the names of purchasers and sellers of a security in which they were the registered specialists."

So far as the major accounting firm is concerned, the SEC itself undertook administrative proceedings under Rule 2-E of Rules of Practice. The specific cases in point were acquisitions by Westec which involved conditional sales agreements of one kind or another. Although contrary to acceptable accounting practice, the earnings of these conditional acquisitions were incorporated into reported income on a pooling-of-interest basis. The prime issue in this case was whether the accounting firm knew the facts.

Hall, who pleaded guilty to the manipulation attempt and turned state's evidence against Williams, served a federal prison term (together with two close associates). Williams was convicted and appealed his 15-year sentence. Numerous civil suits were still pending at reorganization time.

The Aftermath

The consequence of the questionable behavior was resort to chap. X of the Bankruptcy Act for Westec in late September 1966. Such action was necessitated by the decision of creditors, including the company's bankers, to cut off lines of credit. Court protection was required to preserve the value of Westec's businesses for the benefit of creditors and shareholders.

As a first step, in early October 1966, the Bankruptcy Trustee, Orville S. Carpenter, former president of Texas Eastern Transmission Corporation, arranged a $2 million credit line (at 7 percent and secured by stock in Westec subsidiaries) for the remainder of 1966 with Chase Manhattan Bank and First City National Bank of Houston. An additional $1.5 million (at 6.75 percent interest and maturing on July 1,1967) subsequently was obtained from the same two banks.

As a second step, Eastman Dillon Securities Co. was appointed consultant to report on the possible sale of Westec assets. Fees initially set at $60,000 for financial advice and payments up to $500,000 in the event of sale

---

[9] Joseph Petta, 62, the AMEX specialist in Westec, sustained a $2 million loss because of a 30,000-share position in Westec at the time of its suspension. A large portion of his specialist activities was assumed by another specialist group, although Petta *continued* to make markets for several AMEX stocks after receiving new financing. In the words of Petta, "All I can say is that I think I'm a damn fool to have been involved in this at this stage of my life."

TABLE A4-3 SELECTED FINANCIAL DATA FOR WESTEC CORPORATION

	Dec. 31, 1966, $	Dec. 31, 1967, $	Dec. 31, 1968, $	June 30, 1969, $
Current assets	23,825,902	16,490,000	15,342,000[a]	n.a.
Current liabilities	17,405,237	6,442,000	2,769,000[a]	n.a.
Total assets	54,409,130	n.a.	n.a.	n.a.
Sales	32,729,581[b]	30,800,000[c]	n.a.	13,000,000[f]
Income (loss)	(2,575,623)[b]	(3,900,000)[c,d]	(140,000)[e]	425,000[f]

[a] Projected.
[b] First 8 months, 1966.
[c] 8/31/66 to 12/31/67.
[d] Includes (1) a charge of $1.4 million representing the net of gains and losses arising from the sale of certain subsidiaries and other assets of the company and recoveries from claims and settlements, and (2) provision for losses on sale of part of Camerina's assets ($2.4 million) and of Pan Geo Atlas's assets ($1.5 million).
[e] Inclusive of trustee's expenses and legal fees, which totaled $652,000.
[f] Six months, 1969.

or merger were changed to $6,000 per month for 12 months, plus a flat fee of $300,000 in equal payments. As a third step, a new auditor (Price Waterhouse & Co.) was hired to replace Ernst and Ernst Accountants.

Losses reported during the 16 months ending December 31, 1967, approached $4 million (Table A4-3). Deductions from income included (1) a charge of $1.4 million representing—in the words of Mr. Carpenter, the trustee—"the net of gains and losses arising from the sale of certain subsidiaries and other assets of the company and recoveries from claims and settlements," and (2) provisions for losses on sales of assets of Camerina Petroleum Corp., a subsidiary, of $2.4 million and Pan Geo Atlas Corp., another subsidiary, of about $1.5 million. Net income for operating subsidiaries continued to be acceptable, although lower than hoped.

By the end of 1967, $11.2 million had been realized from sales of unprofitable operations and had been largely applied to debt reduction.[10] Seacat-Zapata Offshore Co., which owned an offshore drilling rig, was reacquired from Westec by Zapata Offshore Co. for $500,000 plus 98,765 Westec shares. Orphan Mine, a uranium mine, was sold to Cotter Corp. for $975,000, thus relieving Westec of monthly expenses of $25,000. Westec's sales included Engineers and Fabricators Co. (for $5,446,299) and oil and gas properties of Weco Petroleum Co. (for $350,000) both to Aberdeen Petroleum Corp.

The organization plan, proposed in early 1968, called for the formation of a new company to control eight Westec subsidiaries. Proposed steps included the sale of Pan Geo Atlas Corp. to Dresser Industries for

[10] As early as May 1967, 85 claims—totaling more than $32 million—had been filed against Westec.

$6,040,000, the sale of Camerina Petroleum Corp. for $5,100,000, the use of the proceeds to repay borrowings of $1,168,000 and other debts (and to finance the new company), and settlement of the lawsuit with Chemetron.[11] Chemetron, the former owner of Pan Geo Atlas, would receive $1 million in cash, $1.5 million in subordinated debentures, and 10,000 shares of a new 6 percent preferred stock (with full voting rights and a liquidation value of $1 million). Carpenter, the trustee, proposed to retain 20 percent of the common stock of the reorganized company and other assets in a fund for payment and prosecution of claims and for administrative fees. The remaining stock was to be distributed to current Westec shareholders whose claims were approved by the court.

The last major claims blocking the proposed reorganization were settled in November 1968. Commercial Discount Corp. was permitted to retain ownership of 251,000 Westec shares in return for dropping claims ($4 million) against the trustee. Mr. McGregor, the intermediary in the acquisition of Engineers and Fabricators Co., also dropped claims ($7 million) and agreed to cancelation of his 24,900 Westec shares in return for relief from certain debts to Commercial Discount Corp. Less than $1 million of the total claim that exceeded $30 million was never settled.

The SEC filed its advisory report with the bankruptcy court in January 1969. Hearings were held, and final court approval for the reorganization was given in late April 1969. Trading was permitted to resume on May 5, 1969, after a hiatus of over 32 months. Book value per share approximated $2.50 as of that date. Unaudited profit in the first half of 1969 came to $425,000 on sales of $13 million. The closing stock price in 1969 was $4\frac{7}{8}$; the 1969 range was from $4\frac{3}{8}$ to $11\frac{3}{4}$.

As early as August 1969, Westec was back on the acquisition trail. A proposed merger called for the issuance by Westec of 3.5 shares of its common stock for each of Telecom Corporation's 1,613,220 shares. Telecom, which owns Red Ball Motor Freight Co., is a manufacturer of valves and food-processing machinery and has operations in outdoor advertising, communications, and water supply to the oil industry. A subsidiary, Texas Capital Corporation, is a small business investment company. The union of Westec and Telecom would produce an operating company with annual revenues of $85 million.

See Table A4-4 for a summary of Westec's acquisitions prior to its bankruptcy. Table A4-5 lists the major lawsuits, convictions, and jail sentences brought against Westec's executives for their irresponsible behavior which led to the bankruptcy.

---

[11] The sale of Pan Geo Atlas, completed in early July 1968, was defended on the ground that it required several million dollars in the next 3 years for research and development and for equipment replacement if Pan Geo were to survive.

TABLE A4-4 WESTEC ACQUISITIONS

Date	Acquisitions consummated	Fraction acquired, %	Terms	Comments
1964				
Apr.	Geo Space Corporation	100	3.7 shares of Geo Space for 1 share of Western Equities	
1965				
Mar.	Trak Microwave Corp.	89.5		
Mar.	BECO Inc.	100		
Mar.	Doliver Corp.	100		
	Camerina Petroleum	97	$8,900,000	
	Pan Geo Atlas Corp. (completed in 1966)	87	411,866 com. shs. and $3,000,000 of conv. prfd.	Conv. at $18 a share into 166,667 shs. of Westec common stock.
Late	Jet Set Corp. (116,000 shs. acq.)	100	30,000 com. shs. and 270,000 shs. contingent on Jet earnings	
	Metric Systems, Inc.	100	180,000 com. shs.	
	Datamatics Intl., Inc.	100	$200,000 in stock	
1966				
	Engineers & Fabricators, Inc.	100	85,545 com. shs.	A third corp. (McGregor's Tupper Lake Corp.) borrowed money to purchase E. & F. stock and then swapped E. & F. shs. for Westec stock (pledged as collateral for loan).
	Carey Machine & Supply, Inc.	100	$1,000,000 in stock	
	Seacat-Zapata Offshore Co. S.A.	100	$6,000,000 in stock	Former Seacat stockholder to receive between 30 & 50% of Seacat's profit for management services.
	Acquisitions not consummated			
June	Aberdeen Petroleum		$3.8 million in stock	Purchase by Camerina (April 1966) of all 200,000 shs. of Class B stock to obtain board control.
July	Belinas Co.		$4.8 million in stock	
Aug.	Aircraft Mechanics		$5 million in stock	Would not assume $1.2 million of liabilities.
	Independent Coal & Coke Co.		$4.6 million in stock	

TABLE A4-5 LEGAL ACTIONS

Shareholder and other suits

Date	Plaintiff	Defendants
1966		
Sept.	Ada Elster	Westec directors and Ernst & Ernst Accountants

"Had the true facts concerning Westec's earnings and prospects been known, the price that she and others would have had to pay for Westec shares on the American Stock Exchange would have been very much lower." The suit asked that Westec and other defendants be required to pay Mrs. Elster and other stockholders "the damages each has suffered as a result of the alleged wrongs."

Sept.	Rafkind & Co.	Westec,† Hall, Pan Geo Atlas Corp.,† Williams

Purchase of $499,100 of stock in Scurry Rainbow on basis of order from Mr. Williams for pension fund of Pan Geo Atlas Corp. Unpaid stock sold at loss of $146,100. (On the same day, Scurry Rainbow officials placed an order for Westec stock in the same dollar amount.)

Sept.	Westec	Hall, Williams

Court asked to decide whether Mr. Hall and Mr. Williams could be held liable to the company in a declaration judgment (in which the court gives its opinion on a question of law or tells a party what his legal rights are without ordering that anything be done).

Sept.	1. Steven E. Leber 2. Daniel E. Schneider 3. Norman Lettmon	Westec, officers, and directors, G. C. Haas and Co.

Suits charge that Westec and its officers and directors manipulated the price of the stock and overstated Westec earnings; the actions seek damages for losses allegedly suffered by the stockholders.

Sept.	Beulah Curtis	Westec, officers and directors, Chase Manhattan Bank, brokerage houses, and Ernst & Ernst Accountants

Suit charges that officers and directors "caused the preparation, attestation, public filing and dissemination of false and misleading reports and press releases concerning defendant Westec's financial earnings and outlook." Suit also alleges that defendant stockbrokers "permitted trading in Westec stock without proper supervision of accounts upon improper trading authority in violation of the 'know-your-customer' rule and by false or negligent request for customer payment extensions." Plaintiff asks that defendants return profits and pay damages and that Westec itself not defray any costs.

Oct.	Westec stockholder	Westec management and Hall

Suit charges that Mr. Hall's transaction with Mr. Mize (to help him take control of Zapata Offshore Co.) was a "violation" of his "fiduciary obligation" to Westec.

Oct.	Cosmo Bank	Ernest Hall, Jr., James Williams, Lester Lilley (in May 1967, also filed suit against David C. Bintleff)

Suit for $335,030 allegedly due on a defaulted loan made with 12,166 shares of Westec common stock as collateral (money loaned to Lester Lilley and guaranteed by Mr. Hall, dropped because defendants had no assets in New York).

Oct.	F. W. Blackman (Westec stockholder)	A. G. Becker and three employees

Suit charges that A. G. Becker was "a substantial seller" of Westec stock just before the sharp drop of August 14 and that Mr. Pogue (who was claimed to have *inside* information), who had been represented as personally owning a large amount of Westec stock, was in fact liquidating his own account and those of his customers. Suit charges that these liquidations occurred while A. G. Becker was advising "many of its customers" to retain their Westec stock. Suit asks $31,701.47 for losses in Westec dealings and $59,000 in punitive damages from each defendant.

† Dropped in June 1968.

TABLE A4-5 LEGAL ACTIONS (continued)

Shareholder and other suits

Date	Plaintiff	Defendants
1967		
Mar.	Westec stockholder (Mrs. Kerstein)	Allen Will Harris

Suit alleges Harris stated "he had vast influence in the control of the price of stock of Westec Corp.," that Westec had "discovered in Manitouwadge, Canada, 80 million pounds of molybdenum, having a value of over $400 million," and that "the price of Westec would soar" due to acquisitions. Plaintiff seeks $13,000 in damages from losses and $200,000.00 compensation for alleged losses to her reputation and health.

Aug.	Chemetron	57 individuals and companies

Suit asserts that the purpose of the conspiracy to rig the stock price "was to use such inflated stock unlawfully to acquire cash or other valuable property from Chemetron and other innocent purchasers and unjustly to enrich the conspirators."

1968		
May	Orville S. Carpenter (Westec trustee)	J. W. Williams, Digital Data Systems, Inc. and three officials of Digital Data (employees of Geo Space until late 1966)

Civil antitrust suit ($2,250,000) alleges that defendants conspired to "cripple" Geo Space Corp. and eliminate it as a competitor. Suit charges that defendants as Geo Space negotiators sabotaged contract with Pan American Petroleum and defendants enticed key Geo Space employees to join Digital Data.

Aug.	Westec's trustee	93 individuals and firms

The complaint supplants a civil suit filed against Hall and Williams in October 1967.

Grand jury indictments and sentences are summarized below:

Date	Defendant	Charge
1967		
Dec.	Lester L. Lilley	Charged Lilley and others acted together to defraud brokers and Westec stockholders by purchasing about 470,000 shares of Westec common between May 1, 1966 and August 25, 1966.
	Action: Pleaded guilty	
1967		
Dec.	Ernest Hall, James Williams, Malcolm Baker	Seven counts: (1) On three occasions, Williams filed false reports of his Westec ownership to SEC; (2) three false reports to SEC by Hall; (3) all accused of conspiracy.
1968		
Jan.	E. Hale, J. Williams, M. Baker, F. Hall, M. Hall, D. McGregor	Nine counts, including sale of unregistered shares and purchasing of stock in various names (without disclosing that neither the defendants nor the persons in whose name the stock was ordered had funds to pay for such stock). All charged with conspiracy.
Jan.	J. Williams, E. Hall, F. Hall, H. Belcher	Twenty counts, including (1) conspiring to sell unregistered shares and (2) making and distributing false and misleading statements about Westec's financial condition
May	Ernest Hall pleaded guilty on two counts of conspiring to manipulate Westec stock price and of filing false earnings statements of Westec with the SEC.	

TABLE A4-5 LEGAL ACTIONS (continued)

Grand jury indictments and sentences (continued)

Date	Plaintiff	Defendants
1968		
June	After Ernest Hall's guilty plea, the judge ordered separate trials for the remaining defendants.	
July	James W. Williams, found guilty on one count of conspiracy to file false financial reports and 12 counts of related mail fraud.	
Aug.	Former Westec aide Malcolm Baker pleaded guilty to a criminal information alleging manipulation of Westec shares.	
Oct.	Sentencing: J. W. Williams, 15 years; E. M. Hall, 8 years; M. G. Baker, Jr., 18 months; L. L. Lilley, 1 year.	
1969		
Mar.	H. G. Watson, J. J. Donovan, J. M. Pogue	Beginning in early 1965, the three obtained funds from the Rolling Meadows Bank with intent to defraud. The bank alleged that Pogue "would delay the settlement of the stock purchased through the joint trading account with A. G. Becker & Co. so that the stock would increase in value before delivery," and then "make false entries on the books, reports and statements of the Bank of Rolling Meadows and cause the same to be made to persons other than themselves."

APPENDIX B TO CHAPTER 4
Equity Funding Cases[1]

On March 27, 1973, the New York Stock Exchange halted trading in shares of Equity Funding Corporation of America (EFCA). This action followed an 8-day period in which the stock dropped from $24.875 to $14.375. The following day, the SEC halted trading in the company's securities until April 8 (initially) and began a formal investigation of EFCA and its subsidiary, Equity Funding Life Insurance Co. (EFLIC).

In the days that followed, it became evident that (1) EFLIC had sold bogus policies to reinsurers, (2) assets of the parent (EFCA) included some $77.7 million of fictitious loans to fictitious policyholders, (3) the company's auditor had close ties with management, and (4) a so-called tippee had informed his clients rather than the SEC. These disclosures led to (1) the early resignation of three top officers in the parent and its subsidiary, (2) a court-designated petition for financial reorganization under Chapter X,

[1] Prepared from public sources by James E. Walter, Professor of Finance, The Wharton School, University of Pennsylvania.

(3) the refusal of Salomon Brothers to honor sales of Equity Funding shares by funds alleged to possess inside information, and (4) numerous suits.

Background

Incorporated in Delaware as Tongor Corporation (September 2, 1960), Equity Funding Corporation of America assumed its present name on January 19, 1961. Acquisitions included Wendell Christenson Estate Program Associates of San Francisco (1967), Crown Savings & Loan Association (1967), Presidential Life Insurance Co. of America (1967), Presidential Life Insurance Agency, Inc. (1967), Salik Management Corp. (1968), Insurance Planning Corp. of America (1969), Pension Life Insurance Co. of America (1969), Ankony Angus (1969), Independent Securities Corp. (1970), Liberty Savings & Loan Association (1971), Bankers National Life Insurance Co.

TABLE B4-1 EQUITY FUNDING CORPORATION OF AMERICA: CONSOLIDATED BALANCE SHEET FOR 1970 AND 1971 (AS OF DECEMBER 31)

Assets	1971	1970
	(in 000's)	
Cash and equivalents	$ 39,593	$ 20,855
Investments	188,002	171,560
Receivables	140,675	108,604
Insurance premiums	9,925	9,265
Inventories, etc.	5,632	7,165
Def. policy acquisition lost	40,636	29,352
Net property	27,351	21,533
Excess cost (acquisitions)	23,032	23,195
Equity in unconsolidated subsidiaries	9,067	9,026
Other assets	12,782	12,441
Total	$496,695	$412,996

Liabilities and net worth	1971	1970
Long-term debt	$ 49,728	$ 50,739
Notes payable	33,972	23,924
Subordinated debt	64,687	26,187
Accounts payable	16,283	19,045
Income tax liability	34,903	30,413
Insurance reserves	148,250	139,036
Policyholders funds	19,704	17,773
Other liabilities	11,506	7,797
Minority interest	—	275
Deferred income	—	1,468
Common stock ($.30)	2,314	2,241
Preferred stock	3,649	6,497
Paid-in surplus	61,156	54,553
Retained earnings	50,555	33,060
Reacquired stock	(12)	(12)
Total	$496,695	$412,996

(1971), Northern Life Insurance Co. (1972), and Realty Insurance Associates and Nash Agency (1972). Presidential Life became EFLIC on June 10, 1970.

EFCA offered diversified financial services through its Insurance, Investment Management, Natural Resources, Finance and Real Estate, and Savings and Loan Divisions. Wholly owned subsidiaries sold mutual fund shares and life insurance, either separately or in coordinated purchase plans. An objective of the plans was to allow the investor to use the appreciation, if any, in the value of mutual fund shares, together with dividends or capital gains distributions, to help offset the principal and interest on loans that recur yearly as premiums come due. Other subsidiaries engaged in oil and gas exploration and in the breeding, buying, and selling of cattle.

As of December 31, 1971, consolidated assets reportedly approached $500 million and total revenue and net income respectively surpassed $130 million and $21 million for 1971. (See Tables B4-1 and B4-2.) Proof sheets of EFCA's unpublished 1972 annual report placed year-end assets at $737

TABLE B4-2 EQUITY FUNDING CORPORATION OF AMERICA: CONSOLIDATED INCOME ACCOUNT FOR 1970 AND 1971 (YEAR ENDED 12/31)

Income	1971	1970
	(in 000's)	
Commissions		
Security sales	$ 14,824	$ 16,022
Insurance sales	62,482	56,540
Interest, etc.	20,314	15,160
Real estate operations	18,996	6,731
Investment management	1,712	1,446
Natural resources operations	10,532	7,668
Other income	1,281	326
Unconsolidated subsidiaries	810	520
Total income	$130,951	$104,413
Expenses		
Securities commissions	$ 5,021	$ 5,341
Interest, etc.	9,325	6,964
Operating expenses		
Natural resources	7,236	4,795
Real estate	14,472	7,740
Insurance benefits paid	16,959	16,685
Increase in reserve	14,657	13,463
Insurance commissions	10,260	9,065
Selling expense	19,907	19,006
Policyholder dividends	3,478	2,874
Minority interest		76
Income tax	7,304	6,513
Extraordinary charges	1,140	1,021
Total expenses	$109,759	$ 93,543
Net income	$ 21,192	$ 10,870

TABLE B4-3 EQUITY FUNDING CORPORATION OF AMERICA: SELECTED DATA

Year	Stock price High	Low	Per share earnings†	Average number of common shares (000)†
1972	$46.50	$31.75	$2.81	n.a.
1971	47.00	23.875	2.31	7,883
1970	59.00	12.75	1.72	7,453
1969	81.625	47.125	1.79	7,018
1968‡				
New	66.00	40.875	1.53	6,015
Old	92.50	31.625		
1967 (old)	34.875	11.125	.53	5,294

† Adjusted for split.
‡ Two for one split, Nov. 1, 1968.

million and yearly profits at $22.6 million. Earnings per share reached $2.81 in 1972, up from $.53 in 1967. (See Table B4-3.)

Discovery

The bubble burst on March 6, 1973, when Ronald Secrist, a discharged EFCA employee, notified both the New York Department of Insurance and Raymond Dirks, an insurance specialist and senior vice president at Dela-field Childs, Inc., that EFLIC was involved in massive fraud. New York proceeded to contact California, where EFCA is headquartered, and California then alerted Illinois, where it is registered. Dirks in turn commenced calling institutions, starting on March 12 with Boston Co.'s affiliate, Institutional Investors, Inc., to warn them of the disaster.

The Illinois Insurance Department responded by instituting a surprise audit and was joined by examiners from Mississippi and California. In short order, there were, as one EFLIC employee indicated, "teams of auditors competitively going over the same files, microfilming the same materials, running around trying to talk to the same people. There isn't any coordination. The money being wasted is terrific."

Institutions responded to Raymond Dirks's information with block sales. Boston Co. sold 36,500 shares at $26 on March 15, Bankers Trust sold 98,850 shares at $23.50 on March 19; Boston Co.'s Institutional Investors liquidated its entire holding of 371,500 shares on March 21.

At the insistence of Institutional Capital Corp., Mr. Dirks traveled to the West Coast on March 20 to confront Equity officers. On March 26, he called John W. Bristol, Loew's, Sears Roebuck, Chemical Bank, Morgan Guaranty Bank, and the Steinhardt Hedge Fund. That same day, Bristol sold 445,000 shares at $17.50. The next day, Chemical Bank sold 24,000 shares, while Loew's sold 102,000 of its recently acquired shares. The approximate sequence of block trading is given below; the unusual crash of the stock's price is easy to see in the market data.

Date	Block trades	Price
March 12	17,000	$28\frac{5}{8}$
	10,000	28
March 15	36,500	26
March 19	98,850	$23\frac{1}{2}$
	10,000	$23\frac{3}{8}$
March 21	371,500	$19\frac{1}{4}$
March 23	51,900	$19\frac{3}{4}$
	20,000	19
March 26	445,400	$17\frac{1}{2}$
	17,000	$17\frac{1}{2}$
	77,000	$17\frac{1}{4}$
March 27	102,000	17
	24,000	17

Chapter X Proceedings

The rapidity with which EFCA fell into eclipse was astonishing. Shortly after the story broke in early April, Messrs. Goldblum (president and chairman of EFCA), Levin (executive vice president of EFCA), and Lowell (president of EFLIC) resigned; and an interim three-man management team was named. The Washington State Insurance Commissioner froze the assets of Northern Life, an EFCA subsidiary, until May 1. Illinois officials prohibited EFLIC from writing new policies.

On the basis of an SEC suit, the Los Angeles district court granted the request for appointment of (1) a special investigator with wider powers, and (2) Touche, Ross & Co. to audit EFCA's books. The court order also provided for the appointment of a new, independent board of directors. Other concurrent events included the firing of six other EFLIC officials and the threat of lending banks to impound EFCA's cash balances. In New Jersey, the six EFCA-connected directors of Bankers National Life were replaced. The three EFCA funds terminated their management contracts with EFC Management Corp.; officials connected with Equity Funding were fired; and I.D.S. (a large unrelated mutual fund) agreed to serve temporarily as investment manager.

Less than 48 hours after the initial court plan, Federal Judge Pregerson ordered EFCA to petition for protection under Chapter X of the Bankruptcy Act. The apparent objective was to eliminate ambiguity regarding jurisdictions and to protect EFCA against creditors. Robert M. Loeffler, who resigned as senior vice president and general counsel of I.D.S., was appointed trustee.

Bogus Business

Preliminary estimates placed bogus insurance at some two-thirds of the 3 billion dollars alleged by EFLIC to be in force at the end of 1972. The bogus policies reportedly numbered 56,091 of 92,111 claimed on the books. Premiums on phony policies were estimated at $25.4 million.

Fictitious insurance, referred to as "y" business or "department 99," had antecedents in (1) the creation of phony packages involving both life insurance and mutual fund shares, and (2) the extension of "special class" or "employee franchise" insurance policies to employees and their families with free premiums during the first year. The *package deal* entailed the purchase of fictitious life insurance for fictitious mutual fund holders with fictitious loans that EFCA claimed to finance. The net effect was to generate bogus profits (over which EFCA had absolute control) to the end of inflating EFCA stock price and of facilitating major acquisitions for stock. As a bookkeeping exercise, the process required no *real* money to support the fictitious loans.

Although precise magnitudes remain buried in the computer, some clues exist. Whereas Pennsylvania Life's prospectus (June 1967) indicated that EFCA had produced $58.6 million of life insurance for Penn Life in 1966, an Equity Funding prospectus (May 1967) reported that EFCA had sold $226.3 million (face amount) of life insurance in the same year, the "greater part" through Penn Life. The portion of outstanding loans, which EFCA claimed to finance internally and which were apparently phony for the most part, grew from $2.2 million in 1965 to $63.3 million in 1970 and $117 million in 1972.

Special class insurance was promoted by EFCA with coinsurance in mind. Many employees bought as much as $50,000 each for themselves and their wives and $25,000 for each child. Much of this insurance was either canceled or sharply reduced in the second year. By that time, EFLIC had mixed the dubious special class policies with good policies (to keep the overall lapse rate acceptable) and sold them to reinsurers.

Further impetus for "y" accounts came in 1970 when, with the erosion of the stock market, EFCA's mutual fund salespersons faced growing resistance to the added detriment of insurance sales. The drop in package sales threatened the corporate objective of consistent growth in earnings.

EFLIC reported sales of ordinary life insurance totaling 18,650 policies, with a face amount of $828.6 million, for all 1970. Since parent company reports showed new life insurance sales with a face value of $370 million through mid-November, sales representatives — in the words of a young executive — apparently "wrote more in the last 6 weeks of the year than they did in the previous 46." Another employee who saw the undoctored premium figures for 1970 remembered that they were "maybe around half of what we actually reported."

Alleged production in 1970 just about equaled total insurance and number of policies in force at the year's outset. Profit projections were apparently met by opening the books again after December 31 and by plugging into the general ledger (maintained on magnetic tape) business salted with bogus policies and sold to coinsurers after the year-end.

Factors Retarding Discovery

Company computers were a key factor in enabling EFCA executives to commit massive and prolonged fraud. Neither standard auditing procedures nor Wall Street analyses were sufficiently sophisticated to uncover the bogus insurance. In the words of Gleeson Payne, head of the California Insurance commission, "Under the old hard-copy methods of keeping insurance records, you sure as hell couldn't build up bogus policies in this kind of volume or in this kind of time. But our examiners aren't equipped to check out a computer-run and find out if it's authentic."

The fictitious policies were mixed with genuine ones and dispersed through EFLIC's master-tape files. Printouts thus confirmed their "reality." Faked death certificates were even programmed into the computer. Secret coding numbers prevented leaks from the master tapes.

The standard practice of drawing samples from the tapes for verification against original hard copies failed to uncover the swindle. At least two auditing firms obtained — and supposedly checked — printouts that included bogus policies. Hard-copy files were created overnight, as needed, to match the printouts.

In the words of accounting professionals, "The company made it look valid, and the accountants believed the computer. All in all, it was a beautiful job of programming."

The threat of exposure was minimized by (1) limited familiarity with computer output, (2) close ties between EFCA and its auditors, and (3) limited insurance department budgets. "If an auditor isn't knowledgeable about computers," argues an accounting executive, "he must rely on someone who is." That "someone" is likely to be employed by the *audited* firm, "and this poses a very real threat."

Wolfson Weiner, a small accounting firm with offices in Beverly Hills and New York until it merged with Seidman & Seidman (February 1, 1972), had audited EFCA throughout its public history. In 1972, the firm also assumed from Haskin & Sells the audit of EFLIC.

Several pieces of evidence exist to support the notion that both EFCA and Wolfson Weiner regarded the latter as *inside* — rather than *outside* — auditors. One, Julian Weiner, the head of Wolfson Weiner, publicly stated that the mutual fund insurance package was his idea. Two, EFCA allegedly accounted for some three-fifths of Wolfson Weiner billings in recent years. Three, the merger agreement between Wolfson Weiner and Seidman & Seidman provided that the previous auditors, headed by Solomon Block (who became a CPA on April 27, 1973), were to remain on the EFCA audit. Four, Mr. Block's name was shown in the EFCA directory with no indication of his function.

State insurance examinations tended, moreover, to focus upon the smaller companies. The Illinois department had last undertaken a full-scale examination of EFLIC, formerly Presidential Life, in 1968, and the examination scheduled for 1972 had been delayed. Had a timely examination been conducted, it is highly doubtful whether any discrepancy would have been discovered. Even the New York department, perhaps the most expert, acknowledged that it must "still rely on the integrity of the company's electronic procedures and programming techniques" until its computer training was further along. The California department noted that "our examiners aren't equipped to check out a computer run and find out if it's authentic," and retained Peat, Marwick, Mitchell & Co. to "prepare for the future" and advise whether its techniques could have prevented the alleged fraud.

Affected Parties

The full magnitude of tangible and intangible losses sustained in the collapse of EFCA will probably never be ascertained. The common stock had a market value of $113.5 million at time of trading suspension, down from over $200 million a month earlier. Outstanding debt securities showed a book value in excess of $80 million. Bank loans came to $50 million, while money put up by coinsurers exceeded $25 million.

Major Wall Street firms assigned EFCA shares a zero value for collateral purposes subsequent to the trading halt. The common stock may turn out to have some value after reorganization, but any specific value is problematic.

Details that only the courts can clarify cloud the legitimacy of trades executed after March 6. Salomon Brothers filed suit on April 11 against the Boston Company and 69 of its clients charging that the Boston Company and its affiliate, John W. Bristol & Co., had sold $8.3 million of EFCA stock and $255,000 of its bonds without informing Salomon of their awareness of Mr. Dirks's (the tippee's) findings.[2] The investment banking house, which had paid for the bonds but not for the stock, indicated that its basic objective was to rescind the entire transaction. In presenting its counterclaim, the Boston group denied that the selling was prompted by "inside" information, and argued that Salomon "held itself out as expert and sophisticated in the buying and selling of blocks of stocks and as a company in which Bristol Co. and the public could place trust and confidence" and owed a fiduciary duty to complete the transactions.

Lost in the EFCA shuffle were holders of some $23 million of $5\frac{1}{4}$ percent convertible debentures sold in Europe, $38.5 million of $5\frac{1}{2}$ percent convertibles sold in the United States, and $22 million of $9\frac{1}{2}$ percent subordinated debentures. Following the precepts of the debenture indenture agreement, for example, Chemical Bank, the trustee of the $9\frac{1}{2}$ percent debentures, stated in its letter to holders that it had declared EFCA to be in default and demanded payment on the debenture issue. The bank commented that the "true facts are unclear and uncertain."

In a market letter dated early April, James Heidell of First Manhattan Co. suggested that "perhaps no bond should be bought of an enterprise

---

[2] A similar suit was later instituted against the Sears Fund.

that has not been functioning in its present form for a period of years—say five or eight." He went on to consider the function of the trustee of a public bond, asking whether the role should not be refined and expanded. As contrasted with "continuous monitoring" by direct lenders, "once the homework has been done, a prospectus assembled, and the bond sold, . . . no entity is charged with in-depth supervision."

Collateralized bank loans under a June 1972 revolving credit agreement were placed in jeopardy when the lead bank in the four-member bank group temporarily returned a key part of the loan collateral to EFCA without prior approval of the other banks. The collateral at issue was a certificate representing almost 100 percent of the shares of Northern Life Insurance Company. Other collateral included all outstanding shares of Bankers National Life Insurance Co. and 60 percent of the stock of EFLIC.

Coinsurers were left holding the bag. Investigations prior to coinsuring tended to be less than thorough.

Legitimate policyholders apparently remained unaffected.

Six Months Later

As of early October 1973, EFCA won provisional court approval to dispose of Bishop Bank and Trust Co., Ltd., Nassau (for $12.8 million) and Liberty Savings and Loan Association (for $12.6 million), as the trustee endeavored to streamline the company. Staff had been reduced by one-third, and the advertising department eliminated. Mr. Loeffler indicated that EFCA would probably continue in existence as a "small life insurance holding company with some funding programs and some tax-shelter ventures."

The fate of EFLIC was in doubt. Of 97,000 policyholders known on the concern's books, only 34,000 were confirmed as real. With 7,000 policy lapses, the net remaining was 27,000. The stated intent of the Illinois department was to sell blocks of the business to other insurance companies and to induce existing reinsurers to assume coinsured policies. As a first step, National Investors Life agreed to assume in its own name 918 policies formerly coinsured with EFLIC.

EFLIC's overhead was reduced to $50,000 a month. Monthly premium income was at a comparable level. About $6 million in EFLIC assets had been uncovered.

Some 58 civil suits were pending against EFCA by 1974. The United States court's panel on multidistrict litigation consolidated these suits in one judicial district. Lengthy investigations involving the U.S. Attorney's office in Los Angeles, the SEC, the FBI, and the Illinois and California departments of insurance, and the Illinois attorney general culminated in November 1974 with a 105-count indictment by a Los Angeles federal grand jury. Twenty of the twenty-two persons charged with conspiring to commit felonies were former executives and employees of EFCA. Also indicted were two members of EFCA's independent accounting firm. Upon the release of the federal indictments, earlier indictments by a Dupage County, Illinois, grand jury were made public.

Trading in EFCA stock remained suspended throughout 1973. In November 1973, 22 people were indicted for charges including conspiracy, bank fraud, mail fraud, securities fraud, interstate transportation of stolen securities, electronic eavesdropping, and filing of false documents with the SEC. The trials and appeals resulting from the indictments will drag on, and it will be several years before final sentences are all handed down.

Five

Taxes

Taxes generally have a sizable effect on the profitability of investments. An understanding of some tax law is therefore essential to maximize investment profits. This chapter endeavors only to give an understanding of tax laws affecting investment decisions. Tax laws are so numerous and complex that it would be hopeless to try to produce an expert in the field in just one chapter. It is hoped, however, that the reader will learn enough to know when to consult an expert—an accountant or a tax attorney. The major taxes affecting investors and reviewed in the following pages include the federal personal income tax, the federal corporate income tax, and federal estate and gift taxes for the United States.

5-1 FEDERAL PERSONAL INCOME TAX

The present federal income tax first became a reality in 1913 after passage of the Sixteenth Amendment to the Constitution. Tax rates have gradually increased since that time to their present high levels. Table 5-1 illustrates the progressive personal income tax rates. The reasoning behind this structure is based on the theory that a person's ability to pay increases at a faster rate than his income. These steeply progressive rates make wise tax planning imperative for the middle- to high-income investor.

Personal Income Tax Structure

The amount of tax due is figured from the *taxable income* of the individual. The general form from which the taxable income figure is derived is shown in Table 5-2.[1]

[1] For a more detailed explanation, see the current edition of *Your Federal Income Tax,* published annually by the Internal Revenue Service and sold for a nominal price.

TABLE 5-1 FEDERAL INCOME TAX SCHEDULE FOR MARRIED TAXPAYERS FILING JOINT RETURNS AND CERTAIN WIDOWS AND WIDOWERS

If taxable income is:		The tax owed is:	
Over	But not over		of excess over
$1,000	$2,000	$140 + 15%	$1,000
$2,000	$3,000	$290 + 16%	$2,000
$3,000	$4,000	$450 + 17%	$3,000
$4,000	$8,000	$620 + 19%	$4,000
$8,000	$12,000	$1,380 + 22%	$8,000
$12,000	$16,000	$2,260 + 25%	$12,000
$16,000	$20,000	$3,260 + 28%	$16,000
$20,000	$24,000	$4,380 + 32%	$20,000
$24,000	$28,000	$5,660 + 36%	$24,000
$28,000	$32,000	$7,100 + 39%	$28,000
$32,000	$36,000	$8,660 + 42%	$32,000
$36,000	$40,000	$10,340 + 45%	$36,000
$40,000	$44,000	$12,140 + 48%	$40,000
$44,000	$52,000	$14,060 + 50%	$44,000
$52,000	$64,000	$18,060 + 53%	$52,000
$64,000	$76,000	$24,420 + 55%	$64,000
$76,000	$88,000	$31,020 + 58%	$76,000
$88,000	$100,000	$37,980 + 60%	$88,000
$100,000	$120,000	$45,180 + 62%	$100,000
$120,000	$140,000	$57,580 + 64%	$120,000
$140,000	$160,000	$70,380 + 66%	$140,000
$160,000	$180,000	$83,580 + 68%	$160,000
$180,000	$200,000	$97,180 + 69%	$180,000
$200,000	. . . . . .	$110,980 + 70%	$200,000

TABLE 5-2 DERIVING TAXABLE INCOME

Gross income (includes wages, salaries, rent, etc., but excludes such things as interest on municipal bonds, gifts, social security benefits, and most life insurance proceeds)
Less: Necessary business expenses, certain moving expenses, etc.
Equals: Adjusted gross income
Less: Itemized personal deductions† such as:
1. Interest expense
2. Charitable contributions (with certain limitations)
3. Various state and local taxes
4. Medical expenses (in excess of 3% of adjusted gross income) and drug expenses (in excess of 1% of adjusted gross income)
5. Casualty losses (in excess of $100 per loss)
6. Various miscellaneous deductions
Less: Exemption of $750 for each allowable exemption
Equals: Taxable income

† Instead of itemizing deductions, the taxpayer may take the standard 15 percent of adjusted gross income up to a maximum of $2,000.

Assume the taxable income figure for Mr. and Mrs. Taxpayer, filing a joint return, to be $18,900.[2] They would use the schedule shown in Table 5-1 and compute their tax burden as follows:

Income	Tax
$16,000	$3,260
+2,900 × 28% =	812
Totals: $18,900	$4,072

If, for this particular year, there were an income tax surcharge levied, say 10 percent as was the case in 1969, Mr. and Mrs. Taxpayer would add $407.20 (10 percent of $4,072) to arrive at a final tax burden of $4,479.20.

Maximum Tax and Minimum Tax

The Tax Reform Act of 1969 included two fundamental departures from the graduated tax on taxable income. The first reform — the maximum tax — set a maximum tax rate of 50 percent on "earned taxable income," that is, wages, salaries, professional fees, and compensation for personal services. However, the maximum rate of 70 percent, as shown in Table 5-1, still exists for "other taxable income," and since the other income earned is considered the last income earned, it is subject to the highest marginal rates. The high maximum rate is particularly relevant to the investor since investment income (except for long-term capital gains) is considered "other taxable income" and therefore subject to the 70 percent of maximum.

The 1969 Tax Reform Act also imposed a 10 percent minimum tax (in addition to other taxes) on certain preference items of an individual or a corporation. Congress believed that these preference items allowed special tax advantages to certain individuals and corporations but not to others and that a 10 percent additional tax on these items would redistribute the tax burden more equitably. Some of the tax preference items are capital gains, stock options, the excess of accelerated depreciation over straight-line depreciation, and percentage depletion. In figuring the 10 percent tax, the taxpayer is allowed to reduce the total tax preference items by (1) a $30,000 exemption ($15,000 for a married person filing a separate return) and (2) the income tax on taxable income.

Capital Gains and Losses

Capital gains and losses arise out of exchanges of capital assets. Capital assets include such things as securities, realty holdings, and some personal

[2] The other tax rate schedules available include (1) unmarried individual returns, (2) head-of-household returns, and (3) separate returns (for married taxpayers). For married taxpayers the joint return has the effect of splitting income equally between spouses (even if one spouse has earned all the income). This equal splitting of income reduces the applicable tax rate and amount of tax owed in nearly all circumstances.

assets. Since long-term capital gains are allowed preferential tax treatment (approximately one-half the ordinary tax rate), investors may increase their rates of return by seeking long-term capital gains in preference to short-term capital gains, which are taxed at ordinary rates. Holding time differentiates short-term from long-term. If the asset is held less than 6 months, it is short-term; more than 6 months, long-term. The favorable effect on the after-tax one-period rate of return on a common stock with a *long-term capital gain* may be illustrated as follows:

$$r_t = \frac{(p_{t+1} - p_t)(1.0 - t_g) + d_t(1.0 - t_0)}{p_t} \qquad \text{where } t_g < t_0 \qquad (5\text{-}1)$$

and where p_t is the market price of the stock at the beginning of the period, d_t is the tth period's cash dividend, t_g is the capital gains tax rate, and t_0 is the ordinary income tax rate. In contrast, the after-tax one-period rate of return on a common stock with a *short-term capital gain* would be

$$r_t = \frac{(p_{t+1} - p_t)(1.0 - t_0) + d_t(1.0 - t_0)}{p_t} \qquad (5\text{-}2)$$

To compute the amount of capital gains tax, first the amount of long-term capital gains and long-term capital losses must be combined to arrive at a single *net* long-term capital gain or loss figure. Then the amount of short-term capital gains and capital losses must be merged to arrive at a single *net* short-term capital gain or loss figure. If the two final figures are both positive, the net short-term gain is taxed at the ordinary rate and the net long-term gain is taxed at the preferred rate. If the two final figures are both negative, 50 percent of the long-term loss can offset ordinary income up to a maximum of $1,000 and all the short-term loss can offset ordinary income up to a maximum of $1,000. The total offset (including short-term and long-term) may not exceed $1,000 for a given year. If the capital loss exceeds $1,000 for a given year, however, the individual taxpayer is allowed to carry forward (but not backward) the loss indefinitely.[3] Finally, suppose there is a net long-term capital gain and a net short-term capital loss. Then the two are combined, and any excess of long-term capital gain over short-term capital loss is taxed at the preferential rate. On the other hand, an excess of short-term capital gain over long-term capital loss is taxed at the ordinary rate.

There are two methods of computing the amount of long-term capital

---

[3] A complete explanation of how the amount of carry-over is computed and how and when the excess losses should be taken is beyond the scope of this text. If interested, the reader should consult a complete volume on federal income taxes, such as the current edition of Hoffman and Anderson's *Income Tax Principles and Procedures* (New York: McGraw-Hill) or the current edition of the Internal Revenue Service's *Your Federal Income Tax* (Washington: Government Printing Office).

gains tax owed. The taxpayer, of course, should use the method that results in the least tax. Let us assume that John Taxower is married and has ordinary income of $28,000 and a net long-term capital gain from the sale of common stock of $5,000. From Table 5-1 we see that his income tax would be $7,100 before the capital gain. The first method of computing the tax on the capital gain allows Mr. Taxower to apply his marginal tax rate, 39 percent, to only 50 percent of his $5,000 gain. Thus

$$39\% \times \$2,500 = \$\ \ 975 \quad \text{(capital gains tax)}$$
$$\underline{+7,100} \quad \text{(ordinary income tax)}$$
$$\text{Total tax} = \$8,075$$

The second method of computing the capital gains tax is beneficial only if the married taxpayer's income exceeds $52,000 (or the unmarried taxpayer's income exceeds $38,000), that is, if the taxpayer's tax bracket is greater than 50 percent. This alternative method sets a 25 percent maximum tax rate on the first $50,000 of net long-term capital gains and a 35 percent maximum on gains in excess of $50,000.

Tax Preferences and Investment Planning

Most investors endeavor to structure their portfolios in a way that will minimize their total tax burden. In doing so, the investor should understand the tax effects of interest, cash dividends, stock dividends, marketable government securities, and the timing of capital gains and losses.

Interest. In all cases except for municipal bond interest (discussed below), interest income is given no preferential tax treatment. It is taxed at ordinary rates.

Cash dividends. The Revenue Act of 1954 entitles each taxpayer up to $100 per year in corporate dividends free of any federal income tax. For a joint return the total exclusion available is $200, if $100 can be attributed to stock owned by the husband and the other $100 to stock owned by the wife, or if the stock is held in joint names. Neither husband nor wife may use any portion of the $100 exclusion not used by the other. Therefore, in order to gain full benefit of the exclusion, some stock should be held in joint names or husband and wife should own separately a roughly equal amount of stock paying dividends. This dividend exclusion encourages all individuals to own some stock in order to benefit from this small amount of tax-free income. Dividends in excess of the exclusion are taxed at ordinary rates.

Stock dividends. Stock dividends are in general not taxable. This is the case simply because, although owners receive additional stock certificates, the value of their ownership interest is unchanged. They merely have more pieces of paper representing the same proportion of total ownership. Since they have received nothing of value, there is nothing on which to be taxed. If the investors finally sell their total shares (original and dividend) for a greater amount than they paid for the original shares, the difference is taxed at the preferential capital gains rate (if owned over 6 months). Essentially, the Internal Revenue Service recognizes that stock dividends alone convey no change in the value of the investment or in the investor's income.

Government bonds. To finance its debt, the United States government issues large quantities of bonds. The investor who is interested in receiving preferential tax treatment in the purchase and sale of government bonds will be most interested in marketable issues (bills, certificates, notes, and bonds) as opposed to nonmarketable issues (which include the familiar Series E savings bonds). From nonmarketable savings securities the investor receives only interest income that is taxed at ordinary rates. From marketable securities the bondholder also receives interest income taxed at ordinary rates, but may, in addition, be able to sell the bond for more than its price and realize a long-term capital gain on the difference (which is taxed at the preferential capital gains tax rate rather than at one's ordinary tax rate).

Bonds issued by local governments to finance their debts are called *municipal bonds* or simply *municipals.* They are of particular interest to investors in high personal income tax brackets since the interest income from them is tax-exempt. For example, a person in the 50 percent tax bracket would net after taxes as much interest from a municipal bond earning 8 percent as from another taxable interest-bearing security earning 16 percent. And the very wealthy individual, paying taxes at the 70 percent rate, would need a taxable interest-bearing security yielding about 27 percent to be as well off as if holding a municipal bond yielding 8.1 percent.

16%	taxable interest income	27%	taxable interest income
×.5	(1 − tax rate of 50%)	×.3	(1 − tax rate of 70%)
8%	after-tax interest income	8.1%	after-tax interest income

As inflation pushes incomes upward into higher marginal tax rates, municipal bonds become attractive to more investors. Perhaps the municipal bond mutual funds currently being established are a testament to this fact. Of course, the primary disadvantage of municipal bonds is that they offer relatively low yields because of their tax-exempt status. However, as one's tax rate rises, this disadvantage is ameliorated.

Timing of capital gains and losses. If John Taxower's income is subject to fluctuation, he should take capital gains in low-income years and capital losses in high-income years in an effort to stabilize his income from year to year and avoid the high marginal tax rates. Even if he is not subject to wide fluctuations in income, he may do the following (which is only a small sampling of his options) to maximize after-tax income:

1 To reduce the tax rate, he may hold capital assets which have increased in value until the gains become long-term (that is, over 6 months).

2 If the investor realizes short-term gains, he should, if he has unrealized losses in his portfolio for which the future looks dim, realize the capital losses to offset the short-term gains. He should, of course, make sure in advance that the cost of shifting investments is less than the tax savings generated by the shift.

3 If the taxpayer plans to sell real estate or a business interest at a large profit, he should have an installment sale contract drawn in order to spread the payments and, therefore, the gain over several taxable years. This will prevent small taxpayers from being elevated into a very high tax bracket in the year of sale; it also allows them to realize possible capital losses in their portfolios over a number of years to offset the capital gains from installment sales.

4 The taxpayer may wish to make a large charitable gift that qualifies for tax deduction in a year of unusually high income. Marketable securities which have appreciated substantially may be used as gifts. If so, the gift is valued at the current appreciated price rather than the lower purchase price.

5-2 CORPORATE INCOME TAX

Corporate investing is becoming increasingly widespread as more corporations establish employee pension funds and invest excess cash in short-term marketable securities. Thus we should consider the effect of the corporate income tax on these investment decisions.

Rate Structure

The federal corporate income tax rate structure is very simple in comparison with the personal income tax. The first $25,000 of taxable income is taxed at a 22 percent rate, and any excess, whether $100 or $1 million, is taxed at a 48 percent rate. For example, if a corporation's net income were $500,000 for the current year, its tax would be computed as follows:

$$22\% \times \$\ 25,000 = \$\ \ 5,500$$
$$48\% \times \$475,000 = \underline{\$228,000}$$
$$\text{Total tax} = \$233,500$$

Net Operating Carry-Back and Carry-Forward

The rules for carrying back and carrying forward operating losses are nearly identical for sole proprietorships (individuals) and corporations. An operating loss may be carried back for 3 years and carried forward for 5. The Internal Revenue Service stipulates the sequence of years to which the loss should be transferred: (1) carry the loss back to the third year preceding the year in which it was sustained; (2) if there is any excess loss not used, then carry it to the second preceding year; and so forth. Carry-backs, of course, necessitate recomputation of the tax liability for the year to which the loss is carried.

The purpose of this loss averaging is to avoid penalizing corporations whose incomes fluctuate widely. However, the carry-back, carry-forward right has also been useful to successful firms in the acquisition of unprofitable ones. By merging one firm's losses with another firm's profits, a corporation with a $10 million loss, for example, could save an acquiring firm over $5 million in taxes. The practice of acquiring firms for the sole purpose of providing a tax loss credit has been somewhat curtailed by the following restrictions: (1) no more than 50 percent of the stock may change hands within 2 years after purchase, and (2) the acquired corporation must remain in the same line of business.

Corporate Capital Gains and Losses

The capital assets of a firm are considered those assets not ordinarily bought and sold in the normal course of business. Therefore, a firm's inventory is not regarded as a capital asset, but the machinery used for assembly is.

As for individuals, corporate long-term capital gains (from assets held more than 6 months) are subject to special tax treatment. The maximum tax rate for long-term capital gains is 30 percent if the corporation has total taxable income in excess of $25,000. If the corporation's total taxable income (including capital gains) is $25,000 or less, it is subject to the 22 percent tax rate.

Unlike individuals, corporations are not allowed to deduct any part of a net capital loss against ordinary income. To compensate for this difference in treatment, the corporation is allowed to carry back capital losses to offset capital gains for a period of 3 years (as long as the amount carried back does not cause or increase a net operating loss in the carry-back year). The individual taxpayer does not have this carry-back option—only carry-forward. The corporation is allowed to carry forward a capital loss for 5 years; the individual, indefinitely.

Intercorporate Dividend Payments

Eighty-five percent of dividends received by one corporation from another are exempt from taxation. This works out to be an approximate $7\frac{1}{2}$ percent (that is, about 50 percent of 15 percent) effective tax rate for intercorporate dividends. Thus, this provision in effect encourages intercorporate investments. Furthermore, if Corporation X owns 80 percent or more of Corporation Y, dividends received by X from Y are totally tax-exempt (because Y is viewed as being part of X and not a separate investment).

Improper Accumulation

The tax law considers $100,000 or less a reasonable amount of earnings for a firm to retain (that is, not to pay out in dividends). If a corporation wishes to retain an amount greater than $100,000, it should be prepared to show a bona fide business reason for doing so. If the U.S. Treasury should prove improper accumulation of earnings, the corporation is then subject to a penalty tax rate of 27.5 percent on the first $100,000 improperly accumulated and 38.5 percent on all amounts over that. Only the first $100,000 retained is considered reasonable and exempt from any penalty tax. The amount over $100,000 that may be retained for purposes other than avoiding income tax depends on the corporation's opportunities for growth and the urgency of competitive needs.

From the point of view of corporations with wealthy stockholders, not paying out dividends is very advantageous in terms of avoiding double taxation (that is, 48 percent corporate tax and as high as 70 percent individual income tax on dividends). Rather than be doubly taxed at high rates or pay the penalty tax for improper accumulation, some corporations with stagnating earnings have chosen to merge with rapidly growing businesses that can justify earnings retention. Stockholders may then enjoy the preferred capital gains tax rate when they sell their shares of stock.

5-3 FEDERAL ESTATE AND GIFT TAXES

The federal estate tax is steeply progressive and therefore has a serious impact on large estates. Table 5-3 indicates that the tax reaches its top marginal rate at 77 percent for net taxable estates of $10 million and more. Thus, it is important for the wealthy investor to be aware of the federal estate and gift tax structures and their implications for long-range planning.

Determining the Net Taxable Estate

To minimize estate taxes, the individual should be aware of items not included in the taxable estate. A brief outline for deriving the amount of federal estate tax due is shown in Table 5-4.

Because of the flat $60,000 exemption, a federal estate tax return need not be filed on estates valued at $60,000 or less. The combination of the $60,000 exemption and the marital deduction in effect means that adjusted gross estates of $120,000 or less are not subject to estate taxes for married persons providing that at least one-half the estate is left outright to the surviving spouse. To illustrate the computation of the federal estate tax, assume that a net taxable estate is $250,000. According to Table 5-3, the federal estate tax would be $65,700. Assume also that the deceased was a resident of Florida, which taxes its residents the maximum credit allowed by the U.S.

TABLE 5-3 U.S. ESTATE TAX

A Net taxable estate	B Estate tax on column A	C % on excess over column A
$ 0	$ 0	3
5,000	150	7
10,000	500	11
20,000	1,600	14
30,000	3,000	18
40,000	4,800	22
50,000	7,000	25
60,000	9,500	28
100,000	20,700	30
250,000	65,700	32
500,000	143,700	35
750,000	233,200	37
1,000,000	325,700	39
1,250,000	423,200	42
1,500,000	528,200	45
2,000,000	753,200	49
2,500,000	998,200	53
3,000,000	1,263,200	56
3,500,000	1,543,200	59
4,000,000	1,838,200	63
5,000,000	2,468,200	67
6,000,000	3,138,200	70
7,000,000	3,838,200	73
8,000,000	4,568,200	76
10,000,000	6,088,200	77

Source: U.S. Treasury Department.

TABLE 5-4 OUTLINE FOR DETERMINING FEDERAL ESTATE TAX

Gross estate includes:
1. Life insurance proceeds owned by the decedent on his own life
2. Personal and real property

Less miscellaneous deductions:
1. Charitable gifts
2. Funeral and medical expenses for last illness
3. Debts
4. Administrative expenses

Equals: Adjusted gross estate
Less: Marital deduction (up to a maximum of one-half of the adjusted gross estate)
Less: $60,000 exemption
Equals: Net taxable estate
Total tax due: Figured from Table 5-3
Less credits of:
1. State death taxes (up to maximum allowed)
2. Gift taxes paid as a result of gifts made in contemplation of death

Balance: Federal estate tax

Treasury for state death taxes.[4] The maximum state death tax credit allowed on a taxable estate of $250,000 is $3,920.[5] Therefore, after deducting the credit, the balance of federal estate tax owed would be

$$\$65,700 - \$3,920 = \$61,780$$

If the deceased had made any "death-bed" gifts (gifts given within a 3-year period prior to death with the intent of escaping federal estate tax), the gifts would be added back into the gross taxable estate. However, the gift taxes paid on any gifts made in contemplation of death would also be credited against the $61,780 balance due in this example.

Federal Gift Taxes

A major way of reducing one's gross estate and thereby avoiding much of the estate tax is by making lifetime gifts. The federal tax rate for gifts is three-fourths of the federal estate tax rate. Compare Tables 5-3 and 5-5 for verification.

Another advantage of lifetime giving is that there are several deductions allowable before any gift tax is due. The deductions that may be made from the taxpayer's cumulative total of gifts include:

1 *The annual $3,000 exclusion.* The donor may give $3,000 per year to as many people as desired without paying any tax at all. Since this exclusion is available to both husband and wife, together they may give as much as $6,000 per year to any person.[6]

2 *The lifetime exemption of $30,000.* In addition to the $3,000 annual exclusion, the donor is also allowed a single $30,000 exemption during his or her lifetime. The exemption may be taken all in 1 year or over a period of years. Whenever a donor wishes to give to one individual an amount greater than the $3,000 exclusion, the excess can be credited against the $30,000 exemption until it is all used. A married couple together, of course, have a $60,000 lifetime exemption. Therefore, a husband and wife, using both of their annual exclusions and both of their lifetime exemptions, could give as much as $66,000 to one (but only one) person in 1 year tax-free, assuming no part of their lifetime exemption had ever been used.[7]

---

[4] Other states, such as New York, have death taxes in excess of the federal estate tax credit. Thus, the total taxes on the estate would be greater than the amount shown in Table 5-3.
[5] The U. S. Treasury publishes a table for calculating maximum credit.
[6] In order to qualify for the annual exclusion, the gift must be of "a present interest." That is, the donee must be able to immediately use, enjoy, or benefit from the gift. Thus, if a gift is made in the form of a trust, the income and principal of which the donee does not have immediate access the gift may be considered in certain circumstances to be "future interest" and does not qualify for the annual exclusion.
[7] The lifetime exemption, unlike the annual exclusion, may be applied to gifts of "future interest," such as trusts, to which the donee does not have immediate access.

TABLE 5-5 U.S. GIFT TAX

A Net taxable gift	B Gift tax on column A	C % on excess over column A
$ 0	$ 0	2¼
5,000	112	5¼
10,000	375	8¼
20,000	1,200	10½
30,000	2,250	13½
40,000	3,600	16½
50,000	5,250	18¾
60,000	7,125	21
100,000	15,525	22½
250,000	49,275	24
500,000	109,275	26¼
750,000	174,900	27¾
1,000,000	244,275	29¼
1,250,000	317,400	31½
1,500,000	396,150	33¾
2,000,000	564,900	36¾
2,500,000	748,650	39¾
3,000,000	947,400	42
3,500,000	1,157,400	44¼
4,000,000	1,378,650	47¼
5,000,000	1,851,150	50¼
6,000,000	2,353,650	52½
7,000,000	2,878,650	54¾
8,000,000	3,426,150	57
10,000,000	4,566,150	57¾

Source: U.S. Treasury Department.

3 *The marital deduction.* Under this provision one-half of any gift made by one spouse to the other is free of gift tax. The deduction is in addition to both the annual exclusion and lifetime exemption. In effect, one spouse can give the other $6,000 per year tax-free; the marital deduction reduces the taxable portion of the gift to $3,000, and the annual exclusion further reduces the taxable gift to zero.

4 *Charitable gifts.* Charitable gifts are exempt not only from gift taxes but also from income taxes up to certain specified maximums.

A further advantage of lifetime giving is that it removes the property given from the top brackets of the graduated estate tax to the lower ranges of the graduated gift tax. For example, assume a man has a taxable estate of $500,000. According to Table 5-3, the federal estate tax rate on the last $100,000 is 32 percent or $32,000. If he gave the $100,000 as a gift (assuming no exemption or exclusions), Table 5-5 shows the tax would be only $15,525 with a top rate of 21 percent.

Lifetime giving may be advisable from purely a tax standpoint. However, tax avoidance should not be the only consideration in planning one's estate. It should be remembered that a true gift is irrevocable; recipients are almost always grateful at the moment, but that gratitude may be short-lived. Moreover, no one person can be totally immune to a general economic recession, depression, or personal financial misfortune. In short, the planner of an estate should have a clearly defined list of priorities. For most individuals, financial security and independence probably have a higher priority than tax avoidance.[8]

Planning for an Adequately Liquid Estate

Assume an individual's net taxable estate is $100,000. This means, according to Table 5-3, that $20,700 must be liquidated from the estate for the federal estate tax. However, if much of the estate is tied up in assets not readily marketable (for example, a family-owned business), sizable losses can be incurred in an attempt to obtain funds for the $20,700 tax payment. The 1958 Revenue Act mitigated the problem somewhat by allowing an estate whose assets are concentrated in a closely held business to pay the tax in 10 annual installments as long as 4 percent interest is paid on the unpaid balance. Nevertheless, estates for which this provision does not apply still have liquidity problems.

One method of alleviating the problem is through life insurance policies. Another way to provide liquidity which can be considerably more profitable, although more risky, is to purchase a properly diversified portfolio. A portfolio of various marketable securities (such as stocks, bonds, and options) can be expected to yield about three times the return of life insurance, and adequate liquidity can be built into the portfolio to meet anticipated liabilities with virtually no problem. However, few people are familiar enough with death taxes, the various types of securities required, and the diversification techniques (which are explained in Chap. 15) to develop such a portfolio.

5-4 EPILOGUE ON FEDERAL TAXES

Discussions such as the preceding brief outline of federal taxes typically elicit at least two reactions from those who have not previously studied tax law. First, the laws seem inequitable; that is, they distribute the tax burden over different classes of taxpayers in such a way as to hurt certain groups and benefit other groups. Second, the tax system seems overpowering. The

---

[8] Gifts made in trust can overcome some of the disadvantages of outright gifts. There are so many possible provisions for living trusts and testamentary trusts that the subject is avoided in this chapter. For a full discussion, see chap. 12 of Robert Brosterman's *The Complete Estate Planning Guide* (New York: McGraw-Hill, 1964); and/or chap. 13 of Harry Sauvain's *Investment Management* (Englewood Cliffs, N.J.: Prentice-Hall, 1967).

complex array of tax regulations requires specialized training in order to operate under them without overpaying. Nearly everyone has these two reactions in some form.

Equity of the Tax Laws

Wealthy taxpayers feel that the progressive taxes are confiscatory and kill their incentive to work hard. The less affluent taxpayer, on the other hand, often concludes that taxes are not progressive enough and help "the rich to get richer while the poor get poorer." It is beyond the scope of this text to analyze these issues. The standard welfare economics course (offered by most economics departments) devotes a large segment of time to analyzing the incidence upon society of alternate tax systems. The interested reader should take the course. As might be expected, the conclusion is reached that the present tax system in the United States does not result in an optimal allocation of resources.

Array of Tax Laws Is Overpowering

The overpowering array of tax laws as well as any inequity may be attributed to the legislative process in the United States. The tax laws grew from proposals made by various special interest groups. The original proposals are usually changed and compromised by opposing special interest groups before they become law. As a result, this country's tax laws are a patchwork with loopholes in it. They do not always result in an optimum allocation of resources and almost never result in an income redistribution with which everyone is pleased. Presumably, however, the laws were not opposed by more than 49 percent of the voters' representatives in the Congress when they were enacted. This is no small achievement in a nation as large and diverse as the United States.

The tax law may be a bit overpowering but it is nevertheless the law. For those who do not care to pursue the standard series of accounting and tax courses and master the subject for themselves, a simple alternative is available. Tax specialists may be hired to prepare income tax returns. A competent tax accountant typically saves the client more than enough taxes to pay the accountant's fee.

QUESTIONS

1 Name at least four allowable deductions from adjusted gross income in arriving at taxable income.

2 What is meant by "minimum tax" and what is the rationale for its inclusion in the IRS code?

3 Assume the taxable income (not including capital gains and losses) of Mr.

and Mrs. Taylor, filing a joint return, is $20,000. The Taylors, during the taxable year, also incurred $5,000 in long-term capital gains, $3,000 in short-term capital gains, $2,000 in long-term capital losses, and $1,000 in short-term capital losses. Figure the Taylors' tax due.

4 How is the corporate federal income tax rate structured?

5 For how long may an individual carry forward a capital loss and for how long may a corporation do the same?

6 Jack Lind has a marginal tax rate of 48 percent and must choose between a tax-free municipal bond paying 9 percent and a taxable security paying 15 percent. Assuming all other factors as equal, which security should he choose? Why?

7 Samuel Hardigal died in 1976. His wife received life insurance proceeds of $80,000. His real and personal property were valued at $350,000. Mr. Hardigal had no outstanding debts; his hospital bills and medical expenses for his last illness were fully covered by insurance. Funeral expenses totaled $8,000, and administrative expenses for his estate totaled $4,000. He willed $50,000 to his alma mater. The state death taxes on his estate (which may be credited in full against the federal estate tax) totaled $1,000. What amount of federal estate tax is due?

8 Name three advantages of lifetime gift giving in estate planning.

SELECTED REFERENCES

Brosterman, Robert, *The Complete Estate Planning Guide* (New York: McGraw-Hill, 1964).
> An easy-to-read book that explains the creation and conservation of an estate. Arithmetic examples, but no math.

Prentice-Hall, *Federal Tax Course* (Englewood Cliffs, N.J.: Prentice-Hall, 1972).
> A comprehensive text, frequently revised, that explains with numerous examples the tax law. No math.

U.S. Treasury Department, Internal Revenue Service, *A Guide to Federal Estate and Gift Taxation,* Publication 448 (Washington: Government Printing Office).
> A concise summary of federal estate and gift taxes. Examples are sparse; legal terms are plentiful. No math.

U.S. Treasury Department, Internal Revenue Service, *Tax Guide for Small Business*, Publication 334 (Washington: Government Printing Office, annual).

Explains the tax laws that apply to a business, including sole proprietorships, partnerships, and corporations. No math.

U.S. Treasury Department, Internal Revenue Service, *Your Federal Income
Tax,* Publication 17 (Washington: Government Printing Office, annual).
Explains many specific problems and gives examples. No math.

Six

Sources of
Investment Information

One of the oldest and best pieces of investment advice is: Investigate before you invest. A thorough investigation of most assets should begin with an inquiry into world affairs. Wars and plagues in foreign countries and international tensions affect nations' economies and securities markets. After the financial analyst has developed a forecast about world conditions, he must estimate the impact of these factors on the national economy in which he is interested. Once the analyst has projections for the national economy, he may focus upon certain industries. Labor negotiations, changes in legislation, sales, and the competition within the industry must be forecast. Only after all this background investigation is completed is the financial analyst ready to focus on a particular firm. Obviously, a good financial analyst must consult many sources of news and information.

The purpose of this chapter is to list and describe some sources of financial news and information. These sources of information are not only useful to professional financial analysts; they can be helpful to amateurs. By reading or subscribing to a few of the sources of financial information described in this chapter, the amateur investors can gain insights and broaden their experience.

6-1 FINANCIAL NEWSPAPERS

Three of the most popular financial newspapers in the United States are *The Wall Street Journal, The New York Times,* and *Barron's.*

The Wall Street Journal (WSJ)

The WSJ is published 5 days each week. It is written for a national audience interested in finance and, in particular, investments. WSJ subscriptions cost $42 per year.[1]

The WSJ reports world, national, and financial news and news about industries and firms. It does not publish analytical research, but it does report the verbal opinions of economists and various financial personnel who have definite ideas about the course of future events.

Regular items in the WSJ which are useful to investors include columns and feature-length articles such as "Outlook," "Labor Letter," "Tax Report," "Insider Information," "Dividend News," "Earnings Digest," "Heard on the Street," "Abreast of the Market," and "Bond Markets." The paper also reports price and volume data daily for assets traded on the New York Stock Exchange (NYSE), the American Stock Exchange (AMEX), the over-the-counter markets, various regional and foreign security exchanges, the commodity markets, the bond markets, foreign exchange markets, and other markets.

The New York Times (NYT)

The NYT is a daily newspaper noted for its objective coverage of the news. It has a business and finance section toward the back of the paper which some people prefer to the WSJ. This section reports financial news, market data from various markets, and some stories about individual firms. With the exception of certain regular features, the NYT carries about the same financial news as the WSJ.

Barron's

Barron's is a weekly business and financial newspaper which makes no attempt to report world, national, or local news. *Barron's* "Statistical Section" typically fills about half this 50-page paper. Figures on mutual funds, security quotations, and volume data from all the major markets, bond quotations, the "Market Laboratory," and the "Pulse of Industry and Trade" fill out the "Statistical Section." The name "Statistical Section" is misleading, however, because only raw data are published.

The Dow Jones Averages

Dow Jones & Company publishes the WSJ and *Barron's* financial newspapers and prepares the Dow Jones Industrial Average (DJIA), the Dow Jones Transportation Average (DJTA), and the Dow Jones Utilities Average (DJUA).

---

[1] Instructors who are interested in using the WSJ in class may contact Educational Service Bureau, Dow Jones & Co., P.O. Box 300, Princeton, N.J. 08540, to obtain student subscription programs and various free teaching materials.

TABLE 6-1 DOW JONES SECURITY MARKET AVERAGE

The 30 stocks used in the Dow Jones Industrial Average are:

Allied Chemical	Goodyear
Aluminum Company	International Harvester
American Brands	International Nickel
American Can	International Paper
American Telephone & Telegraph	Johns-Manville
Anaconda	Owens-Illinois
Bethlehem Steel	Procter & Gamble
Chrysler	Sears Roebuck
Du Pont	Standard Oil of California
Eastman Kodak	Texaco
Esmark (Swift & Co.)	Union Carbide
Exxon (St. Oil of N.J.)	United Aircraft
General Electric	U.S. Steel
General Foods	Westinghouse Electric
General Motors	Woolworth

The 20 stocks used in the Dow Jones Transportation Average are:

American Airlines	Penn Central
Burlington North	St. Louis—San Francisco
Canadian Pacific	Santa Fe Industries
Consolidated Freight	Seaboard Coast
Eastern Airlines	Southern Pacific
Louisville & Nashville	Southern Railway
Norfolk & Western	Trans World Airlines
Northwest Airlines	UAL Incorporated
Pacific International Express	Union Pacific Corporation
Pan American World Airlines	U.S. Freight Company

The 15 stocks used in the Dow Jones Utility Average are:

American Electric Power	Niagara Mohawk Power
Cleveland E Illinois	Pacific Gas & Electric
Colum-Gas System	Panhandle EPL
Commonwealth Edison	Peoples Gas
Consolidated Edison	Philadelphia Electric
Consolidated Natural Gas	Public Service Electric and Gas
Detroit Edison	South California Edison
Houston Light & Power	

Table 6-1 lists the securities which form these Dow Jones averages. The three Dow Jones averages are very old, very popular, and receive wide coverage through the firm's newspapers.

6-2 SECURITY MARKET INDICES

An *index* is an indicator. A market index is an indicator of activity in some market. Security market indices usually indicate the level which security prices are following in some market.

Market Indices Differ

Many security market indices are published, some of which are:

> The Dow Jones Industrial Average
> The Dow Jones Transportation Average
> The Dow Jones Utility Average
> Moody's Industrial Average
> Moody's Railroad Stock Average
> Moody's Utility Stock Average
> Standard & Poor's Stock Averages from 90 different industrial categories
> Standard & Poor's 425 Industrial Stocks Average
> Standard & Poor's Railroad Stocks Average
> Standard & Poor's 55 Utility Stocks Average
> Standard & Poor's Composite 500 Stocks Average
> *The New York Times* Index
> Value Line Average
> New York Stock Exchange Average
> Center for Research on Security Prices (CRSP) Index
> National Quotation Board Index of Over-the-Counter Stocks
> American Stock Exchange Index
> Dow Jones 40 Bonds Index
> *Barron's* 50 Stock Average
> Dow Jones Indices of Spot Commodity Prices
> Dow Jones Futures Commodity Index

These indices are indicators of different things and are therefore useful for different purposes. For example, someone who is searching for a growth industry would be more interested in Standard & Poor's indices of stocks from 90 different industrial categories than in the Standard & Poor's composite average of 500 stocks from all industries. Figure 6-1 lists values for the Standard & Poor's indices, which are published with other information weekly in its publication *The Outlook*.

Some indices are leading indices and some are lagging indices. For example, the bond markets sometimes lead the stock markets in their price movements. Commodities, on the other hand, have some tendency to move concurrently with or lag slightly behind stock prices. And the level of the general economy, as measured by the gross national product (GNP) or other indicators of national income and production, tends to lag behind movements in stock prices by as much as a year.

Uses of Indices

Market indices furnish a handy summary of historical price levels in some market. This type of information has several uses. First, a person who owns several securities in some given market or industry can quickly get an indication of how market movements have affected the market value of his or

S. & P. INDEXES OF THE SECURITY MARKETS

Weekly Stock Price Indexes — 1941-43 = 10

	Close July 24	Close July 17	% Change	1974 Range High	1974 Range Low
500 Stocks, Combined	84.99	83.70	+ 1.5	99.80	79.89
425 Industrials	95.92	94.65	+ 1.3	111.65	90.22
15 Railroads	37.04	35.50	+ 4.3	47.36	33.65
60 Utilities	36.64	35.21	+ 4.1	49.44	34.33
110 Capital Goods	97.60	95.47	+ 2.2	111.33	89.87
185 Consumer Goods	81.68	82.14	− 0.6	93.92	79.15
*25 High Grade Common	78.00	77.07	+ 1.2	88.77	73.90
*20 Low Price Common	78.92	76.90	+ 2.6	95.14	74.90

INDUSTRIALS

	Close July 24	Close July 17	% Change	1974 Range High	1974 Range Low
8 Aerospace	38.72	37.54	+ 3.1	42.72	35.37
3 Air Freight [a]	28.88	28.74	+ 0.5	33.71	26.02
7 Air Transport	39.26	39.57	− 0.8	51.05	34.71
4 Aluminum	87.12	86.14	+ 1.1	100.07	74.87
3 Atomic Energy [a]	30.36	30.08	+ 0.9	36.19	24.93
4 Automobile	61.14	60.11	+ 1.7	70.72	59.30
Excl. General Motors	25.06	25.16	− 0.4	28.15	21.65
4 Auto Parts—After Market	37.60	37.40	+ 0.5	50.37	36.30
5 Auto Parts—Original Equipment	51.00	48.48	+ 5.2	57.25	45.95
3 Auto Trucks & Parts	38.19	38.50	− 0.8	47.12	37.19
4 Beverages: Brewers	115.56	116.70	− 1.0	139.82	107.85
4 Distillers	159.90	156.13	+ 2.4	196.96	154.42
5 Soft Drinks	110.23	116.45	− 5.3	146.85	•110.23
Building Materials Composite	36.09	35.73	+ 1.0	46.54	34.54
4 Air Conditioning [e]	15.51	15.93	− 2.6	25.52	•15.51
6 Cement	19.84	19.18	+ 3.4	28.54	19.09
2 Heating & Plumbing	27.00	26.49	+ 1.9	•27.00	18.28
6 Roofing & Wallboard	50.71	49.95	+ 1.5	62.52	47.67
11 Chemicals	65.29	63.48	+ 2.9	68.80	58.53
Excl. du Pont	55.67	53.99	+ 3.1	56.68	46.62
3 Coal: Bituminous	273.65	282.44	− 3.1	382.11	261.84
3 Confectionery	19.94	20.01	− 0.3	26.91	19.72
9 Conglomerates [a]	8.98	8.50	+ 5.6	11.33	8.10
5 Containers: Metal & Glass	27.98	27.12	+ 3.2	30.53	26.06
6 Paper Containers	104.68	103.45	+ 1.2	124.02	101.63
6 Copper	35.95	33.37	+ 7.7	45.77	32.45
5 Cosmetics [e]	45.96	46.94	− 2.1	71.68	•45.96
11 Drugs	199.76	205.75	− 2.9	226.51	194.77
5 Electrical Equipment	234.40	234.08	+ 0.1	298.70	226.15
6 Major Electrical-Electronic	72.58	72.25	+ 0.5	97.46	67.63
3 Household Appliances	157.54	156.44	+ 0.7	188.64	155.23
6 Electronics	582.75	586.87	− 0.7	712.00	576.02
3 Finance Companies	68.53	68.43	+ 0.1	91.85	62.52
5 Small Loans	58.66	57.04	+ 2.8	98.85	54.89
Food Composite	54.95	54.88	+ 0.1	65.70	52.79
6 Canned Foods	76.77	74.41	+ 3.2	91.76	70.35
4 Dairy Products	69.86	68.32	+ 2.3	85.26	68.32
3 Meat Packing	34.93	34.45	+ 1.4	41.87	34.19
7 Packaged Foods	74.47	76.33	− 2.4	89.82	71.90
6 Forest Products [f]	19.36	19.88	− 2.6	23.26	18.14
4 Gold Mining	135.85	118.15	+15.0	•135.85	102.03
4 Home Furnishings	21.66	21.88	− 1.0	30.35	21.01
3 Hospital Supplies [f]	36.47	37.64	− 3.1	44.81	36.03
4 Hotel-Motel [f]	17.48	18.04	− 3.1	30.07	17.37
3 Lead & Zinc	18.48	16.17	+14.3	22.29	15.64
6 Leisure Tme [f]	13.07	12.25	+ 6.7	17.51	11.58
6 Machine Tools	26.50	24.63	+ 7.6	37.88	24.63
3 Machinery: Agricultural	46.78	45.38	+ 3.1	56.81	42.78
Machinery Composite	162.07	159.54	+ 1.6	222.70	154.83
5 Construction & Materials Hand.	258.87	256.66	+ 0.9	322.20	256.66
6 Industrial	115.29	111.66	+ 3.3	139.69	103.85
6 Oil Well Mach. & Services	571.81	560.52	+ 2.0	796.82	541.14
5 Specialty	20.24	20.52	− 1.4	27.76	19.81
3 Steam Generating	132.07	134.44	− 1.8	332.46	123.32
5 Metal Fabricating	68.32	65.17	+ 4.8	79.14	60.70
5 Metals—Miscellaneous	58.47	54.46	+ 7.4	71.76	51.90
3 Mobile Homes [f]	42.74	43.85	− 2.5	66.45	36.07
4 Motion Pictures	42.79	43.01	− 0.5	48.24	35.05
8 Office and Business Equipment	1054.36	1040.23	+ 1.4	1198.48	948.44
Excluding IBM	331.45	328.04	+ 1.0	381.10	301.89
4 Offshore Drilling [f]	39.55	37.59	+ 5.2	77.49	34.48
Oil Composite	119.66	112.33	+ 6.5	153.81	107.08
4 Crude Producers	180.63	178.96	+ 0.9	365.45	166.87
9 Integrated: Domestic	126.39	120.99	+ 4.5	172.41	114.10
6 International	113.06	104.63	+ 8.1	135.97	100.50
8 Paper	197.17	192.27	+ 2.5	221.11	179.04
4 Pollution Control [a]	10.03	9.97	+ 0.6	24.57	9.32
8 Publishing	103.79	97.95	+ 6.0	120.39	94.80
6 Radio-TV Broadcasters	216.95	212.83	+ 1.9	232.48	177.47
4 Radio-TV Manufacturers	162.25	163.47	− 0.7	209.72	155.00
5 Railroad Equipment	37.94	37.74	+ 0.5	57.15	36.37
5 Real Estate [f]	9.80	9.13	+ 7.3	16.41	9.03
6 Real Estate Inv. Tr. [h]	2.72	2.68	+ 1.5	6.45	2.42
5 Restaurants [f]	21.41	20.75	+ 3.2	28.29	18.39
Retail Stores Composite	102.83	103.39	− 0.5	118.17	100.94
9 Department Stores	147.33	148.00	− 0.5	169.20	142.22
3 Discount Stores [b]	5.94	5.96	− 0.3	7.75	5.93
8 Food Chains	51.00	48.81	+ 4.5	60.35	47.07
3 Mail Order & Gen. Chains	189.23	187.51	+ 0.9	215.75	185.02
5 Variety Stores	57.98	62.72	− 7.6	73.68	•57.98
4 Sav. & Loan Holding Cos. [g]	10.52	10.42	+ 1.0	19.67	8.81
3 Shoes	23.44	23.06	+ 1.6	31.01	22.69
5 Soaps	181.11	181.14	0	188.45	157.50
9 Steel	51.17	48.50	+ 5.5	49.90	42.94
Excluding U. S. Steel	49.27	46.61	+ 5.7	49.63	41.99
3 Sugar—Beet Refiners	16.68	15.79	+ 5.6	19.40	14.12
7 Textiles: Apparel Mfrs.	15.22	15.00	+ 1.5	21.27	14.20
2 Synthetic Fibers	49.28	46.54	+ 5.9	54.69	42.80
6 Textile Products	42.59	43.11	− 1.2	48.98	40.12
4 Tires and Rubber Goods	127.23	125.16	+ 1.7	146.64	113.83
4 Tobacco: Cigarette Mfrs.	58.47	57.39	+ 1.9	61.10	53.88
3 Toys [f]	5.50	5.04	+ 9.1	7.58	4.79
10 Truckers [c]	90.18	90.88	− 0.8	101.63	80.83
5 Vending Machines [e]	27.78	27.98	− 0.7	30.02	24.34

PUBLIC UTILITIES

	Close July 24	Close July 17	% Change	1974 Range High	1974 Range Low
35 Electric Companies	24.99	24.22	+ 3.2	34.17	23.83
13 Natural Gas Distributors	47.07	45.83	+ 2.7	61.39	44.82
7 Pipelines	84.23	79.56	+ 5.9	112.55	73.47
6 Telephone	19.99	19.73	+ 1.3	24.04	19.01
Excluding AT&T	30.71	28.43	+ 8.0	37.78	27.46

* BANKS, INSURANCE, INVESTMENT COMPANIES

	Close July 24	Close July 17	% Change	1974 Range High	1974 Range Low
9 New York City Banks	54.28	51.03	+ 6.4	69.33	45.03
16 Banks, Outside N. Y. C.	79.06	74.41	+ 6.2	111.81	66.61
10 Life Insurance	138.81	133.50	+ 4.0	207.01	128.71
5 Multi-Line Insurance [d]	8.86	8.85	+ 0.1	12.95	8.03
10 Property-Liability Insurance	70.52	72.03	− 2.1	116.73	•70.52
9 Investment Cos. (Closed-End)	43.22	42.64	+ 1.4	54.41	41.50

THE MARKET LAST WEEK

Daily Stock Price Indexes (1941-43 = 10)

	July 26	July 25	July 24	July 23	July 22	July 19
425 Industrials						
H...	94.90	96.64	96.66	96.71	95.44	95.71
L...	92.42	93.76	94.38	94.56	93.36	93.70
C...	92.85	94.72	95.92	95.60	94.76	94.44
15 Rails						
H...	37.42	37.79	37.22	36.95	36.36	36.62
L...	36.80	36.79	36.63	36.14	35.72	35.87
C...	36.99	37.20	37.04	36.67	36.07	36.20
60 Utilities						
H...	36.64	37.06	36.90	36.59	35.66	35.66
L...	35.82	36.01	35.92	35.33	34.74	34.78
C...	36.15	36.40	36.64	36.17	35.22	35.11
500 Composite						
H...	84.17	85.67	85.64	85.63	84.44	84.67
L...	82.00	83.13	83.61	83.67	82.59	82.87
C...	82.40	83.98	84.99	84.65	83.81	83.54

	July 24	July 17	1974 High	1974 Low	1973 High	1973 Low
425 Industrials						
P-E Ratio	10.44	10.30	13.15	9.83	20.56	12.45
Yield (%)	3.94	4.00	4.17	3.29	3.46	2.43
****Range of Price Index**			113.16	89.32	136.27	101.84
15 Rails						
P-E Ratio	8.12	7.79	11.36	7.46	12.65	7.99
Yield (%)	5.87	5.84	6.09	4.37	6.15	4.32
****Range of Price Index**			48.12	33.52	46.22	32.25
60 Utilities						
P-E Ratio	6.86	6.59	9.04	6.43	11.98	8.16
Yield (%)	9.29	9.62	9.86	7.08	7.81	5.38
****Range of Price Index**			49.90	33.88	62.00	43.51
500 Composite						
P-E Ratio	10.09	9.94	12.72	9.50	19.47	12.00
Yield (%)	4.29	4.35	4.54	3.56	3.77	2.65
****Range of Price Index**			101.05	79.08	121.74	91.05

Preferred Stocks	Close as of July 24	Close as of July 17	1974 High	1974 Low	1973 High	1973 Low
Price, Dollars per share	82.1	83.0	94.7	•82.1	102.7	88.6
Yield, per cent	8.52	8.43	•8.52	7.39	7.90	6.82

Weekly Bond Yields %

	July 24	July 17	1974 High	1974 Low		July 24	July 17	1974 High	1974 Low
Composite					**Industrials**				
AAA	8.30	8.32	8.32	7.69		8.10	8.12	8.12	7.51
AA	8.73	8.70	•8.73	7.87		8.28	8.30	8.30	7.67
A	8.69	8.73	8.73	8.08		8.39	8.41	8.41	7.82
BBB	9.56	9.54	•9.56	8.63		8.98	9.00	9.00	8.53
Railroads					**Utilities**				
AAA	— DISCONTINUED —					8.50	8.52	8.52	7.87
AA	9.23	9.11	•9.23	7.85		8.68	8.70	8.70	7.99
A	8.89	8.95	8.95	8.09		8.80	8.81	8.81	8.12
BBB	10.59	10.51	•10.59	8.81		9.10	9.12	9.12	8.36

	Yields July 24	Yields July 17	Yields 1974 High	Yields 1974 Low	†Prices July 24	†Prices July 17	†Prices 1974 High	†Prices 1974 Low
Corp. AAA	8.30	8.32	8.32	7.69	58.38	58.24	62.60	58.24
Government:								
Long Term	6.58	6.75	6.78	6.18	66.20	64.97	69.19	64.75
Intermediate	7.94	8.17	8.24	6.70	72.48	71.52	78.46	71.11
Short Term	7.95	8.29	8.56	6.51	85.13	84.21	89.17	83.48
Municipal	6.26	6.65	6.80	5.14	74.42	70.96	85.86	69.68

Miscellaneous Indexes

	Latest Week	Week Ago	Year Ago	1974 High	1974 Low
[1]**Industrial Raw Material Prices**	228.1	220.5	180.2	245.0	214.1
[2]**Weekly Business Index**	125.8	125.7	126.2	126.5	124.1

•Indicates a new high or low. Range for 500 stocks, 425 industrials, 15 rails and 60 utilities is based on daily closing indexes. †Converted from average yield to maturity, assuming an appropriate coupon and maturity. *Not included in composite indexes. a1965=10; b1957=10; c1955=10; these special base indexes not included in composite indexes. d1968=10; e1957 = 10; f1965 = 10; g1959 = 10; h1970 = 10. **Based on intraday high and low prices. [1]BLS Index (1967 = 100). [2]Business Week Index (1967 = 100).

FIG. 6-1 Standard & Poor's market indices as reported in *The Outlook,* July 29, 1974, p. 643.

her portfolio merely by checking the appropriate index and determining the percentage change in it. This is much faster than checking the prices of each security separately. Second, indices are useful for historical analysis. By analyzing market indices and other economic indicators, an analyst can detect some consistent relationships between different indices and sectors of the economy. These types of relationships can be useful. If an index is a dependable leading index, it may be useful for forecasting.

Some people suggest that indices have other important uses. Some believe, for example, that by charting an index over time it is possible to detect patterns which are repeated at various phases of the market's rise and fall. Then the patterns from this one index can be used to forecast that market's future direction. These charting activities, called *technical analysis*, are discussed in some detail in Chap. 20.

Construction of Indices

Every market index is constructed differently. A well-constructed market index will give an indication of the prices of the entire population under consideration. A poorly constructed index will indicate what only an unrepresentative sample of the population is doing. If a population is fairly homogeneous, even a poorly constructed index will give a good indication of its movement. In the selection of a market index with which to work, or in the design of a new index, the following factors should be considered.

1 *Sample size.* The sample should not be an insignificant fraction of the population studied. On the other hand, if the sample is very large, it will be too costly to compile.

2 *Representativeness.* The sample should contain heterogeneous elements representing all sections of the population. For example, a sample of securities should not contain only large firms or firms which are all in the same industry.

3 *Weighting.* The various elements in the sample should be assigned weights which correspond to the actual opportunities in the population under study. For example, a security's weight in some index might be proportional to the fraction of total market value represented by all the firms' shares which are outstanding, or equal weights could be used to represent random sampling.

4 *Convenient units.* An index should be stated in units which are easy to understand and which facilitate answering relevant questions.[2]

Let us compare the popular DJIA with the Center for Research on Security Prices (CRSP) Index in light of these criteria.

---

[2] Other factors should be considered in the design of a sample or an index, but they are beyond the scope of this discussion. The interested reader may find entire courses and books on the subject of experimental design and sampling. See H. A. Latane, D. L. Tuttle, and Wm. E. Young, "Market Indices," *Financial Analysts Journal,* September–October 1971, pp. 75–85. This article also discusses the development of market indices.

Sample size. The DJIA is an average of 30 securities listed on the NYSE. The CRSP index is an average of all securities listed on the NYSE (approximately 1,300). Thus, the DJIA samples only about 2.3 percent of the population ($\frac{30}{1,300} = .023$), whereas the CRSP samples all of it.

Representativeness. The DJIA contains only securities of the large, old, blue-chip firms listed in Table 6-1. No small firms and no new firms are in the sample. The CRSP includes all securities listed on the exchange.

Weighting. The CRSP weights each security equally. Thus, if 1,300 securities are listed on the NYSE at a given date, the CRSP assigns each a weight of $\frac{1}{1,300}$. The DJIA presently uses a weighting system which is arbitrary. In 1928 when the DJIA was expanded to 30 stocks, the 30 market prices were simply summed up and divided by 30 to obtain the DJIA. Thus, equal weights ($\frac{1}{30}$) were assigned to the 30 securities used in 1928. Over the years, however, as some of the 30 securities underwent stock splits and stock dividends, the weights of $\frac{1}{30}$ for each asset became inappropriate. To adjust for these changes, the weights of all 30 shares were increased. Let us assume, for example, that the first of the 30 securities to be split was split 2 for 1. This split would leave two shares, each worth half as much;[3] so the prices of the 29 original shares plus one of the new smaller shares would be summed up and the total would be divided by $29\frac{1}{2}$ instead of 30. This weighting system is equivalent to selling the split share and investing the proceeds evenly in all 30 remaining shares.

This adjustment was rational in 1928, but it became obsolete as some securities in the sample grew more than others. By 1966 the 30 securities in the average were divided by 2.245, and the DJIA was in the 800s while the average price of the 30 shares was about $65. As a result, the weights which are used in the DJIA do not relate to any relevant market proportions or market opportunities. The equal weights used in the CRSP, on the other hand, represent the proportions which would result if a portolio were selected in a random manner, for example, with an unaimed dart.

Convenient units. The DJIA has ranged between 500 and 1,000 "points" in recent years. The Dow Jones Company has explained that each of these "points" equals about a 7-cent change in the market value of an "average share of stock." The "points" themselves are void of any intrinsically meaningful economic interpretation. The CRSP contains market prices, percentage changes in the prices, and rates of return including dividends.[4] Since

---

[3] Split shares usually increase in value; but this is due to retained earnings or growth in earnings and is unrelated to the split. The effects of stock splits and stock dividends, analyzed in Chap. 22, are seen to be nil, on average.

[4] The file is actually a magnetic computer tape which contains price relatives (PR) rather than rates of return r. The relationship between price relatives and rates of return is shown below.

$$\text{PR}_t = \frac{P_{t+1}}{P_t} = 1 + r_t$$

the rate of return is the most important outcome for most investments and since it is the best standard for investment comparisons, the percentages and rates of return are quite convenient.

In view of the various shortcomings of the DJIA, it should not be used in analytical financial studies. The CRSP, on the other hand, is one of the best market indices available.[5]

6-3 INVESTMENT INFORMATION SERVICES

Syntheses of fundamental financial information about individual firms are published by investment services. These firms offer subscriptions to their daily, weekly, and monthly publications. The cost of a subscription to an investor is a deductible expense from the investor's income according to the federal personal income tax regulations. Large public libraries usually carry one or more of these services, which may be consulted free of charge. The leading services are:

> Moody's Investor Services, Inc.[6]
> Standard & Poor's Corporation[7]
> The Value Line Investment Survey[8]

Most of Standard & Poor's (SP) and Moody's information is based on reference volumes: *SP Corporation Records* and *Moody's Industrial Manuals*. *Moody's Industrial Manuals* are thick bound volumes that give complete investment data for a period of years and a financial history for hundreds of companies. They are specialized, with different books published for industrials, transportation, utilities, banks and financial, and government securities. *SP Corporations Records* are also thick volumes, but, unlike *Moody's Manuals*, they are alphabetically arranged by the names of the companies rather than by industrial fields. Frequent bulletins keep the six-volume set of *SP Corporation Records* up to date. Twice weekly Moody publishes a report to keep its manuals current.

Standard & Poor's (SP)

The massive *SP Corporation Records* discuss the affairs of each company, using the following topic headings: Capitalization and Long-Term Debt; Corporate Background, with topic subheadings such as sales backlogs, sub-

---

[5] L. Fisher and J. Lorie, "Rates of Return on Investments in Common Stock," *Journal of Business*, January 1964, pp. 1–21. This article explains the CRSP file and presents some of the data. Professor Fisher has also prepared some additional indices, published in "Some New Stock Market Indexes," *Journal of Business*, January 1966, pp. 191–225.

[6] 99 Church St., New York, N.Y. 10007.

[7] 345 Hudson St., New York, N.Y. 10014. Standard & Poor's is a subsidiary of McGraw-Hill, Inc.

[8] 5 E. 44th St., New York, N.Y. 10017.

MASTER LIST OF RECOMMENDED ISSUES

GROUP 1: FOUNDATION STOCKS FOR LONG-TERM GAIN

These issues are basic building blocks for the portfolio. They offer the prospect of long-term appreciation, along with moderate but growing income. The investor seeking to build an estate should start with stocks from this list, augmenting them with issues from other groups according to his objectives and temperament.

Earnings Per Share ($) 1972	1973	E1974	Indi- cated Div. $	1973-74 Price Range	Recent Price	P/E Ratio	Yield %		Annual Growth Rates —for Latest 5 Years— Sales	Earn.	Div.	▼Price Action vs. Mkt. 5-26-70 to 1-11-73	Since 1-11-73	Last Ref. Page
1.78	2.36	2.55	1.18	37⅜-27¼	28	11.0	4.2	Campbell Soup (July)	8%	9%	3%	0.74	1.09	754
¹1.26	¹1.61	¹1.90	¹0.82	19⅜-14⅛	15	7.9	5.5	Canadian Pacific	5	16	4	0.94	1.17	810
⁴1.78	⁴2.14	⁴2.45	0.80	51½-33⅝	37	15.1	2.2	Citicorp	—	⁴14	7	1.62	1.21	819
6.83	10.90	12.00	4.55	103¾-69⅞	73	6.1	6.2	Exxon Corp.	12	17	2	0.99	1.07	775
2.91	3.21	3.30	1.60	75⅞-46¾	49	14.8	3.3	General Electric	7	17	2	1.37	0.88	862
7.50	8.34	4.00	²3.40	84⅝-44⅞	51	12.8	6.7	General Motors	10	13	3	0.78	0.81	726
2.30	3.60	4.50	1.75	57 -33	48	10.7	3.7	International Paper	7	13	3	0.83	1.52	841
2.53	2.82	3.10	1.50	40½-20¾	23	7.4	6.5	Lone Star Gas	8	12	6	1.22	0.77	858
5.65	8.34	8.50	3.20	75½-40	41	4.8	7.8	Mobil Oil	12	17	6	1.06	0.75	834
3.49	6.90	8.60	2.40	75¾-43⅛	67	7.8	3.6	Monsanto	7	27	2	1.06	1.64	696
3.45	5.50	6.50	1.98	56¾-32⅝	38	5.8	5.2	Union Oil of Calif.	10	13	3	0.96	1.24	697

GROUP 2: STOCKS WITH PROMISING GROWTH PROSPECTS

These stocks promise to enjoy well above average growth rates in earnings per share for the foreseeable future. Stocks in the second category carry a higher degree of risk, but by the same token offer greater reward potential. Income is not a consideration here.

Established Growth

Earnings Per Share ($) 1972	1973	E1974	Indi- cated Div. $	1973-74 Price Range	Recent Price	P/E Ratio	Yield %		Latest 5-Year Growth Rates Sales	Earn.	No. of Earn. Gains '69-'73	Interim ▪Earn. Trend	▼Price Action vs. Mkt. 5-26-70 1-11-73	Since 1-11-73	Last Ref. Page
1.08	1.25	1.40	0.80	48¾- 35	43	30.7	1.9	Amer. Home Products	12%	11%	5	+ 15	1.34	1.36	819
2.60	3.16	3.55	1.52	71¾- 40⅝	54	15.2	2.8	Bristol-Myers	10	9	4	+ 20	0.83	1.01	847
3.30	4.05	4.20	⁶1.56	151¾- 96⅝	111	26.4	1.4	Eastman Kodak	9	13	5	+ 1	1.44	1.00	734
8.82	10.79	12.50	5.12	365¼-209⅝	216	17.3	2.4	Int. Business Machines	10	13	5	+ 31	0.97	0.87	834
1.58	1.90	2.30	0.68	68⅝- 45	45	19.6	1.5	Schlitz (Jos.) Brewing	14	19	5	+111	0.56	1.07	867
3.96	4.33	4.55	1.81	123¼- 78¼	87	19.1	2.1	Sears, Roebuck (*Jan.)	8	10	5	+ 4	1.33	0.96	751
1.50	1.52	2.25	0.40	64¼- 23⅛	45	20.0	0.9	•Syntex (July)	16	15	4	+ 61	2.04	1.49	751

More Speculative Growth

Earnings Per Share ($) 1972	1973	E1974	Mill. Shs. Outst.	1973-74 Price Range	Recent Price	P/E Ratio	Yield %		Latest 5-Year Growth Rates Sales	Earn.	No. of Earn. Gains '69-'73	Interim ▪Earn. Trend	▼Price Action vs. Mkt. 5-26-70 to 1-11-73	Since 1-11-73	Last Ref. Page
0.70	1.05	1.50	18.6	26 - 11¼	19	12.7	1.8	MAPCO	18	25	5	+ 60	3.63	1.23	705
†2.06	†2.26	†2.70	15.8	39⅛- 7½	12	4.4	3.3	Warner Communications	5	10	5	+19	0.95	0.43	766
3.94	4.65	7.00	9.9	77 - 39	58	8.3	0.7	Williams Companies	26	12	5	+50	1.90	1.41	775

EARNINGS are for calendar years or for fiscal years ending as indicated after names. Unless otherwise noted, they are based on common and common share equivalents, excluding nonrecurring items and including restatements. E—Estimated. *Of the following year.

INDICATED DIVIDENDS include actual or possible extras. PRICE/EARNINGS RATIOS are based on latest shown estimated or actual earnings.

Stocks are listed on the New York Stock Exchange, except as indicated. • American Stock Exchange.

▼A figure above 1.0 indicates that the stock outperformed the S & P industrial stock price index in this period. It is computed by taking the ratio of the stock's price at the end of the period vs. the beginning of the period and dividing it by the corresponding ratio of the index.

▪This column compares share earnings of the latest six months with those of the corresponding year-earlier period.

FIG. 6-2 Standard & Poor's weekly buy recommendations from *The Outlook*, June 24, 1974, pp. 700–701. These reports were up to date during the week they were issued. Subsequent events would alter these recommendations, however. (*Source:* Standard & Poor's, 345 Hudson Street, New York, N.Y., 10014.)

GROUP 3: CYCLICAL/SPECULATIVE STOCKS

This group comprises stocks selected for high reward potentials stemming from a variety of considerations—including emerging opportunities, turnaround situations, stocks to benefit from cyclical upswings, and the like. Readers can expect to see frequent changes in this list as likely price objectives are reached, or (as must realistically be expected in some cases) anticipated price appreciation or earnings recovery lags. The risk factor in some of the issues in this group may be high and the stocks recommended may not be suitable for those concerned with income or with investment grade securities.

Earnings Per Share ($) 1972	1973	E1974	Indicated Div. $	1973-74 Price Range	Recent Price	P/E Ratio	Yield %		Remarks
2.39	3.45	4.10	1.50	54¼-28½	39	9.5	3.9	**Allied Chem.**	Active oil exploration program adds speculative kicker.
3.56	4.19	4.50	1.80	51¼-22¾	30	6.7	6.0	**Bendix (Sept.)**	Cost efficiency aiding earnings.
[3]3.80	[3]4.01	[3]6.00	1.50	49⅞-26¾	37	6.2	4.1	**Burlington Northern**	Oil, gas, coal and land holdings add to potentials.
4.27	4.80	2.25	1.40	44¼-14⅝	17	7.6	8.2	**Chrysler**	Good small-car position; stock cheap for long haul.
[5]4.36	[5]4.84	[5]5.15	2.40	43⅝-30⅞	32	6.2	7.5	**Continental Corp.**	Strong advance in investment income lifting over-all results
2.58	2.20	3.00	1.50	58⅜-24¼	36	12.0	4.2	**Joy Mfg. (Sept.)**	Coal mining gear in strong demand due to energy shortage.
1.17	2.52	2.90	0.15	24⅜-10⅝	15	5.2	1.0	**Louisiana-Pacific**	Strong pulp and chip markets aiding results.
2.76	3.13	2.70	1.10	47⅜-14⅝	15	4.3	7.3	**Macy (R.H.) (July)**	Possible turnaround at New York division would be major plus.
d2.68	3.00	3.60	0.72	46¼-26⅜	33	9.2	2.2	**‡NCR Corp.**	Speculative appeal based on new products, labor cost savings.
3.99	4.48	4.00	1.70	47 -20½	26	6.5	6.5	**PPG Industries**	Modest valuation underrates favorable long-range outlook.
2.48	5.06	5.65	1.50	80½-31¼	52	9.2	2.9	**→Pullman Inc.**	Enjoying booming demand (see page 723).
2.59	3.03	3.50	[7]0.80	39⅞-21⅜	33	9.4	2.4	**Raytheon**	Energy-related services spurring earnings gains.
1.86	2.06	2.50	0.36	17⅞- 6¼	7	2.8	5.1	**Rockower Bros.**	Store expansion to support record earnings.
1.94	2.88	3.75	1.20	37½-23¾	26	6.8	4.6	**St. Regis Paper**	Strong supply-demand relationship enhances prospects.
1.04	1.28	1.65	0.20	52⅛-21¾	27	16.4	0.7	**Santa Fe Intl.**	North Sea oil adds plus to offshore drilling, construction.
[3]3.95	[3]4.47	[3]5.40	1.92	52¾-29¾	45	8.3	4.3	**Southern Railway**	Aided by area growth, profit-oriented management.

GROUP 4: LIBERAL INCOME WITH INFLATION PROTECTION

If high yield alone were the goal, it would be simple to devise a list of high-quality bonds yielding 8% or more. But the individual who must rely to a major extent on his investments for income must take into account the prospect of continuing inflation. Accordingly, this group presents a list of quality high-yielding stocks which in our opinion offer the prospect of dividend growth at least sufficient to compensate for inflation over a period of time.

Earnings Per Share ($) 1972	1973	E1974	Indicated Div. $	1973-74 Price Range	Recent Price	P/E Ratio	Yield %		Dividend History 10-Year Growth Rate	No. of Ann. Incr. 1964-73	10-Year Avg. Payout	Latest Increase	Inflation Hedge Ratio††	Last Ref. Page
4.34	4.98	5.30	3.08	55 -45⅜	47	8.9	6.6	**American Tel. & Tel.**	4%	7	61%	1- 2-74	1.04	738
[4]4.65	[4]5.02	[4]5.50	2.88	54⅛-35¼	35	6.4	8.2	**Chemical N. Y.**	5	6	51	1- 1-71	1.03	705
5.32	5.89	6.40	2.68	55¾-36½	45	7.0	6.0	**Reynolds (R.J.) Indust.**	5	9	53	9- 5-73	1.07	751
[3]4.06	[3]3.77	[3]4.25	2.16	44⅝-28	31	7.3	7.0	**Southern Pacific**	5	9	49	1-20-73	1.07	751
3.27	4.75	5.75	2.00	43⅛-24⅞	26	4.5	7.7	**Texaco**	5	9	48	3- 8-74	1.16	762

††A figure of 1.0 indicates that dividend growth exactly offset the impact of inflation in the 1964-73 period; a higher ratio indicates the degree to which the growth in annual dividend payments exceeded the rise in the Consumer Price Index in this period.

[1]Canadian currency. [2]Estimated rate. [3]Consolidated, GAAP accounting basis. [4]Net operating earnings. [5]Assumes conv. of pfd. shares. [6]Excluding extras. [7]Company plans to raise rate from $0.70 on June 26. †Fully diluted. ‡Formerly National Cash Register.

Changes since May 27: → Addition: Pullman (Group 3). Deletion: Cenco Inc. (Group 3).

FIG. 6-2 *(Continued)*

sidiaries, affiliates, principal properties, capital expenditures, employees, officers, directors, and executive offices; Bond Descriptions, with topic subheadings such as trustee, purpose of issue, sinking fund, redemptions, security, dividend restrictions, and price range; Stock Data, with subtopics on voting power, capital changes, capital stock offered through rights, stock issued under convertibles, capital stock sold, stockholders, transfer agent, listings, and dividends; and Earnings and Finances, with subtopics entitled auditors, consolidated earnings statements, adjusted earnings, quarterly sales, property account analysis, maintenance and repairs, consolidated income statement, and consolidated balance sheet.

The Outlook is a weekly publication of SP. It surveys market conditions and makes recommendations as to common stocks investors might buy. It contains special articles, on-the-spot reports on individual firms, stocks now in favor, a report on overall business conditions, a market forecast and recommendations, and sometimes a "stock for action." A special annual issue of *The Outlook* is published with a forecast for the coming year. This forecast is divided into categories such as best low-priced stocks, candidates for dividend increases, rapid growth stocks for long-term profits, and stocks for action in the year ahead. Figure 6-2 shows a sample of the recommendations from Standard & Poor's *The Outlook*. Market indices, too, are tabulated and published in *The Outlook* each week (see Fig. 6-1). Moody's *Stock Survey* is a weekly publication similar to *The Outlook.*

SP publishes a monthly pocket-size *Stock Guide* and a similar *Bond Guide*. Each is a concise summary of investment information about various issues. Figure 6-3 shows two continuous pages of the *Stock Guide.* Figure 6-4 contains an explanation of SP's stock ratings. The *Stock Guide* also lists "stock for potential appreciation," "recommended stocks primarily for appreciation," "candidates for dividend increases," "candidates for stock splits," and "25 of the best low-priced stocks." The back page of the *Stock Guide* lists "quality ratings of utility preferred stocks" and "industry classifications with stock ratings." Figure 6-5 shows a page from SP's *Bond Guide.* Figure 6-6 explains the bond ratings used by SP.

Moody's

The voluminous *Moody's Industrial Manuals* contain fundamental financial information for hundreds of firms. For each firm information is presented under the following heads and subheadings: Capital Structure, with subheads on long-term debt and capital stock, history, subsidiaries, business and products, and principal plants and properties; Management, with subheadings for officers, directors, general counsel, auditors, stockholders, employees, general office address, and unfilled orders; Income Accounts, with subheadings entitled comparative income account, supplementary P & L data, comparative balance sheets, property account, and depreciation reserve; Financial and Operating Data, with subheads entitled statistical records, data adjusted for stock splits and stock dividends, financial and operating ratios and analysis of operations; Long-Term Debt, with subheads such as authorized debt, call dates, sinking fund, security, sales and leasebacks, dividend restrictions, rights on default indenture modification, term loans, notes payable, revolving credit agreement and other notes; and Capital Stock, with subheads entitled authorized stock, dividend restrictions, voting rights, preemptive rights, transfer agent, registrar, stock subscription rights, and debenture subscription rights.

Moody's Handbook of Widely Held Common Stocks is issued four times a year and gives a brief summary of about 1,000 firms. Figure 6-7 shows a sample page. For each firm the price is charted and compared with the industry's price trend. Financial background, current developments, and future prospects are all reported along with the financial statistics for several years. SP's counterpart to *Moody's Handbook* is the *Stock Market En-*

STANDARD & POOR'S CORPORATION

INDEX	Ticker Symbol	STOCKS NAME OF ISSUE (Call Price of Pfd. Stocks) / Market	Earns &Div Rank-ing	Inst.Hold Cos	Inst.Hold Shs.(000)	Par Val.	PRINCIPAL BUSINESS	1960-72 High	1960-72 Low	1973 High	1973 Low	1974 High	1974 Low	Mar. Sales in 100s	Mar High	Mar Low	Mar Last	% Div. Yield	P-E Ratio
1	BIRD	Bird & Son....OTC	B+	1	25	No	Bldg mtl: paperboard prods	43	5⅛	34½	16½	28	18½	135	28	23¼	26¾ B	e5.2	5
2	BDK	Black & Decker Mfg...NYS,Bo,PB	A+	803	3680	50¢	Mfr portable electric tools	36⅜	2½	42⅜	31	28	27¾	4795	39⅜	34⅜	34⅞	5.1	37
3	BHPL	Black Hills Pwr & Lt...OTC	B+	1		1	Elec util: S.D.::Montana,Wyom	52½	20¼	37¼	29¾	36¼	33½	58	36¼	35	35½ B	6.2	5
4	BJ	Blair (John) & Co...NYS	B+	8	133	1	Radio & TV station adv agent	30½	7½	37⅜	4½	13	7⅞	216	7½	6⅞	6⅝	6.2	5
5	BCO	Blessings Corp...ASE,Bo,PB	B+	2	13	3.20	Diaper rental: disp med sup	25	2⅞	10⅞	3½	5¼	3⅞	583	5	4½	4⅞	8.2	5
6	BLI	Bliss & Laughlin Ind...NYS,MW	B+	7	233	2½	Constr:steel:ld dev,hm furn	32⅜	8¼	19⅜	12	15¼	12½	137	15¼	13⅜	13⅜	7.5	5
7	HRB	Block (H & R), Inc...NYS	NR	230	2075	No	Nationwide income tax serv	42⅜	8¾	17	5⅜	15¼	12½	3228	14	11¼	12¼	2.6	12
8	BLOCA	Block Drug, Cl A...OTC	B-	9	124	10¢	Denture, dental care pr: drugs	26⅜	18¾	27¾	9⅜	14⅜	10⅛	1003	14½	13	13 B	3.7	12
9	BLOK	Block Engineering...OTC	NR	1	13	10¢	Electro-optical, bio medical	11⅜	2½	4⅜	4⅛	3⅜	1⅝	121	3⅜	2½	3 B		6
10	BLT	Blount, Inc...ASE	NR			10¢	Gen constr:fabrication,piping	11¾	2½	4⅜	2½	2¼	2	202	2¾	2	2 B	3.2	6
11	BBL	Blue Bell...NYS	B+	34	644	3⅓	Diversified apparel mfr	52¾	4¾	38	12¼	21½	13¾	2094	21½	17⅞	19⅜	e3.9	7
12	BLUE	Blue Chip Stamps...OTC	NR	51	1004	No	Trading stamps:candy shops	25	1	15¾	7¼	8¼	7	188	8¼	7⅞	8 B	3.0	7
13	BBX	Bluebird, Inc...ASE	NR	4	459	25¢	Pork processing:canned meats	16½	¾	4⅜	2⅜	4¼	2⅞	356	4	3⅜	3⅜		5
14	WS	Wrrt (Purch 1 com at $10.75)					bacon and smoked meats	4¾		1⅜					⅞	⅝	B		
15	BFLD	Bluefield Supply...OTC	B	1	2	2	Distr construction, other eq	22	6½	13¾	8	11½	9	113	10½	9¾	9¾ B	6.2	6
16	BLYVY	Blyvoor Gold Mng ADR...OTC	NR	31	1032	$0.25	Gold & uranium, So. Africa	7½	2⅜	10¾	2⅛	15¼	10¼	6857	15¼	12	15⅛ B	4.3	14
17	BMAC	BMA Corp...OTC		18	411	2	Insur hldg: Bus Men's Assur	44⅜	13¾	32¾	17⅛	22	16⅛	422	18½	16½	16½ B	3.5	4
18	BOBE	Bob Evans Farms...OTC	NR			No	Pork sausage:ages 13-29	35¾	5⅝	34¾	17	24	18⅛	80	24	23	23 B		9
19	BBK	Bobbie Brooks...NYS,Bo,MW	B	5	128	No	Fashion apparel,ages 13-29	39⅞	8	9⅜	2⅜	3⅜	2⅜	635	3½	3¼	3		3
20	BDN	Bodin Apparel...ASE,Bo,PB	B	1	51	10¢	Knitted apparel for women	26⅜	9	29⅜	7	9½	6⅞	1131	9⅞	6⅞	7⅜	5.6	10
21	BA	Boeing Co...NYS,Bo,Cl,De,MW,PB,PS	NR	53	1975	5	Mfr jet airplanes: missiles	112¾	11½	26¾	11¾	15¾	11¾	2621	15¼	13¾	14⅜	4.2	6
22	BHK	Bohack Corp...ASE				No	Food supermarkets in N.Y.	24⅜	1⅝	11¾	7⅜	6¾	4⅛	397	6¼	5⅞	5⅞		
23	BOHM	Bohemia Inc...OTC	NR	2	32	No	Mfr & sale of lumb, plywood	30¾	10¾	13¾	6¾	21	15⅜	827	21	18¾	19¾ B	$2.5	5
24	BCC	Boise Cascade...NYS,Bo,Cl,De,MW,PB,PS	B	53	2675	2½	Bldg mtls & paper products	75¾	6⅜	34	13⅛	18¾	14½	9759	18¾	15¾	15¾ B	1.6	9
25	BBN	Bolt Beranek & Newman...ASE,Bo,PB	NR	3	76	No	Research, consulting services	30¾	3⅛	12⅝	5	9½	6¾	66	8⅞	7⅞	7⅞ B		9
26	BNZA	Bonanza Int'l...OTC	NR	10	360	No	Steak restaurants nationwide	47¼	1⅜	17⅛	4⅞	8¾	5¾	3482	6¾	5⅝	5⅝ B		17
27	BND	Bond Indus...NYS,PS	B-	2	12	1¼	Apparel stores: clothing mfr	24⅜	6⅜	7⅞	3⅜	6⅝	4	231	6⅞	5⅝	5⅝		d
28	BOK	Book-of-Month Club...NYS	B+	11	202	5	Sells selected books by mail	37⅜	9¼	29	15¼	18¼	16¼	145	18	16¾	17⅞ B	8.1	7
29	BNEW	Booth Newspapers...OTC	B+	6	118	50¢	Daily, Sunday newspap's: TV	40¼	12¼	34	12	17	16¼	173	18	15¼	15¼ B	5.2	7
30	BOOZ	Booz, Allen & Hamilton...OTC	NR			25¢	Mgmt consultants: R&D sv	25¼	6¼	8¾	5	5¾	3⅞	153	5⅞	4¾	4¾ B	2.5	7
31	BN	Borden, Inc...NYS,Bo,De,MW,PB,PS	A	104	3861	3¾	Dairy & food prod, chemicals	39¼	17⅜	31¼	19	25¼	21	4097	25¼	22¾	24	5.0	10
32	BOR	Borg-Warner...NYS,Bo,Cl,De,MW,PB,PS	A-	46	1613	2½	Widely diversified products	39¼	16	36¾	16⅜	25⅜	18	2178	24	19¾	19¾ B	6.8	10
33	BRF	Borman's Inc...NYS,De				No	Detroit supermkts:drug stores	30¼	4	6	4⅜	6	2⅜	209	3⅜	3	3⅜ B		d
34	BSTNB	Boston Co., Cl B...OTC				No	Subsid: fiduciary, gen bank'g	32	13¾	28	13¼	16¾	15¼	62	15½	15¼	15¼ B	6.8	6
35	BSE	Boston Edison...NYS,Bo,Cl,De,PB	A-	40	360	10	Electric utility: Boston	51	23¾	39¾	24	29¾	26	992	28¾	27¾	27¾	9.0	9
36	Pr	8.88% cm Pfd...NYS[60]	A	4	11	100	& vicinity served: steam	116	101½[60]	103	107½	107½	103	16	107½	104	104½	8.5	
37	BOU	Bourns, Inc...NYS,PB,PS	NR	2	47	50¢	Mfr electronic circuit equip.	32¾	4⅜	21	10¼	17⅝	13¾	259	17⅞	14⅞	14⅜		7
38	BVS	Bovis Corp Ltd...TS,VS	NR			No	Heavy constr'n:eq sup:land	1	⅞	⅞	⅜	2⅛	1⅝	1033	2⅛	1⅞	1⅞		7
39	BVI	Bow Valley Indus...#ASE,TS	NR	57	1008	1	Serves oil & gas ind: Canada	49⅜	2⅜	55	24⅜	33¾	26⅜	326	33¾	26¾	29¼ B	♦0.3	97
40	BWTRY	Bowater Corp Ltd ADR...OTC,MS,TS	B			1£	Newsprint & other papers	9¾	2⅜	5¼	5⅜	3¼	2⅝	109	3¾	3	3 B	4.3	10
41	BOM	Bowmar Instrument...ASE,Bo,PB	B	3	218	No	Semiconductors:hand calcul'r	23⅜	1½	44¾	19¼	24¾	14⅜	1999	19¾	14⅜	14⅜		9
42	BNE	Bowne & Co...OTC	B	2	61		Finance & corp'n printing	40¾	7¼	28¾	6⅝	6⅞	5½	127	6⅞	6¼	6½ B	3.3	6
43	BOZZ	Bozzuto's Inc...OTC	NR				An IGA grocery wholesaler	15¾	2⅜	4	2⅜	5⅞	5½		6¾	5½	6¼ B	4.5	7
44	BRD	Brad Ragan...ASE	NR	1	143	1£	Tire retreading: retail strs	49¾	6½	26¾	5¼	11¼	8½	1533	11¾	6½	9¾		7

Uniform Footnote Explanations—See Page 1. Other: [51]⑤$2.40,'73. [52]Adj: As computed by S&P. [53]☐$1.54,'71. [54]☐$6.26,'72. [55]△$0.24,'69. [56]☐$0.11,'70. [57]☐$0.70,'71. [58]☐$2.28,'73.
[59]71%,'73 non-taxable. [60]To 10-31-77,scale to $102 in'87. [61]Approx.

FIG. 6-3 Pages from Standard & Poor's *Stock Guide*, April 1974.

COMMON AND PREFERRED STOCKS

INDEX	Some Divs. Ea. Yr. Since	DIVIDENDS — Latest Payment — Per $	Date	Ex. Div.	$ So Far 1974	Total Ind. Rate	$ Paid 1973	FINANCIAL POSITION — Mil-$ — Cash& Equiv.	Curr. Assets	Curr. Liabs.	Balance Sheet Date	CAPITALIZATION — Long Term Debt Mil-$	Shs. 000 — Pfd.	Com.	Ended	$ Per Shr—EARNINGS—$ Per Shr — Years — 1969	1970	1971	1972	1973	Last 12 Mos.	INTERIM EARNINGS OR REMARKS — Period	$—Per Share—$ 1972	1973	INDEX
1◆	1924	Q0.35	4-10-74	3-18	0.70	e1.40	†1.28	9.29	43.3	14.6	12-31-73	1.54	23	1559	Dc	△0.70	1.09	□4.13	□5.06	5.89	5.89				1
2◆	1937	Q0.10	3-25-74	3-4	0.10	0.40	0.346	9.50	260.	132.	9-30-73	36.0	...	40146	Sp	0.51	0.55	0.61	0.71	0.87	0.93	3 Mo Dec	0.16	0.22	2
3	1942	Q0.55	3-1-74	2-8	0.55	2.20	2.20	0.58	2.91	3.23	10-31-73	18.4	35	470	Oc	2.77	2.58	3.48	□3.29	3.91	3.95	12 Mo Jan△	□3.66	3.95	3
4◆	1955	Q0.12	5-15-74	4-8	0.24	0.48	0.48	2.34	20.5	9.00	12-31-72	★9.00	...	2403	Dc	1.65	1.50	□1.04	1.27	P1.31	1.31				4
5◆	1962	Q0.10	3-1-74	2-4	0.10	0.40	0.55	1.27	10.1	4.41	4-28-73	3.97	10	1238	Ap	0.86	△1.06	1.31	1.24	1.17	0.81	36 Wk Jan△	0.80	0.44	5
6◆	1939	Q0.25	3-31-74	2-26	0.25	1.00	0.977	9.30	57.9	19.0	12-31-73	35.0	...	3111	Dc	2.29	△1.84	1.52	□2.09	[51]2.62	2.62				6
7◆	1962	Q0.08	3-15-74	2-8	0.08	0.32	0.28	53.3	56.1	25.7	4-30-73	0.08	...	11361	Ap	0.32	0.58	0.80	0.66	1.01	1.06	9 Mo Jan△	d0.20	d0.15	7
8	1971	Q0.12	4-1-74	2-25	0.24	0.48	0.46	19.2	41.9	12.8	3-31-73	....	...	±8132	Mr	±0.73	±0.80	±0.90	±1.00	....	1.08	9 Mo Dec	±0.74	±0.82	8
9	.....	None Paid			....	Nil	....	1.34	4.81	1.48	5-31-73	1.36	...	1605	My	△d0.05	□d0.53	□d0.08	•0.13	•0.36	0.34	6 Mo Nov	•0.20	0.18	9
10	1971	Q0.02	4-23-74	4-2	0.04	0.08	0.06¼	12.9	79.7	66.2	2-28-73	12.3	.4	±8364	Fb	d0.12	0.26	0.30	0.42	....	0.44	9 Mo Nov	0.28	0.30	10
11◆	1923	Q0.18½	3-1-74	2-8	0.18½	e0.74	†0.718	7.46	219.	99.5	9-30-73	42.8	...	6054	Sp	1.57	1.90	2.42	2.51	2.51	2.63	3 Mo Dec	0.34	0.46	11
12◆	1969	Q0.06	2-5-74	1-9	0.06	0.24	0.24	149.	171.	113.	3-3-73	33.8	...	5180	Fb	□1.53	□1.72	□1.15	□1.58	P1.58	1.58				12
13	.....	0.07½	12-29-61	12-18	....	Nil	....	5.16	37.8	19.7	7-28-73	22.2	...	5434	Jl	0.39	□0.27	0.47	0.30	0.58	0.71	6 Mo Jan△	0.26	0.39	13
14	.....	Terms&trad.basis should be checked in detail						Warrants expire Apr 9,1974				....	...	600	Jl	....	....	....	....	....	....	Expire April 9th			14
15◆	1934	Q0.15	3-29-74	3-11	0.15	0.60	0.60	1.36	36.8	9.83	12-31-73	10.2	...	1253	Dc	1.01	1.47	1.89	△1.49	1.77	1.77				15
16	1955	0.43	2-20-74	12-21	0.43	0.671	0.392	22.6	27.4	22.7	j6-30-73	....	...	24000	Je	0.48	0.49	0.49	0.52	0.87	1.09	3 Mo Sep	0.15	0.37	16
17	1924	S 0.29	2-28-74	2-7	0.29	0.58	0.50	Book Value $21.53			[52]6-30-73	108.	...	5972	Dc	1.25	1.43	•1.81	•2.03	2.37	2.37				17
18◆	1964	Q0.15	3-1-74	2-4	0.15	0.60	0.60	1.13	2.70	1.36	4-27-73	....	...	654	Ap	1.24	1.02	1.98	2.22	2.24	2.51	9 Mo Jan△	1.83	2.10	18
19	.....	0.17½	1-16-67	12-27	....	Nil	....	3.04	87.2	41.1	4-30-73	31.7	...	4501	Ap	□0.20	•0.58	□0.68	0.87	□0.66	0.30	9 Mo Jan△	□0.76	0.40	19
20◆	1972	Q0.10	2-15-74	1-24	0.10	0.40	0.25	0.86	11.5	5.13	7-31-73	2.50	...	2040	Jl	0.15	0.30	0.83	1.21	2.26	2.20	6 Mo Jan△	0.98	0.92	20
21	1942	Q0.15	3-11-74	2-1	0.15	0.60	0.40	51.0	1463	725.	12-31-72	503.	...	21546	Dc	0.47	1.02	△1.04	1.40	P2.38	2.38				21
22◆	.....	3%Stk	10-24-69	9-29	....	Nil	....	2.23	35.1	31.7	1-27-73	29.9	1	p1210	Ja	1.04	1.31	□d0.15	0.25	....	0.05	9 Mo Oct	0.07	□d0.13	22
23◆	1965	Q0.12½	4-3-74	3-7	s0.246	0.485	s0.409	2.79	22.8	16.1	4-30-73	16.6	...	1684	Ap	3.29	2.58	△0.68	2.64	4.84	8.66	9 Mo Jan△	3.10	△6.92	23
24◆	1935	Q0.06¼	5-1-74	3-11	0.12½	0.25	0.06¼	83.6	425.	281.	p12-31-72	604.	85	p29548	Dc	△2.35	1.08	[53]□d1.20	[54]□0.78	P△2.89	2.89				24
25	.....	None Paid			....	Nil	....	1.53	6.84	3.22	6-30-73	....	...	1213	Je	△[55]0.31	□[56]0.32	□[57]0.09	0.64	□0.80	0.87	6 Mo Dec	△0.38	0.45	25
26	.....	None Paid			....	Nil	....	3.07	5.78	3.54	12-31-72	★10.6	...	4684	Dc	d0.49	d0.06	•0.10	•0.20	P0.32	0.32				26
27◆	.....	0.167	10-15-70	9-21	....	Nil	....	3.09	52.9	16.5	7-28-73	5.33	...	1720	Jl	1.04	0.18	d1.13	d1.07	d0.72	d1.03	6 Mo Jan△	0.15	d0.16	27
28	1927	Q0.36	4-1-74	3-11	0.72	1.44	1.38½	10.7	31.9	7.79	6-30-73	1.47	...	1423	Je	1.45	1.90	2.22	2.51	2.49	2.52	6 Mo Dec	0.95	0.98	28
29◆	1914	Q0.20	4-1-74	3-18	0.40	0.80	0.80	19.8	29.0	8.14	12-31-72	....	...	4902	Dc	1.79	1.52	1.75	□1.93	P2.26	2.26				29
30	1969	Q0.03	4-10-74	3-14	0.06	0.12	0.12	8.09	24.7	11.6	9-30-73	2.00	...	3377	Sp	0.96	0.92	0.45	0.55	•0.69	0.73	3 Mo Dec	0.16	0.20	30
31	1899	Q0.30	3-1-74	2-4	0.30	1.20	1.20	93.4	716.	369.	12-31-73	★335.	704	30045	Dc	□1.73	1.83	2.00	2.18	∫[58]2.37	2.37				31
32	1928	Q0.33¾	5-15-74	4-15	0.67½	1.35	1.35	25.3	642.	308.	12-31-73	135.	310	18266	Dc	2.65	2.25	2.45	•3.02	∫3.70	3.70				32
33	.....	0.10	1-11-71	12-15	....	Nil	....	7.25	40.7	27.8	1-27-73	9.18	...	2927	Ja	1.55	0.41	□0.16	△0.24	Pd0.21	d0.21				33
34◆	1965	Q0.26	4-26-74	4-5	0.52	1.04	0.98	Book Value $19.05			12-31-72	....	...	±1239	Dc	2.15	△1.71	△1.81	□2.22	P□2.67	2.67				34
35	1890	Q0.61	5-1-74	4-4	1.22	2.44	[59]2.44	14.4	77.3	128.	12-31-73	523.	830	p9535	Dc	3.10	3.31	3.51	△3.55	2.88	2.88				35
36	1971	Q2.22	5-1-74	4-4	4.44	8.88	8.88	Red restr to 11-1-77				....	400	...	Dc	....	32.46	38.18	40.44	36.79	....				36
37	.....	None Since Public			....	Nil	....	12.8	39.0	13.7	12-31-72	3.71	...	3197	Dc	1.46	1.01	1.10	△1.47	P2.09	2.09				37
38	.....	g 0.20	10-1-65	9-14	....	Nil	....	6.74	21.6	8.28	j12-31-72	3.36	...	13686	Dc	0.10	d0.10	0.12	□0.17	P0.26	0.26				38
39	1956	gS 0.05	11-30-73	11-2	....	0.10	g0.10	0.78	20.1	18.0	j5-31-73	14.5	182	p4850	My	△0.47	0.32	□0.01	△0.09	△0.27	0.30	6 Mo Nov	0.13	0.16	39
40	1947	[61] 0.09½	7-15-74	4-25	[61]0.09½	0.14½	0.11½	28.2	230.	145.	j12-31-72	235.	7394	104056	Dc	0.37	0.31	0.15	0.24	....	0.33	6 Mo Jun	0.09	0.18	40
41◆	.....	None Since Public			....	Nil	....	2.53	42.7	30.1	9-30-73	★8.11	...	1978	Sp	d0.28	0.02	△0.08	•0.82	3.75	4.38	3 Mo Dec	•0.55	1.18	41
42	1941	Q0.05	3-27-74	3-8	0.05	0.20	0.20	3.77	14.1	4.50	10-31-73	0.06	41	2000	Oc	1.30	0.97	□1.07	1.47	∫0.86	0.70	3 Mo Jan△	0.28	0.12	42
43◆	1965	Q0.07	3-1-74	2-8	0.07	0.28	0.25	0.04	7.80	5.87	9-30-73	1.85	...	p624	Sp	0.60	1.19	1.02	1.00	1.02	1.11	12 Wk Dec	△0.16	0.25	43
44◆	.....	None Paid			....	Nil	....	4.44	24.0	10.4	4-30-73	3.57	...	2209	Ap	•0.38	•0.55	0.66	1.06	0.98	1.26	9 Mo Jan△	0.73	1.01	44

◆ **Stock Splits & Divs By Line Reference Index** [1]3-for-1,'72. [2]3-for-2,'70:Adj to 4%,'72:3-for-1,'74. [4]2-for-1,'69. [5]5-for-4,'71. [6]10%,'73. [7]5-for-4,'69:2-for-1,'71. [11]3-for-2,'70:2-for-1,'71. [12]2-for-1,'69. [15]2-for-1,'71. [18]10%,'70. [20]3-for-2,'73. [22]Adj to 3%,'69: 3-for-2,'71. [23]2-for-1,'69,adj to 3%,'74. [24]Adj to 2%, '71. [27]3-for-2,'70. [29]2-for-1,'71. [34]2-for-1,'69:50%,'72. [41]2-for-1,'72. [43]Adj to 3%,'71. [44]2-for-1,'71.

FIG. 6-3 *(Continued)*

EARNINGS AND DIVIDEND RANKINGS FOR STOCKS

The relative "quality" of common stocks cannot be measured, as can that of bonds, which depends upon the degree of protection for interest and principal. However, there are differences in the nature of stocks and some of them are well worth measuring and comparing.

Standard & Poor's Rankings are designed to indicate by the use of symbols the relative stability and growth of earnings and the relative stability and growth of dividends. These measures of past records have a considerable bearing on relative quality, but do not pretend to reflect an examination of all other factors, tangible and intangible, that also bear on a stock's quality. *Under no circumstances should these rankings be regarded as a recommendation to buy or sell a security.*

The Common Stock Formula

Standard & Poor's point of departure is a scoring system based upon earnings and dividend records. The first step is to examine the earnings record of the past eight years. In measuring earnings stability, a basic score is given for each year in which net per share equals or exceeds that of the preceding year. For any year in which earnings declined, the score is reduced by the percentage of that decline. The average of these eight annual scores, weighted for frequency of earnings declines, becomes our first "basic earnings index."

This stability index is then multiplied by a growth index, based on the square root of the percentage by which earnings increased between the base years period and the most recent three years. To prevent growth in extreme cases from dominating the rating, the growth factor is "topped" at 150%.

Scoring for dividend stability and growth is similar, with the principal exception that a longer period is used and results are weighted for recency. A dividend reduction fifteen years ago is obviously a less serious current investment consideration than one that was voted recently. A further weighting is applied for frequency of dividend reductions, because an erratic dividend policy is a matter affecting investment standing. The result is multiplied by a growth factor similar to that for earnings.

When this is completed, the two factors—earnings and dividends—are combined into a single numerical ranking. All the common stocks so graded are then grouped into seven classes. To these we have assigned an easy-to-understand code, as follows:

A+ Highest   B+ Average   C Lowest
A High   B Below Average
A− Above Average B− Low

These mathematically determined positions are modified in some instances by special considerations. Non-recurring costs, windfall profits, etc., must sometimes be allowed for. These are certain other exceptions. In the oil industry, for example, so-called "cash flow" is used rather than final net profit in order to avoid the distortions that might be caused by differences in accounting practices.

Since earnings and dividends of regulated public utilities characteristically are more stable than those of most non-regulated industries, numerous other factors must be considered. Among these are capital structure, amount of depreciation reserves, condition of properties, growth potentialities for individual service areas, the regulatory environment, and the rate of return.

These scorings are not to be confused with bond quality ratings, which are arrived at by a necessarily altogether different approach. Additionally, they must not be used as a substitute for market recommendations; a high graded stock may at times be so over-priced as to justify its sale, while a low score stock may be attractively priced for purchase. Rankings based upon earnings and dividend record are no substitute for analysis. Nor are they quality ratings in the complete sense of the term. They cannot take into account potential effects of management changes, internal company policies not yet fully reflected in the earnings and dividend record, public relations standing, recent competitive shifts, and a host of other factors that may be relevant to investment status.

N.R. signifies No Ranking possible, because of insufficient data, non-recurring factors, or some other reason.

*Preceding ranking denotes railroad guaranteed stock quality rating based on S&P bond rating scale.

Preferred Stock Ratings

Quality ratings on preferred stock are expressed by symbols like these used in rating bonds. They are independent of Standard & Poor's bond ratings, however, in the sense that they are not necessarily graduated downward from the ranking accorded the relative security of dividends, and—what is thereby implied—the prospective yield stability of the stock. These ratings are as follows:

AAA Prime   BBB Medium Grade   C Sub-Marginal
AA High Grade   BB Lower Grade
A Sound   B Speculative

FIG. 6-4 Standard & Poor's explanation of its stock ratings. (From Standard & Poor's *Stock Guide*.)

Title-Industry Code & Co. Finances (In Italics) / Individual Issue Statistics, Exchange ↓	Ind / Interest Dates	Chgs. 1971 / S&P Quality Rating	Eligible ↓	Times Earn. 1972 / Bond Form	Times Earn. 1973, Yr. End / Legality C M N N N t a H J Y	Cash & Eqv / Redemption Provisions: Refund Earliest/Other	Current Assets / Call Price For S.F.	Liabs, Date (Million $) / Call Price Regular	L. Term Debt (Mil $) / Out-st'd'g (Mil $)	Debt % Prop / Underwriter Firm	Year	Interim Period / Price Range 1960-72 High	1960-72 Low	Times Earn. 1973 / 1973 High	Times Earn. 1974 / 1973 Low	1974 High	1974 Low	Mo. End Price Sale(s) or Bid	Curr Yield	Yield to Mat.
• ***Beneficial*** Deb 7½s '98	Mn15	AA	X	R	- - - - -	z[1]101.80	....	[2]102.60	75.0	B7	'73	....	....	100¼	96½	91	90⅝	82	9.15	9.40
• Deb 7.45s 2000	Fa	AA	X	R	- - - - -	z[3]102.80	....	[4]103.10	75.0	E1	'72	102	98	101½	92	95	80	76	9.80	10.08
• Deb 7½s 2002	jJ15	AA	X	R	- - - - -	z[3]101.80	....	[4]102.60	75.0	E1	'72	103¼	99½	102	90½	95	84⅝	A87	8.62	8.75
Beneficial Finance	***26a***	***Now Beneficial Corp.,see***																		
• Deb 5s '77	mN	AA	X	CR	- - - - -	....	....	100	50.0	E1	'57	105¾	73	94	84¼	92	87½	85⅛	5.87	10.39
• Deb 4⅞s '81	Jd	AA	X	CR	- - - - -	....	....	±100.77	50.0	E1	'60	105⅛	68	86¼	79¼	84	77	77⅛	6.32	9.45
Deb 4.45s '88	Jd	AA	X	CR	- - - - -	z±101.175	....	±102.35	50.0	E1	'62	102¾	53	75	68	70⅝	63⅝	63⅝	6.99	9.11
Deb 5s '90	mN	AA	X	CR	- - - - -	z±101½	....	±±103	30.0	E1	'65	101½	61	78⅜	70½	73⅛	65¾	65¾	7.60	9.05
Deb 4½s '92	Ms	AA	X	CR	- - - - -	z±100.80	....	±101.60	100	E1	'64	100	54¼	72⅜	63	66⅞	58	59	7.63	9.25
Deb 4¾s '93	Mn15	AA	X	CR	- - - - -	z±101.40	....	±102.80	50.0	E1	'65	100⅝	55½	73¼	64	68½	59¼	61	7.79	9.11
Deb 6¾s '94	fA	AA	X	CR	- - - - -	z[5]101.85	....	[1]102½	50.0	E1	'68	102	71	95⅛	85⅛	88⅜	78	78	8.65	9.16
Bethlehem Steel Corp.	***66a***	***4.87***		***4.51***	***6.31 Dc***	***479***	***1376***	***713 12-73***	***663***	***30.8***		***3 Mo Mar***		***5.72***	***4.99***					
• SF Con J 2¾s '76	mN15	AA	X	CR	- - - - √	....	100	±100¼	16.3	K5	'46	88	70	90	87	86½	86½	85	3.24	10.01
• SF Con K 3s '79	Jj	AA	X	CR	- - - - √	....	100⅛	100⅜	24.3	K5	'49	87½	65	80⅞	77	79¼	76	s76¾	3.91	9.46
• Deb 3¼s '80	Mn	AA	X	C	- - - - -	....	100	±100⅛	3.15	K5	'55	181	62	79⅞	74¾	77½	75	74	4.39	9.09
• Deb 5.40s '92	Jj15	AA	X	R	- - - - √	[3]102½	100	±103¼	128	K5	'67	103¾	66	83¼	75	80½	69¼	s69¼	7.80	8.89
• Deb 6⅞s '99	Ms	AA	X	R	- - - - -	[6]103¾	[5]100	±105	100	K5	'69	102	80	97	84⅛	89½	82	s82½	8.33	8.59
• Deb 9s 2000	Mn15	AA	X	R	- - - - -	[7]104	[8]100	±107	150	K5	'70	113¾	99	113¾	103½	108¼	97½	s98	9.18	9.20
• Sub Deb 4½s '90	Jj	A	X	R	- - - - -	....	100	±103.30	102	Pfd	'64	100¾	61	76⅛	67	71⅜	64	64⅛	7.02	8.77
Birmingham Electric	***72a***	***Mgr into Alabama Pwr,: see***																		
1st 3s '74	fA	A	X	CR	√- √- √	....	100	100	2.73	B7	'44	95½	77	97¼	94⅜	99⅞	97¼	99⅞	3.00	Mat
Blackstone Valley Elec.[9]	***72a***	***1.86***		***2.01***	***1.39 Dc***	***2.84***	***8.66***	***46.7 3-74***	***9.20***	***20.0***		***12 Mo Apr***		***1.83***	***1.30***					
1st CT 6½s '97	Jd	A	X	R	√- √√-	....	±101.81	±106.45	7.00	E1	'67	102½	74	89	79¼	82	69⅜	69⅜	9.37	9.90
1st CT 4⅛s '83	Ms	A	X	CR	√- √√-	....	±101	±101½	2.20	0	'53	98	67	77½	72	74⅜	67⅞	67⅞	6.12	9.79
[10]***Boeing Airplane Co.***	***2a***	***1.40***		***1.54***	***2.31 Dc***	***51.5***	***1057***	***593 12-73***	***165***	***47.2***										
SF Deb 5s '78	fA	BBB	X	CR	- - - - -	....	100	±100½	7.26	H4	'58	102	52	87½	81	88	83	84½	5.92	9.68
Boise Cascade Credit	***26***	....		....	.... ***Dc***				***162***											
• Deb 10s '75	Jd15	BBB	Y	R	- - - - -	....	....	NC	67.3	B7	'70	110⅜	95	102¾	96½	103	99¼	s99¾	10.03	10.28
Borden (Co.) Inc.	***27***	***4.90***		***5.13***	***5.12 Dc***	***93.4***	***716***	***369 12-73***	★***335***	***45.3***										
• SF Deb 2⅞s '81	Ms	A	X	CR	- √- √√	....	*100	±100.40	26.9	M9	'51	87	57	77½	71½	73½	71⅞	65½	4.39	10.11
• SF Deb 4⅜s '91	jD	A	X	CR	- √- √√	....	100	±102¼	32.0	M9	'61	104⅛	62	73¾	68	70¼	62	65⅛	6.72	8.16
• SF Deb 5¾s '97	Jd15	A	X	R	- √- √√	[3]103¼	[1]100	±104¼	75.0	M9	'67	101⅜	68½	87	73⅝	79	73⅝	70½	8.16	8.75
• SF Deb 8½s 2004	Ao	A	X	R	- - - √-	[11]105¼	[12]100	±108¾	100	M9	'74	....	....	....	....	100¼	98	A99	8.59	8.59
Borg-Warner Acceptance	***26e***	***1.31***		***1.31***	***1.20 Dc***	***34.0***		***12-73***	***156***											
• Sr Deb 9½s '75	jJ	A	X	R	- - - - -	....	....	NC	25.0	d1	'70	108	100⅜	106⅜	100⅞	103⅛	99	s99½	9.55	10.03
• Sr Deb 7⅞s '91	aO	A	X	R	- - - - -	z[8]102.845	[3]100	[13]103.504	30.0	G2	'71	102⅝	98	101½	97	88½	84¼	84½	9.32	9.74
• Sr Deb 7½s '93	Jj15	A	X	R	- - - - -	z[1]102.66	[6]100	[2]103.42	25.0	G2	'73	....	....	100	98	87	87	A86½	8.67	9.01
Sr SubDeb 7.80s '93	Jj15	BBB	X	R	- - - - -	z[1]102.78	[1]100	z[2]103.58	12.5	G2	'73	....	....	100	94	96¼	84½	84½	9.23	9.60
Borg-Warner Corp.	***8***	***3.48***		***4.16***	***4.07 Dc***	***25.3***	***642***	***308 12-73***	***135***	***33.9***										
• SF Deb 5½s '92	Ms	AA	X	R	- √√√√	[3]102¾	100	±103.58	61.4	H16	'67	102½	70	84⅛	80½	83	73	70¾	7.77	8.79

Uniform Footnote Explanations—See Page 1. Other: [1]From 1978. [2]From 1983. [3]From 1977. [4]From 1982. [5]From 1975. [6]From 1979. [7]From 1980. [8]From 1976. [9]Subsid E.Util.Assoc. [10]Now Boeing Co. [11]From 1984. [12]From 1985. [13]From 1981.

FIG. 6-5 Page from Standard & Poor's *Bond Guide,* July 1974.

STANDARD & POOR'S BOND RATINGS

CORPORATE BONDS

BANK QUALITY BONDS—Under present commercial bank regulations bonds rated in the top four categories (AAA, AA, A, BBB or their equivalent) generally are regarded as eligible for bank investment.

AAA Bonds rated AAA are highest grade obligations. They possess the ultimate degree of protection as to principal and interest. Marketwise they move with interest rates, and hence provide the maximum safety on all counts.

AA Bonds rated AA also qualify as high grade obligations, and in the majority of instances differ from AAA issues only in small degree. Here, too, prices move with the long term money market.

A Bonds rated A are regarded as upper medium grade. They have considerable investment strength but are not entirely free from adverse effects of changes in economic and trade conditions. Interest and principal are regarded as safe. They predominantly reflect money rates in their market behavior, but to some extent, also economic conditions.

BBB The BBB, or medium grade category is borderline between definitely sound obligations, and those where the speculative element begins to predominate. These bonds have adequate asset coverage and normally are protected by satisfactory earnings. Their susceptibility to changing conditions, particularly to depressions, necessitates constant watching. Marketwise, the bonds are more responsive to business and trade conditions than to interest rates. This group is the lowest which qualifies for commercial bank investment.

BB Bonds given a BB rating are regarded as lower medium grade. They have only minor investment characteristics. In the case of utilities, interest is earned consistently but by narrow margins. In the case of other types of obligors, charges are earned on average by a fair margin, but in poor periods deficit operations are possible.

B Bonds rated as low as B are speculative. Payment of interest cannot be assured under difficult economic conditions.

CCC-CC Bonds rated CCC and CC are outright speculations, with the lower rating denoting the more speculative. Interest is paid, but continuation is questionable in periods of poor trade conditions. In the case of CC ratings the bonds may be on an income basis and the payment may be small.

C The rating of C is reserved for income bonds on which no interest is being paid.

DDD-D All bonds rated DDD, DD and D are in default, with the rating indicating the relative salvage value.

Canadian corporate bonds are rated on the same basis as American corporate issues. The ratings measure the intrinsic value of the bonds, but they do not take into account exchange and other uncertainties.

MUNICIPAL BONDS

Standard & Poor's Municipal Bond Ratings cover obligations of all states or sub-divisions. In addition to general obligations, ratings are assigned to bonds payable in whole or in part from special revenues.

AAA-Prime—These are obligations of the highest quality. They have the lowest probability of default. In a period of economic stress the issuers will suffer the smallest declines in income and will be least susceptible to autonomous decline. Debt burden is not inordinately high. Revenue structure appears adequate to meet future expenditure needs. Quality of management would not appear to endanger repayment of principal and interest.

AA-High Grade—The investment characteristics of bonds in this group are only slightly less marked than those of the prime quality issues. Bonds rated AA have the second lowest probability of default.

A-Upper Medium Grade—Principal and interest on bonds in this category are regarded as safe. This rating describes the third lowest probability of default. It differs from the two higher ratings because there is some weakness, either in the local economic base, in debt burden, in the balance between revenues and expenditures or in quality of management. Under certain adverse circumstances, **any one such weakness** might impair the ability of the issuer to meet debt obligations at some future date.

BBB-Medium Grade—This is the lowest investment grade security rating. Under certain adverse conditions, several of the above factors could contribute to a higher default probability. The difference between A and BBB ratings is that the latter shows **more than one** fundamental weakness, whereas the former shows only one deficiency among the factors considered.

BB-Lower Medium Grade—Bonds in this group have some investment characteristics, but they no longer predominate. For the most part this rating indicates a speculative, non-investment grade obligation.

B-Low Grade—Investment characteristics are virtually non-existent and default could be imminent.

D-Defaults—Interest and/or principal in arrears.

INVESTMENT SECURITIES REGULATIONS

Effective Sept. 12, 1963, the Comptroller of the Currency issued the following regulations applying to the purchase for its own account of investment securities by a national bank or a State member bank of the Federal Reserve System.

Definitions.

The term "investment security" means a marketable obligation in the form of a bond, note or debenture which is commonly regarded as an investment security. It does not include investments which are predominantly speculative in nature.

The term "public security" includes obligations of the United States and general obligations of any State of the United States or of any political subdivision thereof.

The term "political subdivision of any State" includes a county, city, town or other municipal corporation, a public authority, and generally any publicly owned entity which is an instrumentality of the State or of a municipal corporation.

The phrase "general obligation of any State or of any political subdivision thereof" means an obligation supported by the full faith and credit of the obligor. It includes an obligation payable from a special fund when the full faith and credit of a State or any political subdivision thereof is obligated for payments in connection with the obligation. It implies an obligor possessing resources sufficient to justify faith and credit.

Limitations and restrictions on purchase and sale of securities.

A bank may deal in, underwrite, purchase and sell for its own account a public security subject only to the exercise of prudent banking judgment, and with no limitation as to amount.

A bank may purchase an investment security for its own account when in its prudent banking judgment (which may be based in part upon estimates which it

FIG. 6-6 Standard & Poor's explanation of its bond ratings. (From Standard & Poor's *Bond Guide*.)

BOEING COMPANY

LISTED	SYMBOL	INDICATED DIV.	RECENT PRICE	PRICE RANGE (1974)	YIELD
NYSE	BA	$0.60	17	18 - 12	3.5%

STRONG DEMAND FOR MILITARY AIRCRAFT AND WEAPONS SYSTEMS IS OFFSETTING THE SLIGHT DECLINE IN 727 ORDERS. THE STOCK IS SPECULATIVE GRADE.

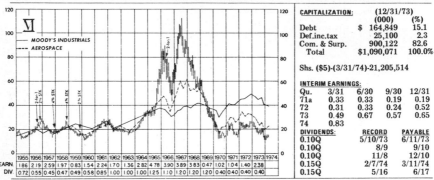

| EARN. | 1.86 | 2.19 | 2.59 | 1.97 | 0.83 | 1.54 | 2.24 | 1.70 | 1.36 | 2.82 | 4.78 | 3.90 | 3.89 | 3.83 | 0.47 | 1.02 | 1.04 | 1.40 | 2.38 | |
| DIV. | 0.72 | 0.55 | 0.45 | 0.47 | 0.49 | 0.58 | 0.85 | 1.00 | 1.00 | 1.00 | 1.25 | 1.10 | 1.20 | 1.20 | 1.20 | 0.40 | 0.40 | 0.40 | 0.40 | |

CAPITALIZATION:

| | (12/31/73) | |
	(000)	(%)
Debt	$ 164,849	15.1
Def.inc.tax	25,100	2.3
Com. & Surp.	900,122	82.6
Total	$1,090,071	100.0%

Shs. ($5)-(3/31/74)-21,205,514

INTERIM EARNINGS:

Qu.	3/31	6/30	9/30	12/31
71a	0.33	0.33	0.19	0.19
72	0.31	0.33	0.24	0.52
73	0.49	0.67	0.57	0.65
74	0.83			

DIVIDENDS:

	RECORD	PAYABLE
0.10Q	5/10/73	6/11/73
0.10Q	8/9	9/10
0.10Q	11/8	12/10
0.15Q	2/7/74	3/11/74
0.15Q	5/16	6/17

BACKGROUND:

Boeing is the largest manufacturer of commercial airliners; current production includes the 707, 727, 737 and 747 aircraft series. For the government, Company is modifying a large fleet of B-52 bombers and producing Sea Knight and Chinook helicopters. 1973 sales breakdown: Commercial, 56.1%; missile and space, 20.6%; military aircraft, 20.0%. Vertol Aircraft was acquired in 1960. In Dec., 1970, Company established its computer services business as a separate subsidiary. Boeing was the prime contractor for development of the Super Sonic Transport (SST) program. $19,780,000 was recovered from the government for the termination of the program.

RECENT DEVELOPMENTS:

Consolidated sales during the first quarter of 1974, rose 33.4% to $841.3 mill. as net income climbed 65% to $17.6 mill. Sales during 1973 gained 40.8% to $3.3 bill., as net income rose 68% to $51.2 mill. The Company continued to experience strong demand for its 727. By year end, a total of 1,100 model 727's had been ordered since the program's inception. Production rate on the 727 program rose from 5½ airplanes per month in January 1973 to its current rate of 8½.

PROSPECTS:

Overcapacity in the airline industry will restrict the short-term order rate for 727's. However, the long-term outlook for 727's remains bright. The demand for the Comany's military aircraft and weapon systems including, airborne warning and control system aircraft, short range attach missiles, air-launched cruise missiles and 747 superjets remains strong. Government contracts, including modification of the B-52 bomber fleet, NASA developmental work will add stability to earnings. Earnings in 1974 could reach $3.00 a share.

STATISTICS:

YEAR	GROSS REVS. ($ MILL.)	OPER. PROFIT MARGIN %	NET INCOME ($ 000)	WORK CAP. ($ MILL.)	SENIOR CAPITAL ($ MILL.)	NO. SHS. OUT. (000)	EARN. PER SH. $	DIV. PER SH. $	DIV. PAY. %	PRICE RANGE	PRICE X EARN.	AVG. YIELD %
64	1,969.5	4.7	45,324	251.7	109.7	16,074	2.82	1.00	36	35₂ - 18₁	9.6	3.7
65	2,023.4	6.8	78,268	260.3	98.3	16,374	4.78	1.25	26	70 - 30₄	10.5	2.5
66	2,356.6	5.5	76,133	434.3	466.5	19,497	3.90	1.10	28	91₃ - 44₆	17.4	1.6
67	2,879.7	5.1	83,938	358.3	480.5	21,597	3.89	1.20	31	112₂ - 61₄	22.4	1.4
68	3,274.0	4.7	82,972	467.0	470.5	21,647	3.83	1.20	31	90₁ - 52₂	18.6	1.7
69	2,834.6	0.1	10,230	610.5	632.5	21,683	0.47	1.20	—	61₇ - 27	94.0	2.7
70	3,677.1	1.2	22,090	656.6	623.8	21,683	1.02	0.40	39	31₂ - 12₄	21.5	1.8
71	3,039.8	0.8	a22,430	694.8	527.6	21,683	a1.04	0.40	38	25₆ - 13	18.6	2.1
72	2,369.6	1.8	30,405	738.5	502.6	21,689	1.40	0.40	29	26₇ - 19₆	16.3	1.7
73	3,335.2	1.6	51,215	463.8	164.8	21,296	2.38	0.40	17	26 - 11	8.1	2.1

Note: Adjusted for 2-for-1 stock split 5/66. a-Excl. special items; 1971, $19.8 mill. ($0.91 a share) credit.

TAX FREE IN PENNA.

INCORPORATED:	July 19, 1934—Delaware	TRANSFER AGENT:	First National City Bank, N.Y.	OFFICERS
PRINCIPAL OFFICE	7755 E. Marginal Way So. Seattle, Washington 98124			CHAIRMAN: T.A. Wilson
		REGISTRAR:	Bankers Trust Co., N.Y.	PRESIDENT: M.T. Stamper
ANNUAL MEETING:	First Monday in May			SECRETARY: J.E. Prince
NUMBER OF STOCKHOLDERS:	74,486	INSTIT. HOLDINGS:	NO.: 53 SHS.: 1,981,568	TREASURER: J.B.L Pierce

FIG. 6-7 Page from Moody's *Handbook of Widely Held Common Stocks* (second quarter, 1974 edition). (*Source:* Moody's, 99 Church Street, New York, N.Y., 10007.)

Disney (Walt) Productions

DIS[1] **755**

Stock—	Price Mar. 13'75	Dividend	Yield
COMMON	44¼	[2]$0.12	[2]0.3%

RECOMMENDATION: This major factor in the leisure-time field derives the bulk of revenues from its activities as an amusement park operator and producer-distributor of motion pictures. The shares could still face some periods of weakness over the near-to-intermediate term in view of a still relatively high price-earnings multiple.

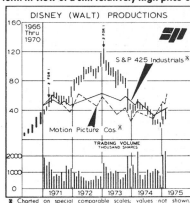

✗ Charted on special comparable scales; values not shown.

TOTAL REVENUES (Million $)

Quarter:	1974-5	1973-4	1972-3	1971-2
Dec.	90.77	78.88	[4]69.04	58.43
March		92.21	87.20	75.42
June		108.23	103.06	86.17
Sept.		150.58	125.77	[4]109.42

Revenues for the fiscal year ended September 30, 1974, rose 12% from those of the prior year. Park volume was up 8.0%, as higher per capita spending, particularly for lodging at Walt Disney World, and increased food and merchandise prices more than offset declines in attendance at Disneyland (down 4.5%) and Disney World (down 6.5%). Film rentals gained 19% and sales of ancillary products were ahead 20%. While theatrical operations improved significantly, reduced profits at the theme parks (particularly the one in Florida), a higher ratio of low-margined ancillary product sales, and higher interest, selling, and other general expenses put pressure on earnings. Net income advanced 1.2%, to $1.63 a share from $1.61 (both adjusted).

For the quarter ended December 31, 1974, revenues rose 15%, year to year, reflecting gains in all major lines of business. Net income was up 21%.

[3]COMMON SHARE EARNINGS ($)

Quarter:	1974-5	1973-4	1972-3	1971-2
Dec.	0.24	0.20	0.17	0.19
March		0.31	0.35	0.31
June		0.42	0.46	0.35
Sept.		0.70	0.63	[4]0.53

PROSPECTS

Near Term—Further revenue progress is expected for the fiscal year ending September 30, 1975, from the $429.9 million reported for 1973-4. In the amusement park group, a series of major price increases implemented in June, 1974, at the two parks, ranging from 8% to 15%, should boost dollar volume. While some moderation in inflationary consumer costs would probably be necessary to stimulate a worthwhile recovery in attendance, comparisons for the second quarter should continue favorable, with the absence of last year's travel restrictions. Total film and television revenues should show continued strength.

Margins should benefit from better attendance at the amusement park group, particularly in the first half of the fiscal year, coupled with the full-year inclusion of the price increases. Improved profits are expected from film rentals, with profits from foreign film operations continuing to grow at a faster rate than the domestic business. Overall, earnings for 1974-5 should be up moderately from the $1.63 a share (adjusted) of 1973-4, barring any severe restrictions on the use of gasoline. Cash dividends, currently at $0.03 quarterly, have frequently been supplemented by an annual stock distribution (2% in January, 1975).

Long Term—Disney's large film library, established leadership in the family-entertainment market, and potentialities of profitable land development support the company's long-term prospects.

RECENT DEVELOPMENTS

In December, 1974, DIS said that it was discussing with Mitsui & Co. Ltd., Mitsui Real Estate Development Co. and Keisei Electric Railway Co. Ltd. the possibility of jointly developing an amusement theme park on a 600-acre peninsula in Tokyo Bay.

DIVIDEND DATA

Payments in the past 12 months were:

Amt. of Divd. $	Date Decl.	Ex-divd. Date	Stock of Record	Payment Date
0.03	May 28	Jun. 4	Jun. 10	Jul. 1'74
0.03	Aug. 27	Sep. 4	Sep. 10	Oct. 1'74
0.03	Nov. 26	Nov. 29	Dec. 5	Jan. 1'75
2%Stk.	Nov. 26	Nov. 29	Dec. 5	Jan. 1'75
0.03	Feb. 12	Mar. 4	Mar. 10	Apr. 1'75

[1]Listed N.Y.S.E.; also listed Pacific S.E. & traded Midwest & PBW S.Es. [2]Indicated rate; also 2% in stk. on Jan. 1, 1975.
[3]Based on com. & com. sh. equivalents; fully diluted earns. in 1971-2; adj. for 2-for-1 split in fiscal 1973 & stk. divs. of 2% each in fiscal 1975, 1974 & 1972. [4]Incl. foreign subs. for 12 mos.

Vol. 42, No. 54 Wednesday, March 19, 1975 Sec. 10

FIG. 6-8 Report from *Standard & Poor's Stock Market Encyclopedia.*

755 DISNEY (WALT) PRODUCTIONS

[1]INCOME STATISTICS (Million $) AND PER SHARE ($) DATA

Year Ended Sept. 30	Total Revenues	% Oper. Inc. of Total Revs.	Oper. Inc.	Depr.	Net Bef. Taxes	[4]Net Income	—[2]Common Share ($) Data— [4]Earns.	Divs. Paid	[3]Price Range	Price-Earns. Ratios HI LO
1975--	-----	---	-----	----	----	----	---	0.08⅞	45¾-21¼	-----
1974--	429.89	29.3	125.84	29.60	88.53	48.33	[5]1.63	0.11⅝	53⅜-16⅝	33-10
1973--	385.07	30.3	116.56	26.55	85.17	47.77	[5]1.61	0.11	119⅛-39	74-24
1972--	329.44	30.6	100.70	24.49	74.39	40.29	[5]1.39	0.09⅜	113⅞-63⅞	82-46
1971--	175.61	32.1	56.35	7.83	48.52	26.72	[5]0.98	0.08⅜	68¾-32⅝	69-33
1970--	167.10	30.9	51.59	7.88	43.71	21.76	[5]0.88	0.06⅞	36½-20⅞	41-24
1969--	148.37	26.9	39.91	7.40	32.50	15.80	[5]0.78	0.06⅞	30⅝-15⅜	39-23
1968--	137.15	23.7	32.47	6.85	25.62	13.11	[5]0.67	0.05⅞	20¼- 9⅛	30-14
1967—	117.49	23.3	27.41	7.85	18.67	10.37	0.55	0.04¼	13⅝- 8⅛	25-15
1966--	116.54	25.2	29.36	5.80	22.49	12.39	0.67	0.04⅛	9 - 4¼	13- 6
1965--	109.95	27.0	29.68	7.47	21.53	11.38	0.62	0.03⅞	6⅜- 4½	10- 7

[1]PERTINENT BALANCE SHEET STATISTICS (Million $)

Sept. 30	Gross Prop.	Capital Expend.	Cash Items	Inven-tories	Receiv-ables	——Current—— Assets	Liabs.	Net Workg. Cap.	Cur. Ratio Assets to Liabs.	Long Term Debt	[2]($) Book Val. Com. Sh.
1974--	752.62	67.24	16.24	46.84	20.81	91.28	57.61	33.67	1.6-1	60.80	19.02
1973--	687.01	85.75	9.56	38.32	15.92	69.09	67.46	1.63	1.0-1	44.41	17.45
1972--	602.07	142.84	12.31	27.49	14.82	58.49	52.05	6.44	1.1-1	53.56	15.73
1971--	459.66	229.34	36.74	35.69	14.84	87.27	45.99	41.28	1.9-1	102.82	12.01
1970--	223.52	69.68	40.13	31.55	17.81	89.49	36.13	53.36	2.5-1	0.79	8.78
1969--	157.57	32.51	88.55	26.61	9.26	124.42	31.72	92.70	3.9-1	51.00	6.54
1968--	125.35	18.04	41.65	29.67	6.27	77.59	25.03	52.56	3.1-1	42.14	4.71
1967--	106.88	23.26	4.71	34.45	4.27	43.43	22.02	21.41	2.0-1	13.70	3.95
1966--	84.80	22.01	3.42	32.44	2.23	38.09	21.18	16.91	1.8-1	6.45	3.38
1965--	71.03	13.09	12.59	27.28	3.64	43.50	21.93	21.57	2.0-1	8.04	2.75

[1]Data for 1973 as originally reported; data for each yr. prior to 1973 as taken from subsequent yr.'s Annual Report; incl. foreign subs. aft. 1971. [2]Adj. for 2-for-1 splits in fiscal 1973, 1971 1968 & for stk. divds. of 2% each in fiscal 1975, 1974, 1972, 1971, 1970 & 1969 & 3% each in fiscal 1968, 1967, 1966 & 1965. [3]Cal. yrs. [4]Bef. spec. cr. of $0.05 a sh. in 1967. [5]Based on com. & com. sh. equivalents (stk. options); fully diluted sh. earns. were $1.35 in 1972, $0.98 (unchanged) in 1971, $0.85 in 1970, $0.66 in 1969 & $0.61 in 1968.

Fundamental Position

Walt Disney Productions and subsidiaries operate the Walt Disney World and Disneyland amusement parks, produce and distribute motion pictures for world-wide exhibition in theatres, produce and market film series for television exhibition, and exploit and market, throughout the world, characters, music and other related values arising from motion pictures.

In fiscal 1973-4 the amusement park group accounted for 66% of revenues and 40% of operating profits, theatrical films and television 21% and 41%, respectively, and ancillary activities (publishing, licensing merchandise, music and records) 13% and 19%.

Periodic reissue of many films, which are essentially timeless in story content, provides substantial profits. Wholly owned Buena Vista Film Distribution Co. distributes all company theatrical films domestically. Films reissued periodically include "Sleeping Beauty," "Snow White and the Seven Dwarfs," "Pinocchio," "Peter Pan" and "Bambi". "Mary Poppins," the company's most successful live action feature, was rereleased in 1973.

Television films are principally one hour shows. NBC-TV, under a long-term contract, televises the company's color TV show, Wonderful World of Disney.

The Disneyland exhibition and amusement park, operated in Anaheim, California, contains educational, scientific, and amusement features. Park attendance in 1973-4 declined 4.5%. More than 60% of the vistors were indicated to have come from within the state of California.

On October 1, 1971, Disney World, a $400,-000,000, 27,400 acre amusement and resort complex, was opened near Orlando, Florida. Disney World features an amusement park similar to Disneyland. Other features include various sporting recreational facilities, hotel and motel facilities, and a transportation system. **In addition, Disney plans to develop a residential community through its recently formed Buena Vista Land Co. subsidiary. The Florida amusement-resort complex generated revenues of $182,519,000 in fiscal 1973-4, an 8.5% increase over the prior year; attendance declined 6.5%.**

In February, 1974, Disney announced the formation of a division which would consult in master planning of new short-range intra-city mass transportation systems and develop and license systems for those applications.

Dividends, initiated in 1957, are on a highly conservative basis.

Employees: 14,000. Shareholders: 55,000.

Finances

In January, 1975, Disney announced that the Government had withdrawn its appeal from a decision of U. S. District Court that the company was entitled to an investment tax credit on motion picture negatives produced and released during Disney's fiscal years from 1963 through 1969. This had the effect of making final the judgment against the Government in favor of the company in the amount of $6,629,540 plus interest thereon in the approximate amount of $3,-200,000.

CAPITALIZATION

LONG TERM DEBT: $60,801,000.

COMMON STOCK: 29,755,362 shs. ($1.25 par).

Incorporated in Calif. in 1938. **Office**—500 So. Buena Vista St., Burbank, Calif. 91505. **Pres**—E. C. Walker. **Secy**—L. R. Marr. **VP-Treas**—L. E. Tryon. **Dirs**—D. B. Tatum (Chrmn), W. H. Anderson, S. C. Beise, S. T. Black, R. E. Disney, R. W. Miller, R. T. Morrow, E. C. Walker, R. L. Watson. **Transfer Agents**—Bankers Trust Co., NYC; Bank of America, San Francisco. **Registrars**—Morgan Guaranty Trust Co., NYC; Bank of America, San Francisco.

FIG. 6-8 (*Continued*)

cyclopedia, which also covers about 1,000 stocks. Figure 6-8 shows a report from SP's *Encyclopedia.*

Along with its monthly *Bond Guide,* SP publishes a weekly *Bond Outlook* and Moody publishes a weekly *Bond Survey.* Both cover similar data about the corporate and municipal bond markets, attractive convertibles and new issues, changes in the respective bond ratings, bonds called for payment, and similar items.

Value Line

The *Value Line Investment Survey* differs somewhat from the Moody and SP publications. Value Line reports on 1,400 stocks in 60 industries, covering each stock in detail once every quarter. Figure 6-9 shows one of Value Line's quarterly reports for a firm. Supplements are issued to Value Line subscribers each week to keep the financial reports updated. About 85 stocks are typically included in the brief, three- or four-page supplement. Once per quarter Value Line issues industry reports, the one shown in Fig. 6-10 being typical.

One of the unique features of Value Line's services is its investment scoring system to facilitate investors' selections. Value Line rates every stock from 1 to 5 with respect to four factors: quality, performance in the next 12 months, appreciation potential in 3 to 5 years, and income from dividends. Value Line suggests that the investor select securities with the highest weighted average rating. The investor selects the weights to be assigned to each rated item to reflect his or her personal investment preferences.

A second distinctive feature about Value Line is the quality of its investment advice. Essentially, Value Line recommends common stocks with low price-earnings ratios which have high earnings growth rates (the meanings of these terms are explained in Chap. 10). In studies to determine the profitability of the investment advice given by various brokerages and investment advisors, Value Line ranks as one of the better ones. On the average, Value Line's recommendations yield a portfolio which earns a few percentage points more return per year than could be earned by picking a large portfolio randomly (for example, the Standard & Poor's 500 Composite Stocks Average returns).[9]

Caveat about Financial Information

Various financial services have published erroneous and misleading information. For example, in 1960, 1961, and 1962 several financial services recommended purchase of stock in Atlantic Research Company (ARC) based on favorable profits. Standard & Poor's and Moody's, among others, pub-

---

[9] Fisher Black, "Yes, Virginia, There Is Hope: Tests of the Value Line Ranking System," *Financial Analysts Journal,* September–October 1973.

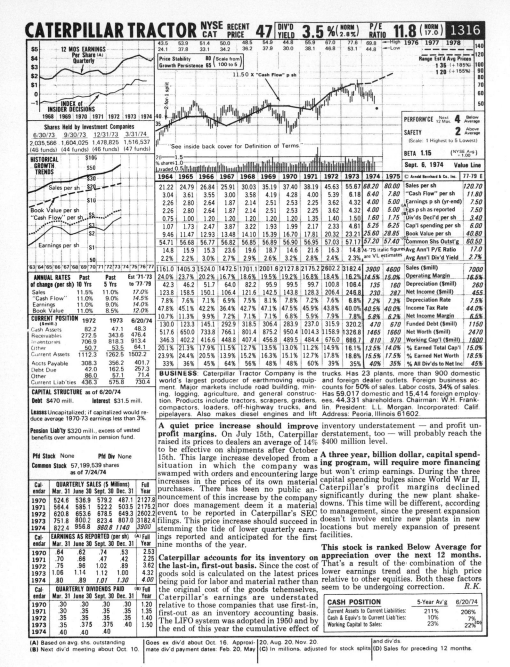

FIG. 6-9 Report from *Value Line Investment Survey*, September 6, 1974. (*Source:* Value Line, 5 East 44th Street, New York, N.Y., 10017.)

Sept. 6, 1974   # MACHINERY INDUSTRY   `1302`

Earnings of most of these companies continued to show good year-to-year gains in the second quarter. But market prices of the stocks went further downhill.

There is some evidence of a slowdown in spending by industry for new plant and equipment — an important source of sales and profits for most of these companies. The downturn is most evident in planned construction of new generating plants by electric utility companies.

Colt Industries and *Omark Industries* will probably show the best performance relative to the market in the 12 months ahead. Fourteen other issues are ranked better than average in this respect. There is wide selection among the group for investors interested primarily in high current yield or potential capital appreciation over the period to 1977-79.

Earnings Are Maintaining Good Growth

Second quarter earnings of the 70 companies in this industry which have reported to date averaged a gain of 24% over the comparable period year. This is about the same increase which was posted in the first quarter, although well below the 33% in the final quarter last year. Only 11 of the companies failed to register an advance in earnings in the second quarter.

While most of the companies were demonstrating the ability to increase earnings, the market was looking the other way, as it was doing for most stocks. The aggregate market price of the shares of the machinery companies has dropped 14% since our last review three months ago. During this period, the Dow Jones Industrial Average (30 stocks) declined by 16% and the Value Line Industrial Average (more than 1,300 stocks) slumped 19% . On average, prices of the machinery stocks stand 44% below this year's highs.

Capital Spending: To Taper Off?

A survey of large U.S. companies made by McGraw-Hill early in 1974 indicated that planned expenditures for new plant and equipment this year were 19% higher than the 1973 level. Reports by the National Industrial Conference Board reveal that capital appropriations by the 1,000 largest U.S. manufacturers in the first quarter of this year were 0.6% below those in the final quarter of 1973 (the first downturn in 11 quarters) but in the second quarter were 39% higher than in the first quarter. The U.S. Department of Commerce figures show that actual capital spending in the first quarter was 11.5% above that in the comparable period one year earlier, and that estimated expenditures would rise by 13.1% in the second quarter, 12.2% in the third quarter and 11.9% in the fourth quarter.

Many of the machinery companies depend heavily on capital spending by industry for sales and profits. But a reduction in appropriations for future spending might have little immediate effect. Most of the companies have record backlogs of unfilled orders — enough to keep their plants humming for some time into the future regardless of the amount of new authorizations for spending by industry.

Electric Utilities are Trimming Capital Spending Budgets

The most visible slowing down in future capital spending plans is in construction of generating plants by electric utility companies. In the past few months, announcements of cancellations and stretchouts in building new generating units have come rapidly on top of one

another, because of the utilities' difficulties in raising the massive amounts of funds required at the present time of high interest rates and low market prices of common stocks. The machinery companies which will feel the cutbacks the most are the major suppliers of steam generating equipment — *Babcock & Wilson, Combustion Engineering* And *Foster Wheeler*. But the full impact of the cutbacks will be years in developing. At June 30th, the combined order backlogs of the three companies totaled more than $8.4 billion — 52% higher than one year ago and equal to nearly three times the aggregate sales of the companies in 1973.   *F.G.*

AIR POWER INDUSTRY

Sales Booming but Margins Slim

Next to electricity, air power systems run by compressors are the most widely used source of power in U.S. industry. Business recently has been almost too good to be true for companies like *Ingersoll-Rand* (the fields dominant factor), *Gardner-Denver*, and *Aro*, so good, in fact, that managements have been checking constantly to see if the end of these good times is in sight. So far it hasn't shown up. Indeed, question a customer about possible cancellations and as likely as not you'll get back a plea to speed up deliveries.

The rich harvest, however, has some chaff in it: profit margins are far from what they should be if the past is any guide. Part of the reason is that producers have had to play catch-up with prices. In some cases, suppliers, especially second tier companies, raised the price of components faster than the industry's members could pass this along to their customers. Many of the products are long lead time manufacturing items, and air power companies have been stuck with delivering goods at prices that were set before the hyper-inflation spiral took hold. A variety of means have been achieved to offset this, including escalator clauses and pricing effective at delivery rather than on order date. The most effective method, however, will simply be the passage of time and the hefty increases instituted after price controls were removed this Spring.

The outlook for next year is unclear. The morbid suspicion that good times won't continue indefinitely has to be balanced with the favorable effect on margins of the recent price increases. On balance we're looking for a slightly down year in unit volume and in profits but under conditions of record, inflation-fed, dollar sales.   *R.K.*

OIL SERVICE COMPANIES

Top Dogs

The stocks of the oil service companies have held up relatively well over the last three months. While the average price of the stocks in this group has fallen 14% since our June 7th review, the Value Line Industrial Average is off 23%. The performance of the oil service stocks is especially noteworthy because the 14 stocks in the group have a high average Beta, 1.35. Thus, a 23% tumble in the market might have been expected to induce a 30% drop in the market value of the group. We think that two factors account for the continued relative market strength of the oil service stocks: large institutional support and highly visible future earnings growth. We continue to expect that most of the stocks in this group will perform at least as well as the market due to excellent quarterly earnings gains.

Rough Seas Ahead

New commitments in the drilling stocks should be deferred. Based on the rig building anticipated over th'

FIG. 6-10 Industry report from Value Line, September 6, 1974.

next three years, the number of semisubmersible drilling vessels in operation by 1977-79 will triple the current fleet size. The only present market for these high cost vessels, the North Sea, will not be able to utilize fully the new rigs. Unless major new oil fields are discovered in rough water areas, there will be an oversupply of semisubmersible rigs 3 to 5 years hence. Price competititon may develop. The drillers' profit margins and return on investment could shrink. Among the companies surveyed, *SED-CO* and *Zapata* are most heavily committed to semisubmersible rig construction.

Inflation may pose another problem for both the ocean drillers and the marine contractors. A piece of drilling or construction equipment which may have cost $20 million a year ago now cannot be built for less than $25 million. We estimate that the replacement value of the contractors' offshore drilling equipment is 80% higher than the undepreciated gross value recorded on their books. The higher value of the equipment will equate to higher day rates. But, as companies seek to add new vessels or replace older equipment, internally generated cash flow will be insufficient to meet these needs. They will need to draw down additional debt. Over the long term, the higher level of financial leverage will increase earnings volatility and probably lower the P/E multiples accorded the drilling and marine construction stocks.

The stocks of oil tool companies could prove the best buys in the oil service group. They are not faced with the problems of overcapacity. Their capital investment per dollar of sales is much lower than that of the drillers. The tool companies' external financing needs will not be great and their depreciation schedules seem adequate. Since most of their revenues are derived domestically, the tool companies' earnings comparisons will not be hampered by possible changes in the U.S. tax laws concerning unremitted foreign profits. They also do not risk being placed at a competitive disadvantage by the protectionist policies of the North Sea producing nations. Of the group, *Baker Oil* and *Smith International* seem to be especially good picks for long term capital gains potential. *D.P.J.*

STEEL FORMING MACHINERY

The two major domestic manufacturers of steel forming machinery, *Wean United* and *Mesta Machine*, have had rough going so far this year. Raw material shortages are causing shipment delays and a stretchout of the normal manufacturing cycle. Profits have suffered since they are recognized on the basis of units completed within each contract and on the percentage of completion method. Operating costs are rising due to the increasing cost of raw materials and production inefficiencies as both companies work down their bulging order backlogs, more than half representing foreign business.

Labor negotiations are currently underway. During the third quarter, both companies have three-year contracts expiring with the United Steelworkers Union. We expect an agreement will be reached along the settlement terms between the union and domestic steel producers earlier this year.

The major domestic steel producers have already announced plans to add over half of the widely-quoted figure of 25 million tons of new additional raw steel capacity that will be needed by 1980 to close the gap between supply and demand. Most of these projects consist of rounding out existing facilities in relatively small steps. A number of mill modernization programs are on the front burner and it's likely that *Wean* and *Mesta* are putting in

Companies Active in Machinery but Followed Under Industries Other than Machinery or Machine Tool

Company	Classification
Alaska Interstate	Conglomerates
Allen Group	Auto Parts
Allis-Chalmers	Agricultural Equipment
American Standard	Building
AMF, Inc.	Recreation
Amsted Industries	Railroad Equipment
Apache Corp.	Petroleum
Chromalloy American	Conglomerates
Conrac Corp.	Precision Instruments
Copeland Corp.	Elec. Eq./Electronics
Crown Cork	Conglomerates
Culligan International	Chemical
Cutler-Hammer	Elec. Eq./Electronics
Deere & Co.	Agricultural Equipment
Eagle-Picher Industries	Conglomerates
Eaton Corporation	Auto Parts
Emerson Electric	Elec. Eq./Electronics
Fansteel Inc.	Metal Fabricating
Federal-Mogul	Auto Parts
Federal Sign & Signal	Elec. Eq./Electronics
Ford Motor	Auto & Truck
General Electric	Elec. Eq./Electronics
Hoover Ball & Bearing	Auto Parts
International Harvester	Agricultural Equipment
1-T-E Imperial Corp.	Elec. Eq./Electronics
LFE Corp.	Elec. Eq./Electronics
Litton Industries	Conglomerates
Massey-Ferguson	Agricultural Equipment
Microdot, Inc.	Fastener
Portec, Inc.	Railroad Equipment
Reliance Electric	Elec. Eq./Electronics
Republic Corp.	Conglomerates
Rockwell International Corp.	Conglomerates
Rucker Co.	Elec. Eq./Electronics
Sparton Corp.	Elec. Eq./Electronics
Sperry Rand	Office Equip./Comp.
Studebaker-Worthington	Conglomerates
Sundstrand Corp.	Aerospace
UMC Industries, Inc.	Personal Service
Westinghouse Electric	Elec. Eq./Electronics
White Motor	Auto & Truck

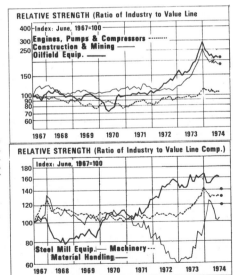

FIG. 6-10 (*Continued*)

lished income statements for ARC which reported profits. During this same period, however, ARC filed certified financial statements with the SEC showing losses instead of profits.[10] This difference was due to the fact that ARC publicly released unconsolidated statements showing profits while filing consolidated statements with the SEC showing losses.

6-4 PERIODIC ACADEMIC AND PROFESSIONAL JOURNALS

The business schools of some universities and some professional organizations publish periodicals containing articles which are relevant to financial investing. Some of the more prominent journals are briefly discussed here.

Journal of Finance

The *Journal of Finance* (JF) is published five times each year by the American Finance Association, a professional organization for finance professors, financial executives, economics professors, and others. The $12.50 annual membership dues entitle members of the association to receive the JF.[11]

The JF typically contains about a dozen papers written by finance professors, about a half-dozen comments pertinent to previous articles, abstracts of doctoral dissertations pertinent to finance, and reviews of recent finance books. The papers range from sophisticated mathematical models to descriptive pieces. They deal with all phases of finance—corporation finance, investments, consumer finance, insurance, international finance, money and banking, public finance, and real estate finance. Therefore, not all are relevant to investments.

Financial Analysts Journal

The *Financial Analysts Journal* (FAJ) is a bimonthly publication of the Financial Analysts Federation, which is an association of financial analysts and others devoted to the professional advancement of investments management and security analysis.[12]

The FAJ addresses itself to the field of financial investments. It typically contains articles under each of the following divisions: economic viewpoint, investment management, and investment analysis. It also publishes articles about industry reviews, corporation finance, bond analysis,

---

[10] The SEC cited this particular case in a special study which concluded that the free investment information provided by the SEC was not adequately utilized.
[11] Subscriptions may be obtained by writing to Dr. Robert A. Kavesh, Executive Secretary, Graduate School of Business, New York University, 100 Trinity Place, New York, N.Y. 10006; or see the inside cover of any recent issue for the address.
[12] Subscriptions are $16 per year and may be obtained from Financial Analysts Journal, 219 E. 42d St., New York, N.Y. 10017.

accounting, and similar investments topics. The articles are written primarily by finance professors, finance executives, and financial technicians. The FAJ is particularly appropriate reading for those who are preparing to take the examinations to obtain the Chartered Financial Analyst (CFA) designation.

Journal of Financial and Quantitative Analysis

The *Journal of Financial and Quantitative Analysis* (JFQA) is a quarterly academic journal which is published jointly by the Western Finance Association and the Graduate School of Business Administration of the University of Washington. All members of the Western Finance Association receive the JFQA.[13]

The JFQA usually contains about six articles written by professors from the finance, economics, and quantitative analysis departments of university business schools. The articles are analytical—advanced mathematics is used in some. The JFQA articles deal with the whole range of financial areas, but investments articles are found in nearly every issue, and occasionally a special edition has been devoted to an investment topic.

Journal of Financial Economics

The Journal of Financial Economics (JFE) is a bimonthly academic journal published by the North-Holland Publishing Company. Professors of finance and economics at various universities make up the editorial staff. The journal typically contains five articles by finance and economics professors. Advanced mathematics is used in the articles. The *Journal* usually contains several investments articles.[14]

Journal of Business

The *Journal of Business* (JB) is a quarterly publication of the Graduate School of Business of the University of Chicago.[15]

The JB publishes articles on topics from every department of the business school. Thus, finance and, in particular, investments articles make up only a fraction of the dozen or so articles in any given issue. The articles tend to be analytical and use advanced mathematics; most are written by business and economics professors.

---

[13] Subscriptions are $10 per year and may be obtained from Journal of Financial and Quantitative Analysis, DJ–10, Mackenzie Hall, University of Washington, Seattle, Wash. 98195.
[14] Individual subscriptions cost $14 per year and may be obtained from North-Holland Publishing Co., Journal Division, P.O. Box 211, Amsterdam, The Netherlands.
[15] Subscriptions, at $11 per year, may be obtained from The Journal of Business, The University of Chicago Press, 5801 Ellis Ave., Chicago, Ill. 60637.

6-5 INFORMATION ABOUT INVESTMENT COMPANIES

Information about mutual funds (that is, open-end investment companies) and closed-end investment companies is published by several sources. The investment companies themselves, especially the mutual funds, are always eager to mail out copies of their prospectuses and other promotional literature. And there are firms which provide information about investment companies, two of the more prominent being Arthur Wiesenberger Services, Inc., and Vickers Associates, Inc.

Arthur Wiesenberger Services

Arthur Wiesenberger Services, Inc., a division of the Nuveen Corporation, primarily sells information about open-end and closed-end investment companies. The firm annually publishes a large book entitled *Investment Companies.* Several early chapters of *Investment Companies* are devoted to explaining the differences between open-end and closed-end investment companies, regulations pertaining to investment companies, pertinent tax laws, and other facts. The greater part of the book is a description of the management, holdings, and history of the large investment companies. It describes individual investment companies, shows their performances (Fig. 6-12), and compares some of the mutual funds' performances (Fig. 6-11).

Wiesenberger Services also publishes *Charts and Statistics,* a companion volume to *Investment Companies; A Guide to Mutual Fund Withdrawal Plans,* a review of the income withdrawal plans of various investment companies; *Dividend Calendar, Reinvestment Prices, Range of Offering Prices, Mutual Affairs, Investor Aids,* and other books and pamphlets which are sold primarily to sales representatives for investment companies. Wiesenberger also sells two expensive ($1,000 per month) security selection services, *Findings and Forecasts* and *Wiesenberger 333 Stock Service.* Full information may be obtained by writing the company.[16]

Vickers Associates

Vickers Associates, Inc., publishes *Vickers Guide to Investment Company Portfolios,* which contains information about each of the large investment companies. Vickers Associates also publishes monthly pamphlets showing in detail the purchases and sales of the large investment companies.[17]

Portfolio Transactions by 75 Leading Investment Companies, Vickers Favorite Fifty, Over-the-Counter Favorites, and *Industry Group Summary* are summaries of current investment activity which are sold to investors

---

[16] Arthur Wiesenberger Services, Inc., 1 New York Plaza, New York, N.Y. 10004.
[17] Vickers Associates, Inc., 48 Elm St., Huntington, N.Y. 11743.

Approximate Per Cent Change in Net Assets per Share

RECORDS FOR INDIVIDUAL YEARS

	ANNUAL RESULTS									
	1973	1972	1971	1970	1969	1968	1967	1966	1965	1964

I. GROWTH FUNDS

A. Objective: Maximum Capital Gains

	1973	1972	1971	1970	1969	1968	1967	1966	1965	1964
Acorn Fund	−23.7	+ 8.6	+31.2							
Admiralty Fund—Growth Series	−25.4	− 22.1	+18.1	−36.0	−34.7	+10.0	+ 75.6	+ 2.9	+41.6	+ 6.6
Afuture Fund	−35.2	+ 19.1	+67.5	−26.8	−16.7					
Alpha Fund	−31.9	+ 27.4	+28.1	− 9.0	− 8.4					
American Express Special Fund	−21.2	− 2.6	+16.7	−13.8						
American Investors Fund	−15.3	+ 10.7	+ 4.3	−29.3	−29.3	+10.8	+ 45.9	+ 3.4	+49.8	+ 15.0
American National Growth Fund	−37.1	+ 3.0	+28.3	− 1.4	−13.8	+20.7	+ 53.5	−12.5	+28.1	+ 11.7
Axe Science Corp.	−19.6	+ 11.9	+15.2	− 8.6	−29.7	+ 2.1	+ 87.5	+ 3.8	+36.9	+ 16.3
Burnham Fund	−25.7	+ 8.2	+27.0	+ 5.2						
Channing Special Fund	−18.3	+ 6.2	+30.4	−41.5	−26.6	+20.9	+ 73.2	− 6.7	+67.9	+ 2.9
Channing Venture Fund	−38.8	+ 28.8	+61.1							
Chase Frontier Capital Fd. of Boston	−46.5	+ 17.9	+30.7	−23.3	−14.1					
Chase Fund of Boston	−31.2	+ 5.6	+29.5	−24.8	−17.1	+20.6	+ 81.6	− 4.5	+43.8	+ 8.7
Chase Special Fund of Boston	−33.3	+ 0.5	+28.3	− 8.8		+10.0	+ 71.9	**	**	**
Colonial Equities	−31.4	− 3.4	+20.3	−16.6	−24.1					
Colonial Ventures	−49.4	+ 2.2	+24.1	−33.3	−15.3	+81.6				
Columbia Growth Fund	−25.5	+ 5.9	+36.2	−13.5	− 2.9	+37.9				
Competitive Capital Fund	−30.3	− 6.4	+10.6	−19.2	−25.8					
Comstock Fund	−17.1	− 0.9	+12.5	−17.4	−18.9					
**Constellation Growth Fund (1971)	−16.3	+ 5.8	+ 2.0	−48.3	− 6.5	+16.0	**	**	**	**
Crown Western-Dallas Fund	−28.1	+ 10.4	+19.1	−40.3	−19.0	+56.4	+ 67.6	− 7.2	+16.8	+ 4.2
Delta Trend Fund	−33.8	− 7.9	+21.4	−19.0	−14.9					
Directors Capital Fund	−32.8	+ 11.0	+31.6							
Dreyfus Leverage Fund	−15.4	+ 12.6	+28.8	+ 0.6						
Eaton & Howard Growth Fund	−33.6	+ 23.4	+27.0	−11.6	− 7.0					
Eaton & Howard Special Fund	−32.3	+ 3.8	+28.2	−21.7	−33.7					
Edie Special Growth Fund	−40.4	+ 16.5	+34.3	− 1.7						
Edie Special Institutional Fund	−38.5	+ 15.9	+35.3	− 2.8						
Enterprise Fund	−20.5	+ 6.4	+23.5	−26.1	−25.9	+44.3	+116.9	+ 4.0	+43.3	+ 24.5
Equity Growth Fund of America	−22.0	+ 1.9	+17.4	− 4.5	−13.5	+26.0	+ 60.2			
Equity Progress Fund	−28.7	− 1.0	+17.5	−22.3	−27.4	+ 4.8	+ 79.8	− 7.4	+14.5	− 1.5
Explorer Fund	−26.2	+ 21.1	+24.6	−25.7	−11.7	+16.7				
Fairfield Fund	−28.2	+ 5.2	+20.2	−17.1	−29.3	+ 7.2	+ 67.8	+ 5.2	+41.7	+ 5.0
Financial Dynamics Fund	−15.3	+ 17.4	+13.6	−40.0	−16.6	+33.0				
Financial Venture Fund	−26.1	+ 22.4	+15.3	−52.9						
First Investors Discovery Fund	−37.7	− 3.4	+15.4	−19.3						
First Investors Fund for Growth	−29.7	+ 6.5	+29.8	−15.1	− 3.2	+ 2.1	+ 34.8			
Fleming Berger Fund	−33.7	+ 14.5	+34.7	−11.6						
Founders Growth Fund	−24.9	+ 16.2	+24.5	− 7.4	−28.2	+17.2	+ 68.5	−13.3	+37.3	+ 26.8
**Founders Special Fund (1969)	−19.1	+ 25.2	+35.5	+21.1	**	**	**	**	**	**
Franklin Custodian—DynaTech Series	−35.2	+ 16.0	+25.5	−20.0	−27.4					
Fund of America	−17.8	+ 10.1	+ 6.0	−12.8	−16.5	+ 5.3	+ 50.3	−14.0	+31.4	+ 2.9
Hamilton Growth Fund	−30.1	+ 5.4	+16.0	−19.7	−10.8					
Herold Fund	−35.5	− 4.1	+32.1	− 8.5	− 6.5					
IDS New Dimensions Fund	− 2.8	+ 27.1	+48.5	−19.3	−12.8					
IDS Progressive Fund	−28.3	+ 11.2	+44.1	−20.6	− 2.0					
Impact Fund	−21.3	+ 14.8	+20.8	−16.6						
Independence Fund	−10.4	+ 23.7	+27.8	−43.0	−26.3	+ 9.4	+ 67.0			
ISI Growth Fund	− 7.8	+ 16.3	+ 8.5	−27.1	−18.3					
Ivest Fund	−32.1	+ 11.7	+21.5	− 4.5	− 7.9	− 2.2	+ 47.4	− 2.2	+41.3	+ 20.4
Janus Fund	−16.0	+ 33.9	+41.5							
Keystone Apollo Fund	−39.1	+ 15.1	+43.2	− 3.9						
Keystone (S-4) Spec. Common	−40.5	+ 13.0	+35.2	−21.1	−20.8	+12.1	+ 66.0	− 6.7	+30.1	+ 21.1
Knickerbocker Growth Fund	−30.6	+ 1.4	+23.8	−20.8	− 9.6	+12.3	+ 48.5	+ 9.1	+42.5	+ 2.8
Lexington Growth Fund	−43.6	+ 13.6	+27.2	−16.8						

** This symbol, when appearing at the left of a fund name, indicates a change of management or policy occurred in the year shown in parentheses. When ** appears under a column heading, it indicates that figures have been omitted because the fund, while in existence throughout the period, was not readily available for purchase by the public, or that a complete change of policy makes earlier figures not meaningful.

FIG. 6-11 Comparison of mutual fund performances. (From Arthur Wiesenberger Services, Inc., *Investment Companies,* 1974 edition.)

With Capital Gains (Reinvested) and Income Dividends (Added Back)

FOR PERIODS OF TWO TO TEN YEARS ENDED DECEMBER 31, 1973

	1972 2 years	1971 3 years	1970 4 years	1969 5 years	1968 6 years	1967 7 years	1966 8 years	1965 9 years	1964 10 years	% Change in Net Asset Value† Not 10 Years	% Change in Net Asset Value† 10 Years	Total Income†† Not 10 Years	Total Income†† 10 Years
I. GROWTH FUNDS													
A. Objective: Maximum Capital Gains													
Acorn Fund	− 16.8	+ 9.2								*+ 5.4*		*+ 3.8*	
Admiralty Fund—Growth Series	− 41.9	− 31.4	− 56.1	− 71.3	− 68.4	− 44.1	− 42.2	− 17.7	− 12.1		− 16.6		+ 4.5
Afuture Fund	− 22.8	+ 29.3	− 5.4	− 21.2						*− 21.2*		*0*	
Alpha Fund	− 13.0	+ 11.8	+ 1.6	− 7.0						*− 11.8*		*+ 4.8*	
American Express Special Fund	− 23.1	− 9.7	− 21.7							*− 29.1*		*+ 7.4*	
American Investors Fund	− 6.2	− 2.1	− 30.8	− 50.9	− 45.3	− 20.1	− 17.3	+ 24.0	+ 40.7		+ 33.2		+ 7.5
American National Growth Fund	− 35.0	− 16.1	− 17.0	− 28.1	− 12.9	+ 33.8	+ 18.0	+ 49.1	+ 65.7		+ 42.0		+ 23.7
Axe Science Corp.	− 9.8	+ 4.1	− 4.9	− 33.1	− 31.2	+ 29.6	+ 34.3	+ 83.3	+ 112.0		+ 83.5		+ 28.5
Burnham Fund	− 19.6	+ 2.1	+ 7.8							*+ 5.3*		*+ 2.5*	
Channing Special Fund	− 13.1	+ 13.4	− 33.8	− 51.1	− 40.8	+ 2.8	− 4.1	+ 61.0	+ 65.4		+ 56.0		+ 9.4
Channing Venture Fund	− 21.2	+ 27.0								*+ 27.0*		*0*	
Chase Frontier Capital Fd. of Boston	− 36.9	− 17.5	− 36.6	− 45.7						*− 47.0*		*+ 1.3*	
Chase Fund of Boston	− 27.3	− 5.6	− 29.0	− 40.7	− 28.1	+ 31.5	+ 25.0	+ 80.2	+ 95.3		+ 75.9		+ 19.4
Chase Special Fund of Boston	− 32.9	− 13.5	− 20.9							*− 23.5*		*+ 2.6*	
Colonial Equities	− 33.6	− 19.7	− 32.7	− 48.6	− 43.0	− 1.8	**	**	**	*− 10.4*		*+ 8.6*	
Colonial Ventures	− 48.3	− 35.6	− 56.8	− 63.2	− 33.2					*− 36.1*		*+ 2.9*	
Columbia Growth Fund	− 20.9	+ 8.2	− 6.4	− 9.2	+ 25.2					*+ 19.9*		*+ 5.3*	
Competitive Capital Fund	− 34.7	− 26.9	− 40.7	− 55.7						*− 59.0*		*+ 3.3*	
Comstock Fund	− 17.4	− 6.5	− 22.6	− 37.1						*− 44.3*		*+ 7.2*	
**Constellation Growth Fund (1971)	− 11.4	− 9.6	− 53.5	− 55.7	− 48.5	**	**	**		*− 50.5*		*+ 2.0*	
Crown Western-Dallas Fund	− 20.3	− 4.8	− 43.1	− 53.7	− 26.6	+ 23.5	+ 14.2	+ 33.2	+ 36.7		+ 15.9		+ 20.8
Delta Trend Fund	− 39.0	− 25.3	− 39.4	− 47.8						*− 51.5*		*+ 3.7*	
Directors Capital Fund	− 25.5	− 1.9								*− 1.9*		*0*	
Dreyfus Leverage Fund	− 4.7	+ 22.7	+ 22.9							*+ 18.8*		*+ 4.1*	
Eaton & Howard Growth Fund	− 18.0	+ 5.0	− 7.3	− 13.8						*− 18.0*		*+ 4.2*	
Eaton & Howard Special Fund	− 29.6	− 8.9	− 28.4	− 52.4						*− 55.9*		*+ 3.5*	
Edie Special Growth Fund	− 30.3	− 6.1	− 7.6							*− 12.0*		*+ 4.4*	
Edie Special Institutional Fund	− 28.5	− 2.8	− 5.0							*− 10.3*		*+ 5.3*	
Enterprise Fund	+ 15.2	+ 5.2	− 22.3	− 42.4	− 16.7	+ 80.7	+ 87.4	+ 168.0	+ 233.1		+195.3		+ 37.8
Equity Growth Fund of America	− 20.4	− 5.9	− 10.1	− 22.2	− 1.9	+ 57.1				*+ 45.9*		*+ 11.2*	
Equity Progress Fund	− 29.4	− 16.4	− 34.7	− 52.6	− 49.2	− 8.3	− 14.5	+ 3.6	− 4.9		− 15.4		+ 10.5
Explorer Fund	− 10.6	+ 11.5	− 17.3	− 26.8	− 14.0					*− 21.0*		*+ 7.0*	
Fairfield Fund	− 24.5	− 8.9	− 24.4	− 46.5	− 42.7	− 3.8	+ 1.2	+ 43.4	+ 50.3		+ 41.7		+ 8.6
Financial Dynamics Fund	− 0.3	+ 13.2	− 32.2	− 43.1	+ 24.1					*− 29.8*		*+ 5.7*	
Financial Venture Fund	− 9.0	+ 5.1	− 50.6							*− 54.4*		*+ 3.8*	
First Investors Discovery Fund	− 39.9	− 30.2	− 43.6							*− 44.7*		*+ 1.1*	
First Investors Fund for Growth	− 25.1	− 2.8	− 17.4	− 20.0	− 18.2	+ 10.4				*+ 8.0*		*+ 2.4*	
Fleming Berger Fund	− 24.0	+ 2.8	− 9.2							*− 13.3*		*+ 4.1*	
Founders Growth Fund	− 12.6	+ 8.9	+ 0.5	− 27.8	− 15.2	+ 43.0	+ 23.8	+ 69.8	+114.9		+ 87.7		+ 27.2
**Founders Special Fund (1969)	+ 1.4	+ 37.4	+ 66.6	**	**	**	**	**	**	*+ 60.0*		*+ 6.6*	
Franklin Custodian—DynaTech Series	− 24.6	− 5.0	− 24.1	− 44.7						*− 47.1*		*+ 2.3*	
Fund of America	− 9.0	− 3.2	− 15.5	− 29.3	− 25.4	+ 12.3	− 3.5	+ 26.9	+ 30.3		+ 14.6		+ 15.7
Hamilton Growth Fund	− 26.2	− 14.3	− 31.0	− 38.0						*− 41.7*		*+ 3.7*	
Herold Fund	− 38.1	− 17.1	− 23.8	− 3.0						*− 9.2*		*+ 6.2*	
IDS New Dimensions Fund	− 9.0	+ 35.2	+ 8.7	− 5.3						*− 8.6*		*+ 3.3*	
IDS Progressive Fund	− 19.6	+ 16.0	− 8.0	− 9.4						*− 14.0*		*+ 4.6*	
Impact Fund	− 9.6	+ 9.2	− 9.1							*− 11.7*		*+ 2.6*	
Independence Fund	+ 10.8	+ 41.5	− 19.6	− 40.6	− 34.6	+ 9.5				*+ 3.6*		*+ 5.9*	
ISI Growth Fund	+ 7.4	+ 16.4	− 15.4	− 30.7						*− 36.5*		*+ 5.8*	
Ivest Fund	− 23.8	− 7.1	− 11.1	− 18.1	− 19.8	+ 18.3	+ 15.7	+ 63.3	+ 96.5		+ 80.5		+ 16.0
Janus Fund	+ 12.4	+ 59.0								*+ 53.1*		*+ 5.9*	
Keystone Apollo Fund	+ 29.9	+ 0.7	− 3.1							*− 4.6*		*+ 1.5*	
Keystone (S-4) Spec. Common	− 32.8	− 9.0	− 28.2	− 43.0	− 35.7	+ 7.2	− 0.2	+ 30.2	+ 56.3		+ 45.8		+ 10.5
Knickerbocker Growth Fund	− 29.6	− 12.6	− 30.7	− 37.1	− 29.2	+ 5.2	+ 14.8	+ 63.4	+ 64.3		+ 55.4		+ 8.9
Lexington Growth Fund	− 36.2	− 35.7	− 32.3							*− 33.4*		*+ 1.1*	

† Including value of shares accepted as capital gains distributions.
†† As a per cent of asset value at the beginning of the period.

FIG. 6-11 (*Continued*)

T. ROWE PRICE GROWTH STOCK FUND, INC.

One Charles Center, Baltimore, Maryland 21201

The Baltimore investment counsel firm, T. Rowe Price Associates, Inc., organized this fund in 1950 and acts as its investment manager. The shares are sold directly by the fund. A number of its officers and directors serve Rowe Price New Horizons Fund, Rowe Price New Era Fund and Rowe Price New Income Fund (initially offered in 1973) in similar capacities.

Major objectives of the Growth Stock Fund are to seek long-term appreciation of capital and increased future income through investment in common stocks believed to have favorable prospects for continued growth in earnings and dividends. A reasonably fully-invested position is usually maintained, but the fund may establish or increase reserves of cash and dollar obligations to take advantage of subsequent buying opportunities.

At the 1973 year-end, the fund had 90% of its assets in common stocks, of which a substantial proportion was concentrated in five industry groups: business & office equipment (13.6% of assets), energy sources (8.4%), food & beverage (6.7%), electronic & electrical equipment (6.4%), and pharmaceutical & health (5.3%). IBM, at 4% of assets, was the fund's largest investment, followed by Xerox (3.8%), Utah International (2.6%), National Cash Register (2.4%), and Polaroid (2.3%). The rate of portfolio turnover during the year was 13.1% of average assets. Unrealized depreciation was 4.3% of year-end assets.

Special Services: An open account system provides for *accumulation* and *automatic dividend reinvestment;* minimum initial investment is $500, subsequent investments must be at least $50. A monthly or quarterly *withdrawal plan* is available to accounts worth at least $10,000; minimum withdrawal payment is $50. There is a *Keogh Plan* custody agreement available as well as a prototype corporate retirement plan.

Statistical History

	Total Net Assets	Number of Share-holders	% of Assets in—Cash & Equivalent	Bonds & Preferreds	Common Stocks	Net Asset Value Per Share	Yield	Income Dividends	Capital Gains Distributions	Expense Ratio	Offering Price High	Offering Price Low
1973	$1,121,029,445	198,438	9%	1%	90%	$11.91	1.1%	$0.14	$0.54	0.51%	$16.81	$11.19
1972	1,370,912,433	181,236	6	1*	93	16.66	0.7	0.12	0.32	0.49	17.22	14.55
1971	1,000,368,709	147,660	5	3*	92	14.81	1.0	0.15	0.20	0.53	14.94	11.41
1970	657,535,808	128,886	5	4*	91	11.55	1.8	0.21	0.29	0.54	13.18	8.78
1969	612,968,446	111,291	11	3	86	13.07	1.4	0.20	0.39	0.50	13.42	11.28
1968	514,121,107	95,140	8	...	92	13.23	0.7	0.20	...†	0.52	13.71	10.74
1967	393,319,029	73,774	5	1	94	12.29	1.6	0.20	0.27	0.55	12.35	10.03
1966	246,601,321	56,703	11	...	89	10.05	1.8	0.19	0.25	0.58	11.20	8.87
1965	196,818,741	42,401	12	1*	87	10.58	1.6	0.17	0.30	0.60	10.84	8.76
1964	128,928,224	32,316	6	...	94	8.80	1.7	0.15	0.17	0.61	9.19	8.19
1963	104,196,714	28,560	5	...	95	8.15	1.7	0.14	0.14	0.65	8.27	7.87

Note: Figures adjusted for 2-for-1 split effective May 1, 1973.
* This percentage includes a substantial proportion in convertible issues.
† Beginning with the year ended December 31, 1968, realized securities profits were paid in February of the following year.

Directors: Charles W. Shaeffer, Chmn.; E. Kirkbride Miller, Pres.; Austin H. George, V. P.; Cornelius C. Bond, Jr., V. P.; Donald E. Bowman; Richard W. Case; Albert Keidel, Jr.; John K. Major; J. H. Pearlstone, Jr.; D. Reid Weedon, Jr.

Investment Adviser: T. Rowe Price Associates, Inc. Compensation to the Adviser is ½ of 1% annually of first $50 million of average net assets; 4/10 of 1% of next $100 million; 35/100 of 1% of the next $850 million, and 3/10 of 1% on assets in excess of $1 billion, payable quarterly.

Custodian and Transfer Agent: The Bank of New York, New York, N. Y.

Distributor: None. Shares are sold directly by the fund.

Sales Charge: None. Shares are issued at net asset value. Minimum initial investment is $500. Minimum subsequent investment is $50.

Dividends: Income dividends are paid semi-annually in the months of February and August. Capital gains, if any, are paid in February.

Shareholder Reports: Issued quarterly. Fiscal year ends December 31. The 1973 prospectus was effective in May.

Qualified for Sale: In all states, D. C. and P. R.

An assumed investment of $10,000 in this fund, with capital gains accepted in shares, is illustrated below. The explanation on page 173 must be read in conjunction with this illustration.

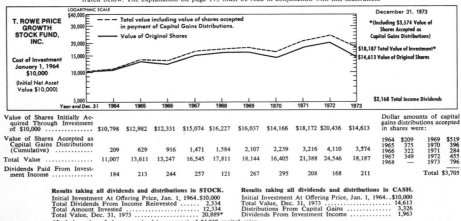

Value of Shares Initially Acquired Through Investment of $10,000	$10,798	$12,982	$12,331	$15,074	$16,227	$16,037	$14,166	$18,172	$20,436	$14,613
Value of Shares Accepted as Capital Gains Distributions (Cumulative)	209	629	916	1,471	1,584	2,107	2,239	3,216	4,110	3,574
Total Value	11,007	13,611	13,247	16,545	17,811	18,144	16,405	21,388	24,546	18,187
Dividends Paid From Investment Income	184	213	244	257	121	267	295	208	168	211

Dollar amounts of capital gains distributions accepted in shares were:

1964	$209	1969	$519
1965	375	1970	396
1966	322	1971	284
1967	349	1972	455
1968	—	1973	796
		Total	$3,705

Results taking all dividends and distributions in STOCK.

Initial Investment At Offering Price, Jan. 1, 1964	$10,000
Total Dividends From Income Reinvested	2,334
Total Amount Invested	12,334
Total Value, Dec. 31, 1973	20,889*

*Includes value of shares received in payment of $4,030 capital gains.

Results taking all dividends and distributions in CASH.

Initial Investment At Offering Price, Jan. 1, 1964	$10,000
Total Value, Dec. 31, 1973	14,613
Distributions From Capital Gains	3,326
Dividends From Investment Income	1,963

FIG. 6-12 Report on a mutual fund. (From Arthur Wiesenberger Services, Inc., *Investment Companies,* 1974 edition.)

Mar.31 1969	Dec.31 1972	Dec.31 1973	Mar.31 1974	STOCKS	$ Value (Millions)	No.Fds. Holding	Number Shares Held	Net Change In Holdings	% Outst. Stk.Held by Fds.
				RANK BY $ VALUE					
1	1	1	1	INTERNATIONAL BUSINESS MACHINES	1712	408	7,263,100	+43,900	5.0
2	4	2	2	EXXON CORPORATION	855	229	10,512,200	-352,400	4.7
7	7	4	3	AMERICAN TELEPHONE & TELEGRAPH	744	192	14,918,300	+1,254,100	2.7
8	3	3	4	XEROX CORPORATION	652	188	5,672,500	+23,700	7.2
13	6	6	5	EASTMAN KODAK COMPANY	477	181	4,490,200	+74,700	2.8
9	11	7	6	BURROUGHS CORPORATION	465	128	4,547,300	-280,700	11.7
28	8	5	7	PHILIP MORRIS, INC. (new)	451	76	9,148,700	-432,500	16.5
4	27	8	8	ATLANTIC RICHFIELD COMPANY	355	128	3,764,100	-107,100	8.1
3	14	10	9	TEXACO INC.	351	145	12,550,200	-263,300	4.6
11	2	12	10	GENERAL MOTORS CORPORATION	337	162	6,775,700	-636,600	2.4
35	5	17	11	FORD MOTOR COMPANY	336	100	6,846,200	-307,700	7.3
30	20	14	12	E. I. DU PONT DE NEMOURS	328	118	1,984,300	-30,100	4.1
-	23	9	13	KERR-McGEE CORPORATION	328	83	4,291,700	-142,100	17.2
-	13	11	14	McDONALD'S CORPORATION	326	92	6,200,400	-88,800	15.6
34	-	16	15	WEYERHAEUSER COMPANY	311	61	7,467,800	-121,100	5.8
-	47	27	16	DIGITAL EQUIPMENT CORPORATION	285	87	2,696,500	+153,900	22.8
21	21	23	17	MINNESOTA MINING & MANUFACTURING	262	94	3,526,600	+107,500	3.1
-	50	32	18	SCHERING-PLOUGH CORPORATION	247	74	3,517,100	+111,900	6.7
-	34	22	19	CITICORP	246	81	6,066,700	+165,400	5.0
23	-	29	20	INTERNATIONAL PAPER COMPANY	239	78	4,659,400	-242,300	10.6
16	9	13	21	GENERAL ELECTRIC COMPANY	237	150	4,370,300	-771,400	2.4
20	26	18	22	STANDARD OIL COMPANY OF CALIFORNIA	231	90	7,891,300	-301,500	4.7
-	-	-	23	**DOW CHEMICAL COMPANY	225	69	3,747,800	+341,900	4.1
5	10	30	24	POLAROID CORPORATION	225	88	3,452,500	-138,300	10.5
-	-	20	25	HALLIBURTON COMPANY	222	87	1,447,100	+33,600	7.6
37	16	21	26	S. S. KRESGE COMPANY	218	83	6,941,400	-1,306,100	5.9
42	-	41	27	MERCK & COMPANY	218	83	2,690,000	+297,000	3.6
29	33	19	28	AETNA LIFE & CASUALTY COMPANY (new)	216	83	6,941,100	-720,100	13.2
-	-	28	29	SYNTEX CORPORATION	214	90	4,332,300	-170,900	21.1
-	32	36	30	WARNER-LAMBERT COMPANY	214	55	5,933,800	+98,500	7.6
-	38	25	31	UNION PACIFIC CORPORATION	213	47	2,631,600	-241,000	11.6
50	44	15	32	PHILLIPS PETROLEUM COMPANY	211	98	3,966,200	-584,000	5.3
17	17	26	33	MOBIL OIL CORPORATION	207	126	4,549,100	436,800	4.5
-	48	38	34	GENERAL TELEPHONE & ELECTRONICS	200	105	8,264,000	+210,200	7.0
39	-	-	35	**INTERNATIONAL NICKEL OF CANADA	195	158	5,459,200	1912,800	7.3
-	25	33	36	TEXAS INSTRUMENTS, INC.	194	81	2,031,000	-165,400	8.9
-	-	31	37	ALCAN ALUMINIUM LTD.	194	131	5,833,100	-305,900	17.0
24	28	24	38	CONTINENTAL OIL COMPANY	192	65	4,546,600	-334,000	9.0
-	-	-	39	**MONSANTO COMPANY	190	85	3,289,700	+265,700	9.9
-	29	34	40	TRAVELERS CORPORATION	188	64	6,301,600	-394,700	14.3
-	31	-	41	**UNION CARBIDE CORPORATION	187	96	5,044,000	-143,200	8.3
12	41	35	42	SPERRY RAND CORPORATION	183	81	4,622,400	-384,400	13.5
-	-	-	43	**AMERICAN HOME PRODUCTS	181	72	4,624,100	+395,800	3.0
-	-	39	44	ALUMINUM COMPANY OF AMERICA	178	75	3,794,000	-237,900	11.5
19	15	42	45	AVON PRODUCTS, INC.	178	82	3,324,600	+301,800	5.7
-	-	45	46	STANDARD OIL COMPANY (INDIANA)	176	75	1,898,300	+105,400	2.7
22	19	-	47	**SEARS, ROEBUCK & COMPANY	174	95	2,098,900	-62,200	1.3
-	-	49	48	BETHLEHEM STEEL CORPORATION	173	51	5,468,100	+19,000	12.6
-	-	37	49	SCHLUMBERGER, LTD.	170	68	1,641,100	+23,400	4.5
-	-	-	50	**R. J. REYNOLDS INDUSTRIES	167	54	3,804,800	-37,600	9.0

**RETURNEE				DISPLACED:	Allied Chemical Co.	-	Deere & Co.	-
Getty Oil Co.	-	Louisiana Land & Exploration	-	Pfizer, Inc.	-	Phelps Dodge Corp.	-	Upjohn Co.	-

FIG. 6-13 *Vickers Favorite Fifty,* showing stocks selected by institutional investors during August 1974.

SUMMARY OF FAVORITE FIFTY BY INDUSTRY

dollar value of stocks by industry to total dollar value of favorite fifty

	3/31/74	12/31/73	12/31/72	3/31/69
OIL & NATURAL GAS..	21.6%	26.2%	15.9%	28.7%
OFFICE EQUIPMENT	21.6	20.6	21.0	24.5
CHEMICALS & DRUGS..	14.3	11.7	8.3	4.1
LEISURE..	6.7	6.7	9.4	5.8
UTILITIES..	6.2	5.7	4.2	3.3
MOTORS..	4.4	3.8	9.2	5.0
FINANCE..	4.3	4.7	5.5	2.4
METALS & MINING..	3.7	3.7	-	2.2
MISCELLANEOUS	17.2	16.9	26.5	24.0
	100.0%	100.0%	100.0%	100.0%

CANDIDATES

STOCKS	$ Value (Mil.)	No. Fds. Holding	Number Shares Held	STOCKS	$ Value (Mil.)	No. Fds. Holding	Number Shares Held
Eli Lilly & Co.	166.9	64	2,367,100	Squibb Corp.	119.7	44	1,418,900
Hercules, Inc.	166.8	46	4,667,000	Procter & Gamble Co.	119.0	54	1,344,200
Allied Chemical Corp.	163.4	54	3,844,400	AMP, Inc.	118.2	42	2,954,400
Phelps Dodge Corp.	163.1	51	4,076,300	CBS, Inc.	117.8	52	3,463,300
Federal Natl. Mortgage Assn.	156.0	66	9,316,300	Union Camp Corp.	117.1	40	2,081,000
Pfizer, Inc.	154.4	71	4,143,800	Air Products & Chemicals	113.0	38	2,103,100
Upjohn Co.	153.6	63	2,353,400	Standard Oil Co. (Ohio)	112.9	68	1,963,900
U. S. Steel Corp.	149.6	48	3,519,900	Hewlett-Packard Co.	110.3	41	1,281,100
Johnson & Johnson	145.2	59	1,332,300	St. Regis Paper Co.	110.0	31	3,548,700
Delta Air Lines, Inc.	144.0	46	2,969,400	Marathon Oil Co.	106.4	40	2,467,800
Sony Corp. (ADR)	141.6	48	4,924,500	PepsiCo, Inc.	106.1	36	1,769,100
Deere & Co.	140.7	92	3,473,600	National Cash Register Co.	102.4	46	2,785,900
Northwest Airlines, Inc.	140.5	52	6,073,800	Caterpillar Tractor Co.	101.9	62	1,726,700
Intl. Telephone & Telegraph	139.1	89	5,982,800	Domtar, Ltd.	98.8	35	3,559,600
Bristol-Myers Co.	137.6	54	2,851,000	Williams Cos.	97.9	57	1,764,400
Imperial Oil, Ltd. 'A'	132.9	81	3,363,500	Newmont Mining Corp.	96.4	48	3,240,700
MGIC Investment Corp.	132.7	67	3,932,600	Baxter Laboratories	96.4	50	2,416,500
Getty Oil Co.	131.5	45	954,400	Colonial Penn Group	95.5	30	2,916,000
Georgia-Pacific Corp.	131.3	30	2,984,100	American Metal Climax	95.4	50	2,198,300
Motorola, Inc.	130.9	65	2,402,600	G. D. Searle & Co.	95.2	40	3,907,200
Utah Intl., Inc.	130.8	46	2,998,700	Gulf Oil Corp.	93.6	69	4,089,700
Crown Zellerbach Corp.	130.7	43	3,643,800	Superior Oil Co.	92.4	24	437,100
Kennecott Copper Corp.	127.6	87	3,219,700	Westinghouse Electric Corp.	91.3	75	4,452,200
Louisiana Land & Exploration	123.4	36	3,269,100	UAL, Inc.	91.1	64	3,660,500
Coca-Cola Co.	122.8	57	1,114,900	Shell Oil Co.	90.5	27	1,536,300

COMMENTS

SCOPE: The 79th issue of Vickers Favorite 50 covers the common stock holdings of about 1025 United States and Canadian Investment Companies with combined assets of approximately $65 billion. Investment company holdings of the 50 favorites total 250 million shares with a market value of $15.3 billion as of March 31, 1974, versus $16.8 billion as of December 31, 1973.

VICKERS FAVORITE 50 INDEX: Vickers Favorite Index stood at 1569.5 on March 31, 1974, against 1692.7 on December 31, 1973, a decrease of 7.3%. This compares with a decrease of 0.5% in the Dow-Jones Industrial Average from 850.9 to 846.7 during the same period. For the year, the VFFI lost 11.4% against a decrease of 11.0% in the DJIA.

SUMMARY BY INDUSTRY GROUP: OIL & NATURAL GAS and OFFICE EQUIPMENT continued their battle for 1st place with OIL winning out by a fraction. However, holdings dropped 4.6% while OFFICE EQUIPMENT rose 1.0%. MOTORS edged ahead of FINANCE but the remaining industries retained their relative positions.

STOCKS BOUGHT AND UP IN RANK: A.T.& T. was way out in front as the most popular stock during this uncertain period... funds purchased 1,254,100 shares worth $62.5 million. MERCK jumped up 14 places on buying of 297,000 shares worth $24.0 million and DIGITAL EQUIP rose 11 places on an in-

crease of 153,900 shares worth $16.3 million. Although buying of AVON PRODUCTS totalled 301,800 shares worth $16.2 million, a price drop of almost 16% caused it to fall 2 places.

STOCKS SOLD AND DOWN IN RANK: G.E., on the downswing for the past two years, lost another 771,400 shares worth $41.8 million and fell to 21st place. Close behind was KRESGE, off 1,306,100 shares worth $41.0 million. Capitalization owned is now at the lowest it has been in ten years. PHILLIPS PETRO. was the biggest oil casualty, -584,000 shares worth $31.1 million. Selling in the two motor stocks, GENERAL MOTORS (-$31.7 million) and FORD (-$15.1 million), was outweighed by good market which moved them up in rank.

RETURNEES: INTL. NICKEL (+$32.6 million), DOW (+$20.5 million), AMER. HOME PRODUCTS (+$15.5 million) and MONSANTO (+$15.3 million) returned to the Favorite 50 on good buying and fairly stable market. The three other Returnees, UNION CARBIDE, SEARS ROEBUCK and REYNOLDS, although nominally sold, made the grade because of adverse action in other stocks rather than any positive action in them.

DISPLACED: Bad market was the biggest factor in the downfall of the Displaced stocks. However, GETTY was also a casualty of large selling, -$35.3 million, as were UPJOHN, DEERE and LA. LAND to a lesser extent.

FIG. 6-13 (Continued)

seeking "hot tips." *Vickers Favorite Fifty* lists stocks which are or were popular with investment companies at various dates (see Fig. 6-13). In addition to information about the holdings of investment companies, Vickers sells information about the portfolios of college endowment funds and insurance companies.

6-6 BROKERAGE HOUSES

Brokerage offices usually carry one or more of the leading investment surveys which their customers may use. However, large brokerages maintain their own research department that provides information for their customers. The broker's research department disseminates publications, usually in the form of market newsletters or reviews, upon request. It makes analyses of industries and individual companies. Upon request some research departments will also analyze portfolios and make specific recommendations tailored to the customer's investment goals. A brokerage that is too small to maintain a research staff may use one of the research companies, such as Argus Research or Data Digests; sometimes they even use a newsletter from one of the larger brokerage houses.

All the leading brokerage houses have research departments. Some of the brokerages are:

Bache & Co.
Dean Witter & Co.
Kidder Peabody & Co.
Loeb Rhoades & Co.
Merrill Lynch, Pierce, Fenner & Smith (MLPFS)
O'Brien Associates, Inc.
Paine, Weber, Jackson & Curtis
Reynolds Securities, Inc.
Shearson Hayden Stone
Smith, Barney & Co.
Walston & Co.

Nearly every large city in the United States has a branch sales office of at least one of these firms. Each brokerage firm's research department produces slightly different reports. These booklets are mailed to anyone requesting them at no cost to attract customers.

Some brokerages have reputations as being "retailers," as opposed to being primarily an institutional brokerage or an investment banker. These retail brokerages sell primarily to the individual investor, the "little guy." In order to attract the small investor, they provide numerous services either free or at a minimum charge. MLPFS is the most prominent retail brokerage. Such firms frequently provide free services for their customers such as safe-deposit storage of securities, up-to-the-minute financial news, information about commodities and bonds as well as common stock, and collection of coupon interest on bonds held in safekeeping.

Although the large retail brokerages strive to maintain their good reputation for fair dealing, their salespeople's advice should not be followed with blind faith. Dishonest salespeople may "churn" their customers' accounts in order to maximize sales commissions. And brokerages have been known to push stocks that they have had a hand in underwriting, making them seem better than they actually are, or to place them ahead of more desirable securities with which the brokerage is not involved. The brokerages' publications enable the investor to get a quick look at the market and the particular brokerage's feelings about it. The wise investor, however, will never take the report of just one firm or investment service as "gospel" but will compare varying views before investing.

6-7 THE ISSUERS OF SECURITIES

One of the greatest sources of financial information is the firm itself. The filing, registration, and other statements required by the NYSE, the Securities and Exchange Commission,[18] the government agencies in charge of regulating various industries (such as the Civil Aeronautics Board, Interstate Commerce Commission, and Federal Communications Commission), and other institutions provide detailed information. Companies usually do not publish this information in their annual and quarterly reports. Such detailed information is of little real value to the casual investor but can be very useful to the professional analyst. Details about expenses, maintenance, interest, receivables, inventories, depreciation, sources and application of funds, employment costs, wasting assets, and treatment of nonrecurring special items are only a few of the things that are required by the SEC.

8-K, 9-K, 10-K, and Registration Statements

In accordance with regulation S-X dealing with "complete disclosure," the SEC requires four kinds of reports from firms whose securities are traded publicly. These forms deal with registration, periodic reporting, insider trading, and proxy solicitations. The 8-K form is a report which firms registered with the SEC are required to file each month in which any action occurs affecting the debt, equity, amount of capital assets, voting rights, or other aspects of the firm. The 9-K form is an unaudited report, required every 6 months, containing revenues, expenses, gross sales, and special items. The 10-K form is an annual version of the 9-K which must be certified by a certified public accountant.

The information in the 8-K, 9-K, and 10-K forms is only a portion of the information which a firm is required to register with the SEC when it plans to "go public." When preparing a primary issue of securities, the firm is required by the Securities Act of 1933 to make a full disclosure of additional information about the issuance of the new securities, the purpose for which the new capital is to be used, information about the management, and professional opinions about various aspects of the new undertaking. The firm is required to file a registration with the SEC at least 20 days

---

[18] For example, see Carl W. Schneider, "SEC Filings—Their Use to the Professional," *Financial Analysts Journal*, January–February 1965, pp. 33–37.

before it may sell its new securities. The first part of this registration statement is the *prospectus*. Prospectuses are available free to the public. The law requires that every investor who buys shares in a new issue be given a prospectus.

Bias in Annual Reports

Investors may also obtain information about a firm by reading its annual report or interviewing its executives. However, both these sources may be biased. Only events which have a favorable impact on the firm's prospects are discussed in most cases. Management is reluctant to publicize its errors.

6-8 ECONOMIC SUMMARIES AND FORECASTS

Much of the price movement in the average security is attributable to movements in the price level of the entire securities market.[19] Thus, if the level of the market indices can be forecasted, much information about the future prices of most securities will be provided. The turns in the market indices tend to lead the turns in the national economy by 2 to 6 months, sometimes more. Thus, forecasting the level and direction of the national economy accurately a year in advance will yield extremely useful information in predicting the direction of security price movements.

Bank Newsletters

The large banks publish newsletters on economic conditions. These reports usually focus on the general economic outlook, but they often also refer to the expected effects of their economic forecast upon the securities markets. Chase Manhattan Bank's *Business in Brief,* the Bank of New York's *General Business Indicators,* First National City Bank's *Monthly Economic Letter,* and Morgan Guarantee Trust Company of New York's *Morgan Guarantee Survey* are given away free upon request.

The *Federal Reserve Bulletin* is a monthly economic summary of economic data published by the Federal Reserve Board.[20] The *Bulletin* is one of the easiest sources to use for raw economic data on many topics. The St. Louis Federal Reserve Bank also publishes weekly and monthly economic newsletters which it sends to subscribers. These publications contain some of the best monetary economic analyses available to the public, and they are free of charge.

These bank newsletters are easy to read. Graphs and tables of numbers

[19] B. F. King, "Market and Industry Factors in Stock Price Behavior," *Journal of Business,* January 1966, pp. 139–190.
[20] Annual subscriptions cost $20 and may be obtained by writing to Division of Administrative Services, Board of Governors of the Federal Reserve System, Washington, D.C. 20551.

may be included, but mathematics and technical economics terms are used sparingly, if at all. The Federal Reserve Board also sells a *Historical Chart Book* and a *Monthly Chart Book* for $1.25 per copy. They contain over 100 pages of readable charts of economic and financial time series.

United States Government Summaries of Economic Data

Several summaries of macroeconomic data may be obtained from United States government sources. These studies furnish ready-made time series which can be used as a data base for forecasting.

The Department of Commerce publishes a monthly *Survey of Current Business* (SCB). The first part of the SCB is an evaluation of business conditions and developments. The second part is a statistical summary covering prices, wages, production, business activity, and many other factors. Subscriptions are $9 per year.

The investor can find a summary of the SCB data in *Long Term Economic Growth* (LTEG). The LTEG volume, published by the Census Bureau, contains numerous time series relating to economic conditions and is over 250 pages long. Copies may be obtained from the Department of Commerce for $2.75.[21]

The National Bureau of Economic Research (NBER) studies business cycles through its widely publicized indicators. Its findings are published by the Department of Commerce's Census Bureau. Each month *Business Conditions Digest* (BCD) publishes the NBER's table of economic indicators and charts their values along with other business data. The 30 leading indicators, 15 coincidental indicators, 7 lagging indicators, and 7 international comparisons are published in the first part of the issue along with other economic information and primary data. Analytical measures of diffusion, direction, and rate of change are found in BCD. The final section examines trends, cyclical indicators, and other data. Figure 6-14 shows the "Key to the Business Cycle Series," and Fig. 6-15 shows some of the data from the BCD. A 1-year BCD subscription costs $55.25.

The monthly *Economic Indicators* is a compendium of economic time series data and graphs sold for $3 per year. Figure 6-16 shows a typical page from *Economic Indicators*. It and the *Annual Economic Review* are published by the President's Council of Economic Advisers to discuss present economic conditions.

The Federal Trade Commission and the Securities and Exchange Commission publish the *Quarterly Financial Report for Manufacturing Corporations* (QFRMC). It contains aggregate balance sheet and income statement information for all manufacturing corporations. The "profits per dollar sales"

---

[21] SCB and LTEG may also be obtained from Superintendent of Documents, U.S. Government Printing Office, Washington, D.C. 20402.

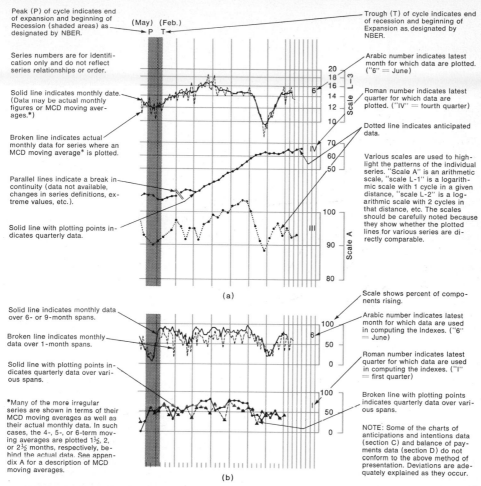

Peak (P) of cycle indicates end of expansion and beginning of Recession (shaded areas) as designated by NBER.

Series numbers are for identification only and do not reflect series relationships or order.

Solid line indicates monthly date. (Data may be actual monthly figures or MCD moving averages.*)

Broken line indicates actual monthly data for series where an MCD moving average* is plotted.

Parallel lines indicate a break in continuity (data not available, changes in series definitions, extreme values, etc.).

Solid line with plotting points indicates quarterly data.

Trough (T) of cycle indicates end of recession and beginning of Expansion as. designated by NBER.

Arabic number indicates latest month for which data are plotted. ("6" = June)

Roman number indicates latest quarter for which data are plotted. ("IV" = fourth quarter)

Dotted line indicates anticipated data.

Various scales are used to highlight the patterns of the individual series. "Scale A" is an arithmetic scale, "scale L-1" is a logarithmic scale with 1 cycle in a given distance, "scale L-2" is a logarithmic scale with 2 cycles in that distance, etc. The scales should be carefully noted because they show whether the plotted lines for various series are directly comparable.

(a)

Solid line indicates monthly data over 6- or 9-month spans.

Broken line indicates monthly data over 1-month spans.

Solid line with plotting points indicates quarterly data over various spans.

*Many of the more irregular series are shown in terms of their MCD moving averages as well as their actual monthly data. In such cases, the 4-, 5-, or 6-term moving averages are plotted 1½, 2, or 2½ months, respectively, behind the actual data. See appendix A for a description of MCD moving averages.

Scale shows percent of components rising.

Arabic number indicates latest month for which data are used in computing the indexes. ("6" = June)

Roman number indicates latest quarter for which data are used in computing the indexes. ("I" = first quarter)

Broken line with plotting points indicates quarterly data over various spans.

NOTE: Some of the charts of anticipations and intentions data (section C) and balance of payments data (section D) do not conform to the above method of presentation. Deviations are adequately explained as they occur.

(b)

FIG. 6-14 *Business Conditions Digest's* explanation of how to read its charts. (*a*) Basis data; (*b*) diffusion indices. (*Source:* U.S. Dept. of Commerce, U.S. Government Printing Office.)

and "annual rate of profit on stockholder's equity at end of period" are classified by industry and by asset size. When an investor is comparing different industries, this information can be quite helpful.

Most of the government publications are oriented toward the national economy and the effects of its cycles and fluctuations upon various industries. Such information is extremely useful to the trained investor in predicting the impact of future movements of the economy on security prices.

Economic Forecasts

Economic forecasts may be purchased from various consultants. One economic forecasting service is Wharton Econometric Forecasting Associates,

| Chart B8 | NBER SHORT LIST

Leading Indicators

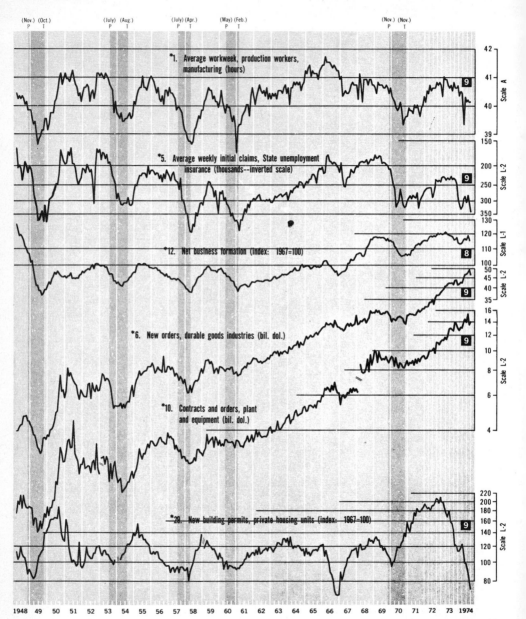

FIG. 6-15 Cyclical indications: Selected indicators by timing. National Bureau of Economic Research, short list. (From *Business Conditions Digest*, October 1974.)

GROSS NATIONAL PRODUCT OR EXPENDITURE

In the third quarter gross national product (seasonally adjusted) rose at an annual rate of 8.3 percent reflecting an inflation rate of 11.5 percent and a decline of 2.9 percent in real GNP.

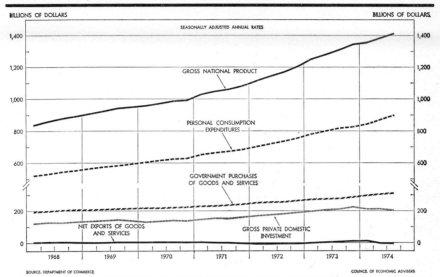

Period	Total gross national product in 1958 dollars	Total gross national product	Personal consumption expenditures	Gross private domestic investment	Net exports of goods and services	Government purchases of goods and services					Implicit price deflator for total GNP, 1958=100[2]
						Total	Federal			State and local	
							Total	National defense[1]	Other		
	Billions of dollars; quarterly data at seasonally adjusted annual rates										
1964	581.1	632.4	401.2	94.0	8.5	128.7	65.2	50.0	15.2	63.5	108.85
1965	617.8	684.9	432.8	108.1	6.9	137.0	66.9	50.1	16.8	70.1	110.86
1966	658.1	749.9	466.3	121.4	5.3	156.8	77.8	60.7	17.1	79.0	113.94
1967	675.2	793.9	492.1	116.6	5.2	180.1	90.7	72.4	18.4	89.4	117.59
1968	706.6	864.2	536.2	126.0	2.5	199.6	98.8	78.3	20.5	100.8	122.30
1969	725.6	930.3	579.5	139.0	1.9	210.0	98.8	78.4	20.4	111.2	128.20
1970	722.5	977.1	617.6	136.3	3.6	219.5	96.2	74.6	21.6	123.3	135.24
1971	746.3	1,054.9	667.1	153.7	−.2	234.2	97.6	71.2	26.5	136.6	141.35
1972	792.5	1,158.0	729.0	179.3	−6.0	255.7	104.9	74.8	30.1	150.8	146.12
1973	839.2	1,294.9	805.2	209.4	3.9	276.4	106.6	74.4	32.2	169.8	154.31
1973: I	832.8	1,248.9	781.7	199.0	−.8	269.0	106.4	75.0	31.4	162.6	149.95
II	837.4	1,277.9	799.0	205.1	.5	273.3	106.2	74.0	32.2	167.1	152.61
III	840.8	1,308.9	816.3	209.0	6.7	276.9	105.3	73.3	32.0	171.6	155.67
IV	845.7	1,344.0	823.9	224.5	9.3	286.4	108.4	75.3	33.1	177.9	158.93
1974: I	830.5	1,358.8	840.6	210.5	11.3	296.3	111.5	75.8	35.7	184.8	163.61
II	827.1	1,383.8	869.1	211.8	−1.5	304.4	114.3	76.6	37.7	190.1	167.31
III[2]	821.1	1,411.6	899.9	204.6	−4.1	311.2	116.4	78.8	37.7	194.8	171.92

[1] This category corresponds closely with budget outlays for national defense, shown on p. 36.
[2] Gross national product in current dollars divided by gross national product in 1958 dollars.

Source: Department of Commerce.

FIG. 6-16 A page from *Economic Indicators*, showing gross national product (GNP). (U.S. Government Printing Office, October 1974.)

Inc. (WEFA), a nonprofit corporation owned by the Wharton School of the University of Pennsylvania. WEFA offers a range of services based on its various econometric models. The cost varies with the service provided. For $1,500 per year annual forecasts, going into some detail, can be obtained. For $11,000 per year, WEFA furnishes a detailed quarterly forecast complete with consulting and educational services.

There are also commercial economic consulting services. For example, Data Resources, Inc., in Lexington, Massachusetts, sells its forecasting services. DRI, essentially a consulting firm for Harvard economics professors, has grown and employs people who are not affiliated with a university. DRI also has a time-sharing facility which may be leased by a user. This facility contains raw data and econometric software packages which enable users anywhere in the world to construct econometric models. Rapidata and Interactive Data Services, two other econometric time-sharing companies, are discussed below.

In addition to the academically related economic consultants, there are numerous purely commercial firms. Chase-Econometrics is a subsidiary of Chase Manhattan Bank's Holding Company, with its office in Bala Cynwyd, Pennsylvania. Lionel D. Edie & Co., Inc., a subsidiary of Merrill Lynch, Pierce, Fenner and Smith Brokerage with offices in New York City, specializes in investment counseling.

The commercial economic consultants typically specialize in speechmaking, answering questions, or solving specific problems, and they do not do much pure research. The academically related consultants are more research-oriented and specialize in forecasting and model-building. All these services are costly—they can easily purvey $20,000 worth of services per year. However, such a service is not costly when compared with the average business economist's salary, which alone was $30,000 per year (in 1973), and such economists are probably less competent than many consultants.

6-9 DATA FILES FOR COMPUTERS

As computers have progressed from the first-generation vacuum tube models through the third-generation models using integrated circuits, the cost per computation has dropped. During the same years the equipment and programs have advanced, making them easier to use. As a result, financial analysis in various forms is now being done by computer. Various firms market financial information in a form which may be read directly into a computer as raw input data.

The CRSP File

The Center for Research in Security Prices (CRSP) file is a magnetic tape which may be read on the tape-drive unit of a computer as raw input data. The tape contains monthly prices and quarterly dividends for every firm listed on the NYSE since 1926. The tape may be purchased from Standard & Poor's.[22] It can be updated periodically for an additional fee.

---

[22] 345 Hudson St., New York, N.Y. 10014.

ISL Tape

Interactive Data Corporation (IDC)[23] sells a quarterly magnetic computer tape with daily stock-trading volumes and prices, quarterly dividends and earnings for all NYSE and AMEX securities, and some OTC securities; it is called the ISL tape. The ISL tapes may be purchased and updated periodically. Data management can be a problem with the ISL tapes because, for example, 20 tapes must be used to obtain 5 years of observations on one stock.

Microfiche

Leasco Information Products has microfilmed the 10-K forms containing the annual audited financial information that firms file with the SEC. These microfilms are called Microfiche. The 10-K forms for over 5,000 firms can be obtained by purchasing the Microfiche service. Input devices for computers are available which can randomly access microfilm and read it as raw data.

Compustat Tapes

Investors Management Sciences, Inc. (IMSI)[24] sells a financial data file, called Compustat, on magnetic tape to be read by a computer's tape-drive input. The Compustat tapes contain over 20 years of annual data for more than 3,500 stocks. Quarterly data on 2,700 stocks from 1962 are also available. There are 60 balance sheet and income statement items for each company on the tapes. The tapes can be updated with current information each quarter for a fee.

PDE File

Investors Management Sciences, Inc., also has the PDE file which contains monthly stock prices, quarterly dividends per share, quarterly earnings per share, monthly trading volume, stock dividend or split information, book value per share, the stock exchange where the stock is traded, the Compustat file code number, the CUSIP number, industry number, and stock exchange ticker symbol for about 3,000 stocks. The tape also contains price, dividend, and earnings data on the various Standard & Poor's stock market indices. Purchasers of the Compustat annual and quarterly tapes may obtain the PDE tape almost free—the PDE data are essentially all taken from the Compustat tapes.

Wells Fargo Tape

The Trust Department of Wells Fargo Bank (a large California bank) has prepared a magnetic computer tape file of daily stock prices [in price plus

---

[23] 122 E. 42d St., New York, N.Y. 10017. IDC is a subsidiary of Chase Manhattan Bank.
[24] 7400 S. Alton Court, Englewood, Colo. 80110. IMSI is a subsidiary of McGraw-Hill Book Co.

dividend relative form, that is, $(p_t + d_t)/p_{t+1} = 1 + r_t]$ adjusted for stock splits for use in its investment management activiites. Copies of this tape, containing about 7 years of data from the 1960s, are used for research outside the bank. The Wells Fargo tape is essentially a well-organized ISL tape without the data on trading volume.

6-10 SOFTWARE SERVICES FOR COMPUTERS

In order to utilize exotic computer hardware and data files, computer programs (sometimes called software packages) are available to do routine tasks. Most of these programs can use one of the data files discussed in Sec. 6-9 as raw input data. The program reads the data file, performs the requested work, and prints out the results.

These software packages can usually be adapted to different computer systems. They calculate financial ratios, make interfirm and interindustry comparisons, do correlation and regression analysis, and perform other tasks which are essentially repetitive in nature.

Statistical Package for the Social Sciences (SPSS)

The Statistical Package for the Social Sciences (SPSS) is a large, well-documented package of computer programs for statistical analysis. The package contains routines to calculate descriptive statistics and make contingency tables, to do correlation analysis of various kinds, to plot scatter diagrams, and to do simple and multiple regression, discriminant analysis, analysis of variance, factor analysis, and scaling. These programs are written in various forms so that they are ready for use with IBM, CDC, Univac, or Xerox Sigma computers of various sizes. McGraw-Hill Book Company publishes a large paperback book documenting practically every phase of the SPSS package; the book is in its second edition and is easy to read.

The Bio-Med Package

The Bio-Med package, prepared for medical research at the University of California, Los Angeles (UCLA), is a widely used software package containing programs to do simple and multiple regression, analysis of variance, analysis of covariance, and linear multiple discriminant analysis. The excellent book of documentation which accompanies the Bio-Med programs rounds out a useful package which is employed in many business schools. It may be obtained at a low cost from UCLA.

Time-sharing Services

Time-sharing services are organizations which connect subscribers' computer terminals to their own computers via telephone lines. The services lease time and storage space on their computers and access to their own specialized software and raw data, and provide consulting assistance with which subscribers may do their own number-crunching (a popular nickname for numerical and/or statistical analysis). There is no fixed fee for connections to most time-sharing services, which charge only for services rendered. These services allow small users around the world to use multimillion-dollar computers, software, and data assemblies for a few thousand dollars per year.

Rapidata[25] and Interactive Data Corporation[26] are two large time-sharing services specializing in economic and financial work. Both firms have raw economic data bases consisting of daily, weekly, monthly, quarterly, semiannual, and annual series of observations on thousands of economic time series reaching in some cases years back into the past. Furthermore, if a subscriber acquires a data base not owned by the time-sharing organization (for example, the Compustat tapes explained earlier), the service will mount that data base onto its system for the subscriber's private use.

Rapidata and Interactive Data Corporation also have sophisticated econometric software packages to perform various tasks. And they have simple systems for noneconometricians. Thus, a business analyst can simply type a phrase as simple as "REGRESS STOCK MARKET INDEX ONTO GNP MONTHLY FROM MARCH 1965 TO 1975" into the office computer console and, within seconds, the computer will print out the statistics. Large city banks (such as Chase Manhattan), large brokerages (such as Merrill Lynch, Pierce, Fenner and Smith), large life insurance companies (such as Prudential), large economic research organizations (such as The Conference Board), governmental agencies (such as some Federal Reserve Banks), management consultants (such as McKinsey & Co.), mutual funds (such as Investors Diversified Services), and investment counseling firms (such as Value Line), are subscribers to time-sharing services.

Computer Services for "Soft Dollars"

Some stock brokerage firms, such as O'Brien Associates, Inc.,[27] specialize in econometric stock market research. And some large brokerages, such as Merrill Lynch, Pierce, Fenner and Smith, have departments headed by vice presidents in charge of econometric investments services for their customers. Such brokerages will provide econometric studies if the portfolio managers who are their customers sign an agreement to provide them a certain amount of commission income (called *soft dollars,* since portfolio managers must incur commission expenses to operate whether or not they receive the research).

---

[25] 350 Fifth Ave., New York, N.Y. 10001.
[26] 122 E. 42d St., New York, N.Y. 10017.
[27] 717 Third Ave., New York, N.Y. 10017.

QUESTIONS

1 "The financial newspapers contain analytical studies aimed at determining the cause and effect relationships between various economic variables." True, false, or uncertain? Explain.

2 Write an essay which (*a*) explains the construction of the New York Stock Exchange index and the SP composite index; and (*b*) compares and contrasts these two indices. This task will require outside research.

3 Select some publicly traded security and compare the reports on that firm found in (*a*) *Standard & Poor's Stock Market Encyclopedia,* (*b*) *Moody's Handbook of Common Stocks,* and (*c*) *Value Line Survey.* Write a page explaining significant differences in these three reports. This assignment will require outside research.

4 Write a short essay explaining and contrasting Moody's Aa bond rating with Standard & Poor's AA bond rating. This will require outside research.

5 If an investor were interested in buying shares in a mutual fund, where could she find some information upon which to base her decision?

6 If you have to prepare a graph of AAA-grade corporate bond yields showing the path of this interest-rate time series monthly for the last 10 years, where could you find the raw data quickly, easily, and inexpensively?

7 Assume you are the senior vice president in charge of the trust department at a very large commercial bank (such as the Wells Fargo Bank in California or the Mellon National Bank in Pittsburgh, which have both already faced this question). How would you effectively manage the multimillion dollars of OPM (the popular term for "other people's money") entrusted to your department at a charge of one-half of 1 percent of the total value of these assets per year, and keep your research costs low enough to show a profit?

PART TWO

BOND PRICES

The preceding six chapters focused on the institutional arrangements which compose the investment setting in the United States. An investor should possess a familiarity with these arrangements in order to know *where* to invest, *who* the people in the investment industry are, *what* alternative investments are available, and *what* rules govern the conduct of investors. After these who, what, and where questions are answered, the *why* questions arise. These questions are more difficult because their answers require abstract concepts. The remaining chapters deal with the *why* questions.

Two of the most basic *why* questions are, "Why does a security have a particular price?" and "Why does a security's price change?" Chapters 7 and 8 answer these valuation questions for the type of security whose price is simplest to explain — bonds.

The price of a bond equals the present value of all the income coming to the bond's owner — it is that simple. Thus, the prices of bonds can be understood once the present value concept is understood. The present value concept is explained in Mathematical Appendix D rather than in the chapter itself because many readers learned present value theory in a previous finance or economics course. Chapter 7 shows how the present value concept is applied to bond valuation and discusses the determination of a bond's quality rating. Then Chap. 8 explains the determination of market interest rates. An understanding of the market interest rates is essential because they are the discount rates which are used in determining the present value of bonds. Part 3 (Chaps. 9 through 12) explains the more complicated factors determining the prices of common stocks. Essentially, however, stock prices are the present value of their income too. Thus, Chap. 7 and Mathematical Appendix D should be mastered before proceeding to common stock valuation.

Seven

Bond Valuation

One of the major problems of investment management involves determining whether the market prices of individual securities are too high or too low. If an asset is purchased for more than it is worth, its rate of return will be too low for the amount of risk it bears, investors will sell it, and it will probably suffer capital losses. On the other hand, underpriced assets are likely to experience capital gains and have rates of return which are unusually high. If investment managers are to avoid the overpriced assets and profit from the underpriced assets, they must be able to estimate the value of a security so that they will be able to tell if it is overpriced or underpriced.

Various formulas and models which show how to estimate the value of an asset are presented in this text. The models and formulas grow increasingly sophisticated as the chapters progress. To begin with, the simplest valuation model—the formulas for valuing a certain stream of cashflows such as might be received from a U.S. Treasury bond, for example—is explicated.

Before even the simplest valuation model is presented, however, a common element found in all valuation models must be understood. Either implicitly or explicitly, all valuation models consider the *time value of money*. Therefore, the *present value* calculations resulting from the fact that money has time value should be reviewed by those who are not already familiar with such computations. Mathematical Appendix D at the end of this book discusses the present value concept.

7-1 VALUING A RISKLESS BOND

There is a large and flourishing market in marketable U.S. Treasury bonds (which are different from the nonmarketable U.S. savings bonds). The prices of these marketable pieces of the national debt vary from day to day; they are published daily in many newspapers. Figure 7-1 is an excerpt from *The Wall Street Journal* which shows the prices of marketable Treasury bonds.

The first column of the newspaper excerpt gives each bond issue's coupon interest rate. The coupon interest rate, denoted i, applies to the bond's face value. Many U.S. Treasury bonds are sold in $1,000 denominations; that is, their face value, denoted F hereafter, is $1,000. Thus, a $1,000 face value bond (that is, $F = \$1,000$) which has a $3\frac{1}{2}$ percent coupon rate (namely, $i = 3.5$ percent) pays $35 interest ($iF = 3.5$ percent $\times$ $1,000) per year every year until it matures and repays its principal of $F = \$1,000$ to its owner. The bond's maturity dates are the year and month shown in the second and third columns of the newspaper excerpt.

The fourth and fifth columns in Fig. 7-1 give the bid (that is, the highest price a potential buyer has bid) and ask (the lowest offering) prices stated as fractions of each bond's face value. The numbers to the right of the decimal places in the bid and asked prices are the number of thirty-seconds of a percentage point. For example, suppose the bid price of some bond is shown as 72.8 in Fig. 7-1. This refers to $72\frac{8}{32}$ percent of the bond's face value. Thus, the bid price of the $1,000 bond is $72\frac{8}{32}$, or 72.25 percent of its face value. So, a $1,000 face value bond is bid at $722.50; similarly, a $10,000 face value denomination is bid at $7,225. The sixth column is the change in the asked price since the close of the previous trading day. A +.4 change, for example, means the bid price is up four thirty-seconds of a percentage point over the previous day. The seventh column gives the bond's yield to maturity.

A bond's yield to maturity can be interpreted as the bond's average compounded rate of return if it is bought at the current asked price and if all interest receipts are immediately reinvested at a rate equal to the yield to maturity and held there until the bond matures and the face value is repaid. That is, the *yield to maturity* is the discount rate that equates the present value of all cashflows to the purchase price of the bond (like the internal rate of return in capital budgeting).

To show how to determine the value of a bond, a hypothetical U.S. Treasury bond like the $3\frac{1}{2}$'s of 1998 will be analyzed.[1] This bond's present

---

[1] If the bond were purchased between the dates when the semiannual interest payment occurred, the seller would receive accrued interest from the party purchasing the bond. For example, if the bond were sold 3 months after a semiannual interest payment, the purchaser would pay the market price of the bond on that date plus half the $17.50 interest earned but not yet received by the party selling the bond. Consideration of accrued interest will not be discussed in this chapter for the sake of simplicity. Ignoring the accrued interest introduces an approximation into the calculations.

Thursday, March 27, 1975

Over-the-Counter Quotations: Source on request.
Decimals in bid-and-asked and bid changes represent
32nds (101.1 means 101 1-32). a-Plus 1-64. b-Yield to call
date. d-Minus 1-64.

Treasury Bonds and Notes

Rate	Mat	Date		Bid	Asked	Bid Chg.	Yld.
5⅞s,	1975	May n	....	99.30	100.2	.....	5.24
6s,	1975	May n	....	99.31	100.3	.....	5.11
5⅞s,	1975	Aug n	....	99.30	100.2	.....	5.66
8⅜s,	1975	Sep n	....	101.4	101.8	− .1	5.79
7s,	1975	Nov n	....	100.19	100.23	.....	5.81
7s,	1975	Dec n	....	100.20	100.24	− .1	5.96
5⅞s,	1976	Feb n	....	99.21	99.25	.....	6.14
6¼s,	1976	Feb n	....	99.31	100.7	.....	5.99
8s,	1976	Mar n	....	101.21	101.25	+ .1	6.13
5¾s,	1976	May n	....	99.9	99.17	.....	6.19
6½s,	1976	May n	....	100.6	100.14	.....	6.09
6s,	1976	May n	....	99.20	99.22	.....	6.20
8¾s,	1976	Jun n	....	102.24	103.0	.....	6.14
6½s,	1976	Aug n	....	100.2	100.10	+ .1	6.26
7½s,	1976	Aug n	....	101.10	101.18	.....	6.30
5⅞s,	1976	Aug n	....	99.4	99.8	+ .1	6.45
8¼s,	1976	Sep n	....	102.10	102.14	− .2	6.51
6¼s,	1976	Nov n	....	99.15	99.23	− .1	6.43
7¼s,	1976	Dec n	....	100.29	101.0	− .1	6.60
8s,	1977	Feb n	....	102.8	102.16	.....	6.57
6s,	1977	Feb n	....	98.22	98.26	− .1	6.68
6½s,	1977	Mar n	....	99.20	99.22	+ .1	6.72
6⅞s,	1977	May n	....	100.2	100.10	− .1	6.71
9s,	1977	May n	....	104.10	104.18	− .1	6.66
7¾s,	1977	Aug n	....	101.31	102.7	− .1	6.72
7¾s,	1977	Nov n	....	101.30	102.6	− .3	6.82
6¼s,	1978	Feb n	....	98.0	98.8	+ .2	6.93
7⅛s,	1978	May n	....	100.2	100.6	.....	7.05
8¾s,	1978	Aug n	....	104.24	105.0	.....	7.06
6s,	1978	Nov n	....	96.12	96.20	− .1	7.07
7⅞s,	1979	May n	....	101.30	102.6	− .2	7.25
6¼s,	1979	Aug n	....	96.20	96.28	+ .2	7.09
6⅝s,	1979	Nov n	....	97.24	98.0	+ .2	7.14
7s,	1979	Nov n	....	98.30	99.6	.....	7.21
4s,	1980	Feb	....	86.30	87.30	+ .2	6.96
6⅞s,	1980	May n	....	97.23	97.31	+ .1	7.36
9s,	1980	Aug n	....	106.16	106.24	.....	7.45
3½s,	1980	Nov	....	83.16	84.16	.....	6.87
7s,	1981	Feb n	....	97.10	97.18	.....	7.52
7⅜s,	1981	Feb n	....	98.24	98.28	+ .3	7.62
7s,	1981	Aug	....	98.2	99.2	− .2	7.19
7¾s,	1981	Nov n	....	100.10	100.14	+ .3	7.67
6⅜s,	1982	Feb	....	94.10	95.10	− .8	7.25
3¼s,	1978-83	Jun	....	77.8	78.8	+ .4	6.75
6⅜s,	1984	Aug	....	94.26	95.26	+ .2	6.99
3¼s,	1985	May	....	76.18	77.18	+ .4	6.28
4¼s,	1975-85	May	....	79.26	80.26	+ .2	6.92
6⅛s,	1986	Nov	....	91.26	92.26	.....	7.04
3½s,	1990	Feb	....	76.20	77.20	+ .4	5.75
8¼s,	1990	May	....	99.30	100.2	+ .10	8.24
4¼s,	1987-92	Aug	....	77.16	78.16	− .4	6.30
4s,	1988-93	Feb	....	77.2	78.2	+ .2	6.02
6¾s,	1993	Feb	....	88.26	89.26	+ .2	7.81
7½s,	1988-93	Aug	....	94.24	95.24	+ .6	7.94
4⅛s,	1989-94	May	....	77.16	78.16	+ .4	6.04
3s,	1995	Feb	....	76.20	77.20	+ .4	4.75
7s,	1993-98	May	....	89.18	90.18	− .2	7.90
3½s,	1998	Nov	....	76.18	77.18	+ .4	5.15
8½s,	1994-99	May	....	101.30	102.30	+ .10	8.20
7⅞s,	1995-00	Feb	....	96.0	96.8	+ .10	8.26
n− Treasury Notes.							

FIG. 7-1 U.S. Treasury bond data for March 27, 1975. (From *The Wall Street Journal,* March 28, 1975.)

value will be found, assuming that 5 percent is the yield to maturity. That is, the market yield of 5 percent will be used as the discount rate. Let i denote the coupon rate of interest, the annual rate of interest printed on the face of the bond. The dollars of interest per year paid on the bond is i times F (that is, 3.5 percent $\times$ \$1,000), or \$35 per year. This bond pays its $3\frac{1}{2}$ percent coupon rate in semiannual payments of \$17.50 for a bond with a face value of $F = \$1,000$. Thus, the "period" is 6 months. Assume there are exactly fifty 6-month periods until the bond matures and the face value of $1,000 is received. The appropriate market rate of return or discount rate is $k = 5$ percent per annum, or 2.5 percent per 6-month period.[2]

The notation $D_k{}^n$ indicates the discount factor for cashflows received n periods in the future and discounted at a rate k. Symbolically, $D_k{}^n = 1/(1 + k)^n$. Present value tables (for example, Table D-1 in Part 7) contain values for $D_k{}^n$ for numerous values for n and k. The cashflows in the tth period, denoted c_t, are $c_t = \$17.50$ for periods $1, 2, \ldots, 49$ plus $c_{50} = \$1,017.50$ when the bond matures. The present value of these cashflows is calculated in Eq. (7-1). (See Mathematical Appendix A, in Part 7, for an explanation of the summation sign if needed.) Mathematically, the problem is to find the present value, denoted v_0.

$$v_0 = \sum_{t=1}^{50} c_t D_k{}^t$$

$$= \sum_{t=1}^{50} 17.50 D^t_{.025} + \$1,000 D^{50}_{.025}$$

$$= \$17.50 (D^1_{.025} + D^2_{.025} + \cdots + D^{50}_{.025}) + \$1,000 D^{50}_{.025}$$
$$= \$17.50 \ (28.36) + \$1,000 \ (.2909)$$
$$= \$496.33 + \$290.90 = \$787.23$$

The present value of $\$787.23$ will be the asked price of the $3\frac{1}{2}$ percent coupon U.S. Treasury bonds maturing in November 1998 on November 30, 1973 (that is, fifty 6-month periods, or 25 years before maturity) if the market-determined yield to maturity is 5 percent on November 30, 1973. The market price of the bond, denoted p_0, should not deviate 1 cent from this present value if the market interest rate is 5 percent, $r^{25\,\text{years}}_{1978} = 5$ percent, that is, $p_0 = v_0$.

In practice, a bond may actually be traded at any price between the bid and asked prices. The reason is that the actual yield may vary a few hundredths of 1 percent (these hundredths of a percentage point are called *basis points*) from day to day as the market yields vary. But the teaching point has been made and is restated succinctly: Since all the cashflows from a U.S. Treasury bond investment are known in advance, the bond's value (and thus its market price) is determined by the market interest rates, that is, the yield to maturity. The bond's market price will not remain above its value because investors will sell it and drive its price down until the price equals its present value. And likewise, the price will not be below the bond's present value because the price would be bid up until it equaled the present value by investors who know how to calculate bond values.

[2] The rate of 2.5 percent is used in order that printed present value tables for 2.5 percent may be used.

7-2 BOND PRICES AND INTEREST RATES

U.S. Treasury bonds contain no financial risk and offer no opportunity for growth in their contractual income; therefore, these factors do not affect their prices.[3] However, the discount rate k and the term to maturity n do vary and do affect the prices of Treasury bonds and other bonds. The following discussion shows how bond prices are affected by the discount rate and the term to maturity, and how to calculate bond values, using several different methods.

Bond Tables

Tables have been prepared to show the correct price for a bond of any given term to maturity and any appropriate market interest rate. Figure 7-2 shows a page from a book of bond tables for bonds with $3\frac{1}{2}$ percent coupon rates.[4] The values in this table show the percentage of face value for which bonds with a $3\frac{1}{2}$ percent coupon rate should sell if they are to yield the rate shown in the left column.

The values in this table are calculated using Eq. (7-1), as shown in the preceding example. By the use of bond tables, the tedious present value calculations may be avoided. The bond tables may be used for two problems. If the term to maturity is known, the bond tables can be used to look up (1) the bond price if the yield to maturity is known, or (2) the yield to maturity if the market price is known.

Formulas for Bond Yields

When it is necessary to determine the yield to maturity of a bond, three methods may be used. First, if a bond table is available, the yield may be quickly and easily found for a given price and maturity. The second way to determine yields is more cumbersome. The yield to maturity for a bond is the discount rate which equates the present value of all net cashflows to the cost of the investment. Since the coupon interest iF, the face value F, the purchase price p_0, and the cashflows c_t are *known* quantities, Eq. (7-1) may be solved[5] for the exact yield $r_0{}^n$. The term $r_0{}^n$ denotes the yield to maturity at time period $t = 0$ (that is, the "present" time) of a bond which has n

---

[3] No asset is completely riskless. In inflation some government bonds have negative real return sometimes. However, we shall pass over these considerations until later.

[4] Technically, bond tables are appropriate for corporate and municipal bonds but not for U.S. Treasury bonds; the number of days in the semiannual periods are counted slightly differently. However, the differences are worth considering only for transactions involving millions of dollars of short-term bonds. This difference is the reason the present value of the bond in the preceding numerical calculation is $787.23 but is found to be $787.30 if the bond table is used.

[5] Because of the difficulties involved in evaluating an nth root, Eq. (7-1) is usually solved by a trial-and-error procedure using different values of r until the correct one is found which yields the desired equality. Such computations are usually done by computer.

3½%	23 YEARS			24 YEARS				25 YEARS			3½%
Yield	even	3 mo	6 mo	9 mo	even	3 mo	6 mo	9 mo	even	3 mo	6 mo	9 mo
1.00	151.25	151.75	152.24	152.73	153.23	153.71	154.20	154.69	155.18	155.66	156.15	156.63
1.10	148.65	149.12	149.58	150.04	150.50	150.96	151.42	151.88	152.33	152.79	153.24	153.69
1.20	146.11	146.54	146.98	147.41	147.84	148.27	148.70	149.12	149.55	149.97	150.40	150.82
1.30	143.61	144.02	144.43	144.83	145.23	145.63	146.03	146.43	146.83	147.22	147.62	148.01
1.40	141.17	141.55	141.93	142.30	142.68	143.05	143.43	143.80	144.17	144.53	144.90	145.27
1.50	138.78	139.13	139.49	139.83	140.18	140.53	140.88	141.22	141.57	141.91	142.25	142.59
1.60	136.44	136.77	137.09	137.42	137.74	138.06	138.38	138.70	139.02	139.34	139.66	139.97
1.70	134.15	134.45	134.75	135.05	135.35	135.65	135.95	136.24	136.54	136.83	137.12	137.41
1.80	131.90	132.18	132.46	132.73	133.01	133.28	133.56	133.83	134.10	134.37	134.64	134.91
1.90	129.70	129.96	130.21	130.47	130.72	130.97	131.23	131.47	131.72	131.97	132.22	132.46
2.00	127.55	127.78	128.02	128.25	128.48	128.71	128.94	129.17	129.40	129.62	129.85	130.07
2.10	125.43	125.65	125.86	126.07	126.29	126.49	126.71	126.91	127.12	127.33	127.53	127.73
2.20	123.37	123.56	123.75	123.95	124.14	124.33	124.52	124.71	124.90	125.08	125.27	125.45
2.30	121.34	121.51	121.69	121.86	122.04	122.21	122.38	122.55	122.72	122.88	123.05	123.22
2.40	119.36	119.51	119.67	119.82	119.98	120.13	120.29	120.44	120.59	120.74	120.89	121.03
2.50	117.41	117.55	117.69	117.83	117.97	118.10	118.24	118.37	118.51	118.64	118.77	118.90
2.60	115.63	115.75	115.87	115.99	116.11	116.23	116.35	116.47	116.58	116.70	116.81	116.93
2.70	113.64	113.74	113.85	113.96	114.06	114.16	114.27	114.37	114.48	114.57	114.68	114.77
2.80	111.81	111.90	111.99	112.08	112.17	112.26	112.35	112.43	112.52	112.61	112.69	112.78
2.90	110.02	110.09	110.17	110.24	110.32	110.39	110.47	110.54	110.62	110.69	110.76	110.83
3.00	108.26	108.32	108.39	108.45	108.51	108.57	108.63	108.69	108.75	108.81	108.87	108.92
3.10	106.54	106.59	106.64	106.69	106.74	106.78	106.83	106.87	106.92	106.97	107.01	107.06
3.20	104.86	104.89	104.93	104.96	105.00	105.03	105.07	105.10	105.14	105.17	105.20	105.23
3.30	103.21	103.23	103.25	103.27	103.30	103.32	103.34	103.36	103.39	103.40	103.43	103.45
3.40	101.59	101.59	101.61	101.62	101.63	101.64	101.65	101.66	101.68	101.68	101.70	101.70
3.50	100.00	100.00	100.00	100.00	100.00	100.00	100.00	100.00	100.00	100.00	100.00	100.00
3.60	98.44	98.43	98.42	98.41	98.40	98.39	98.38	98.37	98.36	98.35	98.34	98.33
3.70	96.92	96.90	96.88	96.85	96.84	96.81	96.80	96.77	96.76	96.76	96.72	96.69
3.80	95.43	95.39	95.36	95.33	95.30	95.27	95.24	95.21	95.19	95.15	95.13	95.10
3.90	93.96	93.92	93.88	93.84	93.80	93.76	93.72	93.68	93.65	93.61	93.57	93.53
4.00	92.53	92.47	92.43	92.38	92.33	92.28	92.24	92.19	92.14	92.09	92.05	92.00
4.10	91.12	91.06	91.00	90.94	90.89	90.83	90.78	90.72	90.67	90.61	90.56	90.51
4.20	89.74	89.67	89.61	89.54	89.48	89.41	89.35	89.29	89.23	89.16	89.11	89.04
4.30	88.39	88.31	88.24	88.16	88.10	88.02	87.96	87.88	87.82	87.75	87.68	87.61
4.40	87.06	86.98	86.90	86.82	86.74	86.66	86.59	86.51	86.44	86.36	86.29	86.21
4.50	85.76	85.67	85.59	85.50	85.42	85.33	85.25	85.16	85.08	85.00	84.92	84.84
4.60	84.49	84.39	84.30	84.20	84.11	84.02	83.93	83.84	83.76	83.67	83.59	83.50
4.70	83.24	83.13	83.04	82.93	82.84	82.74	82.65	82.55	82.46	82.36	82.28	82.18
4.80	82.01	81.90	81.80	81.69	81.59	81.48	81.39	81.28	81.19	81.09	81.00	80.90
4.90	80.81	80.69	80.59	80.50	80.37	80.26	80.16	80.04	79.95	79.84	79.74	79.64
5.00	79.63	79.51	79.40	79.28	79.17	79.05	78.95	78.83	78.73	78.62	78.52	78.41
5.10	78.48	78.35	78.23	78.11	78.00	77.87	77.76	77.64	77.54	77.42	77.31	77.20
5.20	77.35	77.21	77.09	76.96	76.84	76.72	76.60	76.48	76.37	76.25	76.14	76.02
5.30	76.24	76.10	75.97	75.84	75.72	75.58	75.47	75.34	75.22	75.10	74.98	74.86
5.40	75.15	75.00	74.87	74.73	74.61	74.47	74.35	74.22	74.10	73.97	73.86	73.73
5.50	74.08	73.93	73.80	73.65	73.53	73.39	73.26	73.12	73.00	72.87	72.75	72.62
5.60	73.03	72.88	72.74	72.59	72.46	72.32	72.19	72.05	71.93	71.79	71.67	71.54
5.70	72.00	71.85	71.71	71.56	71.42	71.27	71.14	71.00	70.87	70.73	70.61	70.48
5.80	70.99	70.83	70.69	70.54	70.40	70.25	70.12	69.97	69.84	69.70	69.57	69.44
5.90	70.00	69.84	69.70	69.54	69.40	69.25	69.11	68.96	68.83	68.69	68.56	68.42
6.00	69.03	68.87	68.72	68.56	68.42	68.26	68.12	67.97	67.84	67.69	67.56	67.42
6.10	68.08	67.91	67.76	67.60	67.45	67.30	67.16	67.00	66.87	66.72	66.59	66.44
6.20	67.14	66.98	66.82	66.66	66.51	66.35	66.21	66.05	65.91	65.76	65.63	65.48
6.30	66.23	66.06	65.90	65.74	65.59	65.42	65.28	65.12	64.98	64.83	64.69	64.55
6.40	65.33	65.15	65.00	64.83	64.68	64.52	64.37	64.21	64.07	63.91	63.78	63.63
6.50	64.45	64.27	64.11	63.94	63.79	63.62	63.48	63.32	63.17	63.02	62.88	62.73
6.60	63.58	63.40	63.24	63.07	62.92	62.75	62.62	62.44	62.29	62.14	62.00	61.85
6.70	62.73	62.55	62.39	62.22	62.06	61.89	61.74	61.58	61.43	61.28	61.14	60.98
6.80	61.90	61.72	61.55	61.38	61.22	61.05	60.90	60.74	60.59	60.43	60.29	60.14
6.90	61.08	60.90	60.73	60.56	60.40	60.23	60.08	59.91	59.76	59.60	59.46	59.31
7.00	60.27	60.09	59.93	59.75	59.59	59.42	59.27	59.10	58.95	58.79	58.65	58.49
7.10	59.48	59.30	59.14	58.96	58.80	58.63	58.47	58.31	58.16	58.00	57.85	57.70
7.20	58.71	58.53	58.36	58.18	58.02	57.85	57.69	57.53	57.38	57.22	57.07	56.92
7.30	57.95	57.77	57.60	57.42	57.26	57.09	56.94	56.76	56.61	56.45	56.31	56.15
7.40	57.21	57.02	56.85	56.67	56.51	56.34	56.18	56.01	55.87	55.70	55.56	55.40
7.50	56.47	56.29	56.12	55.94	55.78	55.60	55.45	55.28	55.13	54.97	54.83	54.67
7.60	55.76	55.57	55.40	55.22	55.06	54.88	54.73	54.56	54.41	54.25	54.10	53.95
7.70	55.05	54.86	54.69	54.51	54.35	54.18	54.02	53.85	53.70	53.54	53.40	53.24
7.80	54.36	54.17	54.00	53.82	53.66	53.48	53.33	53.16	53.01	52.85	52.71	52.55
7.90	53.68	53.49	53.32	53.14	52.98	52.80	52.65	52.48	52.33	52.17	52.03	51.87
8.00	53.01	52.82	52.65	52.47	52.31	52.14	51.98	51.81	51.67	51.50	51.36	51.20
8.10	52.35	52.17	52.00	51.82	51.66	51.48	51.33	51.16	51.01	50.85	50.71	50.55
8.20	51.71	51.52	51.35	51.17	51.01	50.84	50.68	50.52	50.37	50.21	50.07	49.91
8.30	51.08	50.89	50.72	50.54	50.38	50.21	50.05	49.89	49.74	49.58	49.44	49.28
8.40	50.46	50.27	50.10	49.92	49.76	49.59	49.44	49.27	49.12	48.96	48.82	48.67
8.50	49.85	49.66	49.49	49.31	49.15	48.98	48.83	48.66	48.52	48.36	48.22	48.06
8.60	49.25	49.06	48.90	48.72	48.56	48.38	48.23	48.07	47.92	47.76	47.63	47.47
8.70	48.66	48.47	48.31	48.13	47.97	47.80	47.65	47.48	47.34	47.18	47.04	46.89
8.80	48.08	47.90	47.73	47.55	47.40	47.22	47.08	46.91	46.77	46.61	46.47	46.32
8.90	47.51	47.33	47.17	46.99	46.83	46.66	46.51	46.35	46.21	46.05	45.91	45.76
9.00	46.96	46.77	46.61	46.43	46.28	46.11	45.96	45.80	45.65	45.50	45.36	45.21

FIG. 7-2 One page from a bond table.

years to maturity. When the superscript equals zero, $r_n{}^0$, the bond matures and its life ends. Mathematically, the problem is to solve Eq. (7-1) for $r_0{}^n$ given p_0, n, F, the c_t's, and i.

$$p_0 = \sum_{t=1}^{n} \frac{c_t}{(1 + r_0{}^n)^t} \tag{7-1}$$

$$= \sum_{t=1}^{n-1} \frac{iF}{(1 + r)^t} + \frac{F(1 + i)}{(1 + r_0{}^n)^n} \tag{7-1a}$$

A third method may be used to find an approximation of a bond's yield. Equation (7-2) approximates the yield per annum to maturity.

$$r_0{}^n = \frac{\text{average capital gain or loss per year} + \text{coupon interest per year}}{\text{average investment}}$$

$$\tag{7-2}$$

$$r_0{}^n = \frac{(F - p_0)/n + iF}{(p_0 + F)/2} \tag{7-2a}$$

where n = number of years to maturity

p_0 = purchase price (also the present value if the bond is correctly priced)

i = coupon rate per annum

For example, for the $3\frac{1}{2}$'s of 1998, the approximate yield to maturity is calculated as shown below, assuming there are $n = 25$ years till it matures and the market price is \$800 for a \$1,000 bond.

$$r_0{}^n = \frac{(\$1,000 - \$800)/25 + 3.5\% \ (\$1,000)}{(\$800 + \$1,000)/2} \tag{7-2b}$$

$$= \frac{\$200/25 \text{ years} + \$35}{(\$800 + \$1,000)/2}$$

$$= \frac{\$8 + \$35}{\$900} = \frac{\$43}{\$900} = .0477 = 4.77\% \text{ approximate yield to maturity}$$

The error of $(.0487 - .0477 = .0010 =)$ 10 basis points is why Eq. (7-2) yields only approximations.

Equation (7-2) may also be solved for p_0 and used to estimate the market price for a given yield.

The Reinvestment Rate

As mentioned above, calculations of a bond's yield to maturity are based on the assumption that all cashflows throughout the bond's life (namely, the

TABLE 7-1 AN 8 PERCENT NONCALLABLE 20-YEAR BOND BOUGHT AT 100 TO YIELD 8 PERCENT

Interest-on-interest						Total
Reinvest-ment rate, %	% of total return	Amount, $	Coupon income, $	Capital gain or discount	Total return, $	realized compound yield, %
0	0	0	1,600	0	1,600	4.84
5	41	1,096	1,600	0	2,696	6.64
6	47	1,416	1,600	0	3,016	7.07
7	53	1,782	1,600	0	3,382	7.53
8†	58†	2,201†	1,600†	0	3,801†	8.00†
9	63	2,681	1,600	0	4,281	8.50
10	67	3,232	1,600	0	4,832	9.01

† Yield from Yield Book.

coupon interest) are immediately reinvested at the yield to maturity. Of course, this assumption is not always true; the interest income might be consumed, for example, rather than reinvested. This is equivalent to reinvesting the funds at a zero rate of return, and the realized yield to maturity will be reduced accordingly.

To see the effects of different reinvestment rates on a bond's realized yield to maturity, Table 7-1 has been calculated. Table 7-1 shows the total realized compounded rate (that is, the effective yield to maturity) for an 8 percent coupon ($i = 8$ percent $= .08$) bond bought at face value 20 years before it matured. This table shows that only 4.84 percent total yield is realized if the coupon interest is not reinvested. But the same bond has a realized total yield of 9.01 percent if the coupons are reinvested at 10 percent. This shows the importance of the reinvestment opportunities and highlights an often-ignored source of a bond risk: the reinvestment rate risk can cause a bond's realized yield to vary.

Bond Price Theorems

Equation (7-1) may be represented graphically for some specific bond. For example, a bond with $i = 3$ percent coupon rate and $F = \$1,000$ face value is graphed in Fig. 7-3 for $0 \leqslant n \leqslant \infty$ and $r = 2$, 3, and 4 percent.

The following five theorems about the relationship of bond prices and yield to maturity may be discerned from graphs[6] such as those in Fig. 7-3.

1 Bond prices p_0 move inversely to bond yields, $\delta p_0 / \delta r_0{}^n < 0$.

2 For any given difference between the coupon rate i and the yield to maturity, the accompanying price change will be greater the longer the term to maturity n.

[6] These theorems were derived formally by B. G. Malkiel, "Expectations, Bond Prices, and the Term Structure of Interest Rates," *Quarterly Journal of Economics*, May 1962, pp. 197–218.

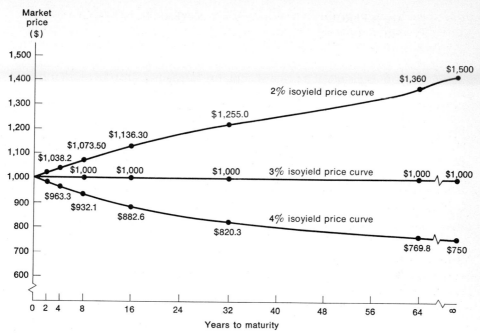

FIG. 7-3 Market prices for a 3 percent coupon, $1,000 face value bond as maturity varies at discount rates of 2, 3, and 4 percent (compounded semiannually).

3 The percentage price changes described in theorem 2 increase at a diminishing rate as n increases.

4 For any given maturity, a decrease in yields causes a capital gain which is larger than the capital loss resulting from an equal increase in yields.[7]

5 The higher the coupon rate i on a bond, the smaller will be the percentage price change for any given change in yields (except for 1-year and perpetual bonds).

Price Speculation with Riskless Treasury Bonds

Figure 7-1 shows that the market price of marketable U.S. Treasury bonds, which are probably the most riskless assets in the world, vary significantly from their face values. For example, the $3\frac{1}{2}$'s of 1998 were selling at the asked price of $762 per $1000 face value on March 27, 1975. This $762 price was deeply discounted below the bond's face value because market interest rates were high above the bond's coupon rate. If purchased for $762 and held to maturity, the bond offered a capital gain of ($1,000 − $762 =) $238. The bond could also be sold to another investor before it matures at whatever the market price is at that time. In any event, there is an opportunity for

---

[7] This assumes yields change from the same starting value whether they move up or down.

price speculators to profit by trading in U.S. government bonds. Let us consider the implications of the five bond price theorems for a speculator.

As theorem 1 stated, the market prices of government bonds move inversely with interest rates. Equation (7-1) and Fig. 7-3 show how this price fluctuation comes about. If a price speculator foresees a drop in market interest rates, he or she infers a rise in the market prices of Treasury bonds (and corporate bonds, too). In this case, the speculator would buy (that is, take a long position in) marketable U.S. Treasury bonds. On the other hand, the speculator who expected a rise in interest rates would expect bond prices to fall. In this latter case, the speculator would sell marketable Treasury bonds short to profit from the expected price fall.

Theorem 2 states that the price fluctuations are larger in bonds which have longer terms to maturity. Figure 7-3 shows this graphically. Speculators in bond prices should prefer long-term to short-term bonds for this reason, but theorem 3 implies that speculators need not go to the very longest term bonds to obtain large price fluctuations.

Theorem 4 implies that speculators can profit more by buying bonds (that is, taking a long position) during a decline in interest rates than by selling short during a period when an equal rise in interest rates (starting from the same level) is expected. Theorem 5 explains that bonds with small coupon rates will undergo larger capital gains (or losses) to attain a high (or low) yield to maturity than similar bonds with higher coupon rates. Thus, bond speculators should prefer bonds with low coupon rates because their prices are more volatile.[8]

7-3 VALUING CORPORATE BONDS

Thus far, the discussion of bond prices has ignored default-risk.[9] When corporate bonds are considered, the default-risk of the bonds and their ratings must be considered. A few ratings are shown on page 154.

Bond ratings essentially rank issues in order of their probability of default. A *defaulted* bond is one that is late in making one or more of its scheduled interest payments. Many defaulted bonds eventually resume their scheduled interest payments. But, for some firms, bond default results from irreversible insolvency and is an early step along the path to bankruptcy and/or reorganization. Bankruptcy is the worst thing that can happen to a corporation which issues bonds, from the bondholder's viewpoint. Bankrupt firms oftentimes have their assets auctioned off at a fraction of their original cost so that there is only enough money left to pay the bondholders a few cents back out of each dollar they loaned the firm. That

---

[8] Table 2-4 shows the market prices of a marketable Treasury bond over a 10-year period as interest rates varied.

[9] The term structure of interest rates is discussed in the following chapter.

is, the holders of *bankrupt* bonds may lose their principal. In contrast, the owners of *defaulted* bonds are missing only their interest payments if the issuing firm avoids bankruptcy.

Bond ratings are determined by a committee at a bond rating agency such as Standard & Poor's, Moody's, or Dun and Bradstreet—all firms which sell financial services. The bond rating committee studies protective provisions in the bond indenture, the collateral, coverage ratios, capitalization ratios, liquidity ratios, and other financial data. When the committee reaches a consensus about the rating of an issue, it is usually made public. Bond rating agencies generally all arrive at identical, or at least very similar, ratings for any given bond. When different bond ratings are assigned to a given issue of bonds by two different bond rating agencies, it is called a *split rating*. Split ratings represent slight differences of opinion.

The Meaning of Bond Ratings

High-quality bonds—that is, bonds with high ratings—have historically defaulted less frequently than lower-quality bonds. Table 7-2 shows the default rates on the various bond rating categories between 1920 and 1939 in the United States. Since about half of all defaulted bonds go bankrupt, the ratings are also an indicator of risk of bankruptcy loss. In recent years the rate at which bonds default has been much less.[10]

One of the problems with bond ratings is that their meaning is not constant over time. That is, any given grade of bonds is less likely to default during an economic boom than during a depression. This is because the bond rating agencies tend to view deterioration in a bond issuer's financial position during a depression as a temporary phenomenon. They try to look at the bond's *longer-run* safety characteristics in assigning ratings. Their tendency to do this was what caused the higher default rates in the 1930–1939 subsample in Table 7-2: the Great Depression was not accompanied by enough downgrading of bond issues to hold the default rates unchanged in each risk-class.

---

[10] Gordon Pye, "Gauging The Default Premium," *Financial Analysts' Journal,* January–February 1974, pp. 49–52.

TABLE 7-2 DEFAULT RATES ON DIFFERENT BOND RATING CATEGORIES IN VARIOUS PERIODS

Period	AAA	AA	A	BBB
1920–1929	$\frac{12}{100}$ of 1%	$\frac{17}{100}$ of 1%	$\frac{20}{100}$ of 1%	$\frac{80}{100}$ of 1%
1930–1939	$\frac{42}{100}$ of 1%	$\frac{44}{100}$ of 1%	1.94%	3.78%
1920–1939	$\frac{30}{100}$ of 1%	$\frac{30}{100}$ of 1%	1.1%	2.3%

Source: W. B. Hickman, *Corporate Bond Quality and Investor Experience* (Washington: National Bureau of Economic Research, 1958).

Determinants of Bond Ratings

Contrary to what some people think, a bond's rating is not dependent upon the value of the issuer's assets or the value of the assets pledged as collateral for the bonds. Collateral values are deemphasized (1) because the assets may not bring a good price at a bankruptcy auction, and more importantly, (2) because an asset's value is a function of its earning power, in addition to its auction value.

Contractual protective provisions written in a bond issue's indenture have some effect on the bond's rating. If, for example, a bond issue's indenture contract says that the bonds are subordinated to another issue, this clause lowers the ratings of the subordinated issue. If hard times befall the firm, it can pay the holders of subordinated bonds only after it has paid off its senior or prior claims. Or, if an indenture gives its bond issue an open-end mortgage on some of the firm's assets, that bond issue will tend to be rated lower than if it had a closed-end mortgage. The open-end mortgage allows more debt to be issued later, using the same assets as collateral; this provision dilutes the bond issue's claim on the collateral assets and thus makes the bonds more risky. In contrast, a bond issue which is protected by the provision of a sinking fund to amortize the bonds will enjoy a higher rating than it would without the sinking fund.

Financial Ratios

Most bond analysts would agree that the main element which determines the rating of a bond issue is its coverage ratio. A bond's *coverage ratio* measures how many times the issuing company's earnings could pay the charges and costs related to the bond issue: it is the ratio of the earnings available for payment of bond charges divided by the bond charges. Table 7-3 shows the rules of thumb used by one bond analyst in evaluating coverage ratios.

In computing coverage ratios, most analysts use as the numerator the firm's before-tax earnings *averaged* over the past 5 to 10 years. This practice partially explains why bond ratings are slow to fall during recessions. But *current* bond charges are used for the denominator. Most bond analysts use the *overall method* of computing coverage ratios. With this method the

TABLE 7-3 EVALUATION GUIDELINES FOR
COVERAGE RATIOS

Coverage ratio	Stability of earnings	Relative quality
6 and over	Cyclical	Very high
4 and over	Stable	Very high
3 to 6	Cyclical	Medium to high
2 to 4	Stable	Medium to high
Under 3	Cyclical	Low
Under 2	Stable	Low

bond analyst assumes that a default on a junior bond issue is just as serious as a default on a senior issue. Therefore, all bond issue charges are combined and one coverage ratio is calculated for the junior and senior issues alike. On the other hand, some analysts use the *cumulative method* to compute coverage ratios. Here, the charges for all senior security issues are combined with charges on the junior security issue and these total charges are divided into the total amount of earnings available to find the coverage ratio of the junior security. For example, the costs on a mortgage bond issue would be combined with the charges associated with debentures, a junior security, before calculating the coverage ratio on the debentures. As a result, junior issues always have lower coverage ratios than senior issues. Use of this method is logical if you believe default of one issue is more or less serious than default of another issue from the same firm.

In addition to coverage ratios, bond analysts examine liquidity ratios. The issuing company's acid-test ratio (that is, cash and liquid securities divided by current liabilities) and current ratio (current assets over current liabilities) are examined to ensure that the firm is not in danger of becoming insolvent. Rules of thumb suggest that a firm's acid-test ratio should exceed unity and its current ratio should be larger than 2 in order for it to have adequate liquidity. However, these rules vary from industry to industry.

Bond Ratings Affect Market Yields

Bond ratings affect the discount rate used to value a bond. The various ratings are listed below.

Moody's ratings	Standard & Poor's bond ratings	Descriptive category	Yields to maturity
AAA AA	AAA AA	High-quality bonds	Lowest
A BAA BA	A BBB BB	Medium-quality bonds	
B CAA CA C	B CCC CC C	Speculative bonds	
	D E	Bonds in default Bonds of bankrupt firms	Highest

The speculative grade, defaulted, and bankrupt bonds are not much different from common stock in risky firms in that their prices are open to negotiation. The financial condition of the issuing firm and of the owner of the bonds and the "haggling power" of the buyer and seller are the main determinants of the prices and yields of these risky bonds.

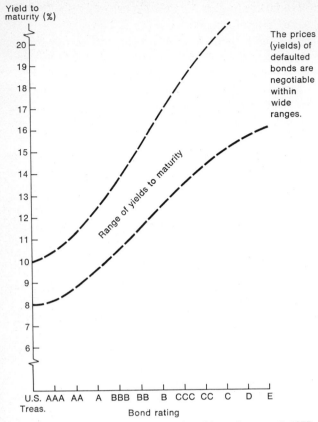

Yield to maturity (%)

The prices (yields) of defaulted bonds are negotiable within wide ranges.

Range of yields to maturity

U.S. AAA AA   A   BBB BB   B CCC CC   C   D   E
Treas.   Bond rating

FIG. 7-4 The risk structure of bond yields on January 3, 1975.

   Figure 7-4 shows the nature of the relationship between bond ratings and the appropriate discount rate or yield to maturity which existed at a particular date. Corporate bonds are discounted at progressively higher discount rates as their ratings deteriorate. Since bond prices are determined by the discount rate, the ratings have a direct effect on bond prices.

   The nature of the relation between the appropriate discount rate k and bond ratings shown in Fig. 7-4 changes over time. Federal Reserve Board policy, fiscal policy, the supply and demand for loanable funds, and other factors which constantly change cause this relation to shift. Figure 7-5 shows the extent to which market yields have varied in recent years. These changing credit conditions can cause bond markets to be speculative markets.

Numerical Examples

Figure 7-6 is an excerpt from *The New York Times* showing the market prices of corporate bonds which were traded on the New York Stock Exchange. In Fig. 7-6 the current yield on the 11's of 88 for AmAirlin, that is, American

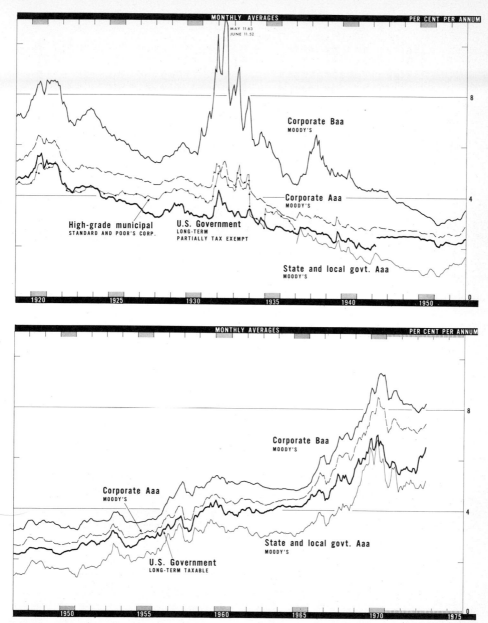

FIG. 7-5 Bond yields.

Airlines bonds maturing in 1988, is shown. This *current yield* is the coupon interest of $110 per year divided by the bond's current market price. The current yield is not a particularly informative number to most investors; the bonds yield to maturity is the more relevant figure.

To show how to use Eqs. (7-1) and (7-2) for corporate bonds, a hypothetical bond will be analyzed here.

THE NEW YORK TIMES, THURSDAY, OCTOBER 23, 1975

New York Stock Exchange Bond Trading

INTER-AMERICAN DEVELOPMENT BANK

Bonds	Current Sales in Yield $1,000	High	Low	Last Chge.	Net
IntBk 8⅜s95	8.6	10	98.16	98.16	98.16 +4.16
IntBk 8.6s85	8.7				
IntBk 8.5	8.5	25	100.8	100.8	100.8 + .24
IntBk 5⅞s93	5.7	5	72.16	72.16	72.16 − .16
IntBk 4½s82	4.8	10	79	79	79 + .12
IntBk 4⅛s79		8	88	88	88

BOND ISSUES TRADED

	WEDNESDAY, OCTOBER 22, 1975			
	U.S. Govt. Bonds	Other Dom. Bonds	Foreign Bonds	Total All Bonds
Day's Sales	$20,200,000	a$520,200,000	$210,000	$20,410,000
Tuesday		a20,180,000	130,000	20,310,000
Year to Date	26,770,000	a4,237,556,000	28,012,500	4,292,338,500
1974	49,864,000	a3,112,754,000	10,818,200	3,173,436,200
a—Includes International Bank Bonds				

	Issues	Advances	Declines	New Highs	New Lows
Oct. 22	764	389	184	21	7
Oct. 21	778	338	219	19	7
Oct. 20	786	335	222	30	6

CORPORATION BONDS

(Corporate bond listings; columns: Bonds, Current Sales in Yield $1,000, High, Low, Last, Net Chge.)

FIG. 7-6 Corporate bond price data for the New York Stock Exchange on October 22, 1975. (From *The New York Times*, Oct. 23, 1975.)

Assume that American Airlines, Inc., bonds maturing in 1988 with a coupon rate of $i = 11$ percent were selling at 90 percent of their face value 10 years before they matured; that is, a $1,000 bond was selling for $900 in 1978. Standard & Poor rates this issue as BBB grade. This low rating is primarily because American Airlines, like most airlines, tends to be heavily leveraged and has cyclical sales and profits.

The yield to maturity on AmAirlin's 11's of 88, or any other bond, can be approximated using Eq. (7-2a). The calculations below are based on a purchase in 1978 when the bond had $n =$ twenty 6-month periods (rather than 10 years, because the coupon interest is paid semiannually).

$$r_0{}^{20} = \frac{(F - p_0)/n + iF}{(p_0 + F)/2}$$

$$= \frac{(1,000 - 900)/20 + \frac{110}{2}}{(900 + 1,000)/2}$$

$$= \frac{\$5 + \$55}{\$950} = \frac{\$60}{\$950} = .0632 = 6.32\% \text{ per 6-month period}$$

The approximate yield to maturity of 6.32 percent per 6-month period is equivalent to 12.64 percent per year. To tell whether the bond is correctly priced, the *exact* yield to maturity should be used as the discount rate to find the bond's present value.

The cashflows from AmAirlin's 11's of 88 are $55 [.5iF = .5(.11)(\$1,000)]$ every 6 months, denoted $c_1 = c_2 = \cdots = c_{20} = \$55$. In addition, the principal of $1,000 is repaid at the end of the twentieth period so $c_{20} = \$1,055$. The present value of these 20 cashflows discounted at 6 percent per 6-month period is calculated below. The 6 percent was used as a discount rate instead of 6.32 percent because 6 percent present value tables with which the interested reader can check the calculations are easier to find than 6.32 percent tables. Furthermore, 6.32 percent is only an approximate estimate of the true yield.

$$v_0 = \sum_{t=1}^{20} \frac{c_t}{(1 + k)^t} \tag{7-1}$$

$$= \sum_{t=1}^{20} c_t D_{.06}^t$$

$$= \sum_{t=1}^{20} \$55 D_{.06}^t + \$1,000 D_{.06}^{20}$$

$$= \$55 \sum_{t=1}^{20} D_{.06}^t + \$1,000 D_{.06}^{20}$$

$$= \$55(11.470) + \$1,000(.3118)$$
$$= \$630.85 + \$311.80 = \$942.65$$

The present value of $942.65 will be the bond's market price 10 years before it matures if market yields are 12 percent per annum then.

Yield Differences within a Grade

The AmAirlin's 11's of 88 are priced to yield a higher-than-average yield for BBB bonds. The market demands this higher-than-average BBB-grade yield because: (1) AmAirlin is a low-grade BBB bond (that is, it is near the BB-grade quality); (2) the bond is not selling at a deep discount so it will not provide large capital gains, which are taxed at a lower rate than ordinary interest income; and (3) the bond is callable at the issuer's discretion. If it were not for these undesirable features, the AmAirlin's 11's of 88 would have lower yields to maturity.

In valuing corporate bonds, Eq. (7-1) yields close estimates of the bond's market price only if various factors *in addition to* the bond's rating are taken into consideration. This is because there is a range of discount rates shown for each corporate bond rating in Fig. 7-4 rather than a single discount rate. The call features, the sinking fund provision, the coupon rate, the financial condition of the issuer, money market conditions, and other subjective considerations must be evaluated to know which discount rate to use for a particular bond at any given moment. When the discount rate which represents the bond market's consensus is found, however, it may be used in Eq. (7-1) to find the exact market price for a bond.

Price Speculation with Corporate Bonds

The market prices of corporate bonds fluctuate as much or more than the prices of marketable Treasury bonds. Therefore, bond price speculators may profit from speculating on corporate bond prices, too. As with the Treasury bonds, the level of market interest rates is a major determinant of the bonds' present value or market price. However, there are additional factors which affect corporate bond yields and prices. As Fig. 7-4 shows, there is a range of yields (and prices) appropriate for a corporate bond of any given risk-class. In addition to all the factors which affect the yields of marketable U.S. Treasury bonds, there are factors relating to corporate bonds which affect their yields and prices such as the bond's rating, the callability of the bond, and the issuing firm's financial outlook. Thus, investors in corporate bonds must consider not only the level and structure of interest rates but also the factors peculiar to each corporate bond issue.

Bond Investing

In the final analysis, the beauty of bond investment (as opposed to bond price speculation) is that investors can be relatively free from worry about interest income fluctuations if they so desire. By simply buying a high-grade bond with little risk of default which offers contractual interest payments and repayment of the principal at specified times, the investor can have peace of mind and earn a yield to maturity which is known in advance. For this reason many bond buyers are investors rather than speculators.

7-4 CONCLUSIONS ABOUT BOND VALUATION

The value of a bond or any other asset is the present value of all the income flowing from it. It is easy to tell what the income from bonds will be. Bonds are essentially contracts to pay fixed periodic interest payments and the face value of the bond when it reaches maturity. Determining the appropriate discount rate to use in finding a bond's present value, on the other hand, is not so easy. The credit conditions and bond ratings which determine market interest rates change daily. Furthermore, various provisions to protect corporate bondholders may be specified in the indenture contract; these provisions can also have an effect on the appropriate discount rate for corporate bonds. In general, the more risk which is associated with an asset and its income stream, the higher the discount rate which should be used in finding its present value. Since present values vary inversely with the discount rate, a corporate bond would have a lower present value than a U.S. Treasury bond which offers the identical stream of cashflows.

It is possible to make large speculative profits by trading bonds when market interest rates are changing because the present value (and equivalently, the market price) of a bond varies inversely with market interest rates and with other factors.

QUESTIONS

1 If the discount rate is 10 percent, find the present value of the following opportunities to:
  a Receive $100 in 2 years
  b Receive $100 in 2 years and another $100 in 3 years
  c Receive $250 at the end of each of the next 10 years

2 If you make investments earning 10 percent, find your terminal wealth if you:
  a Invest $100 and leave it for 10 years
  b Invest $100 now and another $100 a year from now and withdraw the proceeds 2 years from now

3 Find the value of a corporate bond maturing in 5 years which has a 5 percent coupon rate, $1,000 face value, and is rated AA. What is its value if it is rated A? The graph below shows the effect of the bond rating on the appropriate discount rate for this problem.

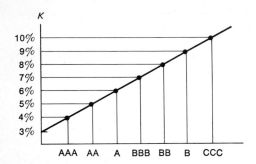

4 What is the yield to maturity if you pay $800 for a U.S. Treasury bond maturing in 4 years that has a face value of $1,000 and a coupon rate of 4 percent if the coupon interest is reinvested at a rate equal to the yield to maturity?

5 Look up the U.S. Treasury 3's of 1995 in Fig. 7-1 and determine the amount and the frequency of the coupon interest payments.

6 What was the yield to maturity (not the current yield) for American Telephone and Telegraph's (ATT) $3\frac{7}{8}$'s of 1990 bonds shown in Fig. 7-6?

7 Compare and contrast the ATT $3\frac{7}{8}$'s of 1990 bonds with the American Airline's 11's of 1988 bonds in terms of risk and return. Explain the reasons for these differences in risk and return.

SELECTED REFERENCES

Fisher, Lawrence, "Determinants of Risk Premiums on Corporate Bonds," *The Journal of Political Economy,* June 1959, pp. 217–237.
> An empirical study using regression analysis to show that bond yields increase with risk.

Homer, Sidney, and M. L. Liebowitz, *Inside The Yield Book* (Englewood Cliffs, N.J.: Prentice-Hall, 1972).
> A thorough discussion of bond valuation, bond yields, bond swaps, yield to call for bonds, and present value. Elementary algebra used.

Pinches, G. E., and K. A. Mingo, "A Multivariate Analysis of Industrial Bond Ratings," *Journal of Finance,* March 1973, pp. 1–32.
> An empirical study which uses multiple discriminant analysis (MDA) to group bonds into quality-rating categories.

APPENDIX A TO CHAPTER 7
Multiple Discriminant Analysis of Bond Rating Categories

Professors Pinches and Mingo (P & M)[1] have shown how to use a statistical procedure called multiple discriminant analysis (MDA) to estimate bond ratings based on six statistics for a firm. Essentially P & M fit four linear equations like Eq. (A7-1) to classify bonds into one of five categories.

$$z_j = f_{i1}x_{1j} + f_{i2}x_{2j} + f_{i3}x_{3j} + f_{i4}x_{4j} + f_{i5}x_{5j} + f_{i6}x_{6j} \qquad \text{(A7-1)}$$

for $i = 1, 2, 3, 4, 5$ ratings and $j = 1, 2, \ldots, n$ bond issues.

The six explanatory variables are defined below for firm j's bonds:

x_{1j} = subordination of the issue is measured by setting x_1 to zero or unity to indicate whether or not it is subordinated

x_{2j} = years of consecutive cash dividends, a measure of stability

x_{3j} = size of the bond issue, a measure of the issue's marketability

x_{4j} = 5-year average of net income divided by interest expense, a coverage ratio (as explained in Table 7-3)

x_{5j} = 5-year average of long-term debt over net worth, a leverage measure

x_{6j} = net income over total assets, a measure of profitability for the jth company

The f_i coefficients in Eq. (A7-1) are numbers estimated statistically so that the discriminant score, denoted z_j for the jth bond, would give the best indication of whether or not that bond issue is in the ith quality rating. For example, for the first category ($i = 1$), which is the AAA grade rating, if a bond issue's discriminant score is not high enough, that bond is not classified in the first category. Instead, the bond's discriminant score is next calculated for the second function ($i = 2$) to see whether it is high enough to qualify the bond to be in category 2 (that is, an AA-grade bond). This process goes on through the third and fourth discriminant scores, respectively. If a bond's discriminant score is not high enough to qualify for any of the first four categories (that is, $i = 1, 2, 3,$ or 4), the bond is assigned to category five, which is grade B and below.[2]

In testing their model, P & M correctly classified 92 out of a sample of 132 bonds; that is, 70 percent were correctly classified. Multiple discriminant analysis appears to be a new and useful tool for rating bonds.

[1] G. E. Pinches and K. A. Mingo, "A Multivariate Analysis of Industrial Bond Ratings," *Journal of Finance*, March 1973, pp. 1–32.

[2] R. A. Eisenbeis and R. B. Avery, *Discriminant Analysis and Classification Procedures* (Lexington, Mass.: Lexington Books, 1972).

APPENDIX B TO CHAPTER 7
Bond Duration

Macaulay's bond duration is defined as the period of time which elapses before the stream of payments from a bond (namely, the coupon interest and principal repayment) generates one-half the bond's present value.[1] Hicks called duration the *average period of the stream* and described it as being "the average length of time for which the various payments are deferred from the present, when the times of deferment are weighted by the discounted values of the payments."[2] For a bond which pays no coupon interest (that is, a bond purchased at discount from its redemption value to provide a yield from capital gains), the bond's duration is identical to its term to maturity. But for bonds paying interest before maturity, as most bonds do, duration is less than the term to maturity.

A bond's duration is calculated by weighting the present value of each future cashflow by the number of periods until its receipt and then dividing by the current price of the bond. More concisely, Eq. (B7-1) defines a bond's duration, denoted d.

$$d = \frac{\sum\limits_{t=1}^{n} \dfrac{c_t t}{(1 + r_0^n)^t} + \dfrac{Fn}{(1 + r_0^n)^n}}{\sum\limits_{t=1}^{n} \dfrac{c_t}{(1 + r_0^n)^t} + \dfrac{F}{(1 + r_0^n)^n}} \qquad (B7\text{-}1)$$

$$= \sum\limits_{t=1}^{n} \frac{[c_t t/(1 + r_0^n)^t] + [Fn/(1 + r_0^n)^n]}{p_0} \qquad (B7\text{-}1a)$$

where c_t = the contractual coupon interest payment (if any) on the bond (or other asset) to be paid in time period t

F = the bond's redemption value, face value, or maturity value, or the amount repaid to the lender at maturity of the bond (if it does not default)

t = the time period in which the payment or interest rate occurs

r_0^n = the yield to maturity on a bond with n periods (namely, years) to maturity observed in the market at time period $t = 0$

n = the number of periods in the bond's life until it matures and is repaid

p_0 = the present value of the bond at period $t = 0$

In essence, Macaulay's bond duration is a weighted average of the time periods $t = 1, 2, \ldots, n$ in which each payment is to be made; the present values of the payments are used as the weights. Thus, a bond which pays

[1] F. R. Macaulay, *Some Theoretical Problems Suggested by the Movements of Interest Rates, Bond Yields and Stock Prices in the U.S. since 1856* (New York, 1938).
[2] J. R. Hicks, *Value and Capital*, 2d ed. (Oxford Press, 1965), p. 186.

more interest sooner (that is, a high coupon bond), will have a shorter duration than another bond which has the same term to maturity and the same yield to maturity but a lower coupon interest rate.

Duration and term to maturity are two different ways of measuring the time structure of a bond or similar asset. The term to maturity provides information about the bond's final payment, and is not effected by the size or timing of the interest payments. In contrast, duration considers every payment and the point in time when it occurs. Thus, many financial economists view duration as the superior measure of a bond's time structure, while term to maturity is seen as a mere legal and bookkeeping technicality.[3]

As a first approximation, bond duration increases monotonically in a nonlinear fashion with term to maturity for any given bond (although the relationship is not quite monotone for bonds selling at discount). Table B7-1 shows the duration of a bond yielding 6 percent if held to maturity at several different coupon rates (compounded semiannually) and different terms to maturity. The table shows that long-term bonds are not as long-term as they may appear if the time structure of the cashflows is considered. The numbers in the table also show that duration varies inversely with a bond's coupon interest rate, all other things being equal, for bonds with finite lives.

Duration can be a useful concept to managers of bond portfolios. Bank vice-presidents, portfolio managers of mutual funds with investments in bonds, high-level officials at the U.S. Treasury and Federal Reserve, pension fund managers, and others who manage multimillion-dollar bond portfolios can measure a portfolio's duration as a way of observing and controling its riskiness. The bond price theorems in Chap. 7 explained how

---

[3] M. H. Hopewell and G. G. Kaufman, "Bond Price Volatility and Term to Maturity: A Generalized Respecification," *American Economic Review*, September 1973, pp. 749–753.

TABLE B7-1 BOND DURATION IN YEARS FOR BOND YIELDING 6 PERCENT UNDER DIFFERENT TERMS

Years to maturity	Various coupon rates			
	.02	.04	.06	.08
1	0.995	0.990	0.985	0.981
5	4.756	4.558	4.393	4.254
10	8.891	8.169	7.662	7.286
20	14.981	12.980	11.904	11.232
50	19.452	17.129	16.273	15.829
100	17.567	17.232	17.120	17.064
∞	17.167	17.167	17.167	17.167

Source: L. Fisher and R. L. Weil, "Coping with the Risk of Interest Rate Fluctuations: Returns To Bondholders from Naive and Optimal Strategies," *Journal of Business*, October 1971, p. 418.

variability in the market prices (that is, the market risk) of bonds increase directly with term to maturity and inversely with coupon interest rates. Bond duration also increases positively with term to maturity and inversely with coupon interest rate. Thus, a bond's duration is one number which can be used as a measure of the risk resulting from the combined effects of term to maturity and the size of the coupon rate. Because of changes in market interest rates, bonds with long duration will experience more fluctuation in their market prices than bonds with short duration regardless of their maturities and coupon rates. Some people who manage bond portfolios calculate a portfolio's weighted average term to maturity to gauge its exposure to the price fluctuations associated with changes in market yields. The portfolio's duration would provide a better measure of this risk exposure because duration is also a price elasticity.[4]

[4] J. B. Yawitz, G. H. Hempel, and W. J. Marshall, "The Use of Average Maturity as a Risk Proxy in Investment Portfolios," *Journal of Finance,* May 1975, pp. 325–335. R. A. Haugen and D. W. Wichern, "The Elasticity of Financial Assets," *Journal of Finance,* September 1974, pp. 1229–1240. Hicks, *op cit.* The implications of duration for constructing yield curves is discussed in J. L. Carr, P. J. Halpern, and J. S. McCallum, "Correcting the Yield Curve: A Re-Interpretation of the Duration Problem," *Journal of Finance,* September 1974, pp. 1287–1294. Also J. H. McCulloch, "Measuring the Term Structure of Interest Rates," *Journal of Business,* January 1971, pp. 19–31.

Eight

Determinants of Market Interest Rates

Most bond price fluctuations are the result of market interest changes. Therefore, Chap. 8 addresses itself to explaining the level and the structure of market interest rates.[1]

Chapter 7 showed how to determine the value of a bond after the appropriate discount rate is known. However, that chapter offered only a partial explanation of what determines the appropriate discount rate, since only the yield spreads (or risk premiums) between bonds with different default-risk ratings were discussed. The appropriate discount rate to use in valuing a given bond is the *current market interest rate* for a bond having the quality rating and protective provisions of that bond. Explaining bond values is easy after the appropriate discount rate is known—just use Eq. (7-1).

8-1 THE LEVEL OF INTEREST RATES

The term *structure of interest rates* (that is, the shape of the yield curve) refers to the relationship between bond yields for bonds which are identical in every respect except their term to maturity. It deals with questions like "Why are the yields of some issuers' bonds which have 20 years to maturity usually higher than the same issuers' bonds with fewer years to maturity, if all other factors are equal?" Such questions are addressed in Sec. 8-2. This section deals with the level, but not the structure, of interest rates. It

---

[1] Do not become confused about bonds' one-period rates of return as defined in Eq. (2-1) on page 15. Chapter 8 discusses only bonds' yields to maturity and these are different from the one-period rates of return.

answers questions about why all interest rates are high or low, or rising, or falling.

Market yields to maturity are determined by many things. The most basic determinant of interest rates is the *marginal productivity of capital,* or the rate at which capital reproduces itself in the real or physical sense. For example, if 10 coconut trees produce enough nuts and leaves to maintain the fertility of their soil, sustain the people who tend them, and increase to 11 coconut trees in a year, the trees have a marginal productivity of capital of 10 percent per year. The marginal productivity of capital is unrelated to price level changes. Economists call this basic rate of interest the marginal physical efficiency of capital, the marginal physical productivity of capital, or the real rate of interest. Whatever it is called, it is represented by the symbol *m* in the remainder of this chapter.

In addition to the *m*, interest rates are affected by the risk-premium. In order to undertake risky investments, lenders require a *risk-premium,* denoted θ (the Greek letter theta), to be paid over and above the marginal productivity of capital to induce them to invest or lend their funds when the risk of loss exists. The determination of risk-premiums for bonds and the relationship between bond yields and bond ratings were explained in Fig. 7-4 and the accompanying discussion (see page 198).

Since interest rates and loans are typically in nominal money quantities rather than real physical quantities, the nominal interest rate must contain an allowance for the rate of price change so that lenders' wealth will not be eroded away by inflation. For example, if a lender loans $100 for a year at 5 percent interest, the lender will be repaid $105. But, if inflation at a rate of 10 percent exists, $E(\Delta P/P) = 10$ percent, this $105 will have the purchasing power a year later of $\frac{1}{1.1} = 90.9$ percent of $105, or $95.44 due to the inflation.[2] Thus, the lender must charge 5 percent interest plus 10 percent inflation allowance, or 15 percent per year to allow for the inflation. In this case, the lender will be repaid $115 [= $100 \times (100$ percent $+ 5$ percent $+ 10$ percent)]. After 10 percent inflation, the $115 has a real purchasing power of $\frac{1}{1.1} = 90.9$ percent of $115, or $104.54. The lender thus gained only a $4.53 increase, or 4.53 percent, in purchasing power by loaning money at 15 percent interest during a year in which inflation was 10 percent. This shows that lenders need to raise interest rates by at least the rate of inflation in order to maintain the real purchasing power of their wealth. This inflation adjustment is called the *Fisher effect,* named after Irving Fisher, who first explained it decades ago.[3]

---

[2] The symbol E denotes the mathematical expectation, defined in Mathematical Appendix E. The delta, Δ, means "change." The symbol P might represent the Consumer Price Index (CPI), for example. So ΔP means price change and $E(\Delta P/P)$ represents an expected percentage price change, that is, the expected inflation rate.

[3] Irving Fisher discussed the effects of inflation on market interest rates in *Appreciation and Interest* (New York: Macmillan, 1896), pp. 75–76. The ideals were expanded later in Fisher's book *The Theory of Interest* (New York: Macmillan, 1930).

The manner in which the three essential determinants of interest rates (that is, the marginal productivity of capital, risk-premiums, and the rate of expected price change) are combined to influence market interest rates is summarized symbolically in Eq. (8-1).

$$r = m + \theta + E\left(\frac{\Delta P}{P}\right)$$ (8-1)

Equation (8-1) is a model of how the *level* of interest rates are determined.

The level of interest rates refers to how high all interest rates tend to be. For example, suppose that the marginal productivity of capital is 4 percent per year ($m = 4$ percent $= .04$), that lenders require a 2 percent risk-premium for loans of some given risk-class ($\theta = 2$ percent $= .02$), and that expected inflation is 2 percent per year [$E(\Delta P/P) = 2$ percent $= .02$]. According to Eq. (8-1), this implies that the nominal interest rate for loans of this given risk-class is (4 percent + 2 percent + 2 percent =) 8 percent per year. If inflationary expectations rise from 2 to 4 percent per year, Eq. (8-1) implies that nominal interest rates will rise to (4 percent + 2 percent + 4 percent =) 10 percent per year. This increase from 8 to 10 percent is a change in the *level* of interest rates which would affect all interest rates similarly.

Inflationary Expectation's Effects

An economist named William Gibson, among others, has recently published scientific evidence showing how the public's inflationary expectations, $E(\Delta P/P)$, determine market interest rates.[4] Gibson estimated a series of regression of the form shown in Eq. (8-2).

$$_i r_t{}^n = A_i + B_i\left[E\left(\frac{\Delta P}{P}\right)_t\right] + \mu_{it}$$ (8-2)

In Eq. (8-2) $_i r_t{}^n$ represents the market interest rate (or yield to maturity) of the ith bond issue in time period t, and $E(\Delta P/P)_t$ denotes inflationary expectations in period t. The A_i and B_i terms are the regression intercept and slope coefficients (see Mathematical Appendix H about regression) for the ith bond issue. Regression equation (8-2) is trying to explain the market yield of the ith bond in the tth period in terms of the rate of inflation which was expected in that period.

---

[4] W. E. Gibson, "Interest Rates and Inflationary Expectations: New Evidence," *American Economic Review*, December 1972, pp. 854–865. A more sophisticated study is by W. P. Yohe and D. S. Karnosky, "Interest Rates and Price Level Changes, 1952–69," *Review*, St. Louis Federal Reserve Bank, December 1969. This readable survey and empirical test is available free in pamphlet form as Reprint No. 49 from the St. Louis Fed. A more esoteric study is by M. Feldstein and O. Eckstein, "The Fundamental Determinants of the Interest Rate," *Review of Economics and Statistics*, November 1970, pp. 303–374. Most recently, see E. Fama, "Short-Term Interest Rates as Predictors of Inflation," *American Economic Review*, June 1975, pp. 269–282.

TABLE 8-1 GIBSON'S REGRESSION STATISTICS FOR EQUATION (8-2)

i	Yields (r's) from:	Intercept A_i	Slope B_i	$\bar{R}^2$
1	3-month Treasury bills	2.20	.93	.76
2	6-month Treasury bills	2.04	1.09	.78
3	9- to 12-month Treasury bills	2.19	1.06	.79
4	3- to 5-month Treasury notes	2.92	.89	.83
5	10-year Treasury bonds	3.23	.67	.85

Gibson used surveys of dozens of economists' inflation forecasts for one year in the future to find the consensus of inflationary expectations. Surveys of United States economists from coast to coast were taken every 6 months for 18 years; $E(\Delta P/P)_t$ denotes their average forecast for the tth period's inflation. Table 8-1 shows the regression results.

Regression Eq. (8-2) was fitted for five different bond issues. The coefficients of determination, denoted $\bar{R}^2$ in Table 8-1, measure the percentage of variation in the bond yields to maturity explained by the concurrent inflationary expectations variable, $E(\Delta P/P)_t$. Since the lowest $\bar{R}^2$ is $.76 = 76$ percent (for 3-month Treasury bills), this means that over three-quarters of the changes in interest rates can be explained with inflationary expectations. All five slope coefficients, B_i, approximate unity, indicating that if the rate of inflation changes by a certain amount, interest rates change by about the same amount. The smaller regression slope coefficients for the bonds with longer terms to maturity may be interpreted to mean that one year's inflation expectations have a smaller effect on long-term bond yields than on the yields of short-term bonds. The intercept terms A_i in Eq. (8-2) are estimates of the marginal productivity of capital (m) plus the risk-premium ($\theta = 0$ for U.S. Treasury bonds) in Eq. (8-1). For example, for Treasury bonds with 10 years and over to maturity the intercept, ($m + \theta$), equals 3.23 percent during the sample period.

These regression statistics attest to the primary importance of inflationary expectations in the determination of market interest rates. Figure 8-1 is a graph which shows further evidence of this interaction.

Supply and Demand for Credit

Although Fig. 8-1 shows that rising rates of inflation have been the main force pushing up interest rates since the 1960s, there are still some wiggles in the interest rate graph which are not related to inflationary factors. These are the result of changes in the supply of and demand for loanable funds caused by intermediation or disintermediation and other factors.[5]

---

[5] *Intermediation* refers to the activity of financial intermediaries like banks and savings and loan associations (S&Ls) as they intermediate between savers and investors. Financial intermediaries accept many small savings deposits, pool them, and then make large loans to finance business expansions and home building. *Disintermediation* is the reverse—savers withdraw their savings from financial intermediaries and thus cause a reduction in loanable funds.

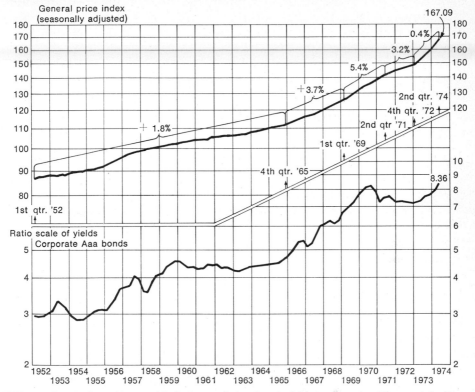

FIG. 8-1 Comparison of rate of inflation and Aaa bond yields to maturity. The straight lines drawn above the graph of the price index measure the trends in the inflation rate over various periods. (From Federal Reserve Bank of St. Louis *Review*).

The business cycle affects credit conditions by affecting the supply of and the demand for funds. Business economists at banks, bond portfolio managers, and others who must forecast day-to-day changes in interest rates study flow-of-funds tables which show where credit inflows (namely, savings) and credit outflows (that is, borrowings) originate in an effort to ascertain the effects of short-run changes in the supply and demand for loanable funds. During a period of economic expansion, the unemployment

---

Rising interest rates cause disintermediation because banks and savings and loan associations are forbidden by law to pay high interest rates on their savings accounts. Credit crunches are a result of interest rates pushed up by inflation rather than the cause of the high interest rates.

In 1969–1970, nonprice rationing of loanable funds resulting from disintermediation occurred when market interest rates were pushed by inflation to levels in excess of the legal ceilings (imposed by the Federal Reserve's Regulation Q, for example) that savings institutions could pay. As a result, savers withdrew their savings and invested them in market securities with higher yields. The so-called credit crunch of 1969–1970 resulted. Similar credit crunches occurred in 1966 and 1959 and almost occurred at other recent times.

rate falls, business activity quickens, and businesses borrow money to build bigger plants and buy more equipment. The resulting credit demands bid up interest rates. In contrast, during slow-downs and recessions, unemployment increases, manufacturing activity slows, and demand for credit shrinks, and so interest rates fall.

The level of inflationary expectations and the phase of the business cycle are the main factors usually affecting interest rates. The business cycle supply and demand factors tend to play a secondary role to inflation in the determination of interest rates. But the supply and demand for credit do have pronounced effects on yield spreads.

Yield Spreads

Yield spreads are the differences between the yields of any pair of bonds — usually U.S. Treasury bonds and other more risky bonds — as defined in Eq. (8-3) for the tth time period.

$$\text{(Yield on risky bond)}_t \text{ less (U.S. Treasury bond yield)}_t$$
$$= \text{(yield spread)}_t \quad (8\text{-}3)$$

Yield spreads are also called *risk-premiums* because they measure the additional yield that risky bonds pay to induce investors to buy risky bonds rather than riskless bonds. Table 8-2 shows some yield spread statistics. Over the 1955 to 1971 period, AA-grade corporate bonds, for example, paid an average risk-premium of 0.6 percent, or 60 basis points over similar (intermediate-term) U.S. Treasury bonds.

The data in Table 8-2 show that yield spreads averaged larger in the 1964-to-1971 sample period than they did in 1955 through 1963. However, Table 8-3 shows that yield spreads vary with the business cycle over a wider range. The right-hand column of Table 8-3 shows, for example, how the average risk-premiums on BBB-grade bonds varied over the business cycle. Other yield spreads may be calculated from the data. The data show that all risk-premiums tend to be larger at economic troughs than at peaks.

Risk-premiums are higher at economic troughs for two main reasons. First, unemployment, fear of job loss, and risk-aversion are higher during recessions. Therefore, most investors demand larger risk-premiums to induce them to buy risky bonds. Second, the corporations which issue bonds typically experience reduced sales and profits during recessions. Since the issuers are more subject to bankruptcy during recessions, investors require larger risk-premiums.[6] These changes in risk-premiums, denoted θ in Eq. (8-1), are one more reason that changes in market interest rates occur.

---

[6] Lawrence Fisher, "Determinants of Risk Premiums on Corporate Bonds," *Journal of Political Economy*, June 1959, pp. 217–37.

TABLE 8-2 AVERAGE YIELDS AND OTHER STATISTICS OVER
SEVERAL PERIODS

	1955–1963 Average yield	1964–1971 Average yield	1955–1971 Average yield
Corporate bonds:			
AAA-grade bonds	4.00%	6.00%	4.93%
AA-grade bonds	4.12%	6.19%	5.09%
A-grade bonds	4.30%	6.40%	5.28%
BBB-grade bonds	4.82%	6.81%	5.74%
Treasury bonds:			
Long-term	3.63%	5.30%	4.41%
Intermediate-term (I.T.)	3.60%	5.51%	4.49%
Short-term	3.36%	5.25%	4.24%
Yield spreads:†			
AAA–I.T.	.40%	.49%	.44%
AA–I.T.	.52%	.68%	.60%
A–I.T.	.70%	.89%	.79%
BBB–I.T.	1.21%	1.29%	1.25%
Financial ratios (national average):			
Return on equity	10.28%	11.56%	10.88%
Current assets/current liabilities	2.50 times	2.14 times	2.33 times
Quick ratio	.53 times	.29 times	.42 times
Equity/debt	4.14 times	2.92 times	3.57 times
Economic statistics:			
Inflation rate	2.05%	3.64%	2.78%
Unemployment rate	5.40%	4.40%	4.93%

† I.T. denotes intermediate-term U.S. Treasury bond yields.
Sources: Standard & Poor's *Trade and Securities Statistics,* 1973; *Federal Reserve Bulletins;*
and *Quarterly Financial Report for Manufacturing Corporations.*

TABLE 8-3 MARKET RATES AND YIELD SPREADS, IN PERCENT,
AT ECONOMIC PEAKS AND TROUGHS

Date	AAA	AA	A	BBB	I.T.†	BBB-I.T.
July 1957 peak	4.00	4.17	4.30	5.00	3.87	1.13
April 1958 trough	3.62	3.82	4.03	4.82	2.58	2.24
May 1960 peak	4.45	4.56	4.74	5.36	4.23	1.13
February 1961 trough	4.27	4.40	4.66	5.21	3.74	1.48
November 1969 peak	7.29	7.51	7.86	8.34	7.04	1.30
November 1970 trough	7.40	7.84	8.35	9.08	6.52	2.86

† I.T. denotes intermediate-term U.S. Treasury bond yields.
Source: National Bureau of Economic Research, Peaks and Troughs.

8-2 THE TERM STRUCTURE OF INTEREST RATES

The combined effects of (1) changes in inflationary expectations and (2) changing credit supply and demand factors which result in changing risk premiums cause the *level* of market yields to vary over a wide range from year to year. However, these facts reveal nothing about the term structure of interest rates. Different bonds have different terms to maturity. For example, the U.S. Treasury, corporations such as American Telephone and Telegraph (ATT), and other organizations which borrow in the bond markets have different bond issues outstanding with maturities ranging from 3 months to over 30 years. And any given bond issuer usually has, on any given day, *different yields* on its various bond issues which differ only with respect to their *terms to maturity*. For a given bond issuer, the structure of yields for bonds with different terms to maturity (but no other differences) is called the *term structure of interest rates. Ceteris paribus,* the term to maturity of a bond, will affect its yield. Thus, Eq. (8-1) can be rewritten as (8-4) to reflect the effects of varying a bond issue's number of periods until maturity, denoted n.

$$r_i = m + \theta_i + E\left(\frac{\Delta P}{P}\right) + f(n_i) \tag{8-4}$$

where $f(n_i)$ denotes some function of the ith bond issue's term to maturity which increases or decreases that issue's market yield. The purpose of this section is to examine $f(n_i)$; that is, the manner in which a bond's term to maturity affects its yield to maturity. Figure 8-2 shows graphs of several yield curves.

The rest of this chapter focuses on the term structure of interest rates. By eliminating all variables which do not affect this term structure, the analysis is simplified and expedited. This can be done by limiting the discussion to the various maturities of U.S. government bonds. All U.S. Treasury bonds have identical default-risk premiums (of zero). By restricting discussion to marketable U.S. government bonds we have, in financial parlance, limited our discussion to the *yield curve.*

The *term structure of interest rates* for U.S. government bonds, or the *yield curve,* may be defined as the relationship between yields and maturities for a given issuer's bonds. The yield curve changes a little every day, and there are different yield curves for each risk-class of bonds. The yield curve for AAA corporate bonds, for example, is different from the yield curve for U.S. Treasury bonds on any given day. But the yield curves for riskier classes of bonds are at a higher *level* than the yield curve for less risky bonds—the difference in levels is due to the difference in risk premiums. And the yield curves for riskier bonds are not so stable as the yield curve for U.S. Treasury bonds. Therefore, we shall confine our attention to the yield curve for U.S. Treasury bonds throughout the remainder of this chapter to expedite the discussion.

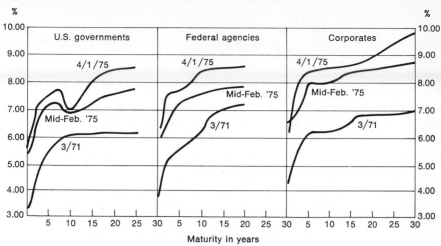

FIG. 8-2 Actual yield curves for government, agency, and corporate taxable bonds. Governments are based on seasoned issues yielding 6 percent or more. Agency yields are from representative seasoned issues. Corporates are from 3-month paper; 1-year CD's; 5-, 10-, and 30-year AA utilities; and 15-year AA railroad equipment bonds. (From "Comments on Values," a weekly newsletter prepared by Salomon Brothers, New York, April 3, 1975, p. 20.)

Three Main Theories about Determination of Yield Curves

There are three main theories about how the shape of the yield curve is determined:

1 The *liquidity premium theory* asserts that long-term yields should average higher than short-term yields. This theory maintains that investors pay a price premium (resulting in lower yields) on short maturities to avoid the risk of principal which is more prevalent in the long maturities. Thus, an upward sloping yield curve is considered "normal."

2 The *expectations theory* asserts that long-term yields are the average of the short-term yields prevailing during the intervening period. This implies that if all investors expected rates to (*a*) rise, the yield curve would slope upward; or (*b*) remain unchanged, the yield curve would be horizontal; or (*c*) fall, the yield curve would slope downward.

3 *The segmentation (or hedging) theory* asserts that the yield curve is composed of a series of independent maturity segments. For example, commercial banks predominantly demand short maturities, savings and loans mainly demand intermediate maturities, and long-term bonds are purchased mostly by life insurance companies. Thus, yields on each segment of the yield curve are determined independently by the supply and demand conditions existing in that maturity segment.

Five bond price theorems were discussed in some detail in Chap. 7 (on page 192). With these bond pricing theorems as a background, consider each of the three theories about the term structure of interest rates in some depth. After these theories have been explained, a discussion will integrate them into one unified theory. It should be pointed out, however, that some people adhere rigorously to only one of these theories and believe that it alone explains the term structure of interest rates.

Liquidity Premium Hypothesis

Assuming that risk is related to dispersion of market value, it appears from a glance at Fig. 7-3 that risk increases with term to maturity. As a matter of fact, the prices of long-term bonds do fluctuate more than the prices of shorter-term bonds (even though long-term rates fluctuate less than short-term rates). The large price fluctuation in the longer-term bonds is the basis for the liquidity premium hypothesis. According to this hypothesis, the yield curve should be typically sloping upward at higher maturities because investors demand higher returns to hold the risky long-term bonds.

> Liquidity preference produces asymmetry in the relationship between short-term and long-term rates at cycle peaks and troughs. It accounts for the failure of short-term rates to exceed long-term rates at peaks by as much as they fall below long-term rates at troughs.[7]

Advocates of the liquidity premium theory support their opinion by taking yield curves from each phase of the last few business cycles and showing that the average of short-term Treasury bond rates is less than the average of long-term Treasury bond rates. Graphically speaking, this means that, on average, the yield curve is upward sloping at the longer maturities. Although this is usually true, it is not conclusive proof of the validity of the liquidity premium theory; there are reasons to doubt this theory.

Four reasons why the liquidity premium theory might be reversed (that is, why higher rates should be observed for short-term bonds) have been suggested by those who doubt the theory.[8] First, with the passage of time, short-term rates fluctuate in an uncertain manner. Investors in short-term maturities must, therefore, face a series of reinvestments at risky and uncertain returns. Second, increased transaction and information costs required to refinance frequently in the short-term maturities (instead of in fewer longer-term bond issues) reduce net returns from such investments. Third, investors in long-term bonds can reduce their risk by hedging (that is, by synchronizing their assets and liabilities to mature simultaneously). For example, there is no uncertainty about the maturity value or maturity date of long-term high-quality bonds. Thus, long-run fund requirements

---

[7] R. Kessel, *The Cyclical Behavior of the Term Structure of Interest Rates,* National Bureau of Economic Research, Occasional Paper No. 91, 1965.

[8] F. Modigliani, Richard Sutch et al., *Supplement to Journal of Political Economy,* August 1967. B. P. Malkiel's book *The Term Structure of Interest Rates* (Princeton, N.J.: Princeton, 1966) also discusses the liquidity premium hypothesis.

can be hedged by buying long-term bonds which mature when the investor expects the funds will be needed. Fourth, the yield curve could slope downward because investors expect lower inflation premiums, and consequently, lower interest rates, in the future than at present. Here, then, are four possible reasons why the long-term bonds might sell at higher prices and lower yields. Although the case for the existence of liquidity premiums is weakly made, it still contains some truth and most economists believe it.

The Expectations Hypothesis

The expectations hypothesis asserts the long-term rates are the average (or, more precisely, the geometric mean) of the short-term rates expected to prevail between the current period and the maturity date of the bonds. For example, using the simple arithmetic average, if 1-year rates are now 1 percent and are expected to be 3 percent next year, then rates on 2-year bonds today will be approximately 2 percent.

$$2\% = \frac{1\% + 3\%}{2 \text{ years}} = 2\text{-year average}$$

In developing the expectations hypothesis, two general types of interest rates will be discussed—they are sometimes referred to as the spot and the future rates. The terms *spot* and *future* are used in the same way they are used in discussing commodity markets to distinguish between items for current delivery and items for future delivery. Future rates, denoted r_t^n, refer to the yield to maturity for bonds which are expected to *exist in the future*. More specifically, r_n^1 denotes the yield to maturity (or market interest rate or future rate) which is currently expected to apply to some future 1-year bond which will exist during period n. Spot rates, denoted r_0^t, refer to the interest rates for bonds which currently exist and are being bought and sold. More specifically, r_0^n denotes the market interest rate (or yield to maturity) for a currently existing bond which matures n periods (usually years) in the future. By the use of these mathematical conventions, a rigorous statement of the expectations theory is given in Eq. (8-5).

$$
\begin{aligned}
1 + r_1^1 &= 1 + r_1^1 \\
(1 + r_1^2)^2 &= (1 + r_1^1)(1 + r_2^1) \\
(1 + r_2^3)^3 &= (1 + r_1^1)(1 + r_2^1)(1 + r_3^1) \\
& \cdots \cdots \cdots \cdots \cdots \cdots \cdots \\
(1 + r_1^n)^n &= (1 + r_1^1)(1 + r_2^1) \cdots (1 + r_n^1)
\end{aligned}
\tag{8-5}
$$

The forward rates $r_2^1, r_3^1, \ldots, r_n^1$ are implicit; that is, these future rates cannot be observed. But the r_1^n's can be observed—they are printed in the newspapers daily. This means that the implicit future rates can be determined for any future period or series of future years by solving Eq. (8-5) for the appropriate r_t^n. This is not a statement of economic behavior; it is simply a mathematics problem. The implicit market rate of interest for period n can be found by solving Eq. (8-6) for $r_t{}^n$.

$$1 + r_t{}^n = \frac{(1 + r_t{}^n)^n}{(1 + r_{t-1}^{n-1})^{n-1}} \tag{8-6}$$

It is similarly possible to determine the implicit future rates for multiperiod bonds. For a bond with a life of t periods running from the start of period n through period $n + t$, the yield over the life (that is, over the t periods) of this future bond can be derived from Eq. (8-7).

$$\sqrt{(1 + r_t{}^1)(1 + \tfrac{1}{t+1}) \cdots (1 + r_{t+n}^1)} = \sqrt{\frac{(1 + r_t^{n+t})^{n+1}}{(1 + r_t{}^n)^n}} \tag{8-7}$$

where $r_t{}^n$ is the market yield for a bond maturing n periods in the future observed at period t.

The relations suggested by the expectations hypothesis will not hold exactly in the "real world" because transactions costs (especially sales commissions) will inhibit trading. But, ignoring transactions costs, arbitrage ensures that Eq. (8-5) will tend to hold if the majority of bond traders are profit maximizers. Recall that arbitrage is a series of transactions which yield a certain return: arbitrage is not uncertain or risky. Arbitrage between maturities will tend to maintain Eq. (8-5) — that is, the expectations theory. It is an economic theory based on a mathematical equation.

Arbitrage

There are some investors who will rearrange their bond portfolios and cause bond prices and yields to be revised according to Eq. (8-5) because they expect to profit from it. For example, suppose inequality (8-8) occurs — this violates Eq. (8-5).

$$(1 + r_1{}^n)^n > (1 + r_1{}^1)(1 + r_2{}^1) \cdots (1 + r_n{}^1) \tag{8-8}$$

Some profit-seeking investors who have money to invest for n periods will buy the existing long-term bond yielding $r_1{}^n$. This will drive up its price and drive down its yield until (8-8) becomes an equality, in accord with Eq. (8-5).

After profit-maximizing investors purchase the long-term bond yielding $r_1{}^n$, its price may later drop because of changing credit conditions and/or changing expectations. In this case, the investor must hold the long-term bond until it matures to attain the yield $r_1{}^n$. Since it is not always possible for profit-maximizing investors to hold long-term bonds until they mature, they may sell them after their price has fallen and inequality (8-8) exists again. In this case, the sale will lower the bond's price and increase inequality (8-8). As a result of such disadvantageous sales (which even a profit-maximizing speculator may sometimes be forced to make), the arbitrage process cannot be expected to maintain Eq. (8-5) as an exact equality. However, the actions of these profit seekers will tend to make current yields (that is, $r_1{}^n$) a function of expected future yields (that is, the $r_t{}^n$'s) as shown in Eq. (8-5).

One empirical test which supports the expectations theory [as represented by Eq. (8-5)] is simply to compare the interest rate forecasts inherent in the yield curve of some past date with the record of business activity after that date. Assuming that most investors have roughly accurate ideas at any moment about the future level of business activity, and also assuming that they believe the level of interest rates follows the level of business activity, it then follows directly from the definition of the expectations hypothesis that the yield curve should usually slope up preceding economic expansions and down preceding contractions. Without recognizing the implicit reasoning, a Wall Street business executive's version of the expectations theory would be: "Declining business activity during the period of time presented by the yield pattern will result in a negatively sloped yield pattern," or vice versa for rising rates.

The data in Fig. 8-3 tend to bear out this version of the expectations hypothesis. A yield curve constructed at nearly any of the cyclical peaks

FIG. 8-3 Yields on U.S. government securities. Official NBER Peaks denoted P and Troughs denoted T. (From Federal Reserve *Chart Books*.)

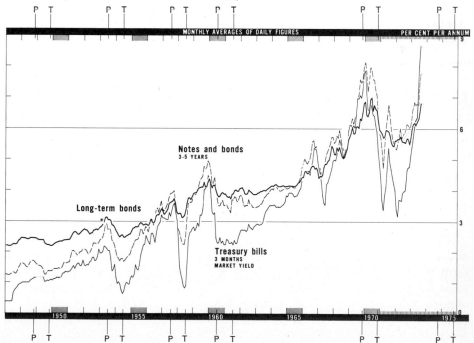

would slope downward, or a yield curve drawn at nearly any of the troughs would slope upward.[9] The yield curves existing at the 1975 economic trough are reproduced in Fig. 8-2. This is the classic upward-sloping yield curve forecasting expectations of rising interest rates. It is seen more frequently than other shapes. This is usually attributed to the predominance of optimism over pessimism. However, it also supports the liquidity premium theory and is the "proof" frequently used to support this theory.

Behavioral Assumptions of the Expectations Theory

The expectations theory has been criticized for crediting investors with too much sophistication. Some writers have erroneously interpreted the theory as assuming that investors must forecast short-term interest rates for years into the future and must continuously calculate the averages of these short-term yields to ensure that they correspond with the appropriate long-term yields. But one writer has correctly pointed out that:

> The fundamental behavioral assumption of the neoclassical theory (that is, the expectations hypothesis) is not that investors calculate long-term rates by averaging short-term rates, but rather that investors will seek to invest in such a way as to maximize their returns on the basis of their expectations about future levels of interest rate and security prices.[10]

The truth of this simple assumption is easily demonstrated by noting that when all yields are high, investors forecasting an equal probability of a rise or a fall in yields will tend to bid prices up and yields down on long-term bonds.[11] This is because the capital gains from a given fall in rates on long maturities exceeds the losses from an equal rise in rates on these maturities (theorem 4). Thus, we need only attribute maximizing behavior (and no particular expectations) to investors in order to explain the downward-sloping yield curve observed at the peak of business activity. If investors see more than a .5 probability of yields falling from peak levels (which they must if they can forecast at all), they will show a stronger tendency to bid long-term prices up, with the result that long-term yields will fall when rates reach a peak. Furthermore, if we take cognizance of the diminishing marginal utility of money, the disutility of a capital loss outweighs the utility of an equal capital gain. So risk-averters will tend to purchase bonds which have prices that are not expected to fall: they will purchase long-term bonds selling at deep discounts, driving their prices up and their yields

---

[9] Peaks and troughs are official National Bureau of Economic Research estimates.

[10] J. W. Conrad, *An Introduction to the Theory of Interest Rates* (Berkeley: University of California Press, 1959), pt. 3.

[11] This result follows directly from assumptions of maximizing behavior and investor knowledge of theorem 4. B. P. Malkiel, "Expectations, Bond Prices and the Term Structure of Interest Rates," *Quarterly Journal of Economics,* May 1962, pp. 206–213.

down. Such risk-averting behavior suggests a third reason to expect the yield curve to slope down during business peaks. Symmetrical but opposite arguments explain why the yield curve will slope up when business activity reaches a trough. The more complex implications of the expectations theory are thus seen not to be sophisticated behavioral assumptions, but rather, to be implications of simple profit-seeking and risk-aversion. This lends further credibility to the theory.

The Segmentation Theory

The pure segmentation theory asserts that lenders and borrowers confine themselves to certain segments of the yield curve for the following reasons:

1 Legal regulations, such as "legal lists," which limit the investments that banks, savings and loan associations, insurance companies, and other institutions are allowed to make

2 The high cost of information, which causes investors to specialize in one market segment

3 The fixed maturity structure of the liabilities which various bond investors tend to have (for example, life insurance companies and pension funds tend to have long-term liabilities which may be forecast by an actuary) and which causes them to hedge their liabilities with assets of equivalent maturity

4 Simply, irrational preferences

As a result, the rates on different maturities tend to be determined independently by the supply and demand conditions in the various market segments.

The segmentation theory is also referred to as the *hedging theory*. The implication of this name is that investors are typically obligated by some particular maturity pattern of liabilities. Given the maturity of an investor's liabilities, he or she can hedge against capital losses in the bond market by synchronizing asset and liability maturities. Thus, each investor is confined to some maturity segment which corresponds to his or her liability maturities. Figure 8-4 shows a grossly simplified conception of how the yield curve might be segmented.

Those individuals who do interpret the yield curve as being completely determined by independent markets dealing in different maturities are usually persons who deal solely in one of those market segments. Such individuals [for example, federal funds officers at banks, Federal Open Market Committee (FOMC) agents and other FOMC officials] cannot help but be impressed by the sheer dollar volume of the transactions and the immediate price reactions which they witness. It is possible that to some extent these persons are victims of their own myopic activities; they may be unaware of the constant activities of professional profit-maximizing arbitragers who are risk-indifferent and view all securities as substitutes.

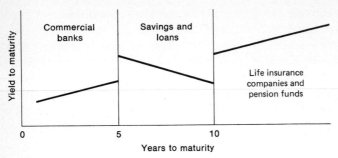

FIG. 8-4 Segmented yield curve.

Such profit-seeking arbitragers earn their living by smoothing out irregularities in the yield curve. Although these professional arbitragers may be few in number, their presence and effectiveness are attested to by the relative smoothness of the yield curve of any date. That is, kinks such as shown in Figs. 8-4 and 8-2 are rare and typically less exaggerated.

8-3 CONCLUSIONS ON TERM STRUCTURE

There is no consensus among business people and economists about which of the preceding theories concerning the term structure is descriptive of reality. There is an undeniable element of logic in each of the three theories, and each is supported to a certain extent by empirical data. In fact, a combination of all three theories probably furnishes the best description of the elements determining the term structure of interest rates.

In essence, expectations of future rates determine a yield curve. However, the yield curve based on pure expectations (denoted *EE* in Fig. 8-5) is unobservable. Liquidity premiums which increase with the term to maturity are superimposed on top of the yields that are purely a function of expectations. Thus, a yield curve such as *YY* in Fig. 8-5, which is observable,

FIG. 8-5 A yield curve determined by expectations and liquidity premiums.

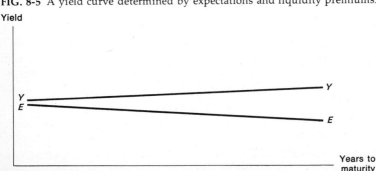

represents a combination of the rates determined by expectations plus liquidity premiums (the liquidity premiums are equal to the vertical distance between YY and EE). This means that the liquidity premium theory is not invalidated by the occasional existence of a downward-sloping yield curve.

The long-term end of the yield curve is determined by investors' expectations and the liquidity premiums they demand to induce them to hold these bonds. The stationary nature of the long-term end of the yield curve over the years reflects the constancy of long-run expectations and liquidity premiums.

The segmentation theory explains the frequent movements in the short-term end of the yield curve. The constant actions of the Federal Reserve's Open Market Committee in controlling the money supply interacting with the liquidity needs of commercial banks are the primary supply and demand forces at work on the short-term end of the yield curve. The wide and frequent swings in this segment of the curve may be largely attributed to changes in these supply and demand factors. The effects of these forces on the yield curve diminish rapidly in the intermediate- and long-term maturities.

Conclusions on the Level of Rates

The factors which determine the level of interest rates are easier to discern. Inflationary expectations have been the single most important factor in the determination of market yields since the mid-1960s. In fact, the studies of Gibson (shown in Table 8-1) and other economists indicate that three-fourths or more of all changes in interest rates can be explained in terms of inflationary expectations. However, at certain times shifts in the credit supply and demand can result in faster interest rate changes than shifting inflationary expectations can. Changes in the risk-premiums which occur as the phases of the business cycle change can contribute significantly to movements in market rates of interest too.

Since bond prices are strongly affected by market interest rates, forecasting interest rates is an important task of a bond portfolio manager. This chapter about the determinants of market interest contains only macroeconomic topics. One message implicit in this content is that bond portfolio managers should be monetary economists as well as bond analysts if they hope to maximize their portfolio's profits.

QUESTIONS

1 Compare and contrast (a) changes in bond prices caused by changes in the level of interest rates with (b) those caused by changes in the structure of interest rates.

2 How should the inflationary expectations of investors in 1-year bonds and investors in 20-year bonds differ?

3 If you managed a bank's multimillion-dollar portfolio of bonds, what would you do if you were convinced a credit crunch was beginning? How might other bond portfolio managers behave if they also expected a credit crunch, and how would their actions affect your job?

4 Plot the yields of an intermediate-term Treasury bond and a bond issued by the Penn Central Railroad monthly from 1965 until it went into reorganization, and see whether you can detect its quality deterioration.

5 Define the term *yield curve*. What financial variables which affect interest rates are held constant throughout the length of the yield curve? Why are these variables held constant?

6 Cut out the section of a recent newspaper which has the yields to maturity for U.S. Treasury bonds. Prepare a yield curve from these data. Write separate paragraphs using each of the following three theories to rationalize this particular yield curve: (*a*) expectations theory, (*b*) liquidity premium theory, and (*c*) segmentation theory.

7 Assume 4-year bonds are currently yielding 7 percent and 3-year bonds are yielding 6 percent. What is the implied yield for 1-year bonds starting 3 years from now? Show your work. HINT: Use the expectations theory.

8 Give two reasons why the yield curve might be expected to slope upward most of the time, and also give two reasons why it might usually slope downward.

9 Why should government economic policymakers care about the yield curve? A portfolio manager? An investment banker?

10 Bond dealers define a bear hedge as a transaction in which "a short sale of longs is hedged by going long shorts"; that is, a short position of long-term bonds is hedged by taking a long position in short-term bonds. Why would a bond dealer enter such a bear hedge? (Refer to Chap. 13 for an explanation of long and short positions.)

SELECTED REFERENCES

Culbertson, J. A., "The Term Structure of Interest Rates," *Quarterly Journal of Economics,* November 1957, pp. 485–517; also, Michaelson, "Comment," ibid., February 1963, pp. 166–174; and J. A. Culbertson, "Reply," ibid., November 1963, pp. 691–696.

    This series of nonmathematical articles articulates the viewpoint of advocates of the segmentation theory.

Fama, E. F., "Short-Term Interest Rates as Predictors of Inflation," *American Economic Review*, June 1975, pp. 269–282.
> Regression analysis is used to analyze the relation between market yields and subsequent inflation rates.

Federal Reserve System, Board of Governors, *Historical Chart Book* (Washington, D.C. 20551).
> This monthly pamphlet may be purchased for 60 cents by writing to the Federal Reserve. It provides a valuable summary of financial and economic data in chart form.

Malkiel, B. G., "Expectations, Bond Prices, and the Term Structure of Interest Rates," *Quarterly Journal of Economics*, May 1962, pp. 197–218.
> A discussion and analysis of the relation between yield changes and bond prices. This article uses differential calculus and utility theory. It develops bond pricing theorems and explains the simple behavioral assumptions behind the expectations hypothesis.

Meiselman, D., *The Term Structure of Interest Rates* (Englewood Cliffs, N.J.: Prentice-Hall, 1962).
> The book explains the expectations hypothesis and supporting data using regression analysis and elementary difference equations.

Yohe, W. P., and D. S. Karnosky, "Interest Rates and Price Level Changes, 1952–69," *Review*, St. Louis Federal Reserve Bank, December 1969.
> A readable survey of relevant literature and explanation of Almon distributed-lag regression analysis which shows the positive relation between inflation and market interest rates.

PART THREE

COMMON STOCK VALUATION

The value of a share of common stock, like the value of a bond, is the present value of all the income flowing to the owner of the stock. But common stockholders are owners of the corporation who receive an uncertain stream of residual income (rather than debtors who receive contractual streams of income). Therefore, common stock valuation must deal with measuring the risk that determines the discount rate to use in finding the stock's present value, the estimation of the stream of residual income a stockholder can expect, and various other problems which are unique to equity valuation. Chapters 9 through 12 explain the concepts of risk and income as they interact to determine the value of a share of stock.

CHAPTER 9 COMMON STOCK VALUATION THEORY deals with the primary conceptual problems encountered in determining the value of common stock.

CHAPTER 10 FUNDAMENTAL COMMON STOCK ANALYSIS explains the widely used practice of multiplying a stock's income per share times its price-earnings multiplier to determine its intrinsic value.

CHAPTER 11 ESTIMATING STOCKHOLDERS' INCOME shows that methods used by accountants are questionable. Instead, the concept of economic income is suggested as the measure of income which is relevant in determining common stock values.

CHAPTER 12 RISK explains in a quantitative fashion how total risk can be divided into two parts called systematic risk and unsystematic risk. Determining the discount rate for a stock from that stock's systematic risk is illustrated.

Each of the four chapters in Part 3 relies on material explained in the preceding chapter; therefore they should be read in the order presented. These chapters show how to estimate the value of an individual asset so the investor will be able to tell if the asset is overpriced or underpriced. The basic valuation model below is used.

Basic Valuation Model

The intrinsic economic value of a market asset is the present value of its future income.

$$\text{Present value} = \sum_{t=1}^{n} \frac{\text{income}_t}{(1+k)^t}$$

Nine

Common Stock Valuation Theory*

Chapters 7 and 8 explained how to find the value of bonds. Bond valuation is simple because a bond's cashflows are unambiguously known in advance and the discount rate can be determined within a narrow range. But several ambiguities and uncertainties frustrate the exact determination of common stock values. This chapter examines the most important of the problems which arise in valuing common stock. Several common stock valuation models will be the focus of this analysis.

9-1 DEFINITION OF A MODEL

Models have been described as simplified versions of reality. The models with which this chapter deals are mathematical models. Like airplane models, they represent reality. They relate certain independent variables, such as dividends and earnings, to a dependent variable, the value of the common stock. Symbolically, the models studied will be of the form $V = f(X_1, X_2, \ldots, X_n)$ where V denotes the value of the asset and X_1, $X_2, \ldots, X_n$ represent those independent variables which determine value. These models will explicitly depict each variable's interaction with the other variables. They are simplified versions of the financial processes that actually determine asset prices.

In an effort to keep things simple, models abstract from many variables and instead focus only on the main determinants. For example, none

---

* Readers who wish to omit the abstract theory and go to more directly applicable common stock analysis techniques may skip Chap. 9 and go on to Chap. 10. But Chap. 7 is needed as background.

of the models contains variables representing presidential assassinations, changes in Federal Reserve monetary and credit policy, the timing and impact of changes in the level of economic activity, and numerous other variables which do not directly affect the value of common stock. All the models do, however, contain a variable representing the asset's income, since income is the most important determinant of value. In this chapter, the important conceptual issues related to the valuation of equity shares in a *nonlevered* firm are explained. Chapters 10 to 12 deal with common stock valuation on a more pragmatic level.

The Basic Valuation Model

The value of a common stock is simply the present value of all the future income which the owner of the share will receive. This valuation model is the same for all stocks and all bonds. It is summarized symbolically in Eq. (9-1).

$$\text{Value} = \sum_{t=1}^{\infty} \frac{\text{income for period } t}{(1.0 + \text{appropriate discount rate})^t} \tag{9-1}$$

Using this valuation model on stocks is more difficult than using it on bonds because of two main problems. First, it is not known in advance what a stock's income will be in each future period. And second, it is not clear what the appropriate discount rate should be for a particular stock. This chapter examines suggested solutions to these problems which have been offered by various financial analysts and economists. Before getting into these different valuation models, however, a brief review of the symbols used is provided.

Symbols

The mathematical models in this chapter use the following symbols which are defined here for easy reference.

v_t = value of one share of common stock at period t

e_t = earnings per share at time period t

d_t = dividends per share at time period t paid to stockholders of record at the start of period t

r_t = *average* internal rate of return of all investments within the firm during time period t

k_t = appropriate discount rate at time t = firm's cost of capital as determined by its risk

f = retention ratio (which is assumed constant) = fraction of e retained

$1 - f$ = payout ratio = dividends/earnings = fraction of e paid out

$g = fr$ = rate of growth in earnings, which is assumed to remain constant

t = an index indicating time period, for example, a quarter or a year

n_t = number of shares of stock outstanding at time period t

$\Delta n_t = n_{t+1} - n_t$ = number of new shares (if any) sold during period t at the ex-dividend price per share

Capital letters are used to denote totals.

V_t = total value of firm at period $t = \overset{n}{\Sigma}\, v_t$

D_t = total dividends paid to all stockholders of record at start of period $t = \overset{n}{\Sigma}\, d_t$

E_t = total earnings of firm in period $t = \overset{n}{\Sigma}\, e_t$

T = last time period or terminal period

I_t = total investment in period $t = E_t - D_t + \Delta n_t V_t$

$D_{t+1,t}$ = total dividends payable at period $t+1$ to stockholders of record at period t (but not to new stockholders) $= n_t d_t$

9-2 CAPITALIZING DIVIDENDS

Dr. Myron Gordon has developed a model relating an equity share's value to its dividend income.[1] He hypothesized that the value v of a stock equals the present value of the infinite ($t = \infty$) stream of dividends d to be received by that stock's owner.

$$v_0 = \sum_{t=1}^{\infty} \frac{d_t}{(1+k)^t} = \frac{d_1}{1+k} + \frac{d_2}{(1+k)^2} + \cdots + \frac{d_\infty}{(1+k)^\infty} \qquad (9\text{-}2)$$

In Eq. (9-2), k is the capitalization rate which is appropriate for the firm's risk-class. Retained earnings are assumed to increase future dividends in this model; thus, it does not ignore retained earnings, but it does treat them indirectly.

The logic of the dividend model is undeniable. Cash dividends are the only income from a share of stock which is held to infinity. So, the value of a share of stock which is held to perpetuity could only be the present value of its stream of cash dividends from now until perpetuity. But what if the share is sold in a few years, you ask? The model includes this possibility.

[1] M. J. Gordon, *The Investment, Financing and Valuation of the Corporation* (Homewood, Ill.: Irwin, 1962).

Selling Shares

If an investor sells a share after, say, three periods, the present value of that share is as shown in Eq. (9-3), according to the logic of the dividend model.

$$v_0 = \sum_{t=1}^{3} \frac{d_t}{(1+k)^t} + \frac{v_3}{(1+k)^3} \tag{9-3}$$

$$= \frac{d_1}{1+k} + \frac{d_2}{(1+k)^2} + \frac{d_3 + v_3}{(1+k)^3} \tag{9-3a}$$

The v_3 term represents the value of the share in period $t = 3$ when it is sold. And, according to the logic of Eq. (9-2), v_3 is the present value of all dividends from period $t = 4$ to infinity; this is represented symbolically as Eq. (9-4).

$$v_3 = \sum_{t=1}^{\infty} \frac{d_{t+3}}{(1+k)^t} \tag{9-4}$$

$$= \frac{d_4}{(1+k)^1} + \frac{d_5}{(1+k)^2} + \frac{d_6}{(1+k)^3} + \cdots + \frac{d_\infty}{(1+k)^\infty} \tag{9-4a}$$

To show how the dividend model encompasses situations in which a share is sold before infinity, Eq. (9-4a) is substituted into Eq. (9-3a) to obtain Eq. (9-3b) below.

$$v_0 = \frac{d_1}{1+k} + \frac{d_2}{(1+k)^2} + \frac{d_3}{(1+k)^3} + \frac{d_4/(1+k)^1 + \cdots + d_\infty/(1+k)^\infty}{(1+k)^3} \tag{9-3b}$$

Since

$$\frac{d_{n+3}/(1+k)^n}{(1+k)^3} = \frac{d_{n+3}}{(1+k)^n(1+k)^3} = \frac{d_{n+3}}{(1+k)^{n+3}}$$

Eq. (9-3b) can be equivalently rewritten as Eq. (9-3c).

$$v_0 = \frac{d_1}{1+k} + \frac{d_2}{(1+k)^2} + \frac{d_3}{(1+k)^3}$$
$$+ \frac{d_4}{(1+k)^{3+1}} + \frac{d_5}{(1+k)^{3+2}} + \cdots + \frac{d_\infty}{(1+k)^\infty} \tag{9-3c}$$

Comparison of Eqs. (9-3c) and (9-2) will reveal that they are equal. This shows the indirect manner in which the dividend model considers retained earnings and capital gains. That is, v_0 includes v_3, the value of the share in the future. And v_3 includes capital gains which result from retained earnings. Thus, the dividend model does not ignore the effects of capital gains or retained earnings.

Definitions and Relationships in Dividend Model

In order to show the interaction of earnings, dividends, retained earnings, and the growth rate of the firm, the model treats these variables explicitly as shown below. Dividends are related to earnings by defining dividends to be equal to the payout ratio $(1-f)$ times earnings, as shown in Eqs. (9-5) and (9-5a).

$$D_t = (1-f)E_t = \text{total cash dividends} \tag{9-5}$$

$$d_t = (1-f)e_t = \text{cash dividends per share} \tag{9-5a}$$

Retained earnings of fE dollars are assumed to be reinvested within the all-equity firm at a rate of return of r. This allows earnings to grow at the rate of $g = fr$ per period as shown in Eq. (9-6), assuming no new outside capital is invested.

$$\left. \begin{array}{l} E_t = (1+g)^t(E_0) \\ = (1+fr)^t(E_0) \end{array} \right\} \text{total earnings growth} \tag{9-6}$$

$$\left. \begin{array}{l} e_t = (1+g)^t(e_0) \\ = (1+fr)^t(e_0) \end{array} \right\} \text{per-share earnings growth} \tag{9-6a}$$

As long as the retention ratio is a positive number $(f > 0)$, dividends per share will grow as shown in (9-7) if no new shares are issued.

$$\begin{array}{ll} d_t = (1-f)(1+fr)^t(e_0) & \tag{9-7} \\ = (1-f)(1+g)^t(e_0) & \tag{9-7a} \\ = (1-f)(e_t) & \tag{9-7b} \end{array}$$

In the case where some fraction f of earnings is retained and earns a return of r within the firm, the present value of a share of stock is determined by substituting Eq. (9-7) into (9-2) to obtain (9-8).

$$v_0 = \sum_{t=1}^{\infty} \frac{e_0(1-f)(1+fr)^t}{(1+k)^t} \tag{9-8}$$

Since Eq. (9-2) may be rewritten equivalently as (9-9),

$$\sum_{t=1}^{\infty} \frac{d_0(1+fr)^t}{(1+k)^t} = \sum_{t=1}^{\infty} \frac{d_0(1+g)^t}{(1+k)^t} = \frac{d_0}{k-g} \tag{9-9}$$

Eq. (9-8) may be rewritten equivalently as (9-9a) by substituting $e_0(1-f)$ for d_0 in Eq. (9-9), as shown below.

$$v_0 = \sum_{t=1}^{\infty} \frac{e_0(1-f)(1+g)^t}{(1+k)^t} \tag{9-8}$$

$$= \frac{d_0}{k-g} \tag{9-9}$$

$$= \frac{e_0(1-f)}{k-g} \tag{9-9a}$$

One of the advantages of the dividend model is that it may be rewritten equivalently in different forms. For example, Eqs. (9-2), (9-8), (9-9), and (9-9a) are all useful representations of the same model. Equation (9-8) explicitly shows the relationship of current earnings e_0, dividend policy f, internal profitability r, and the firm's cost of capital k in the determination of the value of the stock. This model may be used to determine the value per share by defining all the variables on a per-share basis as shown, or the model may be used to value the entire firm by using the total quantities represented by the variables in capital letters.

The Effects of Dividend Policy

Equation (9-9b) is particularly useful for studying the effects of dividend policy (as represented by the variable f) on value. First, consider the normal firm where the internal rate of return on new investment equals the discount rate (that is, $r = k$).

$$v_0 = \frac{e_0(1-f)}{k-fr} = \frac{e_0(1-f)}{k-g} \qquad \text{since } g = fr \tag{9-9b}$$

$$= \frac{e_0(1-f)}{k(1-f)} \qquad \text{if } r = k$$

$$= \frac{e_0}{k} \tag{9-10}$$

Equation (9-10) shows that regardless of the firm's initial earnings e_0 or riskiness (which determines k), the firm's value is not affected by dividend policy. That is, when $r = k$, dividend policy is irrelevant since f, which represents the firm's dividend policy, cancels completely out of Eq. (9-10). Equation (9-10) is also proof that capitalizing earnings is equivalent to capitalizing dividends when $r = k$, regardless of the payout ratio. Equation (9-10), which capitalizes only earnings, was derived from (9-8). Equation (9-9), which capitalizes dividends, was also derived from (9-8). This shows the equivalence of capitalizing dividends and capitalizing earnings when $r = k$. When $r = k$, the quantity $1/k$ is the same as the price-earnings ratio (or earnings multipliers shown in Table 10-3).

Table 9-1 uses the dividend model equation (9-9b) to show the effects

TABLE 9-1 NUMERICAL SOLUTIONS FOR DIVIDEND MODEL

$$V = \frac{e_0(1-f)}{k-fr} \qquad\qquad (9\text{-}9b)$$

Growth firm, $r > k$	Declining firm, $r < k$	Normal firm, $r = k$
$r = 15\%$	$r = 5\%$	$r = 10\%$
$k = 10\%$	$k = 10\%$	$k = 10\%$
$e_0 = \$5$	$e_0 = \$5$	$e_0 = \$5$
If $f = 60\%$, $v = \$200$.	If $f = 60\%$, $v = \$28.57$.	If $f = 60\%$, $v = \$50$.
$v = \dfrac{5(.4)}{.1 - (.6)(.15)}$	$v = \dfrac{5(.4)}{.1 - (.6)(.05)}$	$v = \dfrac{5(.4)}{.1 - (.6)(.1)}$
$= \dfrac{2}{.01} = \$200$	$= \dfrac{2}{.07} = \$28.57$	$= \dfrac{2}{.04} = \$50$
If $f = 20\%$, $v = \$57.14$.	If $f = 20\%$, $v = \$44.44$.	If $f = 20\%$, $v = \$50$.
$v = \dfrac{5(.8)}{.1 - (.2)(.15)}$	$v = \dfrac{5(.8)}{.1 - (.2)(.05)}$	$v = \dfrac{5(.8)}{.1 - (.2)(.1)}$
$= \dfrac{4}{.07} = \$57.14$	$= \dfrac{4}{.09} = \$44.44$	$= \dfrac{4}{.08} = \$50$
Conclusion: v increases with the retention rate f for firms with growth opportunities, $r > k$.	Conclusion: v increases with the payout ratio $(1-f)$ for declining firms $r < k$.	Conclusion: v is not affected by dividend policy when $r = k$.

of various dividend policies, as represented by the value assigned to f, on the value of a hypothetical share. The values in Table 9-1 are computed on the assumption that earnings per share are $e_0 = \$5$, the firm's cost of capital is constant at $k = 10$ percent, and the internal profitability of the firm varies, that is, $r = 5$, 10, and 15 percent.

Table 9-1 shows the effect of various values of r, k, d, and e in determining v. Inspection of Eq. (9-9b) and Table 9-1 reveals that the optimal dividend policy depends on the relationship between the firm's internal rate of profit r and its discount rate k.

Growth Stock

Firms which earn a return on invested funds r that is higher than their cost of capital or discount rate k are *growth firms*. Growth firms have $r > k$ and maximize their value by retaining all earnings for internal investment. For example, Polaroid and IBM were growth stocks during the 1950s and 1960s because of technological breakthroughs combined with patents that gave them temporary monopolies on superior products. During these years the firms could raise capital at a cost of k percent per year and reinvest it internally at a higher rate of r percent per year. Firms with such profitable investments available would be foolish not to reinvest all their earnings if they could not raise capital externally. The model accurately depicts this situation and shows that paying dividends would decrease such a firm's value.

Declining Firms

Firms which do not have profitable opportunities to invest may be called *declining firms*. A firm typically declines because its product becomes obsolete, its sales continue to decline, and no further investment within the firm is profitable. Examples of declining firms can be found in the buggy-whip and fruit-jar industries from 1930 to 1960. They have so few, if any, profitable investment opportunities that their return on investment r remains below their cost of capital or discount rate k. In this case, the firm maximizes its value by paying out whatever it earns in dividends. Furthermore, the firm should liquidate itself and pay one big final cash dividend. In a capitalistic system, the recipients of these dividends will either spend them or search out better investments. Either way, the capital will be used more productively.

Normal Firms

The vast majority of firms have precious few growth opportunities (that is, investments with $r > k$). These firms are in a static equilibrium where their internal rate of return from their investments just equals their cost of capital or discount rate, $r = k$. For these firms, dividend policy has no effect on value in the dividend model. That is, the value of the firm is unchanged whether it pays out 10 percent of its earnings as dividends, or 90 percent, or any other percentage.

Growth in Size Not Equivalent to Growth in Value

It is easy to be deceived into thinking that a firm which is getting bigger is a growth firm. For example, consider a hypothetical railroad which experiences an increase in its total sales, has a bigger labor force, increases profits, and sees its stock price rise. Does this make the railroad's stock a growth stock? No, not necessarily. The railroad may be getting physically larger by retaining earnings and selling new issues of bonds and stock to the public. These funds are raised at a weighted average cost of capital of k. Then, they are reinvested and earn a rate of return of r. But, if $r = k$, the *present* value of dollars invested does not grow. The value of funds invested in the railroad tends to increase only enough to compensate investors for bearing the risk and inconvenience of postponing consumption in order to make the investment (that is, at rate k).

Increases in the railroad's share prices are due to earnings retention. The retained earnings earn a rate r, causing earnings and dividends per share to grow. But future dividends and capital gains must be discounted at the appropriate discount rate k to find their present value. As long as $r = k$, the *present value* of future dividends and capital gains just equals the present value of the earnings which were retained to finance this expansion. Thus, the railroad gets physically bigger in size and the price of its shares rise but the *present value* of an investment in it does not increase. If it paid out 100 percent of its earnings in dividends, the firm could still continue to get bigger by issuing new securities instead of retaining earnings. Either way, the present value of the benefits received from a dollar invested would be unchanged because $r = k$. Therefore, simply getting bigger does not make a corporation a growth firm.

Simplifications in Dividend Model

The dividend model is a valuable teaching device to show the effects of dividend policy on an all-equity firm under different assumptions about profitability. However, the simplified nature of the model can lead to conclusions which are true for the model but not true *in general*. Consider the simplifying assumptions which underlie the dividend model.

1 There is no external financing. The dividend model contains no debt and interest expense variables or allowance for new shares to be issued. As a result, every penny of dividends comes directly out of retained earnings in the model. And since retained earnings are the only source of funds with which the firm may expand, dividend policy and investment compete for the firm's earnings.

2 The internal rate of return r of the firm is constant. This ignores the diminishing marginal efficiency of investment which would normally reduce r as investment was increased.

3 The appropriate discount rate k for the firm remains constant. Thus, the model ignores the possibility of a change in the firm's risk-class and the resulting change in k.

4 The firm and its stream of earnings are *perpetual,* so t goes to infinity.

5 No taxes exist. This simplification will be relaxed later.

6 The growth rate $g = fr$ is constant forever.

7 $k > fr = g$. If $g > k$, the value of a share would be infinite.

8 The firm's dividend policy, as represented by the symbol f, is presumed to remain fixed to infinity.

Consider the problems which are introduced by these eight assumptions. The analysis will provide a review of capital budgeting and financing (that is, corporation finance) and of how such matters affect dividend policy and the value of the firm.

No outside financing. The dividend model confounds dividend policy with the investment program of the firm. Since the model does not include sources of funds from external financing, every dollar of dividends takes

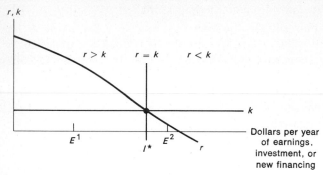

FIG. 9-1 A firm's investment opportunities.

away a dollar from earnings retained for investment. When such a situation exists, either the firm's investment program, its dividend policy, or both will be suboptimal. This problem is represented graphically in Fig. 9-1. A review of the optimum investment program shows the result of ignoring external financing.

Figure 9-1 shows dollars per year on the horizontal axis and the values of r and k on the vertical axis. The exhibit depicts some hypothetical firm's investment opportunities as it makes its financial plans for the next year. Both the corporation's total profit and its total investment are measured on the horizontal axis in dollars per year. The firm's marginal cost of capital equals its average cost of capital k, as represented by the horizontal line at k percent per year.[2] The rates of return r on each investment open to the firm are shown as decreasing as more investment occurs; this reflects the assumption that the most profitable investments will be made first and the poorer investments made last. The total dollar value of the annual investments is also measured along the horizontal axis. In Fig. 9-1, I^* dollars of investment occurs where $r = k$. I^* is the optimal investment regardless of whether the capital to finance this investment is raised by selling stock, bonds, or preferred stock, by retaining earnings or by obtaining a loan (assuming k does not change).

To the left of I^* dollars of investment, the internal rate of return is larger than the firm's cost of capital, $r > k$, and the firm could increase its value by expanding investment to I^*. If earnings are only E^1, I^* still is the amount of investment which will maximize the firm's value. The firm should invest I^* if it has to sell new securities to raise the needed funds. However, in the dividend model, outside financing is not included. Thus, for this situation the model would show that the owner's wealth (that is, v) was maximized by retaining and investing the firm's total earnings of E^1 and paying no dividends. In a more comprehensive model allowing for outside financing, the firm should sell new securities to finance I^* investment; only this investment would truly maximize the owner's wealth. A more comprehensive model which allows new financing is explicated later in this chapter.

Constancy of r.   Assuming that the most profitable investments are made first, common sense indicates that eventually no more profitable investments will be left. This is correctly represented graphically in Fig. 9-1 by a declining investment r curve. But the dividend model assumes that r is constant (an assumption which is true only for small investments, if ever).

If total earnings in Fig. 9-1 were E^2 dollars, for example, the dividend model indicates that they should all be paid out in dividends because $r < k$ at E^2. In a more comprehensive model which recognizes that r declines, the optimal policy would be to retain earnings of I^* for investment and pay dividends of $(E^2 - I^*)$ dollars. Since the model always indicates that the optimal dividend payout is zero, 100 percent, or irrelevant, the dividend policy which actually maximizes the owner's wealth will rarely be indicated.

Constancy of k.   A firm's cost of capital or appropriate discount rate k varies directly with the risk of the firm. Figure 9-2 is a graph of the security market line (SML) which shows that as the risk of a firm (or any asset) increases, the appropriate discount rises too. The present value of the firm's income moves inversely with the discount rate. By assuming that the discount rate k is constant, the model abstracts from these effects of risk on the value of the firm. Risk measurement and the SML are discussed in Chap. 12.

FIG. 9-2 The discount rate k is determined by risk.

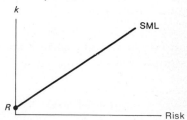

Infinite life. It is usually realistic to assume that a modern corporation endures perpetually. It will have new managements, and probably new products, too, as time passes. But the corporate shell can live forever.

No taxes. This unrealistic simplifying assumption is relaxed in a more comprehensive model developed later in this chapter. The differential tax rates on dividends and capital gains are considered.

Constant growth rate. This assumption is merely a simplification of reality. It can be easily changed without changing the conclusions. The assumption that g does not change is made merely to simplify the mathematics of the model.

Cost of capital exceeding growth rate, $k > g$. This assumption is realistic. Although a firm could sustain very high growth rates over the period of a few years, no firm could double or triple its earnings indefinitely. If a firm's earnings doubled annually for very many decades, its total profit would grow to exceed the gross national product of the United States.

Constant dividend payout ratio $(1 - f)$. The assumption that the firm has a constant retention rate f is merely another effort to simplify the mathematical form of the model. If f did change far in the future, the conclusions of the model would not be changed because the present value of future dollars is smaller. Furthermore, this assumption is fairly realistic. Most firms do tend to maintain a fixed retention rate when it is averaged over several years.

Beginning social scientists should not become discouraged about the dividend model because it is built on eight more-or-less (mostly less) realistic assumptions. Remember, a model is supposed to be a simplified version of reality. The simplifications were made for good reasons: to keep the mathematics as simple as possible, and to focus on only the main issues in the valuation theory of equity shares. And the model yielded some fascinating insights; for example, would you have believed that dividend policy does not affect the value of most normal firms? This issue is analyzed further below.

Gordon's Bird-in-the-Hand Model

Dr. Gordon has studied the effects of relaxing the simplifying assumptions of the dividend model, and he has performed econometric tests using empirical data.[3] He concludes that dividend policy is irrelevant when $r = k$ and all the simplifying assumptions are maintained. But when these assumptions are realigned to conform more closely with reality, Dr. Gordon

---

[3] M. J. Gordon, op. cit., chaps. 6–14.

concludes that dividend policy *does* affect the value of a share even though $r = k$. The introduction of risk into the model is Gordon's way of reaching the conclusion that dividend policy does matter in the "real world."

With the introduction of risk and uncertainty, the appropriate discount rate k *varies* as risk and uncertainty vary.[4] Gordon suggests that risk and uncertainty increase with futurity; that is, the further one looks into the future, the more uncertain things (namely, dividends) become. Therefore, Gordon suggests that k should not be held constant. Rather, k increases further in the future. Future dividends should be discounted at a higher discount rate than current dividends. Symbolically, Gordon says $k_t > k_{t-1}$ for $t = 1, 2, \ldots, \infty$ because of increasing risk and uncertainty in the future. He rewrites his basic model (9-2) as (9-11) with a subscript on the discount rates to represent uncertainty by specifying that $k_t > k_{t-1}$. The subscripts on k change to represent Gordon's assumption that k changes in the future.

$$v_0 = \sum_{t=1}^{\infty} \frac{d_t}{1 + k_t}$$

$$= \frac{d_1}{1 + k_1} + \frac{d_2}{(1 + k_2)^2} + \frac{d_3}{(1 + k_3)^3} + \cdots + \frac{d_t}{(1 + k_t)^t} + \cdots \quad (9\text{-}11)$$

Equation (9-11) is sometimes lightly referred to as the "bird-in-the-hand" model since near dividends are valued above distant dividends. If the average of the discount rates in Eq. (9-11) equals the constant discount rate in Eq. (9 2), then Eq. (9-2) and the "bird-in-the-hand" model, Eq. (9-11), are equal. But it is unlikely the k_t's average out to equal k in Eq. (9-2).

To show the impact of uncertainty on dividend policy, Dr. Gordon suggests that dividend d_1 in (9-11) be *retained and reinvested* to earn a constant internal rate of return r into perpetuity. The earnings from this reinvestment are rd_1 dollars per period per share into perpetuity. If these additional earnings are paid out as increases to the other regular dividends (that is, $d_2, d_3, \ldots$), the value of the stock is represented by (9-12).

$$v_0' = \frac{0}{1 + k_1} + \frac{d_2 + rd_1}{(1 + k_2)^2} + \frac{d_3 + rd_1}{(1 + k_3)^3} + \cdots + \frac{d_t + rd_1}{(1 + k_t)^t} + \cdots \quad (9\text{-}12)$$

Even though r equals the average of all the k_t's, the value of the stock in Eq. (9-12) is less than the value of the stock in (9-2) and (9-11). Symbolically, $v_0 > v_0'$ because the average of the k_t's for $t = 1, 2, \ldots, \infty$ is a smaller average discount rate than the average of the k_t's for $t = 2, 3, \ldots, \infty$.

If the discount rate had remained constant as in (9-2), the value of the

---

[4] Risk and uncertainty are used synonymously in this book to refer to probabilistic outcomes where the probability distribution is known. Uncertainty is not used here in the Knightian sense that the probability distribution is not known.

firm would be unchanged by shifting dividends timewise. Equation (9-13) shows the present value of the income from the reinvested d_1 if $r = k$.

$$\sum_{t=1}^{\infty} \frac{rd_1}{(1 + k)^t} = \frac{rd_1}{k} = d_1 \qquad \text{if } r = k \tag{9-13}$$

Thus, if $r = k_t$ for all time periods, shifting d_1 to a later period does not affect v_0 because the present value of the perpetual income rd_1 is d_1. But when $k_t > k_{t-1}$, as in (9-12), the income from the reinvested dividend (that is, rd_1) is discounted at a higher average discount rate since the average of k_t for $t = 2, 3, \ldots, \infty$ is larger than the average of k_t for $t = 1, 2, 3, \ldots, \infty$. Thus, $v_0' < v_0$, which shows how dividend policy can affect value in a world of uncertainty.

By merely introducing uncertainty into the model, Gordon has shown how dividend policy can affect the value of stock.[5] Uncertainty explains why some investors value a dollar of dividend income more than a dollar of capital gains income. These investors value dividends above capital gains because dividends are easier to predict, less uncertain, and less risky, and are therefore discounted with a lower discount rate. When uncertainty of the type shown in (9-11) exists, the present value of a dollar of dividends is larger the sooner the dividend is received.

9-3 MM's DIVIDEND IRRELEVANCE ARGUMENT

Two financial economists, Dr. Franco Modigliani and Dr. Merton Miller (called MM hereafter, for brevity), disagreed with Dr. Gordon's bird-in-the-hand model which shows that a firm's dividend policy affects its value.[6] So, MM constructed the simpler one-period dividend valuation model developed below from Eq. (9-2) as a basis for their dividend irrelevance argument.

One-Period Dividend Valuation Model

The multiperiod dividend valuation model, Eq. (9-2) or (9-3c), can be simplified to a one-period dividend valuation model by assuming the share of stock is sold after period $t = 1$, as shown below in Eq. (9-14):

$$v_0 = \frac{d_1}{1 + k} + \frac{d_2}{(1 + k)^2} + \cdots + \frac{d_\infty}{(1 + k)^\infty} \tag{9-3c}$$

$$v_0 = \frac{d_1 + v_1}{1 + k} \tag{9-14}$$

[5] M. J. Gordon, "Optimal Investment and Financing Policy," *The Journal of Finance*, May 1963, pp. 264–272.
[6] M. H. Miller and F. Modigliani, "Dividend Policy, Growth and the Valuation of Shares," *Journal of Business*, October 1961, pp. 411–433.

because, if a share is sold at $t = 1$, the term v_1 can be substituted in place of the share's future dividends, $\sum\limits_{t=1}^{\infty} \dfrac{d_{1+t}}{(1+k)^t}$.

To find the value of the entire firm in period t, MM merely multiply both sides of Eq. (9-14) by the number of shares outstanding in period t, denoted n_t, to obtain Eq. (9-14a), as shown below.

$$v_t = \frac{d_t + v_{t+1}}{1 + k_t} \tag{9-14}$$

$$n_t v_t = V_t = \frac{n_t(d_t + v_{t+1})}{1 + k_t} = \frac{D_t + V_{t+1}}{1 + k_t} \tag{9-14a}$$

To expedite mathematical manipulation, MM base their model on the following simplifying assumptions:

1 *Perfect capital markets.* In a perfect capital market no buyer or seller is large enough for his or her individual transactions to affect prices; financial information is freely available to everyone so that uninformed investors may be ignored; and no taxes, brokers' commissions, or other transfer costs exist to deter investors from seeking a profit-maximizing equilibrium.

2 *Investors' value dollars of dividends and dollars of capital gains equally.* This assumption is partially the result of assuming that no tax differential exists between dividends and capital gains.

3 *No risk or uncertainty.* Investors can forecast future prices and dividends with certainty, and therefore one discount rate is appropriate for all securities and all time periods. In this case $r = k = k_t$ for all t.

MM Fundamental Principle of Valuation

Under the assumptions just listed, the price of each share must adjust so that the rate of income (that is, the rate of dividends plus capital gains) on every share will be equal to the appropriate discount rate and be identical for all assets over any given interval of time. This *fundamental theorem of valuation* means that the rate of return from a share of common stock, as defined in Eq. (9-15), is equal for all firms over any given period of time.

$$\begin{aligned} r_t &= \frac{d_t + v_{t+1} - v_t}{v_t} \\ &= \frac{\text{dividends} + \text{capital gains or loss}}{\text{purchase price}} \end{aligned} \tag{9-15}$$

The fundamental theorem says that the rate of economic income defined in Eq. (9-15) will be equal for all shares in perfect markets which are at equilibrium when no differences in risk exist. This fundamental valuation model is true because MM assumed away everything which might interfere with its validity.[7]

The important implication of MM's fundamental principle of valuation is that all firms in all periods will have the same cost of capital k. This is true because a firm's cost of capital k equals the investor's rate of return r. So, if all firms' r_t's must be equal by the fundamental principle of valuation, their k_t's must all be equal too ($r = k$). The quantities r and k are just the two sides of the same coin.

MM's Proof of Dividend Irrelevance

If a firm has a change in the number of shares outstanding, this change is denoted $\Delta n_t = n_{t+1} - n_t$. In the case that new shares are issued (or old ones repurchased as treasury stock), Eq. (9-14a) should be rewritten as Eq. (9-16) to reflect possible changes in the value of the firm.

$$V_t = \frac{D_t + V_{t+1} - \Delta n_t v_{t+1}}{1 + k} \tag{9-16}$$

The quantity $(\Delta n_t)(v_{t+1})$ is subtracted from V_{t+1} in the numerator of (9-16) to reflect the change in the number of shares outstanding. The total value of all of these *new* shares is defined in (9-17).

$$\begin{aligned} \Delta n_t v_{t+1} &= n_{t+1} v_{t+1} - n_t v_{t+1} \\ &= v_{t+1}(n_{t+1} - n_t) \end{aligned} \tag{9-17}$$

Since MM's model allows for the issuance (or retirement) of shares, the firm can raise (or repay) capital to pay dividends and *also* undertake the optimal investment program (as explained in Fig. 9-1). Thus, dividend and investment policies are not perversely intertwined in MM's model as they were in Eq. (9-2), the multiperiod dividend model. As a result, MM's model yields more general conclusions than the dividend model.

Changes in the firm's investment in total assets, denoted I_t, may be financed through either earnings retention ($E_t - D_t$) or the issuance of new shares ($n_t v_{t+1}$). It follows that the proceeds of any new issue equal the new investment less any retained earnings, as shown by Eq. (9-18).

$$\begin{aligned} \Delta n_t v_{t+1} &= I_t - (E_t - D_t) \\ &= I_t - E_t + D_t \end{aligned} \tag{9-18}$$

---

[7] Some people object to models which social scientists like MM build because the models are based on simplifying assumptions. However, the people should not object. Social scientists have as much right to seek basic economic truth by assuming away realistic details like taxes and uncertainty as physical scientists have to conduct their gravity experiments in sealed vacuum chambers where winds do not blow and birds do not fly.

If Δn_t is negative, this represents the case where assets are sold or earnings are retained to purchase outstanding shares (that is, treasury stock).

Using these symbols, MM show that the value of the firm is unaffected by its dividend policy by substituting Eq. (9-18) into (9-16) to obtain (9-19), as shown below.

$$V_t = \frac{D_t + V_{t+1} - \Delta n_t v_{t+1}}{1 + k_t} \tag{9-16}$$

$$= \frac{D_t + V_{t+1} - (I_t - E_t + D_t)}{1 + k_t}$$

$$= \frac{V_{t+1} - I_t + E_t}{1 + k_t} \tag{9-19}$$

The restatement of the total value of the firm with external financing in (9-19) is consistent with the previous statement of the firm's value in (9-16) and (9-14a). But since it is possible to restate the value of the firm (9-19) without dividends (D_t), this proves that dividends have no effect on the value of the firm when external financing is used. As shown in Fig. 9-1, dividends affect the firm's value only when the firm finances all investment *internally*. When external financing is utilized, dividend policy has no effect on the value of the firm under MM's simplifying assumptions.

Subjective Arguments for Dividend Relevance

Some students of finance are not impressed by Modigliani and Miller's dividend irrelevance model. So, to supplement Dr. Gordon's bird-in-the hand model, these people have dissented with MM by offering the following subjective arguments for the relevance of dividend policy in valuing equity shares.

Resolution of uncertainty. Some advocates of dividend relevance have supported the bird-in-the-hand model by pointing out that investors prefer to receive cash dividends because the payout resolves their uncertainty. If a firm retains its earnings, there is uncertainty about when and if those retained earnings will cause capital gains.

Informational content. Many people have argued that information is conveyed from a corporation's top management to its stockholders through the firm's dividend policy. Stockholders are viewed as outsiders who are not fully aware of what is going on in their firm. Therefore, they look for signals about their firm, and its dividend policy is one of the easiest places to find information from top management. For example, if a firm has paid increasing cash dividends for decades and then announces a dividend reduction, many shareholders will interpret this change as evidence that the firm's earning power has been reduced. So these shareholders may sell the stock because they think its earnings can be expected to be less.

Clientele theory. The popular clientele theory is a third subjective theory which suggests that dividend policy affects stock prices. It asserts that certain stocks attract certain kinds of investors because the investors prefer the firm's dividend payout policies. For example, widows who are counting on their investment income to keep them out of the poorhouse are supposed to buy public utility stocks which tend to pay good cash dividends. In contrast, high-income investors are assumed to want growth stocks which pay no cash dividends and instead have large capital gains which enjoy a preferential income tax.

The differential tax treatment of capital gains and dividends requires that the before-tax rate of return as defined in Eq. (9-15) be rewritten thus:

$$_{at}r_t = \frac{d_t(1 - T_0) + (v_{t-1} - v_t)(1 - T_g)}{v_t} \qquad T_0 > T_g \qquad (9\text{-}20)$$

where $_{at}r_t$ denotes the after-tax rate of return at period t, T_0 is the tax rate on ordinary income, and T_g is the capital gains rate.

Since MM's fundamental principle of valuation and all their models are based on the definition of the rate of return, dropping the assumption of no taxes will change all their models. MM freely state that "the tax differential in favor of capital gains is undoubtedly the major systematic imperfection in the market."[8] Nevertheless, MM still conclude that dividend policy has no effect on share values.

MM reason that the lower capital gains tax is not important for several reasons. First, many investors' capital gains and dividends are taxed equally (namely, charitable and educational institutions, foundations, pension trusts, and low-income retired people). Second, MM begin their own clientele theory by pointing out that all stocks have a long-run average payout ratio between zero and 1. Figure 9-3 shows a hypothetical relative-frequency distribution of the payout ratios *supplied* by all the firms issuing

[8] M. H. Miller and F. Modigliani, op. cit., p. 432.

FIG. 9-3 Hypothetical relative-frequency distribution of payout ratios supplied by firms.

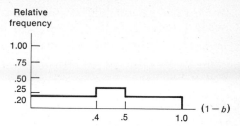

FIG. 9-4 Hypothetical relative-frequency distribution of payout ratios desired by investors.

stock. If investors have preferences for given payout ratios, they could be surveyed and the clientele for each payout ratio could be ascertained. Figure 9-4 shows a hypothetical relative-frequency distribution of payout ratios *desired* by investors. A comparison of the supply and demand for various payout ratios represented by Figs. 9-3 and 9-4 reveals a shortage of payout ratios in the 40 to 50 percent range and an oversupply of all other payout ratios.

MM reason that the market prices of stocks with payout ratios in the scarce 40 to 50 percent range will be bid up. The other firms' prices will be relatively lower because of lack of demand. If the managements of these firms are perceptive, they will note how much more demand exists for firms whose payout ratios are in the 40 to 50 percent range, and they will change their payout ratios until supply equals demand at each payout ratio. Thus, each firm will attract a clientele of investors who prefer its payout policies. For example, a consistent dividend-paying firm like American Telephone and Telegraph (ATT) would not have as many high-income investors who prefer capital gains as Polaroid, Litton, or IBM. MM go on to point out that:

> Even if there were a shortage of some particular payout ratio, investors would still normally have the option of achieving their particular savings objectives without paying a premium for the stocks in short supply by buying appropriately weighted combinations of the more plentiful payout ratios.[9]

Investors' liquidation costs. A final argument in support of cash dividends as a means of increasing owners' wealth is based on stockbrokers' commissions. If a shareholder must liquidate some shares to obtain needed cash, a brokerage commission must be paid to sell the shares. Many of the commission costs could be avoided if firms would all pay cash dividends regularly.

Arguments Favoring Dividend Retention

Among those who believe that a firm's dividend policy does affect the value of its shares there is a group that argues *for* and another group which argues *against* cash dividends. The latter group disagrees with the subjec-

[9] Ibid.

tive arguments that cash dividends are desirable because they resolve uncertainty, convey information, and provide cashflows for needy clientele. This group offers the following points in support of earnings retention (which tends to cause capital gains).

Tax differential. The most powerful and undeniable argument against cash dividends is the fact that they are taxed at a higher rate than capital gains [see Eq. (9-20)]. This tax differential is a good rationale for earnings retention.

The flotation costs of issues. Those who favor earnings retention point out that the firm can expand on retained earnings instead of on new security issues. This allows the firm to avoid paying a fee to an investment banker to float new security issues to raise capital with which to finance expansion.

Sale of stock at lower price. A subjective argument favoring dividend relevance is that new shares of stock which are sold to replace money paid out in cash dividends will drive down the market price of the outstanding shares.[10] The point of this position is that investors should prefer the stock of firms which retain earnings. The value of the shares will not be depressed by diluting sales of new shares to obtain cash with which to pay cash dividends.

Conclusion about Dividend Policy

The preceding discussion embraced many aspects of the intellectual discussion about dividend policy. Valuation models were introduced. And models showing the relevance and the irrelevance of dividend policy were analyzed. The arguments for and against cash dividend payment were reviewed. What is the final answer? Are dividends really irrelevant?

MM's dividend irrelevance model is more general than Gordon's bird-in-the-hand model because the MM model allows external financing. And MM's clientele theory (see Figs. 9-3 and 9-4) is more logical than stories about widows' cash needs and other subjective arguments. However, the burden of heavier taxation on cash dividends is difficult to dismiss. Overall, it seems that dividend policy is probably irrelevant—but investors in high tax brackets logically dislike cash dividends. The problem with reaching this conclusion is that most business persons and amateur investors believe the opposite—they think cash dividends are desirable. So, alas, the dividend debate continues unresolved.

In a different vein, an important common stock valuation question which can be answered fairly quickly is: What do investors capitalize?

---

[10] John Lintner, "Dividends, Earnings, Leverage, Stock Prices, and the Supply of Capital to Corporations," *Review of Economics and Statistics,* August 1962.

9-4 DIFFERENT APPROACHES TO VALUATION

Finance professors, fundamental security analysts, economists, and others have suggested several approaches to determining the values of an asset. Three of the more popular approaches involve capitalizing (that is, finding the present value of) three different streams of money.

> **1** *The cashflow approach.* The advocates of this approach, mostly finance professors and economists, suggest that the value of a security is the present value of the cashflows it produces. Chapter 7 stressed this approach in valuing bonds, since their cashflows are known in advance.

> **2** *The dividend approach.* This approach suggests that the value of a common stock is the present value of all its expected cash dividends.

> **3** *The stream-of-earnings approach.* This approach suggests that the value of a security is the present value of all its future earnings. This approach is supported by many fundamental security analysts.

At this point, the obvious question is: What do investors capitalize—net cashflows, dividends, or earnings? MM have shown that, properly formulated, all three approaches are identical.

MM start to equate these three seemingly divergent valuation approaches by extending (9-19) to cover longer time spans. Equation (9-19) may be rewritten as (9-19a) and (9-19b).

$$V_t = \frac{E_t - I_t + V_{t+1}}{1 + k} \tag{9-19a}$$

$$= \frac{E_t - I_t}{1 + k} + \frac{V_{t+1}}{1 + k} \tag{9-19b}$$

Looking past one period to T periods in the future causes (9-19b) to expand to (9-20) below.

$$V_0 = \sum_{t=1}^{T-1} \frac{E_t - I_t}{(1 + k)^t} + \frac{V_T}{(1 + k)^T} \tag{9-20}$$

When T is infinitely large, $V_T/(1 + k)^T$ becomes zero and (9-20) can be rewritten as Eq. (9-21):

$$V_0 = \sum_{T=1}^{T=\infty} \frac{E_t - I_t}{(1 + k)^t} + 0 \tag{9-21}$$

The Cashflow Approach

The cashflow in period t, denoted C_t, is the difference between inflows and outflows. More specifically, the cashflow from a firm is its earnings less investments necessary to maintain the firm, as shown in Eq. (9-22).

$$C_t = E_t - I_t \tag{9-22}$$

According to the advocates of the discounted cashflow approach, the value of the firm is given by Eq. (9-23).

$$V_0 = \sum_{t=1}^{\infty} \frac{C_t}{(1+k)^t} \tag{9-23}$$

Substituting (9-22) in (9-23) yields (9-21). This shows the equivalence of the cashflow valuation model to (9-21) and its predecessors—Eqs. (9-19), (9-14), and (9-16).

The Stream-of-Earnings Approach

Those who do not approve of the discounted stream-of-earnings approach typically attack it on two points. First, these detractors charge that stockholders cannot withdraw earnings from the corporation as they are earned—they must wait for cash dividends to be paid. When $r = k$ and markets are perfect, this argument is empty. In this case the market value of a share increases by an amount equal to retained earnings. Thus, stockholders who want their earnings can have them by liquidating some of their holdings.

Second, the earnings approach is sometimes attacked for "double counting." The double-counting advocates charge that all earnings are counted as income when they are earned. Then, *earnings on retained earnings* are counted as income again later. The problem with some double-counting advocates is that they define income inappropriately. The earnings E_t less new investments I_t required to maintain future earnings, as defined in Eq. (9-24), correspond with economists' definition of truly *consumable* income.

$$\text{True economic earnings} = E_t - I_t \tag{9-24}$$

Economists and many others correctly assert that the retention of accounting profits in the firm to maintain its future income (but not increase it) is not the retention of true income, although the accounting profession calls it "retained earnings." Thus, the stream-of-earnings approach, properly formulated, says the value of the firm is the present value of all *true economic earnings* as defined in (9-21).

$$V_t = \sum_{t=1}^{\infty} \frac{E_t - I_t}{(1+k)^t} \tag{9-21}$$

Thus, MM show that if it is properly formulated (that is, if earnings are defined properly), the stream-of-earnings approach is equivalent to the other valuation approaches. In practical applications, it is the responsibility of the financial analyst to adjust accounting profit to conform to the true economic income if the stream-of-earnings approach is to be used.

To see the necessity of adjusting accounting earnings to conform to the concept of economic income, consider, say, the color television industry. When RCA went into mass production of color television sets in the 1960s, its television competitors who wanted to maintain their future income undiminished had to invest much or all their *accounting profit* internally in assets to produce color TV sets. The depreciation flows provided by the firms' old assets were not sufficient to finance these new assets for color television production. This investment of accounting profit most certainly is not the retention of true income. These so-called retained earnings could not be withdrawn from the firm and consumed without decreasing the firm's ability to compete and earn in the future. Any television manufacturer that did not move into the production of color sets in the 1960s would more than likely lose market share and income in the television industry of the 1970s. This example shows (1) the need for the financial analyst to adjust reported accounting income; (2) the rationale behind valuation equation (9-21); and (3) the weakness of the accounting definition of income as it compares with the economic concept of income.

The Dividend Approach

The dividend approach, properly formulated, says that the discounted value of the dividends coming to *a given share* of stock equals the value of that share. This is equivalent to taking the present value of *all* future dividends of the firm only if *no* new shares were issued nor old ones retired. Let $D_{(t,1)}$ denote total dividends of the firm *paid in period t to stockholders of record at period t = 1*. Dividends paid on new shares issued after $t = 1$ should not be included in present value of $D_{(t,1)}$, $D_{(t+1,1)}$, $D_{(t+2,1)}$, $D_{(t+3,1)}$, . . . , $D_{(\infty,1)}$. The present value of the firm to stockholders of record at $t = 1$ is given by Eq. (9-25).

$$V_1 = \sum_{t=1}^{\infty} \frac{D_{(t,1)}}{(1 + k)^t} \tag{9-25}$$

$$= \frac{D_{(t,1)}}{1 + k} + \sum_{t=2}^{\infty} \frac{D_{(t,1)}}{(1 + k)^t}$$

$$= \frac{1}{1 + k} \left[D_{(t,1)} + \sum_{t=1}^{\infty} \frac{D_{(t+1,1)}}{(1 + k)^t} \right] \tag{9-25a}$$

The present value at $t = 2$ of the future dividend stream $D_{(t,1)}$ equals the present value at $t = 2$ of the dividend stream $D_{(t,2)}$ times a fraction $[1 - (\Delta n_1)/n_2]$ representing the ratio of the number of shares outstanding at $t = 1$ to the number of shares outstanding at $t = 2$. Equation (9-26) represents this symbolically.

$$\sum_{t=1}^{\infty} \frac{D_{(t+1,1)}}{(1+k)^t} = \left[\sum_{t=1}^{\infty} \frac{D_{(t+1,2)}}{(1+k)^t}\right]\left(1 - \frac{\Delta n_1}{n_2}\right) \qquad (9\text{-}26)$$

Substituting (9-26) into (9-25a) yields (9-27).

$$V_1 = \frac{1}{1+k}\left\{D_{(1,1)} + \left[\sum_{t=1}^{\infty} \frac{D_{(t+1,2)}}{(1+k)^t}\right]\left(1 - \frac{\Delta n_1 v_2}{n_2 v_2}\right)\right\} \qquad (9\text{-}27)$$

Multiplying the quantity inside the brackets by the quantity inside the large parentheses in (9-27) yields

$$n_2 v_2 \left(1 - \frac{\Delta n_1 v_2}{n_2 v_2}\right) = V_2 - \Delta n_1 v_2$$

by using the definitions below in (9-28).

$$V_2 = n_2 v_2 \qquad (9\text{-}28)$$
$$= \sum_{t=1}^{\infty} \frac{D_{(t+1,2)}}{(1+k)^2}$$

Substituting the quantity $V_2 - \Delta n_1 v_2$ in place of the product of the quantity in brackets and the quantity in parentheses in (9-27) yields (9-29).

$$V_1 = \frac{1}{1+k}\,(D_{1,1} + V_2 - \Delta n_1 v_2) \qquad (9\text{-}29)$$

$$V_t = \frac{D_t + V_{t+1} + \Delta n_t v_{t+1}}{1+k} \qquad (9\text{-}16)$$

Since $D_{1,1} = D_t$ at $t = 1$, Eq. (9-29) is equivalent to the basic valuation equation (9-16), from which Eq. (9-21) and others were derived. Thus, MM show that, properly formulated, the dividends approach is equivalent to the earnings and net cashflow approaches.

9-5 SUMMARY AND CONCLUSIONS

The theory of finance is not definitive about the effect of dividend policy on the value of an equity share. Dr. Gordon's model shows how uncertainty about the future can make a share which pays cash dividends more valuable than a share which is identical in every way, except that its dividend policy is more restrictive. Doctors Modigliani and Miller, in turn, developed a more general dividend valuation model which permits external financing. MM, using their model, prove that dividend policy has no effect on the value of a share. The fact that MM's model is more general (that is, it allows outside financing) weights in favor of accepting it over more restricted models. But, when differential income taxes on dividends and capital gains are considered, a good case can be made for retaining all earnings to maximize the value of normal and growth firms. Thus, the theory is at odds with the popular notion among many business executives that cash dividends have a profound effect on the value of common stock.

Theoretical analysis of several commonly used valuation models was highly informative. Valuation models based on cashflows, earnings, and dividends were all shown to be equivalent when properly formulated. And the analysis of these models was helpful in clarifying exactly how they should be formulated to yield consistent results. In the next chapter, the dividend valuation model embraced by Gordon, MM, and other analysts as well — that is, Eq. (9-2) — is reformulated in a more pragmatic manner, and fundamental security analysis methods which have been popular on Wall Street for decades are analyzed within the context of this model.

QUESTIONS

1 Define the phrase *financial model.*

2 For a firm with earnings per share of $10, dividends per share of $6, a cost of capital of 10 percent, and an internal rate of return of 15 percent, calculate its value using the dividend model.

3 Discuss the simplifying assumptions which MM's and Gordon's models have in common. Can any problems arise from using such simplifications?

4 Do investors capitalize dividends or earnings in estimating the value of a stock? Explain.

5 "Dividend policy is irrelevant." True, false, or uncertain? Explain.

6 Compare and contrast the importance of dividend policy with and without the preferential tax rates on capital gains using any model you prefer. Assume that the internal rate of return r equals the firm's cost of capital k and that capital gains are taxed at half the rate for ordinary income.

7 How can the present value of a share's cash dividends be equal to the present value of the share's earnings when dividends are almost always less than earnings?

8 Critically analyze the proposition on which Gordon's bird-in-the-hand model is based — that is, that uncertainty increases with futurity.

9 Why do Modigliani and Miller use the same discount rate k to find the value of three different income streams — dividends, earnings, and cashflows?

SELECTED REFERENCES

Friend, Irwin, and Marshall Puckett, "Dividends and Stock Prices," *American Economic Review,* September 1954, pp. 656–682.

> An empirical test to determine if investors capitalize dividends or earnings. Regression analysis is used.

Gordon, M. J., *The Investment, Financing, and Valuation of the Corporation* (Homewood, Ill.: Irwin, 1962).

> A full discussion of Gordon's model for capitalizing dividends and a review of some of the literature. Some calculus used, mostly algebra.

Miller, M. H., and F. Modigliani, "Dividend Policy, Growth, and the Valuation of Shares," *Journal of Business,* October 1961, pp. 411–433.

> The theory of valuation for shares in an all-equity corporation is analyzed with some analysis and review of relevant theories. Freshman college algebra used.

Modigliani, F., and M. H. Miller, "The Cost of Capital, Corporation Finance and the Theory of Investment; Corporate Income Taxes, and the Cost of Capital: A Correction," *American Economic Review,* June 1958, pp. 433–443.

> The valuation of equity shares in a corporation which uses debt is explained. Freshman college algebra used.

Ten

Fundamental Stock Analysis

The job of security analysts is to estimate the value of securities. This is the basis for rational investment decisions. If a security's estimated value is above its market price, the security analyst will recommend buying the stock. Or, if the estimated value is below the market price, the security should be sold before its price drops. This buying and selling are what determine securities prices. Underpriced stocks are purchased until their price is bid up to equal their value. And overpriced stocks are sold, which drives their price down until it equals the security's value. Thus, in an efficient securities market, prices always equal values. But the values of securities are continuously changing as new news about the securities becomes known, and this flux is what makes life exciting for security analysts. They must keep up-to-date value estimates for the securities with which they are working or they will make bad (that is, unprofitable) buy and sell recommendations and perhaps lose their jobs.

This chapter explains how fundamental common stock analysts—that is, analysts who study the fundamental facts affecting a stock's value rather than follow fads or charts—do their investment research. Fundamental analysts delve into companies earnings, their managements, the economic forecast, the firm's competition, market conditions, and many other factors. However, all their research is based on the valuation model explained below.

10-1 THE PRESENT VALUE OF CASH DIVIDENDS

The true economic value or *intrinsic value* of a share of common stock, like the value of a bond, is the present value of all cashflows from the share. Letting d_{it} denote the ith shares' (for example, General Motors) cash dividends per share paid in the tth time period (say, the third quarter of 1985 might be as one of the time periods), and letting k_i represent the ith stock's risk-adjusted discount rate (or cost of equity capital or equity capitalization rate) means that the ith share's value, denoted p_i, is given by the present value formula (10-1), or equivalently by (10-1a) and (10-1b).

$$p_{io} = \sum_{t=1}^{\infty} \frac{d_{it}}{(1 + k_i)^t} \tag{10-1}$$

$$= \sum_{t=1}^{\infty} \frac{d_{io} (1 + g_i)^t}{(1 + k_i)^t} \qquad \text{since } d_{it} = d_{io} (1 + g_i)^t \tag{10-1a}$$

$$= \frac{d_{i1}}{k_i - g_i} \tag{10-1b}$$

The growth rate for dividends, the g symbol, is presumed constant in writing Eqs. (10-1a) and (10-1b), so $d_t = d_{io} (1 + g_i)^t$. This simplification allows the algebraic manipulation necessary to derive (10-1b) and (10-1a).[1]

---

[1] If dividends grow at some constant rate, denoted g, then future dividends are related to current dividends as shown below. First note that Eq. (10-1a) can be rewritten as (F1).

$$p_0 = \sum_{t=1}^{\infty} \frac{d_0(1 + g)^t}{(1 + k)^t} \tag{F1}$$

$\Sigma d_0 x = d_0 \Sigma x$ because d_0 is a constant. This relation means that Eq. (10-1a) or (F1) may be rewritten as shown below.

$$p_0 = d_0 \sum_{t}^{t=1} \frac{(1 + g)^t}{(1 + k)^t} \tag{F2}$$

$$= d_0 \left[\frac{1 + g}{1 + k} + \frac{(1 + g)^2}{(1 + k)^2} + \frac{(1 + g)^3}{(1 + k)^3} + \cdots \right] \tag{F3}$$

Multiplying (F3) by $[(1 + k)/(1 + g)]$ yields (F4).

$$p_0 \frac{1 + k}{1 + g} = d_0 \left[1.0 + \frac{1 + g}{1 + k} + \frac{(1 + g)^2}{(1 + k)^2} + \cdots \right] \tag{F4}$$

Subtracting (F3) from the preceding equation yields Eq. (F5).

$$\left(\frac{1 + k}{1 + g} - 1 \right) p_0 = d_0 \tag{F5}$$

By assuming that $k > g$, the preceding equation can be rearranged as

$$\frac{(1 + k) - (1 + g)}{1 + g} p_0 = \frac{k - g}{1 + g} p_0 = d_0 \tag{F6}$$

(Continued on next page.)

10-2 FUNDAMENTAL ANALYSTS' MODEL

Most common stock analysts prepare their estimates of intrinsic value per share by multiplying the ith stock's normalized earnings per share, denoted e_{it} for the tth period, times the share's earnings multiplier, m_{it}, as shown in Eq. (10-2).

$$p_{io} = e_{it}m_{it} \qquad (10\text{-}2)$$

The security analyst gets the earnings per share from the corporation's accountants and then normalizes it, as explained in Chap. 11, to obtain e_{it}. The earnings multiplier is obtained simply by dividing both sides of Eq. (10-1) or (10-1a) by normalized earnings per share, e_{it}, as shown below in Eq. (10-3).

$$m_{it} = \frac{p_{it}}{e_{it}} = \sum_{t=1}^{\infty} \frac{d_{it}/e_{it}\,(1+g_i)^t}{(1+k_i)^t} \qquad (10\text{-}3)$$

$$m_{it} = \frac{p_{it}}{e_{it}} = \frac{d_{it}}{e_{it}} \sum_{t=1}^{\infty} \frac{(1+g_i)^t}{(1+k_i)^t} \qquad (10\text{-}3a)$$

$$m_{it} = \frac{d_{i1}/e_{io}}{k_i - g_i} \qquad (10\text{-}3b)$$

The earnings multiplier is frequently called the *price-earnings ratio*.[2] The ratio d_{it}/e_{it} in Eqs. (10-3) and (10-3a) is called the *dividend payout ratio*. It averages about 60 percent for most firms.

The remainder of this chapter focuses on the pragmatic approaches security analysts use to estimate a stock's appropriate earnings multiplier as defined in Eqs. (10-3) through (10-3b) and the intrinsic value of the share.

Multiplying the right-hand side by $1 + g$ yields Eq. (F7):

$$p_0\,(k-g) = d_0\,(1+g) = d_1 \qquad (F7)$$

where $d_0\,(1+g)^1 = d_1$ denotes "next period's" dividends per share. Equation (10-1b) can be obtained by rearranging the preceding equation as follows:

$$p_0 = \frac{d_1}{k-g} \qquad (10\text{-}1b)$$

---

[2] The equity share valuation model represented by Eqs. (10-1), (10-2), and (10-3) has been developed by B. G. Malkiel in the following literature. "Equity Yields, Growth, and the Structure of Share Prices," *American Economic Review,* December 1963, pp. 1004–1031; "The Valuation of Public Utility Equities," *Bell Journal of Economics and Management Science,* 1970, pp. 143–160; and by B. G. Malkiel and J. G. Cragg in "Expectations and the Structure of Share Prices," *American Economic Review,* September 1970, pp. 601–617.

The factors which determine a security's dividend growth rate g are explained first. However, the primary topics for the remainder of the chapter are the factors which cause securities markets to value a stock like, say, American Telephone and Telegraph at 10 times its earnings per share in 1973 after valuing the same share at 22 times its earnings in 1961. However, before discussing earnings multipliers, a more direct approach to the valuation of a corporation is considered, that is, simply appraising its assets to find their sales value. This approach is not recommended because a corporation should not be considered to be merely a collection of physical assets. A viable corporation is one that produces some product of value and earns income. If the corporation's assets cannot produce income, they have no economic value to businessmen.

Asset values. The asset value of a security is determined by estimating the liquidating value of the firm, deducting the claims of the firm's creditors, and allocating the remaining net asset value of the firm over the outstanding junior securities (namely, stock). The asset value of a firm is usually estimated by (1) consulting a specialist in appraising asset values and/or (2) consulting an accountant about the book value of the firm.

Asset values are important in determining the market value of a company usually only when it may go bankrupt. In that case the firm's income and dividends will probably not be continued and will therefore have negligible value: the firm's value is dependent upon the prices its assets

TABLE 10-1 SELECTED FINANCIAL DATA FOR AMERICAN TELEPHONE & TELEGRAPH (ATT) COMMON STOCK ON A PER SHARE BASIS

Year	Book value, $	Range of market price, $	Per share earnings, $	Average price-earnings ratio	Per share cash dividend, $	Dividend payout ratio, %
1975						
1974	52.70	53–39	5.27	8.7 times	3.16	59.9
1973	56.54	55–45	4.98	10.1	2.80	56.2
1972	50.31	53–41	4.34	10.9	2.65	61.0
1971	47.52	53–40	3.99	11.9	2.60	65.1
1970	45.52	53–40	3.99	11.8	2.60	65.1
1969	43.88	58–48	4.00	13.3	2.40	60.0
1968	42.17	58–48	3.74	14.2	2.40	64.1
1967	40.57	62–49	3.79	14.8	2.20	58.0
1966	38.84	63–49	3.67	15.4	2.20	59.9
1965	37.06	70–60	3.39	19.3	2.00	58.9
1964	36.02	75–65	3.18	22.1	1.95	61.3
1963	33.61	70–57	3.02	21.2	1.80	59.6
1962	31.80	68–49	2.86	20.5	1.80	62.9
1961	30.87	70–51	2.72	22.3	1.73	63.6
1960	28.55	54–39	2.72	17.3	1.65	60.6
1959	27.92	44–37	2.60	15.7	1.58	60.7

will bring at sale. But for prosperous firms asset values need not be considered. The intrinsic value of a prosperous firm or "going concern" typically far exceeds its asset value.

Table 10-1 shows some of the data for American Telephone and Telegraph (ATT) which would be used in estimating the intrinsic value of a share of the firm's common stock. The lack of relationship between book asset values and market values is apparent in these data—this is typical. In most cases, asset values may be ignored when valuing common stock (except for a nonoperating asset which may be sold without affecting the firm).

10-3 EARNINGS MULTIPLIERS: A PRAGMATIC APPROACH

Much of the fundamental security analyst's work centers on determining the appropriate capitalization rate, or equivalently, the appropriate multiplier to use in valuing a particular security's income. The main factors which must be considered in determining the correct multiplier are (1) the risk of the security, (2) the growth rate of the dividend stream, (3) the duration of any expected growth, and (4) the dividend payout ratio. Also, as the national economy and credit conditions change, interest rates, capitalization rates, and multipliers change. Table 10-2 suggests the general nature of the relationship between capitalization rates, multipliers, and risk when growth in income is zero. With this general background in mind, the determinants of intrinsic values are examined below. First, earnings multipliers are analyzed.

Earnings Multipliers

In determining the price-earnings ratio to use in valuing a firm's securities, three factors which must be estimated are the capitalization rate, the dividend growth rate, and the dividend payout ratio. As shown in Fig. 10-1,

TABLE 10-2 CAPITALIZATION RATES AND THEIR EQUIVALENT MULTIPLIERS WHEN INCOME IS CONSTANT

Capitalization rate (k), %	Riskiness	Equivalent multiplier ($1/k$)
1	Negligible risk	100
2		50
4		25
6		16.7
8		12.5
10	Medium risk	10
15		6.7
20		5
25		4
33		3
50	High risk	2

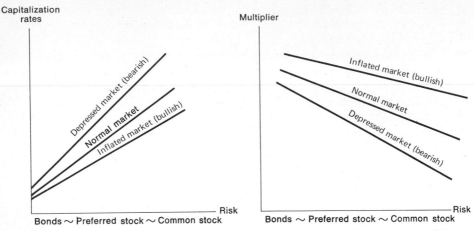

FIG. 10-1 Capitalization rates and multipliers are affected by risk and economic conditions.

capitalization rates vary with the firm's risk-class and the prevailing market conditions. This inquiry into earnings multipliers begins with the multipliers for a normal market; later, the effects of bull (that is, inflated) or bear (falling) markets will be examined.

A *normal market* is a market in which most security prices are experiencing slow, steady growth and the average price-earnings ratio is in the low to mid teens. Figures 10-2, 10-4, and 10-5 show the cyclical fluctuations in the stock market and some market-related economic statistics during recent years. When average earnings multipliers drop below 13 times, many market prices are deflated. When average earnings multipliers rise above approximately 18, it is the result of a bull market and many stocks are overpriced. The definitions of bear and bull markets are not based on particular market levels alone, however, but, rather, on the *direction of change* as well as the *level* of the market.

Since future expectations are influenced by past experience, a good way to estimate a firm's risk-class is to examine historical data. Studies of securities listed on the New York Stock Exchange (NYSE) have shown that their historical average earnings capitalization rate varies directly with the security's volatility coefficient (measuring systematic risk). Figure 10-3 depicts the relationship.[3] The fundamental analyst can measure the risk of the company in recent periods, adjust these historical risk statistics for any expected changes, and then use these forecasted risk statistics to obtain capitalization rates from Fig. 10-3. Chapter 12 explains how to measure a stock's risk in more detail.

---

[3] The security market line (SML) in Fig. 10-3 is the author's subjectively adjusted estimate based on empirical regressions. Empirical estimates of the SML may be found in F. Black, M. C. Jensen, and M. Scholes, "The Capital Asset Pricing Model: Some Empirical Tests," in M. C. Jensen (ed.), *Studies in the Theory of Capital Markets.*

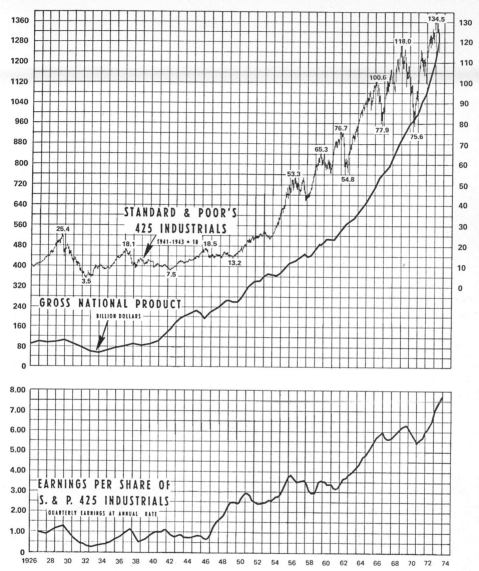

FIG. 10-2 Some stock market–related economic statistics.

The capitalization rates in Fig. 10-3 are for normal markets. If the analysis is being performed during an inflated market, for example, the capitalization rates in Fig. 10-3 should be adjusted downward to increase the earnings multiplier in line with prevailing conditions. The reverse is true if pessimism prevails and the market is depressed. After the capitalization rate has been determined, the growth rate in dividends per share must be estimated.

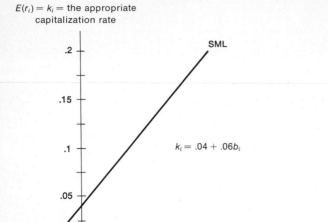

$E(r_i) = k_i = $ the appropriate capitalization rate

$$k_i = .04 + .06b_i$$

$b_i = $ systematic risk index = the beta volatility coefficient

FIG. 10-3 The security market line (SML) for normal market conditions.

Estimated Growth Rates Affect Multipliers

If a security is expected to become more valuable in the future, this antici- pated rise will tend to make it more valuable now. In order to place a cur- rent value on future growth in value, that growth must be estimated before it occurs. The growth rate in dividends or earnings per share is a good measure of growth in a firm's earning power in most cases. It is usually fairly simple to estimate the growth rate in cash dividends or earnings per share. Measuring these growth rates is discussed in Sec. 11-6 (pages 302 to 308).

It is important to develop accurate estimates of the firm's dividend growth rate and the period of time this growth may be expected to con- tinue. Table 10-3 shows that the growth rate and the expected duration of growth in dividends have an important influence on the earnings multipli- ers. In fact, the growth rate is as important as the capitalization rate in es- timating multipliers.

Estimating intrinsic value with zero earnings growth. To see how the multipli- ers in Table 10-3 are used to estimate intrinsic values, consider a hypotheti- cal example. Suppose that security markets were normal and that a security analyst had estimated the risk and growth statistics for the ABC Company. Assuming ABC's beta systematic risk coefficient, which measures its vola- tility, was estimated to be $b = 1.0$, Fig. 10-3 implies that the appropriate capitalization rate for the firm is about $k = 10$ percent.

Two different security analysts' estimates of a security's beta system- atic risk coefficient should not differ appreciably since the betas tend to be

TABLE 10-3 PRICE-EARNINGS RATIOS FOR VARIOUS RISK-CLASSES AND VARIOUS RATES OF DIVIDEND OR EARNINGS GROWTH IN NORMAL MARKETS

Type of risk	Capitalization rate (k), %	Growth rate in div. (g), %	Appropriate P/E ratio if earnings growth continues for:					
			5 years	10 years	15 years	20 years	25 years	Forever
Outcome fairly certain, low risk; example: high-quality preferred stock	2	0	50 (d/e)	50 (d/e)	50 (d/e)	50 (d/e)	50 (d/e)	50 (d/e)
		1	52.4 (d/e)	54.8 (d/e)	57 (d/e)	59.0 (d/e)	61.1 (d/e)	100 (d/e)
	4	0	25 (d/e)	25 (d/e)	25 (d/e)	25 (d/e)	25 (d/e)	25 (d/e)
		1	26.2 (d/e)	27.2 (d/e)	28 (d/e)	28.8 (d/e)	29.5 (d/e)	33.3 (d/e)
		2	27.4 (d/e)	29.6 (d/e)	31.6 (d/e)	33.3 (d/e)	35 (d/e)	50 (d/e)
Some uncertainty, medium risk; example: an established business	6	0	16.7 (d/e)	16.7 (d/e)	16.7 (d/e)	16.7 (d/e)	16.7 (d/e)	16.7 (d/e)
		2	18.2 (d/e)	19.5 (d/e)	20.5 (d/e)	21.4 (d/e)	22.1 (d/e)	25 (d/e)
		4	19.9 (d/e)	22.8 (d/e)	25.5 (d/e)	27.9 (d/e)	30 (d/e)	50 (d/e)
	10	0	10 (d/e)	10 (d/e)	10 (d/e)	10 (d/e)	10 (d/e)	10 (d/e)
		3	11.3 (d/e)	12.3 (d/e)	13 (d/e)	13.5 (d/e)	13.8 (d/e)	14.3 (d/e)
		6	12.8 (d/e)	15.1 (d/e)	17 (d/e)	18.6 (d/e)	20 (d/e)	25.0 (d/e)
	14	0	7.1 (d/e)	7.1 (d/e)	7.1 (d/e)	7.1 (d/e)	7.1 (d/e)	7.1 (d/e)
		4	8.3 (d/e)	9 (d/e)	9.6 (d/e)	9.8 (d/e)	9.9 (d/e)	10 (d/e)
		8	9.7 (d/e)	11.7 (d/e)	13.2 (d/e)	14.3 (d/e)	15.2 (d/e)	16.6 (d/e)
High degree of uncertainty, high risk; example: new business	20	0	5 (d/e)	5 (d/e)	5 (d/e)	5 (d/e)	5 (d/e)	5 (d/e)
		4	5.8 (d/e)	6.1 (d/e)	6.3 (d/e)	6.3 (d/e)	6.3 (d/e)	6.3 (d/e)
		8	6.6 (d/e)	7.6 (d/e)	8.2 (d/e)	8.3 (d/e)	8.3 (d/e)	8.3 (d/e)
	26	0	3.8 (d/e)	3.8 (d/e)	3.8 (d/e)	3.8 (d/e)	3.8 (d/e)	3.8 (d/e)
		4	4.4 (d/e)	4.6 (d/e)	4.6 (d/e)	4.6 (d/e)	4.6 (d/e)	4.6 (d/e)
		8	5 (d/e)	5.5 (d/e)	5.6 (d/e)	5.6 (d/e)	5.6 (d/e)	5.6 (d/e)
		12	5.7 (d/e)	6.7 (d/e)	7.2 (d/e)	7.2 (d/e)	7.2 (d/e)	7.2 (d/e)

Formulas to derive multipliers

$$M = \left[\sum_{y=1}^{p} \frac{(1+g_1)^y}{(1+k)^y} + \sum_{t=p+1}^{\infty} \frac{(1+g_2)^t}{(1+k)^t}\right]\left(\frac{d}{e}\right) \quad \text{where } g_1 \neq g_2$$

$$M = \frac{d/e}{(k-g)}$$

fairly stationary over time.[4] However, when a difference does occur, the security analyst must rely on experience and judgment in selecting a capitalization rate if the discrepancies cannot be attributed to errors in the risk forecasts. Usually two estimates of the appropriate capitalization rate will not diverge very much, and the analyst can simply use their average as a capitalization rate. But if there is a significant divergence which cannot be rationalized, the analyst may have found a security whose price is significantly out of equilibrium. Such disequilibrium situations can result in considerable profits for an investor who is willing to assume the risks associated with such uncertainties. The analysis of risk is of such importance that Chap. 12 is devoted to explaining it in some detail.

For ABC Company (the same hypothetical firm), the security market line (SML) in Fig. 10-3 indicated a capitalization rate of 10 percent. If no dividend growth is expected for ABC, the appropriate earnings multiplier from Table 10-3 is 10 times the payout ratio d/e. The price-earning ratio was derived by finding the present value of unity each year to infinity and multiplying this value by the payout ratio, as shown in Eq. (10-4).

$$\text{Zero growth earnings multiplier} = \sum_{t=0}^{\infty} \frac{1}{1 + \text{capitalization rate}} \left(\frac{d}{e}\right) \tag{10-4}$$

$$= \frac{d/e}{\text{capitalization rate}} \tag{10-4a}$$

Equation (10-4a) is a simplified but equivalent version of (10-4).

Assume that ABC's normalized earnings per share are currently $4 per year and that its average payout rate is 50 percent of earnings. Applying the earnings multiplier of ($\frac{1}{.1}$ =) 10 times to these earnings implies that the intrinsic value of ABC is about (10 × $4 × .5 =) $20 per share.

Of course, there are numerous places where errors may creep into estimates of normalized earnings—the dividend payout ratio, the capitalization rate, and the dividend growth rate. Therefore, it is not certain that the intrinsic value is exactly $20 per share. It is possible that an error of plus or minus 10 percent from the true intrinsic value would occur in a carefully prepared analysis of a mature company. So, it is expected that the intrinsic value is $20 plus or minus 10 percent, which is the range from $18 to $22. Therefore, if the stock were selling at $15, it would seem to be underpriced and therefore a good buy. But if it were selling at $18.50 or $21.75, it might be correctly priced and thus not as interesting.

Estimating intrinsic value with perpetual earnings growth. If it is assumed that ABC's earnings are currently $4 per share but will grow with cash divi-

---

[4] M. Blume, "On The Assessment of Risk," *Journal of Finance*, March 1971, pp. 1–10. W. F. Sharpe and G. M. Cooper, "Risk-Return Classes of NYSE Common Stocks, 1931–67," *Financial Analysts Journal*, March–April 1972, 46 pp.

dends forever at, say, 3 percent per year, the intrinsic value estimate will be quite different from what it was with zero growth. Table 10-3 shows that for a capitalization rate of 10 percent and a growth rate of 3 percent, the correct multiplier is 14.3 times d/e. This multiplier is derived by finding the present value (using a capitalization rate of $k = .1 = 10$ percent) of a stream of numbers starting at unity and growing at a rate of $g = 3$ percent per year into infinity. Equation (10-5) shows the mathematical model representing these computations.

Earnings multiplier for perpetual growth

$$= \sum_{t=0}^{\infty} \frac{(1 + \text{earnings growth rate})^t}{(1 + \text{capitalization rate})^t} \left(\frac{d}{e}\right) \qquad (10\text{-}5)$$

$$= \frac{d/e}{\text{capitalization rate} - \text{growth rate}} = \frac{d/e}{k - g} \qquad (10\text{-}5a)$$

Equation (10-5a) is equivalent to (10-5). Note that Eq. (10-5a) is also equal to Eq. (10-4a) when the earnings growth rate is zero.

For beginning earnings of $4 per share and a price-earnings multiplier of half (that is, $d/e = .5$), the intrinsic value estimate is ($14.3 \times \$4 \times .5 =$) $28.60 per share. Allowing for errors, estimate the intrinsic value to be in the range from (28.60 ± 10 percent $=$) $25.74 to $31.46.

Estimating intrinsic value with temporary growth. It is not likely that a well-managed firm's growth will remain zero, nor is it likely that a firm can maintain its dividend growth at a high level forever. Therefore, suppose ABC's dividends are expected to grow at 3 percent for 5 years and then level off. In this case, Table 10-3 indicates that the appropriate price-earnings multiplier is 11.3 times d/e. This implies that a most likely estimate of the intrinsic value is ($.5 \times 11.3 \times \$4 =$) $22.60. But the intrinsic value could range from (22.60 ± 10 percent $=$) $20.34 to $24.86, allowing the 10 percent margin for error.

As seen above, the intrinsic value of ABC is highly dependent on its dividend growth. Zero growth implies ABC is worth $20 per share, while perpetual growth at 3 percent implies a value of $28.60. Between these two extremes a value of $22.60 is implied if dividends grow at 3 percent for 5 years and then level off.

The Payout Ratio and the Multiplier

The preceding examples demonstrated the effect that the size and duration of the growth rate in dividends can have on the earnings multiplier.[5] The effects of the dividend payout ratio is more direct than the effect of the

[5] Robert A. Haugen and Dean W. Wichern, "The Elasticity of Financial Assets," *Journal of Finance*, September 1974, pp. 1229–1240.

growth rate and thus easier to see. If other things remain constant, reducing a corporation's dividend payout cuts its multiplier and thus its intrinsic value proportionately. The important question related to the payout ratio is how to evaluate it. That is, since corporations' dividends per share are a different percentage of their earnings per share practically every quarter, what is the best estimate of a firm's payout ratio? A glance at the right-hand column of Table 10-1, for example, shows how ATT's payout ratio fluctuated from 56.2 to 65.1 percent within the 3 years from 1971 through 1973. Most corporations' payout ratios fluctuate more than this because the firms endeavor to maintain a constant rate of undiminished cash dividends while their earnings fluctuate violently at times. And when a corporation incurs a loss (that is, negative earnings per share), its payout ratio is simply undefined for that period.

Estimating the payout ratio which a stable public utility like ATT seeks to maintain is simple. Table 10-1 shows that no losses were incurred and the payout ratio fluctuates symmetrically around 60 percent from year to year. For a more risky company, it is necessary to estimate the corporation's *normalized earnings* per share averaged over the complete business cycle. Earnings analysis is investigated in Chap. 11 and the procedure for finding normalized earnings is explained there. After a share's normal earnings are estimated, all that need be done is divide normalized earnings per share into the corporation's regular cash dividend per share to find the payout ratio for use in the determination of an earnings multiplier. Unfortunately, there are a few cases where this straightforward procedure is inappropriate.

Litton Industries has followed the policy of reinvesting all its earnings to maximize internally financed growth—that is, its dividend policy is to have a zero payout ratio. Although this payout ratio is logical if Litton has profitable investment opportunities, it means Eq. (10-3) cannot be used for Litton's multiplier without some adjustments. Other pathological cases exist for which the model in Eq. (10-3) also will not work. For example, what if a corporation keeps borrowing funds with which to pay cash dividends that bear no relation to its earnings? Penn Central Railroad did so when it continued to pay cash dividends quarter after quarter until its bankruptcy in the early 1970s. For these unusual cases, the fundamental security analyst must use the corporation's past earnings multipliers as a starting point. Then past multipliers can be adjusted to derive earnings multipliers with which to estimate a share's intrinsic value. Past earnings multipliers are useful in estimating future earnings multipliers for corporations like Litton, that have unusual payout ratios because the past multipliers implicitly contain the market's estimate of the payout. Even normal corporations with positive dividend payout policies and dividend payments that are highly positively correlated with earnings, as shown in Fig. 10-4, may be analyzed more effectively sometimes by making reference to historical earnings multipliers.

Subjective Factors Affect Multipliers

In the estimation of a stock's intrinsic economic value, there are many subjective considerations. Care must be taken in weighting the different impacts of these subjective factors on d_t, e_t, f, g, and k so as not to double-count the effect of one change in d_t, or e_t, or f, or g, or k unless it truly affects more than one of these variables. Unfortunately, many changes (for example, the addition or deletion of a product line, mergers, or a new competitor) can affect the expected values of d_t, e_t, f, g, and k simultaneously—this is the time when special care must be used to incorporate the change into all the affected variables properly without double-counting or overcompensating. The firm's management and financial position are two of the more important factors which involve subjective evaluations that can effect d_t, e_t, f, g, and k.

Management evaluation. In forecasting the risk and earnings of a given corporation, fundamental analysts also consider management. The depth and experience of management; its age, education, and health; the existence of personalities that are bottlenecks in an organization; and management's ability to react effectively to changes all affect the firm's risk and its future income. The research and development (R&D) program should also be considered. For example, if a company has new discoveries or advanced technology which will give it a competitive advantage in the future, the potential benefit tends to have a favorable effect on the forecasted intrinsic value of its securities by decreasing risk and/or increasing earnings growth.

Assessing the ability of management and the value of ongoing research is difficult. Capable managers do not fit an easily recognizable stereotype, and the most trivial technological development can be extremely profitable. Making such evaluations is more of a personal skill than a science. The more widely educated, experienced, and sensitive the analyst is, the better he or she will be able to recognize significant factors and assess their value.

Analysis of financial ratios. In an effort to forecast earnings, dividends, and their multipliers, financial statements must be considered. Financial analysis can also shed light on how well-managed the firm is, its growth areas, and how risky it is. These factors affect the multipliers used to derive the intrinsic value estimates. Financial analysis starts by adjusting the financial statements to overcome inconsistencies and "window-dressing" gimmicks. In Chap. 11 some cases are analyzed in which large, well-known corporations misrepresent their annual income by millions of dollars. These deceptive accounting practices must be detected and corrected so meaningful financial ratios can be calculated and evaluated. The more common financial ratios are discussed below.

Working capital ratios (such as the current ratio and inventory turnover ratio) are used to determine the firm's liquidity and measure the efficiency of its current assets. Capitalization ratios (such as the debt-to-equity ratio) measure the proportions of borrowed funds and equity used to finance a company. A firm which is heavily in debt will have poor capitalization ratios, high fixed-interest expense, a high break-even point, less financial flexibility, and more volatile profit rates, and it will generally be more risky than an all-equity corporation. All these factors tend to lower the multipliers used in valuing the firm.

Income ratios (for example, the rate of return on assets and return on equity) measure the productivity of the money invested in the enterprise and are useful in detecting ineffective uses of capital. If the income ratios are all high, the firm is in the enviable position of having weak or nonexistent competition. On the other hand, low income ratios indicate low productivity of capital and a significant possibility that the firm might default on its debt contracts. Low income ratios will tend to lower the firm's multipliers.

Standards of comparison for financial ratios. After financial ratios are calculated, they are of more value if they can be measured against some standard of comparison. The common standards against which financial ratios are measured are (1) the firm's own historical ratios, (2) competitors' ratios, and (3) published industry average ratios. Competitors' ratios and industry ratios may be used to detect significant deviations from the normal way of doing business. A historical trend in a firm's ratios indicates that some change is occurring within the firm. Once these items of interest are detected, additional analysis will reveal the source of the deviation and whether the deviation is desirable.[6]

A simplified common-sized income statement is shown in Table 10-4 for a hypothetical firm which is experiencing a rise in its raw materials

---

[6] Altman has shown how to use financial ratios to foretell bankruptcy: Edward I. Altman, "Corporate Bankruptcy Potential: Shareholder Returns and Share Valuation," *Journal of Finance*, December 1969. Also see Altman's "Financial Ratios, Discriminant Analysis, and the Prediction of Corporate Bankruptcy," *Journal of Finance*, September 1968.

TABLE 10-4 COMMON-SIZED INCOME STATEMENT

	Year $t - 2$	Year $t - 1$
Sales	100%	100%
Minus cost of goods sold	− 60	− 65
Gross margin	40	35
Minus operating expenses	− 20	− 20
Operating profit	20	15
Minus taxes	− 10	− 7.5
Net income	10%	7.5%

costs. This may be due to improved quality of the product, poor purchasing management, thievery from inventory, or an excessive number of faulty assemblies which were later rejected. In any event, it is a trend that can change the value of the firm, and it should be investigated. Common-sized statements are quite useful in detecting shifts over time in the makeup of either the income statement or the balance sheet.

The important financial ratios are already calculated for most publicly traded firms. The ratios are published in Moody's *Industrial Manuals,* Standard & Poor's *Corporation Records, Value Line Investment Survey,* and other sources. These sources also reach some conclusions about the implications of their analysis.

Factors Affecting Intrinsic Value

Numerous studies of varying degrees of sophistication have sought to determine the major factors which determine stock prices. One study used a mathematical statistics process called *multivariate analysis.* This study of 63 firms listed on the NYSE found that, on the average, 31 percent of the variation in a stock's price could be attributed to changes in the level of the whole stock market; 12 percent to industry influences; 37 percent to special industry subgroups; and 20 percent to changes peculiar to each firm which were assumed to come from within the firm. These percentages varied from industry to industry. The average percentages for six industries are shown in Table 10-5. This study indicates the necessity for the fundamental analyst to look beyond the firm itself in estimating future earnings, dividends, and multipliers.

Figure 10-4 shows how total corporate profits and dividends in the United States varied over recent years. Figure 10-5 shows how the average capitalization rates for dividends and earnings varied over recent years. The aggregated data conceal many radical fluctuations which affected some firms' multipliers and earnings. Nevertheless, these two figures show that

TABLE 10-5 PROPORTION OF STOCK PRICE VARIATION DUE TO VARIOUS FACTORS, 1927 TO 1960

Industry	Firm	Market	Industry	Industry subgroups
Tobacco	.25	.09	.17	.49
Oil	.15	.37	.20	.28
Metals	.15	.46	.08	.31
Railroad	.19	.47	.08	.26
Utilities	.22	.23	.14	.41
Retail	.27	.23	.08	.42
Overall	.20	.31	.12	.37

Source: B. J. King, "Market and Industry Factors in Stock Price Behavior," *Journal of Business,* January 1966, pp. 139–190.

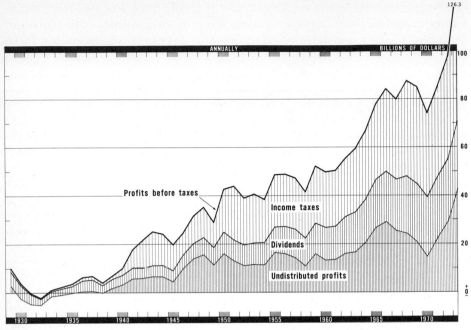

FIG. 10-4 Aggregate corporate profits, taxes, and dividends in the United States.

FIG. 10-5 Stock yields.

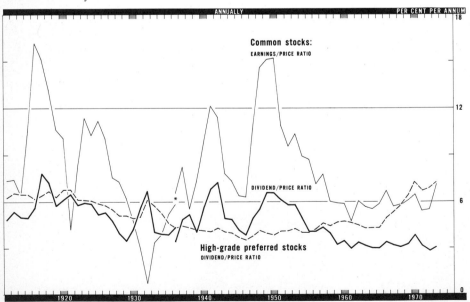

earnings, dividends, and the reciprocals of their multipliers all vary considerably. Fundamental analysts must be able to forecast these and the other factors which introduce this volatility into the determinants of market value if they are to *time* their purchases and sales advantageously.

10-4 TIMING OF STOCK PURCHASES AND SALES

Some investors buy securities whose market prices are at or below the intrinsic value they estimate and then hold these securities to obtain the long-run price appreciation and the dividends normally attained from common stocks. This is called a *buy-and-hold strategy.* It involves no attempt to "buy low and sell high" or otherwise outguess the market. Most life insurance companies, for example, follow a buy-and-hold strategy. They have thousands of dollars of cash premiums flowing in every day, and they invest these funds as they come in and hardly ever liquidate. In contrast, some investors are *traders;* they try to outguess the rises and falls in the market so they will earn more profits by buying at cyclically low prices and selling at cyclically high prices. Traders hope to beat the buy-and-hold strategy.

Over the past years securities markets in the United States have periodically fallen precipitously, offering traders who can anticipate these turns ample opportunity to profit from timely security trading. Table 10-6 lists eight bear markets which have occurred in the United States in the more recent past.

The evidence plainly shows that a trader who buys at market low points and sells at market high points can avoid capital losses and earn larger trading profits than a buy-and-hold strategy would earn. However, this is easier said than done. For example, studies of the performance of mutual funds which have the published objective of maximizing their investors' income by using "professional management" to trade actively reveals that they have been unable to earn a significantly higher rate of return than has been earned with a naive buy-and-hold strategy.[7] Mutual fund

[7] William F. Sharpe, "Mutual Fund Performance," *Journal of Business,* January 1966, supplement, "Security Prices," pp. 119–138.

TABLE 10-6 BEAR MARKETS

Year	% decline in DJIA	Duration of decline, months
1946	23	5
1949	16	11
1953	13	8
1957	18	6
1960	16	10
1962	27	6
1969–1970	53	15
1973–1974	42	19

performance is examined in Chap. 19. Here, the difficulties in forecasting the market's turns and the timing of security purchases and sales so as to earn trading profits are examined.

The purpose of this section is to discuss the tools a fundamental analyst who is an active trader can use to try to forecast the rises and falls in security markets. To predict the timing of security price movements, economic forecasts are utilized. Other approaches also are employed to anticipate the timing of rises and falls in security prices. A group of security analysts called *technical analysts* study charts of stock prices in order to predict the market's turns; they tend to ignore fundamental financial and economic factors. Technical analysis is explained in detail in Chap. 20. Of these two approaches to the timing problem, that of the economic analyst is considerably more difficult because it requires formal training in macroeconomic forecasting. However, to utilize economic forecasts the security analyst need not be capable of actually preparing them.

Leading Indicators

It is important to be able to predict the course of the national economy because it affects corporate profits, investor optimism, and therefore security prices. Figures 10-2 and 10-4 show the manner in which gross national product (GNP), aggregate corporate profits after taxes, and Standard & Poor's 500 stocks average have varied together over time. These economic time series do not move exactly concurrently across time, however. Several economic variables rise and fall some months ahead of similar changes in the GNP; they are called *leading economic indicators.*

The number of private housing starts, new durable goods orders, the number of hours in the average workweek, and the level of SP's 500 stock average are four economic indicators which anticipate changes in GNP with fairly dependable consistency. Table 10-7 shows the range of advance notices (which is greater for downturns than for upturns) offered by these four leading indicators.

Economic Forecasts

After viewing Table 10-7 and noting that the stock market *leads* the national economy, an investor may seem well advised not to bother to forecast

TABLE 10-7 ECONOMIC INDICATORS WHICH LEAD GNP

Indicator	Recent lead times ahead of GNP, months
Private housing starts	2–37
New durable goods orders	1–30
Average workweek	0–20
SP's 500 stock average	4–11

Source: Jesse Levin, "Prophetic Leaders," *Financial Analysts Journal,* July–August 1970, p. 89.

the national economy but simply to follow those indicators which lead stock prices. This can be a valuable forecasting tool—especially in predicting bear markets. Housing starts, durable goods orders, and the number of hours in the average workweek all usually turn down several months before a bear market begins. However, obtaining the most valuable information for making timing decisions in security trading requires a detailed sector forecast of the national economy which extends at least a year into the future.

Since the significant rises and falls (that is, the major bull and bear markets) in security prices have preceded the associated turns in the national economy by as much as 11 months in recent years, a forecast of the economy must extend more than 11 months into the future if it is to be useful in anticipating turns in the stock market. This prediction should be broken down into a series of quarterly figures to give more insight into the timing of the expected changes. Table 10-8 shows a quarterly economic-sector forecast extending 2 years into the future.[8]

A good economic forecast which discloses the timing of changes and provides some detail about inflation and other matters is useful in investment decisions. Much more detailed economic forecasts may be purchased from economic consultants. For example, the organization which prepared Table 10-8 also prepares 10-year economic projections showing the quarterly development of the United States economy broken down into intricate detail. These forecasts can usually predict the dollar amounts of economic activity in various sectors of the economy for a year into the future with only small errors. Such details are quite useful in pinpointing growth industries and other facts necessary for profitable investment timing decisions.

Ultimately, the ability of an economic model to predict dollar quantities is not so important to the security analyst as its ability to foretell the *timing* and *direction* of the changes in the various rates of economic growth. Indications of shifts in the direction of the economy are most useful in anticipating similar changes in the stock market. This type of information allows portfolio managers to assume a defensive position when bear markets are foreseen and to be aggressive when bullish conditions are expected.

Basis for economic forecasts. Economic forecasts which extend very far into the future and/or show very much detail within the national economy are always based upon a fairly detailed set of basic assumptions about the world situation and its impact on the fiscal and monetary policy of the nation. Assumptions about the particular industry in which a company is located and its competitors are also important to a security analyst who is

---

[8] *Wharton Quarterly*, University of Pennsylvania, Wharton School of Finance and Commerce, Summer 1975.

TABLE 10-8 WHARTON MARK IV QUARTERLY MODEL (JUNE 11, 1975: CONTROL SOLUTION): SELECTED MAJOR ECONOMIC INDICATORS FORECAST 8 QUARTERS (DOLLARS IN BILLIONS)

Item	1975.1†	1975.2	1975.3	1975.4	1976.1	1976.2	1976.3	1976.4	1977.1
Gross national product, $	1417.1	1429.7	1450.0	1489.6	1531.5	1572.1	1613.5	1664.7	1710.1
% chg: GNP	-3.80	3.61	5.79	11.37	11.73	11.04	10.94	13.31	11.37
Real gross national product, $	780.2	773.6	774.0	784.2	796.7	806.9	816.7	828.7	840.6
% chg: real GNP	-11.33	-3.32	0.19	5.35	6.55	5.25	4.94	5.99	5.89
National income, $	1149.8	1156.8	1173.2	1208.9	1243.9	1279.0	1314.4	1359.2	1397.9
Personal income, $	1193.4	1213.9	1228.1	1254.0	1280.3	1310.3	1345.6	1387.1	1423.1
Implicit price deflator—GNP	181.6	184.8	187.3	190.0	192.2	194.8	197.6	200.9	203.4
% chg: implicit GNP deflator	8.53	7.13	5.60	5.72	4.87	5.50	5.73	6.91	5.17
Implicit price deflator—private GNP	174.4	177.5	180.0	182.1	184.3	186.9	189.6	192.4	194.9
% chg: private GNP deflator	8.05	7.35	5.68	4.72	5.04	5.71	5.95	5.95	5.37
Chg: Consumer price index, %	7.46	6.38	4.75	4.09	4.74	5.38	5.31	4.85	4.26
Chg: Wholesale price index, %	-0.08	2.33	2.15	0.96	3.06	2.48	4.18	4.03	4.61
Pvt. output per manhour	5.77	5.77	5.82	5.91	5.99	6.03	6.06	6.10	6.13
% chg: pvt. output per manhour	0.87	0.21	3.11	6.15	5.53	2.91	2.03	2.47	2.18
Private comp. per manhour	5.80	5.91	6.00	6.10	6.21	6.31	6.43	6.54	6.67
% chg: pvt. comp. per manhour	10.99	7.89	6.36	6.55	7.24	7.09	7.35	7.53	7.91
Unemployment rate, %	8.35	9.06	9.36	9.37	9.02	8.64	8.29	7.92	7.55
Net exports, current, $	9.3	5.8	5.8	3.6	2.6	1.2	-1.5	-2.9	-3.7
Money supply—M1, $	284.3	288.0	292.9	298.5	305.1	311.4	318.2	325.4	332.6
% chg: money supply—M1	1.13	5.38	6.91	7.95	9.07	8.49	9.16	9.35	9.07
Money supply—M2, $	621.5	637.6	655.8	673.6	690.9	707.9	726.7	744.6	761.4
% chg: money supply—M2	6.49	10.76	11.91	11.30	10.67	10.25	11.02	10.21	9.36
3-month Treasury bill rate	5.75	5.12	4.69	5.52	6.12	6.33	6.02	7.00	7.49
Corp. AAA utility bond rate	9.23	9.56	8.95	9.07	9.07	9.10	8.90	8.82	8.73
4- to 5-month commercial paper rate	6.56	5.74	5.25	5.80	6.46	6.77	6.57	7.26	7.88
Moody's total corp. bond rate	9.39	9.56	9.41	9.37	9.35	9.35	9.27	9.18	9.10
Personal savings rate, %	7.47	11.03	9.15	8.78	8.38	8.15	8.03	8.09	8.09
Corporate profits before tax, $	100.3	100.1	100.9	114.0	128.8	139.0	147.6	156.7	164.2
Federal surplus, NIA basis, $	-54.7	-105.6	-85.7	-82.0	-73.1	-68.2	-65.6	-64.9	-61.7

† First quarter figures are from the U.S. Office of Business Statistics.

Source: U.S. Dept. of Commerce.

estimating the impact of economic developments on a given industry or firm. Figure 10-6 shows the series of decisions which form the basis for any given forecast of the intrinsic value of a corporation's shares.

Since forecasting models rest squarely on assumptions about international, national, and industry conditions, a fundamental analyst trying to relate the effects of economic developments to security prices should take part in the formulation of these assumptions. This participation will ensure that factors such as large government contracts, labor relations, and technical development, all of which affect security prices, are considered. The economic forecasting services allow their customers to suggest their own assumptions on which to base a forecast (although an added fee may be charged).

Varying the assumptions. Working with the economic forecasters allows the security analyst to ask the "what if" questions that are so important in investment timing decisions. For example, in 1969 when the United States began reducing its involvement in Vietnam, it was desirable to make different assumptions about the rate of U.S. withdrawal from that war. Each different assumption implied a different economic forecast and a different set of intrinsic values in U.S. securities markets. As shown in Fig. 10-6, a

FIG. 10-6 The basic assumptions underlying economic forecasts have impact on intrinsic value estimates.

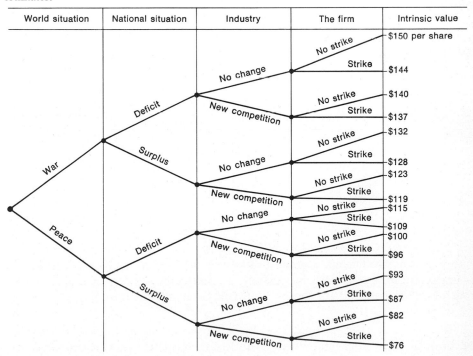

wide array of intrinsic values are forecast for a given firm's share, depending upon the underlying assumptions about the world and the economy. Interaction between the security analyst and the economist will facilitate preparation of the best possible intrinsic value estimates. Multiple forecasts allow security traders to make immediate investment decisions as news is released because they will have estimates of the price implications of various possible economic developments.

Crux of the Timing Question

In forecasting the times when any given security's price will rise above or fall below the intrinsic value which will prevail under normal market conditions, the fundamental analyst must ultimately estimate both (1) what each quarter's earnings per share will be, and (2) what the earnings multipliers will be in each quarter.

Forecasting earnings per share. Chapter 11 discusses the measurement of historical growth in a firm's earnings. Methods are suggested to adjust historical growth rates so they can be used to forecast earnings. The following basic relation is suggested for forecasting earnings:

$$e_t = (1 + g)^t e_0$$

where e_t = earnings per share in period t
g = estimated earnings growth rate

This technique can be used to furnish one forecast of earnings per share. A second earnings forecast can be derived using the economic forecast.

Detailed economic forecasts showing the quarter-by-quarter economic activity in the various industries comprising the national economy can be obtained. These industry sales forecasts can be broken down by company using historical data on market shares and current information about new competitive developments. These sales forecasts can yield information about expected earnings. For example, the graph in Fig. 10-7 shows how the sales of ATT have varied with its earnings per share over the decade from 1964 to 1973. When stationary sales-earnings relationships exist, they can be used along with an economic forecast and sales projection to provide a second earnings forecast.

It should be noted that ATT, whose data were used to prepare Fig. 10-7, has more stationary growth rates and sales-earnings relationships than most companies. Finally, information gained from interviews with the executives of a firm and its competitors can be useful in forecasting earnings.

Forecasting earnings multipliers. The advance notice given by the leading economic indicators (shown in Table 10-7) reveals that security prices have

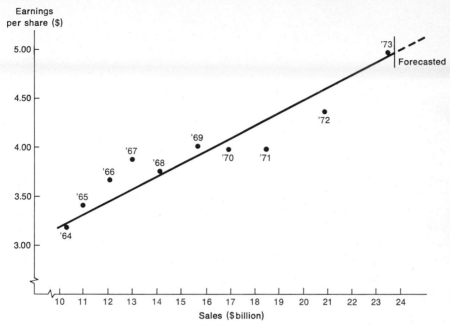

FIG. 10-7 Scatter diagram that is useful in forecasting earnings per share.

anticipated the economy from zero to 11 months in the United States in recent years. This fact implies that an economic forecast for 1 year into the future can be expected to lead changes in the level of security prices from 1 to 11 months. Since the time lag between changes in a 1-year economic forecast and the associated changes in security prices varies from zero to 11 months, even the best economic forecasts cannot be expected to pinpoint the turn in the securities markets within much less than a 3-month range. However, the economic forecast is still quite useful in indicating the direction of the market and in giving information about the extent of coming changes.

Forecasts of the market levels can be expressed most usefully for security analysis by stating them in terms of the average price-earnings ratio for the market. A study of past price-earnings ratios for some market average and the then-prevailing economic conditions will aid the fundamental analyst in converting the economic forecast into a forecast of the market's average earnings multiplier. Table 10-9 shows how the Dow Jones Industrial Average earnings multiplier has varied in recent years.

After the analyst has forecast an average earnings multiplier, a scatter diagram such as the one shown in Fig. 10-8 can be used to convert this market forecast into earnings multipliers for individual securities. The price-earnings ratio may be viewed as an index of investor confidence. Since investors' confidence in all securities tends to rise and fall with the level of the market, useful relationships between the market's average

TABLE 10-9 PRICE-EARNINGS RATIOS FOR SELECTED FIRMS

Industry	1963	1964	1965	1966	1967	1968	1969	1970	1971	1972	1973
Airlines											
American	11.6	10.9	12.9	10.9	16.3	17.2	16.3	loss	loss	18.0	loss
Pan American	7.4	13.0	12.6	13.4	15.2	17.1	loss	loss	loss	loss	loss
Northwest	9.5	8.8	10.2	15.9	17.0	14.8	13.9	10.3	30.5	51.2	11.2
Automobiles											
Chrysler	7.8	9.3	10.1	11.0	10.2	9.8	24.2	loss	17.7	8.2	6.1
Ford	11.4	12.2	8.9	8.5	61.7	9.5	9.4	9.9	10.1	8.3	6.6
General Motors	13.4	14.9	13.8	13.9	13.9	13.5	12.5	33.9	12.2	10.4	7.8
Photographic equipment											
Eastman Kodak	27.9	30.4	31.3	loss	31.6	32.4	30.6	28.5	33.1	35.8	31.5
Polaroid	58.4	34.0	47.0	46.7	56.5	59.5	64.7	48.9	51.9	90.6	66.0
Petroleum											
Exxon (Standard Oil of N.J.)	14.2	17.2	17.0	14.2	11.7	12.8	12.6	10.5	11.1	11.5	8.6
Shell	14.1	16.1	16.2	14.8	14.7	14.3	13.3	12.2	13.2	13.2	11.5
Standard Oil of Indiana	10.9	13.8	14.7	13.2	12.8	13.5	12.4	9.7	12.3	13.9	12.3
Standard Oil of California	14.0	14.2	14.3	12.9	11.4	12.0	11.5	8.7	9.4	10.6	7.2
Steel											
Bethlehem	15.0	12.7	11.7	9.2	12.1	8.5	8.7	12.2	8.1	9.9	6.4
U.S. Steel	15.3	14.7	11.0	9.9	13.8	8.9	10.2	12.4	10.7	10.7	5.4
Rubber											
Goodyear	16.2	15.7	16.2	14.8	13.5	13.2	13.6	15.0	13.4	11.3	8.8
Goodrich	16.8	15.1	13.5	11.7	20.4	13.8	17.2	31.6	14.7	8.4	5.3
Communications											
American Telephone & Telegraph	21.2	22.1	19.3	15.4	14.8	14.2	13.3	11.8	11.9	10.9	10.1
Electronics											
Texas Instruments	25.4	21.6	29.4	35.3	58.2	41.7	38.7	36.1	34.2	35.4	29.1
Fairchild	58.1	39.3	29.3	36.4	loss	loss	loss	loss	loss	17.9	7.9
International Telephone & Telegraph	18.0	16.6	16.9	21.6	loss	20.8	18.4	14.3	16.4	14.8	10.2
Office equipment											
Burroughs	18.5	16.1	19.7	32.1	39.4	41.6	41.8	34.7	33.0	39.9	36.3
IBM	36.6	35.2	35.0	43.1	42.5	40.2	40.2	34.1	34.7	34.4	27.8
Mining											
Homestake	23.8	21.4	24.2	26.5	39.3	66.1	57.4	36.1	45.8	19.1	11.7
Dow Jones Industrial Average	18.5	19.0	18.0	15.5	16.0	17.0	14.5	14.6	16.7	16.1	11.5

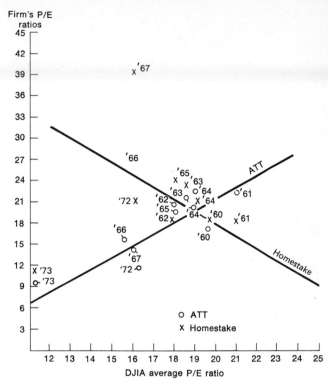

FIG. 10-8 Scatter diagram showing relationship of firms' price-earnings ratios to market average price-earnings ratios. (Data from Table 10-9.)

earnings multiplier and individual securities earnings multipliers, such as the ones shown in Fig. 10-8, are not uncommon.

Conclusions about Timing

Because of the uncertainties involved in forecasting quarterly earnings per share, earnings growth rates, the risk of the firm, and the exact date when the market will begin expected changes in its direction, it is difficult, if not impossible, to earn short-term trading profits which will exceed the returns from a buy-and-hold strategy after the forecasting expenses and commissions are deducted. To be more precise, it is usually not possible to earn trading profits over many trades by buying securities, holding them for less than 6 months, and selling them. Such short-term trading can yield a positive return. However, after the commissions are deducted, trading profits are almost always less than the return attainable with a buy-and-hold strategy based on fundamental analysis.

In Chap. 21, evidence is presented which suggests that short-term security price changes are unpredictable random movements—this is sometimes called the *random-walk theory* of security prices. Many securities sales-persons and managers of "go-go" mutual funds disagree with this theory. However, their opinions are biased because of the fact that they derive their income from investors who seek short-term trading profits. In spite of the advertisements implying the contrary,[9] few mutual funds earn a better rate of return than investors using a naive buy-and-hold strategy, as pointed out earlier. It seems that people who work around security trading are frequently the victims of their own myopic viewpoint — that is, they reach subjective generalities based on the few impressive security trades they recall rather than on objective statistical analysis of thousands of transactions.

For the long run, say, for securities which are held over 6 months, forecasting security prices in order to make advantageously timed trades is easier and more profitable. After 6 months, market turns which were soundly forecast will usually come to pass, short-run random security price fluctuations will tend to average out to zero, and fundamental analysis will be profitable for those who are experienced professional fundamental security analysts. If these professional analysts are provided with good economic forecasts and the other information they need, they should be able to escape losses in bear markets and avoid the securities of corporations which go bankrupt. Thus, they should be able to earn returns on their portfolios in the long run which exceed the returns attainable from a naive (for example, selecting stocks with a dart) buy-and-hold strategy. However, only well-trained professional fundamental security analysts who are provided with good forecasts can expect to earn profits from trading in securities. The part-time or amateur security analyst simply cannot expect to earn higher long-run returns than are attainable from a naive buy-and-hold strategy (or if an amateur earns such returns, he should consider himself lucky).

10-5 CONCLUSIONS ABOUT FUNDAMENTAL SECURITY ANALYSIS

As might be expected, it is not easy to find underpriced and overpriced securities. Professional fundamental analysts have usually forecasted changes in a corporation's income fairly accurately, and security prices have adjusted to the new intrinsic value before the latest income figures are announced to the public.

When significantly different earnings and dividends which were *not* expected are announced by a corporation, some analysts will reach buy or sell decisions immediately. By merely applying recent multipliers to the

---

[9] The Investment Company Institute ran several advertisements in *Time* and *Business Week* which proclaimed "What! You still don't own any mutual funds?" See, for example, *Business Week*, Jan. 25, 1969, p. 96. These ads seemed to disappear after the 1969–1970 bear market in which mutual funds did poorly.

new income data and then comparing the intrinsic value estimates with the market price, it is possible to get some indication as to whether the security is priced correctly. This explains why security prices sometimes react noticeably to announcements of changed levels of income and/or dividends.[10]

Regardless of how sophisticated the techniques used, a complete, painstaking fundamental analysis, based on relevant facts, is a logical way to estimate the true value of a going concern. Understandably, fundamental analysis is the most widely used method of estimating security prices. Erroneous intrinsic value estimates can be attributed to several facts: (1) The analyst did not have all the relevant information, (2) the analyst simply did not thoroughly do the necessary work, or (3) the market was in a temporary disequilibrium (for example, President Kennedy's assassination caused the stock market to drop temporarily, although fundamental values were unchanged). Hindsight is always better than foresight in these matters. But even under ideal conditions, fundamental analysis can suggest only a range of prices rather than a specific value.

QUESTIONS

1 "A fundamental analyst's estimate of intrinsic value is different from the present value of all income." Is this statement true, false, or uncertain? Explain.

2 Compare and contrast the earnings multiplier with the dividend multiplier. Why do they differ?

3 Does an increase in a firm's growth rate of earnings always mean an increase in its intrinsic value? Explain.

4 Why is the growth rate in dividends per share not a good measure of the firm's growth rate?

5 Can factors which are external to the firm, such as national economic conditions, affect the intrinsic value of a share of stock? Explain.

6 "An increase in a firm's liquidity ratios means the firm is well managed and safe. This will always increase its multipliers." Is this statement true, false, or uncertain? Explain.

7 Can fundamental analysis be used for quick, short-range value forecasts, or is it useful only for determining long-run equilibrium values? Explain.

8 Will accounting gimmicks (like accelerating depreciation) affect or distort the intrinsic value estimates made by fundamental analysts?

[10] P. Brown and R. Ball, "An Empirical Evaluation of Accounting Income Numbers," *Journal of Accounting Research*, Autumn 1968, pp. 159–178.

9 An experienced fundamental security analyst claims that the intrinsic value estimating procedures used by members of the profession lead to realistic estimates of true value which are based on "all the facts" and realistic assumptions. Comment on this claim.

10 The Blume Company is a small, growing manufacturer of lawn equipment which is planning to go public for the first time. Assume that Mr. Blume, the president of the firm, has hired you as a financial consultant to estimate the price per share at which the stock should be sold. The Westerfield Corporation and the Pettit Corporation are also young lawn equipment manufacturers which have recently gone public and have similar product lines (they all even have the same accountant). Data on these three corporations are:

Earnings per share	Westerfield	Pettit	Blume's totals
Earnings per share, 1975	$ 5	$ 11	$1,000,000
Average EPS, 1970–1975	$ 5	$ 8	$ 780,000
Median market price, 1975	$29	$145	?
Average price, 1970–1975	$27	$110	—
Dividends per share, 1975	$ 3	$ 7.20	$ 500,000
Average dividends, 1970–1975	$ 2.80	$ 6.50	$ 390,000
Book value per share, 1970	$81.23	$112.10	$ 131,500
Growth in EPS, 1970–1975	0	5%	6%
Debt/equity ratio, 1970	9%	42%	45%
Current assets/current liabilities	3.1	1.9	2.0
Employees	180	90	80
Sales	$17,000,000	$9,800,000	$8,800,000

The sales, earnings, and stock prices of all lawn equipment manufacturers have followed rates of change in national income (that is, GNP) in the past few years. Historical data show that the two public firms have beta coefficients (of systematic risk) of about 1. The future for the lawn equipment industry is bright. Because of increased suburban living and rising affluence, it is expected that the market for lawn equipment will continue to expand. The economic outlook promises steady growth, and securities markets are normal. What data above will you ignore in pricing Blume's stock? If Blume issues 1 million shares, what price per share would you recommend?

11 The Archer Corporation has a beta volatility coefficient (measuring its systematic risk) of 1, and, as Table 10-3 leads us to expect, the market has been applying a $k = 10$ percent capitalization rate in valuing its earnings. Archer's normalized earnings of $2 per share are all paid out in cash dividends. Per-share earnings have been growing at 3 percent per annum for some time, and the current market price of $28.60 reflects this growth experience. However, because of a technological breakthrough, Archer's earnings are expected to grow at the increased rate of 6 percent per year for the foreseeable future. What effect do you think this technological innovation will have on Archer's market price per share when the news becomes public?

SELECTED REFERENCES

Brealey, R. A., *An Introduction to Risk and Return from Common Stocks* (Cambridge, Mass.: M.I.T., 1969).
> A readable, nonmathematical summary of various studies. Chapters 5 to 9 throw light on some issues relevant to fundamental analysis.

Graham, B., D. Dodd, and S. Cottle, *Security Analysis,* 4th ed. (New York: McGraw-Hill, 1962).
> This nonmathematical book is used by most fundamental analysts; it should be read by anyone who aspires to be a fundamental analyst.

Malkiel, B. G., "The Valuation of Public Utility Equities," *The Bell Journal of Economics and Management Science,* 1970.
> A statistical test of the valuation model equation (10-3).

Whitbeck, V., and M. Kisor, "A New Tool in Investment Decision Making," *Financial Analysts Journal,* May–June, 1963.
> An empirical study of earnings per share and multipliers.

APPENDIX TO CHAPTER 10
Econometric Models for Determining Multipliers

The discussion of fundamental analysis has touched upon numerous factors which the security analyst must consider in forming intrinsic value estimates. The factors that affect earnings estimates may be quantified by considering their effect on future growth rates, costs, and profits. However, the interrelated impact of these numerous variables on earnings multipliers is more ambiguous.

General Form of a Model

The following variables are determinants of the multipliers which are frequently considered:

$X_1 = $ risk of the firm
$X_2 = $ forecasted earnings
$X_3 = $ growth rate for earnings
$X_4 = $ sponsorship—the number of institutional investors
$X_5 = $ competitive position and management ability
$X_6 = $ economic and credit conditions

Through some complex but partially unspecified process, represented in mathematical notation by Eq. (A10-1), all these variables are considered simultaneously in determining the earnings and dividends multipliers.

$$\text{Multiplier} = f(X_1, X_2, X_3, X_4, X_5, X_6) \tag{A10-1}$$

In words, (A10-1) says the multiplier is some unspecified mathematical function with X_1, X_2, X_3, X_4, X_5, and X_6 as its determinants.

Students of psychology learn that the human mind—even the mind of a genius—cannot simultaneously consider six variables. To overcome these difficult conceptual problems, mathematical statistics can be usefully employed in determining multipliers. A multiple regression of the form shown in (A10-2) may be fit to recent financial data.[1]

$$M = b_0 + b_1X_1 + b_2X_2 + b_3X_3 + b_4X_4 + b_5X_5 + b_6X_6 + u \tag{A10-2}$$

where b_0 is the average multiplier for the industry under normal conditions, b_i is the multiple regression coefficient of X_i, the X_i's are the independent variables listed above, and u is an unexplained error.

An Econometric Model in Three Variables

One published study suggested that three independent variables largely determine the price-earnings multiplier. The variables used in this study are defined as follows:

$\left(\dfrac{P}{E}\right)_i$ = the ith firm's price-earnings multiplier, the dependent variable to be predicted by the model

g_i = historical growth rate in the ith firm's earnings (as measured from its cashflows)

$\left(\dfrac{d}{e}\right)_i$ = the ith firm's average dividend payout ratio

b_i = the ith firm's beta coefficient, measuring its systematic risk

[1] Fitting a model such as Eq. (A10-2) presents technical statistical problems which are beyond the scope of this discussion. See J. Johnston, *Econometric Methods* (New York: McGraw-Hill, 1963).

TABLE A10-1 ECONOMETRIC MODELS FOR EXPLAINING THE DETERMINATION OF PRICE-EARNING MULTIPLIERS

Year	Multiple regression model	Correlation
1961	$(P/E)_i = 15.52 + 1.82g_i - 1.75\,(d/e)_i - 1.53\,B_i$	.70
1962	$(P/E)_i = 12.42 + 1.02g_i + 4.28\,(d/e)_i - 2.87\,B_i$	.73
1963	$(P/E)_i = 9.20 + 1.28g_i + 6.84\,(d/e)_i - 1.21\,B_i$	.69
1964	$(P/E)_i = 14.37 + .96g_i + 3.29\,(d/e)_i - 3.54\,B_i$	.66
1965	$(P/E)_i = 7.47 + 1.52g_i + 5.58\,(d/e)_i - .95\,B_i$	.80

Source: B. G. Malkiel and J. G. Cragg, "Expectations and the Structure of Share Prices," *American Economic Review*, September 1970, p. 610, table 3.

With a sample of over 150 firms, multiple regression was used to fit the econometric models shown in Table A10-1.

An examination of the econometric models in Table A10-1 reveals several things. First, these regression models are able to predict fairly well (as indicated by the correlation coefficients which are all significantly different than zero). Second, earnings growth (as measured by g_i) always tends to have a positive effect on the multipliers. The effect of the dividend payout is not clear [since the coefficient of $(d/e)_i$ erratically changed signs in 1961]. Third, systematic risk (as measured by b_i) has a negative effect on the multiplier. And finally, the model is not perfectly stationary over time. This last finding means that the changing regression coefficients should be reestimated at least once per year if the model is to be kept current and useful for predicting.[2]

[2] B. G. Malkiel and J. G. Cragg, "Expectations and the Structure of Share Prices," *American Economic Review*, September 1970, pp. 615–616.

Eleven

Estimating Stockholders' Income

The value of any asset is the present value of all the income from that asset. Symbolically,

$$\text{Present value} = \sum_{t=1}^{\infty} \frac{\text{income}_t}{(1 + \text{discount rate})^t}$$

In Chap. 10 it was explained that to use this model to value common stocks or other risky assets, one must answer two questions. First, what discount or capitalization rate k should be used? Chapter 12 goes into some detail in aswering this question. The second question is, how does the investor measure the income from common stocks which, unlike bonds, do not clearly specify the stream of income payments in advance? Discussion of this income question is the subject of this chapter. The economist's concept of income is explained; then it is suggested that the concept of economic income is generally more suitable than reported accounting income for fundamental security analysis.

11-1 THE ECONOMIST'S DEFINITION OF INCOME

Economists define a firm's *income* as the maximum amount which can be consumed by the owners of the firm in any period without decreasing their future consumption opportunities. This is more than a definition; it is an important concept[1] which financial analysts should keep in mind when

---

[1] This concept of income is discussed in J. R. Hicks, *Value and Capital*, 2d ed. (New York: Oxford University Press, 1965), chap. 14.

they analyze income statements. The economist's definition of income is in-tuitively more appealing than the accountant's definition because it relates directly to the owner's real *consumption*. After all, what good is income that some accountant says you have if you cannot consume it?

The periodic income statements issued by a firm's accountants are the most highly visible and well-known source of income measurements. Therefore, this chapter starts by examining the accountant's procedure for determining income. Accountants provide the basic figures an analyst typically uses when estimating a firm's economic income and intrinsic value.

11-2 THE ACCOUNTING INCOME STATEMENT

Table 11-1 outlines the essentials of the model underlying accountants' in-come statements. Despite the model's seeming simplicity, in practice many questions arise concerning the definitions and measurements of the various items determining income. For decisions on these questions, the accounting profession can turn to several sources.

In most cases, acceptable accounting procedures are determined by the general acceptance of the practicing accountants. As the phrase *general acceptance* readily suggests, more than one procedure may exist for re-porting the same type of business transaction; that is, accounting principles are inexact. There are, however, limitations. The American Institute of Cer-tified Public Accountants (AICPA), through its Accounting Principles Board, hands down opinions on which practices are acceptable and which are unacceptable. Often these opinions eliminate the less desirable (that is, the extreme or the completely ambiguous) alternatives while still allowing several accounting choices. The result is a narrowing of practices but not the creation of uniform accounting. Thus, the same economic event often can legitimately be reported in several different ways.

TABLE 11-1 MODEL OF ACCOUNTING INCOME STATEMENT

Sales	Sales
Less: Cost of goods sold	− COGS
Gross operating margin	GM
Less: Selling and administrative expenses and depreciation	− Op. Exp.
Net operating income (earnings before interest and taxes)	NOI (EBIT)
Less: Interest expense	−Int.
Taxable income	T. Inc.
Less: Taxes	− Tax
Net income	NI
Less: Dividends on preferred stock	−P. Div.
Net income for common equity	C. Inc.
Less: Dividends to common equity	−C. Div.
Retained earnings	Ret. E

Another body sometimes limiting the range of choice is the Internal Revenue Service (IRS). The IRS can say, and has said, "If a given accounting procedure is used by a firm for tax purposes, it also must be used in the published financial statements of that firm." Such rulings by the IRS increase the consistency of the accounting statements given to shareholders and the IRS in any given year, but they do not cause published financial statements of firms to be identical with their tax return statements. The IRS also may contest the propriety of certain generally acceptable accounting procedures when they tend to evade income taxes. But such questions do not necessarily tend to align a firm's reported income with its economic income. In the final analysis, the responsibility to ferret out a firm's economic income lies with the fundamental security analyst.

Persons unfamiliar with the complexity of accounting procedures understandably obtain the erroneous impression that the accounting income is a narrowly defined quantity. The neatly published financial statements in annual reports seem to imply that they are the last word and are not open to dispute. However, reference to an accounting textbook will reveal a multiplicity of generally accepted accounting procedures which may be used in many situations.

The following quotation opens the chapter entitled "Measuring and Reporting Income" in a widely used intermediate accounting textbook.

> Arriving at an estimate of the periodic income of a business enterprise is perhaps the foremost objective of the accounting process. The word *estimate* is, unfortunately, proper because income is one of the most elusive concepts in the business and economic world. The art of accounting has not progressed (and never will) to the point where periodic business income can be measured with certainty.[2]

Although this quotation may come as a shock to neophyte accountants and fundamental analysts, experienced accountants and analysts have long recognized the vagaries in accountants' procedures for determining income.

The latitude of alternative generally accepted procedures which the accountant may follow in deriving a firm's income is often not the cause of income reports by accountants which differ significantly from the firm's economic income. The accountant needs some leeway in order to use a procedure which most clearly reports the true economic consequence of a business transaction. When accountants produce income statements which fundamental analysts find necessary to alter significantly in order to obtain income estimates, the cause is usually (1) the accountant's use of an accounting procedure which is inappropriate for the relevant economic transaction and/or (2) pressure brought to bear on the accountant from top management to minimize the firm's income taxes. In order to explain most

[2] W. D. Meigs, C. E. Johnson, and T. F. Keller, *Intermediate Accounting* (New York: McGraw-Hill, 1963), p. 87.

of the adjustments the analyst may find it necessary to make in a firm's income statement, a numerical example is explained below.

11-3 CONTRAST OF INCOME STATEMENTS OF IDENTICAL FIRMS

Table 11-2 shows income and expense statements for two companies which are identical in every way except for their accounting procedures. The statement on the left, for Firm B, tends to minimize taxable income. The income statement for Firm A, on the right, represents the economic income from both firms. The divergent accounting procedures followed in developing the income statements for Firms A and B are legal, commonplace, and generally accepted by practicing accountants. In essence, both income statements are correct on the basis of accounting practices, but only income statement A is correct in the sense that it provides a true picture of the economic results of the firm's transactions.

TABLE 11-2 TWO INCOME STATEMENTS FOR THE SAME YEAR

	Company B, $, 000 omitted		Company A, $ 000 omitted		Key (see text)
Sales revenue		$ 9,200		$ 11,000	
Less: Returns and allowances		−1,000		− 1,000	
Net sales		8,200		10,000	(1)
Beginning inventory	2,000		2,000		
Purchases and freight in	6,000		6,000		
Net purchases	8,000		8,000		
Less: Ending inventory	−2,000		−3,000		(2)
Cost of goods sold		6,000		5,000	
Gross margin		2,200		5,000	
Operating expenses					
Selling costs	1,500		1,500		
Depreciation	500		300		(3)
Research costs	100		20		(4)
Pension costs	200		50		(5)
Salaries	200		200		
Bonuses	100		100		
Total operating expenses		−2,600		− 2,170	
Net operating income (loss)		(400)		2,830	
Less: Interest		− 100		− 100	
Taxable income (loss)		(500)		2,730	
Less: Federal taxes (50%) (refund)		(250)		− 1,365	
Net income from operations (loss)		(250)		1,365	
Other income		100		200	(6)
Capital gains (after tax)		100		100	
Net profit (loss)		$ (50)		$ 1,665	
Earnings per share†		($.05)		$1.66½	

† 1,000,000 shares outstanding.

Firms A and B may be thought of as being two identical manufacturers whose identical sales are expected to remain constant in the future.[3] The firms are assumed to be equally well managed, have identical labor forces and identical assets, and to be carrying on identical research and development programs in search of cost reductions in their manufacturing process. Or the reader may contrive any other fact situation which is consistent with the discussion that follows.

Many firms prepare two different income statements, each statement being completely rational, legal, and compatible with the other. One income statement which minimizes taxable income may be prepared for the IRS, and a second income statement may be kept confidential and used by management as a basis for decision making. Presumably, this second statement would be the better reflection of the firm's economic income. The two income statements A and B in Table 11-2 may alternatively be regarded, if so desired, as two different statements for the same firm instead of different statements for two identical firms.

The six items where statements A and B differ are keyed at the right margin of Table 11-2. These differences are explained below; they are a representative but far from exhaustive list of points where confusion and deception can enter into income measurements.

Sales (1)

Statement A includes in its sales item both cash sales and all current sales made on installment contract. Both firms factor their accounts receivable as soon as they arise and thus realize the cash proceeds of the installment contract sales immediately. But Company B does not recognize these sales until the customer's final cash payment is actually received and the factoring company has no potential bad debt claims against it. Both practices of installment sales recognition are acceptable. However, the procedure shown in statement A is a truer reflection of the actual sales transaction and cashflow and should thus be used to obtain estimates of the firm's economic income. There are, however, some conditions which must be present before a cash-collection method may be used.

It is acceptable accounting practice to realize sales as early as the date the sales order is signed, and this is now common in installment contracts sales. Or, as with some long-term construction contracts, the sale may not be recognized until as late as the day the delivery is made; this may be years after the contract is signed. Between these extremes are many points in time when the accountant may choose to recognize the sales revenue in the financial statements.

Sometimes production companies have credit subsidiaries which facilitate recognizing sales at a certain point in time. For example, General

---

[3] Growth firms—that is, firms whose income and value are growing—will be dealt with later in this and other chapters.

Motors Acceptance Corporation and Ford Motor Credit Corporation buy installment contracts on auto sales. This permits the auto dealer and auto manufacturer to receive cash from the credit subsidiary and recognize the sales revenue when the car is sold although the cash payments from the consumer flow in over several years.

Credit subsidiaries not only speed up the recognition of sales and profits; they can also help "window-dress" the manufacturer's balance sheets. The debts of these credit companies would make the manufacturers appear to be more heavily in debt. But the detail of the credit corporation's balance sheet may be excluded from the parent corporation's balance sheet. Accounting practice allows the parent company to show only its *net* investment in the credit subsidiary as an asset. The parent's share of the dividends of the subsidiary is also included in the parent firm's income statement. These are factors for which the diligent analyst will make adjustments in the reported financial statements.

Inventory (2)

Statement A uses the FIFO (that is, first in, first out) method of inventory valuation while B uses the LIFO (last in, first out) method. During periods of inflation the FIFO method tends to result in higher reported profits.

Perhaps the easiest way to understand LIFO and FIFO is by an example. Imagine that 1-ton steel ingots are the inventory items and that one ingot is always carried in inventory. Assume that, early in the accounting year represented in Table 11-2, the cost of ingots rose from $2,000 apiece to $3,000. The inventory is valued at cost, and the beginning inventory value of the one-ingot inventory is assumed to be $2,000 whether LIFO or FIFO is used. This value is shown in Tables 11-2 and 11-3.

If the newest ingots are assumed to be used in production first, then the LIFO method is appropriate to value the inventory. Thus, during the inflationary accounting period when ingot prices rose 50 percent and only one ingot was carried in stock, the value of the inventory was constant; that is, the value of the ingot in ending inventory is assumed not to change. Thus, relative to the year's ending market prices of $3,000 per ingot, LIFO undervalues ending inventory, overestimates the cost of goods sold, and accordingly underestimates profit during inflation. Table 11-3 depicts this LIFO process.

TABLE 11-3 LIFO DURING INFLATION (FIRM B)

	Inventory value
Beginning inventory (1 ingot at $2,000)	$ 2,000
Plus: Purchases (2 ingots at $3,000 each)	6,000
Cost of goods available for sale	$ 8,000
Less: Ending inventory (1 ingot at $2,000)	−2,000 (undervalued)
Cost of goods sold	$ 6,000 (overvalued)

If FIFO had been used, the ending inventory (of one ingot purchased for $3,000) would be valued at $3,000. This means the cost of goods sold in Table 11-3 would be $5,000 if FIFO had been employed instead of LIFO.

Some consideration of these methods reveals that FIFO incorporates inventory capital gains or losses into regular income, LIFO does not. Thus, the FIFO method often causes profit to be more volatile than the LIFO method. FIFO is assumed to be the most realistic (although least advantageous for tax purposes) method of inventory valuation in this case for two main reasons. First, most manufacturers usually sell the oldest items in their inventories first. Second, profits and losses on the inventory are reflected in reported income as they occur.

Not only does the use of LIFO versus FIFO have different effects on income, switching from one of these inventory valuation techniques to the other can result in some spectacular changes. Chrysler Corporation's 1970 income statement provides good examples of (1) how to detect that a company reports a substantially different set of books to its stockholders from the one it reports to the Internal Revenue Service (IRS); and (2) what switching from LIFO to FIFO can do to reported earnings.

Comparison of the federal income taxes a company reports paying to see whether they are about 50 percent of its reported pre-tax income is a good way to detect if the company keeps "two sets of books." Thus, when Chrysler reported a $34 million loss before taxes in early 1970 and, at the same time, showed an $80 million asset on its balance sheet with the title "Refundable U.S. Taxes on Income," some deception was suspected. Some scrutiny to determine Chrysler's economic income revealed that the company's losses were probably over $74 million rather than the $34 million which was reported by its accountants and certified by its CPAs. This deception was accomplished by switching from LIFO to FIFO, as explained below.

In 1970, Chrysler switched some of its inventory from LIFO to FIFO with the result that consolidated inventories were revised upward from $110 to $150 million. This $40 million bookkeeping gain was then added to Chrysler's accounting profit, or, more precisely, subtracted from the losses its accountants reported to its shareholders. Thus, Chrysler's actual loss was probably somewhere between the $34 million reported loss and the ($34 million + $40 million =) $74 million loss before the change in inventory valuation methods.

In its second set of books, that is, in those it keeps for the IRS, Chrysler reported the economic loss of $74 million plus some other things so that it could get a larger income tax refund. These tricks entitled Chrysler to the $80 million of "Refundable U.S. Taxes on Income" which appeared as a balance sheet asset and first called attention to the deception.[4]

---

[4] Abraham Brilhoff, *Unaccountable Accounting* (New York: Harper & Row, 1972), pp. 36–39.

Depreciation (3)

Assuming that no new technology or unusually heavy use is likely to depreciate the value of the assets used by Firms A and B before they are worn out, the straight-line depreciation used by Firm A is more honest (but less desirable for tax purposes) than the accelerated sum-of-the-digits depreciation procedure employed by B.

Several depreciation techniques may be used:

1 Straight-line method
2 Units of production method
3 Double declining balance method
4 Sum-of-the-digits method

The third and fourth methods are accelerated methods of depreciation. The second method may be used to accelerate depreciation during a period of rapid production. To understand how depreciation affects profit, a numerical example using the first and fourth methods will be used.

Imagine an asset that costs \$1,000 with an expected life of $n = 3$ years. By use of the straight-line method, depreciation is \$333.33 ($= \$1,000/3 = \text{cost}/n$) for each of the 3 years. By use of the sum-of-the-digits method, the annual depreciation starts large and diminishes each year, because a decreasing fraction is multiplied by the cost of the asset (a stable amount) to determine each year's depreciation. The numerator of this fraction decreases by 1 each year as shown below. The numerator represents the number of years left in the life of the asset. The denominator of the fraction remains stable; it is the sum of the years in the life of the asset (for example, if the life expectancy of an asset were 3 years, the denominator would be $1 + 2 + 3 = 6$).

Year	Depreciation as fraction of cost	Sum-of-the-digits annual dollar depreciation, \$
1	$\dfrac{\underset{n=3}{n}}{\sum\limits_{i=1}^{} i} = \dfrac{3}{6}$	500
2	$\dfrac{\underset{n=3}{n-1}}{\sum\limits_{i=1}^{} i} = \dfrac{2}{6}$	333.33
3	$\dfrac{\underset{n=3}{n-2}}{\sum\limits_{i=1}^{} i} = \dfrac{1}{6}$	166.66
	1.0	$\overline{1,000}$ = cost

Accelerated depreciation increases depreciation costs in the early years of a new asset's life; it thereby decreases profit, income tax, and net accounting profit when the asset is new. Accelerated depreciation postpones taxes on income. Postponing taxes is like obtaining an interest-free loan from the federal government. The total depreciation expense is un-changed; only the timing is altered. As Table 11-2 shows, however, it can affect any particular year's reported accounting income significantly.

Research and Development (4)

Statement A capitalizes current research and development (R&D) costs and then amortizes this balance sheet asset over a period of years. Statement B treats R&D cost as a current expense and deducts it all from current rev-enue. The year-to-year fluctuations and the total amount spent on R&D de-termine the effects on income of these two accounting treatments. On the assumption that the two firms' R&D efforts yielded some valuable in-sights which will improve their long-run incomes, amortizing the R&D cost over a period of years will align reported income more closely with their economic income. Thus, the fundamental analyst need not adjust Firm A's treatment of R&D costs.

There are many items which the accountant may either (1) write off as current expenses, or (2) capitalize and then amortize over a period of years. For example, moving-picture production costs, oil well exploration costs, advertising campaign costs, and many other items simply are not clearly either an expense or an asset: these are matters of managerial discretion which the fundamental analyst should scrutinize.

Pension Costs (5)

Statement B reflects the maximum allowable pension cost and statement A the minimum. The maximum is the normal cost for current employee ser-vices, plus 10 percent of any unpaid past employee service costs and/or 10 percent of any change in prior service costs.[5] The minimum is the normal cost, plus the equivalent of an interest payment on any unfunded prior employee service costs. The maximum allowable cost is based on the notion that pension payments are due to individual employees. The minimum cost is based on the idea that payments are put into a pension fund from which all present and all future retired employees can draw payment. The former recognizes prior services' expense during the life span of individuals (short time span), whereas the latter spreads it over the life of the pension plan (perhaps to infinity). On the assumption that the firms have a youthful labor force with few men near the age when they will draw retirement benefits, Firm A's treatment of pension costs is the more forthright ap-proach (although, again, it furnishes the least income tax shelter).

There are several methods of determining pension costs. For pension funds established in advance of the actual payment of the employees' benefits, these costs must be estimated. Usually an actuary analyzes a com-pany's contractual pension liabilities, its labor turnover, the age pattern of

[5] Accounting Principles Board, Opinion No. 8, pp. 85–86.

the employees, and mortality rates of the pensioners. Based on these data, future costs are estimated. The pension costs deducted in any given year thus depend on both the accounting procedure and the actuary's estimates.

Other Income (6)

Statement A shows $100,000 more as "other income" than statement B because A included its capital gain from the sale of an old warehouse. The old building had been depreciated down to a book value of $1 while its market value rose with inflation. Then, when the building was sold for $140,001, the $140,000 excess of the sale price over the book value (less $40,000 capital gains tax) was reported as "other income" by A. This $100,000 was merely added to the net worth on B's balance sheet and it never appeared on B's income statement. Since old assets sold for cash proceeds in excess of their depreciated book values yield consumable cash, statement A's handling of this source of income is a better reflection of the transaction's economic income. However, not all firms' sales of assets result in other income that is consumable economic income. In fact, the "other income" category sometimes includes some elaborate misrepresentations of the economic facts.

An example of bookkeeping which bolstered a firm's "other income" by $2.1 million, but cost the company $1.7 million cash, is one of Occidental Petroleum's land deals in 1970. As the first quarter of 1970 drew to a close, some of Occidental's executives wanted to do something to increase reported profits. So about March 31, 1970, Occidental bought 1,240 acres of land from the Rhodell Company for $2.5 million *cash*. Then, on the same day, Occidental sold 1,000 of these newly purchased acres to Arizona Construction Co. for $4.1 million, with accountants reporting the $2.1 million difference as part of Occidental's profit. On the surface, this appeared to be a last-day-of-the-quarter deal which netted a tidy $2.1 million gain.

Closer examination of this Occidental land deal revealed that a Mr. Rhodes had sold the 1,240 acres to Occidental. The same Mr. Rhodes also owned Arizona Construction. So, in effect, Mr. Rhodes bought 1,000 of the 1,240 acres back from Occidental on the same day he sold them, and he paid almost twice the price he had sold them for earlier in the day. To understand why Mr. Rhodes was apparently running a charitable giveaway for Occidental, it is enlightening to learn that Occidental loaned Mr. Rhodes the money to buy out his partner in Arizona Construction Co. on that same end-of-the-quarter March 31, 1970. When this busy day was over, Occidental had a net cash outflow of $1.7 million, and it had received mostly promissory notes from Mr. Rhodes to pay for the $4.5 million sell-back to his Arizona Construction Co. But, in spite of the preceding dubious developments, Occidental had $2.1 million accounting profit and could report in accordance with "the accepted accounting conventions" to which its CPAs adhered.[6]

---

[6] Abraham Brilhoff, op. cit., pp. 182–183.

Effects on Accounting Income

Table 11-2 summarizes the six differences in accounting procedures which were just discussed and shows the effects on accounting income. Firm B paid no income taxes; instead, it received a $250,000 federal income tax refund to partially offset its losses. In contrast, Firm A paid $1,365,000 in federal income taxes. These tax differences make it difficult to recall that both firms were identical except for the accounting procedures used. Thus, the taxpayers of the United States and Firm B's shareholders were misled by the accounting income reported by the company. However, the firms would have little difficulty getting a certified public accountant to certify that their income statements were within current "generally accepted accounting principles."

Some financial executives and accountants take advantage of the discretionary leeway in the accounting procedures which were highlighted in Table 11-2. These persons use the variables at their discretion to manipulate their firms' income to suit their current purposes.[7] Even if all financial executives were completely ethical in the exercise of their control over income, the mere changing of financial personnel could result in new accounting procedures. These new procedures could be "generally acceptable" and arrived at following honest deliberations by the new management but still be *inconsistent* with the previous procedures and therefore misleading. Obviously, it behooves the investor to adjust reported accounting income to allow for such changes. However, many investors do not have the time or training to make the proper adjustments in reported income figures. Therefore, the accounting profession should continue to narrow the areas left to the discretion of firms in reporting their own incomes.

The numerical example summarized in Table 11-2 dramatically pinpoints major ambiguities in accountants' procedures for estimating income. The point-by-point discussion keyed to this table suggests how fundamental securities analysts could derive estimates of a firm's true economic income from accounting statements which are misleading.

In interpreting this example, the reader should bear at least two caveats in mind. First, the true economic income which a firm earns may be less than its reported income (as represented by statement B, for example) instead of larger. The example in Table 11-2 is a teaching device and is not intended to show all possible misrepresentations.

Second, the amount of difference between the reported earnings in statements A and B is not meant to be suggestive of some average amount of misrepresentation. In the final analysis, it is difficult to specify the amount of misrepresentation present in the use of any given set of accounting procedures since different analysts may interpret a given situation quite differently. However, well-trained, astute, but unethical financial managers

---

[7] See the Westec and Equity Funding cases in Chap. 4, Appendixes A and B, for other real-life examples of dishonest income reporting.

can manage their accountants' and other affairs to make their firms' reported earnings come out to be any number they wish within a wide range. So analysts should not use firms' reported income figures unhesitatingly.

The main point of this chapter is to stress the importance of using a well-defined income concept in accounting for reported income and in security analysis. Most people's actions seem to imply that, consciously or subconsciously, they equate income with a sustainable level of consumption.[8] The concept of economic income was suggested as a measure of sustainable consumption which is suited for fundamental securities analysis.[9]

11-4 HOW ACCOUNTING INCOME AFFECTS THE BALANCE SHEET

A *balance sheet* is a summary of account balances carried after the appropriate closing of the books. Income statements deal with *flows,* whereas the balance sheets deal with *stocks.* Of course, stocks are merely accumulations of flows. Thus, the vagaries which undermine the estimates of accounting income are cumulated in certain balance sheet items. Furthermore, the balance sheet may be adjusted by entries, such as purchased "goodwill," that are often fairly arbitrary. Table 11-4 shows a model of the balance sheet.

Current assets, current liabilities, and long-term liabilities are typically relatively accurate estimates of the dollar value of the firm's liquid assets and contractual liabilities. In addition, the notes accompanying the financial statements usually contain explanations of the inventory valuation technique used, the nature of contingent liabilities (for example, pending court settlements), and other items needed to estimate or recalculate these balance sheet items. Unless a fraud has been perpetrated, these figures are suitable for decision-making purposes.

The accepted accounting conventions are more likely to distort long-term assets and net worth on the balance sheet than other items. For example, the balance sheet items called *buildings and equipment,* which are a

---

[8] Milton Friedman, *A Theory of the Consumption Function* (Princeton, N.J.: Princeton, 1957).
[9] For a deeper discussion of many of the problems raised here, see R. K. Jaedicke and R. T. Sprouse, *Accounting Flows: Income, Funds and Cash,* Prentice-Hall Foundations of Finance Series (Englewood Cliffs, N.J.: Prentice-Hall, 1965). Any intermediate accounting textbook will explain the details of the various procedures accountants use in handling different transactions.

TABLE 11-4 BALANCE SHEET MODEL

Uses of funds	Sources of funds
Current assets	Current liabilities
Long-term assets	Long-term liabilities
Other assets	Net worth
Total assets	Total liabilities and equity

large part of total assets for most firms, are sensitive to the depreciation method used. Long-term assets and net worth items are also distorted by varying rates of inflation over the years.[10] And the item *retained earnings,* which bulks large on the balance sheet of most older firms, is merely the sum of that portion of past years' accounting income which was not paid out in dividends. As a result of these ambiguous balance sheet items, the book value of equity from the balance sheet bears no relation to the true intrinsic value of most common stocks (as shown in Table 2-2 on page 18).

The preceding conclusions about income statements and balance sheets were reached without delving into one of the richest sources of deception which is allowed within the generally accepted accounting principles—mergers and acquisitions. The accounting guidelines for preparing consolidated financial statements after mergers or acquisitions are so loose that accountants can, and sometimes do, create highly misleading consolidated statements with ease.

The major points at which accountants can use deceptive practices in preparing consolidated statements are too numerous to name. Essentially, accountants simply add two balance sheets together as they see fit to create a consolidated balance sheet. A disaggregated consolidated balance sheet for Leasco Corporation is presented in Table 11-5 as an example of the misrepresentation which can result when Leasco and its subsidiary, Reliance Insurance Company, are added together. Table 11-5 was prepared by Dr. Abraham Brilhoff, a CPA and a professor of accounting.

Leasco is a computer hardware rental corporation which acquired Reliance Insurance Company, an unrelated venture. The first column of figures in Table 11-5 is the 1970 consolidated balance sheet for Leasco including its subsidiary, Reliance. This consolidated statement was prepared and certified by CPAs. Column 2 contains Reliance Insurance Company's balance sheet separate from Leasco's. The third column of Table 11-5 is Leasco's *unconsolidated* balance sheet, after Reliance's assets and liabilities are deleted. Note that Leasco's equity is negative; that is, Professor Brilhoff sees Leasco alone as being *bankrupt* without its subsidiary.

By separating Leasco from Reliance to produce the unconsolidated balance sheet for Leasco, Professor Brilhoff was not merely playing accounting games. There is good economic logic for not combining Leasco and Reliance. Many of the assets of Reliance, an insurance company, are guarded over by the insurance statutes and insurance commissioners of the states in which it operates. Thus, Leasco cannot use many of Reliance's assets freely, although it owns the company.

Balance sheets need to be analyzed not only to detect insolvency and possible bankruptcy; they can also reveal information about the firm's income. Leasco's consolidated income for 1970, for example, was reported as

---

[10] For a detailed discussion of these and other issues, see B. Graham, D. Dodd, and S. Cottle, *Security Analysis,* 4th ed. (New York: McGraw-Hill, 1962), chap. 16.

TABLE 11-5 LEASCO'S CONSOLIDATED BALANCE SHEET ANALYSIS

	Leasco's fully consolidated balance sheet (1)	Reliance Insurance Company (including its life insurance subsidiary) (2)	Leasco excluding Reliance Insurance (cols. 1 minus 2) (3)
	(All amounts in millions)		
Assets			
Common and preferred stock at cost	$ 174	$173	$ 1
Bonds at amortized cost	311	313	(2)†
Cash and certificates of deposit	110	29	81
Accounts and notes receivable	115	68	47
Finance lease receivables	60	—	60
Rental equipment (depreciated cost)	252	—	252
Prepaid expenses	50	47	3
Policy and first-mortgage loans	38	38	—
Real estate—at cost	26	17	9
Computers, furniture, and equipment (depreciated cost)	21	4	17
Goodwill	16	—	16
Other assets	29	38	(9)†
Total assets	$1,202	$727	$475
Liabilities			
Unearned insurance premiums	196	195	1
Unpaid insurance losses	220	218	2
Life policies and reserves	95	99	(4)†
Notes payable	292		292
Accounts payable and accruals	76	24	52
Federal and foreign taxes	21	24	(3)†
Due on purchase of securities‡	33		33
Subordinated and convertible debt	99		99
Minority interests	7		7
Total liabilities	1,039	560	479
Equity	$ 163	$167	$ (4)

† These incongruous balances undoubtedly result from the differences in classification and nomenclature used by Leasco, et al., in the statement presentations.
‡ Represents the balance owing on the reacquisition of Leasco's preferred stock.
Source: Abraham Brilhoff, *Unaccountable Accounting* (New York: Harper & Row, 1972), p. 149.

zero. If Reliance's contribution to this consolidated total income was disaggregated, however, Leasco alone would have shown losses. Furthermore, if the Internal Revenue Service had forced Leasco to write off the intangible asset of goodwill, which was valued at $16 million on Leasco's balance sheet, this ruling would have further diminished Leasco's nonexistent reported earnings.

Sometimes an ethical CPA firm or the IRS or both may put pressure on a company to amortize untangible assets, such as goodwill, which appear on the balance sheet. This might occur if a firm was not amortizing a worthless intangible asset because it did not want to diminish its reported income by the amortization process. That is, the firm's reported earnings would be decreased by the portion of the intangible asset which was written off each year against its earnings. Leasco's income is one possible example. If Leasco were forced to amortize the $16 million of goodwill on its balance sheet over a 10-year period, the corporation's reported earnings would be further decreased by $1.6 million per year for a decade. When such accounting transactions are encountered in analyzing a firm's financial statements, appropriate adjustments must be made to obtain unbiased estimates of the company's earnings.

11-5 HOW TO ADJUST A SERIES OF INCOME STATEMENTS

Since income is so important in determining the value of a security, and since the concept of accounting profit is so vague, it is usually necessary to adjust or normalize the reported income figure to a more realistic value that is defined consistently from year to year.

The key word in analyzing a series of income statements from one firm is *consistency*. Since there are so few clear-cut definitions in income accounting, some definitions must be adopted and used consistently. This is where the economists' concept of *income as an amount of consumption which does not diminish future consumption opportunities* becomes useful.

Definition of Economic Income

A person's economic income is the maximum he or she can consume without diminishing a future period's consumption opportunities.

The financial analyst's job is to detect misleading accounting statements and restate them consistently, using the definition of economic income (rather than some accountant's reported profit which may contain tax gimmicks or window-dressing manipulations). In this manner a company's true earning power can be analyzed and the *trend* in income can be detected. Typically, financial statements for several past years are gathered from the company's 10-K reports.[11] Then, by referring to the notes to the financial statements, the various years' statements can be adjusted so the items in all years are consistently defined. After these adjustments, year-by-year comparisons are possible.

11-6 LONG-RANGE INCOME FORECASTING

The preceding paragraphs explained economic income and how to derive estimates of it from the accountant's income statements. After a firm's past accounting income figures have been normalized to yield a series of consistently defined estimates of the firm's economic income, the firm's *future* economic income may be estimated. It is necessary to estimate a stock's future income because the value of the share is the present value of its *future* economic income.

For short-term forecasts (for example, 1 year or less in the future), a firm's earnings may usually be estimated from discussions with the firm's management and the firm's competitors, and from other publicly available information. Such subjective estimates were discussed in Chap. 10. Here, forecasting techniques useful for longer-run earnings projections are explored. A firm's long-run earning power is ultimately what determines its intrinsic value.

Measuring Past Growth

Before the future growth rate in earnings is forecast, it is usually helpful to start by determining their past growth rate. The most common method is to fit a line through successive values of earnings per share on semilogarithmic graph paper. Consider the normalized earnings-per-share data shown in Table 11-6.

[11] The 10-K report is a detailed financial report which publicly held companies are required to file with the SEC. The 10-K form was discussed in Chap. 6. Corporations' 10-K statements are publicly available at the SEC.

TABLE 11-6 NORMALIZED EARNINGS PER SHARE FOR TWO HYPOTHETICAL FIRMS FROM PAST 5 YEARS

Year	Earnings per share for A, $	Earnings per share for B, $	Years	Status
19X7	4	1	1	Known
19X8	4.25	1.30	2	Known
19X9	4.45	1.50	3	Known
19X0	4.75	1.90	4	Known
19X1	5	2	5	Known
19X2	?	?	6	Unknown

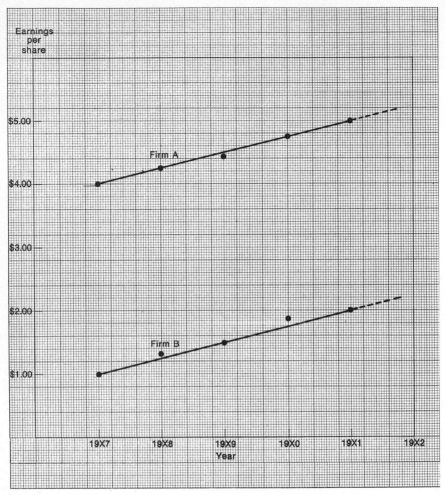

FIG. 11-1 Time series graph of earnings per share, on arithmetic graph paper.

The arithmetic graph in Fig. 11-1 seems to show that Firms A and B are experiencing equal growth since the slopes of the lines fitting through the points are equal. But the semilogarithmic graph in Fig. 11-2 shows that B's earnings are growing much faster (100 percent in 5 years) than A's, which increased only 25 percent in 5 years. This is because the slope of a line on the semilog paper represents the *percentage* increase (that is, the growth *rate*) instead of merely a periodic fixed *dollar* increase. A constant dollar increase per period implies a declining growth rate. The average growth rate in percentage form is more useful than the average dollar growth per period because growth rates measured in percentages are not distorted by changes in the dollar level of the income. Thus, logarithmic time series graphs such as the one in Fig. 11-2 are preferable.

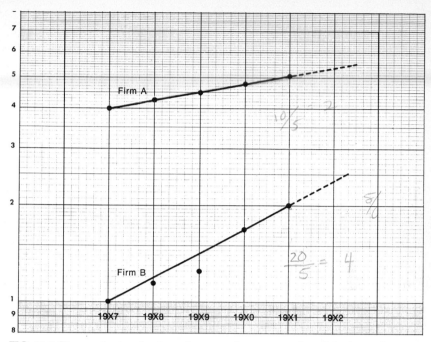

FIG. 11-2 Time series graph of earnings per share, on semilogarithmic graph paper.

After a straight trend line has been fit through 5 or 10 years' earnings-per-share points plotted in semilog paper, as shown in Fig. 11-2, the growth rate per period may be estimated. The growth rate is determined from the earnings-per-share values at the top and bottom ends of the earnings trend line. The relation between a constant growth rate g and the ratio of the ending value of the trend line over the beginning value is given by Eq. (11-1).

$$(1 + g)^t = \frac{V_t}{V_0} = \frac{\text{ending value after } t \text{ periods}}{\text{beginning value}} \qquad (11\text{-}1)$$

Table 11-7 shows the ratios of ending (V_t) over beginning values (V_0) of a trend line which has grown at a constant growth rate for 5, 10, 20, or 40 years. To determine the annual growth rate in Firm B's earnings per share, for example, the end points of its trend line in Fig. 11-2 are first observed to be $V_0 = \$1.00$ per share, and $V_5 = \$2.00$ per share earnings. Substituting these values into Eq. (11-1) yields the values shown in Eq. (11-1a).

$$(1 + g)^5 = 2.0 = \frac{\$2.00}{\$1.00} = \frac{V_5}{V_0} \qquad (11\text{-}1a)$$

Looking up the ratio $V_5/V_0 = 2.0$ for a 5-year period in Table 11-7 shows that $g = 14.9$ percent. That is, $\$1.00$, growing at a constant rate of 14.9 percent for 5 years, will become $\$2.00$.

TABLE 11-7 THE EFFECTS OF DIFFERENT GROWTH RATES OVER 5, 10, 20, AND 40 YEARS OF CONSTANT GROWTH

5 years		10 years		20 years		40 years†	
$(1+g)^5$ $= V_5/V_0$	Rate of change (g), %	$(1+g)^{10}$ $= V_{10}/V_0$	Rate of change (g), %	$(1+g)^{20}$ $= V_{20}/V_0$	Rate of change (g), %	$(1+g)^{40}$ $= V_{40}/V_0$	Rate of change, %
.01	− 60.2	.01	−36.9	.01	−20.6	.01	−10.9
.02	− 54.3	.02	−32.4	.02	−17.8	.02	− 9.3
.03	− 50.4	.03	−29.6	.03	−16.1	.05	− 7.2
.04	− 47.5	.04	−27.5	.05	−13.9	.1	− 5.6
.05	− 45.1	.05	−25.9	.1	−10.9	.2	− 4.0
.07	− 41.2	.1	−20.6	.2	− 7.7	.3	− 3.0
.1	− 36.9	.2	−14.9	.3	− 5.8	.4	− 2.3
.2	− 27.5	.3	−11.3	.4	− 4.5	.6	− 1.3
.3	− 21.4	.4	− 8.8	.5	− 3.4	1.0	0.0
.4	− 16.7	.5	− 6.7	.7	− 1.8	1.5	1.0
.5	− 12.9	.6	− 5.0	.9	− 0.5	2.2	2.0
.6	− 9.7	.7	− 3.5	1.1	0.5	3.2	3.0
.7	− 6.9	.8	− 2.2	1.4	1.7	4.6	3.9
.8	− 4.4	.9	− 1.0	1.8	3.0	6.4	4.8
.9	− 2.1	1.1	1.0	2.3	4.3	8.6	5.5
1.0	0	1.3	2.7	2.8	5.3	12.	6.4
1.1	1.9	1.5	4.1	3.4	6.3	15.	7.0
1.3	5.4	1.8	6.1	4.0	7.2	18.	7.5
1.4	7.0	2.0	7.2	4.7	8.0	22.	8.1
1.6	9.9	2.2	8.2	5.4	8.8	25.	8.4
1.7	11.2	2.4	9.1	5.9	9.3	28.	8.7
1.8	12.5	2.6	10.0	6.4	9.7	31.	9.0
1.9	13.7	2.7	10.4	6.8	10.1	34.	9.2
2.0	14.9	2.8	10.8	7.0	10.2	35.	9.3
2.1	16.0	2.9	11.2	7.1	10.3	36.	9.4
2.2	17.1	3.0	11.6	7.2	10.4	37.	9.5
2.3	18.1	3.1	12.0	7.3	10.5	38.	9.5
2.4	19.1	3.2	12.3	7.4	10.5	39.	9.6
2.5	20.1	3.3	12.7	7.6	10.7	40.	9.7
2.6	21.1	3.4	13.0	7.9	10.9	42.	9.8
2.7	22.0	3.5	13.3	8.3	11.2	44.	9.9
2.8	22.9	3.7	14.0	8.8	11.5	48.	10.2
2.9	23.7	4.0	14.9	9.4	11.9	53.	10.5
3.0	24.6	4.3	15.7	11.	12.7	60.	10.8
3.2	26.2	4.8	17.0	12.	13.2	70.	11.2
3.6	29.2	5.3	18.1	13.	13.7	80.	11.6
4.1	32.6	6.0	19.6	14.	14.1	90.	11.9
4.6	35.7	6.9	21.3	15.	14.5	100.	12.2
5.3	39.6	7.9	23.0	17.	15.2	120.	12.7
6.2	44.0	9.2	24.8	20.	16.2	150.	13.4
7.2	48.4	11.	27.1	22.	16.7	200.	14.2
8.6	53.8	13.	29.2	26.	17.7	250.	14.8
11.	61.5	16.	32.0	30.	18.5	300.	15.4
13.	67.0	19.	34.2	35.	19.5	350.	15.8
16.	74.1	23.	36.8	42.	20.5	400.	16.2
19.	80.2	29.	40.0	50.	21.6	500.	16.8
24.	88.8	36.	43.1	60.	22.7	700.	17.8
30.	97.4	46.	46.6	73.	23.9	1,000.	18.9
38.	107.0	58.	50.1	90.	25.2	1,300.	19.7
49.	117.8	75.	54.0	111.	26.6	1,715.	20.5

† The 40-year growth rate is actually for $39\frac{11}{12}$ years.

Source: L. Fisher and T. Lorie, "Some Studies of Variability of Returns on Investments in Common Stock," *Journal of Business*, April 1970, p. 103.

To solve for the growth rate for Firm A for 5 years, the ratio $V_5/V_0 = \$5/\$4 = 1.25$ is observed to be between the values 1.10 and 1.30 in Table 11-7. Interpolating between the growth rates associated with 1.10 and 1.30 yields a value for g of approximately 4.9 percent per year. Thus, Firm A's earnings grew at about 4.9 percent per anum while B's earnings grew at about 15 percent per year over the 5-year period.[12]

Forecasting Earnings per Share

Once the growth trend has been satisfactorily estimated, future values of earnings per share may be forecasted. First, the earnings trend line on semilog paper may be extrapolated as shown by the dotted segment in Fig. 11-2. If the points do not "fit" fairly closely on the trend line, it may be difficult to determine its slope. In this case a larger sample (change from annual to quarterly data and/or increase in the sample period) may help. Or, Eq. (11-2) may be used.

$$e_t = (1 + g)^t(e_0) \tag{11-2}$$

where e_t denotes earnings per share at period t. These methods should be satisfactory for short forecasts of a few years into the future if no change in the firm's growth rate is anticipated.

Forecasting the Growth Rate for Earnings

Forecasting earnings per share may not be as simple as indicated in the preceding paragraph, if the firm's rate of growth is expected to change. The rate of growth may change for several reasons. Products have life cycles. Figure 11-3 shows how earnings growth might behave over the life cycle of a product. Note that the growth rate is depicted as decreasing in each year. Since the growth rate is such an important factor in determining the price-earnings multipliers, not only its size but its duration must be estimated.[13]

---

[12] Fitting a trend line as described above is equivalent to taking the logarithm of n different periods' earnings per share and using regression analysis to estimate the following equation: $e_t = (1 + g)^t e_0$ for $t = 1, 2, \ldots, n$ periods. This equation is linear in logarithms and t is the independent variable in the regression. Taking the antilog of the regression slope coefficient will yield an unbiased estimate of the $(1 + g)$ quantity. Other techniques of projecting earnings are explained in B. Graham, D. Dodd, and S. Cottle, *Security Analysis*, 4th ed. (New York: McGraw-Hill, 1962), chap. 33. Also see T. E. Johnson and T. G. Schmitt, "Effectiveness of Earnings Per Share Forecasts," *Financial Management*, Summer 1974, pp. 64–72; John Cragg and Burton Malkiel, "The Consensus and Accuracy of Some Predictions of the Growth in Corporate Earnings," *Journal Of Finance*, March 1968, pp. 67–84; Edwin J. Elton and Martin J. Gruber, "Earnings Estimates and the Accuracy of Expectational Data," *Management Science*, April 1972, pp. B409–B424; and R. W. McEnally, "An Investigation of the Extrapolative Determinants of Short-Run Earnings Expectations," *Journal of Financial and Quantitative Analysis*, March 1971, pp. 687–706.

[13] C. C. Holt, "The Influence of Growth Duration on Share Prices," *Journal of Finance*, September 1962, pp. 465–475.

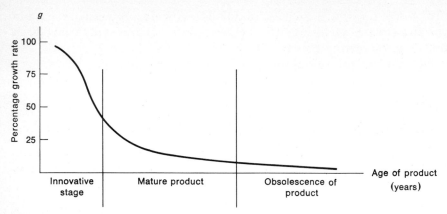

FIG. 11-3 Earnings growth over the life cycle of a product.

If the firm's managers are aggressive and farsighted, they will phase out products which are becoming obsolete and phase in new products which they have developed through a continuing research and development program. In this manner the firm's earnings could grow indefinitely. However, managers frequently become tied to their products, and the company dies as its original product becomes outdated.

Sometimes patents expire, competition becomes more aggressive, economically depressed periods occur, or other factors cause growth rates to drop. One of the purposes of fundamental analysis is to anticipate these factors accurately in order to make a good estimate of the growth rate of a firm's income. To stay abreast of this type of information, professional fundamental analysts typically specialize in one industry. They attend trade conventions for that industry, get to know each firm's products, meet with various firms' managers, follow legislation affecting the industry, and take other steps to ensure that they constantly have up-to-date estimates of the growth rates for most of the firms in the industry. For shorter-range forecasts the earnings figure suggested by Eq. (11-2) is merely adjusted to reflect things which can cause earnings to vary from their long-run trend in the short run, such factors were discussed in Chap. 10.

11-7 CONCLUSIONS ABOUT EARNINGS ANALYSIS

The economic income from an equity share is the maximum amount of consumption which that share can yield during some period such that the consumption opportunities from that share are undiminished at the end of the period. This frequently does not coincide with accountants' concept of income. Therefore, accounting income figures must be adjusted or normalized to obtain as nearly as possible a consistently defined series of economic income. The present value of this latter series is then taken to determine the value of that equity share. The procedures utilized by fundamental securities analysts in determining the intrinsic value of an equity's economic income were explained in Chap. 10.

QUESTIONS

1 Write out the model used by accountants in determining taxable income.

2 How would reported assets, expenses, and accounting income be affected by a switch from LIFO to FIFO inventory valuation during an inflationary period? Explain.

3 Explain why an oil company would show a "dry hole" (that is, a well where no oil was found) as an intangible asset on its balance sheet. Is this ethically right or wrong?

4 Write a one-sentence definition of income as economists define it. What is the difference between accounting and economic income? Which do you think is relevant in determining the value of an asset?

5 List some implicit costs which an accountant would probably ignore in determining the income of a small family-owned and -operated drugstore.

6 If accounting procedures which grossly misrepresent income are followed, what balance sheet items are affected the most?

7 What are the main factors which could cause a firm's historical average growth rate to decrease in future years? To increase?

8 Assume the Bigfirm Corporation acquired the Smallfirm Corporation for cash that is $5 million more than the book value of Smallfirm. Bigfirm could add in $5 million of goodwill as an asset on its new consolidated balance sheet. How would this affect Bigfirm financial statements? How else could this deal be handled by Bigfirm and its accountants?

SELECTED REFERENCES

Brilhoff, Abraham, *Unaccountable Accounting* (New York: Harper & Row, 1972).
> A nonmathematical, case-by-case discussion, giving names of large corporations and large CPA firms, dates, and numerous actual examples of accounting entries which do not reflect the economic realities.

Graham, B., D. Dodd, and S. Cottle, *Security Analysis,* 4th ed. (New York: McGraw-Hill, 1962).
> This book is a standard reference of many practicing fundamental

security analysts. It is a nonmathematical, detailed description of security analysis based on financial statements and other basic facts about the firm. Chapter 33 deals with earnings forecasting.

Jaedicke, R. K., and R. T. Sprouse, *Accounting Flows: Income, Funds and Cash,* 2d ed. (Englewood Cliffs, N.J.: Prentice-Hall, 1973).
   A nonmathematical discussion of the relation of economic income, cashflows, and accounting profit.

Lev, Baruch, *Financial Statement Analysis: A New Approach* (Englewood Cliffs, N.J.: Prentice-Hall, 1974).
   A book which shows new techniques of financial analysis which are oriented toward computer processing of data. Algebra and statistics are used.

Twelve

Risk

Chapter 1 stated the *investment objective* of seeking assets with the maximum expected return in their risk-class, or conversely, the minimum risk for their level of expected return. However, the notion of risk has not yet been examined very closely. Risk is a very important word as it applies to financial investments. In fact, risk is more than just a word—it is a concept. There are different causes for different types of risk. This chapter defines and analyzes investors' risks.

Risk will be defined quantitatively so that it may be treated in an analytical manner. Then a positive relation between risk and a marketable security's expected return, called the security market line (SML), is explained. In Chap. 10 the SML risk-return relationship was used to determine which discount rate to use in finding the present value of a common stock's income after its risk has been estimated. The SML is an important part of security analysis; it will be explained in detail here. In later chapters, risk is also important in portfolio management.

12-1 DEFINING RISK ANALYTICALLY

Webster defines *risk* as "the chance of injury, damage, or loss." This is an intuitively pleasing definition, and few people would disagree with it. However, this verbal definition is not very analytical. Verbal definitions are interpreted in different ways by different people. They can be made clearer only by means of other verbal definitions or by examples which are not always entirely appropriate and are rarely concise. Such definitions do not yield to measurement. Frequently, they are not even exact enough to allow objects possessing the defined characteristic (here, risk) to be ranked in terms of that characteristic. Thus, it seems desirable to develop a surrogate for the dictionary definition of risk which is amenable to quantification.

Quantitative Surrogates

If risk analysis is to proceed, a quantitative risk surrogate is needed.[1] However, if this quantitative risk surrogate is to be intuitively pleasing, it must measure, either directly or indirectly, "the chance of injury, damage, or loss" so that it may be used synonymously with the word "risk." The quantitative financial risk surrogate which will be used is measured from the investment's probability distribution of rates of return.

Probability Distribution of Rates of Return

The rate of return is the single most important outcome from an investment. Therefore, the quantitative risk surrogate focuses on rates of return. Considerations of whether a stock is a growth stock, whether the company's "image is pleasing," or whether the firm's product is "glamorous" are relevant only to the extent they affect its rate of return and riskiness.

In an uncertain world, investors cannot tell in advance exactly what rate of return an investment will yield. However, they can formulate a probability distribution of the possible rates of return. Figure 12-1 shows three probability distributions of returns for ATT, Borden, and Firestone common stock.

A probability distribution may be either subjective or objective. An *objective probability distribution* is formed by measuring objective historical data. A *subjective probability distribution* is formed by simply writing down someone's hunches and assigning probabilities to them. Of course, what occurred historically influences hunches about the future. But if the probability distribution is not fairly stationary over time, historical probability distributions of rates of return are not much help in forecasting the future probability distributions upon which investment decisions are based. Luckily, most firms' probability distributions of rates of return and the statistics describing them do not seem to change very much as time passes.[2] Thus, objective distributions almost always influence the development of subjective distributions and in many cases are good estimates of what the future holds.

---

[1] Quantification is occurring in many fields. For example, a biology student may now major in biometrics at most universities. Biometrics involves measuring biological phenomena. By testing new drugs and detecting subtle cause-and-effect relationships (for example, lung cancer and smoking), biometricians are extending the ability of the medical profession.

Within the social sciences, quantification progress is accelerating, too. Most psychology departments today offer programs in psychometry—that is, the measuring of mental traits. The IQ test is probably the best-known psychometric instrument. However, psychometric tools measure many subtle traits besides intelligence.

Economics departments are offering majors in econometrics. Econometricians develop mathematical economic models which they test statistically. Econometricians are expanding the study of economics from rationalization of observable phenomena to a science of measuring, testing, and predicting.

[2] Marshall Blume, "On the Assessment of Risk," *Journal of Finance,* March 1971, pp. 1–10.

American Telephone
and Telegraph

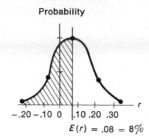

Probability

E(r) = .08 = 8%

i	p_i	r_i
1	.05	.38 = 38%
2	.2	.23 = 23%
3	.5	.08 = 8%
4	.2	−.07 = −7%
5	.05	−.22 = −22%
	1.0	

E(r) = .08 = 8%

Borden

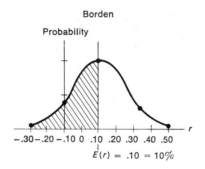

Probability

E(r) = .10 = 10%

i	p_i	r_i
1	.1	.5 = 50%
2	.2	.3 = 30%
3	.4	.1 = 10%
4	.2	−.1 = −10%
5	.1	−.3 = −30%
	1.0	

E(r) = .10 = 10%

Firestone

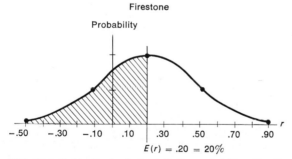

Probability

E(r) = .20 = 20%

i	p_i	r_i
1	.1	.9 = 90%
2	.25	.5 = 50%
3	.3	.2 = 20%
4	.25	−.1 = −10%
5	.1	−.5 = −50%
	1.0	

E(r) = .20 = 20%

FIG. 12-1 Subjectively derived finite probability distributions of rates of return.

Probability distributions of returns are essential in deriving a quantitative financial risk surrogate. Investors tend (consciously or subconsciously) to focus on the probability distribution of rates of return. In particular, investors want to know the average rate of return they can expect from each potential investment and the risk associated with that investment.

Expected Return

The *expected return* is the sum of the products of the various returns times their probabilities. Equation (12-1) defines the expected return symbolically. That is, r_t denotes the tth rate of return from the probability distribution, p_t is the probability that the tth rate of return occurs, and there are n possible rates of return. The calculations are for the Borden probability distribution from Fig. 12-1.

$$E(r) = \sum_{t}^{n} p_t r_t \tag{12-1}$$

$$
\begin{aligned}
&= p_1 r_1 + p_2 r_2 + p_3 r_3 + p_4 r_4 + p_5 r_5 \\
&= (.1)(.5) + (.2)(.3) + (.4)(.1) + (.2)(-.1) + (.1)(-.3) \\
&= .05 + .06 + .04 - .02 - .03 \\
&= .1 = 10\%
\end{aligned}
$$

The expected return is a weighted average return using the probabilities for weights; it measures the average or central tendency of the probability distribution of returns.

Variance and Standard Deviation of Returns

The wideness of a probability distribution of rates of return is a measure of uncertainty or risk. That is, the more an investment's return varies, around its expected return, the larger is the investor's uncertainty. The risk or wideness of the probability distribution can be measured with the variance of returns defined in Eq. (12-2). The calculations are for the Borden Company data from Fig. 12-1.

$$\sigma^2 = \sum_{i=1}^{5} p_i [r_i - E(r)]^2 \tag{12-2}$$

$$
\begin{aligned}
&= p_1[r_1 - E(r)]^2 + p_2[r_2 - E(r)]^2 + p_3(r_3 - E(r))^2 \\
&\qquad\qquad\qquad + p_4[r_4 - E(r)]^2 + p_5[r_5 - E(r)]^2 \\
&= (.1)(.5 - .1)^2 + (.2)(.3 - .1)^2 + (.4)(.1 - .1)^2 \\
&\qquad\qquad\qquad + (.2)(-.1 - .1)^2 + (.1)(-.3 - .1)^2 \\
&= .016 + .008 + 0 + .008 + .016 \\
&= .048 \qquad \text{rate of return squared}
\end{aligned}
$$

The standard deviation is defined in Eq. (12-3); it is the square root of the variance. Borden's standard deviation is calculated.[3]

$$\sigma = \sqrt{\sigma^2} \tag{12-3}$$

$$
\begin{aligned}
&= \sqrt{\sum p_i [r_i - E(r)]^2} \\
&= \sqrt{.048} \\
&= .22 = 22\% = 22 \text{ percentage points rate of return}
\end{aligned}
$$

[3] The first four moments (namely, the variance, skewness, and kurtosis) of a probability distribution are discussed in Mathematical Appendix G. Summation signs, probabilities, and the expected value operator are explained in Mathematical Appendixes A, B, and E, respectively.

The standard deviation is stated in rates of return, but the variance is stated in terms of the "rate of return squared." Since it is more natural to discuss rates of return rather than rates of return squared, risk is sometimes measured with the standard deviation of returns. However, for statistical purposes it is sometimes more convenient to use the variance rather than the standard deviation when discussing risk. Conceptually, either risk definition is appropriate since they are mathematically equivalent.

Symmetric Probability Distribution of Returns

If risk is defined as the chance of loss or injury, it seems more logical to measure risk by the area in a probability distribution which is *below* its expected return. However, this procedure can be difficult, and furthermore, it is unnecessary if the probability distribution is *symmetric.*

Figure 12-2 shows three probability distributions of returns—one skewed left, one symmetrical, and one skewed right. The symmetrical distribution has no skewness. The area on one side of the expected return of a symmetric distribution is the mirror image of the area on the other side of the expected return.

Empirical studies of historical probability distributions of returns indicate they are not significantly skewed if short differencing intervals (for example, if one month elapses between p_t and p_{t+1}) are used.[4] Consequently, it is not important whether variability of returns is measured on one or both sides of the expected return.

Measuring total variability of return (that is, risk) on both sides of the expected return with the standard deviation and variance includes surprisingly good returns (that is, returns above the expected return) in the risk measure. But as long as the probability distributions of returns are fairly symmetric, the way the risk of a group of assets is measured does not change in any meaningful way. Measurements of each asset's *total* variability of return will be twice as large as measurements of that asset's variability below the expected return if its probability distribution is sym-

---

[4] J. C. Francis, "Skewness and Investors' Decisions," *Journal of Financial and Quantitative Analysis,* March 1975. Also, see the first part of the Appendix to Chap. 21 for an intuitive explanation with graphs.

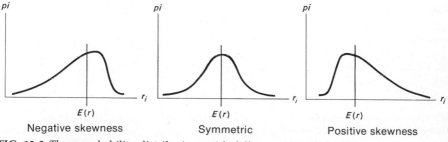

FIG. 12-2 Three probability distributions with different types of skewness.

metric. As long as total variability of return on both sides of the expected return is used consistently as a risk surrogate, the risk measurements of all assets will still result in the same risk rankings for a group of assets. Since the standard deviation and variance are such common statistics and will rank assets' risk in the same order as a more complicated measure (for example, of variability below the expected return), they will be used as quantitative financial risk surrogates.[5] This approach will also be simpler than trying to measure only the lower half of the distribution. Measuring risk by the standard deviation and variance is equivalent to *defining risk as total variability of returns* about the expected return or, simply, as variability of returns.

In essence, it is the accuracy with which future (subjective) probability distributions of rates of returns are forecast that determines the value of the quantitative risk surrogate. Since investment decisions are based on future returns, much care must go into estimating the expected return and expected risk statistics for all assets under consideration. This is the job of the securities analyst.[6]

12-2 TOTAL, SYSTEMATIC, AND UNSYSTEMATIC RISK

The total risk or total variability of return of an asset can be divided into two parts—systematic and unsystematic.

> Systematic risk (or undiversifiable risk)
> +Unsystematic risk (or diversifiable risk)
> _____
> Total risk

Systematic Risk

Systematic risk is that portion of total variability in return caused by factors which *simultaneously* affect the prices of all marketable securities.[7] Changes in the economic, political, and sociological environment which affect securities markets are sources of systematic risk. Systematic variability of return is found in nearly all securities in varying degrees because most securities move together in a systematic manner. Figure 12-3 shows how

[5] H. Markowitz. *Portfolio Selection* (New York: Wiley, 1959), chap. 9. Markowitz explains the use of the variance instead of his semivariance (svr), which measures variability below the expected return. By his definition, svr $= \sum p_t [\text{bar}_t - E(r)]^2$ where bar_t is the tth below average rate of return.

[6] J. C. Francis and S. Archer, *Portfolio Analysis* (Englewood Cliffs, N.J.: Prentice-Hall, 1971). Chapter 3 deals explicitly with procedures the security analyst can use to estimate risk and return statistics.

[7] The simultaneity of systematic stock price movements was documented by J. C. Francis, "Intertemporal Differences in Systematic Stock Price Movements," *Journal of Financial and Quantitative Analysis,* June 1975, pp. 205–219.

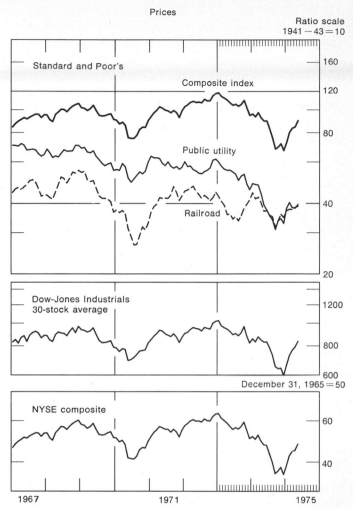

FIG. 12-3 Stock prices and trading. (From Federal Reserve System, *Monthly Chart Book,* September 1975, p. 70.)

averages of 20 railroad stocks, 55 utility stocks, and 425 industrial stocks all tend to vary in price together: this is systematic variability. The *prices* of nearly all individual common stocks tend to move together in the same manner; that is why nearly all stocks listed on the New York Stock Exchange (NYSE) are highly positively correlated with the rate of change in the NYSE index. On the average, 30 percent of the variation in a stock's price can be explained by variation in the market index.[8]

Firms that have high degrees of systematic risk within their total risk include American Zinc, Lead and Smelting Company, Chicago Pneumatic

[8] Marshall Blume, op. cit., p. 4.

Tool Company, Northwest Airlines, Erie-Lackawanna Railroad, B. F. Goodrich Company, Lehigh Valley Railroad, Missouri-Kansas-Texas Railroad, Peoria and Eastern Railroad, U.S. Rubber, Hoffman Machinery Corporation, and PanAm Airlines.

It will be noted that the firms with high systematic risk tend to be those providing basic industrial goods, such as railroads, tool companies, and rubber companies, and highly levered firms which have cyclical sales—like the airlines. As a result, the sales, profits, and stock prices of these firms follow the level of economic activity and the level of the securities markets.

Unsystematic Risk

Unsystematic risk is that portion of total risk which is *unique* to a firm or industry. Changes such as labor strikes, management errors, inventions, advertising campaigns, shifts in consumer taste, and lawsuits cause unsystematic variability of returns in a firm. Unsystematic variations are independent of factors affecting other industries and security markets in general. Since unsystematic risk is caused by factors which affect one firm, or at most a few, it must be forecast separately for each firm.

The proportion of total variability which is unsystematic varies widely from firm to firm. The total risk of a few firms is unsystematic. Coca-Cola, U.S. Tobacco, Wrigley Company, American Snuff Company, ATT, and Homestake Mining Company are firms which have large proportions of unsystematic risk and small proportions of systematic risk.

Many of the firms with low proportions of systematic risk and high proportions of unsystematic risk produce nondurable consumer goods. Sales, profits, and stock prices of these firms do not depend on the level of industrial activity or the stock market. As a result, these firms might have their best years when the economy is in a recession.

12-3 SOURCES OF RISK

There are an infinite number of sources for variability of return. These various sources have been divided into two main groups—systematic causes and unsystematic causes. Within each of these two subdivisions are narrower categories, as shown in Table 12-1.

Interest Rate Risk

Interest rate risk is the variability in return caused by changes in the level of interest rates. All market interest rates tend to move up or down together in the long run. These changes in interest rates affect all securities to some extent and tend to affect all securities in the *same way;* that is, security prices move inversely to interest rates, *ceteris paribus.* This is because a

TABLE 12-1 SOURCES OF RISK CATEGORIZED

1 Systematic sources of risk
    a Interest rate risk
    b Purchasing power risk
    c Market risk
    d Financial leverage risk (cyclical)
    e Operating leverage risk (cyclical)
2 Unsystematic sources of risk
    a Financial leverage risk (noncyclical)
    b Operating leverage risk (noncyclical)
    c Management risk
    d Industry risk

security's value is the present value of the security's income. Since the market rate of interest is the discount rate used in calculating present values of securities, all securities' prices tend to move inversely with changes in the level of interest rates. This was explained in detail in Chaps. 7 and 8.

Interest rate risk affects the prices of fixed-income securities like bonds more than common stock. This is because any change in the rate of return for a fixed-income security must be accomplished solely through capital gain or loss since the interest or dividends from a fixed-income security do not vary as long as the issuing firm is solvent. Consider a bond's one-period (for example, a year) holding period yield, defined in Eq. (12-4), to see this more clearly.

$$r_t = \frac{i_t + (p_{t+1} - p_t)}{p_t} = \text{rate of return during period } t$$

$$= \frac{\text{fixed income} + \text{capital gains or loss}}{\text{purchase price}}$$

(12-4)

where i_t = fixed income such as bond interest
    p_{t+1} = market price of asset at start of period $t + 1$
    p_t = price of asset at start of period t

Equation (12-4) shows that once a security like a bond with a fixed contractual income of i_t per period is purchased at some price p_t, any change in that security's yield to maturity must be accomplished through variations in the future price p_{t+1}. Thus, fixed-income securities may have less business or financial risk than common stock, but they typically have more interest rate risk. Figure 12-4 shows how the prices on a 4 percent coupon U.S. Treasury bond (a bond which has no bankruptcy risk) fluctuates as market interest rates vary from 3 to 4 to 5 percent. Since all security prices are affected in a similar (but probably less dramatic) way by changes in the level of interest rates, it is clear that interest rate changes can systematically affect all securities markets.

Market price of bond

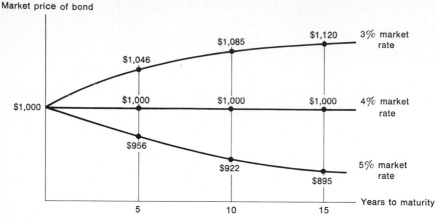

FIG. 12-4 Prices of 4 percent U.S. Treasury bonds as market interest rates vary from 3 to 5 percent.

Some investors believe they can avert interest risk by buying short-term bonds which do not experience the wide swings in market prices that characterize the longer maturities. However, investors in short-term bonds face a series of short-term reinvestments at constantly changing market yields. Thus, the variability of return from interest rate changes cannot be easily avoided.[9]

Purchasing Power Risk

Purchasing power risk is the chance that, because of inflation, the purchasing power of savings or invested wealth will decline. It is uncertainty about the future purchasing power of invested funds.

Purchasing power risk is highest in such investments as savings accounts, cash value life insurance, Christmas savings clubs, bonds, and other contracts that typically pay fixed interest rates. When the rate of inflation exceeds the fixed rates of return, the savings suffer a decline in purchasing power.

The data in Table 12-2 give an indication of the relation between the inflation rate and the yields to maturity on high-quality bonds. Column 2 of the table shows the level of the Consumer Price Index (CPI) for each year, and column 3 shows the percentage change in the CPI from year to year—that is, the rate of inflation. The fourth column shows the average yield to maturity on AAA-grade corporate bonds in each year.

---

[9] More specifically, the *capital risk* can be avoided by using short-term bonds, but the *income risk* of subsequent reinvestments remains. Thus, ignoring income tax differences between capital gains and interest income, the variability of return (that is, total risk) will not be changed by using many short-term bonds rather than a few long-term bonds. Duration is a measure of interest rate risk explained by R. A. Haugen and D. W. Wichern, "The Elasticity of Financial Assets," *Journal of Finance*, September 1974, pp. 1229–1240.

TABLE 12-2 COMPARISON OF NOMINAL MARKET INTEREST RATES AND INFLATION RATES

Year	CPI†	$(CPI_{t+1}/CPI_t) - 1.0 =$ inflation rate, %	AAA yields, %
1975	n.a.	n.a.	n.a.
1974	147.7	10.9	8.2
1973	133.1	6.2	7.4
1972	125.3	3.0	7.2
1971	121.3	4.3	7.6
1970	116.3	5.9	8.5
1969	109.8	5.4	7.0
1968	104.2	4.2	6.3
1967	100.0†	2.8	5.4
1966	97.2	2.8	5.0
1965	94.5	1.7	4.5
1964	92.9	1.3	4.4
1963	91.7	1.2	4.2
1962	90.6	1.1	4.3
1961	89.6	1.0	4.3
1960	88.7	1.5	4.4
1959	87.3	.8	4.5
1958	86.6	2.7	3.6
1957	85.0	3.4	3.9
1956	82.0	1.5	3.2
1955	80.8	1.0	3.0
1954	81.0	.4	2.9

† 1967 is base of 100 for Consumer Price Index (CPI).
Source: Federal Reserve Bulletins.

Equation (12-5) shows the exact relation between a nominal market interest rate, denoted r, the rate of price change, denoted by $\Delta P/P$, and the investor's change in *real* purchasing power, denoted X.

$$X = \frac{1+r}{1 + \Delta P/P} - 1.0 \qquad (12\text{-}5)$$

X represents the percentage change in purchasing power resulting from an investment with a rate of return of r. If the investor's rate of interest just equals the rate of inflation, $r = \Delta P/P$, then the investor's real rate of return is zero, $X = 0$. In a more typical situation, the investor's rate of return might be $r = 10$ percent while inflation is $\Delta P/P = 4$ percent. In this case the investor's purchasing power is increasing at $(1.1/1.04) - 1 = X = 5.7$ percent; this is the investor's *real* rate of return after allowing for inflation. As a first approximation, X equals r less $\Delta P/P$. Comparison of the last two columns in Table 12-2 shows that nominal interest rates on AAA-grade bonds, r, exceeded the rate of inflation, $\Delta P/P$, in most years by only two or three percentage points. That is, $X = 2$ to 3 percent for the bonds. Compare this return with the *real* return from common stock.

Stockbrokers sometimes tell their customers that common stock is an inflation hedge which will *more* than protect them from purchasing power risk. This is generally not true. It is true that common stock tends to suffer less from purchasing power risk than fixed-income investments, but it has not always yielded real increases in purchasing power during inflation.[10] Hence, it is only a partial hedge against inflation.

Table 12-3 compares the real rate of growth in purchasing power, denoted X in Eq. (12-5), of different groups of common stocks with different market rates of return r during recent periods of inflation. The table suggests several conclusions:

1 The Dow Jones and Standard & Poor's common stock indices did not always keep pace with inflation. That is, the rate of inflation ($\Delta P/P$) surpassed corresponding increases in common stock returns r during several inflationary periods so that the real rates of return (X) on common stock decreased during inflation. In fact, in the 1946 to 1948 inflation, the common stock indices were far from being a partial hedge—they were no hedge at all; real rates of return on common stock were negative.

2 Industrial stocks tend to keep pace with inflation better than utility stocks.

3 Over 138 months of inflation, common stocks of all categories earned a rate of return about equal to the rate of inflation. Thus, the common stocks in the sample were a hedge against inflation but they did not increase in purchasing power, as some investment advisors suggest.

The evidence indicates that common stocks are better investments than life insurance or savings accounts during inflationary periods. But some bonds outperform the real returns of stocks. Stockbrokers selling both stocks and bonds are reluctant to point this out even if they realize it, however, because their sales commission rate on bonds is much lower than on stocks.

Market Risk

At summer's end in 1929, a share of U.S. Steel was selling for over $260. Two and a half years later, this same share was selling for $22. By March of 1937, this share had climbed back to $126, only to fall to $38 a year later.

On Friday, November 22, 1963, when news of President Kennedy's assassination reached the NYSE, hysterical selling caused officials to close the exchange early. In the 27 minutes between the arrival of news of the assassination and the closing, many stock prices had dropped as much as $5 or $10 per share. The Dow Jones Industrial Average (DJIA) collapsed 24.5

---

[10] Bruno A. Oudet, "The Variation on the Return of Stocks in Periods of Inflation," *Journal of Financial and Quantitative Analysis*, March 1973, pp. 247–258; N. Biger, "The Assessment of Inflation and Portfolio Selection," and A. H. Chen and J. A. Boness, "Effects of Uncertain Inflation on the Investment and Financing Decisions of a Firm," *Journal of Finance*, May 1975, pp. 451–484.

TABLE 12-3 COMMON STOCKS AS INFLATION HEDGES†

Time period/index	r, %	X, %
From 12/31/65 to 12/31/68 = 36 months of inflation		
DJIA 30 stocks	2.4	− 1.2
SP 425 industrial stocks	7.7	3.9
SP 55 utilities	1.2	− 2.4
SP 500	7.1	3.3
$\Delta P/P$ at annual rate for CPI	3.7	
From 3/31/58 to 12/31/65 = 93 months of fairly stable prices		
$\Delta P/P$ at annual rate for CPI	1.3	
From 3/31/56 to 3/31/58 = 24 months of inflation		
DJIA 30 stocks	− 2.1	− 5.6
SP 425 industrial stocks	− 6.2	− 9.5
SP 55 utilities	7.2	3.4
SP 500	− 3.1	− 6.5
$\Delta P/P$ at annual rate for CPI	3.7	
From 12/31/51 to 3/31/56 = 51 months of fairly stable prices		
$\Delta P/P$	.3	
From 3/31/50 to 12/31/51 = 21 months of inflation		
DJIA 30 stocks	24.9	16.9
SP 425 industrial stocks	31.5	23.1
SP 55 utilities	8.5	1.5
SP 500	28.4	20.2
$\Delta P/P$ at annual rate for CPI	6.9	
From 9/30/48 to 3/31/50 = 18 months of deflation		
$\Delta P/P$ at annual rate for CPI	− 2.6	
From 3/31/46 to 9/30/48 = 30 months of inflation		
DJIA 30 stocks	.2	−11.0
SP 425 industrial stocks	− .7	−11.7
SP 55 utilities	− 5.8	−16.3
SP 500	− 1.5	−12.5
$\Delta P/P$ at annual rate for CPI	12.5	
Weighted average of 138 months of inflation (weighted by length of inflation)		
DJIA 30 stocks	6.6	− .6
SP 425 industrial stocks	9.0	1.7
SP 55 utilities	2.9	− 4.0
SP 500	8.6	1.3

† Symbols all represent annual rates:

$$X = \frac{1+r}{1+\Delta P/P} - 1 = \begin{cases} \text{real rate of return; this represents the growth in actual pur-} \\ \text{chasing power after adjustment for price level changes} \end{cases}$$

$\Delta P/P$ = annual rate of change in Consumer Price Index (CPI)

r = nominal market rate of return (unadjusted for price level changes)

Source: F. K. Reilly, G. L. Johnson, and R. E. Smith, "Inflation, Inflation Hedges and Common Stocks," *Financial Analysts Journal,* January–February 1970, pp. 104–110.

points in the 27 frenzied minutes. However, when the exchange reopened the following Monday morning, the shares had resumed the prices they had had before the tragic news. On the first trading day following the funeral, the DJIA leaped 32 points.

On May 28, 1962, the DJIA opened at 606.88 and rose to a high that day of 609.77. Then the market collapsed and the DJIA fell over 30 points in only a few hours, closing that day at 576.93.

On Monday, May 25, 1970, the DJIA sank 21 points. The market dropped more on Tuesday, the 26th, to close at 631. Then on Wednesday, the 27th, the market rallied and soared 32 points. The DJIA climbed to 700 by the end of the week to mark the end of a bear market which had seen the DJIA drop from near 1,000 down to 631 in the preceding 18 months.

These cases showing the chance of loss due to market fluctuations are examples of *market risk*. In these cases, security prices varied significantly to levels that were out of line with many estimates of the securities' intrinsic values at the time. Even in the depression of the early 1930s, when intrinsic values did fall, market hysteria caused security prices to overreact and fall below their true economic value, in some peoples' opinion. Regardless of whether market risk is always rational or not, its presence is obvious.

Market risk primarily affects common stocks. Bonds and other senior securities are less subject to such fluctuations because their true value may be estimated more accurately than stock values can.

Financial Leverage Risk

A company's financial leverage increases with its use of debt financing relative to equity financing. Financial leverage is usually measured with the debt/equity ratio or the debt/total assets ratio. Holding all other things constant, a shareholder's variability of return increases with the corporation's use of leverage: this is financial leverage risk.[11]

Systematic and unsystematic risk. As a corporation uses more financial leverage, its fixed interest expense rises. This increase raises its break-even point, as shown in Fig. 12-5. The higher break-even point that results from the use of financial leverage increases both systematic and unsystematic risk. *Systematic*, or cyclical, risk is increased because, as a company's sales rise and fall over the business cycle, its profit fluctuations are magnified by the use of leverage.[12] These cyclical gyrations in profits are reflected in systematic stock price swings. The effects of financial leverage on *unsystematic*

---

[11] R. S. Hamada, "The Effect of a Firm's Capital Structure on the Systematic Risk of Common Stocks," *Journal of Finance,* May 1972, pp. 435–452; W. H. Beaver, P. Kettler, and M. Scholes, "The Association Between Market-Determined and Accounting-Determined Risk Measures," *The Accounting Review,* October 1970; and D. E. Logue and L. J. Merville, "Financial Policy and Market Expectations," *Financial Management,* Summer 1972, pp. 37–44.

[12] T. A. Anderson, "Trends in Profit Sensitivity," *Journal of Finance,* December 1963, pp. 637–646.

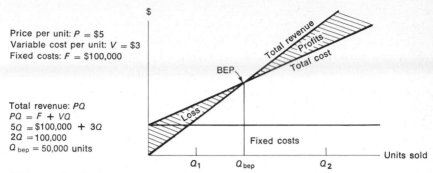

Price per unit: $P = \$5$
Variable cost per unit: $V = \$3$
Fixed costs: $F = \$100,000$

Total revenue: PQ
$PQ = F + VQ$
$5Q = \$100,000 + 3Q$
$2Q = 100,000$
$Q_{bep} = 50,000$ units

FIG. 12-5 Break-even chart.

risk, however, are unrelated to the business cycle. For example, if a firm suffered a traumatic blow (say, the loss of a key customer or the destruction of an inadequately insured plant) that depressed its sales during a period of economic prosperity, it would be more likely to fall below its break-even point if it used financial leverage. As a result, the corporation's stock could fall unsystematically during a bullish period in the stock market. This would be unsystematic financial leverage risk. The following break-even analysis clarifies this situation.

Break-even analysis. If a firm is operating at Q_2 units of output, as in Fig. 12-5, it is earning a profit and has a margin of safety against adverse developments. In this case, the firm has low risk. But a firm operating at or near its break-even point runs considerable chance of default or bankruptcy. For example, a firm selling Q_1 units is not generating enough revenue to cover its costs. A situation like this quickly depletes the firm's liquid assets, and it begins to default on its accounts payable. If this period of default lasts for some time or is irreversible, the firm will be in the bankruptcy courts before long. When this happens, the price of the firm's securities falls. Common stock prices usually suffer more than the prices of senior securities in troubled times because they have the last claim on any assets of the bankrupt firm.

Operating Leverage Risk

Operating leverage is measured by taking the ratio of a company's fixed costs divided by its variable costs. Department stores and steel manufacturers, for example, must have large investments in fixed assets in order to operate; thus, they have higher operating leverage than supermarkets or clothing manufacturers, which typically operate with less fixed assets.

Higher operating leverage results in increased variability of returns for the shareholders. This condition, called operating leverage risk,[13] arises

[13] B. Lev, "On the Association Between Operating Leverage and Risk," *Journal of Financial and Quantitative Analysis,* June 1974.

because the high fixed costs of maintaining fixed assets continue un-diminished whether or not the firm's level of output decreases. Thus, operating leverage increases a firm's break-even point just as the fixed interest expense from using financial leverage does. The manner in which higher fixed costs push up the break-even point and increase profit fluctuations was explained graphically in Fig. 12-5. Actual and potential stockholders observe these profit fluctuations, and some of them speculate on the prospects that the firm is bankrupted by a profit fluctuation below its break-even point. They speculate by buying and selling the stock as profits rise and fall in the hope of earning gains or avoiding losses. As a result, part of the variability of returns from stocks is the result of the profit fluctuations induced by operating leverage.

Operating leverage causes both systematic and unsystematic variability of return. The alternating boom-and-bust phases of the business cycle cause sales and profits to rise and fall with business activity. This cyclical variability in profits causes *systematic* risk. But *unsystematic* risk can also be increased by corporations that raise their operating leverage and then suffer major sales declines even in the midst of a period of economic prosperity. A company's high fixed costs become losses as sales decrease, even though the sales may be moving countercyclically. Unsystematic variability of returns for stockholders is thus induced by the stock purchases and sales which result from these changes in the firm's prospects.

Management Risk

Regardless of a firm's products or its financial position, its management can cause unique and unsystematic variations in the returns to investors. For example, General Motors (GM) is considered by many to be a very well managed company that produces good products and is financially sound. However, GM management was rather unsuccessful in dealing with the consumer movement headed by Ralph Nader. Most analysts would agree that GM lost sales, profits, goodwill, and stock price (not to mention the Corvair and a large out-of-court settlement in Nader's favor) to what can be attributed to management errors.[14] It seems that management is a difficult thing to evaluate.

Obvious management errors and frauds perpetrated by members of management could be cited to indicate the effect management can have on the variability of investors' returns. Westec stock, for example, was suspended from trading on the American Stock Exchange in 1966 (see Appendix A to Chap. 4). Newspapers investigating this case published stories of fraud and deception which can be described only as amazing. Some high-ranking executives went to prison. Investors who owned the stock at the time this fraud became apparent suffered large capital losses.

---

[14] *The New York Times,* Aug. 14, 1970; *The Wall Street Journal,* Aug. 14, 1970, p. 4.

In a different vein, some firms have been nearly bankrupted by honest oversights by management. Management errors which are fairly common include lack of foresight in dealing with the energy crisis, labor strikes for which adequate preparation was not made, loss of plant and equipment which were not properly guarded or insured, loss of sales, and loss of important suppliers for which no substitutes had been developed.

Each firm's management team must be evaluated individually to determine its fitness. This is a difficult and deceptive assignment which only professional fundamental analysts and management consultants carry on with any degree of regularity. However, this appraisal is particularly important to common stockholders whose investment returns are most sensitive to management's actions.

Industry Risk

Sometimes all the firms in one or a few industries experience variability of return due to some common force which does not affect the majority of firms outside that industry in any significant manner. This is called *industry risk.* For example, when a large labor union of one industrial category (say, the United Mine Workers or United Auto Workers) goes on strike, the firms in that industry and their customers and suppliers are affected. If the strike was not anticipated or if it lasts long, the effects can significantly damage the earnings and market values of the firms which are struck and significantly benefit their nonunion competitors.

Industry risk can stem from many sources. One cause may be disruption of raw material supplies. For example, shortages of rubber during World War II caused the tire companies much consternation until they hurriedly developed synthetic rubber. Antipollution laws pose a real threat to paper pulp manufacturers, oil refineries, steel mills, and other industries that generate large quantities of offensive waste materials. Entire industries can wither on the vine if their product becomes obsolete (for example, the buggy whip industry). Foreign competition, such as is offered by the Japanese steel and electronic industries, can quickly disrupt entire domestic industries if they are not competitive and if they are unsuccessful in persuading Congress to erect international trade barriers to protect them. Such industry effects may be small and temporary or large and permanent.

Interaction of Different Forces

Interest rate, purchasing power, market, financial, operating, management, and industry risks all interact in ways which can sometimes be perplexing and impossible to separate. That is, these various sources of variation in security prices can occur simultaneously, and they may exert different forces that tend to offset each other or similar forces that combine to cause large movements in security prices. The bear market of 1969 and 1970 is an interesting case of the latter.

The DJIA fell from a high of 994 in December 1968 to a low of 627 in May 1970. This *large systematic downfall* in security prices was the sum of negative influences from declining purchasing power, higher interest rates, and some market overreaction to these factors. The high rates of inflation (that is, declining purchasing power of the dollar) which existed from 1965 to 1970 caused interest rates to rise as lenders tried to compensate for their loss in purchasing power by raising their rates and as the Federal Reserve Board tightened monetary variables in an effort to stop the inflation. The higher interest rates caused the current value of income from securities to decline, and so security prices started to drop. As fear of falling security prices spread, investors hurriedly liquidated their securities in order to avoid further losses. The selling accelerated the price decline and drove the prices of many securities to values which were below their true intrinsic economic values in many people's opinions.

The bear market of 1969 and 1970, like most other bear markets, was caused by a recession in the national economy which caused many companies to lose sales and suffer losses. As a result, many firms' stock prices also experienced downward pressure from unsystematic factors. Some firms' reduced profits caused them to become insolvent, and the rate of bankruptcies increased in these two years. Firms with poor management suffered stock price declines due to management errors made during these unusually difficult times. And labor unions, demanding higher wages to keep up with inflated prices, struck several industries, causing unsystematic variability of return to firms in those industries. The simultaneous interaction of all these sources of unsystematic and systematic variability caused the bear market of 1969 and 1970.

12-4 CHARACTERISTIC LINE

At the beginning of this chapter it was argued that the standard deviation (or variance) of rates of return was a satisfactory quantitative surrogate for total risk. Then the discussion shifted to a nonquantitative explanation of systematic and unsystematic risks and their sources. It is possible to measure the systematic and unsystematic risks of an asset using quantitative risk surrogates. A statistical tool which we shall refer to as the *characteristic line* is employed to measure systematic and unsystematic risk.

Figure 12-6 shows graphs of the characteristic lines[15] for two firms; they are ordinary least-squares regression lines[16] of the form shown in Eq. (12-6).

$$r_{it} = a_i + b_i\, r_{mt} + e_t \tag{12-6}$$

---

[15] The term *characteristic line* is from Jack L. Treynor, "How to Rate Management of Investment Funds," *Harvard Business Review*, January–February 1965, pp. 63–75.

[16] Mathematical Appendix H, in Part 7, provides a brief review of the definitions of terms such as regression line, correlation coefficient, and standard error.

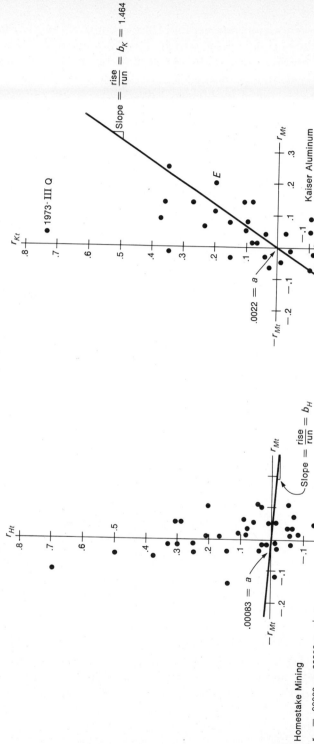

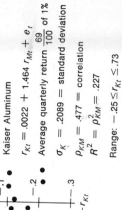

FIG. 12-6 Characteristic lines for Homestake Mining and Kaiser Aluminum.

where a_i and b_i are the regression intercept and slope statistics, and e_t is the random error around the regression line which occurs in period t. A *characteristic line* graphically represents the nature of systematic and unsystematic risks; it shows the relationships of some asset with the market. Each characteristic line is thus a *market model* for one security.

Market Returns: The Characteristic Line's Independent Variable

The action of the stock market is measured along the horizontal axis of Fig. 12-6 in terms of rates of change or rates of return from the market at different time periods, denoted r_{mt}. Equation (12-7) shows how rates of change in the market are calculated, using Standard & Poor's (SP) market index.[17]

$$r_{mt} = \frac{SP_{t+1} - SP_t}{SP_t} \qquad (12\text{-}7)$$

where SP_{t+1} is the dollar amount of the SP index at the beginning of period $t + 1$ and SP_t is the value of the index at the beginning of period t. These period-by-period rates of change in the market index are downward-biased estimates of average returns available in the market because dividends are excluded. There is no reason that dividends should not be included in r_{mt} or that other market indices should not be used in determining characteristic lines. However, once a market index is adopted, it should be used consistently in determination of all characteristic lines if all are to be comparable.

Asset Returns: The Characteristic Line's Dependent Variable

Rates of return for which the characteristic line is being prepared are calculated using Eq. (2-2) for stocks.

$$r_{it} = \frac{p_{t+1} - p_t + d_t}{p_t} \qquad (2\text{-}2)$$

where d_t = cash dividend in period t from stock i
$\qquad p_t$ = market price at beginning of period for ith stock
$\qquad p_{t+1}$ = end-of-period price for period t, or equivalently, the beginning price for period $t + 1$

Returns on the ith asset are the dependent variable on the vertical axis of Fig. 12-6. If the ith asset has any systematic risk, part of its variation in rates of return is dependent upon the independent variable — returns on the market. Monthly, quarterly, semiannual, or annual returns may be used to prepare a characteristic line.

---

[17] The Appendix to Chap. 12 provides some empirical market returns which were calculated with Standard & Poor's 500. Source: *Standard & Poor's Trade and Securities Statistics.*

Estimating a Characteristic Line

The characteristic line is a line of best fit. It may be estimated intuitively or fit to historical data by hand, or ordinary least-squares regression may be used. If historical data are to be used, the first step in estimating the characteristic line for some asset is to calculate the periodic returns on the asset as defined in Eq. (2-2) and the returns on the market as defined in Eq. (12-7). The periods used for calculating returns on the asset and the market should correspond exactly.

Table 12-4 shows the quarterly data used to fit the characteristic line for Homestake Mining. These data can be obtained from the sources of financial information discussed in Chap. 6. After the rates of return on the ith asset and some market index have been gathered, they can be arranged as shown in Table 12-5.

The rates of return from the market and the asset may be plotted as shown in Fig. 12-6. Point E in this figure, for example, is a point where the market return was 20 percent and Kaiser's return was 20 percent during the same time period. Each dot represents the rate of return on the asset and the market during a given time period. A line of best fit can be "eyeballed" through these points, or a regression line can be calculated. The dependent variable r_i is regressed onto the independent variable r_m. It is best to fit the regression line because additional statistics, such as the correlation coefficient, can be obtained once the regression line is determined.

Interpreting the Characteristic Line

Equation (12-8) represents the characteristic line for the ith asset.

$$r_i = a_i + b_i r_m \tag{12-8}$$

The term a_i is called the *alpha coefficient* for security i; it is the intercept point where the characteristic line intercepts the vertical axis. Alpha is an estimate of the ith asset's rate of return when the market is stationary, $r_{mt} = 0$. The term b_i is called the *beta coefficient*; it measures the slope of the characteristic line. The beta coefficient is defined in Eqs. (12-9) and (12-9a).

$$b_i = \frac{\text{cov}(r_i, r_m)}{\sigma_m^2} \tag{12-9}$$

$$= \frac{\text{units of rise}}{\text{units of run}} \tag{12-9a}$$

$$= \text{slope of characteristic regression line}$$

where $\text{cov}(r_i, r_m)$ denotes the covariance[18] of returns of the ith asset with the market and σ_m^2 represents the variance of returns for the market index.

---

[18] Mathematical Appendix C, in Part 7, defines the covariance.

TABLE 12-4 HOMESTAKE MINING DATA†

Year quarter	Raw data Beg. qtr. mkt. pr.	Cash div.	Changes in unit of acct.	Adjusted data Beg. mkt. price	Qtrly. Cash div.	Qtrly. return	Residual error
1964: 1	45.00	.40		22.059	.196	−0.0133	−.0489
2	44.00	.40		21.569	.196	−0.0477	−.0946
3	41.50	.40		20.343	.196	0.1151	.053
4	48.875	.40		22.488	.196	0.1777	.0967
1965: 1	53.625	.40		26.287	.196	−0.082	−.1412
2	52.25	.40		25.613	.196	−0.0617	−.1642
3	48.625	.40		28.836	.196	0.0031	−.0197
4	48.325	.40		23.713	.196	−0.0589	−.1179
1966: 1	45.125	.40		22.120	.196	0.0283	−.0770
2	46.00	.40		22.549	.196	0.0332	−.0943
3	47.125	.40		23.100	.196	−0.0048	−.204
4	46.50	.20		22.794	.098	−0.0763	−.0907
1967: 1	42.75	.20	2% stk. div.	20.956	.098	−0.0480	−.0279
2	40.50	.20		20.250	.100	0.0852	.02
3	43.75	.20		21.875	.100	0.0789	.0517
4	47.00	.20		23.500	.100	0.3074	.2227
1968: 1	61.25	.20		30.625	.100	−0.0171	−.1349
2	60.00	.20		30.000	.100	0.2512	.2383
3	74.875	.20	2 for 1 split	37.438	.100	−0.0624	−.1126
4	35.00	.10		35.000	.100	0.2064	.1334
1969: 1	42.125	.10		42.125	.100	−0.0095	−.1147
2	41.625	.10		41.625	.100	−0.2829	−.3962
3	29.75	.10		29.750	.100	−0.2855	−.421
4	25.50	.10		25.500	.100	0.3392	.2343
1970: 1	16.75	.10		16.750	.100	0.2522	.1247
2	20.875	.10		20.875	.100	0.1425	−.0727
3	23.75	.10		23.750	.100	−0.0642	−.0404
4	22.125	.10		22.125	.100	0.0384	.0564
1971: 1	22.875	.10		22.875	.100	0.2174	.2295
2	27.75	.10		27.750	.100	0.1450	.0262
3	23.625	.10		23.625	.100	0.0306	−.0681
4	24.25	.10		24.250	.100	−0.3103	−.347
1972: 1	18.875	.10		18.875	.100	0.2923	.2561
2	23.00	.10		23.000	.100	0.2543	.1712
3	28.75	.10		28.750	.100	−0.0791	−.1321
4	26.375	.10		26.375	.100	0.0957	.0763
1973: 1	23.75	.10		23.750	.100	0.4989	.3648
2	35.50	.10		35.500	.100	0.3690	.2257
3	48.50	.25		48.500	.250	−0.1365	−.1775
4	41.625	.25		41.625	.250	0.6958‡	.5159

† Regression of $R = a + bM$: $a = 0.0826$, $b = −.0093$. Standard error: .1996. Standard deviation of returns: .1996. Variance of returns: 3.99. Cov. with market: −.363. Var. of market: .3896. Correlation with market: −.283. Arithmetic average return: .075 = 7.5 percent per quarter. Returns on the market from Table A12-1.

‡ The negative beta is largely the result of this 69.5 percent gain while the market was dropping in 1973, fourth quarter.

TABLE 12-5 RETURNS TO CALCULATE CHARACTERISTIC LINE

Time period, t	Independent variable, returns on market	Dependent variable, returns on asset i
$t = 1$	r_{m1}	r_{i1}
$= 2$	r_{m2}	r_{i2}
$= 3$	r_{m3}	r_{i3}
$= 4$	r_{m4}	r_{i4}
.	.	.
.	.	.
.	.	.
.	.	.
.	.	.
$t = n$	r_{mn}	r_{in}

Regression model: $r_{it} = a_i + b_i r_{mt} + e_{it}$ (12-6)

Characteristic line: $r_i = a + b r_m$ (12-8)

The beta coefficient is an *index* of systematic risk. Beta coefficients may be used for (ordinal) rankings of the systematic risk of different assets. However, the beta coefficient is not a (cardinal) measure which may be compared directly with total or unsystematic risk. If the beta is larger than 1, the asset is more volatile than the market and is called an *aggressive asset*. If the beta is less than 1, the asset is a *defensive asset*: it is less volatile than the market. Most assets' beta coefficients are in the range from .5 to 1.5. Figure 12-6 (right panel) shows that Kaiser Aluminum is an aggressive stock with a high degree of systematic risk. Kaiser's beta of 1.46 indicates that its return tends to increase 46 percent *more* than the return on the market average when the market is rising. When the market falls, Kaiser's return tends to fall 146 percent of the decrease in the market. The characteristic line for Kaiser has a lower-than-average correlation coefficient of $\rho = .47$, indicating that the returns on this security do not follow its characteristic line as closely as average. This tendency may be determined by visually noting that the points do not fit the characteristic line very closely.

Partitioning Risk

Statistically, total risk is measured by the variance of returns. This measure of total risk may be partitioned into the systematic and unsystematic components as follows:

$$
\begin{aligned}
\text{var}(r_i) &= \text{total risk of } i\text{th asset} \\
&= \text{var}(a_i + b_i r_m + e) &&\text{substituting } (a_i + b_i r_m + e) \text{ for } r_i \\
&= \text{var}(b_i r_m) + \text{var}(e) &&\text{since var}(a_i) = 0 \\
&= b_i^2 \text{var}(r_m) + \text{var}(e) &&\text{since var}(b_i r_m) = b_i^2 \text{var}(r_m) \quad (12\text{-}10) \\
&= \text{systematic} + \text{unsystematic risk}
\end{aligned}
$$

The unsystematic risk measure, var(e), is called the *residual variance* (or *standard error squared*) in regression language.

The percentage of systematic risk is measured by the coefficient of determination (ρ^2) for the characteristic line. The percentage of unsystematic risk equals ($1 - \rho^2$). More specifically,

$$\frac{\text{Unsystematic risk}}{\text{Total risk}} = \frac{\text{var}(e)}{\text{var}(r_i)} = 1 - \rho^2 \tag{12-11}$$

$$\frac{\text{Systematic risk}}{\text{Total risk}} = \frac{b_i^2 \, \text{var}(r_m)}{\text{var}(r_i)} = \rho^2 \tag{12-11a}$$

Studies of the characteristic lines of hundreds of stocks listed on the NYSE indicate that the average correlation coefficient is $\rho = .5$, approximately.[19] This means that about $\rho^2 = 25$ percent of the total variability of return in most NYSE securities is explained by movements in the whole market; that is, systematic risk averages about one-fourth of total risk for most NYSE stocks.

Average systematic risk $25\% = \rho^2$
Average unsystematic risk $75\% = 1 - \rho^2$
<hr>
Total risk $100\% = 1.0$

The systematic changes are common to all stocks and are nearly impossible to diversify away.

Homestake Mining is a much less risky stock than Kaiser Aluminum in terms of total risk and systematic risk, as indicated by the table below.

	Homestake	Kaiser
Total risk variance of returns = σ^2	.0420	.0436
Unsystematic risk = residual variance	.0396	.0348
Systematic risk measure = $b_i^2[\text{var}(r_m)] = \rho^2[\text{var}(r_i)]$	.0023	.0088
Beta coefficient = index of systematic risk	−.0093	1.464
Percentage of systematic risk = ρ^2	.055 = 5.5%	.227 = 22.7%

Figure 12-6 shows that Homestake has less *total* risk than Kaiser because the points do not vary vertically as much for Homestake.[20] And since the

[19] Mathematical Appendix H discusses correlation, regression, and the characteristic line and defines the residual variance, coefficient of determination, and other regression terms. See also, B. F. King, "Market and Industry Factors in Stock Price Behavior," *Journal of Business*, January 1966, p. 151. King says, in effect, that the average market effect is 50 percent of total risk. This implies $\rho = .7$. Marshall Blume, however, found an average ρ of about .5 in "On the Assessment of Risk," op. cit., p. 4.

[20] Statements about the relative degree of total risk are made in the context of a long-run horizon—that is, over at least one complete business cycle. Obviously, a short-run forecast which says Homestake will go bankrupt next quarter makes it more risky than Kaiser, although the latter has had more historical variability of return.

slope of Homestake's characteristic line is (negative) less than the slope for Kaiser, Homestake also has less *systematic* risk.

Homestake has demonstrated a *very* rare quality, a negative beta. This means that returns on Homestake have a tendency to rise when the rest of the market is falling and vice versa, a very useful quality for diversification purposes. However, the correlation coefficient for Homestake's characteristic line is not significantly different from zero. This can be seen visually by noting the poor fit of the points to Homestake's characteristic line, meaning that the predictive power of Homestake's characteristic line is unusually low—almost nil. However, fundamental analysis of Homestake indicates that there is little reason to expect this stock to follow the market. Homestake is the largest, oldest goldmining firm in the United States. It also mines zinc, lead, and uranium. Because of the nature of its activities, it appears to be a good security with which to diversify away cyclical volatility exhibited by securities of firms manufacturing cyclical industrial products.

TABLE 12-6 BETA COEFFICIENTS

Firm	Time period, month/year	Beta	ρ^2†
Union Oil of California	1/27–6/35	.55	.58
	7/35–12/43	.57	.49
	1/44–6/51	.97	.45
	7/51–12/60	.98	.32
IBM	1/27–6/35	.49	.49
	7/35–12/43	.25	.26
	1/44–6/51	.56	.29
	7/51–12/60	.86	.23
May Department Stores	1/27–6/35	.83	.74
	7/35–12/43	.64	.49
	1/44–6/51	.72	.35
	7/51–12/60	.82	.32
Atlantic Coast Line Railroad	1/27–6/35	1.2	.73
	7/35–12/43	1.26	.7
	1/44–6/51	1.7	.43
	7/51–12/60	1.63	.57

† ρ^2 = coefficient of determination for characteristic regression line
= correlation coefficient squared
= % of variation explained

Source: Marshall E. Blume, "The Assessment of Portfolio Performance: An Application of Portfolio Theory," unpublished doctoral dissertation, University of Chicago, March 1968.

Betas Stationary over Time

The characteristic line of a security contains much information about the risk of the security and can be quite useful for predicting how a given security will react to changes in the market. However, when the points do not fit the characteristic line, its predictive power diminishes accordingly. But even in cases where the points do not fit closely, the security's beta coefficient tends to remain stationary over time. The beta coefficient does vary from decade to decade in all firms. A certain firm's beta may change drastically if, for instance, it undertakes production of new products with a complete new management team. But year after year most firms' probability distributions of returns and betas are nearly the same (that is, they are stationary over time). Table 12-6 shows how the betas for a few firms have behaved with the passage of time. Considering that the data for these calculations span 33 years, the stability of the statistics over time is impressive.[21]

12-5 RISK AND RETURNS

Firms which undergo drastic changes in their product mix, financial structure, and management team will probably experience changes in average return, standard deviation, and systematic risk. But for the majority of firms, the probability distributions of returns are stationary enough that a rational investor should be willing to pay money to find out what they are. This does not imply perfect stability—just sufficient stability to make the information valuable for investment decisions.

Studies of the probability distributions of returns indicate that firms with high total and high systematic risk tend also to have high average rates of return. This is what we would intuitively expect. Investors demand high rates of return to induce them to invest in risky assets, reminding one of the widely quoted axiom that "there is no such thing as a free lunch." This "free lunch" principle asserts that you cannot expect to get something for nothing. Apparently this is also true of investment returns. Investors who want to earn high average rates of return must take high risks and endure the associated loss of sleep, the possibility of ulcers, and the chance of bankruptcy.

The Security Market Line (SML)

In Chap. 1 it was suggested that wealth-maximizing, risk-averting investors will seek investments which have the maximum expected return in their

---

[21] Explicit studies of beta stationarity include Marshall Blume, op. cit.; and W. F. Sharpe and G. Cooper, "Risk-Return Classes of New York Stock Exchange Common Stocks, 1931–67," *Financial Analysts Journal,* March–April 1972. These studies provide information about the movements in stocks' betas from period to period.

risk-class. These investors maximize expected utility which is a function of expected return $E(r)$ and total risk σ. Symbolically, their expected happiness (or utility) from investing is shown below.

$$E(U) = f[E(r), \sigma]$$

Such investors will seek to (1) maximize their expected return in any given risk-class, or conversely, (2) minimize their risk at any given rate of expected return. However, in selecting individual assets, investors will not be particularly concerned with the asset's total risk σ. The unsystematic portion of total risk can be easily diversified away by holding a portfolio of several different securities. However, systematic risk affects all stocks in the market and is therefore practically undiversifiable; clearly, it is much more difficult to eliminate than unsystematic risk.

In the search for assets which will minimize their risk exposure at a given level of expected return, investors will tend to focus on assets' undiversifiable systematic risk. They will bid up the prices of assets with low systematic risk (that is, low beta coefficients). On the other hand, assets with high beta coefficients will experience low demand and market prices that are low relative to the assets' income. That is, assets with high levels of systematic risk will tend to have high expected returns. This may be seen by noting in Eq. (12-12) that the expected return is higher after the purchase price for the asset falls. Obviously, the $E(r)$ ratio will be larger after the denominator decreases.

$$E(r) = \frac{E(p_{t+1}) - p_t + d_t}{p_t} \tag{12-12}$$

$$= \frac{\text{expected income}}{\text{market purchase price}} \tag{12-12a}$$

An asset with high systematic risk (that is, a high beta) will experience price declines until the expected return it offers is high enough to induce investors to assume this undiversifiable risk. This price level is the equilibrium price, and the expected return is the equilibrium rate of return for that risk-class.

Figure 12-7 shows the security market line (SML) which graphically depicts the results of the price adjustments (that is, the equilibrium prices and expected returns) from this risk-averse trading.

The SML is a linear relation in which the expected average rate of return of the ith asset is a linear function of that asset's systematic risk as represented by b_i. Symbolically, Eq. (12-13) represents the SML.

$$E(r_i) = R + cb_i \tag{12-13}$$

where b_i is the independent variable representing the systematic risk of the ith asset and determines the dependent variable, $E(r_i)$, the average ex-

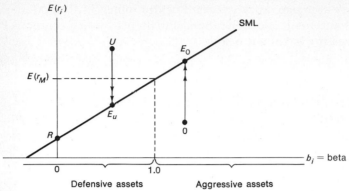

FIG. 12-7 The security market line (SML).

pected rate of return for asset i; R is the vertical axis intercept; and c is the slope of the SML.[22] R is the rate of interest appropriate when risk is zero. United States government bond yields would be a good estimate of R since these bonds come closer to having zero risk than other marketable securities.

Any vertical line drawn on Fig. 12-7 is a *risk-class* for systematic risk. The SML relates an expected return to each level of systematic risk. These expected returns can be interpreted as the appropriate discount rates k or cost of capital investors expect for that amount of systematic risk.

12-6 CAPITAL ASSET PRICING MODEL

Systematic or undiversifiable risk is the main factor risk-averse investors should consider in deciding whether a security yields enough rate of return to induce them to buy it. Other factors, such as the "glamour" of the stock and the company's financial ratios, are important only to the extent they affect the security's risk and return. The SML graphically represents the trade-off of systematic risk for return which investors expect and are entitled to receive. This implies that the SML has asset-pricing implications.

Asset's Price Movements

After an asset's average return and systematic risk have been estimated, they may be plotted in reference to the SML. In equilibrium every asset's

---

[22] The slope of the SML is

$$c = \frac{\text{rise}}{\text{run}}$$

$$= \frac{E(r_m) - R}{b_m} = E(r_m) - R \qquad \text{since } b_m = 1.0$$

$E(r)$ and beta systematic risk coefficient should plot exactly on the SML. To see why this is true, consider Fig. 12-7, which shows two assets denoted O and U. Asset U is underpriced because its average rate of return is too high for the level of systematic risk it bears. Asset O is overpriced because its rate of return is too low to induce investors to accept its undiversifiable risk. These two assets should move to the SML as shown by the arrows to their equilibrium positions at the points marked E.

To see why assets O and U are incorrectly priced, reconsider Eq. (12-12b), which defines the expected rate of return for a common stock.

$$E(r) = \frac{\text{expected capital gains or loss} + \text{expected cash dividends}}{\text{purchase price}}$$

$$(12\text{-}12b)$$

To reach their equilibrium positions on the SML, assets O and U must go through a temporary price readjustment. Assuming the assets' systematic risk remains unchanged, the return of U must fall to E_U and the return of O must rise to E_O. To accomplish this move to an equilibrium rate of return, the denominator of Eq. (12-12b) must rise for asset U and fall for asset O. Assets O and U or any marketable capital asset (such as a portfolio, stock, bond, or real estate) will be in disequilibrium unless its risk and return lie on the SML. Supply and demand will set to work as outlined above to correct any disequilibrium from the SML.

Market Imperfections

The operation of the rational forces of supply and demand can be expected to move assets lying off the SML toward the SML, but, because of market imperfections, all assets' risk-return characteristics never lie exactly on the SML. Some market imperfections which preclude attainment of a complete equilibrium are:

1 *Transaction costs.* The stockbroker's commissions and transfer taxes associated with each security transaction drain away investors' incentive to correct minor deviations from the SML.

2 *Differential tax rates on capital gains.* Since capital gains are taxed differently from dividends and interest, the after-tax rate of return (atr) defined in Eq. (12-14) differs with the investor's tax bracket. Thus, each investor envisions a slightly different SML in terms of after-tax returns.

$$\text{atr}_t = \frac{D_t(1 - T_O) + (P_{t+1} - P_t)(1 - T_g)}{P_t} \tag{12-14}$$

where T_O is the ordinary income tax rate and T_g is the capital gains rate.

3 *Heterogeneous expectations.* Different investors assess the systematic risk of any given asset differently and therefore perceive different equilibrium rates of return for any given asset.

4 *Imperfect information.* Some investors are irrational; some are uninformed; some receive financial news later than others, etc.

Because of market imperfections, all assets are not expected to lie exactly on the SML. Therefore, in practice, the SML is a band instead of a thin line. The width of this band varies directly with the imperfections in the market. As a result, the SML cannot be used to pinpoint an asset's equilibrium price. Instead, it can suggest only a range of prices for an asset.

12-7 EMPIRICAL RISK-RETURN ESTIMATES

The preceding pages of this chapter have explained how to measure total, systematic, and unsystematic risk and expected returns. Economic logic, suggesting that investors should demand higher returns to induce them to buy investments with high systematic risk, was explained, too. The next logical question is: If stocks' betas and average returns are actually measured over a period of time, will the high beta stocks really have higher rates of return? Or, put more crassly: Is this risk-return theory really any good? Empirical tests of the theory were published by William F. Sharpe and Guy Cooper; their work is described in the following paragraphs. Similar studies in which other researchers reached similar conclusions have also been published.[23]

The Sample and the Statistics

In the Sharpe-Cooper study, monthly stock prices for hundreds of NYSE stocks from 1926 to 1967 provided the raw data. Monthly rates of return were first calculated using Eq. (2-2) for every stock and every month. Second, betas were calculated with Eq. (12-9), using 5 years (60 monthly observations) of rates of return. Third, an annual rate of return was calculated for each stock. Fourth, the stocks were all grouped into risk deciles based on their beta coefficients. The risk-classes were based on the 5 years preceding the year in which the annual return was calculated to simulate picking stocks for future investment based on 5 years of past data—a procedure which assumes betas are stable over time.

The procedure was replicated for hundreds of stocks every year from 1931 to 1967. Betas were calculated from 5 years of data, risk deciles formed from the betas, annual returns measured during the sixth year, and then the procedure was repeated for the next year. When the procedure had been repeated once for each $(5 + 1 =)$ 6-year period from 1931 to 1967, the 10 risk deciles from each of the 37 years were averaged to obtain average risk

---

[23] F. Black, M. C. Jensen, and M. Scholes, "The Capital Asset Pricing Model: Some Empirical Tests," in M. C. Jensen (ed.), *Studies in the Theory of Capital Markets* (New York: Praeger, 1972).

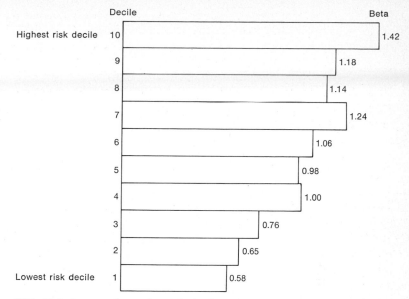

FIG. 12-8 Average betas for risk deciles, 1931–1967. (Redrawn from W. F. Sharpe and G. Cooper, "Risk-Return Classes of N.Y.S.E. Common Stocks, 1931–67," *Financial Analysts Journal*, March–April 1972.)

deciles and average annual returns. Figure 12-8 shows the beta coefficients averaged over all stocks in all years for the 10 risk-classes.

The annual returns averaged over all stocks and all years in each risk decile are shown in Fig. 12-9.

A simple linear regression of the form shown in Eq. (12-15) was fitted through the 10 average betas, denoted $\bar{b}_i$, from Fig. 12-8, and their associated average annual returns, denoted $\bar{r}_i$, from Fig. 12-9, for $i = 1$, 2, . . . , 10 deciles.

$$\bar{r}_i = a + b\,(\bar{b}_i) \tag{12-15}$$

Figure 12-10 shows a graph of the risk-return relationship delineated by the study.

The Sharpe-Cooper study is a scientific investigation which was painstakingly constructed so as to avoid introducing bias. Some sampling error exists in the study as it does in every statistical study, but the statistics do support the theory. In the long run, buying stocks with high (or medium or low) degrees of systematic risk was shown to yield future portfolios with high (or medium or low) average rates of return. On a single-stock basis, this may not occur because the single stock selected may go bankrupt, experience a change in its systematic risk, or undergo some other change which was not representative of most stocks' behavior. But, by

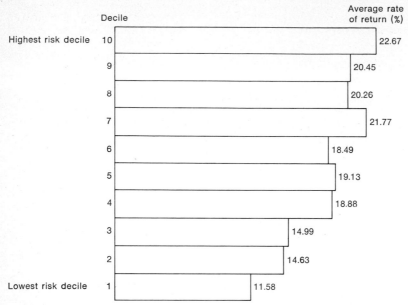

FIG. 12-9 Average annual rates of return by risk deciles, 1931–1967. (Redrawn from W. F. Sharpe and G. Cooper, "Risk-Return Classes of N.Y.S.E. Common Stocks, 1931–67," *Financial Analysts Journal,* March–April 1972.)

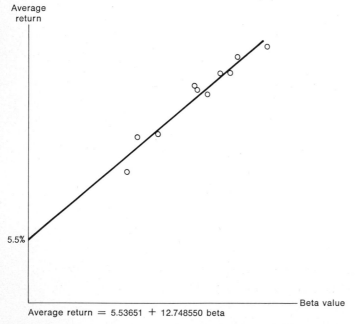

Average return = 5.53651 + 12.748550 beta

FIG. 12-10 Regression line through 10 average betas and 10 average returns. (Redrawn from W. F. Sharpe and G. Cooper, "Risk-Return Classes of N.Y.S.E. Common Stocks, 1931–67," *Financial Analysts Journal,* March–April 1972.)

using hundreds of stocks and decades of data, such sampling problems were averaged out to zero and the market's equilibrium tendency emerges.

12-8 CONCLUSIONS ABOUT RISK

The total risk of any asset can be approximated by measuring its variability of returns. Total risk can be partitioned into two main parts—systematic and unsystematic risk. Both can be estimated by using the characteristic regression line. The characteristic regression line of an asset explains the asset's systematic variability of return in terms of factors related to a market index. The sources of systematic risk include changes in the purchasing power of money, interest rate fluctuations, aberrations in the behavior of security market prices, and/or other cyclical factors.

The portion of total risk which is not explained by an asset's characteristic regression line is called *unsystematic risk.* Unsystematic variability of returns are unique to each asset and are caused by management errors, financial problems in the firm, and/or factors, such as a labor strike, which disturb the firm's industry.

Since unsystematic variations are unique to each firm, they can be easily diversified away to zero by spreading the funds to be invested across the securities of several unrelated firms. Systematic risk, on the other hand, is more difficult to diversify because it is common to all assets in the market to some extent. Within a given market (for example, the stock market), assets with high degrees of systematic risk must be priced to yield high rates of return in order to induce investors to accept high degrees of risk which are essentially undiversifiable within that market. The SML graphically depicts this positive relation between assets' systematic risks and their expected average rates of return: empirical tests support the validity of the theory.

QUESTIONS

1 Write a short essay defining total risk verbally and explain how this definition is consistent with using the variance of returns as a risk surrogate.

2 Make a probability distribution of your starting salary per month when you graduate. What quantitative risk surrogate would you use to measure the risk of these dollar quantities? What problems are presented by simply using the standard deviation of your dollar salary as a quantitative risk surrogate?

3 Write one-sentence definitions of each of the following: (*a*) purchasing power risk, (*b*) interest rate, (*c*) market risk, (*d*) financial leverage risk, (*e*) operating leverage risk, (*f*) management risk, (*g*) industrial risk, (*h*) systematic risk, (*i*) unsystematic risk, (*j*) total risk.

4 Gather 10 years of data for Kaiser Aluminum common stock and for some market index; calculate rates of return for the asset and the market index; estimate the characteristic line for the asset. Is it a defensive or an aggressive asset? Does the characteristic line for the asset have much predictive power? Is the asset good for diversification purposes?

5 How do you expect the total risk of a mutual fund to be divided between systematic and unsystematic risk?

6 Assume that a firm added a new product to its line that decreased the overall riskiness of the firm. For example, a highly cyclical rubber company began producing red ink. How would this affect the value of a share of the firm's stock? Use a diagram of the SML to show the asset-pricing implications of this change in the firm.

7 Could you as a security analyst expect to find any worthwhile information by studying the residual errors in Eq. (12-6)?

SELECTED REFERENCES

Markowitz, H., *Portfolio Selection* (New York: Wiley, 1959).
> This classic book explains portfolio analysis. Chapters 2 through 4 delve into probability distributions, standard deviations, expected returns, and the characteristic line. Chapter 9 discusses the semivariance. Algebra and finite probability are used in these chapters.

Sauvain, H., *Investment Management*, 3d ed. (Englewood Cliffs, N.J.: Prentice-Hall, 1967).
> Chapters 5 through 7 discuss financial, purchasing power, and interest rate risk. No mathematics used.

Sharpe, W. F., "Capital Asset Prices: A Theory of Market Equilibrium under Conditions of Risk," *The Journal of Finance,* September 1964, pp. 425–552. Reprinted in S. Archer and C. D'Ambrosio, *The Theory of Business Finance* (New York: Macmillan, 1967), reading 42; also in J. F. Weston and D. Woods, *Theory of Business Finance* (Belmont, Calif.: Wadsworth, 1967), reading 25.
> This classic article was the first to suggest the asset-pricing implications of systematic risk. Sharpe develops risk-return relationship for portfolios (that is, the capital market line, or the CML) and individual assets (that is, the SML). Calculus is used only in the footnotes. A knowledge of elementary statistics is assumed.

TABLE A12-1 STANDARD & POOR'S 500 STOCKS COMPOSITE AVERAGE

Year: quarter	SP at beginning-of-quarter prices only	Quarterly rate of change in prices, %†	Annualized quarterly dividend, $	Dividend yield, %‡
1973: 4	97.55	−10.44	3.38	3.46
3	108.93	4.47	3.27	3.02
2	104.26	−6.51	3.22	3.09
1	111.52	2.93	3.17	2.84
1972: 4	118.05	6.78	3.15	2.67
3	110.55	3.18	3.08	2.79
2	107.14	−.05	3.07	2.87
1	107.20	10.18	3.07	2.86
1971: 4	97.29	−1.72	3.07	3.01
3	99.00	−3.88	3.09	3.14
2	103.00	10.17	3.10	3.11
1	93.49	10.80	3.11	3.10
1970: 4	84.37	11.42	3.14	3.41
3	75.72	−11.90	3.19	3.79
2	85.95	− 4.82	3.18	4.37
1	90.31	− 2.38	3.17	3.54
1969: 4	92.52	− 5.67	3.16	3.41
3	98.08	− 3.29	3.15	3.21
2	101.42	− 2.42	3.13	3.08
1	103.93	1.04	3.10	2.98
1968: 4	102.86	3.48	3.07	2.98
3	99.40	7.48	3.03	3.04
2	92.48	− 3.78	2.99	3.23
1	96.11	− .22	2.95	3.06
1967: 4	96.32	5.95	2.92	3.03
3	90.91	1.87	2.92	3.33
2	89.24	10.02	2.90	3.24
1	80.38	7.32	2.90	3.60
1966: 4	74.90	−12.51	2.87	3.83
3	85.61	− 4.82	2.89	3.37
2	89.94	− 2.43	2.83	3.14
1	92.18	2.54	2.78	3.01
1965: 4	89.90	6.42	2.72	3.02
3	84.48	− 2.13	2.66	3.14
2	86.32	2.48	2.61	3.02
1	84.23	.18	2.55	3.02
1964: 4	84.08	2.20	2.50	2.97
3	82.27	3.83	2.44	2.96
2	79.24	5.05	2.38	3.00
1	75.43	4.45	2.33	3.08

† Calculated with Eq. (12-7).
‡ Dividend yield = (4 times SP quarterly cash dividend index)/(SP 500 index).
Source: Standard & Poor's Trade & Securities Statistics, an annual booklet of raw economic data for past years. (Data also available in other published reference books.)

APPENDIX TO CHAPTER 12
Data for Standard & Poor's 500
Composite Stock Index

In order to calculate characteristic lines, it is necessary to have rates of change in some market index. Table A12-1 lists quarterly observations on Standard & Poor's (SP) 500 stocks composite average for several years. These data can be used to calculate the rates of price change or rates of return for the market.

The SP 500 index is made up of 425 industrial, 20 railroad, and 55 utility stocks. It is like a portfolio of 500 different common stocks. The weight of each of these stocks is proportional to the total market value of the firm's outstanding securities.

The SP 500 price index may be thought of as the price of a share of stock in a hypothetical portfolio. This price index is constructed so that in 1941 to 1943 it had a base value of 10. The percentage changes in the price index are good estimates of the average rate of price change for marketable common stocks listed on the New York Stock Exchange.

The quarterly dividend series is like a cash dividend paid on one of the hypothetical shares in the SP 500 portfolio. It represents the weighted average cash dividend for all 500 shares in the portfolio. This dividend is divided by the SP 500 price index to obtain the weighted average dividend yield for the 500 firms in the sample. This dividend yield is at an annual rate, that is, 4 times the quarterly rate.

PART FOUR

OTHER INVESTMENTS

CHAPTER 13 SHORT POSITIONS, PUTS AND CALLS, AND OTHER OPTIONS compares and contrasts long and short positions and explains the option securities—puts, calls, strips, straps, spreads, and straddles.

CHAPTER 14 COMMODITIES TRADING starts by listing the commodities and the exchanges where futures contracts are traded. Cash, spot, and futures positions are defined and risk-averting hedges are explained.

The two chapters in Part 4 discuss marketable securities and some institutional arrangements surrounding them which are typically used by more experienced and professional investors in the United States. The securities explained in Chaps. 13 and 14 are useful in constructing well-diversified and profitable portfolios.

Thirteen

Short Positions, Puts and Calls, and Other Options

There are several different positions which the participants in securities markets may assume besides the common position of buying a security, holding it, and hoping for appreciation and /or dividend or interest income. For example, bearish investors can assume short positions to profit from price declines. And short-run speculators who want the breath-taking thrills that accompany highly leveraged positions may buy or sell puts, calls, strips, straps, spreads, straddles, warrants, or some combination of them. Some of these positions are profitable if prices rise, some are profitable if prices fall, some are profitable if prices either rise or fall, and some are profitable if prices do not change at all. Also, some of the positions are best suited for long-term results and some are tailor-made for short-term action. This chapter explains the menu of positions from which participants in securities markets may select.

13-1 LONG AND SHORT POSITIONS

Investors entering the securities markets may assume one or both of two basic positions in a security. A *long position* involves simply buying and holding the security—this is the only position of which most investors are aware. The short position is more complicated.

A *short sale of securities* occurs when one person sells a second person securities the first person does not own. Does it sound unethical—if not illegal? Actually, short sales are routine transactions which just require more explanation than the buy-and-hold position.

Short sellers sell a security short because they expect its price to fall and they want to profit from that price fall. So, the short seller sells a security he or she does not own to a second party who takes a long position in the security; the long buyer expects the price to rise. Thus, a short sale requires a short seller who is bearish (that is, who expects price depreciation) and a long buyer who is bullish (who expects price appreciation) about the same stock at the same time; it is a case of opposites attracting each other in search of profit. The short seller borrows the shares of stock to be sold from a third party in order to make delivery on the short sale. Then, the short seller waits for the security's price to fall so he can purchase it at the lower price he expects and can repay the third party for the shares he borrowed. If the security's price does fall (rise), the short seller profits (loses) by the difference between the price he has paid for the shares to give to the third party and the price at which he earlier sold the shares to the long buyer, less any commission costs. So, aside from the commission costs taken out of the transaction by the stockbroker, the short seller's profit equals the long buyer's loss—or vice versa, if the security's price rises after the short sale. Table 13-1 outlines the parties, suggests some average times, and explains all the transactions in a hypothetical short sale.

Short sales are more complicated than the example in Table 13-1 may seem to indicate for several reasons. First, short sales can be made only on an "up-tick" (that is, after a trade in which the security's price was bid up). This is a New York Stock Exchange (NYSE) rule designed to keep short sellers from accenting a downturn in the price of a stock. A second complication involves dividends. If a common stock which is sold short pays a cash dividend while on loan to the short seller, he must pay that dividend from his own pocket to the third party who lent him the shares. Third, the short seller is required to put up guarantee money equaling as much as 100 percent of the value of the shares he borrowed as collateral for the third party who lent the shares. A fourth problem which can arise with short sales is that the short seller can get "closed out" of his or her short position at any time if the third party who lent the shares demands them back. For example, if the price of the security which was sold short goes up so that the third party who lent the shares wants to sell and recognize a capital gain, the third party can call for the shares to be returned immediately. This can force the short seller, for example, to cover his short position by buying the shares at a disadvantageous higher price. This can throw him for a loss unless the shares can be borrowed elsewhere, which they usually can.

Short sales have been conducted on the floor of the New York Stock Exchange (amidst what is predominantly long buying) for over 100 years. The volume of short sales is reported daily in the financial newspapers under the heading "Short Interest." The short interest is the total number of shares brokers have listed in their accounts as being sold short. The short interest is usually below 5 percent of the total volume of shares traded (and the NYSE specialists do most of it).

Various Reasons for Selling Short

There are different reasons why an individual may take a short position. First, and most obvious, is the desire to make a speculative gain from a

TABLE 13-1 OUTLINE OF THE PARTIES AND TRANSACTIONS IN A HYPOTHETICAL SHORT SALE OF SECURITIES

Date	Mr. First Bull	Mr. Bear	Broker A	Mr. Second Bull
Jan. 15 An independent purchase is made.	First Bull buys 100 shares of XYZ, leaves them in an account with Broker A, and retires to Florida. Broker A holds the shares in the brokerage's name without First Bull's knowing that he is doing so.			
Feb. 10 A short sale occurs.		Mr. Bear expects the price of XYZ to drop, so he calls Broker A and requests a short sale. So 100 shares of XYZ are sold short from Bear's account.	Broker A executes a short sale for Mr. Bear and a purchase for Mr. Second Bull, both for XYZ stock.	Mr. Second Bull buys 100 shares of XYZ through Broker A without knowing they are being sold by a short seller.
Feb. 15 Delivery is made on short sale.	First Bull's 100 shares of XYZ are loaned to Bear by Broker A (without telling First Bull).	Bear makes delivery by borrowing First Bull's shares through Broker A. Now Bear is in a short position	Broker A delivers First Bull's 100 shares of XYZ to Mr. Second Bull, collects cash for the shares, and marks Bear's account short 100 shares which are owed to First Bull.	First Bull's 100 shares of XYZ are received by Second Bull without his knowing he has purchased them from a short seller.
March 3 The short position is covered.		Bear covers his short position by buying 100 shares of XYZ at today's market price and has Broker A return them to First Bull.	Broker A buys 100 shares of XYZ for Bear and places them in First Bull's safe-deposit box. If these shares cost less (more) than the sale price on Feb. 10, Bear gets the profit (loss).	
March 8 Borrowed shares are replaced.	The 100 shares of XYZ are replaced in First Bull's account without his ever being aware they were gone.			

short-term price fall. Second, a *risk-averse* investor may sell short to hedge against possible losses. *Hedging* may be defined in this case as arranging for potential losses to be offset by equivalent profits. For example, a certain investor may own a controlling interest in a corporation which he wishes to maintain. If the investor expects security prices to fall, he may hold his long position and sell short to minimize his anticipated loss.[1] Then, if the price falls, the losses on his long position are matched by gains on his short position. Thus, the investor has maintained control and hedged his loss. Since this investor actually owns the shares (presumably they were in his safe-deposit box) that he sold short, he did what is commonly referred to as *selling short against the box.*

When selling short against the box, short sellers can borrow shares to use for delivery and then purchase shares to repay the loan, or they may simply deliver the shares they hold in their boxes. It is a common procedure to borrow shares. The borrower gives the lender cash to hold equal to the value of the shares borrowed. This protects the lender. The lender of the shares can use this cash at will while still benefiting from income from the shares. The lender of the shares may even be able to charge the borrower a fee for loaning the shares. Many brokers can arrange for such loans of shares in order to complete a short sale—the practice is common.

An investor may sell short against the box in order to carry a taxable gain from a high-income year into a low-income year and thus decrease income taxes. For example, assume an investor is having a high-income year which puts her in the high income tax bracket. If she has a $10,000 price gain on December 15, she might not want to liquidate the shares and take the gain until the next year when she expects to be in a lower tax bracket. However, if this investor fears the price of the securities she holds may decline before the new year, she can sell short against the box. This "locks her into" her gain because the long and short positions' profits and losses cancel each other and any subsequent price decline does not diminish the $10,000 profit. Then after January 1 the investor can deliver her shares against the short sale to terminate both positions. Thus the $10,000 gain occurs and is taxable in the year when the investor anticipates a lower tax rate.

Fourth, a short seller may be short in a security in order to carry on arbitrage. *Arbitrage* involves buying and selling the same asset in order to profit from price differentials. For example, if a particular security is sold in the United States and also in a European market at significantly different prices, arbitrage can be profitable. The arbitrager sells the security short in the market where its price is high and buys the security long in the market where the price is low. As the prices come together, the arbitrage pays off

---

[1] If the security involved in the short selling to maintain control is required to be listed with the SEC (see Chap. 4), then the transaction described is illegal because "insiders" are not allowed to sell short.

regardless of what other price fluctuations occur. Short selling is common in foreign exchange markets and commodity exchanges too, as explained in Chapter 14.

It should be noted from the preceding examples that short sales are not always undertaken in order to attain a speculative profit. Short sales may be used like insurance to hedge away risks. Or they may be used to maintain control, distribute income tax burdens more equitably, or bring differential prices into equilibrium. Therefore, risk-averse investors may desire to use short selling.

Vector Notation for Trading Positions

Sometimes it is desirable to consider the effects of simultaneously holding two (or more) positions in some asset. It can be difficult to conceptualize the net effect of holding multiple positions. Profit position graphs like the ones shown in Fig. 13-1 can be helpful in solving these types of problems. However, graphical analysis is slow and cumbersome. A simplified form of vector notation provides a clear, fast way to conceive of the various trading positions.

The vector notations for various trading positions will all be written as 2×1 vectors containing numbers. These numbers represent gross profits before premiums, transactions, costs, or commissions. The basic form of the vectors is shown below:

$$\begin{bmatrix} \text{Gross profit from a \$1 price increase in the asset} \\ \text{Gross profit from a \$1 price decrease in the asset} \end{bmatrix}$$

In the vectors, $+1$ represents a $1 profit, 0 represents zero profit, and -1 represents a $1 loss. Combinations of positions are represented by adding the vectors representing the various positions. For example, if an investor who has a long position in some asset subsequently sells this asset short, the individual is left with no position in that asset, that is, a perfect hedge, as shown in Eq. (13-1).

FIG. 13-1 Profit graphs. (*a*) Long position; (*b*) short position.

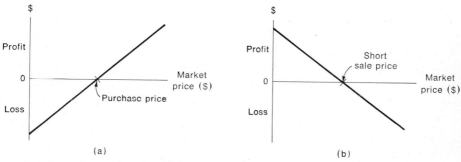

long + short = perfect hedge

$$\begin{bmatrix} +1 \\ -1 \end{bmatrix} + \begin{bmatrix} -1 \\ +1 \end{bmatrix} = \begin{bmatrix} 0 \\ 0 \end{bmatrix} \tag{13-1}$$

The vector notation does not reflect any of the expenses or other features of a position other than the manner in which it profits from price changes. For example, Eq. (13-1) shows that the perfect hedge is equal to holding cash but fails to reflect any commissions which must be paid in such a transaction.

In addition to long and short positions, market participants can buy and sell options. Options are marketable securities which offer high leverage and limited liability to their buyers.

13-2 OPTIONS

Options are contracts giving their holder the right to buy or sell a stated number of shares (usually 100) of a particular security at a fixed price within a predetermined time period. There are two basic types of options. A *put* is an option to sell, that is, an option to "put" shares on someone else. It is a negotiable contract giving the owner (or holder or buyer) the option to sell 100 shares of some security at any time he or she selects within a fixed period at a predetermined price. The predetermined price at which an option is to be exercised is called the *exercise price* or *contract price*. A *call* is an option to buy, that is, an option to call in shares for purchase. It is a negotiable contract giving its owner (or holder or buyer) the option of buying 100 shares of some security at a predetermined price within some specified time interval. Puts and calls are usually written for 30, 60, 90, or 190 days, or 1 year. They may be exercised by the holder at any time before they mature or, being marketable securities until the day they expire, they can be sold.

There are four other kinds of options which are a combination of puts and calls. A *straddle* is a put and a call on the same security at the same exercise price and for the same time period. A *strip* is two puts and one call at the same exercise price for the same period. A *spread* consists of a put and a call option on the same security for the same time period at *different* exercise prices. A *strap* is two calls and one put at the same contracted exercise price and for the same period.

Puts and Calls Markets

About two dozen firms who are members of the Put and Call Brokers and Dealers Association (PCBDA) make an over-the-counter option market. The PCBDA regulates the activities of its members: it investigates complaints, hears the evidence, and may take action against a member. The PCBDA also sets up certain guidelines to facilitate payments and deliveries among its members. The Securities Exchange Act of 1934 (section 9b) authorizes the Securities and Exchange Commission (SEC) to regulate trading in options. Thus the SEC is always "looking over the shoulder" of the PCBDA to see that it does not permit harmful practices. There are also puts and calls dealers who are not members of the PCBDA.

Puts and calls dealers publish lists suggesting premiums for options in the financial newspapers. Interested option buyers and option writers contact the dealer who acts as negotiator, helping a buyer and a writer who are interested in a given security to (1) settle on a mutually satisfactory premium, (2) settle on a *contract price* or *exercise price* at which the security may be put or called, and (3) determine what length of time they want the option contract to cover. To a certain extent these final arrangements depend upon the "haggling power" of the buyer and the writer of the options. However, as a first approximation, the premium on 90-day calls averages about 9 percent of the cost of the 100 shares, while 6-month premiums average about 14 percent of the price of the round lot. Most premiums range from $137.50 to $1,000 per 100-share option.

In 1973 an organized options market, the Chicago Board of Options Exchange (CBOE), began operation. This is America's first options exchange and organized secondary market for options. The CBOE began trading only call options on about two dozen stocks. But trading volume flourished and the CBOE enjoyed almost immediate success. As a result of the CBOE's success, the American Stock Exchange (AMEX) and other securities exchanges followed the CBOE's lead and began trading options too.

If someone wishes to speculate on a stock price change, he or she may buy or sell options through any one of numerous stockbrokers. Speculators need only examine the security prices and/or option prices published daily in most newspapers and, if they want to buy or sell an option on some security, call a few stockbrokers until they find one who will accommodate them. Figure 13-2 shows the prices of call options on various stocks which are traded on the Chicago Board of Options Exchange. Options on securities not traded on the CBOE may be bought or sold through the American Stock Exchange's options market or through one of the over-the-counter options dealers.

Option Premiums

The price for which an option sells is called the option's *premium*. The option buyer pays the premium to some option writer to induce the writer to grant the option. The main factors which determine the price (or synonymously, the premium) the option buyer must pay for an option are discussed below.[2]

---

[2] J. P. Shelton, "The Relation of the Price of a Warrant to the Price of Its Associated Stock," *Financial Analysts Journal,* May–June and July–August 1967. A. J. Boness, "Elements of a Theory of Stock Option Value," *Journal of Political Economy,* April 1964.

Chicago Board Options Exchange

Tuesday, January 21, 1975

Closing prices of all options. Sales unit is 100 shares. Security description includes exercise price.

Option & price	– Jan – Vol.	Last	– Apr – Vol.	Last	– Jul – Vol.	Last	Stock Close
Alcoa .. 30	b	b	14	1¾	7	2⅝	28½
Am Tel 50	22	1-16	90	⅝	26	1 3-16	46¾
Am Tel 45	460	1⅝	233	2¾	20	3⅝	46¾
Am Tel 40	43	6¾	156	7⅛	b	b	46¾
Atl R .. 90	227	⅛	177	3¾	22	7	85¼
Atl R .. 80	68	5¼	80	9	15	12	85¼
Avon .. 30	647	1½	334	3⅞	44	5⅝	31¼
Avon .. 25	158	6⅜	121	7¼	10	8⅜	31¼
Avon .. 20	138	11½	29	11¼	43	11¾	31¼
Avon 35	b	b	459	1⅞	b	b	31¼
Beth S ..30	4	1-16	86	⅝	74	1⅜	27¼
Beth S ..25	98	2½	62	2¾	73	3⅝	27¼
Bruns .. 15	5	1-16	117	3-16	b	b	10
Bruns .. 10	742	3-16	454	1	96	1⅝	10
Citicp .. 40	1	1-16	b	b	b	b	31⅝
Citicp .. 35	114	1-16	b	b	b	b	31⅝
Citicp .. 30	336	1⅝	153	3	57	4⅜	31⅝
Citicp .. 25	73	6⅜	43	6⅞	a	a	31⅝
Delta .. 25	b	b	9	3½	2	5½	27¼
Delta .. 30	b	b	23	1¾	26	2¾	27¼
Dow Ch 50	b	b	13	7¾	2	10¼	54¾
Dow Ch 60	b	b	60	2½	4	4⅝	54¾
Eas Kd 100	a	a	20	⅛	b	b	63⅞
Eas Kd 90	a	a	24	⅜	b	b	63⅞
Eas Kd 80	a	a	156	1	21	2½	63⅞
Eas Kd 70	251	1-16	211	3⅛	54	5⅝	63⅞
Eas Kd 60	155	4	172	8¼	24	10½	63⅞
Exxon .. 80	1	1-16	85	⅝	b	b	67⅜
Exxon ..70	182	1-16	125	2⅞	35	3⅞	67⅜
Exxon ..60	93	7⅜	99	8⅞	30	10	67⅜
F N M 15	b	b	51	4	34	5⅛	18⅜
F N M 20	b	b	521	1¼	107	2	18⅜
Ford 45	a	a	16	3-16	b	b	35⅝
Ford 40	2	1-16	67	½	b	b	35⅝
Ford 35	169	¾	83	1⅞	37	3¼	35⅝
Ford 30	77	5⅝	27	5¾	19	6⅜	35⅝
G M 30	b	b	46	6½	25	7⅛	36½
G M 35	b	b	96	2⅝	59	3⅝	36½
Gen El 30	b	b	1	6⅛	1	7½	34⅝
Gen El 35	b	b	139	2⅝	17	3⅞	34⅝
Glf Wn 25	302	⅛	120	1 11-16	60	2¾	24⅛
Glf Wn 20	78	4¼	28	4¾	5	5⅞	24⅛
Gt Wst 15	974	5-16	414	1 9-16	125	2½	15
Gt Wst 10	166	4⅞	130	5⅜	143	5⅞	15
I B M 220	a	a	289	⅞	b	b	159⅝
I B M 200	5	1-16	326	2⅝	74	5⅞	159⅝
I B M 180	93	1-16	716	6⅛	173	10¾	159⅝
I B M 160	609	2⅛	601	13	130	19¼	159⅝
I N A .. 30	316	1¼	58	2⅝	50	3½	31⅝
I N A .. 25	92	6½	33	6¾	4	7⅜	31⅝
I N A .. 20	5	11⅝	12	11½	b	b	31⅝
I T T .. 20	10	1-16	315	⅜	b	b	16¾
I T T ..15	441	1¾	354	1 15-16	206	2¾	16¾
I T T .. 10	b	b	103	6½	71	6⅞	16¾
In Har ..25	a	a	45	5-16	b	b	20½
In Har 20	325	7-16	169	1 3-16	52	2⅛	20½
In Pap ..30	b	b	10	6	15	7½	35¾
In Pap ..35	b	b	3	2⅝	6	3¾	35¾
Kenn C 35	b	b	27	4⅛	16	5⅝	37
Kenn C 40	b	b	43	1⅞	14	2⅝	37
Kerr M 65	176	¼	111	4⅞	69	7⅞	62⅞
Kerr M 75	a	a	193	1¾	18	4	62⅞
Kerr M 55	16	8½	34	10½	b	b	62⅞
Kerr M 50	3	12⅞	6	15	b	b	62⅞
Kresge ..30	a	a	372	5-16	b	b	20¾
Kresge 25	69	1-16	592	15-16	110	1⅞	20¾
Kresge 20	460	1	328	2½	100	3¾	20¾
Loews ..15	331	5-16	177	1 3-16	79	2	15¼
Loews .. 10	12	5	15	5¼	a	a	15¼
M M M 75	a	a	2	1-16	b	b	45½
M M M 65	a	a	13	5-16	1	1	45½
M M M 55	a	a	83	¾	5	2	45½
M M M 50	b	b	55	1⅞	20	3⅝	45½
M M M 45	b	b	45	3⅞	23	5½	45½
Mc Don 40	a	a	176	¾	b	b	28¾
Mc Don 35	20	1-16	476	1⅜	65	3	28¾
Mc Don 30	508	⅜	554	2⅞	125	4¾	28¾
Mc Don 25	136	3¾	100	6	b	b	28¾
Merck 70	13	1-16	57	1 11-16	16	3¾	58⅞
Merck ..60	296	¾	150	5	66	7⅝	58⅞
Merck .. 50	61	8¾	16	11¼	b	b	58⅞
Monsan 60	5	1-16	59	⅜	b	b	46
Monsan 50	83	1-16	202	1⅜	18	3⅛	46
Monsan 45	81	1¼	90	3¾	8	5⅝	46
Monsan 40	19	6¾	50	7	4	8¾	46
Nw Air 20	a	a	8	¼	b	b	12½
Nw Air 15	4	1-16	123	⅝	65	1 7-16	12½
Nw Air 10	b	b	39	3⅛	49	3⅝	12½
Pnz U ..20	8	1-16	204	¾	92	1⅜	17⅝
Pnz U ..15	221	2½	76	3⅛	19	3¾	17⅝
Polar .. 15	299	¾	498	2⅜	285	3⅜	15½
Polar .. 25	19	1-16	455	7-16	189	15-16	15½
Polar .. 20	32	1-16	928	13-16	515	1⅞	15½
R C A ..15	1	1-16	421	¼	b	b	10½
R C A 10	396	¾	479	1⅛	333	1 11-16	10½
Sears .. 80	a	a	20	⅛	b	b	52⅝
Sears .. 70	a	a	17	⅜	b	b	52⅝
Sears .. 60	2	1-16	84	1½	b	b	52⅝
Sears .. 50	307	2⅞	156	4⅞	14	6⅝	52⅝
Sears .. 45	35	7¾	26	9⅞	8	9¾	52⅝
Sperry ..40	10	1-16	b	b	b	b	25½
Sperry ..35	a	a	29	7-16	b	b	25½
Sperry ..30	4	1-16	165	1	50	2	25½
Sperry ..25	76	¾	74	2¾	17	3¾	25½
Tex In ..90	a	a	12	⅜	b	b	63¼
Tex In ..80	a	a	76	⅞	b	b	63¼
Tex In ..70	52	1-16	168	2⅞	16	6	63¼
Tex In ..60	161	3¾	185	7	4	10¼	63¼
Upjohn ..75	a	a	67	1-16	b	b	35
Upjohn ..65	a	a	82	¼	b	b	35
Upjohn 50	2	1-16	484	¾	187	1⅞	35
Upjohn 45	32	1-16	496	1½	282	2⅞	35
Upjohn 40	b	b	637	2¾	306	4⅜	35
Upjohn 35	b	b	183	4⅜	49	6¼	35
Weyerh 35	a	a	42	15-16	b	b	29⅝
Weyerh 30	46	5-16	140	2¼	54	3½	29⅝
Weyerh 25	11	4¾	9	5½	7	6⅞	29⅝
Xerox ..100	a	a	10	⅛	b	b	56½
Xerox .. 80	1	1-16	53	½	b	b	56½
Xerox .. 70	a	a	137	1⅜	38	3	56½
Xerox .. 60	187	3-16	145	3⅝	75	6⅛	56½
Xerox .. 50	b	b	99	8½	8	11¼	56½

Total volume 37,060. Open interest 585,993..........
a–Not traded. b–No option offered.
Sales in 100s. Last is premium (purchase price).

FIG. 13-2 Price quotations for calls traded on the Chicago Board of Options Exchange (CBOE). (From *The Wall Street Journal*.)

1 *The stock price.* It takes a larger premium to induce the option writer to assume the risks associated with 100 shares of high-priced stock because the possible losses are larger than for 100 shares of low-priced stock. For example, if market prices drop 10 percent, then the decrease in value of 100 shares of a $20 stock is only ($20 × 100 − $18 × 100 =) $200, whereas the 10 percent decrease in value of 100 shares of a $150 stock is ($150 × 100 − $135 × 100 =) $1,500. Thus a put writer charges a larger premium to write puts on high-priced securities.

2 *The length of time the option remains open.* Writers of 6-month options tend to charge about 40 percent larger premiums than they would to write 3-month options on the same security. The charge is higher simply because the probability that the option will be exercised and the writer will lose money increases with the time the option remains open.

3 *The probability of a large price change in the optioned security.* A sizable change can make it profitable for the option owner to exercise the option. Several factors determine a security's potential for price volatility. The most important influences of volatility are:

    a The historical price volatility of the security. For example, Fairchild has always been more volatile than ATT common stock.

    b The trend of the market (that is, bullish or bearish).

    c Recent news which may affect the security's price.

4 *The exercise price.* The exercise price of an option is usually the market price of the security on the day the option was written. But sometimes the exercise price of a put or a call is "points away" from the market price (that is, the exercise price is above or below the market price by several dollars). For example, if the exercise price of a call is several dollars above the current price, there is a decreased probability that the call will be exercised. As a result, the call writer will be willing to accept a smaller premium.

Federal Income Taxes

The cost of an option is a nondeductible capital expenditure, and the option represents a capital asset in the hands of the holder. Gain or loss occurring upon the sale of an option in a closing sale transaction constitutes capital gain or loss, long term or short term depending upon how long the option has been held. If an option is allowed to expire, it is treated as having been sold on the expiration date. Upon the exercise of an option, its cost is added to the exercise price to determine the basic cost of the underlying stock acquired.

    The premium received for writing an option is not included in the writer's taxable income at the time of receipt (when the option is written), but is deferred until such time as the writer's obligation terminates. The writer's obligation may terminate (1) by the passage of time, or (2) by delivery of the underlying stock pursuant to the terms of the option.

    If a writer's obligation terminates by reason of the passage of time, the premium constitutes ordinary income to the writer realized on the day of expiration. If the option is exercised, the premium received by the writer is treated as an increase in the proceeds realized upon the sale of the underlying stock in the exercised transaction. The gain or loss on such a sale constitutes capital gain or loss, long term or short term depending upon how long the stock has been held.

Profits from the Basic Options

The investor who thinks a security's price is likely to move upward may want to buy a call. If the security's price falls, only the premium (which is typically only about 15 percent of the value of the 100 shares) is lost. But if the security's price rises, the buyer of a call can reap all the capital gains. Since the call buyer had only the amount of the writer's premium invested, he or she can earn a very large rate of return on the investment if the price of the stock rises very much. On the other hand, someone who is very bearish about some security may profit from writing a call on it. Of course, another investor who is bullish about this same security must be found to buy the call; it is the job of the puts and calls broker to help the buyer and the writer arrange the contract they desire.

Call. The market position of options buyers and writers can be depicted graphically. Figure 13-3 shows a profit graph for the buyer and the writer of a call. Profit or loss is graphed on the vertical axis, and the market price of the optioned security is on the horizontal axis. The graph of the call option buyer's position shows a loss equal to the premium up to the point where the market price rises above the exercise price (also called the striking price or the contract price). Where the market price exceeds the exercise price by enough to cover the premium, the option buyer's profit is zero if he or she exercises the option; this is point Z in the graphs. The buyer might actually exercise the option at this zero profit point in order to recoup the premium in the belief that the market price would not rise any more. If the market price rises above Z, the buyer reaps a profit (after the cost of the premium) by exercising the call.

FIG. 13-3 Profit graphs for a call option. (*a*) Call buyer; (*b*) call writer.

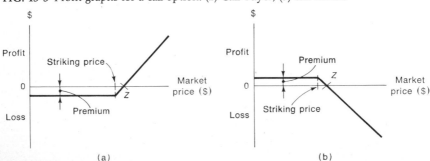

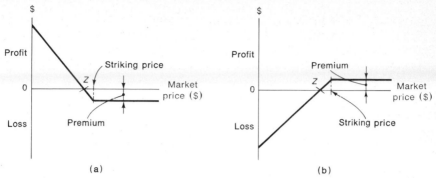

FIG. 13-4 Profit graphs for a put operation. (*a*) Put buyer; (*b*) put writer.

Put. The profit positions of the writer and the buyer of a put option are shown in Fig. 13-4. The buyer of the put hopes the optioned security's price will fall, just as a short seller would. But, unlike the short seller, the buyer has limited losses (that is, only the premium) if the security turns capricious and rises. If the security's price falls, the put owner's profit cannot exceed the exercise price times 100 shares less the premium paid. Thus, the writer of the put has limited losses if the price falls. The put writer cannot lose more than 100 times the exercise price less the premium received. If the price of the security rises, the writer gains the premium and no more. Options writers' gains are always limited to their premiums.

Any investor who wants to speculate that the price of some security will fall must choose between buying a put or selling short. The purchase of a put is usually more desirable than taking a short position for two main reasons. First, the investment in a put is limited to the premium, whereas a short seller usually must invest a larger sum. Second, the holder of a put loses no more than the premium if the price of the optioned security rises, but a short seller's losses are unlimited if the security's price rises.

Summary of Vector Notation for Basic Positions

The seven basic positions discussed so far in this chapter are summarized thus in vector notation.

$$
\begin{array}{cccc}
\text{long} & \text{short} & \begin{array}{c}\text{perfect hedge, hold}\\ \text{cash, or no position}\end{array} & \text{buy call} \\[4pt]
\begin{bmatrix} +1 \\ -1 \end{bmatrix} &
\begin{bmatrix} -1 \\ +1 \end{bmatrix} &
\begin{bmatrix} 0 \\ 0 \end{bmatrix} &
\begin{bmatrix} +1 \\ 0 \end{bmatrix}
\end{array}
$$

$$
\begin{array}{ccc}
\text{write call} & \text{buy put} & \text{write put} \\[4pt]
\begin{bmatrix} -1 \\ 0 \end{bmatrix} &
\begin{bmatrix} 0 \\ +1 \end{bmatrix} &
\begin{bmatrix} 0 \\ -1 \end{bmatrix}
\end{array}
$$

The trading positions discussed in the remainder of this chapter are merely combinations of these basic positions.

Converting Puts and Calls

The price of a call option on some security is more than the premium for a put option on the same security any time the two premiums are compared. Some people hastily attribute this discrepancy to the fact that there are more bullish speculators trying to buy calls than there are bears trying to buy puts, but this assumption is naive. Calls cost more than puts because of the conversion process through which puts are converted into calls, and vice versa. To understand this process, consider the option writer's position in bull and bear market conditions.

During a prevailing bull market, many option buyers want to buy calls. But no option writers want to write calls in a bullish market because they would probably be thrown for losses as their call options were exercised on them (see Fig. 13-3b). However, there are plenty of option writers who would be happy to write puts during a bullish period and enjoy the premium income from the unexercised puts. As a result, conversion specialists buy puts, sell calls, and simultaneously hedge themselves by buying a long position in the same stock, as shown in Eq. (13-2). Thus, conversion specialists can sell calls in a bull market but take no risk of loss because they are perfectly hedged.

$$\text{buy put} + \text{sell call} + \text{buy long} = \text{perfect hedge}$$

$$\begin{bmatrix} 0 \\ +1 \end{bmatrix} + \begin{bmatrix} -1 \\ 0 \end{bmatrix} + \begin{bmatrix} +1 \\ -1 \end{bmatrix} = \begin{bmatrix} 0 \\ 0 \end{bmatrix} \tag{13-2}$$

Rather than have all their invested funds tied up in the long positions necessary to hedge their risks, conversion specialists typically finance these costly inventories of securities with borrowed funds. Therefore, the call premium on any security must exceed the put premium by enough difference to cover the conversion specialists' interest expense or they would not find it profitable to buy puts and convert them to salable calls. This is the reason that prices of calls are higher than prices of puts. An opposite but symmetric line of reasoning will show that calls can be bought and converted into salable puts with the same effect on the premiums.[3]

Straddles, Strips, Spreads, and Straps

Straddle. The buyer of a straddle is betting the premium paid that the price of the optioned security will deviate (either up or down) from the exercise

---

[3] There is a parity between put and call premiums which is maintained by an arbitrage process. This complicated line of reasoning is best explained by Hans R. Stoll, "The Relationship Between Put and Call Option Prices," *Journal of Finance,* December 1969, pp. 801–824.

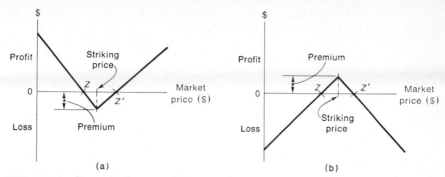

FIG. 13-5 Profit graphs for a straddle option. (*a*) Straddle buyer; (*b*) straddle writer.

price. The writer of a straddle accepts this bet and implicitly asserts confidence that the security's price will not vary before the option matures.

The profit positions of the buyer and the writer of a straddle are depicted in Fig. 13-5. Since a straddle is a put and a call at the same price, the profit positions for the straddle in Fig. 13-5 are merely Figs. 13-3 and 13-4 added for the case when the exercise prices of the put and the calls are identical. In vector notation, straddles are formed as shown below.

buy put + buy call = buy straddle

$$\begin{bmatrix} 0 \\ +1 \end{bmatrix} + \begin{bmatrix} +1 \\ 0 \end{bmatrix} = \begin{bmatrix} +1 \\ +1 \end{bmatrix} \tag{13-3}$$

write put + write call = write straddle

$$\begin{bmatrix} 0 \\ -1 \end{bmatrix} + \begin{bmatrix} -1 \\ 0 \end{bmatrix} = \begin{bmatrix} -1 \\ -1 \end{bmatrix} \tag{13-4}$$

Equation (13-4) and Fig. (13-5) show that the straddle writer loses if the optioned security's price either rises or falls. For taking this large risk, the straddle writer receives a premium which is usually equal to a put premium plus a call premium. In fact, there may be two writers to a straddle, a put writer and a call writer. This could occur if the puts and calls dealer is not able to find one person to write the entire straddle; or the person desiring to buy a straddle might buy a put and a call separately on the same security to attain the desired straddle position.

Strip. The buyer of a strip is betting that the price of some security will change from the exercise price, but the buyer believes that the security's price is more likely to fall than it is to rise. Figure 13-6 represents the profit positions for the buyer and the writer of a strip.

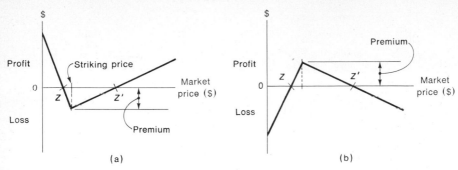

FIG. 13-6 Profit graphs for a strip. (*a*) Strip buyer; (*b*) strip writer.

Since a strip is two puts and a call, the buyer evidently believes a decrease in the price of the optioned security is more probable than an increase. The profit positions of the buyer and the writer of a strip are represented in vector equations (13-5) and (13-6), respectively.

buys 2 puts + buy a call = buy a strip

$$\begin{bmatrix} 0 \\ +1 \end{bmatrix} + \begin{bmatrix} 0 \\ +1 \end{bmatrix} + \begin{bmatrix} +1 \\ 0 \end{bmatrix} = \begin{bmatrix} +1 \\ +2 \end{bmatrix} \tag{13-5}$$

write 2 puts + write a call = write a strip

$$\begin{bmatrix} 0 \\ -1 \end{bmatrix} + \begin{bmatrix} 0 \\ -1 \end{bmatrix} + \begin{bmatrix} -1 \\ 0 \end{bmatrix} = \begin{bmatrix} -1 \\ -2 \end{bmatrix} \tag{13-6}$$

The premium for writing a strip usually equals the premium for writing two puts plus one call. In order for the buyer to recoup this large premium, the market price of the optioned security must either drop to Z or rise to Z' in Fig. 13-6. The drop from the exercise price to Z is only half as far as the rise from the exercise price to Z' because the line through Z has twice as steep a slope as the line through Z'. Figure 13-6, representing the strip, is quite similar to Fig. 13-5 for the straddle. The only differences are in the size of the premium and the slope of the line through point Z'.

Spread. Figure 13-7 represents the profit position of the buyer and the writer of a spread and is similar to Fig. 13-5 for the straddle. The difference between these two figures is attributable to the fact that the exercise price of the spread is "points away" from the market. The exercise price for the put portion of the spread is point A in Fig. 13-7. The market price of the optioned security when the option was written is represented by point B. Point C is the exercise price for the call portion of the spread. The premium on the spread is less than the premium on the straddle because the market price of the security which is optioned with a spread must rise or fall more

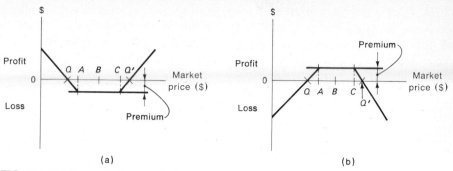

FIG. 13-7 Profit graphs for a spread. (*a*) Spread buyer; (*b*) spread writer.

than if it were optioned with a straddle in order for the option buyer to profit. Graphically, this means the distance from Z to Z' in Fig. 13-5 is less than the distance from Q to Q' in Fig. 13-7. Symbolically, $(Z' - Z) < (Q' - Q)$. Since the vector notation does not account for the differences between the exercise prices in a spread, the vector representations of a spread and a straddle are identical.

Strap. Straps consist of two calls and one put on the same security at the same exercise price. Thus, a strap is like a strip which is skewed in the opposite direction. The buyer of a strap evidently foresees bullish and bearish possibilities for the optioned security, with a price rise being more likely. Graphing the profit positions and developing the vector notation for the buyers and sellers of a strap are left as an exercise.

Writing Options Covered and Uncovered

Sometimes options writers buy the security on which they are writing the option. When they do so, they are said to have *covered* themselves. For example, the writer of a call, say a woman, may buy 100 shares of the security on which she is writing the call if she expects (as the buyer does) that the price will rise. Then, if the security's price does rise and the call is exercised, the writer will simply deliver the shares she has already purchased and not suffer any loss. Assuming that the call writer's interest expense and commissions incurred by covering herself are less than the premiums she received, the call writer and the buyer both profit from the price rise. The profit position of a covered call writer is shown in vector notation in Eq. (13-7).

long + write call = covered call writer

$$\begin{bmatrix} +1 \\ -1 \end{bmatrix} + \begin{bmatrix} -1 \\ 0 \end{bmatrix} = \begin{bmatrix} 0 \\ -1 \end{bmatrix} \tag{13-7}$$

If this call writer has covered herself with securities purchased on margin, she may earn a handsome rate of return on her invested capital. Of course, if the security's price falls, then the call buyer loses the premium and the covered call writer loses on her long position. However, the call writer's losses are offset by the premium she received.

Figure 13-8 represents writing covered calls graphically. At points Z the buyer and the writer have zero profit. Note, however, that point Z for the buyer is above the striking price by the amount of the premium, whereas point Z is below the striking price for the writer.

An option writer who writes a call against some security without owning that security is said to be *writing naked* or *writing against cash*, or *writing uncovered*. Equation (13-8) shows that writing a call naked is similar to selling the security short if the price rises but not if the price drops.

sell short $\neq$ write call uncovered

$$\begin{bmatrix} -1 \\ +1 \end{bmatrix} \neq \begin{bmatrix} -1 \\ 0 \end{bmatrix} \tag{13-8}$$

The right-hand side of Fig. 13-3 shows the profit position for a call writer who was writing naked. That is, this particular call writer had not covered himself by buying the securities for which he wrote the option. In this case, the call buyer's profits are the call writer's losses. A comparison of the call writer's exposure to loss in Figs. 13-3 and 13-8 shows that writing calls naked is risky in a bull (rising) market and writing calls covered is risky in a bear (falling) market.

The writers of options may write any option naked or choose to cover themselves. The final decision depends on the particular option being written and the option writer's beliefs about the direction of the market. In any event, the option writer's profits are limited to the premium, while the potential losses are unlimited. Most dealers require that option sellers who write naked put up a margin of at least 50 percent of the total market value

FIG. 13-8 Profit graphs for a call. (*a*) Call buyer; (*b*) covered writer.

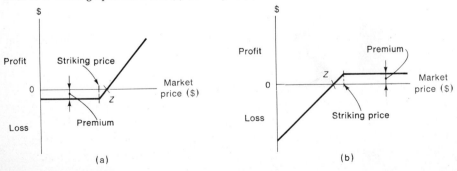

of the 100 shares. Thus the leverage attainable by writing naked is not infinite, but it is more than can be obtained in most other security transactions.

Converting Options

There are many positions which may be created with the use of the long and short positions and options. For example, buying a call and writing a put on the same asset is equivalent to taking a long position, as shown in Eq. (13-9).

buy call + write put = long

$$
\begin{bmatrix} +1 \\ 0 \end{bmatrix} + \begin{bmatrix} 0 \\ -1 \end{bmatrix} = \begin{bmatrix} +1 \\ -1 \end{bmatrix}
\tag{13-9}
$$

A situation in which it might be desirable to write a put after selling a call on the same stock would occur when the person's opinion of downside risk changes. For example, if, after buying a call to obtain its limited downside risk, the call buyer becomes convinced the price of the optioned security will not fall, he can write the put to obtain the writer's premium.

The investor who owns a put option and also purchases a long position in the same security has done what is called converting a put to a call. This would be appropriate if the person's outlook has changed from bearish to bullish. Equation (13-10) represents such a transaction.

buy put + long = buy call

$$
\begin{bmatrix} 0 \\ +1 \end{bmatrix} + \begin{bmatrix} +1 \\ -1 \end{bmatrix} = \begin{bmatrix} +1 \\ 0 \end{bmatrix}
\tag{13-10}
$$

If someone wants a short position but is unable to borrow the securities to deliver on the short sale, it is nevertheless possible to obtain a short position by selling a call and buying a put on the same asset, as shown in Eq. (13-11).

sell call + buy put = short

$$
\begin{bmatrix} -1 \\ 0 \end{bmatrix} + \begin{bmatrix} 0 \\ +1 \end{bmatrix} = \begin{bmatrix} -1 \\ +1 \end{bmatrix}
\tag{13-11}
$$

These are only a small sample of the positions which may be created. A clever risk-averse investor will utilize the various opportunities provided by options to diversify or hedge the risk and increase the returns. A more aggressive, confident speculator will invest directly in options. By investing only the premium on the option, a speculator can attain large amounts of financial leverage which will result in very large rates of return (either positive or negative).

Warrants

Warrants are options to buy shares of stock. They are like calls to the extent that they are options to buy a fixed number of shares at a predetermined price during some specified time period. But warrants are different from calls in certain respects. They are written by the corporation to whose stock they apply rather than by an independent option writer. They are given as attachments to the corporation's issue of bonds or preferred stock. Warrants are "sweeteners" given with an issue of senior securities in order to increase the proceeds of the issue and thereby lower the interest cost. These options may expire at a certain date or they may be perpetual. They are usually detached from the securities with which they were issued and traded as separate securities.

The price stated on the warrant which the owner must pay to purchase the stated number of shares is called the *exercise price*. The minimum value of a warrant, denoted MVW, may be calculated with Eq. (13-12).

$$MVW = (p_s - e)N \tag{13-12}$$

where p_s = market price per share of stock
e = conversion or exercise price
N = number of shares of common stock obtained with one warrant

For example, a warrant which entitles its owner to buy two shares (that is, $N = 2$) of stock at an exercise price of $50 per share ($e = \$50$) while the market price is $60 per share ($p_s = \$60$) has a minimum value of ($60 − $50)2 = $20 per warrant. Figure 13-9 depicts Eq. (13-12) graphically.

Figure 13-9 shows that when the market price of the security, p_s, is above the exercise price e, the warrant has some positive minimum value. The actual market price of the warrant, denoted p_w on the vertical axis, typically follows the dotted line. This shows that warrants typically have a market value p_w above the MVW. The excess of a warrant's price over its minimum value (that is, p_w − MVW) is determined by expectations about future stock prices in the same way as call option premiums are determined by expectations.[4]

Figure 13-9, depicting the determination of warrant prices, is also appropriate to explain the price of call options since call options and warrants are identical except for their original writers and a few other minor details.

[4] John P. Shelton, op cit. D. Leabo and R. L. Rogalski, "Warrant Price Movements and the Efficient Market Model," *Journal of Finance*, March 1975. A. H. Y. Chen, "A Model of Warrant Pricing in a Dynamic Market," *Journal of Finance*, December 1970. A. J. Boness, "Elements of a Theory of Stock-Option Value," *Journal of Political Economy*, April 1964.

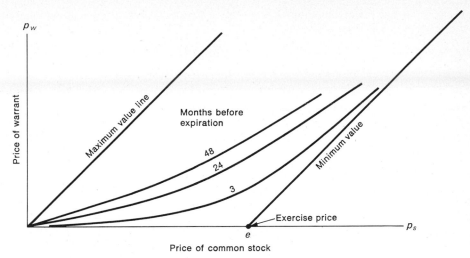

FIG. 13-9 Typical price curves for a warrant or call.

13-3 CONCLUSIONS

Research by one of the Nobel prize winners in economics, Kenneth Arrow, has shown that resources within a nation can be allocated better if there are more different contingent claims on assets than are provided by only the long position.[5] That is, the existence of short positions and options actually increases the nation's average per capita wealth in some small way, whether or not each person owns securities. This scientific finding refutes the naive notion that speculation is some worthless form of gambling.

The spectrum of possible positions which participants in securities markets may assume is wide. For example, a person who thinks that the price of some security will not change and wants to profit from this "knowledge" can do so. By writing strips, straps, and straddles, the person can profit if the security's price remains stationary. Positions exist from which thoughtful individuals may profit from practically every other situation too. The existence of such profitable opportunities encourages good securities research, helps keep securities prices aligned with their true intrinsic values and makes securities markets more efficient allocators of capital.

QUESTIONS

1 "Risk-averters do not sell short. Short selling is done by speculators." Is this statement true, false, or uncertain? Explain.

[5] Kenneth Arrow, "The Role of Securities in the Optimal Allocation of Risk-Bearing," *Review of Economic Studies,* April 1964, pp. 91–96.

2 Who are the parties to put and call options and what function is performed by each party?

3 What are the main factors determining put and call premiums? What are the main factors determining the market price of a warrant?

4 Graph the profit positions and develop the vector notation showing the positions of the buyer and the writer of a strap.

5 Compare and contrast writing a call naked and selling a common stock short.

6 Is it possible to create a short position from options? Explain.

7 Compare and contrast call options and warrants.

8 Does the Chicago Board of Options Exchange ever trade options of any type with the same expiration date but different exercise prices? Why?

9 Should the price of a strip option bear any relation to the prices of put and call options? Explain.

SELECTED REFERENCES

Black, F., and M. Scholes, "The Pricing of Options and Corporate Liabilities," *Journal of Political Economy*, June 1973, pp. 637–654.
>   A seminal mathematical paper which develops a static equilibrium pricing model for options.

Cootner, Paul, *The Random Character of Stock Market Prices* (Cambridge, Mass.: M.I.T., 1964).
>   This is a collection of 22 readings by various authors studying the nature of security price movements. Part 4 contains a series of readings analyzing the pricing of options. Mathematics is used. Some readings use advanced calculus, matrix algebra, and mathematical statistics. Readings 17 through 22 deal with options.

Malkiel, B. G., and R. E. Quandt, *Strategies and Rational Decisions in the Securities Options Market* (Cambridge, Mass.: M.I.T., 1969).
>   This book uses calculus and utility theory to show the economic rationale for options. It also explains the history, institutions, and practices (for example, the income tax treatment) that affect options trading.

Merton, Robert C., "The Theory of Rational Option Pricing," *The Bell Journal of Economics and Management Science*, Spring 1973, pp. 161–183.
>   A mathematical analysis of option prices which summarizes and extends the literature on the subject.

APPENDIX TO CHAPTER 13
The Black-Scholes-Merton Call Pricing Model

Professor Paul Samuelson developed the two boundaries listed below (and others) for the prices of rationally priced calls:[1]

1 Maximum call price: $c_{it} \leq s_{iy}$
2 Minimum call price: $c_{it} \geq \max\ [0,\ (s_{it} - e_{it})]$

The symbol c_{it} denotes the market price of the ith call option on a common stock at the tth instant in time, s_{it} represents the market price at time t of the common stock which may be called by the ith option, and e_i is the exercise price of the ith call (which never changes throughout the call's life). The two call price boundaries should never be violated or riskless profits may be earned by arbitrage.

Professors Fischer Black and Myron Scholes first derived an explicit option valuation theory which lies within Samuelson's boundaries.[2] Then Professor Robert Merton refined the Black-Scholes derivation.[3] The resulting Black-Scholes-Merton (BSM) call valuation model is shown below as Eq. (A13-1):

$$c_{it} = [s_{it}][N(s_{it})] - [e_{it}][\mathrm{antiln}(-i_t d_{it})][N(y_{it})] \qquad \text{(A13-1)}$$

where i_t is the market interest rate per annum on commercial paper on day t; $N(x)$ is a cumulative normal density function of the argument x; x_{it} and y_{it} are defined in Eqs. (A13-2) and (A13-3), respectively; and d_{it} is the duration of the ith call at time t measured as a fraction of one year (for example, $d = .5$ for a call with 180 days life remaining).

$$x_{it} = \left[\frac{\ln(s_{it}/e_i) + (i_t + .5\ \mathrm{var}_i)(d_{it})}{(\mathrm{var}_i)^{1/2}(d_{it})^{1/2}}\right] \qquad \text{(A13-2)}$$

$$y_{it} = x_{it} - [(\mathrm{var}_i)^{1/2}(d_{it})^{1/2}] \qquad \text{(A13-3)}$$

The symbol var_i in Eqs. (A13-2) and (A13-3) is a risk surrogate which measures the variance of the ith optioned stock's rate of stock price change,

[1] Paul A. Samuelson, "Rational Theory of Warrant Pricing," *Industrial Management Review,* Spring 1965, pp. 13–31.
[2] Fischer Black and Myron Scholes, "The Pricing of Options and Corporate Liabilities," *Journal of Political Economy,* June 1973, pp. 637–654.
[3] Robert C. Merton, "The Theory of Rational Option Pricing," *Bell Journal of Economics and Management Science,* Spring 1973, pp. 141–183.

$\text{var}(s_{it}/s_{i,t-1})$, using annualized differencing intervals to calculate the rates of change.[4]

Figure 13-9 is a two-dimensional graph of Samuelson's rational call pricing boundaries. The BSM valuation model is represented by the curves which lie between the maximum value line and the minimum value line (labeled MVW). Figure 13-9 is applicable to both call options and warrants since warrants are essentially call options sold by a corporation on its own stock.[5]

To show an illustrative numerical example of how to use the BSM call valuation model the following data are used: $s_{it} = \$60.00$, $e_{it} = \$50.00$, $d_{it} = .333$ (which represents 120 days out of a 360-day year), $i_t = .07$ (which represents 7 percent per annum), and $\text{var}(s_{it}/s_{i,t-1}) = .144$. The quantity x_{it} is evaluated below:

$$x_{it} = \frac{\ln\frac{60}{50} + [.07 - .5(.144)(.333)]}{\sqrt{.144}\ \sqrt{.333}}$$

$$= \frac{.182 + .0700 - .0239}{(.379)(.577)} = \frac{.228}{.218} = 1.048$$

The quantity y_{it} is evaluated next:

$$y_{it} = x_{it} - (\sqrt{.144}\ \sqrt{.333}) = 1.048 - .218 = .830$$

Substituting the values from above into Eq. (A13-1) yields the figures below:

$$c_{it} = (\$60.00)[N(1.048)] - (\$50.00)\{\text{antiln}[(-.070)(.333)]\}[N(.830)]$$

Looking up the values of the antilog for natural logs and the cumulative normal distribution in tables and completing the calculations yields the results below:

$$c_{it} = (\$60.00)(.851) - (\$50.00)(.9769)(.800)$$
$$= \$51.060 - 39.076 = \$11.98$$

The calculations indicate the ith call option's intrinsic value is $11.98 according to the BSM model. Empirical experience suggests that the ith call's price will be near the value indicated by the BSM model.

---

[4] The variables i_t, d_{it}, and var_i may be stated at annual rates, weekly rates, or any other rate as long as they are consistent.

[5] Warrants differ from calls because (1) they increase the total number of shares outstanding when exercised; (2) when warrants are exercised, earnings per share are diluted; and (3) there are differences in other minor respects.

Fourteen

Commodities Trading

Commodity futures contracts are marketable investment securities that are, in some ways, similar to common stocks.[1] A commodity futures contract is an equity claim to bushels of corn or some other commodity just as a share of stock is an equity claim on some corporation's physical assets. Futures contracts are marketable securities traded every day, and they have their own secondary markets where their market prices fluctuate minute by minute. Thus, commodity futures contracts are securities which portfolio managers may wish to consider. The opportunities to diversify across stocks, bonds, options, and futures contracts are too rich to ignore.

14-1 COMMODITIES TRADING

Commodities include farm products such as cotton, hogs, and their derivatives, like cottonseed oil and hog bellies (that is, unsliced bacon). Other homogeneous raw materials, such as platinum, silver, copper, and lead, are also actively traded commodities. Commodity supplies are subject to all such capricious acts of nature as fire, flood, disease, insects, and drought, plus various unpredictable governmental acts like import-export quotas, subsidies, and foreign exchange revaluations. In contrast to erratic supply, the demand for most commodities is fairly steady. Farm products are traded in fairly perfect markets where there are many small sellers (namely, farmers) and many buyers, none of whom is large enough to affect prices. As a

[1] C. V. Harlow and R. J. Tewles, "Commodities and Securities Compared," *Financial Analysts Journal,* September–October 1972, pp. 64–70.

TABLE 14-1 COMMODITY FUTURES CONTRACTS AND COMMODITY EXCHANGE FACTS (SUBJECT TO CHANGE)

Commodity	Name of exchange (trading hours, Mon. through Fri.)	Contract unit	Minimum fluctuation Per lb, etc.	Per contract	Round turn commission (domestic nonmember)
Beef cattle, (live)	Chicago Mercantile Exchange 10:05 A.M.–1:40 P.M.	25,000 lb	$\frac{2.5}{100}$ ¢	$ 6.25	$25
Choice steers	Chicago Board of Trade 10:10 A.M.–2:00 P.M.	27,600 lb	$\frac{2.5}{100}$ ¢	$ 6.90	$25
Cocoa	New York Cocoa Exchange 10:00 A.M.–3:00 P.M.	30,000 lb	$\frac{1}{100}$ ¢	$ 3	$50 when price is 15¢ to 24.99¢ $60 when price is 25¢ to 34.99¢ $70 when price is 35¢ and above
Coffee (B contract)	N.Y. Coffee & Sugar Exchange 10:30 A.M.–2:50 P.M.	32,500 lb (250 bags)	$\frac{1}{100}$ ¢	$ 3.25	$50 when price is 30¢ to 39.99¢ $60 when price is 40¢ to 49.99¢ $70 when price is 50¢ to 74.99¢ $80 when price is 75¢ and above
Copper	Commodity Exchange, Inc. 10:00 A.M.–2:10 P.M.	50,000 lb	$\frac{1}{100}$ ¢	$ 5	$50 plus $.50 exchange fee
Cotton, #1, #2	New York Cotton Exchange 10:30 A.M.–3:30 P.M.	(100 bales) 50,000 lb	$\frac{1}{100}$ ¢	$ 5	$45 when price is 40¢ or under Add $5 for every 5¢ rise thereafter
Cottonseed oil	N.Y. Produce Exchange 10:20 A.M.–2:30 P.M.	60,000 lb		$ 6	$30 when price is 15¢ or under $33 when price is 15.01¢ to 20¢ $36 when price is over 20¢
Eggs	Chicago Mercantile Exchange 10:15 A.M.–1:45 P.M.	Shell: 18,000 doz. Frozen: 36,000 lb	$\frac{5}{100}$ ¢ $\frac{2.5}{100}$ ¢	$ 9 $ 9	$36

Grain: Chicago (wheat, corn, oats, rye, soybeans)	Chicago Board of Trade 10:30 A.M.–2:15 P.M.	5,000 bu	$\frac{1}{8}$ ¢	$ 6.25	5,000 bushels:
					  Oats: $18
					  Wheat, corn, and rye: $22
					  Soybeans: $24

Commodity	Exchange and hours	Contract size	Minimum fluctuation	Commission	Margin/fee
Grain: Minneapolis (wheat, rye, oats, flaxseed)	Minneapolis Grain Exchange 10:30 A.M.–2:15 P.M.	5,000 bu	$\frac{1}{8}$ ¢	$ 6.25	$22 for all grains except oats ($18)
Grain: Kansas City (wheat, corn)	Kansas City Board of Trade 10:30 A.M.–2:15 P.M.	5,000 bu	$\frac{1}{8}$ ¢	$ 6.25	$22
Hides	Commodity Exchange, Inc. 10:10 A.M.–2:00 P.M.	40,000 lb	$\frac{1}{100}$ ¢	$ 4	$40 plus $.50 exchange fee
Hogs, live	Chicago Mercantile Exchange 10:15 A.M.–1:45 P.M.	20,000 lb	$\frac{2.5}{100}$ ¢	$ 5	$20
Lead	Commodity Exchange, Inc. 10:30 A.M.–2:35 P.M.	60,000 lb	$\frac{1}{100}$ ¢	$ 6	$50 plus $.50 exchange fee
Mercury	Commodity Exchange, Inc. 9:50 A.M.–2:30 P.M.	10 flasks	$1 per flask	$10	$40 plus $.50 exchange fee
Orange juice concentrate	New York Cotton Exchange 10:15 A.M.–3:00 P.M.	15,000 lb	$\frac{5}{100}$ ¢	$ 7.50	$45
Palladium	N.Y. Mercantile Exchange 10:20 A.M.–1:00 P.M.	100 oz	5¢	$ 5	$40 when price is $59.95 or under $50 when price is $60 or over
Platinum	N.Y. Mercantile Exchange 9:45 A.M.–1:15 P.M.	50 oz	10¢	$ 5	$40 when price is $149 or under $50 when price is $150 or over
Pork bellies, frozen	Chicago Mercantile Exchange 10:25 A.M.–2:00 P.M.	30,000 lb	$\frac{2.5}{100}$ ¢	$ 7.50	$36
Potatoes, Maine	N.Y. Mercantile Exchange 10:00 A.M.–1:30 P.M.	50,000 lb	1¢ per hundred lb	$ 5	$23 + $2 clearance fee
Rubber	Commodity Exchange, Inc. 10:05 A.M.–2:55 P.M.	22,400 lb	$\frac{1}{100}$ ¢	$ 2.24	$40 plus $.50 exchange fee
Silver	Commodity Exchange, Inc. 10:15 A.M.–1:30 P.M.	10,000 ozs	$\frac{10}{100}$ ¢	$10	$40 plus $.50 exchange fee

TABLE 14-1 (Continued)

Commodity	Name of exchange (trading hours, Mon. through Fri.)	Contract unit	Minimum fluctuation Per lb, etc.	Per contract	Round turn commission (domestic nonmember)
Soybean meal	Chicago Board of Trade 10:30 A.M.–2:15 P.M.	100 tons	5¢ per ton	$ 5	$30
Soybean oil	Chicago Board of Trade 10:30 A.M.–2:15 P.M.	60,000 lb	$\frac{1}{100}$ ¢	$ 6	$30
Sugar #8, raw (world)	New York Coffee & Sugar Exchange 10:00 A.M.–3:00 P.M.	50 tons (112,000 lb)	$\frac{1}{100}$ ¢	$11.20	$30 when price is under 3¢ Add $5 with each 2¢ increase to 14.99¢; $65 when 15¢ and over
Sugar #10, raw (domestic)	New York Coffee & Sugar Exchange 10:00 A.M.–2.55 P.M.	50 tons (112,000 lb)	$\frac{1}{100}$ ¢	$11.20	$20 when price is under 2¢ Add $5 with each 2¢ increase to 15.99¢; $60 when 16¢ and over
Tin	Commodity Exchange, Inc. 10:20 A.M.–2:45 P.M.	5 long tons	$\frac{5}{100}$ ¢	$ 5.60	$50 plus $.50 exchange fee
Wool, grease	Wool Associates of the N.Y. Cotton Exchange 10:00 A.M.–2:45 P.M.	6,000 lb	$\frac{1}{10}$ ¢	$ 6	$50
Wool tops	Wool Associates of the N.Y. Cotton Exchange 10:00 A.M.–2:45 P.M.	5,000 lb	$\frac{1}{10}$ ¢	$ 5	$50
Zinc	Commodity Exchange, Inc. 10:25 A.M.–1:40 P.M.	60,000 lb	$\frac{1}{100}$ ¢	$ 6	$50 plus $.50 exchange fee

Note: Most commodities have special rates for straddles and day trades.
Source: Gerald Gold, Modern Commodity Futures Trading (New York: Commodity Research Bureau, 1968), pp. 247–249.

result, commodity prices are largely determined by changes in supply and various government actions.

Commodities are traded in cash markets and futures markets. Some cash markets are physically separate and organizationally independent from futures markets. The actual commodities may or may not be present at the commodity exchanges where futures contracts are traded. There is no particular reason for physical commodities to be present where futures contracts are traded, because the contracts do not apply to any specific batch of the commodity covered by the contract. But commodities are physically present at the cash markets or physical markets for commodities. Grain elevators and stockyards where farmers deliver and sell their products for cash are examples of *cash markets.*

Since the supply of commodities is erratic (for example, most harvests come only once per season), some commodities must be stored for future delivery. Contracts to deliver stocks of stored commodities are called commodity *futures contracts,* or simply *futures.* Actually, only contracts which will not fall due for delivery in the current month are called futures contracts. Futures contracts that are near expiration and ready for the commodity to be delivered are called *spot contracts* instead of futures. Both spot and futures contracts are traded on commodity exchanges. Table 14-1 lists the major commodity exchanges in the United States and the commodity futures that are traded at each. The Chicago Board of Trade, now more than a century old, is the largest and oldest commodity exchange in the United States.

Figure 14-1 shows a floor plan of a trading room found in a commodity exchange. There are usually several trading rooms at an exchange, and only the exchange members may enter them. Trading actually occurs in the *trading ring* or *trading pit,* shown in Fig. 14-1. Exchange members who want to buy or sell futures in some commodity go to the appropriate trading room, step into the trading pit, and indicate (by gestures and/or shouting)

FIG. 14-1 Trading floor of a commodity exchange.

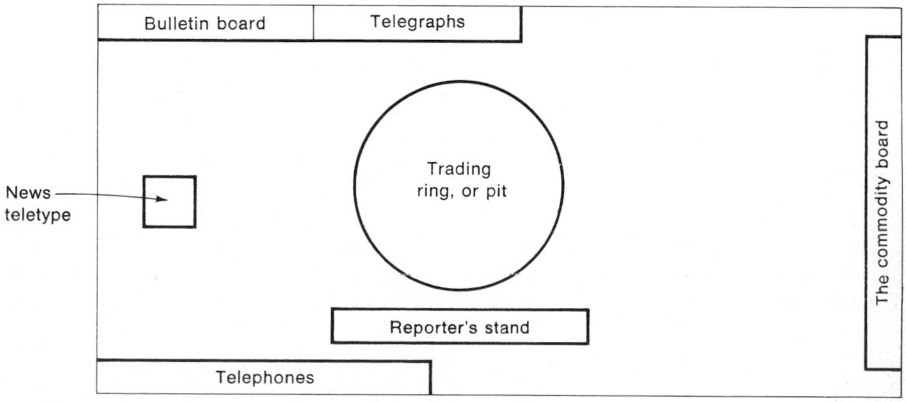

their intention to transact business. This is how commodity buyers and sellers get together to consummate a futures contract. When the buyer and the seller settle on the contract terms, news of the latest price is immediately posted to the board on the trading room wall and also sent out by teletype to the board rooms of brokerage houses around the country.

Floor brokers are self-employed members of the commodity exchange who transact most of the trading. For a commission, they buy and sell futures for their customers. Orders to buy and sell come into the exchange by phone calls and/or telegraph messages to the floor brokers from their customers. The floor brokers step into the appropriate pit, execute the trade, and then notify their customers.

Futures Contracts

The phrase "commodity exchange" can be misleading, because the commodities themselves are not necessarily traded at commodity exchanges. (Some exchanges also have cash markets in some commodities, however.) It is the commodity futures contracts that are actively traded at the exchanges. Futures contracts are standardized, preprinted forms. A different form exists for each commodity which specifies the standard trading unit for the commodity in pounds, bushels, or whatever unit is appropriate; what grade of commodity is to be delivered; where the commodity is to be delivered; and what penalties will be imposed if the delivery is made at another place or in another grade. When a futures contract is signed, the buyer and the seller merely fill in blanks on the contract specifying their names, the date, the price, and the month in which delivery is to be made. Figure 14-2 shows a blank futures contract.

The Commodity Board

For any given commodity there are several delivery months which may be specified in the futures contract. The price of the futures in any given commodity varies with the month in which the commodity is to be delivered. Thus, March #2 soft red winter wheat deliverable at Chicago has a different price per bushel from the price of the same type wheat delivered at the same place in May. As a result, commodity futures prices are listed on a commodity board like the one shown in Table 14-2.

TABLE 14-2 COMMODITY BOARD FOR CHICAGO WHEAT

High and low	190–151	199–170	191–166	179–159	184–160
Trading months	December	March	May	July	September
Previous close	170	$177\frac{1}{8}$	179	155	$163\frac{3}{8}$
Opening today	$171\frac{1}{2}$	177	$178\frac{7}{8}$	153	162
Today's high	171	179	179	153	162
Today's low	$168\frac{5}{8}$	$177\frac{1}{4}$	177	$150\frac{1}{2}$	161
Ticker	169	179	178	150	$161\frac{1}{8}$

CONTRACT "B" (new)
(BRAZIL COFFEE CONTRACT)
(Variable Differentials)
New York _____ 19 _____

_____ (has) this day (sold)
(have) (bought)

and agreed to (deliver to) _____
(receive from)

32,500 lbs. (in about 250 bags) of Brazilian COFFEE shipped through the ports of Santos, Paranagua, Angra dos Reis or Rio de Janeiro, grading from No. 2 to No. 6 inclusive, provide the average grade shall not be above No. 3, nor below No. 5. Nothing in this contract, however, shall be construed as prohibiting a delivery averaging above No. 3 at the premium for No. 3 grade. No premium shall be allowed for Softish Coffee grading above No. 4.

At the price of _____ cents per pound for Santos No. 4, Strictly Soft, Fair to Good Roast, Solid Bean with additions or deductions for grades, ports of shipment and description (quality) according to the differentials established or to be established by the Committee on Coffee of the New York Coffee and Sugar Exchange for the delivery month specified below in accordance with Section 88(8) (a) of the By-Laws of said Exchange. The delivery must consist of Coffee from one port only.

The Coffee to be Fair to Good Roast, Solid Bean, and the description (quality) to be Strictly Soft, Soft, or Softish. No delivery permitted of Hard Coffee.

Deliverable from licensed warehouse in the Port of New York between the first and last days of _____ inclusive, the delivery within such time to be at the seller's option upon either five, six or seven days' notice to the buyer as prescribed by the Trade Rules.

Either party may call for margin as the variations of the market for like deliveries may warrant, which margin shall be kept good.

This contract is made in view of, and is in all respects subject to, the By-Laws, Rules and Regulations of the New York Coffee and Sugar Exchange, Inc.

_____

(Across the face is the following):   *(Brokers)*

For and in consideration of One Dollar to _____
in hand paid, receipt whereof is hereby acknowledged, _____
accept this contract with all its obligations and conditions.

FIG. 14-2 Futures contract for coffee.

The top line of the commodity board gives the highest and lowest prices at which that particular commodity has ever been traded since the crop was harvested. All prices are in cents per bushel for this particular commodity. The second line of the board lists the active trading months. It will be noted that Chicago wheat futures, like most futures, are not available for delivery in every month. The *active trading months* for futures are determined by the commodity exchange. The third line of the board gives the closing price of the commodity on the last day the exchange was open for business. The bottom four lines of the board give the current day's opening price, the highest price attained so far that day, the lowest price for the day, and the current price for the commodity, in each of its active trading months. The board is kept current by clerks employed by the exchange. The current prices are also wired to the board rooms of brokerage houses around the country.

Price Fluctuations

Commodity futures prices have both minimum and maximum price limit fluctuations imposed on them by the commodity exchanges. The fourth column of Table 14-1 lists the minimum price fluctuations on the major commodities. Bids must be larger than the price of the last transaction, and asked prices must be less than the price of the last transaction by at least the amount of the minimum fluctuation limit. Otherwise, the exchange will not accept the new bid or asked price. The minimum price limit fluctuations are designed to prevent effort wasted in haggling over insignificant differences. However, offers to buy or sell at the old price are always accepted — although, of course, they may not result in trades.

Table 14-3 lists the maximum price fluctuations permitted on most commodities. The purpose of these maximum limits is to stop hysterical trading which might result if destabilizing price manipulators somehow generated large price changes. Thus, if a commodity's price rises the day's limit all trading is stopped in that commodity for the remainder of the day, unless its price falls. The next day, trading resumes at the previous day's high price but still cannot rise more than the daily maximum or trading will be halted again. Actually, however, the maximum price fluctuation limits seldom halt trading in any commodity.

The Clearing House

In addition to the buyer and the seller, there is a third party to every futures contract, the *clearing house,* which guarantees that every futures contract will be fulfilled even if one of the parties defaults. Every commodity exchange has a clearing house.

For a small fee, the clearing house agrees to act as buyer if the buyer defaults or as seller if the seller defaults. The clearing house performs an insurance function. It saves part of the fees it collects for insuring futures contracts in a guarantee fund. When one of the parties to a futures contract defaults, the clearing house pays whatever costs are necessary to carry out the contract from this fund. This provision frees futures traders from checking one another's credit every time they sign a contract and makes the futures contract a freely negotiable security.

The clearing house also facilitates secondary trading of futures contracts before they expire and the commodity is delivered. If the original buyer of a future sells the contract and if the second buyers resells the contract to a third buyer, the clearing house keeps track of the current owner of the contract. Then, when the time comes to deliver on the contract, the clearing house arranges for the original seller of the contract to make delivery to the last buyer of the contract. In practice, the clearing house actually splits the futures contract into two separate contracts and substitutes its name into both. That is, the clearing house becomes the seller from which all buyers obtain delivery and the buyer to whom all sellers make

TABLE 14-3 DAILY TRADING LIMITS (SUBJECT TO CHANGE)

Commodity	Limit above or below previous close	Permitted range between day's high and low
Barley	10¢ per bushel	20¢ per bushel
Beef cattle (live) and choice steers	1½¢ per lb	3¢ per lb
Cocoa	1¢ per lb[a]	2¢ per lb[a]
Copper	2¢ per lb[a]	4¢ per lb
Corn	10¢ per bushel	20¢ per bushel
Cotton #2	2¢ per lb[b]	2¢ per lb[b]
Cottonseed oil	1¢ per lb[a]	1¢ per lb[a]
Eggs (Chicago)	2¢ per doz.	4¢ per doz.
Eggs, frozen (Chicago)	1½¢ per lb	3¢ per lb
Fishmeal	$1 per ton	$5 per ton
Flaxseed and rapeseed (WPG)	15¢ per bushel	30¢ per bushel
Hides	2¢ per lb[a]	4¢ per lb[a]
Hogs, live	1½¢ per lb	3¢ per lb
Lead	1½¢ per lb[a]	3¢ per lb[a]
Mercury	$50 per flask[a]	$100 per flask[a]
Oats (U.S.)	6¢ per bushel	12¢ per bushel
Oats (Winnipeg)	8¢ per bushel	16¢ per bushel
Orange juice, concentrate	3¢ per lb[c]	3¢ per lb[c]
Palladium	$5 per 100 oz[d]	$10 per 100 oz[d]
Platinum	$10 per 50 oz[d]	$10 per 50 oz[d]
Potatoes (New York)	35¢ per bag[e]	70¢ per bag[f]
Pork bellies, frozen	1½¢ per lb	3¢ per lb
Propane	¼¢ per gallon[d]	½¢ per gallon[d]
Rubber	2¢ per lb[a]	2¢ per lb[a]
Rye (U.S.)	10¢ per bushel	20¢ per bushel
Rye (Winnipeg)	10¢ per bushel	20¢ per bushel
Silver	20¢ per ounce[a]	20¢ per ounce[a]
Soybeans (US.)	20¢ per bushel	40¢ per bushel
Soybean meal (Chicago)	$10 per ton[a]	$20 per ton[a]
Soybean oil (Chicago)	1¢ per lb[a]	2¢ per lb[a]
Sugar (domestic andworld)	½¢ per lb[d]	1¢ per lb
Sugar (domestic andworld)	½¢ per lb[d]	1¢ per lb[d]
Tin	8¢ per lb[a]	16¢ per lb[a]
Wheat (Chicago, Minn., K.C.)	10¢ per bushel	40¢ per bushel
Wool, tops and grease	10¢ per lb[c]	10¢ per lb[c]
Zinc	1¢ per lb[a]	2¢ per lb[a]

[a] Limit is removed from spot month on first notice day.

[b] Limit is removed from spot month on first day of delivery month.

[c] Limit is removed from spot month on eight day of delivery month.

[d] Limit is removed from spot month on last trading day.

[e] Limit for spot month becomes 50 cents on first day of delivery month. No limit on last trading day.

[f] Maximum range for spot month becomes $1.00 on first day of delivery month. No limit on last trading day.

Source: Gerald Gold, *Modern Commodity Futures Trading* (New York: Commodity Research Bureau, 1968), p. 250.

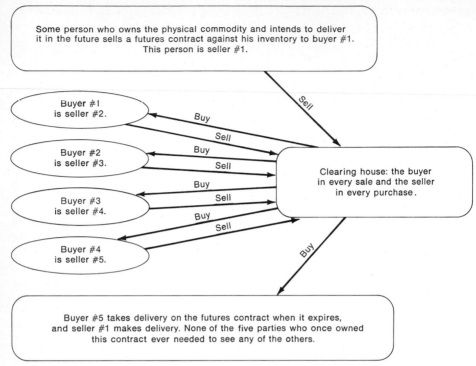

FIG. 14-3 Flow chart of a series of trades of one futures contract.

delivery. Thus, when several subsequent buyers are involved in a given futures contract, these various buyers and sellers never know one another's names. The clearing house keeps track of these details and deals directly with each buyer and seller separately, as shown in Fig. 14-3.

The Mechanics of Trading Commodity Futures

Futures traders need not be involved in a business utilizing the commodities they trade; they need not ever see the commodities; and, in fact, they need not even know what the stuff looks like. Commodity traders usually start by opening a trading account with a brokerage house which deals in commodities. This broker will have a seat on a commodity exchange where his or her agent trades futures contracts, or the broker will make arrangements with a floor trader who is a member of an exchange to carry out the trades.

Commodities are traded only in standardized units. For example, on the Chicago Board of Trade 100 tons is one unit or one contract of soybean meal, a wheat contract is for 5,000 bushels, and a unit of lard is 40,000 pounds. Table 14-1 shows the standard contract units for every major commodity in its third column. To sell a futures contract, the trader notifies his or her broker. The broker obtains all the needed details about whether the customer wants to sell futures (to take a short position) or buy futures (to go long); what the current prices, margin requirements, the relevant unit, and the total costs are; and in what trading months futures may be bought and sold.

The broker prepares the order and transmits it to the commodity exchange. For example, if the customer wanted to go short 200 tons of soybean meal until November, the broker could notify the floor trader at the soybean trading room of the Chicago Board of Trade to "sell two November soybean meals." This message would be transmitted by telephone or direct wire to the floor trader. This floor trader would probably execute the order and send word back to the broker that the transaction had been consummated — all within a few minutes. At that time the customer would be required to pay the 5 to 10 percent margin requirement. In November, when the soybean meal was due to be delivered, the broker's short-selling customer could either buy back the contract in the spot market or buy soybean meal in the cash markets and deliver it to fulfill the contract. If the short seller defaulted on the contract, the clearing house would carry out the contracted delivery of 200 tons of soybean meal as scheduled and initiate a lawsuit against the defaulted short seller.

One-Period Futures Returns and Margins

The one-period rate of return from purchasing a futures contract in period t and selling it in period $t + 1$ is defined in Eq. (14-1). Essentially, the rate of return is the rate of price fluctuation. The price of the futures contract in period t is denoted p_t.

$$r_t = \frac{p_{t+1} - p_t - \text{commissions}}{p_t} \tag{14-1}$$

$$= \frac{\text{net income or loss}}{\text{invested capital (without margin trading)}}$$

Speculators buy and sell futures contracts in the hope of profiting from price changes. They usually never hold a futures contract long enough for the delivery date to arrive. Instead, they trade contracts actively and only make small down payments, called the *margin,* to bind their purchase or sales agreements. Margin requirements are set and enforced by the commodity exchanges to control pyramiding of debt which could cause a market crash. Most commodity exchanges require purchasers of futures or short sellers to put up margin money to guarantee that they perform as contracted. Initial margin requirements of 5 and 10 percent (much lower than the common stock margin requirements set by the Federal Reserve) are common. The initial margin down payment is sufficient to guarantee performance by the speculator unless the margined commodity's price falls by more than the initial margin on a buy-and-hold position (or rises by more than the initial margin on a short position). Then the trader receives a *margin call* to put up the maintenance margin.

Maintenance margin or variation margin requirements are additional amounts of guarantee money that margin traders may be required to pay to their brokerage to ensure their performance of the futures contract if the price of the commodity fluctuates adversely. For example, if a speculator buys a futures contract long on 5 percent initial margin and then the commodity's price falls 5 percent, the speculator's original margin is wiped out. In this case the broker will ask the speculator to put up some maintenance margin money; if he or she does not do so, the broker will liquidate the futures contract being held as collateral on the 95 percent loan granted the speculator to buy the contract. This threat of a *margin call* by the broker will force the speculator to "mark to the market," as it is called in the trade.

The use of margins increases the trader's financial leverage and risk. Equation (14-1) is rewritten as (14-1a) to show mr_t, the one-period rate of return to a margined buyer of a long position when the initial margin is the fraction m of the purchase price.

$$mr_t = \frac{p_{t+1} - p_t - \text{commissions} - \text{interest}}{(p_t)(m_t)} \qquad \text{(14-1a)}$$

The variability of return, or risk, in margin trading increases, as shown by Eq. (14-2). The r_t term was defined in Eq. (14-1).

$$\text{var}(mr_t) = \left(\frac{1}{m_t}\right)^2 \text{var}(r_t) \qquad \text{(14-2)}$$

Equation (14-2) shows that trading on $(m = .1 =)$ 10 percent margin increases the margined trader's variance of returns $[(1/m)^2 = (1/.1)^2 =]$ 100 times. Clearly, margin trading can be breath-taking.

Normal and Inverted Markets

For any given commodity on a given day, the futures price is normally higher than the spot price. The excess of future price over spot price is called the *premium* or *basis*. In *normal markets*, the premium is just sufficient to cover storage, inspection, insurance, and the other carrying charges incurred while holding a commodity for future delivery. This premium is necessary to compensate speculators for buying commodities when their cash prices are low (for example, at harvest time) so that they will store them until their prices are bid higher, at which time they will sell the commodity to fill the excess demand. Such storage by speculators provides a supply of commodities all year long, although the entire crop in the commodity may be harvested in one month of the year. It is so common for futures prices to exceed spot prices by the amount of carrying charges in commodity markets that this situation is frequently called a *normal carrying charge market.*

More generally, the difference between futures and spot prices on the same commodity at a given moment is called the *basis.* If futures exceed spot prices, this situation is called a positive basis or a premium. But a negative basis, or *discount situation,* can also occur.

Occasionally the market in some commodity becomes inverted. In an *inverted market* the futures price is less than the spot price. This excess of spot over future prices is called a *discount.* Futures can sell at a discount to spot, for example, when the current supply of a commodity is short, keeping cash and spot prices high, but when the currently growing crop is expected to yield a large harvest so future supplies will be plentiful and future prices low.

Hedging

People who wish to avoid the risk that future prices may move in a direction that will cause them to lose money may do so by hedging. That is, hedgers cover themselves so they are not later forced to make a disadvantageous purchase or sale. Hedging is not an activity which is designed to maximize profits. In fact, hedging results in less than maximum profits; this is the cost of averting a possible loss. *Hedging* may be defined as arranging (namely, synchronizing) a requirement to coincide with its fulfillment. There are basically three types of hedges—a perfect hedge, a buying hedge, and a selling hedge.

Perfect hedge. Someone who owns identical long and short positions is perfectly hedged. The owner of a perfectly hedged position has contracted to buy and to sell the same goods at the same price at the same time. Thus, future price fluctuations cannot affect holders of a perfect hedge. They are contractually bound to a zero profit and zero loss situation. For example, before July 197X if a silverware manufacturer owned a futures contract to take delivery on 10,000 ounces (one contract) of silver in July 197X, and also was obligated by another futures contract to sell 10,000 ounces of silver in July 197X, this person is perfectly hedged against changes in the level of silver prices and also is assured of needed supply. In effect, a perfectly hedged position is like having no position or holding cash until such time as the hedge is lifted. Before July 197X, the silverware manufacturer can lift the hedge by taking delivery of the silver needed to produce the firm's product and buying back the July 197X futures contract. If the price level of silver has changed, the profits on one position will be exactly offset by the losses on the other position, so the silverware manufacturer will not suffer or gain from the price change in silver.

Buying hedges. A buying hedge is a purchase of futures to protect against price rises. Cereal manufacturers who buy grain commodities, shoe manufacturers who buy hides, and other commodity users frequently use buying hedges to protect themselves from price fluctuations in these commodities. For example, consider the plight of a manufacturer of breakfast cereals who has contracted to deliver fixed quantities of breakfast cereals to supermarkets at a fixed price every month for a year. If the price of grains rises above the price for which the cereal manufacturer has contracted to sell, the seller could go bankrupt. To be free of this risk, the cereal manufacturer need only buy grain futures providing for delivery of the quantity of grain needed to fill the orders at a cost which allows a profit. The cereal manufacturer has thus hedged away the buying risks and can earn the profit needed by concentrating on manufacturing efficiently. The speculator who sold the futures contract bears all risks of an increase in the price of the grain.

If the price of the commodity falls, the hedged buyer cannot gain from it. The speculator who sold the futures contract captures the profit from a price drop or absorbs the loss from a price rise, whichever the case may be. Thus, commodity markets allow specialization of the risk-taking function. The manufacturers who use commodities may hedge away their commodity risks and concentrate on manufacturing efficiently, and the commodity speculators can concentrate on forecasting commodity prices and specialize in assuming the risks of commodity price fluctuation; thus, they perform an insurance function.

Selling hedge. A selling hedge involves selling futures to avoid losses from possible price declines on an item carried in inventory. Commodity handlers who buy commodities in the cash markets frequently use selling hedges to protect themselves from losses in inventory values. For example, the operator of a grain elevator may own the tons of grain which are stored in the company facility. Now suppose that during the spring the elevator operator hears rumors that a foreign country is dumping grain on the domestic markets. To protect the firm from losses if its inventory falls in value, the elevator operator can sell grain futures against its inventories. By selling grain futures equal in quantity to this inventory at a price which will allow a profit, the grain elevator operator has hedged away the selling risks. The speculator who buys the grain futures will assume the risks of a price drop.

Of course, if the price of the grain rises in the future, the hedged sellers will not profit from the rising value of their inventories. Therefore, a selling hedge removes the possibility of profit from a price rise as well as the possibility of loss from a price fall. There are many risk-averse commodity processors who prefer to earn their income from operations rather than commodity speculation and therefore use selling hedges regularly.

Consider how farmers might sell a growing crop before it is harvested to protect themselves from uncertainty. They commonly use the transaction called a selling hedge as a safeguard against losses if the market value of their crop falls. Unfortunately, hedges also keep the hedged farmer from making a profit if the market value of the crop goes up.

Suppose, for example, a wheat producer can profitably produce at least 20,000 bushels of wheat if, at the time of planting, he is assured of a price of $4.50 per bushel. He expects to harvest his crop in late June, and notices that the present futures price of July wheat is $4.50 per bushel. To assure himself of this price, he decides to sell contracts on wheat of 20,000 bushels. Assume that in June when he harvests and markets his crop, the cash price of wheat has fallen to $4.25 per bushel. Since futures and cash prices converge near the contract expiration date, the futures price will also be near $4.25 per bushel. At the same time that the producer sells his crop in the cash market for $4.25 per bushel, he executes a *buy* order in the futures market for the same price, thus canceling his earlier July contract committing him to delivery in July. He realizes a net gain of 25 cents per bushel on his futures transactions while the cash market value of wheat was 25 cents per bushel less than the price upon which he based his planting plans. Excluding the brokerage commissions, the three transactions (the cash sale and the two futures contracts) have the net result that the farmer receives the $4.50 per bushel he anticipated. This is all summarized in Table 14-4. Note that if the farmer had not hedged his harvest against a price change, he would have lost 25 cents per bushel.

A farmer does not necessarily gain from a *hedged,* as compared with an *unhedged,* position. If the cash price *increases* during the production season, as in the similar example shown in Table 14-5, the farmer is worse off than if he had not hedged. The important point is that the farmer has, within fairly narrow limits, protected himself from *downside* price risk by hedging at the time of planting his crop.

If the farmer had not hedged in the rising market example shown in Table 14-5, he would have made 25 cents per bushel additional profit. On

TABLE 14-4 ADVANTAGEOUS SELLING HEDGE

In cash market		In futures market		Farmer's action
October 1 Expected harvest: Expected price: (at harvest)	20,000 bu $4.50/bu	October 1 Sells: Price:	20,000 bu July futures $4.50/bu	Lays down hedge
July 1 Sells: Price: Loss:	20,000 bu $4.25/bu $ .25/bu	July 1 Buys: Price: Gain:	20,000 bu July futures $4.25/bu $ .25/bu	Lifts hedge

Hedged position: No net gain or loss from expected price of $4.50 per bushel because cash losses equal futures gains.

TABLE 14-5 DISADVANTAGEOUS SELLING HEDGE

In cash market		In futures market		Farmer's action
October 1		October 1		Lays down hedge
Expected harvest	20,000 bu	Sells:	20,000 bu July futures	
Expected price: (at harvest)	$4.50/bu	Price:	$4.50/bu	
July 1		July 1		
Sells	20,000 bu	Buys:	20,000 bu July futures	Lifts hedge
Price:	$4.75/bu	Price:	$4.75/bu	
Gain:	$ .25/bu	Loss:	$ .25/bu	

Hedged position: No net gain or loss from expected price of $4.50 per bushel because cash losses equal futures gains.

20,000 bushels, the possible $5,000 profit was lost because of the disadvantageous hedge.[2]

One Risk-Averter Plus One Speculator Equals One Futures Contract

Between most risk-averting hedged sellers and most risk-averting hedged buyers is a risk-taking speculator. This speculator dislikes risk, too. However, like an insurance company, the professional speculator takes many risks in both buying and selling. If the majority of the speculator's decisions are based on correct forecasts, he or she earns a trading profit over many transactions.

Professional speculators may or may not be members of a commodity exchange. They prepare commodity forecasts and then, on the basis of their forecasts, negotiate to buy futures contracts from hedging sellers. Thus one hedging seller and one speculator can create one futures contract. The professional speculators usually liquidate their long futures positions by selling them to hedging buyers, with the result that one speculator and one hedging buyer can create another futures contract.

The final result is that the hedging buyer and the hedging seller have passed the risks they sought to avoid on to the professional speculator (who is probably perfectly hedged and also earned a profit for being the middle link in the chain). However, if the number of hedging buyers does not exactly equal the number of hedging sellers (and it rarely will), the speculator

[2] The hedging example in Tables 14-4 and 14-5 is simplified. It ignores the basis risks of (1) a larger loss if the basis narrows, (2) an undesirable grade of wheat being delivered, (3) delivery on the future being made at an undesirable location, and (4) July not being a desirable delivery month. For an easy-to-read discussion of these finer points of hedging, see G. Gold, *Modern Commodity Futures* (New York: Commodity Research Bureau, 1968), chaps. 13 and 14. Essentially, these points involve speculating on hedges, a common practice called *trading on the basis.*

is left holding some long or short positions which are unhedged. In such situations, speculators hope that the price forecasts on which they based their decisions are correct. The fact that commodity exchanges have been growing for over a century suggests that, typically, the parties to these arrangements profit from them.

Information for Commodity Speculation

Spot and futures prices are largely determined by supply and demand expectations. Since demand is fairly steady, it is usually not too difficult to forecast. Forecasting commodity supplies is more difficult and requires accurate, up-to-date information. In particular, profitable speculation in commodities requires information about inventories held in storage, current harvests, exports and imports, and any changes in the government's policies which will affect supply. The main sources of commodity information are listed below.

Government reports.   The U.S. Department of Agriculture (USDA) issues periodic crop reports and news bulletins for farm commodities. These reports are released to the public and are quite accurate. The USDA also gathers and publishes information from U.S. embassies abroad about the commodity situation in foreign lands. These foreign agriculture bulletins are typically more accurate than official commodity reports issued by the foreign governments themselves.

Situation reports.   Various magazines discuss the major price-making influences in specific commodities. Two of the many situation reports are *The Poultry and Egg Situation* and *The Wheat Situation.* Situation reports are available for every major commodity; they discuss any issue which might affect prices. Since there are so many factors to consider in commodity speculating, most speculators specialize in contracts for only a few commodities.

Commodity research organizations.   Some research companies publish newsletters, price analyses, supply and demand statistics, and analyses of current news, and even buy and sell recommendations about commodities. The Commodity Research Bureau in New York City is the largest of these services. However, there are many other commodity advisory services (not to mention every commodities broker who is eager to earn a commission).

Newspapers.   *The New York Journal of Commerce* has a section devoted to commodities futures. *The New York Times* and *The Wall Street Journal* publish commodity news, too.

Brokerage houses.   Most brokerage houses which handle commodity trading have commodity research departments which issue free newsletters to customers.

In reading these various sources of information, the commodity speculator should watch particularly for news concerning factors which can influence commodity prices. The major news items which affect these prices are cited in the following paragraphs.

Changes in the U.S. government's agricultural program. Changes in government subsidies, acreage allotments, marketing quotas, export programs, and commodity "loan" programs have a major impact on commodity prices.

International news. International tensions have a strong effect on prices of imported and exported commodities. Currency restrictions, war rumors, or loss of imports can touch off a wave of stockpiling which will send prices skyrocketing.

General business conditions. Commodity prices tend to rise and fall with the general price level.

Agricultural production news. Unusual weather in areas where a commodity is produced can cause changes in the price of the commodity. Planting crop reports should be followed closely for news of changes in the number of acres under cultivation, insect damage, or disease in the crop. And harvest reports should be compared with previous expectations to see if the supply and demand expectations upon which current prices are based were correct.

Successful speculation is based on fast and accurate information processing. After all, prices are determined by buyers' and sellers' expectations. Only by studying the information which shapes these expectations can speculation be profitable in the long run.

Simultaneous Determination of Spot and Futures Prices

Highly perishable commodities (for example, lettuce) have no futures market. On the other hand, most commodities that are traded actively on commodity exchanges may be stored safely. As a result, both their spot and futures prices are affected by both current and future supply and demand conditions; that is, spot and futures prices are determined simultaneously rather than one determining the other.

To see the manner in which spot and futures prices are determined simultaneously, consider a hypothetical example of some commodity which is easily stored, such as coffee, sugar, cocoa, or cotton. Imagine that this year's new crop of, say, coffee is very small. The scarcity could occur for several reasons. Nearly all coffee comes from Latin America. If international trade relations with Latin America become poor because of political tensions; if foreign exchange restrictions were raised by Latin America; if Latin American revolutionaries burned the coffee crop; or if the coffee crop was wiped out by insects, drought, disease, or flood, existing inventories would have to last at least two seasons until the next new crop was available. Current coffee inventories would become more valuable as soon as news arrived that the new crop would not be forthcoming.

The rise in spot prices would decrease current coffee consumption and cause coffee processors to process their supplies more carefully to minimize waste. Speculators would bid up coffee futures prices in order to profit from expected price rises. Coffee futures, as a result, would stay at a premium above the rising spot prices, and higher premiums would provide more margin to pay higher coffee storage expenses. As a result, coffee inventories would receive unusually good care. Some coffee inventories might be moved to better leakproof, fireproof, humidity-controlled storage facilities and would be treated with insect repellent. Thus the current supply would be conserved. Spot and futures prices could rise until consumption was cut back to a level which existing inventories could be expected to meet. Then supply and demand would be equated in both the spot and futures markets, and coffee prices would stabilize at a new, higher level.

The speculators who were first to obtain, interpret, and act upon the news indicating that future commodity supplies would be decreased would earn a speculative profit. By buying both spot and futures contracts before the news spread and prices were bid up, they would obtain inventories of the spot commodity and futures contracts which could later be sold at a profit (after news of the shortage spread and prices were bid up).

14-2 IS COMMODITY SPECULATION HARMFUL?

Speculation is a word which has undesirable connotations to some people who do not understand speculation and who may erroneously identify it with market corners or similar activities. Market corners are socially and economically undesirable. These and other price manipulation schemes use the brute force of centrally controlled wealth to destabilize prices and profit therefrom; such results are clearly not beneficial. In fact, laws have been passed making price manipulation and fraud illegal. On the other hand, the legal forms of speculation discussed here are socially and economically desirable. Consider the costs and benifits to the community which result from speculation.

Speculation May Destabilize Prices

Only one issue has been seriously suggested by economists considering the undesirable effects of futures and options speculation; that is, price destabilization. There is an unresolved academic debate on this point.[3] Some

---

[3] M. Friedman, "In Defense of Destabilizing Speculation," in R. W. Pfouts, *Essays in Economics and Econometrics,* pp. 133–141; W. J. Baumol, "Speculation, Profitability and Stability," *Review of Economics and Statistics,* August 1957; L. G. Telser, "A Theory of Speculation Relating Profitability and Stability," ibid., August 1959, pp. 295–301; W. J. Baumol, "Reply," ibid.; J. L. Stein, "Destabilizing Speculation Can Be Profitable," ibid., August 1961.

Market
price

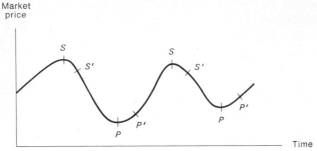

FIG. 14-4 Graph of price fluctuations across time.

economists have argued that profitable speculation in commodities or other investments must stabilize the price of the asset. In essence, this group argues that to earn a profit the speculator must "buy low and sell high" and that this activity will be stabilizing. Purchases made at low prices, such as point P in Fig. 14-4, will tend to drive prices up, and sales at high prices, like point S, will tend to lower prices. The overall effect of such speculation will be to (1) maximize speculators' profits and (2) stabilize prices. It is reasoned that speculators who do not "buy low and sell high" will remain a near-bankrupt, nonpowerful force and that their destabilizing effects will be small.

The second group of economists disagree. They assert that it is possible for speculation to be both profitable and destabilizing at the same time. These economists assert that purchases can be made after prices have started to rise (at points like P' in Fig. 14-4), which accents the price rise. They also point out that sales can be made after prices have started to fall (at points like S' in Fig. 14-4), causing prices to fall faster and perhaps farther. Yet, as long as the purchase price P' is below the sales price S', a speculative profit will result. In this case speculation will be both profitable and destabilizing.

Unnecessarily unstable prices are undesirable because they increase business executives' uncertainty, frustrate planning, discourage long-range investment programs, and cause capital to be allocated to projects which yield only short-run profits with very little risk. The issues involved in this debate are fairly simple. However, no empirical tests have been published to substantiate either claim. The conclusion that can be drawn is that speculation can destabilize prices if the speculator is not adept at maximizing profit (that is, buying at the bottom and selling at peak prices). However, such speculators will probably not become very powerful in the price formation process.

Socially Desirable Effects of Speculation

Several desirable economic benefits result from speculation. For example, society enjoys the following benefits from speculation:

1 Consumption is expeditiously allocated over time.

2 Risks may be hedged away.

3 Free public forecasts are contained in futures prices.

4 Prices adjust efficiently.

5 Resources are allocated efficiently.

6 Liquidity is provided for traders.

7 Arbitrage helps ensure uniform prices.

These points are advantageous in the following ways:

Allocation of consumption over time. Commodities and most investments are items which may be used either now or later. The price at which an item is expected to sell for later, relative to the current price, will largely determine when the item is used. For example, if the premium on some commodity exceeds its carrying costs, it will be profitable to stockpile the commodity for use later.

Speculators prepare the forecasts and conduct the activity which help determine spot and futures prices. Thus, speculators help allocate consumption over time. It is fairly well recognized that futures speculators are necessary to keep farm prices from dropping to near zero at harvest time (that is, during the new-crop month), to store goods for the future, and to sell goods at reasonable prices long after the harvest and during bad years.

Risks hedged away. In the preceding pages, buying hedges and selling hedges were discussed. It was explained how futures contracts are utilized by risk-averters to hedge away risk. Speculators can relieve business executives of their buying and selling risks and leave them free to concentrate on efficient production. Thus, speculation allows separation and specialization of the risk-bearing function, and this expedites efficiency.

Free public forecasts. Speculator's fortunes depend on their ability to forecast. As a result, professional speculators devote considerable time, expense, and effort to forecasting the supply of and demand for commodities and other investments. Such speculators actively search out news. Any new information contains a profit potential if it will affect the price of an asset in which they are prepared to speculate. After the new information becomes public and prices adjust accordingly, the information is worthless to the speculators' efforts to earn a profit. So, in order to maximize their profits, speculators act upon such new information immediately.

Speculators' forecasts and news discoveries enable them to make timely profit-oriented purchases and sales. As a result, the prices of speculative assets reflect the latest information — frequently even before it reaches the public news media. These prices are widely published. Therefore, the general populace may avail itself of a free, up-to-the-minute, expert forecast of the future price of any commodity simply by observing the published prices of futures contracts.

Efficient price adjustment.   Efficient prices may be defined as prices which react immediately and continuously to all relevant information so that prices at every instant fully reflect the latest relevant facts. Efficient prices are characterized by continuous, unpredictable moves. Although seasonal or other trends may be evident in efficient prices, the day-to-day price changes should be random as they adjust to the random arrival of news.

Although unnecessary price movement of the type caused by price manipulation is undesirable, the price movement characterizing efficient markets is valuable. Only if prices reflect all the latest information about supply and demand may resources be allocated in such a manner as to maximize society's welfare. Efficient prices may overreact or underreact to any given piece of information. Nevertheless, it is essential that prices react continuously as they pursue an ever-changing equilibrium price. Efficient prices may be imperfect estimates of equilibrium prices, but they are unbiased estimates which fluctuate around the equilibrium price. Since stable equilibriums with constant prices are impossible in this world of uncertainty, efficient prices are the best that can be hoped for.

Efficient prices are partially the result of profit-maximizing speculators. These persons will uncover the relevant facts about supply and demand and act upon them without delay in an effort to maximize their profits.[4] This action causes continuous, unbiased price adjustments.

Efficient resource allocation.   The supplies of resources which are available in the world at any time are limited. If these resources are not allocated in an optimum manner, the welfare of society cannot attain its full potential. In order for these limited resources to be allocated to the proper place at the proper time, they must be mobile and must react swiftly to changing demands.

In a market economy such as that in the United States, resources tend to go to the highest bidder. Thus, efficient resource allocation requires (1) efficient prices and (2) resources which may be readily shifted between places and time periods. The activities of speculators facilitate these needs by (1) making prices adjust in an efficient manner and (2) making inventories available when and where demand is high.

---

[4] Aggressive forecasting and news prospecting do not necessarily earn a profit for the speculator. These activities are necessary merely to avoid bankruptcy. Only the experts will profit from their forecasts. Empirical research suggesting commodity prices are random has been published. R. A. Stevenson and R. M. Beur, "Commodity Futures: Trends or Random Walks," *Journal of Finance*, March 1970. T. F. Cargill and G. C. Rausser, "Time and Frequency Domain Representations of Futures Prices as a Stochastic Process," *Journal of the American Statistical Association*, March 1972.

Liquidity for traders. The existence of a commodity market provides a place where commodity producers, speculators, and users all can meet and enjoy free entry and exit (perhaps through their brokers) to the market. If the trading activity on the commodity exchange is flourishing, liquidity (of both long and short positions) is increased. This liquidity reduces cash budgeting problems and frees business executives to transact their primary business.

Arbitrage to ensure uniform prices. As explained before, if the prices of a given commodity sold in different markets differ by more than the transportation costs between the two markets, arbitrage will bring the prices together. A speculator can buy the commodity in the market where its price is low and simultaneously sell it where the price is high. This transaction will yield a riskless profit and may be continued until the two prices differ by no more than the transportation costs between the two markets. A uniform price between markets will ensure that a commodity is not in excess supply and being wasted in one place because its price is low while the same commodity is in short supply in another place.

Speculation Is Beneficial

The preceding review of the undesirable and desirable effects of commodity speculation points fairly clearly to the conclusion that speculation is beneficial to the public welfare. The probabilty does exist that prices will occasionally be destabilized by some speculator who *ineptly* tries to maximize profits. However, this seems to be a small cost to pay in comparison with the benefits society derives from speculation. In view of the net benefits that futures markets provide the nation, it is difficult to understand why Congress outlawed futures trading in onions in 1958 and nearly outlawed potato futures a few years after that.

QUESTIONS

1 Compare and contrast selling a futures contract without owning an inventory in the commodity, and selling a common stock short.

2 What functions are performed by the clearing house in a commodity futures contract?

3 Define an inverted market and suggest how it might occur.

4 "Futures prices are determined after spot prices are known. Adding carrying costs to spot prices yields futures prices." Is this statement true, false, or uncertain? Explain.

5 Explain what a selling hedge is and give an example.

6 "Speculation is an evil pastime for wealthy playboys. It destabilizes prices, and misallocates resources, and it should be declared illegal." True, false, or uncertain? Explain.

7 The following data are reported on the commodity prices of wheat futures:

July	$1.49 per bushel
September	1.57
December	$1.69\frac{1}{4}$
March	$1.81\frac{1}{2}$
May	1.88
July	$1.75\frac{7}{8}$
September	1.84

From these data, estimate (*a*) the cost of storing a bushel of wheat per month, and (*b*) the month in which wheat is harvested. Explain how you obtain these estimates.

8 Explain why there are no futures markets for gasoline, coal, raisins, and salt. Does the absence of such markets mean that no speculation in these commodities occurs?

9 If wheat futures were selling at $2 per bushel and some event occurred which changed wheat's new equilibrium price to $2.50 per bushel, what would this do to trading in the relevant wheat future?

SELECTED REFERENCES

Gold, Gerald, *Modern Commodity Futures Trading,* 5th ed. (New York: Commodity Research Bureau, 1968).
> A nonmathematical book that describes in some detail the institutions and procedures of commodities futures markets, hedging, and various practices used by commodity speculators.

Labys, W. C., and C. W. J. Granger, *Speculation, Hedging and Commodity Price Forecasts* (Lexington, Mass.: Heath, Lexington Books, 1970).
> An econometric study of commodity price fluctuations.

Tewles, R. J., C. V. Harlow, and H. L. Stone, *The Commodity Futures Trading Guide* (New York: McGraw-Hill, 1969).
> A nonmathematical textbook that explains various facets of commodity futures trading.

PART FIVE

PORTFOLIO THEORY

CHAPTER 15 EFFICIENT INVESTMENTS AND DIVERSIFICATION explains why and how wealth-seeking, risk-averse investors should diversify. Portfolios, rather than individual securities, are shown to be the objects of choice for rational investors.

CHAPTER 16 CAPITAL MARKET THEORY explicates models for the determination of the prices of risky marketable securities.

CHAPTER 17 DIFFERENT INVESTMENT GOALS rationalizes the coexistence of both daring and timid investors and shows their common, rational grounds by using utility analysis to analyze investment decisions.

CHAPTER 18 MULTIPERIOD WEALTH MAXIMIZATION deals with the problems involved in managing, revising, and updating a portfolio over a period of many years.

CHAPTER 19 PORTFOLIO PERFORMANCE EVALUATION introduces the tools used to evaluate the performance of the managers of investment portfolios; mutual fund data are analyzed.

In Part 5 the focus shifts from individual assets to portfolios of assets. The concepts essential to portfolio management are introduced and analyzed.

Fifteen

Efficient Investments and Diversification

Chapters 7 through 14 explained how to estimate the value of securities in order to tell whether they are over- or underpriced in the market. It is essential to make this estimate before purchasing an investment because an overvalued asset will experience capital losses. Such losses could reduce the investor's rate of return to a level which is not adequate compensation for assuming the accompanying risks. On the other hand, if an undervalued security is found, it will experience unusually large capital gains. These capital gains would tend to raise the investor's return to an unusually high level. Thus, when estimating a security's expected return, some determination must be made as to whether the security's market price equals its intrinsic value. Then, after the security analysts have finished estimating each security's intrinsic value, expected return, and risk statistics, the portfolio management task begins.

In portfolios which are large enough to employ a staff of specialized personnel, the portfolio's manager does not perform the security analysis work explained in Chaps. 7 through 14. The portfolio manager works with the expected return and risk statistics for individual stocks and bonds only in order to develop a diversified portfolio having the maximum rate of return which can be expected at whatever level of risk is deemed appropriate for the portfolio. These risk-return statistics, explained in Chap. 12, should summarize all the security analysts' information about the individual securities, and thus furnish the input information for the portfolio analysis. Chapters 15 through 19 therefore ignore the use of much information about the individual securities being considered for the portfolio and, instead, focus on portfolio analysis and management. As a start, this chapter explains how the portfolio manager should select which assets to buy and how much of each one to buy based only on each assets' risk and expected return statistics.

15-1 DOMINANCE AND EFFICIENT PORTFOLIOS

When a portfolio manager is confronted with the expected return and risk statistics of hundreds of different bonds, stocks, options, mortgages, and whatever other assets that may be in the portfolio, he or she may select the assets worthy of investment by using the dominance principle.

Dominance Principle

The *dominance principle* states that (1) among all investments with any given expected rate of return, the one with the least risk is the most desirable; or (2) among all the assets in a given risk-class, the one with the highest expected rate of return is the most desirable.

Application of the dominance principle to the assets in Table 15-1 reveals that Fairyear Tire and Rubber (*FTR*) is dominated by American Telephone Works (*ATW*) because they both have the same risk ($\sigma = 3$ percent) but *ATW* has a higher expected return than *FTR*. Figure 15-1 shows this graphically. That is, *FTR* can be eliminated from consideration because it is a dominated investment. *ATW* dominates General Auto Corporation (*GAC*); their expected returns are the same, but *ATW* has less risk. So *GAC* is dominated and can be ignored too.

Use of the dominance principle shows *FTR* and *GAC* to be inferior investments. The nondominated assets are Fuzzyworm Tractor Co. (*FTC*), Hotstone Tire Corporation (*HTC*), and *ATW*. Part of the work of investment decision making seems to be done, since the investment choices have been narrowed from five to three.

Efficient Portfolios

Although *HTC* is a nondominated asset, a close examination of Fig. 15-1 shows that its relative risk and return opportunities are somehow not so appealing as those of *ATW* and *FTC*. The reason is that *portfolios* have not been considered.

Suppose a portfolio were constructed of *ATW* and *FTC*. The portfolio's expected return is simply the weighted average of the expected rates of return of the assets in the portfolio. Equation (15-1) defines the expected return for a portfolio, denoted $E(r_p)$, for an n-asset portfolio.

TABLE 15-1 THE RISK AND EXPECTED RETURN OF FIVE ASSETS

Security	Expected return, $E(r)$, %	Risk, σ, %
American Telephone Works (*ATW*)	7	3
General Auto Corporation (*GAC*)	7	4
Fuzzyworm Tractor Co. (*FTC*)	15	15
Fairyear Tire and Rubber Co. (*FTR*)	3	3
Hotstone Tire Corporation (*HTC*)	8	12

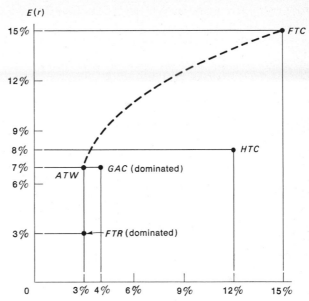

FIG. 15-1 Five assets in risk-return space.

$$E(r_p) = \sum_{i=1}^{n} w_i E(r_i) \tag{15-1}$$

where w_i is the fraction of the total value of the portfolio which is invested in the ith asset (the w_i's are called *weights* or *participation levels*) and $E(r_i)$ denotes the expected rate of return from the ith asset. It is assumed that the weights sum to 1 $\left(\text{that is, } \sum_{i=1}^{n} w_i = 1\right)$, since it is foolish to account for more or less than 100 percent (which is equal to 1.0) of the funds in the portfolio.

To be more specific, suppose that seven-eighths of the portfolio's funds are put into *ATW* and the other one-eighth into *FTC*. In this case $n = 2$; the weight in *ATW* is $w_{ATW} = \frac{7}{8}$; and the weight in *FTC* is $w_{FTC} = \frac{1}{8}$. The computations for this two-asset portfolio's expected return are as shown below.

$$
\begin{aligned}
E(r_p) &= W_{ATW}\ E(r_{ATW}) + W_{FTC}\ E(r_{FTC}) \\
&= \tfrac{7}{8} \quad (7\%) \ + \ \tfrac{1}{8} \quad (15\%) \\
&= .875 \quad (.07) \ + \ .125 \quad (.15) \\
&= .08 = 8\%
\end{aligned}
$$

The two-asset portfolio made of $\frac{1}{8}ATW$ and $\frac{7}{8}FTC$ has the same expected return as *HTC*. The dashed line from *ATW* to *FTC* in Fig. 15-1 represents the risk and return of all possible portfolios which can be formed from various proportions of *ATW* and *FTC*.[1] *HTC* is a dominated asset if portfolios

---

[1] The curvature of the opportunity locus representing portfolios composed of ATW and FTC is due to diversification effects which will be explained later in this chapter.

are considered as possible assets, that is, if the dotted line from *ATW* to *FTC* dominates *HTC*.

It appears that the concept of dominant assets should be extended to include portfolios. Hereafter, dominant assets will be called *efficient portfolios* whether they contain one or many assets. An efficient portfolio, then, is any asset or combination of assets which has:

1 The maximum expected return in its risk-class, or conversely,

2 The minimum risk at its level of expected return.

The objective of portfolio management is to develop efficient portfolios. As the dotted line in Fig. 15-1 shows, there are a number of efficient portfolios. The group of all efficient portfolios will be called the *efficient set* of portfolios, or, simply, the efficient set. The efficient set of portfolios composes the efficient frontier in risk-return space (if borrowing and lending are ignored). The *efficient frontier* is the locus of points in risk-return space having the maximum return at each risk-class.

The efficient frontier dominates all other assets. Consider how different kinds of diversification can be used to reduce a portfolio's risk and improve the efficient frontier from which a rational, risk-averse, wealth-seeking investor will select his or her investments.

15-2 NAIVE DIVERSIFICATION

Naive diversification can be defined as "not putting all the eggs in one basket," or "spreading the risks."

Effects of Naive Diversification

Naive diversification implies that a portfolio made up of 200 different securities is 10 times more diversified than a portfolio make up of only 20 different securities (it will be shown later in this chapter that this is not necessarily true). Naive diversification can usually be expected to reduce the risk of a portfolio somewhat. As the number of securities added to a naively diversified portfolio increases up to 10 or 15, the portfolio's risk will usually decrease toward the systematic level of risk in the market. After the portfolio's assets have been spread across more than 15 randomly selected securities, further decreases in risk usually cannot be attained by buying additional securities.

Several studies have shown that the total risk of most securities, as measured by their variance in rates of return over time, can be divided into two parts of approximately equal size.[2] The exact proportions of systematic

[2] Given the *i*th security's characteristic line, $r_i = a_i + b_i(r_m) + e_i$, the variance of the security's returns can be partitioned as follows:

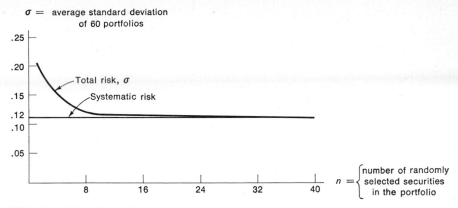

FIG. 15-2 Naive diversification reduces risk to the systematic level in randomly selected portfolios. (From J. H. Evans and S. H. Archer, "Diversification and the Reduction of Dispersion: An Empirical Analysis," *Journal of Finance*, December 1968, pp. 761–767.)

and unsystematic risk vary from security to security and industry to industry, but for a large number of common stocks listed on the New York Stock Exchange (NYSE), systematic risk has been shown to compose about one-quarter of the securities' total risk.

Systematic variability of return	25%
+Unsystematic variability of return	75%
Total variability of return	100% of total risk

Naive diversification will usually decrease the unsystematic portion of total risk toward zero until as many as 15 securities are added to the portfolio, because unsystematic risk is (by definition) uncorrelated with the market. That is, the unsystematic variability in different firms' rates of return are independent with an average value of zero, and therefore they average out to zero when added together into a portfolio. Adding more than 15 securities to a portfolio cannot be expected to reduce its unsystematic risk (or to increase it in most cases either).

Figure 15-2 shows the manner in which naive diversification works. The figure was prepared using empirical data on 470 common stocks from

---

$$\begin{aligned}
\text{var}(r_i) &= \text{var}(a + br_m + e) \\
&= b_i^2 \, \text{var}(r_m) + \text{var}(e) \\
&= \text{systematic risk} + \text{unsystematic risk}
\end{aligned}$$

Here, var(e) is the residual variance, and var(r_i) is the total variance. Independent studies show that systematic risk is typically between one-fourth and one-third of a security's total risk. J. Evans and S. H. Archer, "Diversification and the Reduction of Dispersion: An Empirical Analysis," *Journal of Finance*, December 1968, pp. 761–767. K. H. Johnson and D. S. Shannon have extended the Evans-Archer study in "A Note on Diversification and the Reduction of Dispersion," *Journal of Financial Economics*, December 1974, pp. 365–372.

the NYSE during the period from 1958 to 1967 inclusive. The figure shows that the average standard deviation of returns for all 470 stocks was .21. The level of systematic risk in the market was estimated at .12 (that is, $\sigma_m = 12$ percent).

For preparation of Fig. 15-2, 60 different portfolios of each size were constructed randomly; that is, 60 one-security portfolios, 60 two-security portfolios, 60 three-security portfolios, and so on up to 60 forty-security portfolios were constructed from randomly selected stocks. Then the average standard deviation of returns was calculated for the 60 portfolios of each size. Figure 15-2 shows these average standard deviations at each size of portfolio. From it we can see that, on the average, randomly combining 10 to 15 stocks will reduce the portfolio's risk to the systematic level of variation found in the market average, but spreading the portfolio's assets over twice or three times as many stocks cannot be expected to reduce risk any more.

Diversifying across Industries

Many investment counselors advocate selecting securities from different and unrelated industries to achieve better diversification. It is certainly better to follow this advice than to select all the securities in a portfolio from one industry, but diversifying across industries is not much better than simply selecting securities randomly. Either procedure is naive diversification.

Studies of the rates of return of securities in many industries have shown that nearly all industries are highly correlated with one another. The easiest way to see the meager benefits of diversifying across various industries is to examine the movement of Standard & Poor's indexes for industrial, railroad, and utility stocks. Figure 12-3 shows how these three different indexes move up and down together month after month. This systematic variability of return cannot be naively diversified away merely by selecting securities from different industries.

One study sought to test the effectiveness of diversifying across different industries and also of increasing the number of different assets in the portfolio. Portfolios containing 8, 16, 32, and 128 common stocks, all listed on the NYSE, were formed by two separate techniques. Technique 1 involved simple random selection of assets (for example, with a dart). Technique 2 drew each asset in the portfolio from a different industry. Numerous portfolios were constructed in this study, and statistics were tabulated about the portfolio's rates of return.[3] Table 15-2 presents the findings

---

[3] The study actually investigated wealth relatives, $P_{t+1}/P_t = 1 + r_t$, rather than rates of return. However, the variance of the wealth relatives are the same as the variance of the percentage price change over the same period since $var(1 + r) = var(r)$. See Mathematical Appendix E for proof.

TABLE 15-2 STATISTICS OBTAINED BY USE OF DIFFERENT DIVERSIFICATION TECHNIQUES†

Stocks in portfolio	Technique used to diversify	20th and 80th percentiles (the middle 60%)	Min. wealth relative	Max. wealth relative	Mean wealth relative	Std. dev. of wealth relatives
8	Random	.94 to 1.29	.53	2.64	1.13	.22
	Across industries	.94 to 1.30	.53	2.58	1.13	.22
16	Random	.94 to 1.28	.63	2.21	1.13	.21
	Across industries	.94 to 1.28	.65	2.21	1.13	.21
32	Random	.95 to 1.27	.69	1.98	1.13	.20
	Across industries	.95 to 1.27	.71	1.93	1.13	.20
128	Random	.96 to 1.27	.71	1.76	1.13	.19

Source: L. Fisher and J. Lorie, "Some Studies of Variability of Returns on Investments in Common Stocks," *Journal of Business,* April 1970, p. 112, table 5.
† Wealth relatives equal $p_t/p_{t-1} = 1 + r_t$, but $var(1 + r_t) = var(r_t)$.

of the study. The rates of return were calculated from the twenty 1-year portfolios constructed in each year from 1945 to 1965 inclusive.

The two main conclusions which may be drawn from Table 15-2 are that (1) diversifying across industries is not better than random diversification, and (2) increasing the number of different assets held in the portfolio above eight does not significantly reduce the portfolio's risk. The often-recommended practice of diversifying across industries is evidently just another type of naive diversification.

Superfluous Spreading of Assets Lowers Returns

Naive diversification will ordinarily reduce risk to the systematic level in the market (as indicated by Fig. 15-2). However, portfolio managers should not become overzealous and spread their assets over too many assets. If 10 or 15 different assets are selected for the portfolio, the maximum benefits from naive diversification have most likely been attained. Further spreading of the portfolio's assets is *superfluous diversification* and should be avoided. Superfluous diversification will usually result in the following poor portfolio management practices:

1 *Purchase of lackluster performers.* The search for numerous different assets to buy will ultimately lead to the purchase of investments which will not yield an adequate rate of return for the risk they bear.

2 *Impossibility of good portfolio management.* If the portfolio contains dozens of different securities, the portfolio's management cannot hope to stay informed on the status of all of them simultaneously.

3 *High search costs.* The larger the number of assets to be selected for the portfolio, the more expensive the search for them is.

4 *High transaction costs.* Frequent purchase of small quantities of shares will result in larger broker's commissions than less frequent purchase of larger quantities (especially as the third and fourth markets continue to become more competitive).

Although more money is spent to manage a superfluously diversified portfolio, there will most likely be no concurrent improvement in the portfolio's performance. Thus, superfluous diversification lowers the *net* return to the portfolio's owners. The portfolio should be concentrated in 10 to 15 carefully selected and closely followed securities for better results.

15-3 MARKOWITZ DIVERSIFICATION

Named after its originator, Dr. Harry M. Markowitz,[4] *Markowitz diversification* may be defined as combining assets which are less than perfectly positively correlated[5] in order to reduce portfolio risk without sacrificing any portfolio returns.[6] It can sometimes reduce risk below the systematic level (naive diversification cannot). Markowitz diversification is more analytical than naive diversification and considers assets' correlation (or covariances). The lower the correlation between assets, the more it will be able to lower risk.

Numerical Example

The simplest way to see the benefits of combining securities with low correlations is by numerical example. Consider what happens when two

---

[4] H. Markowitz, "Portfolio Selection," *Journal of Finance*, March 1952, p. 89.
[5] Mathematical Appendix H, in Part 7 defines correlation and discusses it briefly.
[6] There is a trade-off between risk and return in the market. But, at any given level of expected return, Markowitz diversification can reduce risk lower than naive diversification. This reduction in risk need not be accompanied by a reduction in the portfolio's expected rate of return.

TABLE 15-3 NUMERICAL EXAMPLE OF MARKOWITZ DIVERSIFICATION WITH INVERSE CORRELATION

Time period	$t = 1$	$t = 2$	$t = 3$	$t = 4$	var(r)†
Return from X	$r_{x1} = 5\%$	$r_{x2} = 10\%$	$r_{x3} = 15\%$	$r_{x4} = 5\%$	$\sigma_x^2 = .0015$
Return from Y	$r_{y1} = 25\%$	$r_{y2} = 20\%$	$r_{y3} = 15\%$	$r_{y4} = 25\%$	$\sigma_y^2 = .0021$
Return for portfolio of half X and Y	$\dfrac{25 + 5}{2} = 15\%$	$\dfrac{10 + 20}{2} = 15\%$	$\dfrac{15 + 15}{2} = 15\%$	$\dfrac{5 + 25}{2} = 15\%$	$\sigma_p^2 = 0$

† $\text{var}(r_x) = 1/4^4(r_x - .088)^2 = .00612/4 = .00153$
$\text{var}(r_y) = 1/4^4(r_y - .2125)^2 = .0085/4 = 00212$
$\text{var}(r_p) = 1/4^4(r_p - .15)^2 = 0$

assets, denoted X and Y, which have perfectly negatively correlated rates of return, are combined into a portfolio. Table 15-3 shows the results.

The portfolio of half asset X and half Y had zero variability of returns. This complete reduction of risk was due to the perfect negative correlation of the rates of return of X and Y; their returns move inversely.

General Two-Asset Analysis of Markowitz Diversification

Numerical examples represent only specific cases. It is a well-known (but often violated) error in logic to draw general conclusions from specific cases. Therefore, a more general mathematical analysis of Markowitz diversification is needed. Consider the risk and return of a simple two-asset portfolio as the correlation coefficient between the two assets varies. Table 15-4 gives the risk and return of two hypothetical assets denoted A and B.

Formula for portfolio return. For the two-asset portfolio made of A and B, Eq. (15-2) defines the portfolio's expected return.

$$E(r_p) = w_A E(r_A) + w_B E(r_B) \tag{15-2}$$
$$= w_A(5\%) + w_B(15\%)$$
$$= .05w_A + .15w_B \tag{15-2a}$$

The portfolio's return formula is a linear function, since the variables (the weights) in Eq. (15-2) or (15-2a) have exponents of unity.

Risk formula. The risk, as measured by the standard deviation of returns of a portfolio made up of n assets, is defined in Eq. (15-3).

$$\sigma_p = \sqrt{\sum_i^n \sum_j^n w_i w_j \sigma_{ij}} \tag{15-3}$$

$$= \sqrt{w_i^2 \sigma_i^2 + w_j^2 \sigma_j^2 + 2w_i w_j \sigma_{ij}} \quad \text{if } n = 2 \tag{15-3a}$$

In these equations, σ_p denotes the standard deviation of the portfolio's rates of return; $\sigma_i^2 = \sigma_{ii} =$ the variance of returns of the ith asset, that is, the standard deviation squared; and $\sigma_{ij} = \text{cov}(r_i, r_j) =$ the covariance[7] of returns for assets i and j. The covariance is related to the correlation coefficient[8] as shown in Eq. (15-4).

[7] Mathematical Appendix C, in Part 7, explains the covariance.
[8] Mathematical Appendix H explains correlation and the correlation coefficient in more detail.

TABLE 15-4 ASSETS A AND B

Asset	Expected return $E(r)$, %	Risk, %
A	5	20
B	15	40

$$\sigma_{ij} = (\sigma_i)(\sigma_j)(\rho_{ij}) \qquad (15\text{-}4)$$

where ρ_{ij} is the correlation coefficient between variables i and j.

The covariance measures how two variables covary. If two assets move together, their covariance is positive. For example, most common stocks have a positive covariance with each other. If two variables are independent, their covariance is zero. For example, the covariance of the stork population and the human birth rate is zero (despite any stories your grandmother may have told you to the contrary). If two variables move inversely, their covariance is negative.

Equation (15-3) defines a portfolio's risk. For the two-asset portfolio of A and B, Eq. (15-5) gives the standard deviation of returns.[9]

$$\sigma_p = \sqrt{w_A^2 \sigma_A^2 + w_B^2 \sigma_B^2 + 2w_A w_B \sigma_{AB}} \qquad (15\text{-}5)$$

Substituting Eq. (15-4) into (15-5) yields (15-6), which shows exactly how the correlation of assets A and B affects the portfolio's risk.

$$\sigma_p = \sqrt{w_A^2 \sigma_A^2 + w_B^2 \sigma_B^2 + 2w_A w_B \rho_{AB} \sigma_A \sigma_B} \qquad (15\text{-}6)$$

$$= \sqrt{w_A^2 (20\%)^2 + w_B^2 (40\%)^2 + 2w_A w_B \rho_{AB} (20\%)(40\%)} \qquad (15\text{-}6a)$$

$$= \sqrt{.04 w_A^2 + .16 w_B^2 + .16 w_A w_B \rho_{AB}}$$

Figure 15-3 is a graph in risk-return space of the two assets A and B and the portfolios which can be formed from them at three different values for their correlation coefficient, $\rho_{AB} = -1, 0, +1$. This figure was prepared by plotting the risk and return of the various portfolios composed of risky assets A and B for which the participation levels summed to unity (that is, $w_A + w_B = 1$) and for three different correlation coefficients, $\rho_{AB} = -1, 0,$ and $+1$.

The reader should check a few points in Fig. 15-3 by plugging some appropriate numbers into Eqs. (15-2a) and (15-6a) and calculating the portfolio's expected return and risk. For example, for the portfolio which has $w_A = \frac{2}{3}$ and $w_B = \frac{1}{3}$, the expected return is fixed at 8.3 percent regardless of what value the correlation coefficient assumes.

$$E(r_p) = \sum_{i=1}^{2} w_i E(r_i)$$

$$= w_A E(r_A) + w_B E(r_B)$$
$$= w_A (.05) + w_B (.15)$$
$$= \tfrac{2}{3}(.05) + \tfrac{1}{3}(.15) = .083 = 8.3\%$$

---

[9] The portfolio risk formula shown in Eqs. (15-5), (15-6), and elsewhere is derived and explained in Mathematical Appendix I.

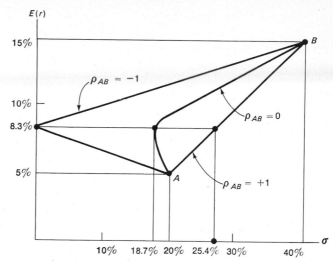

FIG. 15-3 The assets' correlation affects the portfolio's risk.

The risk for this portfolio with $w_A = \frac{2}{3}$ and $w_B = \frac{1}{3}$ varies with the correlation coefficient, ρ_{AB}.

$$
\begin{aligned}
\sigma_p &= \sqrt{w_A{}^2\sigma_{AA} + w_B{}^2\sigma_{BB} + 2w_A w_B \rho_{AB}\sigma_A\sigma_B} \\
&= \sqrt{(\tfrac{2}{3})^2(20\%)^2 + (\tfrac{1}{3})^2(40\%)^2 + 2(\rho_{AB})(\tfrac{2}{3})(\tfrac{1}{3})(20\%)(40\%)} \\
&= \sqrt{.0175 + .0175 + .035(\rho_{AB})} \\
&= \sqrt{.035 + .035(\rho_{AB})}
\end{aligned}
$$

When $\rho_{AB} = +1$, then $\sigma_p = \sqrt{.07} = 26.4$ percent. If $\rho_{AB} = 0$, then $\sigma_p = \sqrt{.035} = 18.7$ percent. But, if $\rho_{AB} = -1$ then $\sigma_p = \sqrt{0} = 0$. Figure 15-3 was constructed by plotting such points in risk-return space.

Markowitz diversification can lower risk below the systematic level if the security analyst can find securities whose rates of return have low enough correlations. Unfortunately, there are only a precious few securities which have low correlations. Therefore, using Markowitz diversification requires a data bank of financial statistics for hundreds of securities, an electronic digital computer, and an econometrician. Private investors with small portfolios must use naive diversification since they typically lack the resources to perform Markowitz diversification.

Markowitz diversification applied on a large scale to hundreds of assets with a computer is called *Markowitz portfolio analysis*. It is a scientific way to manage a portfolio, and its results are quite interesting. Since it considers both the risk and return of dozens, or hundreds, or thousands of different securities simultaneously (the number is limited only by the size of the computer and the number of securities for which one has risk and return statistics), it is a more powerful method of analyzing a portfolio than using one's head or selecting investments with a committee. A person's mind (even the mind of a genius) or an investment committee cannot simultaneously evaluate hundreds of different investment opportunities and balance the risks and returns of them all off against one another to find efficient portfolios which dominate all other investment opportunities. Markowitz portfolio analysis is essentially a mathematics problem which requires that many different equations be solved simultaneously. This can be done on a large scale only by using a computer program which does what is called "quadratic programming." *Quadratic programming* minimizes the portfolio's risk (a quadratic equation) at each level of average return for the portfolio.

The type of portfolio manager who is not sufficiently analytical to use quadratic programming is sometimes lightly referred to as a financial interior decorator.

Financial Interior Decorating

Many investment counselors are "financial interior decorators," meaning that they design portfolios of securities to match the investors' personalities. Thus, an elderly widow completely dependent on the income from a small investment would be advised to invest in low-risk, low-return assets like bonds and utility stocks on the assumption that they would minimize her risk. Little or no consideration would be given to the correlation between these low-risk assets by a financial interior decorator. On the other hand, a young professional man with a promising future would be advised to invest in high-risk, high-return securities such as Fairchild Camera, Northwest Airlines, and Texas Instruments. A financial interior decorator would make this suggestion on the assumption that the high-risk stocks must combine to make a portfolio with the highest long-run rate of return, an assumption which is not necessarily true.

In spite of the intuitive appeal of the financial interior-decorating approach to portfolio management, the preceding analysis reveals its fallacy. A Markowitz diversified portfolio of risky assets will earn a higher average return in the long run than a naively diversified portfolio because it will not experience the large losses which will periodically hurt the long-run performance of a naively diversified portfolio. Or, on the other hand, two high-risk, high-return securities might yield the minimum risk portfolio if they were negatively correlated. That is, the risk-averse elderly widow's needs may be more adequately met by a small portfolio of high-risk assets like Fairchild Camera and Northwest Airlines *if* the assets were negatively correlated (which Fairchild and Northwest are not, unfortunately). The financial interior-decorating approach suggests such a portfolio of high-risk securities would not be satisfactory. The problem with financial interior decorating is that it ignores analytical considerations such as the correlation coefficients among assets. Instead, the financial interior decorators prefer to focus naively on subjective considerations which may or may not be relevant in portfolio construction.

15-4 CONVEXITY OF THE EFFICIENT FRONTIER

If the risk and return of all individual assets on all security exchanges were plotted in risk-return space, they would be dominated by portfolios. Figure 15-4 represents the set of investment opportunities available in the securities markets.

The escalloped, quarter-moon–shaped opportunity set in Fig. 15-4 contains individual assets (stocks and bonds) in the lower right-hand side, represented by dots. The efficient frontier is represented by the heavy dark curve from E to F. Only portfolios will lie along the efficient frontier. Portfolios will always dominate individual assets because of the risk-reducing benefits of diversification which portfolios enjoy. Only the highest return portfolio F in Fig. 15-4 is likely to be a one-asset portfolio.

The opportunity set is constructed of curves which are all convex toward the $E(r)$ axis. This is because all assets have correlation coefficients between positive unity and negative unity. As shown in Fig. 15-3, this fact results in a locus of portfolios that traces a curve which is convex to the $E(r)$ axis in $[\sigma, E(r)]$ space. Only perfectly positively correlated (that is, $\rho = +1$) assets will generate linear combinations of risk and return; and under no circumstances will a portfolio possibility locus ever curve away from the $E(r)$ axis in $[\sigma, E(r)]$ space.

Not all portfolios will lie on the efficient frontier; some will dominate others. For example, Markowitz diversification will generate portfolios which are more efficient than naively diversified portfolios. If Markowitz diversification is applied to all marketable assets, the resulting portfolios

FIG. 15-4 The set of investment opportunities.

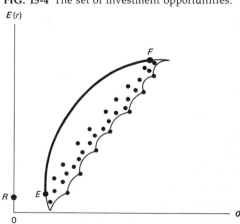

would be the efficient set of portfolios which forms the efficient frontier in Fig. 15-4. Appendixes A and C to Chap. 15 show how to perform the portfolio analysis required to find the efficient frontier when more than two assets are involved.

15-5 DERIVATION OF THE CAPITAL MARKET LINE

In Chap. 12 the analytical concept of risk was developed. It was explained that there was a trade-off of risk for return which could be attained in the securities markets. Earlier in this chapter the concept of the efficient frontier was examined. It was explained that the efficient frontier (which can be constructed without borrowing or lending) is never a straight line. Rather, it is a curve which is convex toward the $E(r)$ axis in risk-return space. However, if borrowing and lending opportunities are included in the analysis, a linear set of investment opportunities called the capital market line (CML) emerges.

One Riskless Asset Assumed

If investors were surveying *all* investment opportunities, they would find that opportunities to borrow and lend existed. Figure 15-4 depicts a *riskless asset* at point R on the expected return axis. Point R might represent U.S. Treasury bonds which are held to maturity. Such an investment yields a low return and has zero variability of return from year to year. Symbolically, $\sigma_R = 0$.

After considering the opportunities shown in Fig. 15-4, a thoughtful investor would realize that it was possible to create more investment opportunities. By combining the riskless asset with a risky asset, new portfolios could be created which are not shown in this figure.

The expected return of a portfolio composed of one risky and one risk-free asset would be given by Eq. (15-7).

$$E(r_p) = w_R R + w_i E(r_i) \tag{15-7}$$

$$= w_R R + (1 - w_R)E(r_i) \qquad \text{since } w_i = 1 - w_R \tag{15-7a}$$

R denotes the expected return of the riskless asset, and $E(r_i)$ is the expected return of some risky asset. The risk of a portfolio of R and a risky asset is given by Eq. (15-8).

$$\sigma_p = \sqrt{w_R^2 \sigma_R^2 + w_i^2 \sigma_i^2 + 2w_R w_i \sigma_{iR}} \tag{15-8}$$

$$= 0 + w_i \sigma_i + 0 \qquad \text{since } \sigma_R = \sigma_{iR} = 0 \tag{15-8a}$$

The opportunity locus in risk-return space representing the portfolios

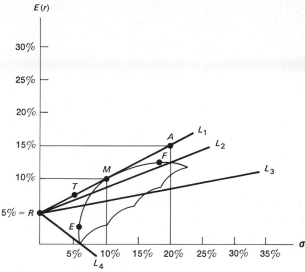

FIG. 15-5 Several portfolio possibility lines for portfolios containing risk-free asset R.

which may be formed from a risky asset and R is a straight line since Eqs. (15-7) and (15-8a) are both linear. Figure 15-5 shows four of the infinite number of opportunity loci representing portfolios containing R and a risky asset. These opportunity loci all start at R and pass through the opportunity set of risky assets.

In Fig. 15-5 the portfolios between R and the efficient frontier (point T, for example) represent portfolios containing both R and the risky asset M; that is, part of the portfolio is invested in the riskless asset. But those portfolios which lie on the section of the opportunity loci that is above point M on the line $RTMAL_1$ (point A, for example) contain negative amounts of R, $w_R < 0$. A negative amount of R may be interpreted as borrowing at interest rate R to buy more of a risky asset like M. Thus, an aggressive investor might create a leveraged portfolio like A in Fig. 15-5 to increase her expected return. Of course, financial leverage also increases the financial risk, as shown in the figure. To understand leveraged portfolios better, consider the following numerical example of how the portfolios along the upper section of L_1 are constructed.

Numerical Example of a Leveraged Portfolio

Suppose one share of investment M cost $1,000 and offered a 50-50 chance of returning either $1,000 or $1,200. The expected return for the holding period is 10 percent, as shown below.

$$E(r_M) = \sum_{i=1}^{2} p_i r_i$$

$$= .5 \left(\frac{1,000 - 1,000}{1,000} \right) + .5 \left(\frac{1,200 - 1,000}{1,000} \right)$$

$$= (.5)(0) + .5(20\%)$$

$$= 0 + 10\% = 10\%$$

The standard deviation of returns is 10 percent for M (still assuming the zero and 20 percent outcomes are equally likely).

$$\sigma_m = \sqrt{\Sigma p_i [r_i - E(r)]^2}$$

$$= \sqrt{.5(0 - .1)^2 + .5(.2 - .1)^2}$$

$$= \sqrt{.5(.01) + .5(.01)}$$

$$= \sqrt{.01}$$

$$= .1 = 10\%$$

Now if an investor borrows $1,000 at $R = 5$ percent and buys a second share of M, $w_m = 2$ and $w_R = -1$. In this case the investor has a 50-50 chance of receiving $950 or $1,350 on his $1,000 of original equity, as shown below.

	Two alternative outcomes	
	First	Second
Original equity	$ 1,000	$ 1,000
Principal amount borrowed at 5%	1,000	1,000
Total amount invested in M	$ 2,000	$ 2,000
Return on two shares of M	$ 2,000	$ 2,400
Repayment of loan principal	⟨1,000⟩	⟨1,000⟩
Payment of interest at 5%	⟨50⟩	⟨50⟩
Net return on original equity	$ 950	$ 1,350
Probability of outcome	.5	.5

Thus, the expected return on M leveraged is 15 percent. The calculations follow.

$$E(r) = \sum_{i=1}^{2} pr$$

$$= .5 \frac{950 - 1,000}{1,000} + .5 \frac{1,350 - 1,000}{1,000}$$

$$= .5(-5\%) + .5(35\%)$$

$$= -2.5\% + 17.5\%$$

$$= 15\%$$

The standard deviation of returns on the leveraged portfolio is 20 percent, as shown below.

$$\sigma = \sqrt{\Sigma p_i[r_i - E(r_i)]^2}$$
$$= \sqrt{.5(-5\% - 15\%)^2 + .5(35\% - 15\%)^2}$$
$$= \sqrt{.5(-20\%)^2 + .5(20\%)^2}$$
$$= \sqrt{.5(.04) + .5(.04)}$$
$$= \sqrt{.02 + .02}$$
$$= \sqrt{.04}$$
$$= .2 = 20\%$$

These results are shown graphically in Fig. 15-5 as portfolios M and A on line L_1. Equations (15-7) and (15-8a) may be checked by substituting in the values from this example.

The CML Emerges

Rational investors who use Markowitz diversification will recognize the various opportunities shown in Fig. 15-5. These investors will also recognize that the opportunity locus designated L_1 dominates *all* other opportunities. The portfolios which can be created from R and risky assets other than M (along lines like L_2, L_3, and L_4, for example) and even most of the efficient set of portfolios (along curve EF) are dominated by the opportunities represented by the line L_1 in Fig. 15-5. Therefore investors will all want the portfolio denoted M in Fig. 15-5 because this is the risky asset which is needed to generate the dominant opportunity locus L_1. Hereafter L_1 will be called the *capital market line,* or merely the CML. The CML is a separate and distinct relation from the security market line (SML) developed in Chap. 12. The SML is a linear relationship between expected return and *systematic* risk for portfolios *and* individual assets. The CML, on the other hand, is a linear relationship between expected return and *total* risk on which *only* portfolios will lie.[10]

The Market Portfolio

Imagine a capital market, such as the ones shown in Figs. 15-5 and 15-6, which is at equilibrium. By the definition of equilibrium in a market, excess demand is zero (that is, supply and demand are equal) for all goods. So every security in the market must be held by some owner. Since all in-

---

[10] The rationale for the CML and SML and the assumptions underlying them both are explained in detail in Chap. 16.

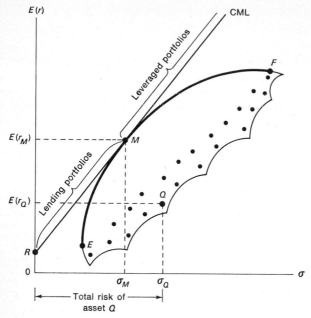

FIG. 15-6 The capital market line (CML) tangent to efficient frontier.

vestors unanimously want M, it follows that, in equilibrium, M must be a huge portfolio containing *all* securities in the proportions w_i^* where

$$w_i^* = \frac{\text{total value of the } i\text{th firm's securities}}{\text{total value of all securities in the market}}$$

In equilibrium, R must be the interest rate which equates the supply of, and demand for, loanable funds. Let M be designated as the *market portfolio*,[11] the unanimously desirable portfolio containing all securities in exactly the proportions in which they are supplied. The return on the market portfolio is the weighted average return on all securities in the market.

In reality there is no market portfolio. However, it is a useful theoretical construct since the return on M is the return the Dow Jones average, Standard & Poor's average, the NYSE index, and others are estimating. The return on M would be the optimum market index.

Lending and Leveraged Portfolios on the CML

In Fig. 15-6, portfolio M is the only portfolio on the CML which is not utilizing the opportunity to borrow or lend at the riskless rate R (that is, $w_R = 0$ for M). The portfolios along the CML between R and M are *lending*

[11] For a discussion of the market portfolio, see E. Fama, "Risk, Return and Equilibrium: Some Clarifying Comments," *Journal of Finance*, March 1968, pp. 32–33.

portfolios. They all have some money invested in the riskless asset R; that is, they are lending money at the rate R. Symbolically, $w_R > 0$ for lending portfolios.

The portfolios above M on the CML are all *leveraged* or *borrowing* portfolios. They were constructed by borrowing at the rate R and investing the proceeds in M, increasing the portfolios' expected returns on equity and risk as shown by the upper portions of the CML. Leveraged or borrowing portfolios on the CML have $w_R < 0$.

Systematic Risk

When borrowing and lending opportunities (at the riskless rate R) are considered, the true efficient frontier is the straight line called the CML. These investment opportunities dominate the portfolios lying on the curve EF in Fig. 15-6. It was shown in Fig. 15-3 that when assets form a linear opportunity locus in risk-return space, they are perfectly positively correlated. This means that the returns from portfolios on the CML must all vary together systematically. These portfolios along the CML have had their unsystematic risk reduced to zero by diversification. Only the undiversifiable systematic risk remains. Their returns are perfectly positively correlated because of *systematic* variability in returns.

Individual assets represented by dots like point Q in Fig. 15-6 are not efficient because their total risk includes both systematic and unsystematic risk. These individual assets have not had their total risk reduced by diversification. The total risk of asset Q is equal to the distance from 0 to σ_Q along the horizontal axis of Fig. 15-6. The total risk can be partitioned into two pieces — systematic and unsystematic risk.[12] As explained in Chap. 12, the systematic part of an asset's total risk is due to market risk, purchasing power risk, and interest rate risk. Managerial risk and industry risk determine how large the unsystematic portion of total risk will be.[13]

CML Is Simplified but Realistic

The preceding analysis is a simplified version of reality. The CML was mathematically derived from the efficient frontier by unrealistically assuming that money could be freely borrowed or lent at the risk-free rate R. Of course, private citizens cannot borrow money at the same low rate as the federal government, that is, at interest rate R. But, by making such assump-

---

[12] Partitioning asset Q's total risk statistically proceeds as shown below:

$$\mathrm{var}(r_Q) = \mathrm{var}(a_Q + b_Q r_m + e) \qquad \text{since } r_Q = a_Q + b_Q r_m + e$$
$$= b_Q{}^2\, \mathrm{var}(r_m) + \mathrm{var}(e)$$
$$= \text{systematic} + \text{unsystematic risk}$$
$$= \text{total risk of asset } Q$$

[13] B. F. King, op. cit., pp. 139–190. King partitions the risk of 316 stocks listed on the NYSE from 89 different industrial categories. Factor analysis is used.

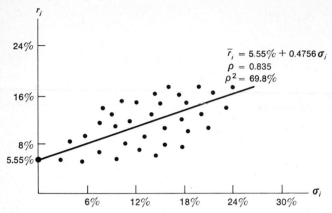

FIG. 15-7 Empirical test of the capital market line (CML). (From William F. Sharpe, "Risk Aversion in the Stock Market: Some Empirical Evidence," *Journal of Finance,* September 1965, pp. 416–422.)

tions, the model may be kept simple and manageable. In spite of the simplifications used to derive the market model shown in Fig. 15-6, it is still realistic. Most portfolios' rates of return are highly positively correlated and lie along a curve like the efficient frontier *EF* in Fig. 15-6.

Table 15-5 lists the risk and return statistics of 34 mutual funds. These portfolios' average returns were regressed on their risk. The results are shown in Fig. 15-7.

The correlation coefficient for the regression line shown in Fig. 15-7 is high and positive. The empirical data indicate the nature of the trade-off of risk for return available in the market. The data also attest to the realism of the model shown in Fig. 15-6.

15-6 CONCLUSION: RATIONAL INVESTORS DIVERSIFY

In the preceding pages of this chapter, it was shown how the dominance principle could be used to delineate desirable assets. Then various diversification practices were reviewed. It was seen that diversification of even the most naive variety (for example, selecting securities with a dart) was beneficial in reducing risk and thereby increasing the portfolio's average rate of return in the long run. Markowitz diversification was seen to be the most effective way of attaining these risk-reducing benefits.

After derivation of the efficient frontier was explained in terms of Markowitz diversification, borrowing and lending opportunities were introduced. It was seen that the dominant assets were always portfolios (as opposed to individual assets) and usually involved lending or leverage. Thus, we reach the conclusion that *diversification is essential* to the investment program of a rational, risk-averse, wealth-seeking investor. Furthermore, Markowitz diversification helps the investor attain a higher level of

TABLE 15-5 PERFORMANCE OF 34 MUTUAL FUNDS, 1954–1963

	Average annual return, %	Std. dev. of annual return, %
Affiliated Fund	14.6	15.3
American Business Shares	10.0	9.2
Axe-Houghton, Fund A	10.5	13.5
Axe-Houghton, Fund B	12.0	16.3
Axe-Houghton, Stock Fund	11.9	15.6
Boston Fund	12.4	12.1
Board Street Investing	14.8	16.8
Bullock Fund	15.7	19.3
Commonwealth Investment Company	10.9	13.7
Delaware Fund	14.4	21.4
Dividend Shares	14.4	15.9
Eaton and Howard, Balanced Fund	11.0	11.9
Eaton and Howard, Stock Fund	15.2	19.2
Equity Fund	14.6	18.7
Fidelity Fund	16.4	23.5
Financial Industrial Fund	14.5	23.0
Fundamental Investors	16.0	21.7
Group Securities, Common Stock Fund	15.1	19.1
Group Securities, Fully Administered Fund	11.4	14.1
Incorporated Investors	14.0	25.5
Investment Company of America	17.4	21.8
Investors Mutual	11.3	12.5
Loomis-Sales Mutual Fund	10.0	10.4
Massachusetts Investors Trust	16.2	20.8
Massachusetts Investors—Growth Stock	18.6	22.7
National Investors Corporation	18.3	19.9
National Securities—Income Series	12.4	17.8
New England Fund	10.4	10.2
Putnam Fund of Boston	13.1	16.0
Scudder, Stevens & Clark Balanced Fund	10.7	13.3
Selected American Shares	14.4	19.4
United Funds—Income Fund	16.1	20.9
Wellington Fund	11.3	12.0
Wisconsin Fund	13.8	16.9

Source: William F. Sharpe, "Mutual Fund Performance," *Journal of Business*, January 1966 suppl., p. 125.

expected utility than any other technique. Thus, rational investors will be concerned with the *correlation* between assets in addition to the assets' expected returns and standard deviations.

After investors somehow (that is, by using either naive or Markowitz diversification) delineate the most dominant investment opportunities to be found (that is, their own most efficient frontier), they still must select one in which to invest their funds. Essentially, once the efficient frontier is delineated, portfolio selection is a personal choice.

QUESTIONS

1 Write a few sentences explaining the mathematical calculations which are used to find the portfolio's expected return.

2 What is assumed about the weights or participation levels of the assets in a portfolio? Why?

3 Define an efficient portfolio.

4 Define naive diversification. Will naive diversification reduce total risk? Unsystematic risk? Systematic risk?

5 Define superfluous diversification. What problems frequently result from superfluous diversification?

6 Define Markowitz diversification. Draw a graph of a two-asset portfolio's risk and return and explain how Markowitz diversification can reduce risk.

7 What does it mean to say that two variables are perfectly positively correlated? Uncorrelated or independent? Inversely correlated? Graph realistic examples of each and explain.

8 Define financial interior decorating and explain the shortcoming of this popular approach to portfolio management.

9 Why are all the curves in the opportunity set drawn convex to the expected return axis?

10 "A portfolio of many different assets from many different industries will be a well-diversified portfolio." Is this statement true, false, or uncertain? Explain.

11 "Apart from negatively correlated stocks, all the gains from diversification come from 'averaging over' the independent components of the returns and risks of individual stocks. Among positively correlated stocks, there would be no gains from diversification if independent variations [unsystematic risk] were absent."[14] Explain this statement.

Note: The following questions are more technical and presume a knowledge of the Appendixes to Chap. 15.

12 What assumptions describe an investor who prefers to use Markowitz portfolio analysis?

13 What is the objective of portfolio analysis?

14 What statistical inputs are required for a portfolio analysis of four assets?

---

[14] J. Linter, "Security Prices, Risk, and Maximal Gains from Diversification," *Journal of Finance*, December 1965, p. 589 (bracketed words added).

15 Expand the following formula for a portfolio's variance of returns for four assets into a form showing all four assets' variances and covariances.

$$\text{var}(r_p) = \sum_i^n \sum_j^n w_i w_j \sigma_{ij}$$

16 Below are the possible returns for two assets:

r_1	r_2	$p(r_1 \text{ and } r_2)$
15%	15%	$\frac{1}{3}$
30%	12%	$\frac{1}{3}$
45%	9%	$\frac{1}{3}$
$E(r_1) = 30\%$	$E(r_2) = 12\%$	1.0

Assume that a security analyst has forecasted these returns, based on three different possible rates of economic growth. He has also calculated the expected return for each asset. Calculate the two variances and $\text{cov}(r_1, r_2)$. If assets 1 and 2 are combined 50-50 into a portfolio, what is the variance of this portfolio? Show your formulas and calculations.

17 Assume that you are analyzing a portfolio made up of three securities with $E(r_1) = 2$ percent, $E(r_2) = 4$ percent, $E(r_3) = 6$ percent, and that the graph below has been completed.

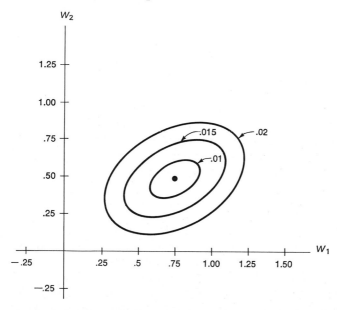

a What are the weights in the minimum variance portfolio as near as you can tell?
b What are the three circular shapes in the graph?
c Graph the isomean lines for $E(r_p) = 4$ and 5 percent.

d Sketch in a small section of the critical line.

e What are the approximate weights in the most efficient portfolio with var(r_p) = .015?

18 Explain the relation between the critical line and the efficient frontier.

19 How do policies against leverage constrain the critical line? Show your answer graphically.

SELECTED REFERENCES

Brealey, R. A., *An Introduction to Risk and Return from Common Stocks* (Cambridge, Mass.: M.I.T., 1969).

A modern nonmathematical review of scholarly literature relevant to investment management. Chapters 10 and 11 discuss financial interior decorating, the set of investment opportunities, and diversification. An appendix rationalizes the use of the standard deviation of returns as a risk surrogate.

Francis, J. C., and S. H. Archer, *Portfolio Analysis* (Englewood Cliffs, N.J.: Prentice-Hall, 1971).

Chapters 2 and 5 develop the CML and other more sophisticated market models. Graphical utility analysis and elementary statistics are used in the chapters.

Markowitz, H., *Portfolio Selection* (New York: Wiley, 1959).

Chapters 1 through 5 present the foundations for portfolio analysis. Chapters 7 and 8 present different techniques for performing portfolio analysis. Algebra is used.

APPENDIX A TO CHAPTER 15
Markowitz Graphical Portfolio Analysis

Dr. Harry Markowitz developed a mathematical procedure to analyze the expected return, risk, and covariance statistics for a group of assets and delineate the efficient frontier which may be expected if these assets are combined into optimum portfolios.[1] These optimum portfolios or efficient portfolios dominate the individual assets in risk-return space and are therefore highly desirable investments. Markowitz portfolio analysis tells what assets are held in each efficient portfolio and their exact proportions in the portfolio. This is the information the portfolio manager needs.

[1] H. Markowitz, "Portfolio Selection," *Journal of Finance*, March 1952, pp. 77–91.

In Chap. 15 Markowitz diversification was discussed in terms of two-asset portfolios. The purpose of that discussion was to introduce the notion of analytical diversification techniques which might be used on an intuitive level by the manager of a small portfolio. However, since that discussion did not extend much beyond the two-asset case, it has limited use for managers of portfolios which contain dozens or hundreds of securities. The purpose of this appendix is to show how to use Markowitz diversification for larger portfolios. The material in the beginning of the appendix explains how to generate the input statistics needed to do portfolio analysis. Then a three-security portfolio is analyzed graphically in order to reveal the "inner workings" of Markowitz portfolio analysis. These are the tools needed to utilize Markowitz diversification in managing a large portfolio. Appendix C extends the portfolio analysis procedure to the general n-asset case.

Assumptions Underlying Portfolio Analysis

Portfolio analysis is a valid optimum-seeking analysis for investors who are described by the following assumptions:

1 The rate of return is the most important outcome of any investment. The "glamour" of the product or other subjective considerations are irrelevant except as they affect the rate of return.

2 Investors visualize the various possible rates of return from any asset in a probabilistic fashion. In essence (either consciously or unconsciously), the investor sees each asset as a probability distribution of returns (with an expected return and a standard deviation, and a correlation coefficient or covariance relating it to other assets).

3 Investors define risk as variability of return and are willing to base their investment decision on only two things—expected return and risk. That is, investors' utility is a function of risk and return. Symbolically, $U = f[\sigma, E(r)]$.

4 Investors prefer to hold the investment with the maximum rate of return in any given risk-class they select, or conversely, investors prefer to minimize risk at whatever expected rate of return they seek.

The preferences of any rational, risk-averse, wealth-maximizing investor will be fairly well described by these assumptions.[2]

Efficient Frontier Varies with the Assets Analyzed

Markowitz portfolio analysis can simultaneously analyze n individual assets where n is any integer larger than 1. Increasing the number of assets

---

[2] Investors preferences will be exactly defined by these assumptions if (1) their utility functions are quadratic in the range of likely returns, or (2) the distribution of returns is a two-parameter distribution which is completely described by the mean and variance. See the Appendix to Chap. 17 for a discussion of this assertion.

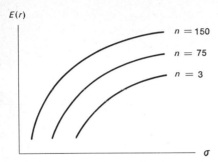

FIG. A15-1 The efficient frontiers typically vary with the number of assets in the analysis.

analyzed usually results in a more efficient frontier. Figure A15-1 shows three different hypothetical efficient frontiers for three different values of n (namely, $n = 3, 75, 150$).

In this appendix, Markowitz portfolio analysis is performed for a three-asset portfolio. Three assets are enough to make the portfolio interesting yet few enough to keep the mathematics at the simplest possible level. The main advantage of studying three-asset portfolios is that the analysis can be represented graphically. If more than four assets are analyzed, advanced mathematical techniques involving calculus or quadratic programming must be used. (Such techniques are discussed in Appendix C to Chap. 15.)

A15-1 SECURITY ANALYSIS FOR PORTFOLIO ANALYSIS

For an n-asset portfolio analysis problem, the security analyst must provide the portfolio analyst with n expected returns, n variances (or standard deviations), and $[\frac{1}{2}(n^2 - n)]$ covariances. These statistical inputs are then analyzed to determine the efficient portfolios. For a three-asset problem, the statistical inputs required for portfolio analysis are shown in Table A15-1.

Formulas for Historical Statistics

To derive the return, risk, and covariance statistics for each asset under consideration, the security analyst can begin by determining the historical values for these statistics. Data for at least several years should be tabulated. If

TABLE A15-1 STATISTICAL INPUTS FOR PORTFOLIO ANALYSIS OF THREE COMMON STOCKS

Asset	$E(r_i)$	$\mathrm{var}(r_i) = \sigma_{ii}$	$\mathrm{cov}(r_i, r_j) = \sigma_{ij}$
Homestake Mining	$E(r_1) = 5\% = .05$	$\sigma_{11} = .1$	$\sigma_{12} = -.1$
Kaiser Aluminum	$E(r_2) = 7\% = .07$	$\sigma_{22} = .4$	$\sigma_{13} = 0$
Texas Instruments	$E(r_3) = 30\% = .3$	$\sigma_{33} = .7$	$\sigma_{23} = .3$

T different periods (for example, months, quarters, or years) of data are analyzed, Eqs. (A15-1), (A15-2), and (A15-3) may be used to calculate historical return, risk, and covariance.

$$\bar{r}_i = \frac{1}{T} \sum_{t=1}^{T} r_{it} \tag{A15-1}$$

$$\sigma_i^2 = \frac{1}{T} \sum_{t=1}^{T} (r_{it} - \bar{r}_1)^2 = \sigma_{ii} = \text{var}(r_i) \tag{A15-2}$$

$$\sigma_{ij} = \frac{1}{T} \sum_{t=1}^{T} [(r_{it} - \bar{r}_i)(r_{jt} - \bar{r}_j)] \tag{A15-3}$$

where r_{it} = rate of return for asset i in period t
$\quad\bar{r}_i$ = arithmetic average historical return for asset i
$\quad\sigma_i^2$ = variance of returns for firm i
$\quad\sigma_{ij}$ = covariance between assets i and j

Sources of Historical Data

The needed historical data may be obtained from any of the following sources:

1 *ISL Daily Stock Price* manuals. Each manual contains daily stock prices, the quarterly dividend, and the quarterly earnings per share for stocks from the New York and American Stock Exchanges.

2 *Moody's Handbook of Widely Held Stocks.* These quarterly paperbacks contain information on quarterly dividends and earnings, annual high and low prices, and stock splits for the three most recent years. Most stocks listed on the NYSE and some stocks from the American Stock Exchange are included.

3 *Standard & Poor's Stock Market Encyclopedia.* This book contains data on quarterly dividends and earnings, stock-split information, and annual high and low prices. Most NYSE stocks are included.

There are other sources for the needed information. A form like the one shown in Table A15-2 may be helpful in gathering the data and adjusting them for stock splits and stock dividends.

The two columns of blanks on the left-hand side of Table A15-2 may be used to record the data reported by the firm. The third column is to record stock splits or stock dividends which change the unit of account (that is, the number of shares outstanding). Columns 4 and 5 can be used to record the data after they have been adjusted for changes in the unit of account. Then the period-by-period rates of return may be calculated and recorded in column 6. Lastly, the average rate of return, variance of returns, and any other statistics desired may be calculated and recorded at the bottom of the table.

TABLE A15-2 FORM FOR GATHERING HISTORICAL SEMIANNUAL DATA
ABOUT COMMON STOCK

Name of firm researched:_____Researcher:_____
Type of security:_____Source of data:_____
Industry:_____

Half years	Reported data			Adjusted data		
	Begin. mkt. price	Semi ann. div.	Changes in unit of account	Begin. mkt. price	Semi ann. div.	Rate of return†
1975, 2	____	____	____	____	____	____
1975, 1	____	____	____	____	____	____
1974, 2	____	____	____	____	____	____
1974, 1	____	____	____	____	____	____
1973, 2	____	____	____	____	____	____
1973, 1	____	____	____	____	____	____
1972, 2	____	____	____	____	____	____
1972, 1	____	____	____	____	____	____
1971, 2	____	____	____	____	____	____
1971, 1	____	____	____	____	____	____
1970, 2	____	____	____	____	____	____
1970, 1	____	____	____	____	____	____
1969, 2	____	____	____	____	____	____
1969, 1	____	____	____	____	____	____
1968, 2	____	____	____	____	____	____
1968, 1	____	____	____	____	____	____
1967, 2	____	____	____	____	____	____
1967, 1	____	____	____	____	____	____
1966, 2	____	____	____	____	____	____
1966, 1	____	____	____	____	____	____

Variance in rates of return:_____Standard deviation:_____
Average rate of return:_____
Regression coefficients for characteristic line: A_____, B_____, ρ_____

† $r_t = \dfrac{p_{t+1} - p_t + d_t}{p_t}$ = rate of return in period t

Adjusting Historical Data Subjectively

Since most securities' probability distributions of returns are fairly stationary over time, the historical statistics will be good estimates of the future in some cases. However, if the security analyst knows of new developments which will tend to change the firms' return, risk, or covariance, the historical statistics should be adjusted subjectively.

A15-2 THE GRAPHICAL PORTFOLIO ANALYSIS PROCESS

The objective of portfolio analysis is to delineate the efficient set of port-folios. Mathematically, the objective is to maximize the portfolio's expected return $E(r_p)$, as defined in (A15-4).

$$E(r_p) = \sum_{i=1}^{n} w_i E(r_i)$$
(A15-4)

at each risk-class, as defined in (A15-5),

$$\text{var}(r_p) = \sum_{i=1}^{n} \sum_{j=1}^{n} w_i w_j \sigma_{ij}$$
(A15-5)

subject to the constraint of (A15-6).

$$\sum_{i=1}^{n} w_i = 1$$
(A15-6)

The w_i's are the weights, percentages, or participation levels of the individual assets in the portfolio.

Weights Are the Variables

The return, risk, and covariance statistics [that is, $E(r_i)$, σ_{ii}, and σ_{ji}] for the individual assets are constants and are not changed by portfolio analysis. The weights of the assets (the w_i's) are the variables which portfolio analysis adjusts in order to obtain the optimum portfolios. By varying these weights, the portfolio's expected return, $E(r_p)$, and risk, $\text{var}(r_p)$, are varied. However, as the weights of the assets are varied, Eq. (A15-6) can never be violated or the analysis has no rational economic interpretation.

Although the weights must always sum to 1, they can assume any value. If a three-asset portfolio has $w_1 = w_2 = w_3 = \frac{1}{3}$, this means that one-third of the portfolio's funds are invested in each asset. If the three weights are $w_1 = 1.5$, $w_2 = -.5$, and $w_3 = 0$, this means that none of asset 3 is held in the portfolio; asset 1 is held in the portfolio in an amount equal to $1.5 = 150$ percent of the value of the portfolio's equity; and debt with the same risk and return as asset 2 has been issued in an amount equal to 50 percent of the equity in the portfolio in order to finance the large holding of asset 1. None of asset 2 has been purchased.

The Steps of the Analysis

The steps in graphing a three-asset portfolio are:

1 Convert the formulas from three variables to two variables (that is, two weights) so the analysis can be done with a two-dimensional graph.

2 Find the minimum variance portfolio (MVP).

3 Graph the isovariance ellipses.

4 Graph the isomean lines.

5 Delineate the weights of the efficient portfolios by drawing the critical line.

6 Determine the expected return and risk of the efficient portfolios and graph the efficient frontier.

The next few pages of this appendix will explain how to perform these steps.

Step 1

For a three-asset portfolio, Eq. (A15-6) may be expanded into (A15-7).

$$\sum_{i=1}^{3} w_i = w_1 + w_2 + w_3 = 1 \qquad (A15\text{-}7)$$

Solving (A15-7) for w_3 yields (A15-8).

$$w_3 = 1 - w_1 - w_2 \qquad (A15\text{-}8)$$

Substituting (A15-8) for w_3 in the return and risk formulas eliminates one variable, w_3. Elimination of the variable w_3 from the formulas for the risk and return of a three-asset portfolio converts the formulas from three variables to two variables which allows them to be graphed in an ordinary two-dimensional graph with w_1 and w_2 on the axes. Equation (A15-4) is rewritten as (A15-9) by substituting (A15-8) for w_3.

$$E(r_p) = \sum_{i=1}^{3} w_i E(r_i) \qquad (A15\text{-}4)$$

$$
\begin{aligned}
&= w_i E(r_1) + w_2 E(r_2) + w_3 E(r_3) \\
&= w_1 E(r_1) + w_2 E(r_2) + (1 - w_1 - w_2) E(r_3) \qquad \text{substituting for } w_3 \\
&= w_1 E(r_1) + w_2 E(r_2) + E(r_3) - w_1 E(r_3) - w_2 E(r_3) \\
&= w_1 [E(r_1) - E(r_3)] + w_2 [E(r_2) - E(r_3)] + E(r_3) \qquad (A15\text{-}9)
\end{aligned}
$$

Substituting the expected returns from Table A15-1 into Eq. (A15-9) yields (A15-10)

$$
\begin{aligned}
E(r_p) &= w_1(.05 - .3) + w_2(.07 - .3) + .3 \\
&= .3 - .25w_1 - .23w_2
\end{aligned}
\qquad (A15\text{-}10)
$$

Equation (A15-10) is the formula for an isomean line stated in two variables, w_1 and w_2. For any given value of $E(r_p)$, Eq. (A15-9) or (A15-10) can be solved for the weights which will yield that expected return for the portfolio, since $E(r_1)$, $E(r_2)$, and $E(r_3)$ are constants.

Substituting (A15-8) into (A15-5) for the three-asset case yields Eq. (A15-11), which defines the risk of the portfolio.

$$
\begin{aligned}
\mathrm{var}(r_p) &= \sum_{i=1}^{3}\sum_{j=1}^{3} w_i w_j \sigma_{ij} \\[4pt]
&= w_1^2\sigma_{11} + w_2^2\sigma_{22} + w_3^2\sigma_{33} + 2w_1w_2\sigma_{12} \\
&\quad + 2w_1w_3\sigma_{13} + 2w_2w_3\sigma_{23} \\
&= w_1^2\sigma_{11} + w_2^2\sigma_{22} + (1 - w_1 - w_2)^2\sigma_{33} \\
&\quad + 2w_1w_2\sigma_{12} + 2w_1(1 - w_1 - w_2)\sigma_{13} \\
&\quad + 2w_2(1 - w_1 - w_2)\sigma_{23} \quad\text{substituting (15-8) for } w_3 \\
&= w_1^2\sigma_{11} + w_2^2\sigma_{22} \\
&\quad + (1 - 2w_1 - 2w_2 + 2w_1w_2 + w_1^2 + w_2^2)\sigma_{33} + 2w_1w_2\sigma_{12} \\
&\quad + (2w_1 - 2w_1^2 - 2w_1w_2)\sigma_{13} + (2w_2 - 2w_1w_2 - 2w_2^2)\sigma_{23} \\
&= w_1^2\sigma_{11} + w_2^2\sigma_{22} + \sigma_{33} - 2w_1\sigma_{33} - 2w_2\sigma_{33} \\
&\quad + 2w_1w_2\sigma_{33} + w_1^2\sigma_{33} + w_2^2\sigma_{33} \\
&\quad + 2w_1w_2\sigma_{12} + 2w_1\sigma_{13} - 2w_1^2\sigma_{13} - 2w_1w_2\sigma_{13} \\
&\quad + 2w_2\sigma_{23} - 2w_1w_2\sigma_{23} - 2w_2^2\sigma_{23} \\
&= w_1^2(\sigma_{11} + \sigma_{33} - 2\sigma_{13}) \\
&\quad + w_2^2(\sigma_{22} + \sigma_{33} - 2\sigma_{23}) + w_1(2\sigma_{13} - 2\sigma_{33}) \\
&\quad + w_2(2\sigma_{23} - 2\sigma_{33}) \\
&\quad + w_1w_2(2\sigma_{33} + 2\sigma_{12} - 2\sigma_{13} - 2\sigma_{23}) + \sigma_{33}
\end{aligned}
$$

(A15-5)

(A15-11)

Substituting the risk and covariance statistics from Table A15-1 into Eq. (A15-11) yields (A15-12).

$$
\begin{aligned}
\mathrm{var}(r_p) &= w_1^2(.1 + .7 - 0) + w_2^2(.4 + .7 - .6) + w_1(0 - 1.4) \\
&\quad + w_2(.6 - 1.4) + w_1w_2(1.4 - .2 - 0 - .6) + .7 \quad\text{(A15-12)} \\
&= .8w_1^2 + .5w_2^2 - 1.4w_1 - .8w_2 + .6w_1w_2 + .7 \quad\text{(A15-12a)}
\end{aligned}
$$

Equation (A15-12) is a formula for an isovariance ellipse in two variables, w_1 and w_2.† For any given value of $\mathrm{var}(r_p)$, Eq. (A15-11) or (A15-12) may be solved for the weights which will yield that amount of portfolio risk (since the variances and covariances for the three individual assets are constants). Several isovariance ellipses are graphed in Fig. A15-2; they are egg-shaped with a common center and orientation.

---

† Mathematical Appendix K discusses isovariance ellipses in some detail and explains shortcuts in this stage of graphical portfolio analysis which require higher mathematics.

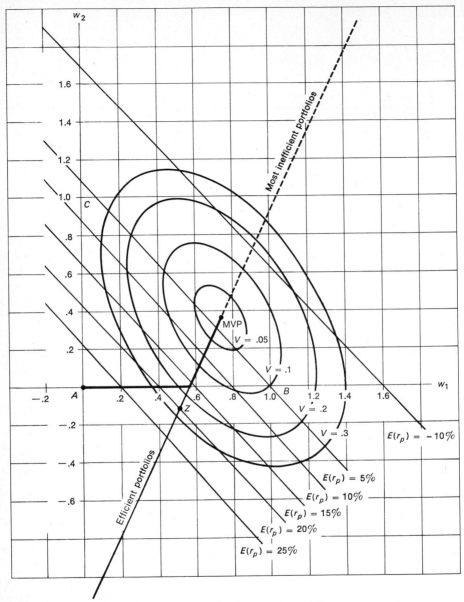

FIG. A15-2 Graphical portfolio analysis of a three-asset portfolio.

A15-3 FINDING THE MVP AND GRAPHING ISOVARIANCES

After the portfolio's return and risk formulas have been reduced to two variables, they are in a form suitable for graphing. Before the graphing begins, however, it is necessary to find the weights of the minimum variance portfolio (MVP).

The MVP

For any three assets, there is one portfolio which has less variance than any other portfolio which can be constructed from those assets—this is the MVP. In order to avoid trying to plot points for portfolios with variances below the MVP, we must find the variance of the MVP.

The derivation of the MVP involves some differential calculus which is omitted.[3] In essence, to find the MVP we must simultaneously solve the two linear equations (A15-13) and (A15-14) for w_1 and w_2.

$$\overbrace{2(\sigma_{11}+\sigma_{33}-2\sigma_{13})w_1}^{a}+\overbrace{2(\sigma_{33}+\sigma_{12}-\sigma_{13}-\sigma_{23})w_2}^{b}+\overbrace{2\sigma_{13}-2\sigma_{33}}^{c}=0$$
$$(\text{A15-13})$$

$$\overbrace{2(\sigma_{33}+\sigma_{12}-\sigma_{13}-\sigma_{23})w_1}^{d}+\overbrace{2(\sigma_{22}+\sigma_{33}-2\sigma_{23})w_2}^{e}+\overbrace{2(\sigma_{23}-\sigma_{33})}^{f}=0$$
$$(\text{A15-14})$$

Use of the compact notation a, b, c, d, e, and f allows (A15-13) and (A15-14) to be rewritten as (A15-13a) and (A15-14a).

$$aw_1 + bw_2 + c = 0 \qquad\qquad (\text{A15-13}a)$$
$$dw_1 + ew_2 + f = 0 \qquad\qquad (\text{A15-14}a)$$

where
$$a = 2(\sigma_{11} + \sigma_{33} - 2\sigma_{13})$$
$$b = 2(\sigma_{33} + \sigma_{12} - \sigma_{13} - \sigma_{23}) = d$$
$$c = 2(\sigma_{13} - \sigma_{33})$$
$$d = 2(\sigma_{33} + \sigma_{12} - \sigma_{13} - \sigma_{23}) = b$$
$$e = 2(\sigma_{22} + \sigma_{33} - 2\sigma_{23})$$
$$f = 2(\sigma_{23} - \sigma_{33})$$

Solving (A15-13a) and (A15-14a) for w_1 and w_2 yields Eqs. (A15-15) and (A15-16).

$$w_1 = \frac{-c}{a - bd/e} + \frac{bf}{ae - bd} \qquad\qquad (\text{A15-15})$$

$$w_2 = \frac{dc}{ae - bd} - \frac{f}{e - bd/a} \qquad\qquad (\text{A15-16})$$

Evaluating a, b, c, d, e, f, bd, ae, bf, and dc for the values from Table A15-1 yields $a = 1.6$, $b = .6$, $c = -1.4$, $d = .6$, $e = 1$, $f = -.8$, $bd = .36$,

---

[3] To find the MVP, take partial derivatives of (A15-12) or (A15-11) with respect to the two variables. That is, find $\partial\mathrm{var}(r_p)/\partial w_1$ and $\partial\mathrm{var}(r_p)/\partial w_2$, set them to zero as shown in (A15-14) and (A15-13), and solve them for w_1, w_2, and $w_3 = 1 - w_1 - w_3$. These are the MVP weights.

$ae = 1.6$, $bf = -.48$, and $dc = -.84$. Substituting these values into (A15-15) and (A15-16) and solving yields the MVP values for w_1 and w_2;

$$w_1 = \frac{+1.4}{1.6 - .36} + \frac{-.48}{1.6 - .36}$$

$$= \frac{+1.4 - .48}{1.24} = \frac{.92}{1.24} = .745$$

$$w_2 = \frac{-.84}{1.6 - .36} - \frac{-.8}{1. - .225}$$

$$= \frac{-.84}{1.24} + \frac{.8}{.775} = -.68 + 1.02 = .34$$

Since $w_3 = 1 - w_1 - w_2$, this implies $w_3 = -.085$ at the MVP. Substituting $w_1 = .745$ and $w_2 = .34$ into Eq. (A15-11) or (A15-12) and solving reveals that the variance of the MVP is .035. The MVP is shown graphically in (w_1, w_2) space in Fig. A15-2.

Graphing Isovariance Ellipses

After the MVP has been determined, the graphing can proceed. Either the isomeans or the isovariances may be graphed first; we shall graph the isovariances first. Isovariances are ellipses with a common center at the MVP, common orientation, and common eggshape. These ellipses are a locus of points which represent portfolios with the same variance. Isovariances are risk isoquants.

To graph isovariances, we must solve Eq. (A15-11) or (A15-12) in terms of one of the variables (that is, one weight) while treating the other variable and the variance as constants. Arbitrarily selecting w_1 as the variable to be solved for, and treating w_2 as a constant, reduces Eqs. (A15-11) and (A15-12) to a quadratic equation in one variable. The quadratic form of an equation in general form is

$$Aw_1^2 + Bw_1 + C = 0 \qquad\qquad \text{(A15-17)}$$

where the w_1 is a variable and the other symbols represent constants. Solution of such second-order equations in one variable may be obtained with the quadratic formula shown as Eq. (A15-18).

$$w_1 = \frac{-B \pm \sqrt{B^2 - 4AC}}{2A} \qquad\qquad \text{(A15-18)}$$

The quantity under the square root sign in the quadratic formula $\sqrt{B^2 - 4AC}$ is called the *discriminant*. The solution of the quadratic equation for w_1 has a rational economic interpretation only if the discriminant is nonnegative.[4]

Equation (A15-19) shows Eq. (A15-11) for the portfolio's risk rearranged as a quadratic equation (A15-17) treating w_2 as a constant.

$$w_1{}^2(\sigma_{11}+\sigma_{33}-2\sigma_{13}) + w_1[2\sigma_{13}-2\sigma_{33}+2w_2(\sigma_{33}+\sigma_{12}-\sigma_{13}-\sigma_{23})]$$
$$+ [w_2{}^2(\sigma_{22}+\sigma_{33}-2\sigma_{23}) + w_2(2\sigma_{23}-2\sigma_{33})+\sigma_{33}-\mathrm{var}(r_p)] = 0 \quad \text{(A15-19)}$$

Equation (A15-19) is in the form $Aw_1{}^2 + Bw_1 + C = 0$ where A, B, and C are defined as follows:

$$A = \sigma_{11} + \sigma_{33} - 2\sigma_{13}$$

$$B = 2\sigma_{13} - 2\sigma_{33} + 2w_2(\sigma_{33} + \sigma_{12} - \sigma_{13} - \sigma_{23})$$

$$C = w_2{}^2(\sigma_{22} + \sigma_{33} - 2\sigma_{23}) + w_2(2\sigma_{23} - 2\sigma_{33}) + \sigma_{33} - \mathrm{var}(r_p)$$

Substituting the values from Table A15-1 into A, B, and C yields

$$A = .1 + .7 - 2(0)$$
$$= .8$$

$$B = [2(0) - 2(.7)] + 2w_2(.7 - .1 - 0 - .3)$$
$$= -1.4 + .6w_2$$

$$C = w_2{}^2[.4 + .7 - 2(.3)] + w_2[2(.3) - 2(.7)] + .7 - \mathrm{var}(r_p)$$
$$= .5w_2{}^2 - .8w_2 + .7 - \mathrm{var}(r_p)$$

Substituting these real values for A, B, and C into the quadratic formula (A15-18) yields (A15-20).

$$w_1 = \frac{-B \pm \sqrt{B^2 - 4AC}}{2A} \quad \text{(A15-18)}$$

$$w_1 = \frac{-(-1.4 + .6w_2) \pm \sqrt{(-1.4 + .6w_2)^2 - 4(.8)[.5w_2{}^2 - .8w_2 + .7 - \mathrm{var}(r_p)]}}{2(.8)}$$

$$\text{(A15-20)}$$

The quadratic formula (A15-20) should never be solved with values of $\mathrm{var}(r_p)$ which are less than the variance of the MVP because imaginary values of w_1 will result. To plot isovariances, set $\mathrm{var}(r_p)$ to some value slightly larger than the variance of the MVP and set w_2 to some value in the vicinity of w_2 for the MVP. Then solve for the two values of w_1. Next, change w_2 a little while holding $\mathrm{var}(r_p)$ constant and solve for two more values of w_1. Continue this process until enough points are derived to plot a few iso-

---

[4] If $B^2 < 4AC$, then w_1 is not a real number. When $B^2 < 4AC$, then w_1 is a complex number. In effect, no isovariance exists at points where $B^2 < 4AC$.

TABLE A15-3 PLOTTING POINTS
FOR ISOVARIANCES

$\text{var}(r_p)$	w_2	First w_1	Second w_1
.05	.2	.85	.75
.05	.3	.875	.65
.05	.4	.84	.61
.05	.5	.75	.63
.1	0	1.0	.75
.1	.1	1.05	.62
.1	.2	1.05	.54
.1	.3	1.04	.49
.1	.4	1.00	.49
.1	.5	.95	.43
.2	−.1	1.23	.59
.2	.1	1.25	.425
.2	.3	1.21	.315
.2	.5	1.125	.25
.2	.7	.99	.23
.2	.9	.78	.3
.3	−.3	.64	1.33
.3	−.1	.44	1.39
.3	.1	.29	1.38
.3	.3	.19	1.33
.3	.5	.125	1.25
.3	.7	.09	1.13
.3	.9	.11	.96
.3	1.1	.22	.70

variances. Table A15-3 shows the results of this procedure when the data from Table A15-1 are used.[5]

Plotting the points shown in Table A15-3 yields isovariance ellipses. Figure A15-2 is a graph of the MVP, isovariance ellipses, isomean lines, and the critical line.

A15-4 GRAPHING ISOMEANS AND FINDING THE CRITICAL LINE

After the MVP is determined and a few isovariances are graphed, the fourth and fifth steps of graphical portfolio analysis can be undertaken.

Graphing Isomeans

Equation (A15-9) gives the general form of all isomean lines. Substituting the expected returns from Table A15-1 into Eq. (A15-9) yields (A15-21).

---

[5] Solving the quadratic formula (A15-20) is quite exacting and tedious. A computer program can be used expeditiously. Appendix B to Chap. 15 shows a Fortran IV computer program which is useful for plotting isovariances.

$$E(r_p) = w_1[E(r_1) - E(r_3)] + w_2[E(r_2) - E(r_3)] + E(r_3) \quad \text{(A15-9)}$$

$$E(r_p) = -.25w_1 - .23w_2 + .3 \quad \text{(A15-21)}$$

By varying the value of $E(r_p)$, a family of isomean lines is generated.

The simplest way to graph a linear equation in two variables like (A15-21) is to set one variable equal to zero and solve for the other variable. This will yield one point where the line crosses an axis. Next, the other variable is set to zero, and the equation is solved for the remaining variable. This yields a point on the other axis which the line passes through. Connecting these two points with a straight line yields the graph of the equation. For example, for the 10 percent isomean, $E(r_p) = .1$, the points where the isomean intersects the two axes are determined as follows:

$$E(r_p) = .1 = -.25w_1 - .23w_2 + .3$$

$$.2 = .25w_1 + .23w_2$$

$$.8 = w_1 \quad \text{if } w_2 = 0 \quad \text{so } (.80, 0) \text{ is one intercept point}$$

$$.87 = w_2 \quad \text{if } w_1 = 0 \quad \text{so } (0, .87) \text{ is the other intercept}$$

Plotting the two points $(w_1, w_2) = (.80, 0)$ and $(w_1, w_2) = (0, .87)$ yields two points on the 10 percent isomean. Running a straight line through these two points yields the 10 percent isomean line. This is shown in Fig. A15-2.

The formulas for the 5, 15, and 25 percent isomean lines are:

$$E(r_p) = w_1[E(r_1) - E(r_3)] + w_2[E(r_2) - E(r_3)] + E(r_3) \quad \text{(A15-9)}$$

$$E(r_p) = .05 = -.25w_1 - .23w_2 + .3$$

$$E(r_p) = .15 = -.25w_1 - .23w_2 + .3$$

$$E(r_p) = .25 = -.25w_1 - .23w_2 + .3$$

Solving these three equations shows the points at which the 5, 15, and 25 percent isomean lines intersect the axes. Table A15-4 shows the points where these and other isomeans intersect the axes.

TABLE A15-4 POINTS WHERE ISOMEAN LINES INTERSECT AXES

$E(r_p)$, %	w_1 when $w_2 = 0$	w_2 when $w_1 = 0$
5	1.0	1.09
10	.8	.87
15	.6	.65
20	.4	.435
25	.2	.217

Graphing the isomeans from the data in this table or with Eq. (A15-9) reveals that all isomean lines are parallel.

The Critical Line

After some isomeans and isovariances have been graphed, the critical line can be determined. The critical line delineates the weights of the efficient set of portfolios and shows the weights of the portfolio in every risk-class which has the maximum expected return. Since each isovariance ellipse represents one risk-class, the point where the highest isomean [that is, maximum $E(r_p)$ line] is just tangent to it shows the weights of the portfolio with the maximum expected return in that risk-class. The locus of all such tangencies between isovariances and isomeans is the critical line.

The critical line is shown in Fig. A15-2. It starts at the MVP and runs downward toward the w_1 axis. The critical line in this particular example extends downward since isomeans for higher expected returns lie below the isomeans for lower expected returns. In a different problem the isomeans would likely have a different slope, and the critical line would therefore extend in a different direction. These points in (w_1, w_2) space represent the efficient set of portfolios.[6] A two-dimensional graph like Fig. A15-2 shows only two of the three weights. The third weight may be determined by substituting the two weights shown in the graph into the constraining equation (A15-7) $w_1 + w_2 + w_3 = 1$ and solving for the third weight.

No Unusual Solutions Exist

Students who are learning Markowitz graphical portfolio analysis are sometimes alarmed when they perform the analysis with three different assets and find a different graph. This should be no cause for alarm. The isomeans are always parallel straight lines, but they may have any slope. The isovariances are always concentric ellipses centered on the MVP; they may, however, be oriented in any direction. The MVP may or may not lie in the positive quadrant (that is, where w_1 and w_2 are both positive). The critical line is always a straight line from the MVP; it may run in any direction. In general, there are no typical slopes which the various parts of the graphical

---

[6] By use of advanced mathematics it is possible to show that the following three linear relationships exist between the weights of the securities in the efficient portfolio and the expected returns of the efficient portfolios.

$$w_1 = .789 - 1.433E(r_p)^*$$

$$w_2 = .447 - 2.790E(r_p)^*$$

$$w_3 = -.236 + 4.223E(r_p)^*$$

where $E(r_p)^*$ denotes the expected return of an efficient portfolio. Note that $w_1 + w_2 + w_3 = 1$ for any given value of $E(r_p)^*$. Appendix C to this chapter shows how these formulas can be derived: it presumes a knowledge of calculus and matrix algebra.

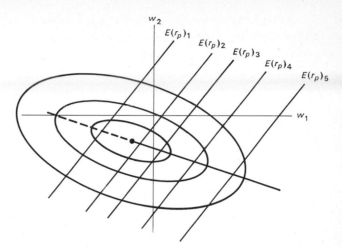

FIG. A15-3 Second example of graphical portfolio analysis.

analysis tend to follow. Figure A15-3 shows an example of a graphical portfolio analysis using three different assets; note that it differs significantly from Fig. A15-2 and that the MVP in Fig. A15-3 has negative values for w_1 and w_2.

Leveraged Portfolios

The critical line in Fig. A15-2 runs downward from the MVP. Where this critical line intersects the w_1 axis, we note that it branches into two critical lines. The second critical line starts off in a different direction; it runs along the w_1 axis to the origin and ends there. This second critical line represents the most efficient *nonleveraged* portfolios. All these portfolios lie within the positive quadrant bordered by points A, B, and C which trace a right triangle in Fig. A15-2. None of these portfolios contains negative weights. Since legal requirements forbid certain public portfolios such as open-end mutual funds from issuing debt, these portfolios are essentially constrained to lie within the triangle bordered by points A, B, and C. If the portfolio is free to issue debt, then it may follow the original, true critical line outside the triangle bordered by A, B, and C. Of course, the unconstrained critical line represents portfolios which dominate the portfolios along the constrained critical line. For example, note that the MVPs in Figs. A15-2 and A15-3 both happen to be leveraged portfolios (that is, one or more of the assets' participation levels is negative).

The Most Inefficient Portfolios

The most inefficient portfolios have the *lowest* expected return at each risk-class; these are the worst portfolios attainable. The most inefficient portfolios are found by extending the critical line in the wrong direction.

In Fig. A15-2 the most inefficient portfolios lie along the dotted portion of the critical line. All the most inefficient portfolios have expected returns below 5 percent, the expected return of the MVP.

A15-5 GRAPHING THE EFFICIENT FRONTIER

The critical line shows the weights of every portfolio on the efficient frontier. After the weights comprising a given portfolio are known, they may be substituted into the risk and return formulas to determine the expected return and risk of that portfolio. For example, let us select the point on the critical line in Fig. A15-2 where $w_1 = .5$ and $w_2 = -.11$. This implies that $w_3 = 1 - w_1 - w_2 = 1 - .5 + .11 = .61$. This is point Z in Fig. A15-2.

Calculating the Expected Return for an Efficient Portfolio

The expected return of the efficient portfolio represented by $w_1 = .5$ and $w_2 = -.11$ may be determined by substituting these values into Eq. (A15-9) or (A15-10).

$$E(r_p) = w_1[E(r_1) - E(r_3)] + w_2[E(r_2) - E(r_3)] + E(r_3) \qquad \text{(A15-9)}$$

$$\begin{aligned}
E(r_p) &= -.25w_1 - .23w_2 + .3 \qquad \qquad \qquad \qquad \text{(A15-10)}\\
&= -.25(.5) - .23(-.11) + .3\\
&= .2 = 20\%
\end{aligned}$$

Thus, we see that point Z in Fig. A15-2 represents an efficient portfolio with an expected return of 20 percent. This is obvious since the 20 percent isomean line passes through point Z.

Calculating the Risk for an Efficient Portfolio

The risk of the efficient portfolio at point Z may be calculated by substituting $w_1 = .5$ and $w_2 = -.11$ into Eq. (A15-11) or (A15-12a).

$$\begin{aligned}
\text{var}(r_p) &= .8w_1^2 + .5w_2^2 - 1.4w_1 - .8w_2 + .6w_1w_2 + .7 \qquad \text{(A15-12a)}\\
&= .8(.5)^2 + .5(-.11)^2 - 1.4(.5) - .8(-.11) + .6(.5)(-.11) + .7\\
&= .20 + .00605 - .70 + .088 - .033 + .7\\
&= .26105
\end{aligned}$$

This calculation shows that the efficient portfolio at point Z has a variance of .26105.

After several pairs of values for w_1 and w_2 have been read off of the critical line and the expected return and risk calculated for each, we have delineated the efficient frontier. Table A15-5 shows weights, expected returns, and risk statistics for portfolios lying on the critical line.

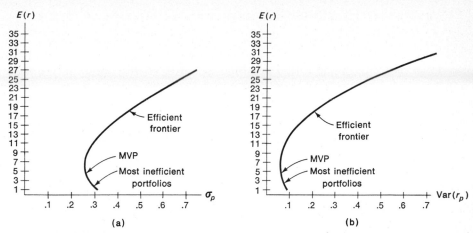

FIG. A15-4 The efficient frontier (a) in $[\sigma, E(r)]$ space; (b) in $[\sigma^2, E(r)]$ space.

Graphing

The efficient frontier is graphed by plotting the return and risk statistics for the portfolios lying along the critical line. Figure A15-4 is a graph of the data for the efficient portfolios shown in Table A15-5. Graphing the efficient frontier completes portfolio analysis.

TABLE A15-5 DATA FOR PORTFOLIOS LYING ON CRITICAL LINE

$E(r_p)$	σ	var(r_p)	w_1	w_2	w_3
.01	.3158	.0997	.7747	.4191	−.1938
.03	.2789	.0778	.7460	.3633	−.1093
.05	.2557	.0654	.7174	.3075	−.0249
.07	.2498	.0624	.6887	.2517	.0596
.09	.2626	.0690	.6600	.1959	.1441
.11	.2916	.0850	.6314	.1401	.2285
.13	.3325	.1106	.6027	.0843	.3130
.15	.3816	.1456	.5741	.0285	.3974
.17	.4361	.1902	.5454	−.0273	.4819
.19	.4941	.2442	.5167	−.0831	.5664
.21	.5547	.3077	.4881	−.1389	.6508
.23	.6170	.3807	.4594	−.1947	.7353
.25	.6806	.4632	.4308	−.2505	.8197
.27	.7451	.5552	.4021	−.3063	.9042
.29	.8104	.6567	.3734	−.3621	.9887
.31	.8762	.7677	.3448	−.4179	1.0731
.33	.9425	.8882	.3161	−4737	1.1576
.35	1.0091	1.0182	.2875	−.5295	1.2420
.37	1.0760	1.1577	.2588	−.5853	1.3265
.39	1.1431	1.3067	.2301	−.6411	1.4110

A15-6 PORTFOLIO REVISION

Portfolio analysis is a "one-period" portfolio optimization technique which uses expected returns, variances, and covariances as the basis for the analysis. In developing the optimum portfolio, security analysts must refine their estimates of the future into probability distributions of returns for some future time period. This future time period is then the horizon — it furnishes an upper limit on the period the resulting portfolio is designed to span. However, as history unfolds and the planning horizon draws nearer, new information becomes available and expectations change. As a result, the existing portfolio becomes suboptimal in terms of the newer expectations. Likewise, when the planning horizon is reached, the portfolio is based on a set of expectations which have most likely become obsolete. As a result of changing expectations, it will be necessary to revise a portfolio.

Even if the security analysts's expectations do not change, because of the dividend income and changes in prices which combine to yield the expected return of assets in the portfolio, the participation levels (the w_i's) of the various securities will become suboptimal as the prices change. Thus, portfolio revision is necessary to consider under almost any circumstance. Portfolio revision and other aspects of multiperiod portfolio management are discussed in Chapter 18.

A15-7 CONCLUSIONS

This appendix has outlined the security analysis and portfolio analysis process which will yield efficient portfolios. Section A15-1 showed how to generate the input statistics needed for portfolio analysis — this is essentially a security analysis function. Then a numerical example was utilized to show how to use graphical portfolio analysis to delineate the efficient frontier for a three-asset portfolio. This graphical exercise provides an excellent teaching vehicle for beginning portfolio analysts. Appendix C shows a more sophisticated mathematical approach to performing portfolio analysis which can analyze portfolios containing any number of assets and, therefore, has more practical value. These are the tools and procedures necessary to implement Markowitz diversification on a meaningful scale (for example, in a large institutional portfolio). If an investor or a portfolio manager utilizes portfolio analysis as it was outlined in this chapter, he or she should be able to manage a portfolio so it will maximize the owner's expected utility.

APPENDIX B TO CHAPTER 15
Fortran IV Program to Plot Isovariance Ellipses for Three-Security Portfolios

The most tedious, exacting, and error-prone phase of graphical portfolio analysis is repetitively solving the quadratic formula to obtain plotting points in (w_1, w_2) space for the isovariances. The Fortran IV program shown in Fig. B15-1 will perform these calculations for one or more three-security portfolios.

One data card with six decimal numbers is required for each portfolio. If three-portfolio problems are to be solved, then three data cards are to be

FIG. B15-1 Fortran IV program to plot points for isovariance ellipses.

```
      REAL                VARP,W2,A,B,C,V1,V2,V3,COV13,COV12,COV23
      REAL                FW1,SW1, SQRT , S,B1,B2,C1,C2,C3,SRS,NFW1,NSW1
      INTEGER VARC,W2C
9     PRINT10
10    FORMAT('1','PROGAM TO PLOT ISOVARIANCES BY DR J C FRANCIS'/)
15    READ(5,16)V1,V2,V3, COV12, COV13, COV23
16    FORMAT(6F10.7)
17    IF( V1.GE.10.)GO TO 135
20    PRINT 21
21    FORMAT('0 ','VARIANCE',6X,'FIRST W1',3X,'SECOND W1',4X,'W2',7X,
     C 'A', 10X, 'B', 12X, 'C' , 9X 'S',9X,'SRS',9X,'NFW1'//)
30    VARP= 0
33    DO 120 VARC=1,8
36    VARP=VARP+ .05
39    W2=-2.5
42    DO 119 W2C=1,30
44    W2=W2 + .1
46    A=V1+V3-COV13*2
48    B1=2*COV13 - 2*V3
50    B2=2*(V3 +COV12 - COV13 -COV23)
52    B=B1 + B2*W2
54    C1=V3 - VARP
56    C2=V2+V3-2*COV23
58    C3=2*(COV23 - V3)
60    C= C1 + C2*(W2**2) + C3*W2
70    S=(B**2)-(4*A*C)
75    IF(S)119,78,78
78    SRS=  SQRT(S)
80    NFW1=  -B+ SRS
82    NSW1= -B-SRS
84    FW1= NFW1/(2*A)
86    SW1= NSW1/(2*A)
90    PRINT91,VARP,FW1,SW1,W2, A,B,C,S,SRS,NFW1
91    FORMAT(' ', 10F11.6)
119   CONTINUE
120   CONTINUE
124   PRINT125,V1, V2, V3, COV12, COV13, COV23
125   FORMAT('  VAR=',F7.4,'VAR2=',F9.6,' VAR3=',F9.6, /
     C        '  COV12=',F9.6 ,'  COV13=',F9.6, '  COV23=',F9.6)
130    GO TO 9
135    STOP
C 136    END OF PROGRAM DATA CARDS FOLLOW, ONE CARD PER PORTFOLIO
       END
```

stacked after the end (that is, after statement 137) of the program. Each data card must conform to the following format:

Field	Columns	Data item
1	1–10	Variance for asset 1, that is, σ_1^2
2	11–20	Variance for asset 2, that is, σ_2^2
3	21–30	Variance for asset 3, that is, σ_3^2
4	31–40	Covariance between 1 and 2, that is, σ_{12}
5	41–50	Covariance between 1 and 3, that is, σ_{13}
6	51–60	Covariance between 2 and 3, that is, σ_{23}

After the last data card, place a card which has a real number larger than 10 in columns 1 through 10; this will end the program.

The printed output from the program is shown in Fig. B15-2. The output data are for the problem solved in the chapter. Only the first four columns of the output data are used to plot isovariances; the rest of the output facilitates checking the program.

FIG. B15-2 Output data for isovariance plotting program.

PROGRAM TO PLOT ISOVARIANCES BY   DR. J. C. FRANCIS

VARIANCE	FIRST W1	SECOND W1	W2	A	B	C	S
0.050000	0.850001	0.749999	0.200001	0.800000	-1.280000	0.510000	0.006400
0.050000	0.875000	0.650000	0.300001	0.800000	-1.220000	0.455000	0.032400
0.050000	0.839564	0.610435	0.400001	0.800000	-1.160000	0.410000	0.033600
0.050000	0.749999	0.625001	0.500001	0.800000	-1.100000	0.375000	0.010000
0.100001	1.000001	0.749999	0.000001	0.800000	-1.400000	0.600000	0.040001
0.100000	1.050000	0.624999	0.100001	0.800000	-1.340000	0.525000	0.115600
0.100000	1.054951	0.545049	0.200001	0.800000	-1.280000	3.460000	0.166400
0.100000	1.036646	0.488353	0.300001	0.800000	-1.220000	3.405000	0.192400
0.100000	1.000000	0.450000	0.400001	0.800000	-1.160000	0.360000	0.193600
0.100000	0.945194	0.429806	0.500001	0.800000	-1.100000	0.325000	0.170000
0.150000	1.109747	0.715252	-0.099999	0.800000	-1.460000	0.634999	0.099601
0.150000	1.154509	0.595491	0.000001	0.800000	-1.400000	0.550000	0.200001
0.150000	1.165610	0.509389	0.100001	0.800000	-1.340000	0.475000	0.275600
0.150000	1.157071	0.442928	0.200001	0.800000	-1.280000	0.410000	0.326400
0.150000	1.133520	0.391479	0.300001	0.800000	-1.220000	0.355000	0.352400
0.150000	1.096651	0.353348	0.400001	0.800000	-1.160000	0.310000	0.353600
0.150000	1.046535	0.328465	0.500001	0.800000	-1.100000	0.275000	0.330000
0.200000	1.179129	0.720870	-0.199999	0.800000	-1.520000	0.679999	0.134401
0.200000	1.230944	0.594056	-0.099999	0.800000	-1.460000	0.584999	0.259601
0.200000	1.250000	0.499999	0.000001	0.800000	-1.400000	0.500000	0.360001
0.200000	1.250000	0.425000	0.100001	0.800000	-1.340000	0.425000	0.435600
0.200000	1.235890	0.364110	0.200001	0.800000	-1.280000	0.360000	0.486400
:	:	:	:	:	:	:	:
0.350000	1.347997	0.102007	0.400001	0.800000	-1.160000	0.110000	0.993600
0.350000	1.303053	0.071946	0.500001	0.800000	-1.100000	0.075000	0.970000
0.400000	1.200002	0.999998	-0.600000	0.800000	-1.760000	0.959999	0.025601
0.400000	1.375000	0.749999	-0.500000	0.800000	-1.700000	0.824999	0.250001
0.400000	1.444077	0.605923	-0.399999	0.800000	-1.640000	0.699999	0.449601
0.400000	1.481369	0.493631	-0.299999	0.800000	-1.580000	0.584999	0.624401
0.400000	1.500000	0.400000	-0.199999	0.800000	-1.520000	0.479999	0.774401
0.400000	1.505295	0.319704	-0.099999	0.800000	-1.460000	0.384999	0.899601
0.400000	1.500000	0.250000	0.000001	0.800000	-1.400000	0.300000	1.000001
0.400000	1.485694	0.189305	0.100001	0.800000	-1.340000	0.225000	1.075600
0.400000	1.463325	0.136675	0.200001	0.800000	-1.280000	0.160000	1.126400
0.400000	1.433437	0.091563	0.300001	0.800000	-1.220000	0.105000	1.152400
0.400000	1.396286	0.053714	0.400001	0.800000	-1.160000	0.060000	1.153600
0.400000	1.351884	0.023116	0.500001	0.800000	-1.100000	0.025000	1.130000

VAR1= 0.100000 VAR2= 0.400000   VAR3= 0.700000
COV12=-0.100000   COV13=-0.000000   COV23= 0.300000

Those who wish to study the computer program in more detail will find the following list of definitions of variables helpful.

VARP = the variance of the portfolio

W1, W2, W3 = the participation levels of the three assets in the portfolio; W1 is output, W2 is a variable in the program, and W3 is implicit and does not appear in the program

V1, V2, V3 = the variances of the three assets

COV12, COV13, COV23 = the covariances between the three assets

S = the discriminant = $B^2 - 4AC$

SRS = the square root of the discriminant

A = coefficients of w_1^2 in $Aw_1^2 + Bw_1 + C = 0$

B = coefficients of w_1 in $Aw_1^2 + Bw_1 + C = 0$

C = constants plus functions of $w_2 = C1 + (C2)[(W2)^2] + (C3)(W2)$

FW1, SW1 = the first and second root of $Aw_1^2 + Bw_1 + C = 0$

NFW1, NSW1 = the numerators of FW1 and SW1

APPENDIX C TO CHAPTER 15
Mathematical Portfolio Analysis

Graphical portfolio analysis, presented in Chap. 15, cannot handle more than four securities. However, it serves well as an introduction to portfolio analysis and, one hopes, permits a better understanding of the analysis and of the solution obtained. A more efficient solution technique for portfolio analysis which uses differential calculus and linear algebra is explained in this appendix.

A Calculus Risk Minimization Solution: General Form

Calculus can be used to find the minimum risk portfolio for any given expected return E^*. Mathematically, the problem involves finding the minimum portfolio variance. That is,

$$\text{Minimize var}(r_p) = \sum_i^n \sum_j^n w_i w_j \sigma_{ij} \tag{C15-1}$$

subject to two Lagrangian constraints. The first constraint requires that the desired expected return E^* be achieved. This is equivalent to requiring the following equation:

$$\sum_i^n w_i E(r_i) - E^* = 0 \tag{C15-2}$$

The second constraint requires that the weights sum to 1. Of course, this constraint is equivalent to requiring the following equation:

$$\sum_i^n w_i - 1 = 0 \tag{C15-3}$$

Combining these three quantities yields the Lagrangian objective function of the risk minimization problem with a desired return constraint:

$$z = \sum_i^n \sum_j^n w_i w_j \sigma_{ij} + \lambda_1 \left(\sum^n w_i E(r_i) - E^* \right) + \lambda_2 \left(\sum^n w_i - 1 \right) \tag{C15-4}$$

The minimum risk portfolio is found by setting $\partial z/\partial w_i = \partial z/\partial \lambda_j = 0$ for $i = 1, \ldots, n$ and $j = 1, 2$ and solving the system of equations for the w_i's. The number of assets analyzed (n) can be any positive integer. Martin solved this problem and has shown the relationship between the solution and the graphical critical line solution in a readable article which the interested reader is invited to pursue.[1]

Calculus Minimization of Risk: A Three-Security Portfolio

For a three-security portfolio, the objective function to be minimized is

$$z = w_1^2 \sigma_{11} + w_2^2 \sigma_{22} + w_3^2 \sigma_{33} + 2w_1 w_2 \sigma_{12} + 2w_1 w_3 \sigma_{13} + 2w_2 w_3 \sigma_{33}$$
$$+ \lambda_1 (w_1 E_1 + w_2 E_2 + w_3 E_3 - E^*) + \lambda_2 (w_1 + w_2 + w_3 - 1) \tag{C15-4}$$

Setting the partial derivatives of z with respect to all variables equal to zero yields equation system (C15-5) below.

$$\frac{\partial z}{\partial w_1} = 2w_1 \sigma_{11} + 2w_2 \sigma_{12} + 2w_3 \sigma_{13} + \lambda_1 E_1 + \lambda_2 = 0$$

$$\frac{\partial z}{\partial w_2} = 2w_2 \sigma_{22} + 2w_1 \sigma_{12} + 2w_3 \sigma_{23} + \lambda_1 E_2 + \lambda_2 = 0$$

$$\frac{\partial z}{\partial w_3} = 2w_3 \sigma_{33} + 2w_1 \sigma_{13} + 2w_2 \sigma_{23} + \lambda_1 E_3 + \lambda_2 = 0 \tag{C15-5}$$

$$\frac{\partial z}{\partial \lambda_2} = w_1 + w_2 + w_3 - 1 = 0$$

$$\frac{\partial z}{\partial \lambda_1} = w_1 E_1 + w_2 E_2 + w_3 E_3 - E^* = 0$$

[1] A. D. Martin, Jr., "Mathematical Programming of Portfolio Selections," *Management Science,* January 1955, pp. 152–166. Reprinted in E. B. Frederickson, *Frontiers of Investment Analysis* (Scranton, Pa.: International Textbook Co., 1965), pp. 367–381.

This system is linear since the weights (w_1's) are the variables and they are all of degree 1; thus the system may be solved as a system of linear equations. The matrix representation of this system of linear equations is shown below as matrix equation (C15-5).

$$\begin{bmatrix} 2\sigma_{11} & 2\sigma_{12} & 2\sigma_{13} & E_1 & 1 \\ 2\sigma_{21} & 2\sigma_{22} & 2\sigma_{33} & E_2 & 1 \\ 2\sigma_{31} & 2\sigma_{32} & 2\sigma_{33} & E_3 & 1 \\ 1 & 1 & 1 & 0 & 0 \\ E_1 & E_2 & E_3 & 0 & 0 \end{bmatrix} \begin{bmatrix} w_1 \\ w_2 \\ w_3 \\ \lambda_2 \\ \lambda_1 \end{bmatrix} = \begin{bmatrix} 0 \\ 0 \\ 0 \\ 1 \\ E^* \end{bmatrix} \qquad \text{(C15-5)}$$
$$C \qquad\qquad\qquad w \quad = \quad k$$

This system may be solved several different ways. With matrix notation, the inverse of the coefficients matrix (C^{-1}) may be used to find the solution (weight) vector (w) as follows:

$$Cw = k$$
$$C^{-1}Cw = C^{-1}k$$
$$Iw = C^{-1}k \qquad\qquad \text{(C15-6)}$$
$$w = C^{-1}k$$

The solution will give the n ($n = 3$ in this case) weights in terms of E^*.

$$w_1 = \alpha_1 + d_1 E^*$$
$$w_2 = \alpha_2 + d_2 E^* \qquad\qquad \text{(C15-7)}$$
$$w_3 = \alpha_3 + d_3 E^*$$

where the α_i and d_i are constants. For any desired E^* the equations give the weights of the minimum risk portfolio. These are the weights of a portfolio in the efficient frontier. By varying E^* the weights may be generated for the entire efficient frontier. Then the risk, var(V_p), of the efficient portfolios may be calculated, and the efficient frontier may be graphed.

As a numerical example, the data from the three-security portfolio problem which was solved graphically in Appendix A of this chapter yield the following coefficients matrix.

$$\begin{bmatrix} 2\sigma_{11} & 2\sigma_{12} & 2\sigma_{13} & E_1 & 1 \\ 2\sigma_{21} & 2\sigma_{22} & 2\sigma_{23} & E_2 & 1 \\ 2\sigma_{31} & 2\sigma_{32} & 2\sigma_{33} & E_3 & 1 \\ 1 & 1 & 1 & 0 & 0 \\ E_1 & E_2 & E_3 & 0 & 0 \end{bmatrix} = \begin{bmatrix} 2(.1) & 2(-.1) & 2(0) & .05 & 1 \\ 2(-.1) & 2(.4) & 2(.3) & .07 & 1 \\ 2(0) & 2(.3) & 2(.7) & .3 & 1 \\ 1 & 1 & 1 & 0 & 0 \\ .05 & .07 & .3 & 0 & 0 \end{bmatrix} = C$$

Multiplying the inverse of this coefficients matrix by the constants vector (k) yields the weights vector ($C^{-1}k = w$) as shown below in matrix Eq. (C15-6).

$$
\overset{C^{-1}}{\begin{bmatrix}
.677 & .736 & .059 & .789 & -1.433 \\
-.736 & .800 & -.064 & .447 & -2.790 \\
.059 & -.064 & .005 & -.236 & 4.223 \\
-1.433 & -2.790 & 4.223 & .522 & -15.869 \\
.789 & .447 & -.236 & -.095 & .552
\end{bmatrix}}
\overset{k}{\begin{bmatrix}
0 \\ 0 \\ 0 \\ 1 \\ E^*
\end{bmatrix}}
=
\overset{w}{\begin{bmatrix}
w_1 \\ w_2 \\ w_3 \\ \lambda_1 \\ \lambda_2
\end{bmatrix}}
\qquad \text{(C15-6)}
$$

Evaluating the weights vector yields the system of Eqs. (C15-7) below.

$$
\left.
\begin{aligned}
w_1 &= .789 - 1.433E^* \\
w_2 &= .447 - 2.790E^* \\
w_3 &= -.236 + 4.223E^*
\end{aligned}
\right\} w_1 + w_2 + w_3 = 1 \text{ for any given } E^* \qquad \text{(C15-7)}
$$

$$
\lambda_1 = .522 - 15.869E^*
$$
$$
\lambda_2 = -.095 + .522E^*
$$

The weights in the three equations (C15-7) sum to unity, are a linear function of E^*, and represent the weights of the three securities in the efficient portfolio at the point where $E(r_p) = E^*$. Varying E^* generates the weights of all the efficient portfolios.

APPENDIX D TO CHAPTER 15
Stochastic Dominance

Stochastic dominance selection rules utilize every bit of information in the probability distributions rather than simply focus on the probability distribution's first two moments. As a result, stochastic dominance selection rules can occasionally yield portfolios which maximize expected utility and are not Markowitz efficient portfolios. Figure D15-1 shows that in terms of the logic of stochastic dominance, inefficient portfolio A is more desirable than efficient portfolio B for example. This demonstrates that portfolio analysis methods which consider only the first two moments may waste some information which could be used to maximize investors' expected utility.

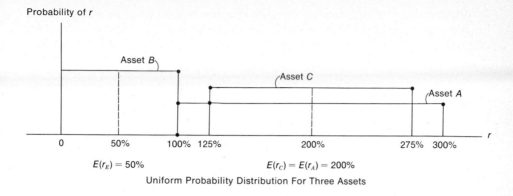

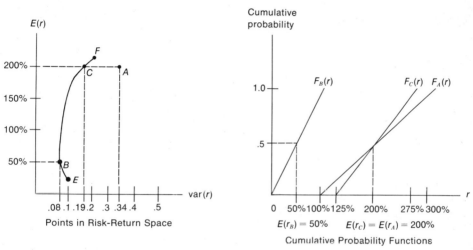

FIG. D15-1 Data for three risky assets. The bases for the graphs are uniform probability distributions from b to c. It is well known that the expected value of such distribution is $E(r) = (b + c)/2$; the variance is $\sigma^2 = (c - b)^2/12$; and the cumulative probability of a return less than or equal to r_0 is $F(r_0) = (r_0 - b)/(c - b)$.

Probability distribution A is said to stochastically dominate probability distribution B if the cumulative probability of achieving any rate of return up to some specified level for distribution A is less than, or equal to, that same cumulative probability for asset B and, at least at one point, the less than inequality holds. In common sense terms, this means that the chances of earning a low rate of return from asset A are lower than the chances of earning a low return from asset B.

Figure D15-1 graphically depicts how portfolio A stochastically dominates portfolio B even though A is an inefficient portfolio. For any given rate of return, the cumulative probability that asset B earns up to that return is larger than the cumulative probability that A earns up to that same return. This is obvious since portfolio A's lowest return (of 100 percent) equals portfolio B's highest possible return.[1]

The advantages of selecting investments with the stochastic dominance criteria instead of risk-return criteria are:

1 Stochastic dominance orderings do not presume a certain form of probability distribution.

2 Fewer restrictions on the investor's utility function are implied by use of the stochastic dominance criteria.

3 Undesirable portfolios, such as those on the lower section of the efficient frontier, can be eliminated from further consideration.[2]

4 The stochastic dominance selection criteria do not waste information about the probability distribution; *every* point is considered.

Although stochastic dominance selection rules are logically superior to other simpler selection criteria, their practical value is dubious since they require knowledge of *every point* on the probability distribution rather than, for example, merely the first two moments. It requires rather heroic confidence to try to estimate *every* point on a probability distribution in this world of uncertainty and changing expectations. The cost of estimating the entire probability distribution not only exceeds the cost of estimating the first two moments, but this cost probably is not justified in terms of the additional benefits it could realistically be expected to yield. This is an empirical question which is not as yet completely resolved.[3]

---

[1] More rigorous mathematical statements are usually used to define stochastic dominance. Some writers distinguish between first degree, second degree, and third degree stochastic dominance. In the interest of brevity these distinctions are not developed here. For a more detailed discussion, see J. P. Quirk and R. Saposnik, "Admissibility and Measurable Utility Functions," *Review of Economic Studies,* 1962. An unpublished paper by R. B. Porter and J. E. Gaumnitz, "Stochastic Dominance versus Mean-Variance Portfolio Analysis," Working Paper no. 37, University of Kansas, School of Business, December 1970, provides some empirical evidence comparing stochastic dominance selection with mean-variance selection.

[2] W. J. Baumol, "An Expected Gain-Confidence Limit Criterion for Portfolio Selection," *Management Science,* October 1963, pp. 171–182.

[3] Interested readers may learn more about stochastic dominance by pursuing the following articles and their references. W. H. Jean compares and contrasts stochastic dominance and the mean-variance criteria (and higher-order moments) in a March 1975 article in the *Journal of Financial and Quantitative Analysis* entitled "Comparison of Moment and Stochastic Dominance Ranking Methods." R. Burr Porter published an empirical analysis entitled "An Empirical Comparison of Stochastic Dominance and Mean-Variance Portfolio Choice Criteria" in the September 1973 *Journal of Financial and Quantitative Analysis.*

Sixteen

Capital Market Theory

Capital market theory concerns asset valuation. The theory considers all marketable investments—that is, thousands of stocks, thousands of bonds, options, commodities, warrants, and other things—simultaneously, and explains how their prices should behave. Parts of this theory have already been introduced in studying individual assets. The notions of a security's total risk, systematic risk, and unsystematic risk were explained and the concept of the security market line (SML) was presented in Chap. 12. Then in Chap. 15, when the discussion turned to portfolios instead of individual assets, the capital market line (CML) emerged as a portfolio pricing model. This chapter pulls all these ideas together and shows how they interact in one unified economic theory about investments markets.

16-1 INVESTMENT OPPORTUNITIES IN RISK-RETURN SPACE

Chapter 15 explained how to determine the efficient frontier for a group of assets. Suppose that all investment assets in the world were analyzed. Stocks, bonds, paintings, entrepreneurships, foreign exchange, commodities, and many other marketable assets would be considered. By use of a large computer and advanced mathematics, it is possible to perform portfolio analysis upon these thousands of assets and thus to determine the efficient frontier. Figure 16-1 shows the investment opportunities which might be shown to exist by such a massive analysis.

The Efficient Frontier

All the thousands of investment opportunities in the world are assumed to be represented by the escalloped quarter-moon–shaped design in Fig. 16-1.

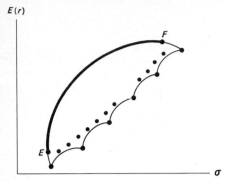

E(r)

F

E

σ

FIG. 16-1 The opportunity set without borrowing and lending opportunities.

The individual assets lie along the *bottom* of this set of investment opportunities and are represented by the dots.

Individual assets (like stocks, bonds, and other securities) contain both systematic risk and unsystematic risk and are not efficient. Only *portfolios* using Markowitz diversification have had the unsystematic risk reduced to zero and can attain the curved efficient frontier. The efficient frontier is represented by the heavy dark curve from *E* to *F* in Fig. 16-1. The portfolios lying on the efficient frontier contain only systematic risk caused by variations in the economic, political, and sociological environment which affect nearly all assets in some way. As a result, the efficient assets along the curve *EF* in Fig. 16-1 are highly positively (but not perfectly) correlated.

Borrowing and Lending at a Riskless Rate

The investment opportunities shown in Fig. 16-1 may be extended by considering the possibilities of borrowing and lending. To keep the model simple and easy to conceptualize, suppose that all investors can borrow or lend at one riskless rate of return, denoted *R*.

Figure 16-2 represents the investment, the borrowing, and the lending opportunities which would exist in equilibrium if all investors were Markowitz portfolio analysts, could borrow or lend at rate *R*, and had homogeneous expectations. The term *homogeneous expectations* means that all investors visualize the same expected return, risk, and correlation statistics for every asset in the world. This assumption allows us to represent the investment opportunities visualized by every investor with just one graph rather than draw separate graphs to represent differences of opinion over risk and return statistics.

The Market Portfolio

Portfolio *M* in Fig. 16-2 is a huge portfolio containing all assets in the world in the proportions w_i^* where

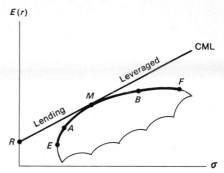

FIG. 16-2 Borrowing, lending, and investment opportunities in a market of Markowitz diversifiers.

$$w_i^* = \frac{\text{total value of the } i\text{th security}}{\text{total value of all securities in the market}}$$

Let M be designated as the *market portfolio*. It contains all securities in exactly the proportions they are supplied in equilibrium because it is the one unique portfolio which all investors would buy. The return on the market portfolio is the weighted average return on all securities in the market.[1]

Of course, there is no real-life analog to the market portfolio, but it is a useful theoretical construct since the return on M is the return that the Dow Jones average, Standard & Poor's average, and the New York Stock Exchange index are estimating.

16-2 ASSUMPTIONS UNDERLYING CAPITAL MARKET THEORY

Capital market theory is based on the assumptions underlying portfolio analysis. The theory consists essentially of the logical, mathematical, and economic implications of portfolio analysis. The assumptions which form the basis for performing Markowitz portfolio analysis to delineate the efficient frontier are the following:

> **1** The rate of return from an investment adequately summarizes the outcome from the investment, and investors see the various possible rates of return in a probabilistic fashion (that is, they visualize a probability distribution of rates of return either consciously or subconsciously).

[1] The market portfolio is E. Fama's concept. See "Risk, Return and Equilibrium: Some Clarifying Comments," *Journal of Finance*, March 1968, pp. 32–33. However, Wm. Sharpe had previously published the conclusions discussed in this chapter before anyone else without the market portfolio notion. See "Capital Asset Prices: A Theory of Market Equilibrium under Conditions of Risk," *Journal of Finance*, September 1964, pp. 425–552.

2 Investors' risk estimates are proportional to the variability of return (namely, the standard deviation or variance) they perceive for a security or portfolio.

3 Investors are willing to base their decisions on only two parameters of the probability distribution of returns, the expected return and the variance (or its square root, the standard deviation) of returns. Symbolically, $U = f(E(r), \sigma)$ where U denotes the investors' utility.

4 For any risk-class, investors prefer a higher rate of return to a lower one. Symbolically, $\partial U/\partial E(r) > 0$. Conversely, among all securities with the same rate of return, investors prefer less rather than more risk. Symbolically, $\partial U/\partial \sigma < 0$.

Investors who conform to the preceding assumptions will prefer efficient portfolios. Such investors will be referred to as *Markowitz diversifiers*. With this background, it is possible to begin to discuss capital market theory. The assumptions necessary to generate the capital market theory are listed below.

1 All investors are Markowitz efficient diversifiers who delineate and seek to attain the efficient frontier (that is, the four assumptions in the preceding list).

2 Any amount of money can be borrowed or lent at the risk-free rate of interest R. The return on short-term U.S. government bonds may be used as a proxy for R. No other borrowing is permitted.

3 Idealized uncertainty prevails; that is, all investors visualize identical probability distributions for future rates of return. They have homogeneous expectations.

4 All investors have the same "one-period" time horizon.

5 All investments are infinitely divisible; fractional shares may be purchased in any portfolio or any individual asset.

6 No taxes and no transaction costs for buying and selling securities exist.

7 No inflation and no change in the level of interest rates exist (or all changes are fully anticipated).

8 The capital markets are in equilibrium.

Readers who are unaccustomed to economic analysis are probably confused and discouraged by a theory which is based upon a list of unrealistic assumptions, but they should not be. The assumptions provide a concrete foundation upon which a theory can be derived by applying the forces of logic, intuition, and mathematics. Without these assumptions, the analysis would degenerate into a polemic discussion of which historical facts, folklore, and institutions are significant, which are insignificant, what their relationships are, and what conclusions might be reached by a "reasonable person." Such discussions are usually not productive.

Traditionally, economists have based their analyses on as few and as simple assumptions as possible. Then a theory is derived with conclusions and implications which are incontestable, given the assumptions. Later the assumptions are relaxed to determine what can be expected in more realistic circumstances. In the final analysis, the test of a theory is not how realistic its assumptions are; rather, it is the predictive power of a model which should be judged. Later in this chapter, the assumptions underlying the capital market theory are aligned with reality in order to see whether the implications of the model are changed. Before this alignment is made, however, the parts of the capital market theory will be examined in a unified presentation.

16-3 THE CHARACTERISTIC LINE: A CLOSER EXAMINATION

The characteristic line describing the period-by-period interaction between the rates of return of asset i and the rates of change in some market index is defined in Eq. (16-1); it is a model of market forces as they affect the ith asset.

$$r_{it} = a_i + b_i r_{Mt} + e_t \qquad (16\text{-}1)$$

where r_{it} is the tth observation of the ith asset's rate of return; r_{Mt} is the tth observed rate of return on the market portfolio or some other market index; e_{it} is the tth random error term (which has an expected value of zero, constant finite variance, and is independent of other e_t's); and a_i and b_i are least-squares regression coefficients.[2] This model may be used to show that variation in r_i is introduced from two sources: variation in r_M and variation in e_t. Taking the variance of both sides of Eq. (16-1) yields (16-2).

$$\begin{aligned}
\text{var}(r_i) &= \text{var}(a_i + b_i r_M + e) \qquad (16\text{-}2)\\
&= \text{var}(a_i) + \text{var}(b_i r_M) + \text{var}(e)\\
&= 0 + \text{var}(b_i r_M) + \text{var}(e)\\
&= \text{systematic risk} + \text{unsystematic risk} \qquad (16\text{-}2a)
\end{aligned}$$

Equation (16-2a) shows clearly that the two sources of variability in r_i are due to systematic and unsystematic risk.

Graphing Characteristic Lines

For prediction purposes, the conditional expectation of (16-1), which is shown in Eq. (16-3), is useful.

---

[2] The assumptions about the error term are merely the usual minimum assumptions which should be fulfilled by any simple, linear regression if the statistics from the regression are to be unbiased.

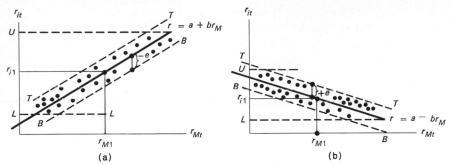

FIG. 16-3 Two different characteristic lines. (*a*) Regression line for an asset with cyclical returns; (*b*) regression line for an asset with countercyclical returns.

$$E(r_i/r_M) = a_i + b_i r_M \qquad (16\text{-}3)$$

Two possible forms that Eq. (16-1) may assume are shown in Fig. 16-3. Equation (16-3) has been fitted to (*a*) a firm which has returns that are positively correlated with the returns on the market, and (*b*) a firm whose returns are negatively correlated with the market. For these two firms, the characteristic lines indicate that when the rate of return for the market portfolio is r_{M1}, the security is expected to earn a return of r_{i1}.

In terms of capital market theory language, the asset in Fig. 16-3a has more systematic risk than the asset in Fig. 16-3b. It has a positive slope coefficient b_i, positive covariance of returns with the returns on M, and positive correlation of returns with returns on M. The firm in Fig. 16-3b has a negative regression slope coefficient b_i, negative covariance, and negative correlation coefficient. Thus the asset in (*b*) will decrease the risk of a portfolio which is correlated with M (as most portfolios are) more than the asset in (*a*). Most simply, the asset in (*b*) is the better candidate for Markowitz diversification purposes. The b_i coefficient is an index of systematic risk; it is variously referred to as the beta coefficient or as an index of market sensitivity or as a volatility index.

Unsystematic Risk Is Residual Variance

Any time Eq. (16-1) results in a correlation coefficient below 1, the observations will not all lie on the regression line; of course, this is the typical case graphed in Fig. 16-3. The vertical deviations of the observations from the regression line are called *residual errors* and are denoted e in Eq. (16-1). Although the least-squares regression technique used to derive Eq. (16-1) minimizes the sum of the squared errors $\left(\min \sum_{t=1}^{n} e_{it}^2\right)$ over all the observations, the sum is still a nonnegative value. The term $\sigma^2(r_i/r_M)$ is called the *residual variance around the regression line* in statistical terms or *unsystematic risk* in capital market theory language.

$$\sigma^2(r_i|r_M) = \frac{\sum\limits_{n}^{n} e_i^2}{n} \tag{16-4}$$

$$= \frac{\sum\limits_{n}^{n} (r_{it} - a - br_{Mt})^2}{n} = \mathrm{var}(e)$$

The residual variance is the squared standard error in regression language, a measure of unsystematic risk.

In Fig. 16-3 the total range over which the returns varied is represented graphically by the vertical distance between the upper (U) and lower (L) horizontal dotted lines. The residual or unsystematic range of variability is represented graphically by the vertical distance between the top (T) and bottom (B) dotted lines which are parallel to the characteristic line. These dotted lines ($U,L,T,$ and B) are not any kind of boundary lines; they are merely added to depict graphically the total risk (between U and L) and unsystematic risk (between T and B).

Comparative Statics for a Change in Profitability[3]

If a firm were to experience a change in earning power, its characteristic line might or might not move. Suppose a technological breakthrough occurred which increased a firm's income at every level of sales. If the increased earnings raised the firm's expected rate of return at any given sales volume by one percentage point, the characteristic line might shift upward by one percentage point on the vertical axis. Figure 16-4 represents one possible shift.

In Fig. 16-4 the rise in the characteristic line is measured by the change in the intercept coefficients ($a_2 - a_1$). If the firm is to continue to yield a higher rate of return to its shareholders, it must experience an increase in systematic risk. This is the equilibrium relation between expected return and systematic risk which was represented by the SML. Thus, the slope of the firm's characteristic line must increase from b_1 and b_2, as shown in Fig. 16-4.

If an increase in systematic risk does *not* accompany the rise in earnings, a once-and-for-all capital gain will result from the increase in earnings. This capital gain will raise the firm's purchase price enough that its expected return will not change although future dividends may be expected to remain higher. That is, both the numerator and the denominator in Eq. (16-5) will increase proportionally so the expected return does not change.

---

[3] Comparative statics involves comparing different static equilibriums. Thus, Fig. 16-4 does not depict the once-and-for-all capital gain and unusually large one-period rate of return which would occur because of the increased earning power.

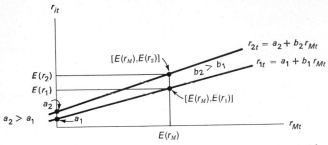

FIG. 16-4 Comparative statics of a change in earning power with a change in systematic risk.

$$E(r) = \frac{E(\text{capital gains} + \text{dividends})}{\text{purchase price}} \tag{16-5}$$

Thus the firm's systematic risk and expected return will be unchanged, and the original characteristic line will still describe the characteristic pattern for the firm's rates of return. Investors who owned the stock at the time the once-and-for-all capital gain occurred will have captured the capitalized value of the earnings increase (that is, the big one-time capital gain).

Firms with Different Systematic Risks

All simple linear regression lines pass through the *centroid* where the expected value (or mean) of both variables occurs. Since the characteristic line is a regression line, it must pass through this point $[E(r_m), E(r_i)]$. The centroids and three different characteristic lines are shown graphically in Fig. 16-5.

FIG. 16-5 Comparison of three firms with different systematic risks.

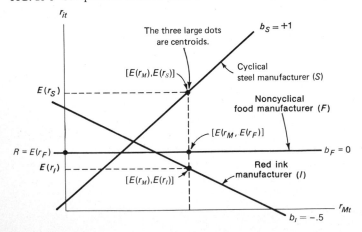

Suppose one firm depicted in Fig. 16-5 is a steel manufacturer, denoted S. Such a firm's sales and profits will likely follow the level of activity in the national economy. As a result, the steel firm has a beta regression slope (systematic risk) coefficient of unity. The second firm is the noncyclical firm denoted F, which might be a food manufacturer; its beta coefficient is zero, and so its returns are not expected to vary owing to systematic risk factors. The third hypothetical firm shown in Fig. 16-5 is a red ink manufacturer denoted I. This firm is unique in that its returns characteristically covary inversely with the rate of return from the market. Supposedly, red ink sells better in recessions and depressions; so the manufacturer has a beta coefficient of $-\frac{1}{2}$.

As a result of the basic difference in the characteristics of each business, the three firms in Fig. 16-5 all have drastically different beta coefficients, $b_S > b_F = 0 > b_I$. Since expected returns are a function of systematic risk for all assets, the three firms' expected returns also differ as follows: $E(r_S) > E(r_F) = R > E(r_I)$, where R denotes the risk-free rate of return. Figure 16-5 depicts these facts graphically.

16-4 THE SECURITY MARKET LINE: A CAPITAL ASSET PRICING MODEL

Thus far in this chapter, the analysis has determined that in an equilibrium situation characterized by the given assumptions, the expected return of *portfolios* is a linear function of the portfolio's standard deviation of returns. This linear relation has been called the CML. The discussion of characteristic lines alluded to the determination of the equilibrium rate of return on *individual* assets and/or portfolios as represented by the SML. Reconsider the rationale lying behind the SML.

The variance of a two-security portfolio is given by Eq. (16-6).

$$\text{var}(r_p) = w_1{}^2 \, \text{var}(r_1) + w_2{}^2 \, \text{var}(r_2) + 2w_1w_2 \, \text{cov}(r_1, r_2) \qquad (16\text{-}6)$$

For an n-security portfolio, the variance is given by Eq. (16-6a).

$$\text{var}(r_p) = \sum_{i=1}^{n} w_i^2 \, \text{var}(r_i) + \sum_{i=1}^{n} \sum_{j=1}^{n} w_i w_j \sigma_{ij} \qquad \text{for } i \neq j \qquad (16\text{-}6a)$$

Note that within the expression for the risk of a portfolio of any size are covariance terms between all possible pairs of securities in the portfolio. The essence of Markowitz diversification is to find securities with low positive covariances or negative covariances. Demand for individual securities or portfolios that have low positive covariance or negative covariance of returns with the market portfolio will be high. Securities that have high covariance with the market portfolio, that is, high systematic risk, will expe-

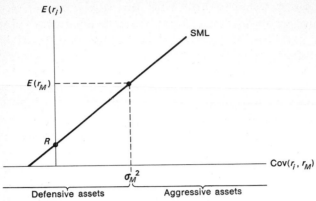

FIG. 16-6 The security market line (SML) in terms of the covariance.

rience low demand. As a result, the prices of securities with high systematic risk will fall, and prices of securities with low systematic risk will be bid up. Since equilibrium rates of return move more inversely with the price of the security, securities having a high covariance with the market will have *relatively* low prices (that is, low relative to their income but not necessarily low in absolute dollars) and high expected returns. Conversely, securities with low or negative covariances will have *relatively* high prices and therefore experience low expected rates of return in equilibrium. This relationship is depicted in Fig. 16-6. Equation (16-7) is a mathematical statement of the SML in terms of the covariance.

$$E(r_i) = R + \frac{E(r_M) - R}{\sigma_M^2} \operatorname{cov}(r_i, r_M) \tag{16-7}$$

where $\dfrac{E(r_M) - R}{\sigma_M^2}$ = slope of SML

R = riskless rate of interest
$\operatorname{cov}(r_i, r_M)$ = ith asset's covariance of returns with market
$E(r_i)$ = equilibrium expected return for ith asset

The expected return $E(r_i)$ is the appropriate discount rate to use in valuing the ith security's income; it is the cost of capital for that security's amount of systematic risk.

Expressed in words, Fig. 16-6 and Eq. (16-7) say that in equilibrium an individual security's *or* a portfolio's expected return is a linear function of its covariance of return with the market. That is, the expected return from *any* market asset is an increasing function of its systematic risk. Since systematic risk is the portion of a security's total risk which hinders rather than helps diversification, this relationship is intuitively appealing. The more risk a security has which cannot be eliminated by diversification, the more return investors will require to induce them to hold that risky security in their portfolios. The locus of equilibrium points in Fig. 16-6 is the SML, a separate and distinct relation from the CML.

In equilibrium, an *individual* security's expected return and risk statistics will lie *on* the SML and *off* the CML. Likewise, in equilibrium, efficient portfolios $[E(r),\sigma]$ pairs will lie *on* the CML, and portfolio $[E(r),\text{cov}(i,m)]$ pairs will lie on the SML. Thus, even under idealistic assumptions and at static equilibrium, the CML will not include all points if portfolios and individual securities are plotted together on one graph. In equilibrium, individual securities and inefficient portfolios will not lie on the CML.

The returns of individual securities and portfolios are not determined by *total* risk. The unsystematic risk of a security is not particularly undesirable since it washes out to zero in a portfolio. Unsystematic risk is the stuff that naive diversification is made of.

Defensive and Aggressive Securities

In Fig. 16-6, the portion of the horizontal axis representing low or negative covariances is marked as including *defensive securities.* These securities are defensive in the sense that they offer the opportunity to reduce portfolio risks by including them in a portfolio which is correlated with M (as nearly all portfolios will be). Defensive assets covary with the market less than average. Symbolically, $\text{cov}(r_i,r_M) < \text{cov}(r_M,r_M) \equiv \sigma_M^2$ for defensive assets.

The *aggressive securities* are securities which offer opportunities for speculation; their dividend and price reactions to changes in market conditions are more dramatic and volatile than the reactions of defensive securities. Aggressive assets have more than average covariances with the market; that is, $\text{cov}(r_i,r_M) > \text{cov}(r_M,r_M) \equiv \sigma_M^2$ for aggressive assets.

The SML Restated

In the discussion of systematic risk in Chap. 12, the regression coefficient b_i from Eqs. (16-1) and (16-3) was suggested as an *index* of systematic risk. The covariance of returns with M was suggested as a *measure* of systematic risk earlier in this chapter. Two methods of defining the SML are possible. In Fig. 16-7a, the SML is defined in terms of the beta regression coefficient b_i. In terms of b_i, defensive and aggressive securities can be delineated more simply. It is intuitively appealing to think of securities with $b_i < 1$ as being defensive and aggressive securities as having $b_i > 1$.

The SML in terms of the $\text{cov}(r_i,r_M)$ is shown in Fig. 16-7b (the right-hand panel). The two presentations of the SML in Fig. 16-7 are equivalent. The only difference between the two graphs of the SML is that the vertical scale of the SML in terms of the beta coefficient is $(1/\sigma_M^2)$ times the length

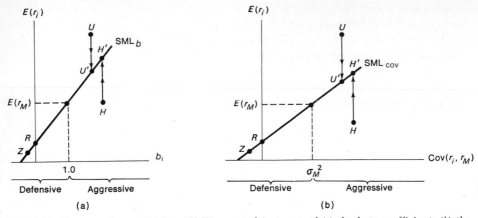

FIG. 16-7 The security market line (SML) restated in terms of (a) the beta coefficient; (b) the covariance.

of the vertical scale of the other graph. This is due to the definition of the slope coefficient shown in Eq. (16-8).

$$b_{(i|M)} = \frac{\text{cov}(r_i, r_M)}{\sigma_M^2} \tag{16-8}$$

$$= \text{cov}(r_i, r_M) \left(\frac{1}{\sigma_M^2} \right) \qquad \text{where } \frac{1}{\sigma_M^2} \text{ is constant for all assets}$$

Equation (16-7) may be equivalently restated in terms of the beta coefficient as shown in Eq. (16-9).

$$E(r_i) = R + \frac{E(r_M) - R}{\sigma_M^2} \text{cov}(r_i, r_M) \tag{16-7}$$

$$= R + E(R_M) - R \frac{\text{cov}(r_i, r_M)}{\sigma_M^2}$$

$$= R + [E(r_M) - R]b_i \tag{16-9}$$

Equation (16-9) is the SML graphed as in Fig. 16-7a and is equivalent to the graph in Fig. 16-7b, which represents Eq. (16-7). Note that when $b_{(i|M)} = 1$, then $\text{cov}(r_i, r_M) = \sigma_M^2$. This relation reveals why the divisions between defensive and aggressive securities in the two graphs in Fig. 16-7 are comparable.

Overpriced and Underpriced Indications

The SML has asset pricing implications for both portfolios and individual securities. Points between the SML and the $E(r)$ axis like point U in Fig. 16-7 represent securities whose prices are lower than they would be in equilibrium. Since points like U represent securities with unusually high returns for the amount of systematic risk they bear, these securities will enjoy strong demand that will bid their prices up until their equilibrium rate of return is driven back onto the SML at point U'.

Likewise, assets lying between the SML and the systematic risk axis represent securities whose prices are too high. The asset at point H in Fig. 16-7 does not offer sufficient return to induce rational investors to accept the amount of systematic risk it bears. As a result, the asset's price will fall owing to lack of demand. The prices of such assets will continue to fall until the denominator of the rate of return formula is low enough to allow the expected return to reach the SML at a point like H'.

$$E(r) = \frac{E(\text{capital gains or losses} + \text{dividends})}{\text{purchase price}}$$

Then the capital loss will cease, and an equilibrium purchase price will emerge until a change in the firm's systematic risk, a change in R, or some other change causes another disequilibrium.

Negative Correlation with Portfolio M

Consider point Z in Fig. 16-7; it represents a defensive security which has an equilibrium rate of return below the return on riskless asset R. Upon observing rates of return which were consistently below R, the traditional financial analyst would typically attribute the low return to a high price for the security, which was bid up in expectation of growth. But capital market theory provides a second rationalization of points like Z: Their price is maintained at high levels by the Markowitz diversification benefits they offer (for example, Homestake Mining stock).

Ex Ante Theory and Ex Post Data

This analysis implies that equilibrium *expected* returns are determined by *expected* risk (the ex ante theory). Historical, or ex post, returns are not used by investors as a basis for their decisions about the future, although their expectations can be affected by ex post behavior. Their investment plans for the future are based on their expectations about the future. Thus it should be noted that a "jump" is made in going from the capital market theory, which is stated in terms of expectations, to actual historical data. If the probability distribution of historical returns has remained fairly stable over time, then historical average returns and variances can be used to estimate expected returns and expected variances. However, historical data play no role in the theory itself.

To test capital market theory, expectations must be observed — an obviously impossible task if conducted on a meaningful scale. Of course, expectations may be formed from historical observations, but unless investors' past expectations were always correct, historical data will not be satisfactory to completely validate the theory.

16-5 RELAXING THE ASSUMPTIONS

The assumptions underlying capital market theory will now be aligned more closely with conditions existing in the "real world." First, assumption 2, that one riskless interest rate exists at which everyone may borrow or lend, will be relaxed.

Multiple Interest Rates

In a more realistic model, the borrowing rate B is higher than the lending rate L. In Fig. 16-8, this is represented by two unchanging rates (that is, $\sigma_L = \sigma_B = 0$) at points L and B. The lines emerging from points L and B represent the dominant lending and borrowing opportunities, respectively. The dotted portions of these two lines do not represent actual opportunities and are included merely to indicate the construction of the figure. Two tangency portfolios, denoted M_L and M_B, are shown for lenders and borrowers, respectively. They replace the market portfolio. The kinked line formed by the solid sections of the two lines and a section of the opportunity locus is the relevant efficient frontier when the borrowing and lending rates differ. As a result, the CML has a curved section between M_L and M_B in Fig. 16-8. The curved section is part of the efficient frontier.[4]

Of course, not all investors can borrow at rate B; those with poor credit ratings must pay a higher borrowing rate than those with good credit ratings. The proverbial "deadbeat" might be able to borrow money only by

---

[4] K. L. Hastie, "The Determination of Optimal Investment Policy," *Management Science,* August 1967, pp. B757–B774. Hastie was the first analyst to study relaxing the assumptions.

FIG. 16-8 The capital market line (CML) when borrowing and lending rates differ.

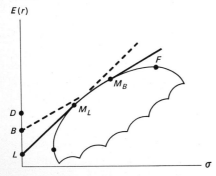

paying rate D in Fig. 16-8. Obviously, the greater the difference between the lending and the various borrowing rates, the greater the curve of the CML. Furthermore, the CML will change for each individual as that person's credit rating changes, and the CML for the market in general will change with credit conditions, that is, as the borrowing and lending rates change. The reader may graph these complications as an exercise.

In Fig. 16-8, points M_L and M_B are two separate tangency portfolios for lending and borrowing, respectively, if one lending rate and one borrowing rate are recognized. The existence of two tangency portfolios creates problems. Equation (16-7) is a mathematical representation of the SML in terms of the covariance.

$$E(r_i) = R + \frac{E(r_M) - R}{\sigma_M^2} \text{cov}(r_i, r_M) \tag{16-7}$$

where $[E(r_M) - R]/\sigma_M^2$ is the slope.

If separate borrowing B and lending L rates are assumed to exist, two SMLs emerge:

$$E(r_i) = B + \frac{E(r_{MB}) - B}{\sigma_{MB}^2} \text{cov}(r_i, r_{MB}) \qquad \text{for } E(r_i) > E(r_{BL}) \tag{16-7a}$$

$$E(r_i) = L + \frac{E(r_{ML}) - L}{\sigma_{ML}^2} \text{cov}(r_i, r_{ML}) \qquad \text{for } E(r_i) < E(r_{ML}) \tag{16-7b}$$

These two SMLs will not only have different vertical axis intercepts; they will have different slopes since $[E(r_M) - R]/\sigma_M^2$ will be different. Also, since their covariances are measured with respect to two different tangency portfolios (namely, M_L and M_B), even their covariances differ. As a result,

FIG. 16-9 Two security market lines (SMLs) when borrowing and lending rates differ.

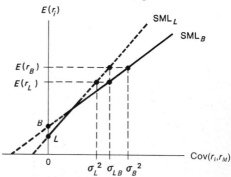

two SMLs emerge. Figure 16-9 shows the relationship between SML_L and SML_B.

Because borrowing and lending rates are divergent, equilibrium prices are not possible for all individual securities. Since further relaxation of assumption 2 would clutter Figs. 16-8 and 16-9 without yielding any additional insights, this task is left to the reader's imagination.

Transaction Costs

If assumption 6 (which assumes away transaction costs) is dropped, the CML and SML have "bands" on their sides, as shown in Figs. 16-10 and 16-11. Within these bands, it would not be profitable for investors to buy and sell securities and generate the price revisions necessary to attain equilibrium; transaction costs would consume the profit which induces such trading. As a result, the markets would never reach the theoretical equilibrium described earlier, even if the other assumptions were retained.

The effects of naive diversification, which were explained in Chap. 15 (see Sec. 15-2), showed that investors need not diversify over many securities to obtain portfolios near the CML. Therefore the effects of transaction costs need not be particularly detrimental to the attainment of equilibrium; that is, the "bands" around the CML and SML will not be wide.

General Uncertainty or Heterogeneous Expectations

To jettison assumptions 3 and 4 about homogeneous expectations over a common planning horizon would require drawing an efficient frontier, CML, and SML composed of "fuzzy" curves and lines. The more investors' expectations differed, the "fuzzier" and more blurred all lines and curves would become. In effect, they would become bands. As a result of general uncertainty, the analysis becomes determinate only within limits. Only major disequilibriums will be corrected. Statements cannot be made with certainty, and predictions must contain a margin for error.

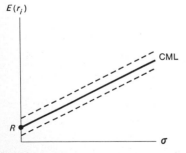

FIG. 16-10 Transaction costs obscure the capital market line (CML).

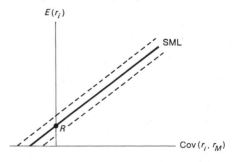

FIG. 16-11 Transaction costs obscure the security market line (SML).

Different Tax Brackets

Recognition of the existence of different tax rates on ordinary income and capital gains would also blur the picture. The after-tax rate of return r_{AT} is defined as follows.

$$r_{AT} = \frac{\text{capital gains} \times (1 - T_G) + \text{dividends} \times (1 - T_0)}{\text{price at beginning of holding period}}$$

where T_G is the capital gains tax rate and T_0 is the tax rate applicable to ordinary income. In terms of after-tax returns, every investor would see a slightly different CML and SML depending on his or her particular tax situation. Thus, a static equilibrium could never emerge under existing tax laws even if all the other assumptions were rigorously maintained.

Indivisibilities

If all assets were not infinitely divisible, that is, if assumption 5 were discontinued, the SML would degenerate into a dotted line. Each dot would represent an opportunity attainable with an integral number of shares. Little profit is to be gained from further examination of this situation.

Inflation and Varying Productivity of Capital

The interest rates observed in reality are nominal interest rates rather than real interest rates. Symbolically,

$$r_t^n = m + E\left(\frac{\Delta P}{P}\right) + \theta + \text{transaction costs} + f(n) \tag{8-4}$$

where r_t^n is the nominal rate of interest in period t for an n-period bond seen in the news media, m is the marginal productivity of capital or real rate of interest per period, $E(\Delta P/P)$ is the expected percentage change in the general price level per period, that is, the expected rate of inflation or deflation, θ is a risk-premium, and f is a function of the term to maturity. This discussion will omit the impact of risk-premiums, transaction costs, and the term structure of interest rates in determining r_t^n. The marginal productivity of capital and the rate of inflation fluctuate with technology, the level of investment, monetary policy, fiscal policy, and consumers' tastes. It follows that r_t^n fluctuates, too.

Relaxing assumption 7 means that even if r_t^n is the interest rate of U.S. short-term government bonds, it must nevertheless vary in both the money and the real sense. Thus, there is no true riskless asset; even default-free

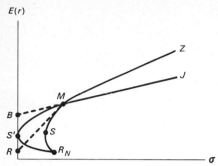

FIG. 16-12 Lack of riskless rate obscures the capital market line (CML).

U.S. government securities will experience some variability of real return.[5] Graphically, this means point R in Fig. 16-12 ceases to exist as a lending possibility and is replaced by a risky nominal interest rate at a point like R_N. The efficient frontier is now the curve from S to Z or from S' to Z, assuming all money is borrowed at rate R_N. Portfolio S or S' is the minimum-risk portfolio—it may or may not contain default-free securities and it may or may not have zero risk, as S' does. A point like S will be the minimum-variance portfolio if returns on R_N and M are uncorrelated but not perfectly negatively correlated.[6] If borrowing at rate B, rather than at rate R, is considered, the efficient frontier becomes SMJ or $S'MJ$, depending on whether S or S' is the minimum-variance portfolio.

Lack of a riskless lending rate blurs the lower section of the SML. Above $E(r_{MB})$, the formula for the SML is given by Eq. (16-10), where B is the borrowing rate.

$$E(r_i) = B + \frac{E(r_{MB}) - B}{\sigma_{MB}^2} \operatorname{cov}(r_i, r_{MB}) \tag{16-10}$$

Figure 16-13 shows the SML, assuming B does not vary. Below $E(r_{MB})$, the locus of equilibrium returns is not defined since a riskless rate and a market portfolio of maximum efficiency for lending are not defined when $\sigma_R > 0$.

[5] K. L. Hastie, op. cit., pp. B-771 and B-772. More recently, Black has extended Hastie's work by developing a portfolio, called the zero-beta-portfolio (ZBP), which is free of systematic risk. Black derived the ZBP mathematically and derived some theorems about it (see Fischer Black, "Capital Market Equilibrium with Restricted Borrowing," *Journal of Business*, vol. 45, 1972, pp. 444–455). Empirical estimates of the returns on the ZBP were also prepared by F. Black, M. C. Jensen, and M. Scholes [see "The Capital Asset Pricing Model: Some Empirical Tests," in M. C. Jensen (ed.), *Studies in the Theory of Capital Markets* (New York: Praeger Publishing Co., 1972)]. Essentially, the ZBP is an all-equity portfolio which has positive variance but zero correlation with the market portfolio; borrowing and lending at some riskless interest rate were not employed in the derivation of the ZBP.

[6] See Fig. 15-3 and the accompanying discussion of how the correlation coefficient determines the degree of convexity.

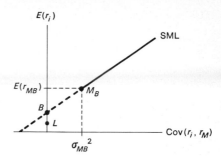

FIG. **16-13** The security market line (SML) obscured by lack of risk-free rate.

Some Investors Are Naive Diversifiers

Thus far, all the assumptions underlying capital market theory except the first have been relaxed. Finally, let us relax the first assumption — that all investors are Markowitz diversifiers. Naively diversified investors would most likely adjust asset prices until returns were proportional to the *total* risk (as measured by its variance or standard deviation) in an asset. They will not delineate the efficient frontier and therefore will not recognize that portfolio M in Fig. 16-2 is the single most desirable portfolio. Only the Markowitz diversifiers will recognize that M is the most desirable asset: they will bid up the price of portfolio M. Consequently, the purchase price of asset M will rise, and its expected return will be lower after these temporary capital gains cease if systematic risk is unchanged (because the expected return moves inversely to the purchase price).

$$E(r) = \frac{E(\text{capital gains} + \text{dividends})}{\text{purchase price}}$$

The prices of portfolios other than M (for example, A and B in Fig. 16-2) will tend to remain constant as they are held by naive diversifiers who do not realize the unique desirability of M. After some temporary capital gains for portfolio M, a new, higher equilibrium purchase price and a lower rate of return emerge. Thus, prices and expected returns are revised, asset M falls downward in $[\sigma, E(r)]$ space, and the CML swings downward until portfolios A, M, and B are all tangent to the CML.

As a result of these price revisions, which occur in a market where some investors are naive diversifiers, a condition represented by Fig. 16-14 emerges. Several portfolios lie along the CML in Fig. 16-14, all those along the line segment AMB. Equilibrium is attained when all assets are included in combinations lying along AMB, and they are included in such proportions as they are supplied to the market.

Consider the implications of the equilibrium shown in Fig. 16-14. It was shown that when two or more assets plot in a straight line in $[\sigma, E(r)]$

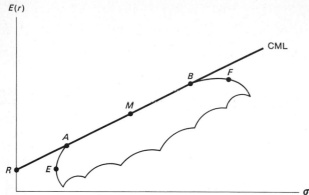

FIG. 16-14 Market equilibrium with naive diversification.

space, they must be perfectly positively correlated. Thus, assets like A, M, and B and all other combinations along AMB must be perfectly positively correlated. The risky combinations of assets along AMB vary owing to some common cause, such as variation in the overall economic, psychological, and market situations. The returns on combinations A, M, and B will vary together *systematically*. All other variability of return (namely, unsystematic risk) due to causes unrelated to movements in market conditions has been reduced by diversification. Only undiversifiable risk remains in the assets on the efficient frontier.

In a capital market partially inhabited by naive diversifiers, an equilibrium such as the one shown in Fig. 16-14 is expected to emerge.[7] In this model the efficient frontier is flattened out along the CML, since naive diversifiers cannot delineate the efficient frontier. This suggests that the regression line shown in Eq. (16-11) should fit the empirical data for portfolios and yield high correlations.

$$\bar{r}_i = R + c\sigma_i \qquad \text{for } i = 1, 2, \ldots, n \text{ portfolios} \tag{16-11}$$

In Eq. (16-11), $\bar{r}_i$ and σ_i are the historical average return and risk statistics for portfolio i, and c is the regression slope coefficient, a positive constant. In fact, it was explained in Chap. 15 (see Fig. 15-7) that such a simple linear regression, using a sample of 34 mutual funds, yielded a $+.83$ correlation

---

[7] If all investors were naive diversifiers who focused only on total risk, all assets (that is, both portfolios and individual assets) would lie on the CML in equilibrium. The SML would cease to exist because naive diversifiers would not recognize the importance of undiversifiable systematic risk.

Empirical data supporting an equilibrium such as the one shown in Fig. 16-14 could also arise from heterogeneous expectations. That is, if each investor delineated a different efficient frontier, each would seek to attain a different market portfolio. As a result, many portfolios could lie along a ray like AMB in Fig. 16-14.

coefficient.[8] The inclusion of individual assets in this regression would decrease the correlation because individual assets are not efficient enough to lie on the CML.

Conclusions about Capital Market Theory

Thus far, all the assumptions underlying capital market theory have been relaxed one at a time. In each case the implications of the model were slightly obscured. If all were relaxed simultaneously, the result would be even less determinate. However, the fact that the analysis is not exactly determinate under realistic assumptions does not mean it has no value. The analysis still rationalizes much observed behavior, explains such hitherto unexplained practices as diversification, and offers realistic suggestions about the directions that prices and returns should follow when they deviate significantly from equilibrium. The theory is a powerful engine for analysis.[9]

QUESTIONS

1 Compare and contrast the two terms *dominant asset* and *efficient asset*. Use graphs to show what you mean.

2 Which of the following graphs is incorrect? Why?

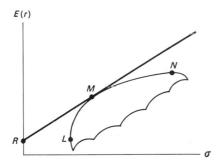
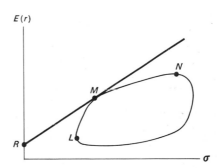

3 Draw a graph in risk-return space showing the various parts of the total risk for some inefficient asset.

4 Define the market portfolio.

5 "Since the assumptions underlying portfolio analysis are unrealistic, the

---

[8] William F. Sharpe, "Risk Aversion in the Stock Market: Some Empirical Evidence," *Journal of Finance,* September 1965, pp. 416–422; W. F. Sharpe, "Mutual Fund Performance," *Journal of Business,* January 1966, pp. 123–125.

[9] Capital market theory has been extended into the international securities markets by Bruno H. Solnik, "An International Market Model of Security Price Behavior," *Journal of Financial and Quantitative Analysis,* September 1974, pp. 537–554.

theory is not a valid description of reality." True, false, or uncertain? Explain.

6 Compare and contrast your conception of the characteristic lines for a highly leveraged tool manufacturer's common stock and a cigarette manufacturer's common stock.

7 Compare and contrast the CML and the SML. What assets lie on both lines in equilibrium? What assets should never lie on the CML?

8 Professor John Lintner says that the "best portfolio will never be the one in the Markowitz efficient set with the lowest attainable risk."[10] Explain Prof. Lintner's remark.

9 Compare and contrast the behavior of aggressive securities and defensive securities in a bear market.

10 Explain how you would find the beta coefficient for some firm using historical data. What data would you need? What would you do with the data? What can you use this beta for? Graph two different models in which the beta coefficient is an important factor and explain them.

11 Given the assumptions underlying capital market theory, rationalize the following separability theorem (ST): The investment decision of which asset to buy is a separate and independent decision from the financing decision of whether to borrow or lend.

12 Consider the (unrealistic) CML and SML graphed below and the data about assets A and B.

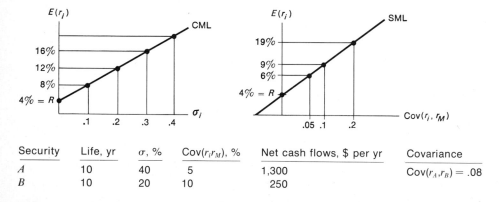

Security	Life, yr	σ, %	$Cov(r_i r_M)$, %	Net cash flows, $ per yr	Covariance
A	10	40	5	1,300	$Cov(r_A, r_B) = .08$
B	10	20	10	250	

(*a*) Find the present value of the two risky assets A and B if they are held separately. (*b*) If a portfolio is constructed containing equal proportions of A and B (that is, $W_A = W_B = .5$), find its present value.

[10] In "Security Prices, Risk, and Maximal Gains from Diversification," *Journal of Finance*, December 1965, p. 589.

13 What does it mean to assume that all investors have "homogeneous expectations" or that "idealized uncertainty" exists? Why is this assumption necessary to capital market theory?

14 Basic Scientific Research, Inc. (BSRI) is composed of a group of scientists working to develop new products which can be patented, manufactured, and sold to obtain large monopolistic profits. Investors in BSRI stock are told that the corporation has a small chance of inventing a highly lucrative product like Xerox or Polaroid. They are also told that, quite frankly, it is much more likely that BSRI will simply consume its original capital with no payoff at all. The best possible outcome is the long shot that BSRI's research will be fruitful and thus will turn their investment into a multimillion-dollar capital gain. Use risk-return analysis to evaluate this investment opportunity.

SELECTED REFERENCES

The reader who wishes to follow the original development of capital market theory is directed to the following four articles, especially the second one by Sharpe. All use calculus and probability theory. This list is not exhaustive.

Sharpe, William F., "A Simplified Model for Portfolio Analysis," *Management Science*, January 1963, pp. 277–293. See especially part 4 on the diagonal model.

_____, "Capital Asset Prices: A Theory of Market Equilibrium under Conditions of Risk, *Journal of Finance*, September 1964, pp. 425–552. Reprinted in Archer & D'Ambrosio, *The Theory of Business Finance* (New York: Macmillan, 1967), reading 42.

Lintner, John, "Security Prices, Risk, and the Maximal Gains from Diversification," *Journal of Finance*, December 1965, pp. 587–615.

Fama, Eugene F., "Risk, Return and Equilibrium: Some Clarifying Comments," *Journal of Finance*, March 1968, pp. 29–40.

Francis, J. C., and S. H. Archer, *Portfolio Analysis* (Englewood Cliffs, N.J.: Prentice-Hall, 1971).
This book derives the risk and return formulas in its appendix to chap. 2. Chapters 3 and 5 deal explicitly with capital market theory. Algebra and statistics are used. The appendix to chap. 5 uses calculus to derive the main propositions of capital market theory.

Jacob, Nancy, "The Measurement of Systematic Risk for Securities and Portfolios: Some Empirical Results," *Journal of Financial and Quantitative Analysis*, March 1971, pp. 815–834.
Different formulations of models from capital market theory are tested empirically, using regression analysis.

Seventeen

Different Investment Goals

When portfolios were first discussed in Chap. 15, the dominance principle was used to explain why investors should prefer investments on the efficient frontier. This chapter delves into the more specific question of exactly which one of the efficient portfolios is the best investment for a specific person. The economic concept of utility is used to analyze the different preferences of individuals.

Utility is a measure of psychic gain. Punishment, for example, is designed to decrease the recipient's level of utility; it yields disutility. Frequently, the recipient would pay money in order to avoid the punishment. On the other hand, eating sweet fruit increases utility for most people. They would pay money for the psychic gain to be derived from eating, say, a grape. Every activity provides some level of utility. If eating an apple is more enjoyable than eating a grape, and eating a grape is preferable to receiving punishment, this situation can be represented symbolically as follows:

$$U \text{ (apple)} > U \text{ (grape)} > U \text{ (punishment)}$$

where U (apple) denotes the utility from an apple, etc.

Investors' basic reason for investment activity is to maximize their personal happiness, or utility. They hope to increase their wealth by investing so they will have more money to buy the things they want. This is summarized in Eq. (17-1), where U denotes an investor's utility, w represents personal wealth, and g is some positive function,[1] so the investor's utility rises as that wealth increases ($dU/dw > 0$).

$$\text{Maximize } U = g(w) \tag{17-1}$$

17-1 MAXIMIZING UTILITY

Maximizing an investor's utility-of-wealth function, Eq. (17-1), is related to the investor's one-period rate of return because the rate of return measures the percentage change in wealth, as shown in Eq. (17-2).

$$\text{Maximize } r_t = \frac{w_t - w_0}{w_0} \tag{17-2}$$

or

$$\text{Maximize } w_t = w_0(1 + r_t) \tag{17-2a}$$

where w_0 is the beginning level of wealth and w_t is the wealth at the end of period t. If $w_t > w_0$, this implies $r_t > 0$. For example, if an investor invests $75 and one period later liquidates the investment for $100, his wealth increases 33 percent.

$$r_t = \frac{w_t - w_0}{w_0}$$

$$= \frac{\$100 - \$75}{\$75} = 33\%$$

If $w_t < w_0$, then $r_t < 0$ and wealth diminished in period t.

In an uncertain world, investors cannot know in advance which investment will yield the highest return. Even if investors have a "hot tip" or "inside information" about an investment, they are still uncertain that this tip is true or precisely how to act upon it. In an uncertain world, investors can maximize only their *expected* utility. Expected utility is determined by expected return and risk. Symbolically, this is summarized in Eq. (17-3).

---

[1] The functional notation may be unfamiliar. Functions f, g, and h are some unspecified functions performed on the variables in parentheses. f, g, and h represent three different functions. Three examples of the form a function in the variable w might assume are

$U = aw \quad$ a linear function denoted $U = f(w)$

$U = a + bw^2 \quad$ a second-degree equation denoted $U = g(w)$

$U = a + b\,[\log\,(cw)] \quad$ a logarithmic function denoted $U = h(w)$

where a, b, and c are some constants in the explicit formulas.

$$\text{Maximize } E(U) = f[E(r),\text{risk}] \qquad\qquad (17\text{-}3)$$
$$= f[E(r),\sigma] \qquad\qquad (17\text{-}3a)$$

where $E(U)$ denotes expected utility, $E(r)$ is expected return, risk is defined as variability of returns and measured by the standard deviation of returns (denoted σ), and f is some mathematical function. An increase in expected return will increase the investor's expected utility if risk does not also increase, or a decrease in risk will increase expected utility if expected return does not decrease simultaneously. In other words, the investor will prefer efficient investments over inefficient ones. Such utility-maximizing behavior is analyzed graphically, using isoquants to measure investor utility in risk, σ, and expected return, $E(r)$, space, as shown in Fig. 17-1.

17-2 INDIVIDUALS' INVESTMENT GOALS

Investment goals are determined in large part by the age and socioeconomic status of the individual investor. For example, consider the fictitious character named Aunt Jane, a poor, little, old, frail widow who is all alone in the world and has bad nerves. Aunt Jane lives modestly on social security and the income from a small portfolio. She is terrified, and rightfully so, of the prospect of decrease in value in her portfolio. But she does not know how to manage the portfolio for herself and has no idea how many more years she will live. In order to conserve her meager wealth, she consumes only the income from her portfolio and none of the principal.

In marked contrast to Aunt Jane is Dr. Swift. Dr. Swift is an aggressive young man who can expect a successful professional career (as a physician, dentist, lawyer, or scientist). Dr. Swift's income began at a comfortable level shortly after he completed his terminal degree, and it can be expected to rise in years to come if he works hard. The financial future for this man is fairly secure.

Dr. Swift has different investment objectives from those of Aunt Jane. He is willing to take risks in order to gain a larger return. If his risky investments are wiped out, his family will not suffer—he may merely have to work a few more years before retirement or do without some luxuries.

FIG. 17-1 Different investment preferences in risk-return space.

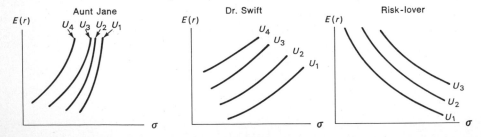

However, Dr. Swift is not a reckless person. He dislikes risk and is willing to assume it only because he wants the high returns which might be attained. Thus, Aunt Jane and Dr. Swift are both risk-averters, but Aunt Jane is the more risk-averse of the two.

Indifference Maps in Risk-Return Space

The investment preferences of these two hypothetical investors are represented graphically in Fig. 17-1, which shows three families of indifference curves representing three investors' investment preferences. Each indifference curve is an expected utility isoquant showing all the various combinations of risk and return which provide an equal amount of expected utility for the investor. Aunt Jane's indifference curves are steeply sloped, reflecting the fact that it would take a large increase in expected return to induce her to assume a small increase in risk. Dr. Swift's indifference curves are less steep, indicating that he is more willing to assume risk to attain an increase in his expected return than Aunt Jane.

The indifference map of a risk-lover is also shown in Fig. 17-1. The risk-lover's indifference curves are curved toward the origin, indicating a willingness to give up expected return in order to gain risk. This author has never actually observed this type of behavior; it is graphed only as an intellectual exercise.

In order to see how the three investment preferences shown in Fig. 17-1 will result in different investments, they must be graphed with some investment opportunities in risk-return space. Figure 17-2 shows a hypothetical set of investment opportunities in $[\sigma, E(r)]$ space. These opportuni-

FIG. 17-2 Selection of an investment in $[\sigma, E(r)]$ space.

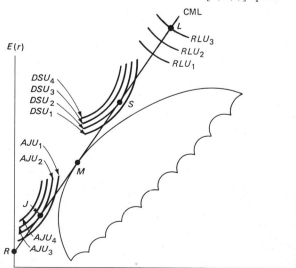

ties might represent all the stocks, bonds, real estate, and art objects in the world at a given point in time, plus the opportunity to borrow or lend at R.

Aunt Jane's utility isoquants are $AJU_4 > AJU_3 > AJU_2 > AJU_1$ and appear in the lower left of Fig. 17-2. Aunt Jane will maximize her expected utility by selecting the low-risk, low-return portfolio at point J on the capital market line (CML). Portfolio J is the weighted average of investments R and M. The previous discussion of diversification and the fallacy of financial interior decorating (in Chap. 15) explained that efficient low-risk portfolios like Aunt Jane's can contain individual assets which are risky when held alone. Thus, the fact that Aunt Jane wants a low-risk portfolio gives us no clue as to whether she should purchase risky stocks until we analyze the risk, return, and correlation statistics of the individual assets in portfolio M.

Dr. Swift maximizes his expected utility higher on the CML by purchasing portfolio S. Portfolio S will provide him with the level of expected utility represented by his indifference curve DSU_2. This is the highest level of utility he can hope to achieve, given the investment opportunities shown in Fig. 17-2.

In contrast with rational investors, risk-loving investors will not maximize their expected utility by holding efficient investments. Instead, these strange fellows' highest attainable indifference curve (RLU_3) is tangent to the opportunity set at point L. Actually, the risk-lovers would fearlessly borrow all they could to leverage themselves as high on the CML as possible.

Thus far, the discussion has focused on investors' preferences at a point in time. People's preferences change with the passage of time; so we shall see how this tendency can affect their investment decisions.

The Typical Family's Changing Investment Preferences

For most young couples, the first three investments are life insurance, an emergency fund, and a home—in about that order.

Life insurance. Most newly married men are advised that they should make provisions to care for their wife, any children, and any large expenses (such as hospital and funeral expenses) in the event that they die or are killed. Working wives are being encouraged to make similar provisions. This is advice which most couples acknowledge. However, the newly married person must be wary not to buy (or be sold) more than necessary to meet family needs.

The amount of life insurance a person should buy is a matter of personal opinion. Although life insurance sales agents usually recommend much more, a policy which will provide the family of the deceased with a death benefit equal to about 2 years' income should be sufficient coverage for most people. Two years' income is typically sufficient to pay all death expenses and leave the survivors with enough money to live without working for up to 1 year. Within a year of the death, the surviving family should

be ready and able to become financially independent, unless some unfortunate extenuating circumstances develop. If the wife has a profession, skill,
or a wealthy family, less coverage may be needed to provide for the family
of a deceased husband.

After the amount of coverage is determined, the question arises as to
whether term insurance or whole-life insurance with cash values is best.
Again, this is a somewhat personal matter. After looking at the facts, many
young persons find that decreasing term insurance which has no cash value
other than the death payment is a good buy. However, life insurance sales
agents prefer to sell whole-life or endowment policies because the sales
commissions are larger than for term insurance. Furthermore, the life insurance company can invest the cash values in a whole-life or endowment policy until the policy is cashed in, while paying the policyholder a small rate
of interest for the funds.

A *term insurance policy* is essentially a bet with the insurance company
that the insured will not die—nothing more, no frills or savings plans. The
insured pays the insurer a premium to issue a contract which legally binds
the insurer to pay the beneficiaries of the insured the face value of the policy if the insured dies within some specified time period. If the insured
does not die within the time span of the policy, the policyholder and the
beneficiaries receive nothing from the insurer. When the term insurance
policy expires, a new policy must be purchased. As the insured grows
older, the probability of dying increases; therefore, the cost of a given
amount of term insurance increases with the age of the insured. When the
insured reaches old age, term insurance will be very expensive, and it
should be discontinued. Table 17-1 shows some typical costs of term insurance at various ages. This is the type of insurance policy which is best for

TABLE 17-1 COSTS PER
$1,000 OF TERM LIFE
INSURANCE PER YEAR AT
VARIOUS AGES

Age	Annual cost per $1,000, $†
20	3.66
25	3.71
30	3.78
35	3.89
40	4.44
45	6.04
50	9.06
55	14.41
60	21.56
65	32.06

† These figures are the averages of
several rates quoted by large insurance companies.

many people; it is the cheapest, simplest type. By purchasing term insurance instead of more expensive policies, the insured will save hundreds of dollars each year. If these savings are saved at compound interest, they will grow to thousands of dollars by the time the insured reaches old age. At that time, the insured can cancel the term insurance because the savings on insurance premiums will exceed the face value of the term life insurance policy.

If the insured does not have the self-discipline to save the difference in cost between term insurance and the whole-life or endowment policies, he or she should consider those policies which include contractual savings plans.

Whole-life and *endowment* insurance policies are a combination of decreasing term insurance and rising cash values. These policies are more expensive than term insurance. Table 17-2 shows the costs of various types of cash value life insurance purchased at different ages. The cash values associated with these policies arise because the insurance company invests the extra revenue from whole-life and endowment policies in the insured's name, and it grows at a low rate of interest. Figure 17-3 graphically depicts how the $123.50 annual premium on a straight-life policy paying a $10,000 death benefit, purchased at age 25, will be divided between actual insurance costs and savings.

The interest paid by the insurer on the cash values is low and may not equal inflation in some years.[2] But the insured who lacks self-discipline to buy term insurance and invest the money so saved should buy these more expensive policies with their automatic savings provisions. In this manner the insured will have a paid-up insurance policy with cash values when old age finally comes.

---

[2] For example, in 1974 the rate of inflation was over 12 percent. At that time the interest which most life insurance companies were paying on cash values was about 5 percent. Savings accounts at banks and savings and loan associations were paying about 6 percent.

TABLE 17-2 ANNUAL PREMIUM COST PER $1,000 OF VARIOUS TYPES OF LIFE INSURANCE WITH CASH VALUES†

Age	5-year term renewable and convertible, $	Straight or ordinary life, $	Life paid up at 65, $	20-pay life, $	20-year endowment, $
25	4.33	12.35	13.86	21.07	41.69
30	4.41	14.65	16.83	23.73	42.01
35	5.04	17.61	20.93	26.93	42.63
40	6.61	21.55	26.68	30.80	43.76
45	9.08	26.58	35.49	35.49	45.67
50	13.40	32.81	49.66	41.19	48.65
55	21.05	40.37	78.10	48.25	53.14

† Averages of several quoted rates.

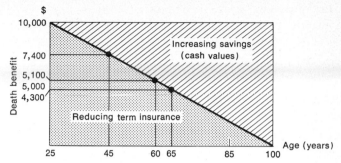

FIG. 17-3 Whole- or straight-life insurance policy is a combination of term insurance and a savings plan. The figures are the average of several quoted rates.

An emergency fund and a home. The new family also needs an emergency fund to cover unforeseen problems not covered by insurance. This fund should be held in a form that is liquid and available if needed. After a new family has life insurance, an emergency fund, and some furniture, it usually invests in a home. Home ownership can be a good investment. There are positive economic benefits from ownership. The mortgage interest and property tax on the home are (unlike rent) tax-deductible; so the costs of home ownership are partially offset by income tax reductions. The home owner builds equity in the home which can be recovered if the house is sold at a price advantageous to the seller. In addition, a home is an inflation hedge because the values of houses tend to rise during inflation while the real value (in terms of purchasing power) of the fixed mortgage debt decreases.

Most of the disadvantages of home ownership are difficult to assess in money terms. Home ownership decreases many people's willingness to move to a new job even if it offers better pay and opportunities. Home and yard care often consumes time which could be used more productively elsewhere. Home owners make "home improvements" which are sometimes poor investments when viewed from a purely financial point of view. Home ownership involves the risk that the neighborhood may depreciate in value. All in all, it is difficult to base home-ownership decisions purely on investment criteria.

One of the purposes of the low-risk, low-return investments of life insurance, an emergency fund, and a home is to assure the young family of some fixed minimum-level financial support and security. After these basic investments are made and if no health or education expenses are straining the family budget, the family's willingness and ability to undertake risky investments increase. Figure 17-4 shows the risk and return preferences for a typical family as it matures.

The investment in life insurance and an emergency fund are represented by point *R*. After the young family has accumulated sufficient

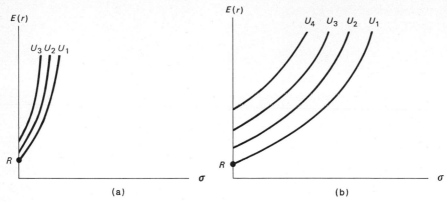

FIG. 17-4 Investment preferences for (*a*) a young family; (*b*) a mature family.

wealth, it typically purchases a home. In the next few years, families mature and their preferences for risk and return shift. The indifference map in Fig. 17-4*b* represents the typical risk-averse, wealth-maximizing behavior of most mature families whose homes are paid for and whose children are educated. At retirement, the families' risk-return preferences will shift again. Most families in retirement will have investment preferences similar to those of Aunt Jane; they become very risk-averse after their income ceases. They move back to an attitude like the one shown in Fig. 17-4*a*.

17-3 INSTITUTIONAL INVESTORS

Many of the marketable securities in the United States are managed by institutional investors such as insurance companies, pension funds, and trusts, although they are actually owned by individuals. Table 17-3 shows the total dollar value of all common and preferred stock owned by various institutional investors. Some of these institutions own more bonds, mortgages, and other financial instruments than they do stock.

Owing to the fact that the institutional investors manage such a large quantity of financial assets, many portfolio management job opportunities exist within these organizations. Consider the type of investments some institutional investors select and the reasons.

Mutual Funds

The Securities and Exchange Commission (SEC) requires that all mutual funds (that is, open-end investment companies) state their investment policies and objectives as explicitly as possible in a report filed with the SEC and also in the prospectuses which they give to prospective investors. The funds are expected to follow these stated objectives so investors will know

TABLE 17-3 MARKET VALUE OF STOCKHOLDINGS OF FINANCIAL
INSTITUTIONS AND OTHER INVESTORS, 1968†

		Percent	Dollars
1.	Private noninsured pension funds	7.8	59.6
2.	Investment companies, total	7.8	59.6
	Mutual funds	6.7	50.9
	Other	1.1	8.7
3.	Life insurance companies	1.7	12.8
4.	Property and casualty insurance companies‡	1.9	14.7
5.	Mutual savings banks	.3	2.3
6.	State and local trust funds	.6	4.8
7.	Common trust funds	.5	4.4
8.	Personal trust funds	10.5	80.1
9.	Foundations	2.0	15.8
10.	College endowments	1.2	9.0
11.	Total institutions (items 1 through 10)§	33.9	257.8
12.	Foreigners¶	3.3	25.5
13.	Domestic individuals (item 14 less item 11 less item 12)	62.8	478.0
14.	Total stock outstanding	100.0	761.3

† Billions of dollars as of end of year.
‡ Excludes holdings of insurance company stock.
§ Excludes holdings of mutual fund shares.
¶ Includes estimate of stock held as direct investment.
Source: Irwin Friend, Marshall M. Blume, and Jean Crockett, *Mutual Funds and Other Institutional Investors: A New Perspective* (New York: McGraw-Hill, 1970), p. 113.

what kind of investment management services they are buying. Three main categories of mutual funds can be delineated by these statements of objectives:

1 *Balanced or income funds.* A balanced fund typically holds one-third of its invested assets in bonds and preferred stocks. The other two-thirds of the fund's investment are usually diversified across over 100 different common stocks. Balanced funds stress risk minimization and conservation of principal. These funds are conservatively managed and do not seek high-return investments that are risky.

2 *Income and growth funds.* The income and growth funds take a middle-of-the-road approach in selecting between high returns and low risks. As their name implies, they keep the vast majority of their invested capital in common stocks. Capital gains and dividend income are sought, but these funds do not invest in high-risk situations in an effort to maximize their returns.

3 *Growth funds.* Growth funds, which are also called "go-go" or performance funds, seek to maximize their returns. The prospectuses of these funds usually refer to the fact that risks will be assumed in pursuit of high capital gains. Dividend income is desired by the performance funds, but it is second to price appreciation.

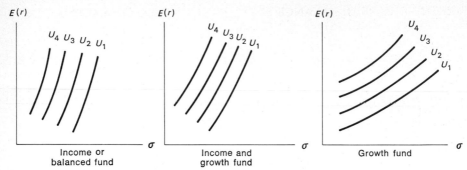

FIG. 17-5 Different mutual fund objectives represented in $[\sigma, E(r)]$ space.

Figure 17-5 shows indifference maps characterizing the risk-return preferences of the three main types of mutual funds. The actual operating performances of mutual funds are analyzed in Chap. 19.

Commercial Banks

The banks' activities are highly regulated because the federal government allows them to create money by making loans against fractional deposits. If banking activities are not stable, the nation's money supply and the national economy cannot be stable either. With the exception of their trust departments, which manage people's investments, banks are practically forbidden from investing in common stocks. In fact, banks are forced into investing heavily in federal, state, and local bonds because of actions taken by the Federal Reserve Board and rules handed down by the Comptroller of the Currency and enforced by bank examiners.

Table 17-4 shows the balance sheet of a typical commercial bank in common-sized percentages. Over one-third of the bank's funds are obtained from demand deposits. The bank must remain liquid in case the owners of these deposits should withdraw their funds simultaneously.

Barring a money panic and a run on the banks, their liquidity needs are determined by loan demand, the volatility of demand deposits, loan maturities, and the business cycle. Banks do not try to hold vault cash equal to their total demand deposits. However, they do hold large primary reserves, highly liquid assets which earn low rates of return and can be used to meet possible large withdrawals of demand deposits. In Table 17-4, the asset items which compose the bank's primary reserves are indicated. They can be liquidated to provide funds.

The main asset on the balance sheet, commercial loans, is only partially controlled by the bank. The quantity of commercial loans demanded by businesses depends on the rate of business expansion and market interest rates. The interest rates on commercial loans are largely determined by economic conditions. Mortgage loans are long-term loans, the demand for which varies with credit conditions and home-building activity. Manage-

TABLE 17-4 TYPICAL BALANCE SHEET FOR A LARGE COMMERCIAL BANK

Assets	Percent	Liabilities and net worth	Percent
Cash, federal reserve balances†		Demand deposits	36
and deposits in other banks	10	Time deposits	54
Commercial loans‡	20	Accounts payable	1
Mortgage loans	17		
Short-term loans‡	18		
Government bonds			
U.S. Treasury bonds†	13		
Tax-exempt municipals‡	15	Equity	9
Other assets	3		
Total assets§	100	Total liabilities and net worth	100

† Primary reserves.
‡ Secondary reserves.
§ Total will not equal 100 percent because of rounding errors.
Source: Federal Reserve Functional Cost Accounting Book, 1973.

ment of those portions of the banks' investments represented by commercial loans and mortgages largely involves evaluating the customers' creditworthiness and collateral at the time the loan is made. These assets are like long-term accounts receivable and are not as liquid as short-term securities. Risk can be assessed only subjectively for most of a bank's assets that are direct loans. Furthermore, some mortgages are insured with the Federal Housing Administration or Veterans Administration. This all makes risk-return analysis difficult.

It is common for banks' liquidity to alternate with economic conditions. During an economically slow period, the bank may be saturated with liquidity for which it cannot find borrowers, whereas during an economic boom, banks may be rationing loans, raising loan rates, and liquidating "secondary reserves" to meet loan demand. The asset items in Table 17-4 which are secondary reserves are indicated. Secondary reserves are about the only true marketable investments over which a bank may exercise continuing control. However, the banks' control over this small part of its total assets is quite important because secondary reserves generate a disproportionately large proportion of the banks' total earnings. In effect, the opportunities open for adept investment management of secondary reserves are limited mainly to anticipating shifts in interest rates in the bond markets and operating so as to minimize federal income taxes. Banks are so highly constrained by regulations that only their trust departments need be concerned with seeking the efficient frontier.

Trusts

A *trust* is a fiduciary agreement in which a trustee or trustees administer assets which are placed in trust by a creator (donor, or grantor). In general, trusts are established to place responsibility for the administration of a person's estate or assets into the hands of someone other than the creator or the beneficiary of the trust. They are managed by trust companies, the trust departments of commercial banks, or insurance companies. Trust contracts are called *fiduciary agreements*.

Personal trusts may be set up by a deceased person's will (a testamentary trust), or a living person may put assets in trust (a living trust) for some designated beneficiary. *Living trusts* may be classed as either revocable or irrevocable. Irrevocable trusts have tax advantages which are not available through revocable trusts.

About one-third of all employee pension funds are set up as common trusts in which the retired employees are the beneficiaries. Some banks' trust departments also have *common trusts* in which many small accounts are commingled and managed as one. *Endowment trusts* are also set up which designate schools, research facilities, libraries, art groups, and others as beneficiaries. Under most of these arrangements, the trustee has the power of attorney to buy and sell the assets of the trust in any manner he or she chooses (1) as long as the transactions are done in accordance with any provisions stated in the trust agreement, and (2) as long as the trustee (man or woman) acts as what the courts interpret to be a "prudent man."[3] Under some personal trusts the trustee acts only as an advisor and caretaker of the trust; in these situations some other person, usually the beneficiary, holds the ultimate decision power over the way the trust is managed. The trustee receives a fee for his or her services which ranges from $\frac{1}{4}$ of 1 percent to 2 percent per year on the value of the assets in trust, depending mainly upon the size of the trust.

The total assets held in trust are much larger than most people realize. For example, the total value of common stock held in all trusts in the United States exceeds the total value of the common stocks owned by all mutual funds by a sizable margin. Trusts are the largest single institutional investor.

In some cases, an entire business or other asset will be turned over to the trustee to administer. However, most assets held in trusts are marketable securities. About 60 percent of all assets in trusts are stocks and about 25 percent are bonds. Trust funds are managed in accordance with the provisions set out in the trust agreement. Most trusts specify maintenance of principal as the main objective. The trustee can violate the trust agreement only under penalty of law; that is, the trustee's own personal risk-return preferences should not affect the manner in which the trust is managed. The risk-return preferences used in trust management are specified by the creator of each trust and usually reflect that creator's risk-return preferences and the purpose for which that trust was created. Thus, no single preference map in risk-return space is suitable for the entire trust portfolio.

---

[3] The "prudent man" legal guidelines which govern trust portfolio managers are discussed in a readable article by C. W. Buck entitled, "Managing Our Trusts as Prudent Men Would Do," *Commercial and Financial Chronicle*, March 3, 1960, New York. Reprinted in H. Wu and A. Zakon (eds.), *Elements of Investments* (New York: Holt, 1965), reading 4.3.

Life Insurance Companies

Most life insurance policies are more than mere insurance policies—they are combinations of insurance and savings plans. As the insureds grow older, their risk of death mounts and their insurance rates rise. But by this time the savings portions of most life insurance policies (other than term insurance) have attained cash values that can offset the purchase of increasingly expensive insurance. The investment activities performed by life insurance companies arise from a need to invest the savings portion of the whole-life or endowment life insurance policies which represent cash values to the insured.

Life insurance companies pay a small fixed rate of dividends or interest on the cash value of the savings. Then they invest these funds at a higher rate of return. Table 17-5 shows the balance sheet of a typical life insurance company.

The balance sheet in common-sized percentages in Table 17-5 shows that life insurance companies invest heavily in interest-income–bearing assets, that is, bonds and mortgages. The companies enjoy a very favorable treatment under the income tax laws which, among other things, make them indifferent between interest and capital gains income. Thus, life insurance companies can earn satisfactory after-tax returns on their investments by specializing in corporate bonds and mortgages rather than by seeking the more risky capital gains.

Life insurance companies buy about half of all corporate bonds in the United States. They are such large purchasers of corporate bonds that they sometimes capture part of the broker's commissions from the bond market by buying entire bond issues directly from the issuer. Direct placements, as these purchases of an entire bond issue are called, allow the issuer to avoid the delays, uncertainties, red tape, and underwriting costs of a public bond issue. Instead, the issuer sells the entire issue directly to a life insurance company at an interest rate which is slightly above the appropriate market rate. Thus, the issuer of the bonds passes along some of the savings of the

TABLE 17-5 TYPICAL BALANCE SHEET FOR A LIFE INSURANCE COMPANY

Assets	Percent	Liabilities	Percent
Cash and short-term U.S. government bonds	1–2	Policy reserves	75–85
Long-term federal, state, and local government bonds	4–7	Dividends and other obligations	10–12
Corporate bonds	35–40	Net worth	
Mortgages	35–40	Contingency reserves	1–3
Policy loans	4–8	Equity and surplus	6–8
Preferred and common stock	4–7		
Real estate	2–4		
Company premises	3–5		
Total assets	100	Total liabilities and net worth	100

Sources: Institute of Life Insurance, *Life Insurance Fact Book;* Treasury Bulletin.

direct placement to the purchasing life insurance company by paying the slightly higher interest rate.

Some large life insurance companies have also developed very efficient mortgage investment operations. These companies employ full-time forces of agents who go into the field and originate mortgages, with the life insurance company lending home buyers the money they need. Small and medium-sized life insurance companies whose volume of mortgage credit in any given area is not large enough to justify the expense of originating their own mortgages simply buy them from mortgage bankers who originate the mortgages and then resell them.

It is interesting to note insurance companies' lack of interest in common stocks.[4] Although even the tightest state restrictions allow life insurance companies to hold up to 5 percent of their total assets in common stocks, some companies do not even approach this proportion (see Table 17-5). Their reluctance to hold common stocks is particularly unusual in view of their lack of need for liquidity. They usually have premium inflows which exceed their outflows for loans, death payments, and operating expenses and thus are in the enviable position of being able to wait for favorable market conditions to buy and sell common stocks. In fact, there is a controversy in the life insurance industry as to whether more or less common stock should be purchased. This discussion revolves around technicalities involving legal reserves and the treatment of capital gains.

Another reason life insurance companies do not invest more aggressively in common stock is the "legal list" restrictions imposed on them. According to state laws (in New York) which govern the majority of life insurance companies, the company can buy only common stocks which (1) have paid dividends continuously for over 10 years and (2) have paid dividends from current earnings rather than borrowed funds. Common stocks which meet these and other restrictions are included on the "legal list" of stocks in which life insurance companies are permitted to invest. Such arbitrary restrictions have caused life insurance companies to invest their funds in other sources. Some have been putting funds into sales-and-lease-back arrangements which involve some risk and a higher return. In any event, the rigid investment restrictions imposed on life insurance companies make it impossible to accurately represent their investment preferences in terms of risk and return.

17-4 CONCLUSIONS ABOUT INVESTMENT PREFERENCES

Investors' preferences about investing can be represented with an indifference map in risk-return space. The point at which an investor's highest

[4] Life insurance companies administer about one-third of all pension fund assets. Most of these portfolios are heavily invested in common stock, but these assets are separate from the assets which provide backing for life insurance policies' cash values. These insured pension fund portfolios can be viewed as being a separate group of assets aside from the insurance companies' own assets.

indifference curve is just tangent to the efficient frontier is the portfolio which will maximize the investor's expected utility. When investment preferences change, this may be represented by drawing a new set of indifference curves in risk-return space.

Institutional investors' investment choices are often severely constrained by federal and state laws (some of which may not be rational or in the interest of the public welfare). It is impossible to represent the investment objectives of these institutions by preference maps in risk-return space. Mutual funds, whose investment practices are only moderately constrained, are one of the few institutional investors whose investment objectives may be represented by an indifference map. Unfortunately, mutual funds' published statements of investment objectives do not always align with the investment preferences implied by their actual investments. This latter problem is one of the points which will be taken up in Chap. 19, where the ability of mutual funds to maximize their shareholders' expected utility is evaluated.

QUESTIONS

1 Draw an indifference map in risk-return space for an investor who is absolutely fearless but loves high returns. Have you ever known anyone who actually had such investment preferences? Explain.

2 "Term insurance is the best buy for the person who has the self-discipline for regular saving." Is this statement true, false, or uncertain? Explain.

3 "Life insurance companies' holdings of common stocks are predominantly in low-risk stocks." Is this statement true, false, or uncertain? Is the investment area, as implied by your answer, the desirable one?

4 Define a trust and explain the roles of the parties to a trust. Do trusts tend to be managed conservatively, or do they tend to seek high risks and high returns?

5 Explain what difficulties you would have in constructing the indifference map for an institutional investor like a bank or life insurance company.

6 Do you think that the legislators and government policymakers who developed the investment regulations for publicly owned institutional investors understood Markowitz diversification? Explain your view.

SELECTED REFERENCES

Badger, R. E., H. W. Torgeson, and H. G. Guthmann, *Investment Principles and Practices,* 6th ed. (Englewood Cliffs, N.J.: Prentice-Hall 1969).

Chapters 21 and 24 through 26 describe the investment practices followed by various groups of private and institutional investors. No mathematics is used.

Cohen, J., E. Zinbarg, and A. Zeikel, *Investment Analysis and Portfolio Management*, rev. ed. (Homewood, Ill.: Irwin, 1973).

Chapters 14 through 26 describe the investment practices followed by different types of investors. No mathematics is used.

Sharpe, William F., *Portfolio Theory and Capital Markets* (New York: McGraw-Hill, 1970).

Chapters 2 and 9 present a discussion of selecting investments in terms of their risk and return. Freshman college algebra is used.

APPENDIX TO CHAPTER 17
Utility Analysis

Utility analysis and decision making in uncertainty are complex. To discuss all the important issues in the field would take several volumes.[1] Therefore, Chap. 17 has merely touched on the main points necessary to understand (1) what utility is; (2) how utility is related to consumption, wealth, and the rate of return; and (3) how a utility map in risk-return space may be used to maximize investor utility. This appendix extends that analysis and shows proof of several of the important assertions made in the chapter about single-period utility maximization. Multiperiod utility analysis is discussed in Chap. 18.

A17-1 GRAPHICAL UTILITY ANALYSIS

The principal elements of utility analysis underlying investments management are explained graphically in the following few pages. To begin with, a utility-of-wealth function is a formula or a graph of a formula which shows how much utility (or how many utils, or how much happiness) a person derives from different levels of wealth. A utility-of-wealth function might be mathematically written as $U = f(w)$ or simply $U(w)$, for example. Figure A17-1 shows a graph of a utility-of-wealth function. The notion of marginal utility is a little more complex; it involves segments of the utility-of-wealth function. In words, *marginal utility* of wealth may be defined as the addi-

[1] Some of the important literature is in the following books: S. Archer and C. D'Ambrosio, *The Theory of Business Finance: A Book of Readings* (New York: Macmillan, 1967), readings 2–4, 39, and 40; Harry Markowitz, *Portfolio Selection*, Cowles Foundation Monograph 16 (New York: Wiley, 1959), chaps. 10–13; and J. L. Bicksler and P. A. Samuelson, *Investment Portfolio Decision-Making* (Lexington, Mass.: Lexington Books, 1974), readings 1–8 and 14–18.

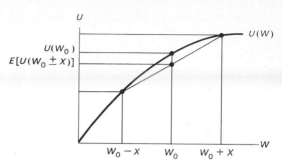

FIG. A17-1 Diminishing marginal utility of wealth.

tional utility a person gets from a change in his or her wealth. Mathematically, marginal utility is the first derivative of the utility function—that is, dU/dw, or $U'(w)$. To determine whether marginal utility is rising or falling, the slope of the utility function or the sign of the second derivative of the utility function must be observed. Decreasing marginal utility is present when the utility function rises at a less steep rate or when the second derivative of the utility function is negative, $d^2U/dw^2 < 0$ or $U''(w) < 0$.

Utility analysis is useful for analyzing the logic, or lack of it, in decisions involving risk. The analysis of such decisions is based on the expected utility principle.

Expected Utility Principle
Decision makers make decisions which maximize their *expected utility*.

Maximizing *expected utility* is different from simply maximizing utility if the possible outcomes are risky. To understand the difference, consider the definition of expected utility. (Mathematical Appendix E in Part 7 explains the mathematical expectation and may be informative.) The expected utility from a decision to undertake some risky course of action is the weighted average of the utils from the possible outcomes which are calculated, using the probability of each outcome as the weights. For example, if you decide to enter into a coin-tossing gamble, you have made a decision to undertake a risky course of action. There are two possible outcomes—heads or tails. The probability of getting heads is denoted $P(\text{head})$ and the probability of a tail is written as $P(\text{tail})$. The utility from the gamble which results if heads turns up is represented by $U(\text{head})$ and the utility of getting the tail is $U(\text{tail})$. Thus, the expected utility of the gamble is written symbolically as

$$E[U(\text{coin toss})] = P(\text{head}) \times U(\text{head}) + P(\text{tail}) \times U(\text{tail})$$

To understand this more clearly, consider some more specific examples.

Diminishing Marginal Utility and Risk-Aversion

Risk-averse behavior will result if the investor has diminishing marginal utility of wealth or returns. Diminishing marginal utility-of-wealth and utility-of-returns functions are graphed in Figs. A17-1 and A17-2, respectively. They are both concave to the horizontal axis.[2]

Diminishing marginal utility of wealth or of returns leads to risk-avoiding behavior since, from any point on the utility-of-wealth or utility-of-returns curve, a risky investment has a lower expected utility than a safe investment with the same expected outcome. That is, if an investment offers a 50-50 chance of increasing or decreasing a given level of starting wealth by X dollars, the loss of utility from the bad outcome is larger than the gain in utility from the favorable outcome. Symbolically, $(.5)U(W_0 - X) + (.5)U(W_0 + X) \leq U(W_0)$. Thus, the person with diminishing utility of wealth would prefer to keep W_0 rather than make a risky investment or bet to attain $(W_0 + X)$ or $(W_0 - X)$ with equal probability. Figure A17-1 represents this situation graphically. Since the utility of the certain starting wealth, $U(W_0)$, is larger than the expected utility of an equal amount of uncertain wealth, $E[U(W_0)]$, the risk-averter prefers not to assume the risk, $U(W_0) > E[U(W_0)]$. The risk-averter prefers simply to hold W_0 cash rather than assume risks in an effort to increase this wealth. If the chance for gains from the risky investment were large enough, however, the risk-averse investor would find it sufficient compensation to assume the risk. Thus, risk-averters may gladly accept risky investments if they feel the odds are in their favor. People everywhere commonly exhibit diminishing marginal utility of wealth; for example, people require higher wages to work overtime.

Equality of Wealth and Return Utility Functions

Utility preference orderings are invariant under a positive linear transformation of the utility function. Graphically speaking, this means that any utility curve (such as the ones in Figs. A17-1 and A17-2) can be raised or lowered (that is, can have a constant added or subtracted), can be scaled down without having its shape changed (that is, can be divided by a positive constant), or can be expanded without changing its curvature (that is, can be multiplied by a positive constant) without changing the way the utility curve would rank the desirability of a set of investment opportunities. These transformations would change the number of utils assigned to any given outcome, but the preference *rankings* would be invariant under a positive linear transformation. Since the one-period rate of return is just a positive linear transformation of the investor's wealth, this implies that a given investor's utility-of-returns function is simply a linear transformation

---

[2] By definition, a function U is concave if and only if $U(X) \geq \alpha U(x - y) + (1 - \alpha)U(x + y)$ for $1 \geq \alpha \geq 0$. A concave (to the horizontal axis) utility function results in risk-aversion.

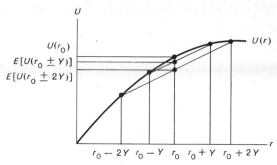

FIG. A17-2 Diminishing marginal utility of returns.

of his or her utility-of-wealth function, and the two will yield the same preference orderings for any given group of investment opportunities. Thus, the investor's utility curves shown in Figs. A17-1 and A17-2 are merely linear transformations of each other and result in identical preferences for single-period changes in wealth or equivalent one-period rates of return. The positive linear transformation between one-period changes in wealth and the rate of return is shown below.

$$r_t = \frac{w_t - w_0}{w_0}$$

where w_0 denotes beginning of period wealth (a positive constant), w_t represents end-of-period wealth (a random variable), and r_t is the one-period rate of return (also a random variable), as explained in Chap. 17.

Graphical Analysis

Suppose, for example, that an investor can earn a rate of return of r_0 with certainty or can invest in a risky investment which will return $r_0 + y$ or $r_0 - y$ with equal probability. Symbolically, $P(r_0 - y) = P(r_0 + y) = \frac{1}{2}$. Both the riskless and the risky investment have an expected return of r_0.

$$
\begin{aligned}
E(r) &= p_1(r_0 + y) + p_2(r_0 - y) \\
&= \tfrac{1}{2}(r_0 + y) + \tfrac{1}{2}(r_0 - y) \\
&= r_0
\end{aligned}
$$

Since the expected returns are the same, a risk-averse investor will prefer the sure return because the risk-averter's diminishing marginal utility will cause the disutility from a return of $r_0 - y$ to exceed the gain in utility from a return of $r_0 + y$.

Furthermore, suppose that this risk-averter had a third investment opportunity in an even riskier investment which was expected to yield either $r_0 - 2y$ or $r_0 + 2y$ with equal probability. This latter investment is riskier (that is, has more variability of return) than the other risky invest-ment, but it offers the same expected return. The calculations below show that the two risky investments have equal expected returns.

$$\overbrace{E(r) = p_1(r_0 - y) + p_2(r_0 + y)}^{\text{Small risk}} = r_0$$

$$\overbrace{E(r) = p_1(r_0 + 2y) + p_2(r_0 + 2y)}^{\text{Larger risk}}$$
$$= \tfrac{1}{2}(r_0 - 2y) + \tfrac{1}{2}(r_0 + 2y) = r_0$$

A risk-averse investor will rank the desirability of the riskiest investment last since its expected return is the same as the other two investments but it entails more risk. Therefore, the riskiest investment will have the least ex-pected utility. Symbolically, $U(r_0) > E[U(r_0 \pm y)] > E[U(r_0 \pm 2y)]$. This is shown graphically in Fig. A17-2.

Expected Utility, Expected Return, and Risk Formulas

In an uncertain world, expected utility is determined by expected return *and* risk.[3] Symbolically, this is summarized in Eq. (A17-1).

$$E(U) = f[E(r), \text{ risk}] \qquad\qquad\qquad\qquad \text{(A17-1)}$$
$$= f[E(r), \sigma] \qquad\qquad\qquad\qquad \text{(A17-1a)}$$

where $E(U)$ denotes expected utility, $E(r)$ is expected return, risk is de-fined as variability of returns and measured by the standard deviation of returns (denoted σ), and f is some mathematical function. An increase in expected return will increase the investor's expected utility if risk does not also increase. Or a decrease in risk will increase expected utility if expected return does not decrease simultaneously.[4] Expected returns and expected utility are defined in Eqs. (A17-2) and (A17-3), respectively.

$$E(r) = \sum_i p_i\, r_i \qquad\qquad\qquad\qquad\qquad \text{(A17-2)}$$

$$E(U) = \sum_i p_i\, U_i \qquad\qquad\qquad\qquad\qquad \text{(A17-3)}$$

---

[3] The standard deviation of returns is, of course, only a risk surrogate rather than a risk syn-onym, as this discussion implies. See Chap. 12 for a more complete discussion of risk. Throughout this book, σ is used as a symbol standing for *total* risk. Sometimes it is convenient to use the variance σ^2 rather than the standard deviation. Both are used interchangeably to denote total risk.
[4] Technically, expected utility is a function of $E(r)$ and σ only if the utility function is quad-ratic or if the distribution of terminal wealth is a two-parameter distribution (such as a normal distribution).

where p_i = probability of ith outcome
$\quad U_i$ = utility of ith outcome
$\quad r_i$ = ith possible rate of return

The expected value is like a weighted average of the possible outcomes where the probabilities are the weights.[5]

Measurement of risk was examined in detail in Chap. 12. Equation (A17-4) shows the formula used to calculate the standard deviation of returns for the ith security from expected rates of return.[6]

$$\sigma = \sqrt{\sum_{t=1}^{T} p_t [r_{it} - E(r_i)]^2} \tag{A17-4}$$

Before the utility analysis of risky investment alternatives can be performed, the investment analyst must be supplied with probability distributions of outcomes and a utility function in order to find the expected utility for each object of choice. For example, in selecting among alternative investments, a probability distribution of returns representing the possible investment outcomes and their probabilities is required. And a utility function assigning utils to each possible rate of return that the investment might earn is also needed. Only after the utility function and the probability distributions are known can utility analysis proceed.

Numerical Example

Consider three objects of choice, say, investments A, B, and C, with probability distribution of returns as defined in Table A17-1.

Figures A17-3 to A17-5 represent the utility functions for a risk-averting, a risk-indifferent, and a risk-seeking investor, respectively. Since

[5] Mathematical Appendix E discusses the mathematical expectation.
[6] When calculating the standard deviation of returns from historical rates of return, the probabilities become relative frequencies, so substitute $p = 1/T$ and rewrite Eq. (A17-4) as (A17-4a).

$$\sigma = \sqrt{\sum_{t}^{T} \frac{1}{T} [r_t - E(r)]^2} \tag{A17-4a}$$

TABLE A17-1 PROBABILITY DISTRIBUTIONS OF RETURNS FOR THREE INVESTMENTS

Investments	Outcomes	-3%	0	3%	6%	9%	$\Sigma p = 1$	$E(r)$	σ
A	Probabilities	.5		+		.5	1	$E(r_A) = 3\%$	$\sigma_A = 6\%$
B			.5	+	.5		1	$E(r_B) = 3\%$	$\sigma_B = 3\%$
C				1			1	$E(r_C) = 3\%$	$\sigma_C = 0$

Investment outcomes and their probabilities / Investment characteristics

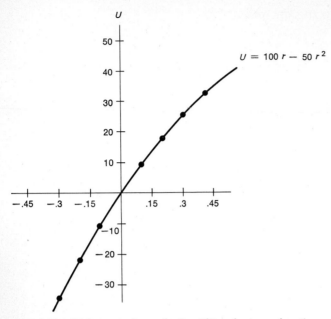

FIG. A17-3 Risk-averter's quadratic utility-of-returns function.

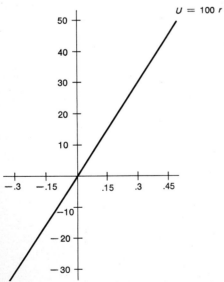

FIG. A17-4 Risk-indifferent investor's linear utility-of-returns function.

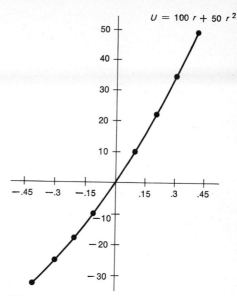

FIG. A17-5 Risk-lover's quadratic utility-of-returns function.

investments A, B, and C all offer the same expected return of 3 percent, it is clear that the three investors will rank these three investments differently *purely* because of their differences in risk.

The risk-averter's expected utility from A, B, and C is calculated thus:

$$E[U(A)] = \sum_{i=1}^{2} p_i U(r_i)$$

$$= \tfrac{1}{2}[U(-.03)] + \tfrac{1}{2}[U(.09)]$$
$$= \tfrac{1}{2}(-3.045) + \tfrac{1}{2}(8.595)$$
$$= 2.785 \text{ utils}$$

$$E[U(B)] = \tfrac{1}{2}[U(0)] + \tfrac{1}{2}[U(.06)]$$
$$= 0 + \tfrac{1}{2}(5.82)$$
$$= 2.91 \text{ utils}$$

$$E[U(C)] = 1[U(.03)]$$
$$= 1(2.955)$$
$$= 2.955 \text{ utils}$$

The risk-averter derives the most satisfaction from investment C, which has the least variability of return.

The risk-indifferent investor's expected utils from the three investments are calculated below:

$$E[U(A)] = \tfrac{1}{2}[U(-.03)] + \tfrac{1}{2}[U(.09)]$$
$$= \tfrac{1}{2}(-3) + \tfrac{1}{2}(9)$$
$$= 3 \text{ utils}$$

$$E[U(B)] = \tfrac{1}{2}[U(0)] + \tfrac{1}{2}[U(.06)]$$
$$= 0 + \tfrac{1}{2}(6)$$
$$= 3 \text{ utils}$$

$$E[U(C)] = 1[U(.03)]$$
$$= 1(3)$$
$$= 3 \text{ utils}$$

Since investments A, B, and C differ only with respect to their risk, the risk-indifferent investor assigns the same utility to all three. Symbolically, $E[U(A)] = E[U(B)] = E[U(C)]$ for the risk-indifferent investor.

The risk-lover's utility calculations follow.

$$E[U(A)] = \tfrac{1}{2}[U(-.03)] + \tfrac{1}{2}[U(.09)]$$
$$= \tfrac{1}{2}(-2.055) + \tfrac{1}{2}(9.405)$$
$$= 3.225 \text{ utils}$$

$$E[U(B)] = \tfrac{1}{2}[U(0)] + \tfrac{1}{2}[U(.06)]$$
$$= 0 + \tfrac{1}{2}(6.18)$$
$$= 3.09 \text{ utils}$$

$$E[U(C)] = 1[U(.03)]$$
$$= 1(3.045)$$
$$= 3.045 \text{ utils}$$

The risk-lover prefers the large variability of return exhibited by investment A. The three investors' expected utilities are summarized in Table A17-2.

Investments A, B, and C all have identical expected returns of 3 percent, $E(r) = 3$ percent; only their variability of returns differs. The lower expected utilities assigned to A and B by the risk-averse investor are due to their larger variability of returns which seems distasteful. And the larger expected utility the risk-lover associates with investments A and B reflects this investor's preference for risk. Thus, the two parameters — mean and variance of returns — are both reflected in expected utility. In all cases, ex-

TABLE A17-2 DIFFERENT INVESTMENT PREFERENCES FOR RISKY INVESTMENTS

Investor	Asset A — most risky $E(r_A) = 3\%$, $\sigma_A = 6\%$	Asset B $E(r_B) = 3\%$, $\sigma_B = 3\%$	Asset C — least risky $E(r_C) = 3\%$, $\sigma_C = 0$
Risk-averter	$EU(A) = 2.785$	$EU(B) = 2.91$	$EU(B) = 2.955$
Risk-indifferent	$EU(A) = 3$	$EU(B) = 3$	$EU(B) = 3$
Risk-lover	$EU(A) = 3.225$	$EU(B) = 3.09$	$EU(B) = 3.045$

pected utility measures the effects of *both* $E(r)$ and σ. Symbolically, $E(U) = f[E(r),\sigma]$.

The preceding numerical example showed how both $E(r)$ and σ affect an investor's expected utility. Now let us see how a rational, risk-averse, wealth-seeking investor will select investments which minimize risk at any given level of expected return and thus maximize expected utility in a world of uncertainty.

Selecting Investments in Terms of Risk and Return

Given the investor's utility function, we have seen how an individual will be able to select investment assets (either consciously or subconsciously) in terms of the investments' expected return and risk. Figure A17-6 shows graphically how an investor will select between investments by examining only their expected returns and risk. The exhibit is a graph in risk-return space of the seven hypothetical securities listed below:

Name of security	Expected return, $E(r)$, %	Risk, σ, %
American Telephone Works (ATW)	7	3
General Auto Corporation (GAC)	7	4
Fuzzyworm Tractor Company (FTC)	15	15
Fairyear Tire & Rubber (FTR)	3	3
Hotstone Tire Corporation (HTC)	7	12
Rears and Sawbuck Co. (RS)	9	13
Treasury IOU's (IOU)	2	0

Figure A17-6 also shows a utility map in risk-return space representing the preference of some risk-averse investor (like the one whose utility of rates

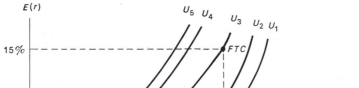

FIG. A17-6 Opportunities and preferences in risk-return space.

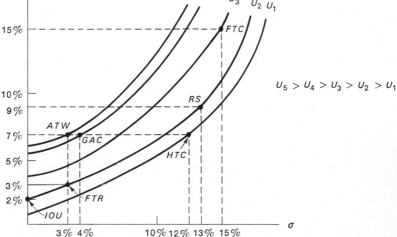

of return curve was shown in Fig. A17-3). In this indifference map the investor's utility is equal all along each curve. These curves are called *utility isoquants* or *indifference curves.* The graph is called an *indifference map in risk-return space.* Since investments RS, IOU, and FTR are all on the same indifference curve (that is, U_2), the investor obtains equal expected utility from them although their expected returns and risk differ considerably.

An infinite number of indifference curves could be drawn for the risk-averter depicted in Fig. A17-6, but they would all be similar in shape and would all possess the following characteristics:

1 Higher indifference curves represent more investor satisfaction. Symbolically, $U_5 > U_4 > U_3 > U_2 > U_1$, because the investor likes higher expected return and dislikes higher risk.

2 All indifference curves slope upward. This is because the investor requires higher expected returns as an inducement to assume larger risks. Consider, for example, the investor's indifference between FTR, IOU, and RS. It is due to the fact that RS's expected return is just enough above the expected return of FTR to compensate the risk-averse investor for assuming the additional risk incurred in going from FTR to RS. Riskless investment IOU has just enough reduction in risk below the risk of FTR to compensate the investor for accepting IOU's lower rate of return and still be as happy as with FTR or RS. Investment IOU is called the *certainty equivalent* of investments FTR and RS because it involves no risk.

3 The indifference curves grow steeper at higher levels of risk. This reflects the investor's diminishing willingness to assume risk as returns become higher.

Given the investment opportunities and the investor preferences shown in Fig. A17-6, we see that the investor prefers ATW over any of the other investments since ATW lies on a higher indifference curve than any other investment. In fact, Fig. A17-6 shows that

$$U(ATW) > U(GAC) > U(FTC) > U(IOU)$$
$$= U(RS) = U(FTR) > U(HTC)$$

Unusual Risk Attitudes

The indifference map graphed in Fig. A17-6 represents rational, normal, risk-averse preferences. Figure A17-6 is implied by a utility-of-returns function like the one in Fig. A17-3. Figures A17-4 and A17-5 represent radically different investment preferences, the preferences of a risk-indifferent investor and of a risk-loving investor, respectively.

Figure A17-7 is simply another way of representing the utility-of-returns function graphed in Fig. A17-4. And Fig. A17-5 results from a utility function like the one in Fig. A17-8. These two pathological cases of investment preferences are presented merely as intellectual curiosities. They do not represent rational, risk-averse behavior.

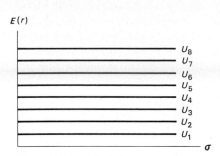

FIG. A17-7 Risk-indifferent wealth max-imizer's preferences in risk-return space.

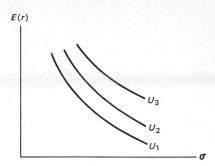

FIG. A17-8 Risk-lover's preferences in risk-return space.

A17-2 MATHEMATICAL UTILITY ANALYSIS

For quadratic utility functions it may be shown that expected utility is de-termined by expected return $E(r)$ and risk (as measured by the variance of returns σ^2, or standard deviation σ). This finding can be generalized to other utility functions if the probability distribution of returns is a two-parameter distribution.

Quadratic Diminishing Marginal Utility Functions

Consider the quadratic utility of wealth and return functions (A17-5) and (A17-6).

$$U = w - aw^2 \qquad w < \frac{1}{2a} \qquad a > 0 \tag{A17-5}$$

$$U = r - br^2 \qquad r < \frac{1}{2b} \qquad b > 0 \tag{A17-6}$$

Equations (A17-5) and (A17-6) are graphed in Figs. A17-9 and A17-10

FIG. A17-9 Diminishing quadratic utility-of-wealth function.

FIG. A17-10 Diminishing quadratic utility-of-returns function.

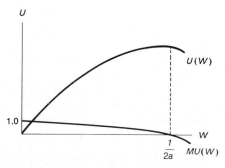

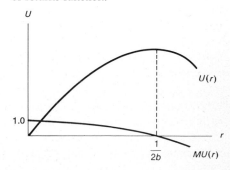

respectively. Figures A17-9 and A17-10 also show the marginal utility curves. The marginal utility diminishes as larger returns are obtained.

The preference orderings of a utility function are invariant under a positive linear transformation of the basic random variable.[7] This implies that the diminishing quadratic utility-of-wealth function (A17-5) is equivalent to the diminishing quadratic utility-of-returns function (A17-6), since one variable is a positive linear transformation of the other.

Expected utility is a function of $E(r)$ and σ for quadratic utility functions. Taking the expected value of Eq. (A17-6) yields (A17-7). (See Mathematical Expectation Theorem E-2 in Part 7 for proof.)

$$
\begin{aligned}
E(U) &= E(r - br^2) \\
&= E(r) - bE(r^2) \\
&= E(r) - b\sigma^2 - bE(r)^2 \qquad \text{since } E(r^2) = \sigma^2 + E(r)^2 \qquad \text{(A17-7)} \\
&= f[E(r), \sigma^2] \qquad\qquad\qquad\qquad\qquad\qquad\qquad\qquad\quad \text{(A17-7a)}
\end{aligned}
$$

Equation (A17-7a) shows that expected utility is a function of expected return and risk as measured by the variance of returns. Expected utility varies directly with $E(r)$ and inversely with risk since

$$
\frac{\partial E(U)}{\partial E(r)} = 1 - 2bE(r) > 0
$$

and

$$
\frac{\partial E(R)}{\partial \sigma^2} = -2b\sigma < 0
$$

for the values to which b and r are constrained. Thus, investors with diminishing quadratic utility of wealth on returns desire both higher $E(r)$ and less risk.

Solving Eq. (A17-7) for σ^2 yields (A17-8).

$$
\sigma^2 = \frac{E(r)}{b} - E(r)^2 - \frac{E(U)}{b} \qquad\qquad\qquad\qquad\qquad\qquad \text{(A17-8)}
$$

$$
= \frac{E(r)}{b} - E(r)^2 - \text{constant} \qquad\qquad\qquad\qquad\qquad \text{(A17-8a)}
$$

Varying the constant term in Eq. (A17-8) generates the quadratic indifference map in $[E(r), \sigma]$ space shown in Fig. A17-11. Figure A17-11 shows that investors whose utility is well approximated by Eqs. (A17-6) and (A17-7) will maximize their expected utility by selecting investments with the maximum return in some risk-class, that is, by selecting efficient portfolios.

---

[7] J. VonNeumann and O. Morgenstern, *Theory of Games and Economic Behavior*, 3d ed. (Princeton, N.J.: Princeton, 1953), pp. 22–24.

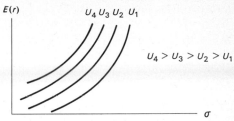

FIG. A17-11 Indifference map for risk-averter.

Quadratic Utility Not Required for $[E(r),\sigma]$ Analysis

It can be shown that if the probability distribution of rates of return or wealth is a two-parameter distribution and the investor has a diminishing single-period utility function, the investor can maximize expected utility by selecting investments with the minimum risk at each rate of return (or, conversely, the maximum return at each risk-class).[8]

$$E[U(r)] = \int U(r)f(r\,|\,m_1,m_2)\ dr \tag{A17-9}$$
$$= F(r\,|\,m_1,m_2) \tag{A17-9a}$$

where $f(r\,|\,m_1,m_2)$ is a two-parameter probability distribution of returns which is completely specified by m_1 and m_2. For example, if Ms. Investor had a logarithmic utility function (that is, diminishing marginal utility) and if the probability distribution was a two-parameter distribution (such as a normal distribution), she would maximize her expected utility by maximizing returns at any given risk-class, since $\partial E(U)/\partial E(r) = \partial F/\partial m_1 > 0$ and $\partial E(U)/\partial \sigma^2 = \partial F/\partial m_2 < 0$. Thus, selection of investments in terms of $E(r)$ and σ does not necessarily imply a quadratic utility function.

A17-3 CONCLUSIONS

This book deals with investors who have diminishing but positive marginal utility of wealth and/or returns. Such investors, this chapter has shown, prefer more wealth to less wealth but prefer less risk to more risk. In an uncertain world, these investors will maximize the expected utility from their investment activities by selecting assets which have (1) the maximum expected return in their risk-class, or conversely, (2) the minimum risk at any particular level of expected return.

The objective of rational investment management, then, is to delineate and select those investments which have the maximum expected return within the risk-class the investor prefers over the investor's single-period

[8] J. Tobin, "Liquidity Preference as Behavior Towards Risk," *Review of Economic Studies*, February 1958; pp. 65–86; and M. K. Richter, "Cardinal Utility, Portfolio Selection of Taxation," *Review of Economic Studies*, June 1960, pp. 152–160.

planning horizon. The investor need not always select an individual asset. He or she can construct a portfolio which yields higher expected utility than an individual asset.

QUESTIONS

1 If people's utility is determined largely by what they consume, how do investors derive utility from the rates of return of their investments? After all, a rate of return cannot be eaten.

2 Draw a graph on the utility-of-wealth function for a risk-lover. What are the characteristics of a risk-lover's marginal utility of wealth?

3 If their risk is the same, is investment A or B better? Show how you choose between them.

	A	B
Cost at time $t = 0$	$W_0 = \$500$	$W_0 = \$40$
Proceeds at time $t > 0$	$W_1 = \$800$	$W_2 = \$95$

4 How does risk affect utility?

5 Rank the desirability of the following investments. Show your work graphically.

Investment	$E(r)$, %	σ, %
A	10	5
B	10	10
C	5	5
D	12	10

6 Write down your social security number. Assume that you can purchase a risky investment which will pay one of two equally likely rates of return. This investment will pay the rate of return indicated by the last digit in your social security number with a .5 probability and the rate of return indicated by the next-to-the-last digit with a .5 probability. Calculate the expected return of this investment. For example, for the social security number 307-38-3152, the expected return is $(.5)(5\%) + (.5)(2\%) = 3.5\% = E(r)$. If you were the risk-averse investor shown in Fig. A17-3, would you rather have a *certain* (that is, one riskless) investment paying the expected return calculated from the last two digits of your social security number, or the risky investment based on the equal probability of the last two digits? Explain. Explain what the risk-indifferent investor in Fig. A17-4 and the risk-lover in Fig. A17-5 would do if confronted with this same choice between a certain expected return and a risky investment with the same expected return.

SELECTED REFERENCES

Friedman, M., and L. J. Savage, "The Utility Analysis of Choices Involving Risk," *The Journal of Political Economy*, August 1948, pp. 279–304.
> A classic paper rationalizing choice in uncertainty with the expected utility hypothesis. Only algebra is used.

Markowitz, H., *Portfolio Selection* (New York: Wiley, 1959).
> Chapters 10 through 13 discuss the utility theory underlying the selection of efficient assets. Most of the mathematics is freshman college algebra.

Eighteen

Multiperiod Wealth Maximization

The preceding chapters about portfolio management are oriented toward "one-period" investment management. That "one period" may be less than a week, or it may be longer than 5 years. But Markowitz portfolio analysis, on which the preceding chapters were based, endeavors to delineate those portfolios which have the maximum *one-period expected return* at each level of risk. Since security analysts have increasing difficulty as they try to estimate expected return and risk statistics further in the future, the length of the one period cannot be extended indefinitely. It is difficult to imagine predicting, for example, a security's expected return and risk statistics as long as 5 years ahead; and 10-year forecasts are even more impossible. So, what does the portfolio manager do in the long run?

When the one-period planning horizon on which a portfolio is constructed comes to its end, the old portfolio is presumably revised on the basis of more current information, and then a new portfolio must be selected. The question to which Chap. 18 addresses itself is: What kind of investment management policy is appropriate for long-run investing over *multiple periods?* For example, suppose you should inherit millions of dollars at age 20 and you expect to bequeath it to charity when you are 70 years old. Or, suppose you manage a multibillion-dollar portfolio for a life insurance company and it is not expected that any of this portfolio ever need be liquidated. In such real-life situations which involve decades—that is, they clearly involve multiple periods—the question naturally arises as to whether the *one-period* Markowitz portfolio analysis procedure is relevant. And if the Markowitz model is relevant for multiple-period investment management, how is portfolio analysis over one period applied to multiple periods?

18-1 UTILITY OF TERMINAL WEALTH

The proper multiperiod or long-run investment policy is assumed to be the one which will maximize the investor's utility (that is, happiness) from his or her consumption in each period, as shown in Eq. (18-1)

$$\max U(C_1, C_2, \ldots, C_T) \tag{18-1}$$

The symbol C_t denotes consumption in the tth period and the Tth period is the last period. For an average fellow, C_1 and C_2 would probably involve more wine and women and less geriatric medical care than C_T, for example. Since a gentleman's acquisition of wine, female companionship, and geriatric medical care, or a lady's desire for furs and antiques and the other things that we may wish to consume during our lifetimes can be expedited with money, economists typically assume that maximizing a person's wealth in each period is equivalent to maximizing the utility from consumption.

If a person owns a portfolio of securities and other market assets, he or she can borrow money for consumption purposes in each period. By pledging the portfolio as collateral, the investment owner can borrow more as the portfolio grows in value. Or the owner can liquidate part of the portfolio. Either way, it is reasonable for economists to assume that maximizing the terminal value w_T of a portfolio at the end of T periods (for example, at the end of someone's lifetime or at the end of an insurance company's long-run planning horizon) as shown in Eq. (18-2) is equivalent to maximizing utility-of-consumption equation (18-1).

$$\max U(w_T) \tag{18-2}$$

The investor's beginning wealth at time period $t = 0$ may be denoted w_0. This allows Eq. (18-2) to be rewritten equivalently as (18-2a), since $w_T = w_0(1 + r)^T$, where r denotes the average compounded rate of return over T periods.

$$\max\{U[w_0(1 + r)^T]\} = \max[U(w_T)] \tag{18-2a}$$

In a world of uncertainty, an investor cannot expect to foresee the future clearly. Therefore, *expected* (rather than known with certainty) utility must be maximized to acknowledge the existence of risk. This is represented by rewriting Eq. (18-2a) with an expectation operator (discussed in Mathematical Appendix E and the Appendix to Chap. 17), as shown in Eq. (18-3).

$$\max\{E[U(w_T)]\} = \max(E\{U[w_0(1 + r)^T]\}) \tag{18-3}$$

Geometric Mean Return

The compounded rate of return, r, equals the geometric mean of the T one-period rates of return, r_t for $t = 1, 2, \ldots, T$, as shown in Eqs. (18-4) and (18-4a). (See Mathematical Appendix J in Part 7 if a more detailed explanation of the geometric mean return is desired.)

$$(1 + r)^T = \frac{w_T}{w_0} \tag{18-4}$$

$$= (1 + r_1)(1 + r_2) \cdots (1 + r_T) \tag{18-4a}$$

Equation (18-4) shows that maximizing the geometric mean return is equivalent to maximizing the ratio of terminal wealth over beginning wealth. More simply, maximizing the geometric mean also maximizes terminal wealth.

Since the geometric mean return, as defined in Eq. (18-4), is a factor in the utility-of-terminal-wealth function, Eq. (18-3), it can be seen that increases either in terminal wealth or in the geometric mean return help increase the investor's expected utility. And, in the special case where initial wealth, w_0, is a fixed constant which is separable and independent from the geometric mean return, maximizing the geometric mean is equivalent to maximizing the investor's expected utility of terminal wealth. In fact, w_0 is separable and independent of r if the investor's utility is logarithmic.[1]

Logarithmic Utility of Terminal Wealth

For the sake of concreteness, assume utility is logarithmic in wealth, or equivalently logarithmic in returns. The investor's beginning wealth, w_0, is separable from the rate of return, r, as shown in Eq. (18-5b).

$$U(w_T) = \ln w_T \tag{18-5}$$
$$= \ln[w_0(1 + r)^T] \tag{18-5a}$$
$$= \ln w_0 + T[\ln(1 + r)] \tag{18-5b}$$

---

[1] Separability occurs in log utility functions

$$U(w) = \ln w$$

as shown in Eq. (18-5). For an analysis of these cases, see E. J. Elton and M. J. Gruber, "On the Optimality of Some Multi-Period Portfolio Selection Models," *Journal of Business*, April 1974, pp. 231–243.

Other cases are analyzed by Samuelson and Merton: Paul A. Samuelson, "Lifetime Portfolio Selection by Dynamic Stochastic Programming," *Review of Economics and Statistics*, August 1969, pp. 239–246; and Robert C. Merton, "Lifetime Portfolio Selection Under Uncertainty: The Continuous Time Case," ibid., pp. 247–257. The papers by Merton and Samuelson are companion pieces.

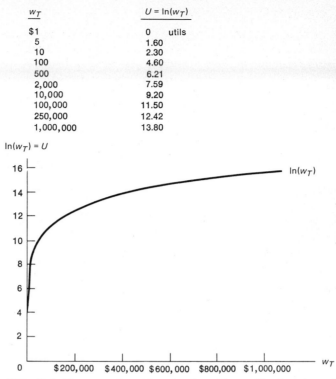

w_T	$U = \ln(w_T)$	
$1	0	utils
5	1.60	
10	2.30	
100	4.60	
500	6.21	
2,000	7.59	
10,000	9.20	
100,000	11.50	
250,000	12.42	
1,000,000	13.80	

FIG. 18-1. The natural or Naperian logarithm utility function of terminal wealth.

Since the rate of return is separable from wealth, this shows that, at least, the Markowitz procedure of confining the analysis to the rate of return and ignoring the dollar value of the investor's wealth is satisfactory for log utility functions.

As the analysis focuses explicitly on the log utility function, the plausibility of this popular form is reviewed before proceeding further. Figure 18-1 shows a graph of Eq. (18-5). This utility function is realistic because, first, it exhibits positive marginal utility of wealth. That is, more terminal wealth always increases utility, a fact meaning that the investors never get tired of more wealth. Second, utility function (18-5) is also realistic because it has diminishing marginal utility of wealth. In other words, each additional wealth increment increases its recipient's happiness less than all preceding increments of the same size. The log utility function possesses other properties which are desirable for analysis, too.[2]

---

[2] J. W. Pratt, "Risk Aversion in the Small and in the Large," *Econometrica*, April 1964, pp. 122–136.

Positive Linear Transformations

The log utility function yields an invariant preference ordering over a set of objects (for example, investments) if the function undergoes any positive linear transformation. That is, if a, b, c, and d are positive constants, Eq. (18-6) is true.

Preference ordering $(\ln w_T)$
$$= \text{preference ordering } [c \ln(aw_T + b) + d] \quad (18\text{-}6)$$

For a directly relevant example, consider the positive constant initial wealth, w_0. If w_0 is subtracted from w_T and the difference is divided by w_0, this is a positive linear transformation of w_T. As shown in Eq. (18-7), it transforms the random variable terminal wealth into a rate of change in wealth.

$$r = \frac{w_T - w_0}{w_0} \quad (18\text{-}7)$$

Equations (18-6) and (18-7) mean that ranking investments based on the log of their expected terminal values or their expected returns will yield identical preference rankings. This is summarized succinctly in Eq. (18-6a).

Preference ordering $[U(\ln w_T)]$
$$= \text{preference ordering } [U[(\ln r)] \quad (18\text{-}6a)$$

Other positive linear transformations can be used to vary the shape of the log utility function. It can even be transformed to create approximations of nonlogarithmic utility functions.[3] Therefore, the conclusions obtained here with the log utility function are also roughly true for some other classes of utility functions. That is, in spite of the fact that a mathematical economist can prove that a quadratic and a logarithmic utility function yield different investment preferences, for example, the differences might be so slight that a pragmatic business executive would not even notice them. Furthermore, many business investment decisions are made by committees, and it is not possible to specify the utility function for a group of people. Thus, selecting efficient portfolios, or any other portfolios, must be done without reference to utility function for group decision making.

Regardless of the numerous business situations for which utility analysis is inappropriate, it is still useful for analyzing the logic of various economic decisions. So, to gain more insights into the proper long-term investment strategy, log utility function (18-5) is rewritten in terms of the one-period rates of return below.

[3] Harry Markowitz, *Portfolio Selection* (New York: Wiley, 1959), pp. 120–122. Markowitz shows how the quadratic function can approximate the log function.

One-Period Returns and Utility of Terminal Wealth

Substituting the logarithmic equation (18-5a) into the investor's long-term expected utility objective function Eq. (18-3) produces Eq. (18-3a).

$$\max E[U(w_T)] = \max E\{U[w_0(1 + r)^T]\} \tag{18-3}$$
$$= \max E\{\ln[w_0(1 + r)^T]\} \tag{18-3a}$$

Substituting Eq. (18-4a) into objective function (18-3a) yields Eq. (18-3b), which shows explicitly how utility of terminal wealth relates to the T different single-period rates of return, r_t for $t = 1, 2, \ldots, T$.

$$\max E[U(w_T)] = \max E\{\ln[w_0(1 + r)^T]\} \tag{18-3a}$$
$$= \max E\{\ln[w_0(1 + r_1)(1 + r_2) \cdots (1 + r_T)]\} \tag{18-3b}$$

One of the insights which can be obtained by restating the investor's long-term objective as Eq. (18-3b) is the effect of taking risks period after period. Suppose that in the tth period the investor selects a risky asset that has a one-period rate of return of $r_t = -100$ percent. The link relative for period t becomes zero since -100 percent $= -1.0$ and thus $(1 + r_t) = (1 - 1) = 0$. This might happen, for example, if an investor becomes too greedy and impatiently invests in ventures which are too risky for his own good in the hope that he can "get rich quick."

As a result of any one link relative becoming equal to zero, the investor loses *all* the wealth he had accumulated up to period t; that is, he goes bankrupt and his utility [namely, Eq. (18-3b)] becomes as low as it can possibly be. This shows that some risk-aversion (that is, the fear of bankruptcy) is essential to maximize expected utility of terminal wealth over multiperiod reinvesting. Merely buying high-risk assets or "taking long shots" at the racetrack will not automatically yield riches. Quite to the contrary, the assumption of high risks period after period means that $r_t = -100$ percent $= -1.0$ may occur in one period and cause the geometric mean return and terminal wealth to become zero. Such outcomes were what caused some Wall Street speculators to jump from their office windows to their deaths on the pavement below during the Great Crash of the early 1930s.

18-2 SINGLE-PERIOD PORTFOLIO MANAGEMENT

Thus far, three long-run investment strategies have been shown to be equivalent: maximizing the logarithmic utility function, maximizing the geometric mean rate of return, and maximizing terminal wealth. The analysis of these multiperiod objectives ultimately focused on the individual one-period rates of return, r_t, which are the focal point of Markowitz single-period portfolio analysis. It was shown that the portfolio manager must undertake some risks of investing in order to obtain some returns with which to increase the portfolio's terminal wealth above its initial wealth $w_T > w_0$. But it was also shown that it was foolhardy to undertake large risks and expect to maximize (or even to have any) terminal wealth. To go a step further and reach a conclusion about exactly how the portfolio manager should select a portfolio, it is necessary to assume that the one-period rates-of-return distribution may be described by the two-parameter normal distribution. In fact, there is a large and growing body of evidence that returns are normally distributed.[4]

The normal probability distribution is completely defined by its two parameters: the expected value (or mean) and the variance (or standard deviation). Information about higher-order statistical moments is irrelevant when analyzing the normal distribution. The rational investment policy is therefore to select a portfolio which has the maximum expected return at whatever level of risk is deemed appropriate, that is, to select an efficient portfolio.[5] The optimum multiperiod strategy is the selection of any efficient portfolio between the low-return-and-low-risk segment and the high-risk-and-high-return segment that seems as if it should maximize terminal wealth in light of the current facts. Of course, this is identical to the optimal single-period investment strategy.

It is not possible to specify in advance exactly how much risk is wise to undertake when seeking to maximize terminal wealth.[6] However, a study by Sharpe and Cooper throws some light on the question.[7] Over a 36-year

---

[4] Randolph Westerfield, "The Distribution of Common Stock Price Changes: An Application of Transaction Time and Subordinated Stockastic Models," *Journal of the American Statistical Association*, 1975, in press; and R. C. Blattberg and N. J. Geonedes, "A Comparison of the Stable and Student Distributions as Statistical Models for Stock Prices," *Journal of Business*, April 1974, pp. 244–280.

[5] Mathematical proof that expected utility of terminal wealth is a function of the expected return $E(r)$ and variance σ^2, if rates of return are normally distributed, is outlined below. Mathematical statisticians will be able to fill in the missing steps of the proof.

$$E[U(w_T)] = \int U(r \mid w_0) f(\tilde{r} \mid E(\tilde{r}), \sigma^2) \, dr$$

$$= E[U(\tilde{r}) \mid w_0, E(r), \sigma^2]$$

where $\tilde{r}$ denotes the rate of return random variable, the vertical bars indicate that the variables after them are given, U is a logarithmic utility function, and $f(\tilde{r} \mid E(r), \sigma^2)$ refers to a normal probability distribution of rates of return. The full proof is omitted because it is lengthy and involves integral calculus. See equations (3.5), (3.6), (3.7), et al., in James Tobin, "Liquidity Preference as Behavior Towards Risk," *The Review of Economic Studies*, February 1958.

[6] Richard Roll, "Evidence on the Growth Optimum Model," *Journal of Finance*, June 1973, pp. 551–566. Harry Markowitz, op. cit., chap. 6.

[7] W. F. Sharpe and G. M. Cooper, "Risk-Return Classes of N.Y.S.E. Common Stocks, 1931–1967," *Financial Analysts Journal*, March–April 1972, p. 46.

TABLE 18-1 BETA SYSTEMATIC RISK COEFFICIENTS AND GEOMETRIC MEAN RETURNS FOR 10 NYSE STOCK PORTFOLIOS, 1931–1967

Risk-class	Portfolio's beta	Geometric mean return, %
1	1.42	14.52
2	1.18	14.21
3	1.14	14.79
4	1.24	15.84†
5	1.06	13.80
6	.98	15.06
7	1.00	14.69
8	.76	12.14
9	.65	12.40
10	.58	9.89

† Highest geometric mean return.

sample, they found that large portfolios of New York Stock Exchange stocks with beta systematic risk coefficients slightly above unity had the highest geometric mean rate of return. Table 18-1 shows the average betas for portfolios made from NYSE stocks which were constructed from homogeneous risk deciles. The table also shows the geometric mean returns for each of the portfolios from the 10 different risk-classes.

The statistics in Table 18-1 tend to indicate that portfolios composed of stocks which had beta coefficients between about 1.0 and 1.25 were the most lucrative. A search for either low-risk stocks with betas below about .6 or high-risk stocks with betas above about 1.3 appears to be a counter productive strategy. However, the stocks for this Sharpe-Cooper study were selected only on the basis of their beta coefficients. Selecting stocks with the aid of an expert security analyst and/or an economic forecaster could change the results in Table 18-1. In the final analysis, the experience of the decision maker and the "luck of the draw" can be significant factors in investment selection.

The only aspect of multiperiod portfolio management left to be discussed is the question, "How and when should the single-period efficient portfolios be revised to take advantage of new information which becomes available during the multiperiod horizon?"

18-3 PORTFOLIO REVISION

As bull- and bear-market periods pass in succession, new stocks are offered, old securities go bankrupt, and the efficient frontier shifts, making portfolio revision necessary. Furthermore, the portfolio will receive cash dividends and interest income which need to be reinvested. Also, new information will arrive continually, causing securities risks and return statistics to change. For these reasons, a multiperiod portfolio strategy will involve portfolio revision even though the investor's utility function may never change.

Investors do not usually desire a portfolio which changes its risk-class, even if it shifts along the efficient frontier. For example, a poor, lonesome, old widow would probably not be happy to have her life savings in a "go-go" mutual fund even if it were efficient. Instead, she would probably prefer a less risky balanced fund even though it was not on the efficient frontier. Thus, the practical objective of portfolio management in most business and personal situations typically becomes one of simple return maximization in a particular risk-class (when the investor's utility map is not known).

For example, suppose a mutual fund has become suboptimal at point A in Fig. 18-2. This portfolio's managers should not seek just any portfolio which has less risk and/or more expected return, such as the portfolios in the triangle bounded by points A, B, and C. Instead, only portfolios in or near the mutual fund's traditional risk-class (that is, σ_A, which its owners presumably prefer) that have higher expected returns should be sought. Such portfolios lie along the dotted line $AC'C$ in Fig. 18-2.

Revision Costs Make True Efficient Frontier Unattainable

Portfolio revision is a costly process. When a portfolio is revised, previously purchased securities which did not perform as expected may have to be liquidated at a capital loss. The expense of updating the risk and return statistics for many securities and the computer operation necessary to determine the new efficient frontier are not trivial, and the commissions on any securities bought or sold must be paid, too.

As a result of these costs, it is not possible for a revised portfolio to attain the true efficient frontier along the curve $EBCF$ in Fig. 18-2. Instead, the constrained efficient frontier along the curve $E'C'F'$ represents the op-

FIG. 18-2 Portfolio revision possibilities.

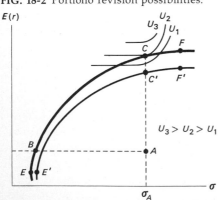

timum attainable investments. The vertical difference between the true efficient frontier curve *EBCF* and the *optimum attainable efficient frontier* curve *E'C'F'* equals the revision costs as a percentage of the portfolio's total assets.[8] In Fig. 18-2, the optimum attainable efficient frontier is closer to the true efficient frontier for low-risk, low-return portfolios than for efficient portfolios with higher returns because the low-risk, low-return portfolios presumably contain many bonds, and the sales commissions for buying and selling bonds are lower than for stock.

In situations like the one depicted in Fig. 18-2, portfolio *A* should be revised to attain point *C'*. Revisions of this nature should occur as often as they are possible—a month, a quarter, or longer after portfolio *A* was originally purchased. There is no optimum time schedule for portfolio revision. Owing to revision costs, it is impossible to attain the most efficient portfolio, *C*, in the desired risk-class, σ_A. But there is no reason that portfolio *C'* should not be obtained directly and immediately if it yields net profit after the revision costs.

18-4 CONCLUSIONS

When all things are considered, there are unusual circumstances which could arise in selecting an investment portfolio that would make a Markowitz efficient portfolio inadvisable.[9] However, as a pragmatic matter, myopically selecting a one-period Markowitz efficient portfolio in each successive period can maximize expected utility of terminal wealth over a planning horizon which extends many periods into the future, or over a single period.

This discussion about long-run portfolio strategies encompassing multiple periods tends to draw attention away from the portfolio managers who are managing small and/or short-term portfolios. These managers must consider liquidating their portfolios and consuming the wealth, using the money for an emergency, using the proceeds to finance some expenditure for which they were accumulating wealth over one period, ad infinitum. These portfolio managers are not in the position to look more than one period into the future. But they too should seek efficient portfolios to maximize their expected utility.[10] Thus, whether portfolio managers are looking one period or multiple periods into the future, they should seek the efficient frontier.

[8] A. H. Chen, F. C. Jen, and S. Zionts, "The Optimal Portfolio Revision Policy," *Journal of Business,* January 1971, pp. 51–61.

[9] Nils H. Hakansson, "Capital Growth and the Mean-Variance Approach to Portfolio Selection," *Journal of Financial and Quantitative Analysis,* January 1971, pp. 517–555.

[10] Eugene F. Fama, "Multiperiod Consumption-Investment Decisions," *American Economic Review,* March 1970, pp. 163–174.

QUESTIONS

1 Why maximize *expected* utility rather than simply the utility of wealth?

2 Find a utility function with positive but diminishing marginal utility which is incompatible with the logarithmic function and graph it. Compare and contrast this function with the logarithmic function. Can you make positive linear transformations on the log function so that it closely approximates the other function?

3 Assume a portfolio manager had taken large risks to attain large returns and had been so successful at this strategy that he had quadrupled his wealth every year for the past 10 years. Now this portfolio manager offers to manage your life savings along with his own funds for free. What do you think of this free chance to get rich quick and retire early?

4 Suppose investor A had as his investment strategy the maximization of a one-period logarithm of returns utility function. In contrast, his twin brother B maximized the log of multiperiod terminal wealth. If A and B were choosing from the same assets from which to form their portfolios, how should their portfolios differ?

5 Compare and contrast the marginal utility of an investor with a log utility function with the quadratic utility function of another investor.

6 If investor P had to pay brokerage fees to trade securities when she revised her portfolio but her twin sister, F, could trade without paying brokerage fees, how should their portfolios differ after a few periods?

SELECTED REFERENCES

Bicksler, J. L., and Paul A. Samuelson, *Investment Portfolio Decision-Making* (Lexington, Mass.: Lexington Books, 1974).

> This is a book of 23 investments readings of a mathematical nature. Readings 1 through 11, 15, and 16 are relevant to questions regarding multiperiod portfolio management.

Chen, A. H. F., F. C. Jen, and S. Zionts, "The Optimal Portfolio Revision Policy," *Journal of Business*, January 1971, pp. 51–61.

> This mathematical article uses calculus and explains portfolio revision in a one-period and a multiperiod context. A dynamic programming solution is formulated.

Elton, E. J., and M. J. Gruber, *Finance as a Dynamic Process,* Prentice-Hall Foundations of Finance series, 1975.

> Chapter 5 presumes a knowledge of utility analysis; it shows that multiperiod investments using Markowitz efficient portfolios are appropriate with logarithmic and exponential utility functions for normally

distributed returns. A readable summary of multiperiod portfolio theory.

Fama, Eugene F., "Multiperiod Consumption-Investment Decisions," *American Economic Review*, March 1970, pp. 163–174.

This article uses integral calculus to show that selecting one-period Markowitz efficient portfolios will yield an optimal multiperiod investment strategy if the investor has current consumption as an alternative to reinvestment each period and if the capital markets are perfect. A knowledge of utility and portfolio theory is presumed.

Nineteen

Portfolio Performance Evaluation

To attain the efficient frontier, or even get very near it, it is necessary to use diversification. In effect, this means that *portfolios* of assets must be held instead of a single individual asset. Chapter 17 showed how different attitudes toward risk resulted in widely different choices along the efficient frontier. But regardless of their preferences, risk-averse investors will still maximize their expected utilities by selecting *efficient portfolios.* There are virtually no circumstances in which investors in a world of uncertainty would be happier with all their funds in a single asset than in a portfolio, if they are rational, risk-averse persons who have no knowledge of future events.

In view of the importance of portfolios, it is essential to know how to evaluate their performance. This chapter will explain analytical tools to compare the performance of different portfolios with different risks and rates of return. In the course of this performance analysis, various operating deficiencies will be revealed. Suggestions will be made to overcome these impediments to achieving an efficient portfolio.

The documented performance of dozens of mutual funds is evaluated in this chapter. Mutual funds are examined rather than other portfolios because, by law, they must publicly disclose their operating results. Also, provisions of the Investment Company Act of 1940 limit mutual funds' use of leverage (that is, issuing debt); buying on margin; taking more than 9 percent of the proceeds from the sales of new shares for sales commissions; selling the funds' shares on margin; selling short; and deviating from the written statement of investment objectives that must be published in every prospectus. These requirements ensure a certain amount of similarity among mutual funds. Because of these similarities, plus their tax-exempt income status, the requirements that they disclose their holdings and income, and their popularity with investors, mutual funds make an interesting subject for study.

As explained in Chap. 2, *open-end investment companies,* or *mutual funds,* as they are more popularly called, sell their shares to the public and redeem them at the current net asset value of the shares. The *net asset value* per share is computed by dividing the total market value of all the mutual fund's holdings (net of any liabilities) by the number of the fund's outstanding shares. The one-period rate of return, r_t, is based on the mutual fund's change in net asset value, nav, plus its cash dividend disbursements, d, and capital gains disbursements, c, as shown in Eq. (2-3).

$$r_t = \frac{(\text{nav}_{t+1} - \text{nav}_t) + d_t + c_t}{\text{nav}_t} \tag{2-3}$$

19-1 RANKING FUNDS' AVERAGE RETURNS

When an investor considers the purchase of shares in mutual funds, the first question to be asked is: "Can the mutual funds earn a higher return for me than I can earn for myself?" Table 19-1 shows data for 39 mutual funds' performances for the decade from 1951 to 1960 inclusive.

Column 1 of Table 19-1 shows the average rate of return for each mutual fund. These returns are what would have been earned if a tax-exempt investor had purchased shares in each fund on January 1, 1951, held them 10 years while reinvesting the dividends, and sold the shares at the end of December 1960. It will be noted that only 18 of the mutual funds (that is, less than half of them) were able to earn a rate of return above the 14.7 percent which the investor could have expected to earn by picking stocks listed on the New York Stock Exchange with a dart or using some other naive buy-and-hold strategy.[1] Of the 39 funds, the best performance exceeded the average by only four percentage points. The data indicate that, on the average, the mutual funds did not earn returns for investors which a naive investor could not attain independently.

Columns 2 through 11 of Table 19-1 show the rankings of the 39 funds' yearly rates of return. The most striking feature of the ranking is their lack of consistency. None of the 39 funds was able to consistently outperform the naive buy-and-hold strategy over the decade.

---

[1] A naive buy-and-hold strategy means randomly selecting securities (for example, with a dart), buying them, and holding them regardless of what information becomes available about them or the market. The naive buy-and-hold strategy is used as a standard of comparison because it represents an investment with average return and average risk. The actual data referred to were computed by Drs. J. Lorie and L. Fisher at the University of Chicago. See "Rate of Return on Investments in Common Stocks: The Year-by-Year Record, 1926–1965," *Journal of Business,* July 1968, pp. 291–316. See Table 22-1, for the actual returns.

TABLE 19-1 YEAR-BY-YEAR RANKING OF INDIVIDUAL FUND RETURNS

Fund	Average annual return (1)	1951 (2)	1952 (3)	1953 (4)
Keystone Lower Price	18.7	29	1	38
T Rowe Price Growth	18.7	1	33	2
Dreyfus	18.4	37	37	14
Television Electronic	18.4	21	4	9
National Investors Corp.	18.0	3	35	4
De Vegh Mutual Fund	17.7	32	4	1
Growth Industries	17.0	7	34	14
Massachusetts Investors Growth	16.9	5	36	31
Franklin Custodian	16.5	26	2	4
Investment Co. of America	16.0	21	15	14
Chemical Fund Inc.	15.6	1	39	14
Founders Mutual	15.6	21	13	25
Investment Trust of Boston	15.6	6	3	25
American Mutual	15.5	14	13	4
Keystone Growth	15.3	29	15	25
Keystone High	15.2	10	7	3
Aberdeen Fund	15.1	32	23	9
Massachusetts Investors Trust	14.8	8	9	14
NYSE Market Average†	14.7			
Texas Fund, Inc.	14.6	3	15	9
Eaton & Howard Stock	14.4	14	9	4
Guardian Mutual	14.4	21	26	25
Scudder, Stevens, Clark	14.3	14	23	14
Investors Stock Fund	14.2	8	28	21
Fidelity Fund, Inc.	14.1	21	26	25
Fundamental Investment	13.8	14	15	31
Century Shares	13.5	14	28	35
Bullock Fund Ltd.	13.5	29	9	21
Financial Industries	13.0	26	15	31
Group Common Stock	13.0	38	8	25
Incorporated Investors	12.9	14	13	37
Equity Fund	12.9	14	27	21
Selected American Shares	12.8	21	15	21
Dividend Shares	12.7	32	7	14
General Capital Corp.	12.4	10	28	9
Wisconsin Fund	12.3	32	26	4
International Resources	12.3	10	37	39
Delaware Fund	12.1	36	23	25
Hamilton Fund	11.9	38	28	9
Colonial Energy	10.9	10	15	35

† The NYSE market average represents what a tax-exempt investor could have expected to earn by randomly picking (for example, with a dart) a large number of stocks listed on the NYSE and holding them 10 years while reinvesting the dividends. The data were published by L. Fisher and J. Lorie. "Rates of Return on Investments in Common Stock," *Journal of Business,* January 1964, pp. 1–21.

Source: Eugene F. Fama, "The Behavior of Stock Prices," *Journal of Business,* table 18, p. 93, January 1965.

1954 (5)	1955 (6)	1956 (7)	1957 (8)	1958 (9)	1959 (10)	1960 (11)
5	3	8	35	1	1	36
8	14	15	2	25	7	4
3	7	11	3	2	3	7
2	33	20	16	2	4	20
19	27	4	5	5	8	1
8	14	4	8	15	23	36
17	9	9	20	5	6	11
11	9	1	23	4	9	4
13	33	20	16	5	9	4
11	17	15	23	15	15	15
27	3	33	1	27	4	23
8	2	20	16	11	13	28
3	14	26	31	20	29	20
22	14	13	16	25	25	4
1	1	1	39	11	13	38
27	23	36	5	27	25	11
25	9	7	10	27	7	30
16	9	15	20	18	32	28
32	23	26	5	27	37	7
17	20	15	13	37	29	17
34	31	29	13	20	15	2
19	27	15	29	9	15	30
22	27	20	23	5	29	23
34	31	29	13	20	15	23
16	9	11	31	18	25	30
25	3	20	23	31	34	2
19	14	9	20	34	34	20
13	19	29	34	20	9	35
27	27	33	8	20	34	17
6	3	13	37	11	18	39
32	31	33	13	31	18	23
31	23	20	23	15	32	30
34	20	32	4	37	37	11
38	35	39	23	34	13	23
37	35	38	10	34	18	7
22	35	1	37	39	1	11
27	39	26	29	9	23	30
34	35	36	10	31	18	17
39	20	4	36	20	39	10

19-2 EFFICIENCY AND RELIABILITY OF
THE FUNDS' PERFORMANCES

One might question whether the mutual funds are really as poor at managing investments as the data in Table 19-1 indicate. After all, the mutual funds might be maximizing their returns in a very low risk-class where high returns were not available. This would mean the funds were efficient investments along the bottom portion of the efficient frontier. Figure 19-1 shows the actual performance of 23 mutual funds in risk-return space relative to the efficient frontier (that is, the curve *EF*) which existed at that time.

Figure 19-1 was prepared from monthly data on the 23 mutual funds from 1946 to 1956. It shows that none of the funds was an efficient asset, only a few had average returns which were within one percentage point of the efficient frontier. It is interesting to note, however, that the funds tended to cluster into groups. The funds which sought growth and were willing to assume risk to attain it formed a cluster which tends to lie above that of the less aggressive funds, and the income-growth funds clearly lie above the risk-avoiding balanced funds. Mutual fund managers evidently are able to distinguish the risk and return characteristics of their investments and stay in some preferred risk-class fairly consistently. Unfortunately, they do not seem to be able to follow their published objective very well, however.

According to the Investment Company Act of 1940, mutual funds must publish a written statement of their investment objectives and make it available to their shareholders. This objective can be changed only if the

FIG. 19-1 Performance of 23 mutual funds from 1946 to 1956 in risk-return space. [From Donald E. Farrar, *The Investment Decision under Uncertainty* (Englewood Cliffs, N.J.: Prentice-Hall, 1962), p. 73.]

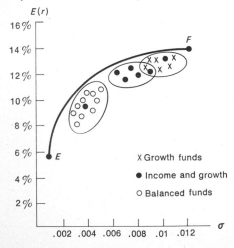

majority of the shareholders consent in advance to the new objective. These investment objectives can be classified into the following four categories:

1 Growth

2 Growth and income

3 Income and growth

4 Income, growth, and stability (a balanced fund)

These objectives are listed in descending order with respect to the aggressiveness with which the fund's management implies it will seek high average rate of return and assume the corresponding risks.

The stated objectives which mutual funds issue to their shareholders are not dependable; that is, there is sometimes no relation between the stated investment objectives and the actual performance of some mutual funds. Although the funds shown in Fig. 19-1 tended to remain in fairly consistent risk-return groupings over time, the risk-return grouping did not align with the funds' stated objectives in some cases. As a matter of fact, quantitative risk measures give a clearer picture of the funds' investment objectives than what the fund management say in their published statements.

Portfolios' Risk-Classes

All portfolios' average rates of return vary widely over time as the market alternates between bullish and bearish periods. Therefore, average rates of return are not satisfactory measures with which to classify mutual funds' risk and return. Certain quantitative risk measures, however, are fairly stationary over time. And, since risk and return are positively related, they also furnish an indication of whether the portfolio can be expected to earn a high, medium, or low rate of return in the long run—that is, over at least one complete business cycle.

Two quantitative risk surrogates are appropriate for measuring the historical risk of portfolios. First, the standard deviation of historical rates of return may be used to measure total risk. Second, portfolios' beta coefficients from their characteristic lines (which were fit with historical data) may be used to measure systematic or undiversifiable risk. Either of these risk surrogates is satisfactory for categorizing portfolio risk. Examples of both will be explained later in this chapter.

Mutual funds' beta coefficients may be classified as explained in Table 19-2. Table 19-3 shows the relationship between the two risk surrogates and the average rates of return for 103 mutual funds. The data for these statistics were gathered from January 1960 to June 1968. Table 19-3 shows the two risk surrogates are highly positively related with each other and with the portfolios' average rates of return.

TABLE 19-2 PORTFOLIO SYSTEMATIC RISK MEASURES DEFINED

Range of beta	Level of funds' risk	Description of price volatility
.5 to .7	Low	Share prices vary about half the rate of the market index.
.7 to .9	Medium	Share prices rise about 80% of the rate of the market index.
.9 to 1.3	High	Share prices vary directly with the rate of change in the market index.

TABLE 19-3 RISK-RETURN RELATIONSHIPS FOR MUTUAL FUNDS

Risk-class	Range of betas	Number of mutual funds	Average beta	Average variance, σ^2	Average rate of return
Low	.5 to .7	28	.619	.000877	.091 = 9.1%
Medium	.7 to .9	53	.786	.001543	.106 = 10.6%
High	.9 to 1.1	22	.992	.002304	.135 = 13.5%

Source: Irwin Friend, Marshall M. Blume, and Jean Crockett, *Mutual Funds and Other Institutional Investors: A New Perspective* (New York: McGraw-Hill, 1970), p. 150.

Table 19-4 compares the portfolios' published investment objectives with their quantitative risk and average return statistics. It shows that the portfolios' standard deviations and beta coefficients were much better indicators of the portfolios' actual performance than their published statements. The data in the table also show that the betas and standard deviations for the portfolio vary together positively.

19-3 SHARPE'S PORTFOLIO PERFORMANCE MEASURE

In assessing the performance of a portfolio, it is necessary to consider *both* risk and return. Ranking portfolios' average returns ignores the skill with

TABLE 19-4 COMPARISON OF MUTUAL FUNDS PERFORMANCES WITH THEIR STATED OBJECTIVES JANUARY 1960 TO JUNE 1968†

Beta coefficient	Number of funds in category				Average rate of return, %			
	Growth	Growth & income	Income & growth	Income, growth, & stability	Growth	Growth & income	Income & growth	Income, growth, & stability
.5 to .7	3	5	4	16	6.9	10.1	9.7	9.1
.7 to .9	15	24	7	7	11.2	10.0	10.0	12.2
.9 to 1.1	20	1	0	1	13.8	9.5		13.5

† Investment objectives as classified by Arthur Wiesenberger Services in 1967.
Source: Irwin Friend, Marshall M. Blume, and Jean Crockett, *Mutual Funds and Other Institutional Investors: A New Perspective* (New York: McGraw-Hill, 1970), p. 150.

which they minimize risk and is therefore an oversimplified performance measure. Determining the relative efficiency of a portfolio, as done in Fig. 19-1, is a more comprehensive analysis of a portfolio's performance. However, it is often desirable to be able to *rank* portfolios' performance. The real need is for an index of portfolio performance which is determined by both the return and the risk of a portfolio.

Dr. William F. Sharpe has devised an index of portfolio performance, denoted S_i which is defined in Eq. (19-1) for the ith portfolio.

$$S_i = \frac{\text{risk premium}}{\text{total risk}} = \frac{\bar{r}_i - R}{\sigma_i} \tag{19-1}$$

where $\bar{r}_i =$ average return on ith portfolio
$\quad \sigma_i =$ standard deviation of returns for portfolio i
$\quad R =$ riskless rate of interest

The numerator $(r - R)$ is called the "risk-premium" for portfolio i. The *risk-premium* is that return over and above the riskless rate which is paid to induce investors to assume risk.

Sharpe's index of performance generates one (ordinal) number which is determined by both the risk and the return of the portfolio (or other investment) being assessed. Figure 19-2 graphically depicts Sharpe's index. S_i measures the slope of the solid line starting at the riskless rate R in Fig. 19-2 and running out to asset i. Thus $S_C > S_B > S_A$ indicates that asset C is a better performer than asset B, and B is better than A. The fact that the portfolios have different average returns or risks does not hinder a direct comparison with Sharpe's performance index.[2]

Sharpe gathered data on the risk and return of 34 mutual funds for the decade from 1954 to 1963 inclusive and ranked their performances. Table

[2] I. Friend and M. Blume, "Measurement of Portfolio Performance under Uncertainty," *American Economic Review*, September 1970, pp. 561–575. This study questions portfolio performance measures.

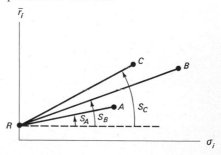

FIG. 19-2 Sharpe's index of portfolio performance measures the ratio of risk-premium to total risk.

TABLE 19-5 PERFORMANCES OF 34 MUTUAL FUNDS 1954–1963

Mutual fund	Average ann. return, %	Std. dev. of ann. return, %	Risk-premium† to std. dev. ratio = S_i
Affiliated Fund	14.6	15.3	.75896
American Business Shares	10.0	9.2	.75876
Axe-Houghton, Fund A	10.5	13.5	.55551
Axe-Houghton, Fund B	12.0	16.3	.55183
Axe-Houghton, Stock Fund	11.9	15.6	.56991
Boston Fund	12.4	12.1	.77842
Broad Street Investing	14.8	16.8	.70329
Bullock Fund	15.7	19.3	.65845
Commonwealth Investment Company	10.9	13.7	.57841
Delaware Fund	14.4	21.4	.53253
Dividend Shares	14.4	15.9	.71807
Eaton and Howard, Balanced Fund	11.0	11.9	.67399
Eaton and Howard, Stock Fund	15.2	19.2	.63486
Equity Fund	14.6	18.7	.61902
Fidelity Fund	16.4	23.5	.57020
Financial Industrial Fund	14.5	23.0	.49971
Fundamental Investors	16.0	21.7	.59894
Group Securities, Common Stock Fund	15.1	19.1	.63316
Group Securities, Fully Administered Fund	11.4	14.1	.59490
Incorporated Investors	14.0	25.5	.43116
Investment Company of America	17.4	21.8	.66169
Investors Mutual	11.3	12.5	.66451
Loomis-Sales Mutual Fund	10.0	10.4	.67358
Massachusetts Investors Trust	16.2	20.8	.63398
Massachusetts Investors—Growth Stock	18.6	22.7	.68687
National Investors Corporation	18.3	19.9	.76798
National Securities—Income Series	12.4	17.8	.52950
New England Fund	10.4	10.2	.72703
Putnam Fund of Boston	13.1	16.0	.63222
Scudder, Stevens & Clark Balanced Fund	10.7	13.3	.57893
Selected American Shares	14.4	19.4	.58788
United Funds—Income Fund	16.1	20.9	.62698
Wellington Fund	11.3	12.0	.69057
Wisconsin Fund	13.8	16.9	.64091

† S_i = (average return − 3 percent)/variability. The ratios shown were computed from original data and thus differ slightly from the ratios obtained from the rounded data shown in the table.
Source: William F. Sharpe "Mutual Fund Performances," *Journal of Business*, Suppl., January 1966, p. 125.

19-5 lists the average return, standard deviation, and Sharpe's performance index for each of the 34 mutual funds. Sharpe also measured the index of performance for the Dow Jones Industrial Average (DJIA) to use as a standard of comparison in evaluating the performance of the funds. The DJIA is a sample of 30 stocks of large, old, blue-chip firms which are popular with investors. Figure 19-3 shows a frequency distribution of the S_i's for the 34 mutual funds listed in Table 19-5 and the DJIA.

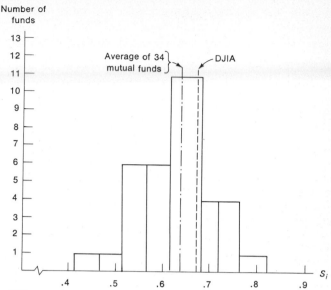

FIG. 19-3 Frequency distribution of Sharpe's risk-premium to risk ratio for a sample of 34 mutual funds, 1954–1963.

Of the 34 funds shown in Fig. 19-3, 11 had risk-premium-to-risk ratios above the .667 of the DJIA.[3] The average of the 34 mutual funds' ratios is .633, which is below .667 for the DJIA. This means that the DJIA was a more efficient portfolio than the average mutual fund in the sample. When one considers that (1) the sales commission of 8 percent paid on the purchase of mutual fund shares exceeds the commissions incurred in purchasing securities directly (that is, creating your own portfolio) and (2) the efficiency of the average mutual fund investment is below that of the DJIA, it follows that most investors would be better off by creating their own portfolios of randomly selected blue-chip stocks than buying mutual funds.

In calculating the data in Table 19-5, which are shown in Fig. 19-3, the management expenses of the mutual funds were deducted to determine net returns to the funds' investors. If the management expenses of the 34 funds are ignored, 19 of them had better performance index scores than the DJIA. The sample data indicate that before management expenses, the average mutual fund performs about as well as a market average such as the DJIA, but the returns to the funds' shareholders (after the funds' operating ex-

---

[3] The average return of the DJIA over the period was 16.3 percent and its standard deviation was 19.94 percent, giving $S_{DJIA} = (16.3 - 3)/19.94 = 13.3/19.94 = .667$. Another study of data for 38 mutual funds from 1958 to 1967 showed similar but not identical results. This study showed that only 18 out of the 38 mutual funds outperformed the Standard and Poor's (SP) 500 stocks average, but the average risk-premium-to-risk ratio for the 38 funds was slightly above the SP 500's ratio. K. V. Smith and D. A. Tito, "Risk Return Measures of Ex Post Portfolio Performance," *Journal of Financial and Quantitative Analysis,* December 1969, pp. 464–465.

penses are deducted but ignoring the sales commission paid by fund investors) were less than those of the DJIA. It seems that mutual fund managers' salaries and other professional management expenses lowered the net returns to shareholders because these costs were larger than the increase in returns they generated.

19-4 TREYNOR'S PORTFOLIO PERFORMANCE MEASURE

Mr. Jack Treynor conceived an index of portfolio performance which is based on systematic risk, as measured by portfolios' beta coefficients, rather than on total risk, like Sharpe's measure. To use Treynor's measure, the characteristic regression lines of portfolios must first be calculated by estimating Eq. (19-2).

$$r_{pt} = a_p + b_p(r_{Mt}) + e_t \qquad t = 1, 2, \ldots, T \tag{19-2}$$

where r_{pt} = rate of return on pth portfolio in tth time period
r_{Mt} = return on market index in period t
e_t = random error term for period t
a_p = intercept coefficient for portfolio p
b_p = portfolio's beta coefficient

Figure 19-4 shows typical characteristic lines for two portfolios with different management policies toward risk.

Chapter 12 discussed characteristic regression lines and the beta coefficient as an index of systematic risk in some detail. As with individual assets, the beta coefficient from a portfolio's characteristic lines is an index of the portfolio's systematic or undiversifiable risk. Using only naive diversification, the unsystematic variability of returns of the individual assets in a portfolio typically average out to zero, and the portfolio is left with only systematic risk. Therefore, Treynor suggests measuring a portfolio's return relative to its systematic risk rather than relative to its total risk, as does the Sharpe measure.

FIG. 19-4 Characteristic lines for portfolios.

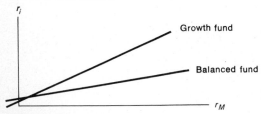

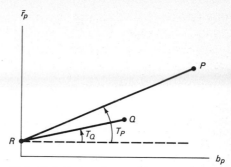

FIG. 19-5 Treynor's portfolio performance measure in $(b_p, \bar{r}_p)$ space.

The Treynor Index

Equation (19-3) defines Treynor's index of portfolio performance, denoted T_p for the pth portfolio.[4]

$$T_p = \frac{\text{risk-premium}}{\text{systematic risk index}} = \frac{\bar{r}_p - R}{b_p} \qquad (19\text{-}3)$$

where $\bar{r}_p$ = average rate of return on portfolio p
b_p = beta coefficient for portfolio p
R = riskless rate

Graphically, T_p is a measure of the slope of the line from R to the pth portfolio as shown in Fig. 19-5. As this figure demonstrates, portfolio P is more desirable than portfolio Q because P earned more risk-premium per unit of systematic risk; that is, $T_P > T_Q$.

Comparison of Sharpe and Treynor Measures

Treynor's portfolio performance index T_p is similar to Sharpe's index S_i, which was defined in Eq. (19-1), since they both use the risk-premium as a numerator. But Treynor's index measures systematic risk as its denominator while Sharpe's index uses total risk. In effect, Sharpe's measure ranks assets' degree of dominance in $[\sigma, E(r)]$ space and Treynor's measure ranks assets' dominance in $[b_i, E(r_i)]$ space. Both risk measures implicitly assume that money may be freely borrowed or lent at R. This is the rationalization for the linear rays out of R.

The two portfolio performance indices yield very similar rankings of the portfolios' performances in most cases. Figure 19-6 shows a plot of points representing rankings of 34 mutual funds with the Sharpe and

---

[4] J. Treynor, "How to Rate Management of Investment Funds," *Harvard Business Review*, January–February 1965, pp. 63–75.

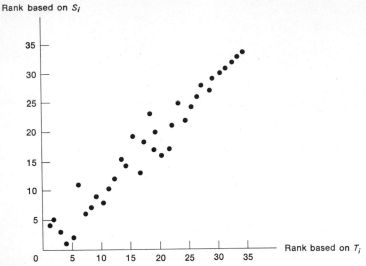

FIG. 19-6 Comparison of portfolio performance rankings in (rank of T_i, rank of S_i) space. (From William F. Sharpe, "Mutual Fund Performance," *Journal of Business*, Suppl., January 1966, p. 129.)

Treynor indices. These two sets of rankings were calculated with the same data used to prepare Table 19-5. Each point represents the ranking of one of the 34 portfolios in terms of both indices. The rank correlation coefficient for the two rankings was .97. Thus, although the Treynor and Sharpe measures differ conceptually, in practice they both tend to rank portfolios' performances similarly.

More Recent Results

Using 120 monthly rates of return from the 1960–1969 decade, Dr. John G. McDonald analyzed the performance of 123 mutual funds. The Sharpe and Treynor performance measures were used in the slightly reformulated manner shown in Eqs. (19-1a) and 19-2a) below.

$$S_i = \frac{E(r_{it} - R_t)}{\sigma_i} \qquad (19\text{-}1a)$$

$$T_i = \frac{E(r_{it} - R_t)}{b_i} \qquad (19\text{-}2a)$$

Dr. McDonald used monthly observations of the 30-day commercial paper rate as a surrogate for the riskless rate; this is why the R's in Eqs. (19-1a) and (19-2a) have subscripts of t for $t = 1, 2, \ldots, 120$ months. These monthly observations of R_t were subtracted from each portfolio's monthly rate of return to obtain monthly risk-premiums, denoted $(r_{it} - R_{it})$. Then the

TABLE 19-6 PORTFOLIO PERFORMANCE STATISTICS, 1960–1969, FOR 123 MUTUAL FUNDS

Fund's stated objective (sample size)	Average beta	Average σ_i	Average $E(r_{it} - R_t)$	Average S_i	Average T_i
Maximum capital gain (18)	1.22	5.90	.693	.117	.568
Growth (33)	1.01	4.57	.565	.124	.560
Growth-income (36)	.90	3.93	.476	.121	.529
Income-growth (12)	.86	3.80	.398	.105	.463
Balanced (12)	.68	3.05	.214	.070	.314
Income (12)	.55	2.67	.252	.094	.458
Total sample (123)	.92	4.17	.477	.133	.510
Market average				.133	.510

Source: John G. McDonald, "Objectives and Performance of Mutual Funds, *"Journal of Financial and Quantitative Analysis,* June 1974, pp. 311–333.

average risk-premium, denoted $E(r_{it} - R_t)$, over the 120 months was divided by the appropriate risk measure to compare the portfolios' performances. Table 19-6 shows a summary of the statistics.

McDonald found that, on average, the funds with more aggressive objectives took more risk and earned higher returns, as was found earlier (see Table 19-3) in the Friend-Blume-Crockett study. The McDonald study also found that a few funds departed from their stated objective; similar results were reported (see Table 19-4) in the Friend-Blume-Crockett study and elsewhere.

Concerning the investment performance of the 123 funds, McDonald's study reported that slightly over half the 123 mutual funds (that is, 67 out of 123) had values for Treynor's performance index which exceeded the stock market average. Using Sharpe's performance measure, about 31.7 percent (that is, 39 out of 123) of the funds outperformed the stock market average. Thus, using a slightly different specification of the Sharpe and Treynor portfolio performance measures, and a more recent sample, did not yield any significantly different conclusions. On average, mutual funds perform about as well as a naive buy-and-hold strategy. All the studies of mutual fund performance reach essentially the same conclusions.

19-5 POOR MUTUAL FUND MANAGEMENT PRACTICES

The poor performances of the samples of mutual funds may be the result of a number of causes. The main causes appear to be (1) incurrence of expenses in an unfruitful search for undervalued securities, (2) superfluous diversification, (3) inability to utilize macroeconomic forecasts, and (4) inflexible utilization of the investment alternatives available. These causes are discussed below.

Searching for Undervalued Securities

Most mutual funds employ fundamental security analysts to search for "good buys"—that is, securities which are undervalued. These security analysts tend to specialize in one or more given industries. They keep files of information on the industries they follow, attend trade conventions, and interview (and in some cases "wine and dine") executives of the firms in the industry in an effort to learn news which would change the intrinsic value of a security.

Some mutual funds also employ technical analysts (that is, chart readers) who prepare and study graphs of the volume of trading and the prices of securities. These technical analysts hope to be able to detect shifts in supply and demand for a security by studying the trading activity in it. Different technical analysts use different charting devices in their work. There are bar characteristics, point-and-figure chartists, confidence index technicians, Elliot's wave theory chartists, and credit balance chartists—just to name a few.

The fundamental analysts and/or technical analysts employed by a mutual fund make buy and sell recommendations to the portfolio manager, who may or may not follow these recommendations. In any event, each mutual fund expends thousands of dollars each year in its search for "good buys." As the data reviewed earlier in this chapter showed, this expense is not paying off. The search for undervalued securities which will yield capital gains has not enabled the average mutual fund to earn returns (before management expenses) which are significantly above what could be achieved with a naive buy-and-hold strategy.[5] However, the cost of the search does reduce mutual funds' net return to their shareholders to below what the shareholders could have expected to earn if they had selected securities randomly.

Superfluous Diversification

Most mutual funds own over 100 different securities. This superfluous diversification lowers the portfolio's performance. In Chap. 15 (see Fig. 15-2) it was shown how owning numerous randomly selected securities can reduce a portfolio's total risk to the systematic level of the market as a whole. With this many securities, the portfolio becomes a market index itself (after all, the DJIA is made up of only 30 nonrandom securities). If the portfolio's individual assets are highly correlated (for example, if all have betas above unity), no amount of spreading the portfolio's funds across different assets will lower the portfolio's risk to the average level of the market. As a result, it is not likely that a naively and/or superfluously diversified portfolio will have risk below the systematic level. Even mutual funds

---

[5] A closer analysis of why chartists cannot be expected to outperform a naive buy-and-hold strategy is undertaken in Chap. 21.

whose stated objective is to minimize risk and maintain principal typically use only naive diversification. Most mutual fund managers do not use Markowitz diversification techniques. They usually consider the recommendations that their fundamental and/or technical analysts make without regard to the security's correlation with the existing portfolio or the market. Such practices explain why mutual funds' risks are not lower.

Superfluous diversification also reduces the portfolio's returns. Large, efficient security exchanges like the NYSE do not contain numerous securities which are underpriced. Only a few securities' prices will typically be low enough that they offer unusually high returns relative to other assets in their risk-class. But, instead of concentrating the portfolio's assets in the few unusually promising securities which they find, nearly all mutual funds hold such superfluously diversified portfolios that a majority of their securities can be expected to turn in only ordinary performances at best.

Not only will portfolios containing dozens of different securities typically fail to minimize risk or maximize returns; they will generate high expenses. The cost of maintaining information files on all the securities in the portfolio and hiring additional portfolio managers will swell the funds' management expenses, slow their decision making, and decrease the net returns to the shareholders.

Some Mutual Funds Too Large

Many of the inadequacies currently experienced by mutual funds and some important potential problems are due to the large size of some of the funds. Over 60 mutual funds have total assets in excess of $100 million. When these large funds become actively involved in trading during periods of market instability or when certain issues are undergoing significant reevaluation, they can destabilize security markets.[6] And, as mutual funds grow larger, whatever destabilizing influences exist now can be expected to increase.

The mutual funds' large size is not only undesirable because of possible destabilizing effects on securities markets; it is also one of the reasons they diversify superfluously. If a large mutual fund spread its assets over as few as a dozen securities, it might exceed its legal limit (according to the Investment Company Act of 1940, funds cannot own more than 10 percent of the outstanding shares of any company), or the fund's liquidity could be impaired.

Outside observers can only speculate why mutual funds seek to grow large. The undesirable side effects of destabilization and superfluous diversification do not seem to be offset by benefits from being large. That is, there are few economies of scale to be attained by increasing the size of

[6] Irwin Friend, Marshal M. Blume, and Jean Crockett, *Mutual Funds and Other Institutional Investors: A New Perspective* (New York: McGraw-Hill, 1970) pp. 24–27.

portfolios which are already large.[7] To the contrary, the difficulties in managing a large portfolio and the potential harm which could come to the market mechanism suggest that society might be better off if the size of mutual funds were limited.

Funds' Inability to Utilize Macroeconomic Forecasts

Portfolio managers can benefit from using economic forecasts of the following macroeconomic variables:

1 Gross nation product

2 Disposable personal income

3 Sector forecasts of the activity in the various industries comprising the nation's economy

4 Unemployment rate

5 Rate of inflation

6 Interest rates

7 Probable actions taken by the monetary (the Federal Reserve System) and fiscal (federal administration and the Treasury) authorities

8 Corporate profits

9 Housing starts

10 Automobile sales

These are the factors which ultimately determine security prices. Various economic forecasting services regularly forecast these and numerous other economic series for years into the future. Security prices react to anticipated changes in these variables up to 12 months in advance of their occurrence. Thus, an accurate economic forecast for at least 12 months into the future is needed to be able to anticipate changes in the securities markets.

Chapter 12 explained that approximately one-third of the price change in the average common stock could be explained by relating changes in some market index to individual securities through the characteristic line, and Sec. 10-4 showed how fundamental security analysts could utilize economic forecasts to obtain advantageous timing in their trading. However, if these tools are to be used to their utmost advantage, a dependable economic

---

[7] With the development of the third and fourth markets, negotiated commissions, increased use of large computers, and sophisticated economic forecasting techniques, there will be economies of scale to be attained in large operations. Several small funds, however, could obtain these economies of scale by using one large, centralized trading office, computer center, and economic forecasting staff. This arrangement would also allow the small funds to enjoy the benefits that can be attained only by a smaller, independent organization and also the economies of scale of a larger operation.

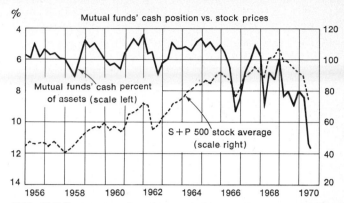

FIG. 19-7 Percentage of total assets held in cash by mutual funds as bear market advanced. (From "Mutual Funds: Positions vs Stock Prices," *United Mutual Fund Selector*, Feb. 12, 1970.)

forecast is required. Unfortunately, many mutual funds apparently do not utilize these tools.

Figure 19-7 shows how the average cash positions of several dozen mutual funds varied during the bear market which lasted through 1969 and hit bottom in May 1970. This figure shows that as the bear market was developing, the average mutual fund in the sample varied its cash holdings between about 5 to 10 percent of its total assets. During 1969 as the market declined continuously, the funds still held about 90 percent of their total assets in securities. As the market neared its bottom in 1970, the funds liquidated only enough of their assets for average cash holdings to reach a maximum of about 12 percent. The funds' failure to disinvest and hold cash during this long, hard bear-market period implies certain things. It seems that either the average mutual fund did not foresee the bear market or that the funds' investments were being shifted from falling stocks to other investments with rising prospects. Figure 19-8 reveals the unfortunate answer to this question.

Figure 19-8 shows the percentage change in various mutual funds preceding and during the 1969–1970 bear market, including 73 funds claiming to seek growth, 49 funds claiming to seek both growth and income, 19 funds claiming to seek primarily income, and 22 balanced funds primarily seeking safety of principal. At the bottom of each grouping are average performance figures for that group. It will be noted that, throughout 1969 and the first half of 1970 when the bear market was declining the most rapidly, most of the funds were *declining faster* than the market average. Only the balanced funds which hold large proportions of bonds were able to decline less drastically than the stock market as measured by the Standard & Poor 500 stock average.

Figure 19-8 shows that nearly all the mutual funds stayed heavily invested in risky securities during a long bear market. They apparently had

FIVE YEARS 1965-69 How Managmt. Performed % Chg.	FIVE YEARS 1965-69 How Investors Fared % Chg.	73 Growth Funds	THREE YEARS 1967-69 How Managmt. Performed % Chg.	THREE YEARS 1967-69 How Investors Fared % Chg.	ONE YEAR 1969 How Managmt. Performed % Chg.	ONE YEAR 1969 How Investors Fared % Chg.	1ST HALF 1970 How Managmt. Performed % Chg.	1ST HALF 1970 How Investors Fared % Chg.
+ 27.3	+ 16.2	Aberdeen Fund	+ 15.2	+ 5.1	− 14.8	− 22.3	− 23.0	− 29.7
+ 83.5	+ 67.4	Admiralty Funds—Growth	+ 26.3	+ 15.2	− 34.7	− 40.4	− 47.7	− 52.3
+ 34.2	+ 22.8	American Growth Fund	+ 22.3	+ 11.9	− 18.8	− 25.7	− 19.4	− 26.3
+ 77.1	+ 77.1	***American Investors Funds**	+ 14.6	+ 14.6	− 29.3	− 29.3	− 42.1	− 42.1
+ 81.9	+ 66.0	Anchor Growth Fund	+ 29.8	+ 18.4	− 16.4	− 23.7	− 32.3	− 38.2
+ 74.2	+ 59.4	Apex Fund	+ 11.3	+ 1.8	− 17.1	− 24.1	− 30.9	− 36.8
+103.3	+ 87.0	Axe-Houghton Stock Funds	+ 48.4	+ 36.5	− 25.6	− 31.6	− 17.9	− 24.5
+ 92.0	+ 76.6	Axe Science	+ 35.8	+ 24.9	− 29.7	− 35.3	− 23.4	− 29.5
+ 51.7	+ 38.4	The Businessman's Fund	+ 24.5	+ 13.6	− 23.4	− 30.3	− 29.8	− 35.9
+ 57.0	+ 43.7	Channing Growth Fund	+ 9.3	+ 0.1	− 27.8	− 33.9	− 32.8	− 38.5
+140.6	+120.1	Channing Special Fund	+ 53.9	+ 40.8	− 26.6	− 32.8	− 49.5	− 54.8
+149.7	+128.5	Chase Fund of Boston	+ 82.7	+ 67.2	− 17.1	− 24.1	− 43.0	− 47.8
+ 81.6	+ 66.2	Chemical Fund	+ 46.6	+ 34.1	+ 5.8	− 3.2	− 22.7	− 29.3
+ 76.5	+ 61.5	Colonial Growth Shares	+ 40.1	+ 28.2	− 16.0	− 23.1	− 28.7	− 34.8
+ 30.5	+ 19.4	Commerce Fund	+ 30.5	+ 19.4	− 13.0	− 20.4	− 20.5	− 27.3
+ 73.0	+ 59.2	Common Stock Fund—SBM	+ 46.2	+ 34.5	− 6.9	− 14.3	− 23.7	− 29.8
+ 73.9	+ 59.1	Delaware Fund	+ 25.9	+ 15.2	− 16.3	− 23.1	− 19.2	− 26.1
+ 83.4	+ 83.4	***deVegh Mutual Fund**	+ 35.7	+ 35.7	− 14.7	− 14.7	− 21.7	− 21.7
+118.7	+118.7	***Drexel Equity Fund**	+ 59.5	+ 59.5	− 14.7	− 14.7	− 29.1	− 29.1
+ 63.1	+ 48.8	Dreyfus Fund	+ 24.6	+ 13.7	− 11.9	− 19.6	− 24.1	− 30.7
+ 60.2	+ 60.2	***Energy Fund**	+ 26.1	+ 26.1	− 14.7	− 14.7	− 21.8	− 21.8
+243.6	+214.4	Enterprise Fund	+132.0	+112.3	− 25.9	− 32.2	− 38.3	− 43.5
+ 89.3	+ 73.2	Fairfield Fund	+ 27.1	+ 16.3	− 29.3	− 35.3	− 33.0	− 38.7
+ 79.2	+ 64.0	Federated Growth Fund	+ 35.9	+ 24.3	− 13.0	− 20.4	− 23.0	− 29.5
+ 76.6	+ 61.6	Fidelity Capital Fund	+ 14.7	+ 5.0	− 14.0	− 21.3	− 19.0	− 25.9
+ 83.8	+ 68.2	Fidelity Trend Fund	− 10.2	− 17.8	− 12.1	− 19.6	− 24.9	− 31.3
+ 62.5	+ 48.7	Florida Growth Fund	+ 64.7	+ 50.7	− 16.7	− 23.8	− 34.7	− 40.3
+ 41.7	+ [illegible]	Foursquare Fund	+ 10.4	+ 1.0	− 19.7	− 26.5	− 21.4	− 28.1
+ 56.2	+ 42.5	Franklin Cust.—Growth	+ 36.9	+ 24.9	− 2.3	− 10.8	− 25.4	− 31.9
+ 49.2	+ 36.5	Fund of America	+ 32.3	+ 21.1	− 16.5	− 23.6	− 27.2	− 33.4
+ 43.4	+ 43.4	***Growth Industry Shares**	+ 31.4	+ 31.4	− 2.1	− 2.1	− 27.8	− 27.8
+ 79.1	+ 79.1	***Hedberg & Gordon**	+ 23.8	+ 23.8	− 13.8	− 13.8	− 26.6	− 26.6
+119.8	+101.1	Invêstors Research Fund	+ 41.3	+ 29.3	− 2.7	− 11.0	− 18.2	− 25.2
+ 38.8	+ 27.[illegible]	Investors Variable Payment Fund	+ 24.2	+ 14.3	− 14.1	− 21.0	− 30.8	− 36.3
+ 83.3	+ 68.6	Ivest Fund	+ 32.8	+ 22.2	− 7.9	− 15.3	− 24.5	− 30.5
+ 82.2	+ 82.2	***Johnston Mutual Fund**	+ 40.7	+ 40.7	+ 0.5	+ 0.5	− 24.3	− 24.3
+ 56.1	+ 43.1	Keystsone (K-2)	+ 23.0	+ 11.3	− 20.3	− 26.9	− 26.8	− 32.9
+ 68.5	+ 54.5	Keystone (S-3)	+ 24.3	+ 14.0	− 13.8	− 21.0	− 23.4	− 29.8
+ 79.0	+ 64.1	Keystone (S-4)	+ 48.5	+ 36.2	− 20.8	− 27.4	− 37.6	− 42.8
+133.7	+113.4	Knickerbocker Growth Fund	+ 50.9	+ 37.8	− 9.6	− 17.5	− 17.0	− 24.2
+ 71.0	+ 56.5	Lexington Research	+ 52.1	+ 39.2	− 7.7	− 15.5	− 25.5	− 31.8
		***Loomis-Sayles Capital Development**	+ 33.5	+ 33.5	− 16.4	− 16.4	− 27.2	− 27.2
+ 65.8	+ 51.7	Mass. Investors Growth Stk. Fund	+ 31.6	+ 20.4	+ 0.2	− 8.7	− 26.8	− 33.0
+ 44.2	+ 51.8	Mid-America Mutual Fund	+ 21.7	+ 11.4	− 10.9	− 18.5	− 30.5	− 36.4
+ 43.7	+ 32.9	Mutual Investing Found. Growth	+ 38.6	+ 28.2	− 16.0	− 22.3	− 28.8	− 34.1
+ 16.2	+ 16.2	***Nassau Fund**	+ 11.5	+ 11.5	− 12.3	− 12.3	− 20.4	− 20.4
+ 46.0	+ 46.0	***National Industries Fund**	+ 12.5	+ 12.5	− 21.1	− 21.1	− 26.6	− 26.6
+ 78.0	+ 62.[illegible]	National Investors Corp.	+ 48.4	+ 35.8	+ 4.4	− 4.5	− 28.1	− 34.2
+ 71.8	+ 57.[illegible]	National Securities Growth Series	+ 40.8	+ 28.8	− 11.7	− 19.2	− 20.0	− 26.8
+ 92.6	+ 76.[illegible]	Oppenheimer Fund	+ 40.8	+ 28.8	− 16.0	− 23.1	− 21.0	− 27.7
+ 30.6	+ 30.6	***Penn Square Mutual Fund**	+ 15.2	+ 15.2	− 16.2	− 16.2	− 12.6	− 12.6
...	...	Philadelphia Fund			− 3.2	− 11.7	− 23.9	− 30.6
+ 74.9	+ 74.9	***Price (T. Rowe) Growth Fund**	+ 41.8	+ 41.8	+ 3.4	+ 3.4	− 27.3	− 27.3
+263.3	+263.3	***Price (Rowe) New Horizons**	+114.3	+114.3	− 6.8	− 6.8	− 33.8	− 33.8
+ 67.8	+ 53.5	Putnam Growth Fund	+ 35.7	+ 24.2	− 13.3	− 20.7	− 20.6	− 27.3
+ 59.5	+ 45.9	Putnam Investors Fund	+ 46.7	+ 34.2	− 0.3	− 8.8	− 22.9	− 29.5
+111.7	+ 93.7	Revere Fund	+ 55.7	+ 42.5	− 22.0	− 28.2	− 34.3	− 39.9
...	...	***Scudder Special Fund**	+ 72.7	+ 72.7	− 18.0	− 18.0	− 23.5	− 23.5
+ 82.4	+ 66.4	Steadman AIF	+ 56.3	+ 42.6	− 16.6	− 23.9	− 44.9	− 49.7
+ 23.2	+ 12.4	Steadman FIF	+ 22.3	+ 11.6	− 16.7	− 24.0	− 23.1	− 29.8
+ 43.8	+ 30.8	Steadman Science & Growth	+ 12.8	+ 2.9	− 28.5	− 34.8	− 42.9	− 47.9
+ 49.3	+ 49.3	***Stein Roe & Farnham Stock Fund**	+ 35.6	+ 35.6	− 7.5	− 7.5	− 26.7	− 26.7
+ 20.6	+ 15.8	Teachers Assn. Mutual Fund	+ 8.8	+ 4.4	− 20.9	− 24.1	− 25.7	− 28.7
+ 61.2	+ 47.9	Technology Fund	+ 30.3	+ 19.6	− 9.3	− 16.8	− 21.9	− 28.3
+ 61.9	+ 48.1	Twentieth Century Growth	+ 17.9	+ 7.9	− 24.6	− 31.0	− 44.9	− 49.6
+ 16.9	+ 6.7	United Accumulative Fund	+ 8.6	− 0.9	− 10.3	− 18.1	− 25.7	− 32.2
+ 51.4	+ 38.2	United Science Fund	+ 22.7	+ 12.0	− 10.2	− 18.1	− 30.0	− 36.1
+ 96.8	+ 80.0	Value Line Fund	+ 55.8	+ 42.2	− 21.1	− 28.0	− 36.2	− 41.8
+163.4	+140.4	Value Line Special Situations	+ 69.9	+ 55.0	− 33.0	− 38.9	− 44.8	− 49.6
+101.3	+ 84.2	Vanderbilt Mutual Fund	+ 76.1	+61.1	− 23.5	− 30.0	− 33.6	− 39.2
+ 92.2	+ 75.9	Western Industrial Shares	+ 45.7	+ 33.3	− 13.6	− 20.9	− 43.0	− 47.8
+ 89.1	+ 73.0	Windsor Fund	+ 53.0	+ 40.0	− 3.7	− 11.9	− 16.1	− 23.2
+105.2	+ 87.8	Winfield Growth Fund	+ 59.9	+ 46.3	− 31.7	− 37.5	− 37.8	− 43.1
+ 76.7	+ 61.6	LOAD FUND AVERAGE	+ 37.1	+ 25.5	− 15.7	− 22.6	− 28.7	− 34.4
+ 78.9	**+ 78.9**	**NO-LOAD FUND AVERAGE**	**+ 37.9**	**+ 37.9**	**− 12.2**	**− 12.2**	**− 26.1**	**− 26.1**
+ 26.0	+ 26.0	STANDARD & POOR'S 500 STOCKS	+ 26.0	+ 26.0	− 8.3	− 8.3	− 19.3	− 19.3

How Managmt. Performed % Chg.	How Investors Fared % Chg.	49 Growth With Income Funds	How Managmt. Performed % Chg.	How Investors Fared % Chg.	How Managmt. Performed % Chg.	How Investors Fared % Chg.	How Managmt. Performed % Chg.	How Investors Fared % Chg.
+ 31.4	+ 21.5	Affiliated Fund	+ 25.6	+ 16.2	− 14.3	− 20.7	− 17.7	− 23.9
+ 46.9	+ 34.4	American Express Stock Fund	+ 26.3	+ 15.6	− 15.7	− 22.9	− 21.6	− 28.3
+ 36.4	+ 24.8	American Mutual Fund	+ 21.2	+ 10.9	− 13.1	− 20.5	− 16.5	− 23.6
+ 30.4	+ 19.3	Broad Street Investing Corp.	+ 31.1	+ 20.0	− 3.7	− 11.9	− 17.1	− 24.1
+ 40.8	+ 28.6	Bullock Fund	+ 33.2	+ 21.7	− 6.8	− 14.9	− 24.2	− 30.8
+ 30.6	+ 19.5	Channing Common Stock Fund	+ 19.5	+ 9.3	− 15.3	− 22.5	− 14.6	− 21.9
+ 29.7	+ 18.7	Colonial Fund	+ 23.0	+ 12.5	− 16.4	− 24.5	− 16.1	− 23.2
+ 32.2	+ 22.3	Commonwealth Fund—Plan C	+ 23.1	+ 13.9	− 15.3	− 21.7	− 18.3	− 24.4
+ 56.4	+ 43.9	Composite Fund	+ 38.6	+ 27.5	−17.4	− 24.0	− 16.3	− 23.0
+ 3.0	− 4.9	Corporate Leaders Trust, Ser. B.	+ 12.6	+ 4.0	− 12.6	− 19.3	− 10.5	− 17.3
+ 56.6	+ 43.3	Crown Western-Diver. Fund	+ 51.1	+ 38.3	− 11.7	− 19.2	− 23.3	− 29.8
+ 29.0	+ 17.8	Dividend Shares	+ 30.2	+ 18.9	− 4.8	− 13.0	− 16.3	− 24.5
+ 24.2	+ 13.6	Eaton & Howard Stock	+ 16.0	+ 6.1	− 13.5	− 20.9	− 21.7	− 28.4
+ 28.8	+ 17.9	Equity Fund	+ 23.9	+ 13.4	− 14.9	− 22.1	− 17.6	− 24.6
+ 57.3	+ 43.9	Fidelity Fund	+ 36.6	+ 25.0	− 7.4	− 15.3	− 17.8	− 24.8
+ 36.2	+ 24.6	Financial Industrial Fund	+ 18.4	+ 8.3	− 14.9	− 22.1	− 22.3	− 28.9
+ 25.8	+ 14.8	First Investors	+ 13.7	+ 3.8	− 11.8	− 19.5	− 18.9	− 26.0
+ 21.1	+ 10.8	Founders Mutual Fund	+ 21.9	+ 11.5	− 10.0	− 17.6	− 18.3	− 25.2
+ 27.2	+ 16.1	Fundamental Investors	+ 16.6	+ 6.4	− 12.7	− 20.3	− 23.4	− 30.1
+ 25.9	+ 15.2	Group Securities—Common Stock Fund	+ 25.4	+ 14.7	− 12.8	− 20.2	− 11.4	− 18.9
+ 43.6	+ 43.6	***Guardian Mutual Fund**	+ 29.8	+ 29.8	− 9.0	− 9.0	− 21.3	− 21.3
+ 18.1	+ 8.1	Hamilton Fund Series	+ 14.9	+ 5.1	− 20.4	− 17.2	− 20.8	− 27.5
+ 45.9	+ 34.2	Imperial Capital Fund	+ 33.4	+ 22.7	− 4.6	− 12.2	− 21.5	− 27.8
+ 70.2	+ 55.7	Investment Co. of America	+ 34.6	+ 23.2	− 10.6	− 19.2	− 19.2	− 26.1
+ 25.7	+ 15.0	Investment Trust of Boston	+ 27.2	+ 16.4	− 8.9	− 16.6	− 18.2	− 25.2
+ 20.2	+ 11.1	Investors Stock Fund	+ 22.4	+ 12.6	− 8.0	− 15.4	− 25.1	− 31.1
+ 83.3	+ 77.8	†Istel Fund	+ 61.0	+ 56.2	− 15.5	− 18.0	− 22.3	− 24.6
+ 23.8	+ 13.5	Keystone (S-1)	+-17.9	+ 8.1	− 5.5	− 23.3	− 18.8	− 25.5
+ 28.8	+ 18.1	Keystone (S-2)	+ 25.5	+ 15.1	− 14.2	− 21.3	− 14.1	− 21.2
+ 33.3	+ 21.7	Knickerbocker Fund	+ 27.0	+ 16.0	− 16.2	− 23.5	− 16.7	− 23.9
+ 19.7	+ 14.9	†Mann (Horace) Fund	+ 20.8	+ 16.0	− 0.4	− 4.4	− 21.2	− 24.4
+ 26.9	+ 16.1	Mass. Investors Trust	+ 26.1	+ 15.4	− 4.8	− 12.9	− 19.6	− 26.4
+ 43.7	+ 32.9	Mutual Investing Foundation	+ 38.6	+ 28.4	− 16.0	− 22.3	− 14.1	− 20.5
+ 30.8	+ 30.8	***Mutual Trust**	+ 27.3	+ 27.3	− 9.0	− 9.0	− 30.0	− 30.0
+ 35.3	+ 23.8	National Securities—Stock	+ 28.0	+ 17.1	− 17.2	− 24.2	− 15.0	− 22.2
+ 44.6	+ 44.6	***One William Street Fund**	+ 30.1	+ 30.1	− 3.9	− 3.9	− 24.9	− 24.9
+ 30.9	+ 30.9	***Pine Street Fund**	+ 24.9	+ 24.9	− 10.0	− 10.0	− 15.3	− 15.3
+ 75.1	+ 60.2	Pioneer Fund	+ 49.7	+ 37.0	− 15.6	− 22.8	− 18.3	− 25.2
+ 19.6	+ 19.6	***Scudder Common Stock Fund**	+ 15.8	+ 15.0	− 15.6	− 15.6	− 30.3	− 30.3
+ 46.6	+ 34.1	Security Investment Fund	+ 35.5	+ 24.0	− 16.3	− 23.4	− 7.1	− 15.0
+ 47.1	+ 36.1	Selected American Shares	+ 22.0	+ 12.9	− 10.0	− 16.7	− 19.8	− 25.2
+ 32.9	+ 21.6	Sigma Investment	+ 21.5	+ 11.1	− 12.3	− 19.8	− 18.3	− 25.2
+ 38.0	+ 27.7	Southwestern Investors	+ 30.1	+ 20.3	− 14.4	− 20.8	− 14.8	− 21.2
+ 16.0	+ 5.9	Sovereign Investors	+ 19.5	+ 9.1	− 11.9	− 19.5	− 10.5	− 18.3
+ 35.3	+ 23.5	United Income Fund	+ 30.4	+ 19.0	− 8.5	− 16.5	− 21.2	− 29.1
+ 24.7	+ 14.7	Varied Industry Plan	+ 12.8	+ 3.8	− 18.1	− 24.7	− 16.8	− 23.5
+ 23.6	+ 13.1	Wall Street Investing Corporation	+ 15.9	+ 6.0	− 9.7	− 17.3	− 17.4	− 24.4
+ 43.0	+ 30.8	Washington Mutual Investors Fund	+ 33.5	+ 22.2	− 13.9	− 21.2	− 15.1	− 22.3
+ 39.3	+ 27.5	Wisconsin Fund	+ 27.7	+ 16.8	− 5.8	− 14.1	− 14.1	− 21.4
+ 35.6	+ 24.6	LOAD-FUND AVERAGE	+ 26.9	+ 17.9	− 11.9	− 19.1	− 17.8	− 24.3
+ 33.9	**+ 33.9**	**NO-LOAD FUND AVERAGE**	**+ 25.4**	**+ 25.4**	**− 9.5**	**− 9.5**	**− 24.3**	**− 24.3**
+ 26.0	+ 26.0	STANDARD & POOR'S 500 STOCKS	+ 26.0	+ 26.0	− 8.3	− 8.3	− 19.3	− 19.3

FIG. 19-8 Mutual fund performances during bear market. † = no-load fund; ‡ = low-load fund. The column "How Management Performed" refers to the change in net asset value without deducting sales commissions. The column "How Investors Fared" refers to the change in the investor's wealth after an allowance for whatever sales commissions he must pay to buy into the fund. (From Arthur Wiesenberger Services, New York.)

19 Income Funds

Fund	How Managmt. Performed % Chg.	How Investors Fared % Chg.	How Managmt. Performed % Chg.	How Investors Fared % Chg.	How Managmt. Performed % Chg.	How Investors Fared % Chg.	How Managmt. Performed % Chg.	How Investors Fared % Chg.
Admiralty Funds—Income Series	+ 37.2	+ 25.2	+ 34.3	+ 22.5	− 20.5	− 27.5	− 6.3	− 14.5
American Express Income	+ 27.9	+ 17.0	+ 28.7	+ 17.8	− 14.6	− 21.9	− 13.0	− 20.4
Anchor Income Fund	+ 22.4	+ 11.7	+ 17.6	+ 7.3	− 14.8	− 22.3	− 15.7	− 23.1
Associated Fund Trust	+ 23.1	+ 12.3	+ 22.6	+ 11.2	− 21.7	− 28.6	− 10.9	− 13.7
Channing Income	+ 37.9	+ 26.2	+ 28.9	+ 17.9	− 13.0	− 20.4	− 8.8	− 16.6
Decatur Income	+ 58.8	+ 45.3	+ 45.1	+ 32.8	− 13.2	− 20.6	− 11.3	− 18.8
Eaton & Howard Income	+ 21.5	+ 11.2	+ 18.5	+ 8.4	− 13.5	− 22.7	− 10.8	− 18.4
Financial Industrial Income	+ 72.0	+ 57.3	+ 58.7	+ 45.2	− 16.3	− 23.4	− 20.2	− 27.0
Income Fund of Boston	+ 19.8	+ 9.3	+ 16.2	+ 6.0	− 13.1	− 20.7	− 7.2	− 15.3
Keystone (K-1)	+ 17.2	+ 7.5	+ 10.8	+ 1.6	− 13.6	− 20.8	− 10.5	− 17.9
Liberty Fund	+ 28.8	+ 17.9	+ 26.8	+ 16.0	− 19.6	− 26.4	− 23.2	− 29.7
Magna Income Trust	+ 19.7	+ 9.5	+ 15.8	+ 6.0	− 15.0	− 22.2	− 7.5	− 15.4
National Securities—Dividend	+ 39.4	+ 27.6	+ 31.9	+ 20.7	− 19.5	− 26.3	− 14.3	− 21.6
National Securities—Income	+ 26.4	+ 15.7	+ 21.7	+ 11.2	− 11.2	− 18.7	− 14.2	− 21.5
*Northeast Investors	+ 15.7	+ 15.7	+ 14.6	+ 14.6	− 9.4	− 9.4	− 4.0	− 4.0
Provident Fund for Income	+ 73.4	+ 58.7	+ 53.6	+ 40.5	− 20.6	− 27.3	− 16.3	− 23.4
Puritan Fund	+ 45.7	+ 33.3	+ 27.4	+ 16.6	− 14.9	− 22.1	− 12.9	− 20.3
Putnam Income	+ 10.1	+ 0.7	+ 8.8	− 0.4	− 18.6	− 25.5	− 16.9	− 18.5
Value Line Income	+ 36.0	+ 24.1	+ 22.8	+ 12.1	− 23.0	− 29.7	− 13.8	− 21.3
LOAD FUND AVERAGE	+ 34.3	+ 22.8	+ 27.2	+ 16.3	− 16.4	− 23.7	− 17.7	− 20.1
NO-LOAD FUND AVERAGE	+ 15.7	+ 15.7	+ 14.6	+ 14.6	− 9.4	− 9.4	− 4.0	− 4.0
STANDARD & POOR'S 500 STOCKS	+ 26.0	+ 26.0	+ 26.0	+ 26.0	− 8.3	− 8.3	− 19.3	− 19.3

22 Balanced Funds

Fund	How Managmt. Performed % Chg.	How Investors Fared % Chg.	How Managmt. Performed % Chg.	How Investors Fared % Chg.	How Managmt. Performed % Chg.	How Investors Fared % Chg.	How Managmt. Performed % Chg.	How Investors Fared % Chg.
American Business Shares	+ 19.5	+ 16.5	+ 16.9	+ 8.1	− 9.7	− 16.5	− 5.7	− 12.6
American Express Investment	+ 24.6	+ 14.0	+ 20.9	+ 10.6	− 10.2	− 17.8	− 16.5	− 23.6
Axe-Houghton A	+ 61.4	+ 48.5	+ 37.8	+ 26.8	− 27.5	− 33.3	− 23.7	− 29.8
Axe-Houghton B	+ 25.9	+ 15.8	+ 15.4	+ 6.2	− 24.7	− 30.7	− 17.9	− 24.5
Boston Foundation Fund	+ 40.0	+ 28.1	+ 25.8	+ 15.1	− 15.0	− 22.2	− 12.7	− 20.1
Boston Fund	+ 3.4	− 5.4	+ 10.0	+ 0.7	− 9.0	− 16.7	− 12.7	− 20.1
Channing Balanced	+ 23.4	+ 11.3	+ 15.0	+ 5.2	− 13.2	− 20.6	− 10.5	− 18.1
Composite Bond & Stock	+ 37.1	+ 26.1	+ 32.1	+ 21.5	− 15.8	− 22.5	− 12.3	− 19.3
*Dodge & Cox Balanced	+ 33.4	+ 33.4	+ 23.4	+ 22.4	− 8.0	− 8.0	− 15.1	− 15.1
Eaton & Howard Balanced	+ 8.4	− 0.8	+ 11.4	+ 1.9	− 9.3	− 17.0	− 13.0	− 20.4
Group Securities—The Balanced Fund	+ 18.8	+ 8.7	+ 19.4	+ 9.3	− 8.5	− 16.3	− 7.1	− 15.0
Investors Mutual Fund	+ 10.4	+ 1.6	+ 14.2	+ 5.1	− 6.4	− 13.9	− 14.5	− 21.3
*Loomis-Sayles Mutual	+ 24.1	+ 24.1	+ 23.2	+ 23.2	− 7.5	− 7.5	− 17.8	− 17.8
Massachusetts Fund	+ 26.2	+ 15.2	+ 19.1	+ 8.7	− 10.5	− 18.3	− 15.6	− 23.0
Nation-Wide Securities	+ 15.5	+ 6.8	+ 16.6	+ 7.9	− 8.0	− 14.9	− 8.7	− 13.5
Putnam (George) Fund	+ 32.1	+ 20.9	+ 22.7	+ 12.3	− 6.6	− 14.5	− 14.8	− 22.0
*Scudder Balanced	+ 5.4	+ 5.4	+ 8.1	+ 8.1	− 6.6	− 6.6	− 4.2	− 17.3
Shareholders Trust Boston	+ 49.9	+ 37.2	+ 43.8	+ 31.6	− 18.8	− 25.7	− 20.8	− 27.3
Sigma Trust Shares	+ 7.1	− 2.0	+ 3.1	− 5.7	− 15.9	− 23.0	− 16.0	− 23.1
*Stein Roe & Farnham Balanced	+ 35.7	+ 35.7	+ 35.7	+ 26.9	− 7.7	− 7.7	− 21.3	− 21.5
Wellington Fund	+ 5.8	− 3.2	+ 7.8	− 1.4	− 7.7	− 15.5	− 12.0	− 22.0
Whitehall Fund	+ 46.4	+ 34.0	+ 45.6	+ 33.2	− 2.3	− 2.3	− 10.5	− 29.5
LOAD FUND AVERAGE	+ 21.0	+ 11.8			− 12.2	− 19.4	− 14.4	− 21.9
NO-LOAD FUND AVERAGE	+ 18.4	+ 18.4	+ 18.4	+ 18.4	− 7.4	− 7.4	− 17.9	− 17.9
STANDARD & POOR'S 500 STOCKS	+ 26.0	+ 26.0	+ 26.9	+ 26.9	− 8.3	− 8.3	− 19.3	− 19.3

FIG. 19-8 (*Continued*)

little or no advance warning of this market decline and took little or no action to shift to investments (for example, cash, puts, or certain bonds) which would be profitable during a general market decline — or at least would resist it. Most mutual funds do not seem to utilize economic forecasting.

Inflexible Utilization of the Investment Alternatives Available

The preceding discussion of mutual funds' reactions to a bear market highlights the nature of their rigid investment policies. Had they shifted from falling common stocks to such investment instruments as short sales, puts, calls, bonds, or commodity future contracts, their action would not only have increased the shareholders' return; it would have reduced their risk exposure.

Various state and federal laws and Internal Revenue Service regulations limit mutual funds' investment alternatives (namely, short sales and options are forbidden). However, the funds are allowed more leeway than they utilize. Their failure to fully utilize the legal investment alternatives which could increase their returns and/or lower their risk again suggests unthinking adherence to inflexible investment policies.

19-6 CONCLUSIONS

The preceding discussion explained certain risk-return portfolio performance tools. These tools were applied to mutual funds to provide examples of their use. Certain conclusions can be drawn regarding mutual funds and the tools used to evaluate portfolio performance.

Conclusions about Mutual Fund Investing

The preceding portfolio performance analysis of mutual funds suggests that many investors who own or are considering buying mutual fund shares could expect higher rates of return and less risk if they invested their own funds by selecting securities blindly with a dart and then simply holding them. This statement does not mean that all mutual fund shares represent poor investment decisions. Mutual funds can perform some valuable services for some investors.

Consider a small, amateur investor who has $6,000 or less to invest. If we suppose that she will purchase only round lots (to avoid paying the higher odd-lot trading cost) and that the securities she buys have an average cost of $30 per share, she would probably be well advised to invest in a good mutual fund. Such an investor would be able to buy only two securities, as the following computations show.

$$\$30 \times 100 \text{ shares} = \$3,000 \text{ per round lot}$$
$$\$6,000 \text{ total investment} = \$3,000 \text{ per round lot} \times 2 \text{ round lots}$$

Since two is too few securities to minimize the portfolio's unsystematic portion of total risk, this investor should probably look for a mutual fund. Furthermore, the small private investor cannot usually find time and/or does not have the skills needed to perform the economic and financial analysis which should precede any investment decision.

Although mutual funds do not typically earn high rates of return, they are usually able to reduce their risk to the systematic level of the market fluctuations. So, the fortunes of a mutual fund investor are not tied to the fortunes of only one or two individual securities. Therefore, unless investors have the resources at their disposal to perform Markowitz diversification (namely, access to an electronic digital computer, a data file for many securities, and the ability to program the computer), they might be better off investing in a mutual fund.

The majority of mutual funds earn long-run average rates of return which exceed the returns paid by insured savings accounts. Thus, investors receive some added return for assuming risk (unless they are forced to liquidate their holdings in a period of depressed prices).

Finally, mutual funds can help an investor stay in some preferred risk-class (although that risk-class is not necessarily the one the fund says it will pursue in its statement of investment objectives). By examining mutual funds' quantitative risk coefficients, an investor can find a fund which will fairly consistently maintain a given level of risk. Table 19-3 explains the risk implications of various portfolio risk measures. As mentioned before, mutual funds do tend to stay in a given risk-class and select assets which earn a mediocre return for that level of risk.[8] This is a valuable service which amateur or part-time investors might not be able to provide for themselves.

Conclusions about Portfolio Performance Measures

Ranking portfolios' yearly rates of return reveals whether any of them are consistently able to outperform their competitors. However, such rankings may make an efficient low-risk portfolio appear to be doing poorly. To evaluate a portfolio adequately, the level of risk it assumes must be considered *with* its rate of return. Unfortunately, some portfolio managers' statements about the degree of risk (and concurrent expected returns) they will seek are sometimes erroneous. In contrast, portfolios' empirically measured risk coefficients furnish stationary indices of the level of risk a portfolio is undertaking. If the standard deviation is used, portfolios' standard deviations and average rates of return may be plotted in $[\sigma, E(r)]$ spaced and compared with the efficient frontier. Sharpe's index of portfolio performance measures the risk-premium per unit of risk borne by individual portfolios. This index considers both risk and return and yields one index number for each portfolio; these numbers may be used to rank the performances of a group of portfolios. Some analysts prefer Treynor's portfolio performance measure. The Treynor index uses portfolios' beta systematic risk coefficients and average returns to compare portfolios' performance in $[b, E(r)]$ space. The two performance measures rank mutual funds similarly.

Conclusions about Portfolio Management Practices

There are several common traps a portfolio manager may fall into which can shackle the portfolio's performance. An aimless search for undervalued securities is not likely to yield returns which exceed those that could be attained by using a naive buy-and-hold strategy. So the portfolio manager should try to limit the portfolio's holdings to a small number of securities so that each one may be watched carefully. Superfluous diversification across dozens of securities is not good diversification, and it reduces the portfolio's flexibility and diminishes the portfolio's expected return. Portfolio management could benefit considerably from an accurate, detailed economic forecast. Such an economic forecast will reveal the growth industries in the economy and furnish various indicators that are necessary to allocate capital in an optimal manner. Finally, a good economic forecast will provide advance warning of economic downturns and thus of the bear markets which precede them. This advance notice will allow the portfolio manager to shift the portfolio's assets to financial instruments that are advantageous to hold in a bear market. In order to be efficient, a portfolio's funds must be shifted among various unrelated securities (such as stocks, bonds, options,

---

[8] R. S. Carlson, "Aggregate Performance of Mutual Funds, 1948–1967," *Journal of Financial and Quantitative Analysis*, March 1970, pp. 1–32.

and commodities) in order to take full advantage of Markowitz diversification and to maximize the expected return. Judging from the performance statistics reviewed above, all mutual fund managers have room for improvement.

Performance Evaluation of Other Portfolios

Today, many billions of dollars of investment capital in the United States are being moved about from one institutional investor to another. American Telephone and Telegraph and the Bell System, for example, have over $10 billion spread across more than 50 commercial banks and 15 investment advisors in more than 100 separately managed pools of capital. Other large corporations have equally large pools of investment funds. The financial managers who control these mobile investment funds are continually searching for and evaluating places to invest their funds productively. But their studies of bank trust departments, investment advisors, mutual funds, life insurance companies' funds management programs, and other institutional investment management organizations are not reported to the general public. Furthermore, since the institutional investment management organizations are not required by law to disclose their performance results (as are mutual funds), they keep their results secret. As a result, the studies of mutual fund performance are much richer and more widely available than similar studies on other institutional investors.

Publicly disseminated scientific studies of various institutional investment management organizations[9] are not sufficiently plentiful to justify detailed conclusions about the relative investment management skills of the various organizations. However, the limited material available suggests that mutual funds do not tend to do significantly better or significantly worse than the trust departments of commercial banks or life insurance companies.

QUESTIONS

1 "Closed-end investment companies redeem their shares at the current net asset value." Is this statement true, false, or uncertain? Explain.

2 How is the income of an open-end investment company taxed?

3 "Rankings of portfolios' average returns show that, although the average mutual fund does not outperform the market, a few truly superior funds consistently beat the market." Is this statement true, false, or uncertain? Explain.

---

[9] W. G. Burns and R. H. Klemm, "Performance of Bank Managers of Trust Funds," R. L. White Center for Financial Research, unpublished manuscript, August 1973. Edward Malca, *Bank-Administered Comingled Pension Funds* (Lexington, Mass.: Lexington Books, 1973). I. Friend, M. Blume, and J. Crockett, op. cit.

4 Why is ranking mutual funds by their rates of return a poor way to evaluate their performance?

5 How well does the mutual fund industry perform relative to some naive buy-and-hold strategy?

6 Assume you have been put in charge of a mutual fund with a large staff of fundamental analysts and millions of dollars of assets spread over more than 100 different securities. The fund's gross return is about average for the industry, but its management expenses are high, so its net yield to its investors is slightly below average. The previous management did not try to specialize as a growth or safety fund, but ran the firm as a general-purpose fund. What do you plan to do with your fund? Explain why.

7 Consider the following investment advice: "Put your money in the trust department of a good commercial bank. Banks will manage your investments better than the mutual funds, and they won't charge you a load fee." Is this statement true, false, or uncertain? Explain.

SELECTED REFERENCES

Fama, E. F., "Components of Investment Performance," *Journal of Finance,* June 1972, pp. 551–568.
>This paper uses mathematical statistics to analyze and extend the Sharpe and Treynor portfolio performance evaluation tools.

Jensen, Michael C., "The Performance of Mutual Funds in the Period 1945–64," *Journal of Finance,* May 1968, pp. 389–416.
>An analysis of the performance of mutual funds which uses regression analysis.

Sharpe, William F., "Mutual Fund Performance," *Journal of Business,* Supplement on Security Prices, January 1966, pp. 119–138.
>This risk-return analysis of mutual fund performance uses correlation, regression, and statistical inference.

Treynor, J. L., and K. K. Mazuy, "Can Mutual Funds Outguess the Market?," *Harvard Business Review,* July–August 1966, pp. 131–136.
>Multiple regression is used to determine if mutual funds outperform the market.

PART SIX

THE BEHAVIOR OF STOCK PRICES

CHAPTER 20 TECHNICAL ANALYSIS shows graphs of stock prices which the chartists use to select investments.

CHAPTER 21 THE BEHAVIOR OF STOCK MARKET PRICES reports scientific studies on how the prices of common stocks move.

CHAPTER 22 ABOUT "BEATING THE MARKET" explains the folly of schemes which try to "get something for nothing."

The three chapters comprising Part 6 deal with security price movements. They analyze some "popular wisdom" (for example, some of the charting techniques explained in Chap. 20) used by untutored investors and go on to show the desirability of using the analytical tools introduced in the preceding chapters to select investments which have the maximum expected return in their risk-class.

Twenty

Technical Analysis

In the past, technical analysis was a euphemistic synonym for charting. That is, technical analysts prepared charts of various financial variables in order to make forecasts about stock prices. Today, however, technical analysis includes the work of some nonchartists who use quantitative rather than graphical tools.[1] Dozens of different techniques are used by professional technical analysts. In this chapter, a few of the more prominent technical analysis tools are explained. Before the tools of technical analysis are examined, however, the notions which are at the core of all technical analysis are reviewed.

20-1 THE PHILOSOPHY OF TECHNICAL ANALYSIS

Technical analysis is based on the widely accepted premise that security prices are determined by the supply of and the demand for securities. The tools of technical analysis are therefore designed to measure supply and demand. Typically, technical analysts record historical financial data on charts, study these charts in an effort to find meaningful patterns, and use these patterns to predict future prices. Some charting techniques are used to predict the movements of a single security; some are used to predict move-

---

[1] One of the new technicians is R. A. Levy, President, Computer Directions Advisors, Inc., Silver Spring, Md. Levy has stated his position in articles and a book. R. L. Levy, "Conceptual Foundations of Technical Analysis," *Financial Analysts Journal*, July–August 1966, p. 83; and *The Relative Strength Concept of Common Stock Forecasting* (Larchmont, N.Y.: Investors Intelligence, 1968). *Fortune* magazine reported that Levy's own work indicated that many technical analysis tools of the traditional charting type were worthless: *Fortune*, September 1970, p. 188.

ments of a market index; some are used to predict both the action of individual securities and the market action.

Edwards and Magee[2] articulated the basic assumptions underlying technical analysis as follows:

1 Market value is determined solely by the interaction of supply and demand.

2 Supply and demand are governed by numerous factors, both rational and irrational.

3 In disregard of minor fluctuations in the market, stock prices tend to move in trends which persist for an appreciable length of time.

4 Changes in trend are caused by the shifts in supply and demand.

5 Shifts in supply and demand, no matter why they occur, can be detected sooner or later in charts of market action.

6 Some chart patterns tend to repeat themselves.

In essence, technical analysts believe that past patterns of market action will recur in the future and can therefore be used for predictive purposes.

In Chap. 10 it was explained how fundamental analysts estimate the intrinsic value of a security. Technical analysts, on the other hand, seek to estimate security *prices* rather than intrinsic *values;* that is, they try to forecast short-run shifts in supply and demand which will affect the market price of one or more securities. They tend to ignore factors such as the firms' risks and earnings growth in favor of various barometers of supply and demand that they have devised.

One text on technical analysis dramatically states that:

It is futile to assign an intrinsic value to a stock certificate. One share of United States Steel, for example, was worth $261 in the early fall of 1929, but you could buy it for only $22 in June 1932. By March 1937, it was selling for $126 and just one year later for $38. . . . This sort of thing, this wide divergence between presumed value and actual value, is not the exception; it is the rule; it is going on all the time. The fact is that the real value of a share of U.S. Steel common is determined at any given time solely, definitely and inexorably by supply and demand, which are accurately reflected in the transactions consummated on the floor of the . . . Exchange.

Of course, the statistics which the fundamentalists study play a part in the supply and demand equation — that is freely admitted. But there are many other factors affecting it. The market price reflects not only the differing fears and guesses and moods, rational and irrational, of hundreds of potential buyers and sellers, as well as their needs and their resources — in total, factors which defy analysis and for which no statistics are obtainable, but which are nevertheless all synthesized, weighted and finally expressed in the one precise

[2] R. D. Edwards and John Magee, Jr., *Technical Analysis of Stock Trends,* 4th ed. (Springfield, Mass.: John Magee, 1958), p. 86.

figure at which a buyer and seller get together and make a deal (through their agents, their respective brokers). This is the only figure that counts.

In brief, the going price as established by the market itself comprehends all the fundamental information which the statistical analysts can hope to learn (plus some which is perhaps secret to him, known only to a few insiders) and much else besides of equal or even greater importance.[3]

The preceding quotation makes some strong assertions, stresses the impact of the investor emotion in an unscientific manner, and is an extremely flattering interpretation of one set of facts; but it does convey the spirit of technical analysis.

In defending their practices, most technical analysts do not accuse fundamental analysts of being illogical or conceptually in error. In fact, many technical analysts would agree with fundamental analysts that security prices do fluctuate around their true intrinsic values. But they assert the superiority of their methods over fundamental analysis by pointing out that technical analysis is easier, faster, or can be simultaneously applied to more stocks than fundamental analysis. This latter claim is certainly true. Of course, if technical analysis does not accomplish what it is purported to do, its relative simplicity does not justify its use.

Many technical analysts would say that fundamental analysis is not worthless, but, rather, that it is just too troublesome to bother with. First, they point out that even if a fundamental analyst does find an underpriced security, he must wait and hope that the rest of the market recognizes the security's true value and bids its price up. Second, fundamental analysis is hard, time-consuming work. Technical analysis, on the other hand, requires less schooling and is easier to use. Third, technical analysts cite the inadequacy of the income statements produced by accountants (as discussed in Chap. 11) which form the basis for much fundamental analysis. Finally, technical analysts point out the highly subjective nature of the earnings multipliers used by fundamental analysts. In view of these deficiencies of fundamental analysis, consider some of the tools used by technical analysts to measure supply and demand and forecast security prices.

20-2 THE DOW THEORY

The Dow theory is one of the oldest and most famous technical tools; it was originated by Charles Dow, who founded the Dow Jones Company and was the editor of *The Wall Street Journal* around 1900. Mr. Dow died in 1902, and the Dow theory was developed further and given its name by members of *The Wall Street Journal* staff. Down through the years, numerous writers have altered, extended, and in some cases abridged the original Dow

---

[3] R. D. Edwards and John Magee, Jr., ibid, p. 3.

theory. Today, many versions of the theory exist and are used; it is the basis for many other techniques used by technical analysts.

The Dow theory rose to a peak of prominence during the 1930s. At that time, *The Wall Street Journal* published editorials written by its staff members which interpreted market action in terms of the theory. On October 23, 1929, *The Wall Street Journal* published a now-famous editorial, "A Turn in the Tide," which correctly stated that the bull market was then over and a bear market had started. This forecast was based on the Dow theory. The horrendous market crash which followed the forecast drew much favorable attention to the Dow theory.

How the Dow Theory Works

The Dow theory is used to indicate reversals and trends in the market as a whole or in individual securities. According to Mr. Dow himself, "The market is always considered as having three movements, all going at the same time. The first is the narrow movement from day to day. The second is the short swing, running from two weeks to a month or more; the third is the main movement, covering at least 4 years in its duration."[4] Dow theory practitioners refer to these three components as: (1) daily fluctuations, (2) secondary movements, and (3) primary trends. The primary trends are commonly called bear or bull markets. Secondary trends last only a few months. The theory asserts that daily fluctuations are meaningless. However, the chartist must plot the asset's price or the market average day by day in order to outline the primary and secondary trends.

Figure 20-1 is a line chart which a Dow theorist might develop. This figure shows a primary uptrend existing from period t to the peak price which occurred just before day $t + j$. On trading day $t + j$, an "abortive

[4] *The Wall Street Journal*, Dec. 19, 1900.

FIG. 20-1 A line chart of daily closing prices with Dow theory signals.

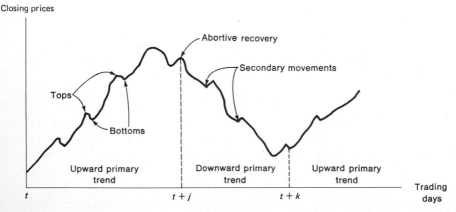

Closing prices

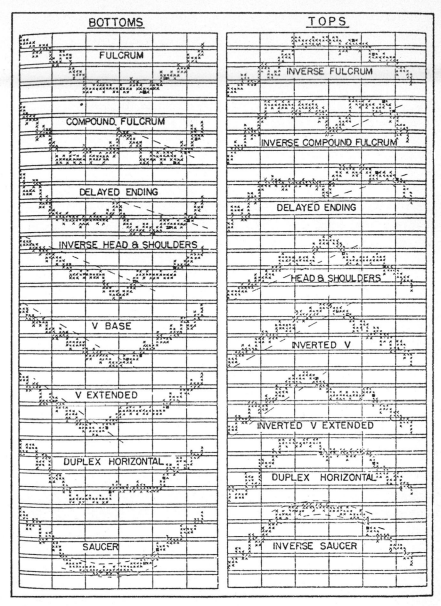

FIG. 20-2 Graphic illustrations of chart formations. (From *Commodity Year Book,* Commodity Research Bureau, Inc., New York.)

recovery'' occurs, signaling a change in the direction of the market's primary movement. An abortive recovery occurs when a secondary movement fails to rise above the preceding top. Before $t + j$, all the tops are ascending but after the abortive recovery, the tops are descending until just before day $t + k$. At $t + k$, a secondary movement fails to reach a new bottom, signaling the start of a bull market. Most Dow theorists do not believe that the emergence of a new primary trend has been truly *confirmed* until the pattern of ascending or descending tops occurs in both the industrial and railroad averages.

Figure 20-2 shows graphs of various price patterns that Dow theorists search for as signs of market tops and bottoms. Some of these patterns are discussed in reference to other technical analysis theories.

20-3 BAR CHARTS

Technical analysts use three basic types of charts: (1) line charts, (2) bar charts, and (3) point and figure charts. Figure 20-1 shows a line chart; lines are used to connect successive days' prices. Figure 20-3 shows a bar chart. *Bar charts* have vertical bars representing each day's price movement. Each bar spans the distance from the day's highest price to the day's lowest price; a small cross on the bar marks the closing price. Most charts usually have a bar graph along the bottom of the chart showing each day's trading volume. The chart in Fig. 20-3 shows such volume data.

Point and figure charts (PFCs) are made of X's and O's and are more complex than line and bar charts; they will be discussed in the next section. Charts of the price movements of both individual assets and the market indices are kept on all three types of charts. The following paragraph discusses, as an example, a pattern called *head and shoulders,* a formation which chartists find in line charts, bar charts, or PFCs and for both individual assets and market indices.

Head and Shoulders Top on a Bar Chart

A head and shoulders top (HST) is a formation which signals that the security's price has reached a top and will decline in the future. As the name indicates, the HST has a left shoulder, a head, and a right shoulder. The market action which forms an HST can be broken down into four phases:

1 *Left shoulder.* A period of heavy buying followed by a lull in trading pushes the price up to a new peak before the price begins to slide down.

2 *Head.* A spurt of heavy buying raises prices to a new high and then allows the price to fall back below the top of the left shoulder.

3 *Right shoulder.* A moderate rally lifts the price somewhat but fails to push prices as high as the top of the head before a decline begins.

4 *Confirmation or breakout.* Prices fall below the neckline, that is, the line drawn tangent to the left and right shoulders. This breakout is supposed to precede a price drop and is a signal to sell. Figure 20-3 shows an HST.

FIG. 20-3 Bar chart of head and shoulders top formation. (From W. L. Jiler, *How Charts Can Help You in the Stock Market,* Trendline, New York, p. 114.)

Other Formations

Technical analysts have described numerous patterns which are supposed to indicate the direction of future price movements. Triangles, pennants, flags, channels, rectangles, double tops, triple tops, wedge formations, and diamonds are only some of the patterns for which chartists search. Figures

20-2 and 20-3 are charts with construction lines that have been added by a chartist to show the presence of some of these patterns.

20-4 POINT AND FIGURE CHARTS

Point and figure charts (PFCs) are more complex than line or bar charts. PFCs are not only used to detect reversals in a trend; PFCs can also be employed to set actual price forecasts, called price targets.

Construction of PFCs

The construction of PFCs differs significantly from the construction of line and bar charts in several respects. First, the construction of the chart varies with the price level of the stock being charted. Only "significant" changes are posted to a PFC. Thus, for high-priced securities only three- or five-point (that is, dollar) price changes are posted, and for low-priced securities only one-point changes are posted. As a result, there are one-point PFCs, two-point PFCs, three-point PFCs, and five-point PFCs.

A second unusual feature of PFCs is their lack of a time dimension. On line and bar charts, each vertical column represents a trading day, but on a PFC, determining the days is sometimes impossible because each column represents a "significant reversal" instead of a trading day. As a result, a trading day in which the direction of the price made two significant reversals would generate two new columns on a PFC. Consider the construction shown in Fig. 20-4. These two pages are from a point and figure chartbook, and they are provided along with the accompanying explanation as a PFC teaching vehicle.

Interpretation of PFCs

To set the price target (that is, forecasted price) which a stock is expected to attain, PFC chartists begin by finding "congestion areas." A congestion area is a horizontal band of X's and O's created by a series of reversals around a given price level. Congestion areas are supposed to result when supply and demand are equal. A breakout is said to have occurred when a column of X's rises above the top of a congestion area. A penetration of the top of a congestion area is a signal for a continued price rise. Penetration of the bottom of a congestion area by a column of O's is a bearish signal.

Figure 20-5 shows PFCs where top and bottom penetrations have occurred. It shows that the PFC of the Standard & Poor's 500 composite average had some sell signals late in the summer of 1969 as the 1969–1970 bear market began. The months of the year are indicated by the numbers from 1 through 12, which are used in place of an X or O when the first significant change occurs in a new month. At the end of 1969, some weak buy signals were given only to be followed by a strong sell signal in December

1969. If investors had followed all these signals, they would have been "whipsawed." That is, securities could have been sold, bought back at higher prices, and then later sold again at even lower prices for a considerable cumulative loss. In December 1969 when the PFC issued a strong sell signal, the bear market of 1969–1970 was already under way; so this signal merely pointed to something which was already obvious.

Establishing Price Targets

To establish estimates of the new prices which a security should attain, PFC chartists measure the horizontal width (called the *horizontal count*) of a congestion area as they watch for a "breakout." *Breakout* refers to a price rise or fall in which the price rises above or falls below the horizontal band which contained the congestion area. When a breakout occurs, the chartist projects the horizontal count upward or downward in the same direction as the breakout to establish the new price target. The reason a particular price target is appropriate is not clear; even the PFC chartists themselves have difficulty explaining the establishment of price targets. John Schulz, a PFC chartist who has written columns for *Forbes* magazine, once wrote that "on the question of where, in actual practice, measurements of lateral action should be taken, we are far from doctrinaire . . . we advocate the utmost flexibility because this tends to obviate the dangerous rigidity of preconceived notions."[5] Such flexibility also tends to obviate use of the technique.

20-5 THEORIES OF CONTRARY OPINION

The odd-lot theory is one of several theories of *contrary opinion*. In essence, the theory assumes that the "man in the street" is usually wrong and it is therefore advantageous to pursue strategies opposite to his thinking. The odd-lot theory is used primarily to predict tops in bull markets, but also to predict reversals in individual securities.

Odd-Lot Theory

In order to find out what the "man in the street" is doing, statistics on odd-lot trading are gathered. It will be recalled that round lots are groups of 100 shares and that odd lots are groups of less than 100 shares. Since the sales commissions on odd lots are higher than the commissions on round lots, professional investors avoid odd-lot purchases. Most odd-lot purchases are made by amateur investors with limited resources—that is, "the man in the street," who is a small, amateur investor.

Odd-lot trading volume is reported daily. The odd-lot statistics are broken down into the number of shares purchased, sold, and sold short.

---

[5] As quoted in D. Seligman, "The Mystique of Point and Figure," *Fortune*, March 1962.

INTRODUCTION

THE ESSENTIAL FEATURE OF A POINT-AND-FIGURE CHART

A line or a bar chart is two-dimensional. The vertical spaces measure price. The horizontal spaces measure calendar time, whether daily, weekly, or monthly.

A point-and-figure chart is one dimensional. Both vertical and horizontal spaces measure price. There is no measurement of arbitrary calendar time. Each successive horizontal space on the chart represents a change of direction in the price, from up to down or from down to up.

WHY A POINT-AND-FIGURE CHART?

A point-and figure chart is indigenous to stock market trading. It originated in the stock market and has been used exclusively in the stock market. It is not a new-fangled idea or method. It was used in stock trading long before line or bar charts were introduced from other fields.

A point-and-figure chart is easier to construct and maintain than any other type of chart. This is because entries do not have to be made on a calendar basis. Days or weeks may go by without any entries being made.

A point-and-figure chart is easier to read and interpret than other charts. It is easier to recognize bases of accumulation and tops of distribution. It is easier to see ascending bottoms and tops and descending tops and bottoms.

READING THE CHARTS CONTAINED IN THIS BOOK

Xs are used when the price of a stock is going up and Os are used when the price of a stock is going down. Rows of Xs and Os alternate-they never appear in the same column. Passage of time is indicated by months. "1" stands for January "2" for February, etc. In charts printed out by computer, "A" is used instead of "10" for October, "B" instead of "11" for November and "C" instead of "12" for December. These figures appear in place of an X or an O.

The charts contained in this book are 3-point or, more correctly, 3-box reversal charts. A full 3 boxes of price change are necessary. before one moves from Xs to Os or from Os to Xs. Once a direction has been established, each one point or 1 box change in the same direction is recorded.

Units of charting -

From 20 to 100, 1 point units are used (each box represents $1)
Above 100, 2 point units are used (each box represents $2)
Below 20, ½ point units are used (each box represents 50 cents)
Below 5, ¼ point units are used (each box represents 25 cents)

TRENDLINES

Each chart in this book contains at least one trendline; 99% of them contain two trendlines. These trendlines are the Bullish Support Line and the Bearish Resistance Line.

The BULLISH SUPPORT LINE is drawn upwards by intersecting each successive higher square on the chart. It does not connect two price points. It is drawn from a low point on the chart immediately after the first upturn. If there are only two columns of price changes above this trendline then it should be considered as tentative. If there are more than two columns then it is a valid Bullish Support Line. This line will disappear when it is touched by a downward price change.

The BEARISH RESISTANCE LINE is drawn downwards by intersecting each successive lower square on the chart. It does not connect two price points. It is drawn from a high point on the chart immediately after the first downturn. If there are only two columns of price changes below this trendline then it should be considered as tentative. If there are more than two columns then it is a valid Bearish Resistance Line. This line will disappear when it is touched by an upward price change.

The Bullish Support Line is a guide to where a downmove may find support and reverse itself. The Bearish Resistance Line is a guide to where an upmove may find resistance and reverse itself. Long term traders may use these trendlines as guides for how long to hold their positions. If they are long of the stock, they may hold as long as the Bullish Support Line is not penetrated. If they are short of the stock they may hold as long as the Bearish Resistance Line is not penetrated.

The best stock to buy is: (1) a stock that has given a buy signal by penetrating a previous top, (2) has a valid Bullish Support Line, and (3) has no valid Bearish Resistance Line.

The best stock to sell short is: (1) a stock that has given a sell signal by penetrating a previous bottom, (2) has a valid Bearish Resistance Line, and (3) has no valid Bullish Support Line.

On page V, there is an exercise in point-and-figure chart construction. We suggest that you go through this practice exercise at your leisure. This will enable you to continue posting the charts in this book without any difficulty. The figures used for such posting are obtained from the daily highs and lows of the stock market tables carried in your newspaper. A complete explanation of point-and-figure charting and interpretation is contained in our book, "How to Use The Three-Point Reversal Method of Point and Figure Trading" which sells for $3.95 a copy.

Before taking positions on any of the chart patterns in this book, please consult the Technical Indicator Review pages. We do not believe that the average trader should trade against the trend of the market. We believe in following the line of least resistance.

NOTES: Each chart is marked with a short term indication of Bullish or Bearish. The figure after the word "Bullish" or "Bearish" is the Price Objective (decimal point is omitted, i.e. 1950 is $19.50). When none appears, none exists or has already been attained.

The eight digit number appearing to the right of the stock name over each chart is the CUSIP number. This is the number assigned by NASDAQ to identify each stock.

The number appearing in the upper right hand corner of certain charts refers to S & P's group index to which that stock is assigned. (See complete listing under Industry Groups in Table of Contents, page 111).

Occasionally throughout the Chartbook you will find two charts for a single stock. This means that the first chart has run off either the top or bottom of the price scale. The second chart shows a new price scale and picks up where the first one left off.

The Chartcraft Weekly Service now supplies the recordable price changes for each of the stocks contained in this book. Thus, by using the service you can bring your charts up-to-date once a week with a minimum of time and effort. The combination rate for the monthly Chart Book and the Weekly Service is $300 per year.

FIG. 20-4 Explanation of point and figure charts from technical analysis book. (From Chartcraft *Chart Book*, Larchmont, N.Y.)

PRACTICE EXERCISE IN CHART CONSTRUCTION

Date	High	Low	Chart Entries
5/2	22-7/8	21	O 22-21
5/3	21	20	(5) 20
5/4	20-3/4	20-1/8	
5/5	19-7/8	19-1/2	O 19½
5/6	20-1/2	19-1/2	
5/9	20-1/2	20-1/4	
5/10	20-1/4	20-1/8	
5/11	20-1/4	20	
5/12	20-1/4	19-7/8	
5/13	21-1/2	20-1/8	
5/16	21-1/2	21	
5/17	21-1/4	20-3/4	
5/18	22-1/2	21-1/2	X 20-21-22
5/19	22-1/2	22	
5/20	22-3/8	21-1/4	
5/23	22	21-1/4	
5/24	22	21	
5/25	21	20-1/4	
5/26	21-1/2	20-1/2	
5/27	22-1/4	21-1/2	
5/31	22-7/8	22	
6/1	24-7/8	24	(6)23-X 24
6/2	25	24	X 25
6/3	24	23-1/4	
6/6	23-3/8	23	
6/7	24-1/4	23-1/2	
6/8	24-1/4	23-3/4	
6/9	24	23-5/8	
6/10	23-5/8	23-1/8	
6/13	23-1/2	23	
6/14	23-3/4	22-1/2	
6/15	22-7/8	21-1/2	O 24-23-22
6/16	22	21-1/4	
6/17	22-1/4	21-5/8	
6/20	22-1/4	21-3/4	
6/21	22-1/4	22	
6/23	21-1/4	20-1/2	O 21
6/24	20-3/4	20-1/2	
6/27	21	20-3/4	
6/28	20-7/8	20-1/4	
6/29	20-1/2	20	O 20
6/30	21-1/8	19-1/2	O 19½
7/1	21-5/8	20-7/8	
7/5	21-1/4	21	
7/6	21	20-7/8	
7/7	20-7/8	20-1/2	
7/8	20-1/4	19-3/4	
7/11	20	19-3/4	
7/12	19-3/4	19-1/4	
7/13	19-3/4	19-3/8	
7/14	20	19-5/8	
7/15	20	19-5/8	
7/18	21	19-3/4	
7/19	20-1/2	20	
7/20	20	20	
7/21	20-1/8	19-7/8	
7/22	19-7/8	19-1/4	
7/25	10-7/8	19	(7) 19
7/26	19-3/4	19	
7/27	19	18-1/2	O 18½
7/28	19	18-1/2	
7/29	19	18-3/4	
8/1	19-1/4	19	
8/2	-	-	
8/3	19-1/2	19	

Date	High	Low	Chart Entries
8/4	19	19	
8/5	19-1/4	19	
8/8	19-1/4	19	
8/9	19-3/8	18-1/2	
8/10	18-1/2	18-1/2	
8/11	19	18-1/8	
8/12	20	19	X 19-19½-(8)20
8/15	20	20	
8/16	20	20	
8/17	19-5/8	19-1/4	
8/18	19-1/8	19-1/8	
8/19	19-1/8	19	
8/22	19-1/4	19-1/4	
8/23	19-1/2	19-1/4	
8/24	19-1/2	19-1/8	
8/25	19-1/4	19	
8/26	19	19	
8/29	18-7/8	18-1/2	O 19½-19-18½
8/30	18-3/4	18-1/4	
8/31	18-1/2	18-1/4	
9/1	20-7/8	19-3/4	X 19-19½-(9)20
9/2	20-3/8	19-7/8	
9/6	19-3/4	19-1/4	
9/7	19-1/4	18-1/4	O 19½-19-18½
9/8	18-1/4	18-1/4	
9/9	19	19	
9/12	18-3/4	18-1/4	
9/13	18-5/8	18-1/4	
9/14	18-5/8	18-1/8	
9/15	18-1/2	18	O 18
9/16	18-1/2	18	
9/19	18-1/4	17	O 17½-17
9/20	17-1/2	17-1/2	
9/21	18	17-1/2	
9/22	18	18	
9/23	18	17-3/4	
9/27	17-3/8	16-1/4	O 16½
9/28	16-1/4	15-1/2	O16-15½
9/29	16	15-5/8	
9/30	17	16-1/4	X 16-16½-17
10/3	17	16-1/4	
10/4	16-7/8	16-1/4	
10/5	16-1/2	16	
10/6	16-1/2	16-1/4	
10/7	16-1/2	16-1/2	
10/10	16-3/4	16-1/2	
10/11	16-3/4	16-1/2	
10/12	17-1/4	16-1/2	
10/13	16-7/8	16-3/4	
10/14	16-5/8	16-5/8	
10/17	16-1/2	16-1/4	
10/18	16-1/4	16-1/4	
10/19	16-1/8	16	
10/20	16	15-1/2	O 16½-16-(A)15½
10/21	15-1/2	14	O 15-14½-14
10/24	14-1/4	13	O 13½-13
10/25	14-1/8	13-1/8	
10/26	14	13-3/8	
10/27	15	14	X 13½-14-14½-15
10/28	15-1/2	14-3/4	X 15½
10/31	14-7/8	14-1/4	
11/1	15-1/4	15	
11/2	15-3/8	15	
11/3	15	15	
11/4	15	15	

Date	High	Low	Chart Entries
11/7	15-3/8	15-1/8	
11/9	15-3/8	15-1/9	
11/10	15-3/4	15-3/4	
11/11	15-3/4	15-3/8	
11/14	15-5/8	15-3/8	
11/15	15-1/2	15-1/4	
11/16	15-3/4	15-1/2	
11/17	15-3/4	15-3/8	
11/18	15-7/8	15-1/2	
11/21	15-3/4	15-3/8	
11/22	16-1/2	16	(B)16-X 16½
11/23	16-3/8	16-1/4	
11/25	17-1/8	16-1/8	X 17
11/28	17-1/4	16-/34	
11/29	17	'16-5/8	
11/30	16-1/2	16-1/2	
12/1	16-1/4	16	
12/2	15-5/8	15-5/8	
12/5	15-5/8	15-1/4	O 16½-16-C15½
12/6	15-1/4	15	O 15
12/7	15	15	
12/8	15-7/8	15-1/8	
12/9	15-1/2	15-1/2	
12/12	15-1/2	15-1/4	
12/13	15-1/2	15	
12/14	16	15	
12/15	16	15-5/8	
12/16	15-3/4	15-5/8	
12/19	15-3/4	15	
12/20	15-1/8	14-3/4	
12/21	15	14-3/8	O 14½
12/22	15-1/2	14-1/2	
12/23	14-7/8	14-1/4	
12/27	14-7/8	14-3/8	
12/28	14-3/4	14-1/2	
12/29	15	14-1/2	
1/3/72	16	14-3/4	X 15-15½-(1)16
1/4	17-1/8	16-1/4	X 16½-17
1/5	16-7/8	16-5/8	
1/6	16-7/8	16-1/2	
1/9	17-1/4	16-1/2	
1/10	18-1/2	17-1/8	X 17½-18-18½
1/11	18-5/8	18-1/4	
1/12	18-1/2	17-7/8	
1/13	18	17-3/4	
1/16	18	17-3/4	
1/17	17 3/4	17 1/2	
1/18	17-1/2	17	O 18-17½-17
1/19	17-3/4	17-1/2	
1/20	18-1/4	17-1/2	
1/23	18-5/8	17-1/2	X 17½-18-18½
1/24	19-3/4	18-1/4	X 19-19½
1/25	18-3/8	18-1/8	
1/26	19	18-1/4	
1/27	20-1/8	19-1/4	X 20
1/30	21-7/8	20-1/4	X 21
1/31	21-7/8	21-1/4	

SAMPLE CHART

If your last chart entry is an X, look at the daily high. If the stock has gone up, enter the additional X or Xs and forget about the lows. If the stock has not gone up, look at the low for a possible 3-box reversal.

If your last chart entry is an O, look at the daily low. If the stock has gone lower, enter the additional Os and forget about the highs. If the stock has not gone lower, look at the daily high for a possible 3-box reversal.

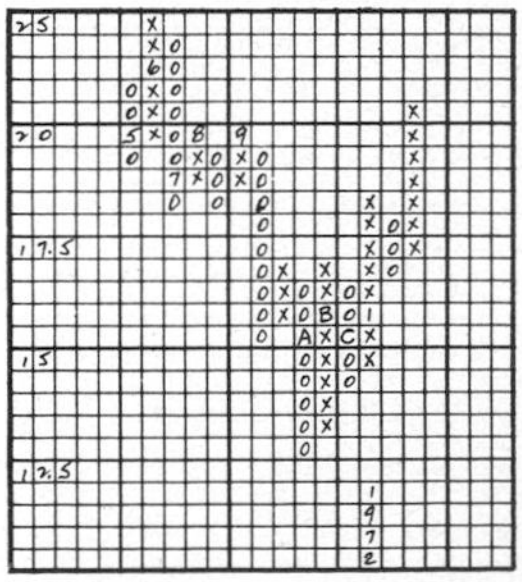

FIG. 20-4 *(Continued)*

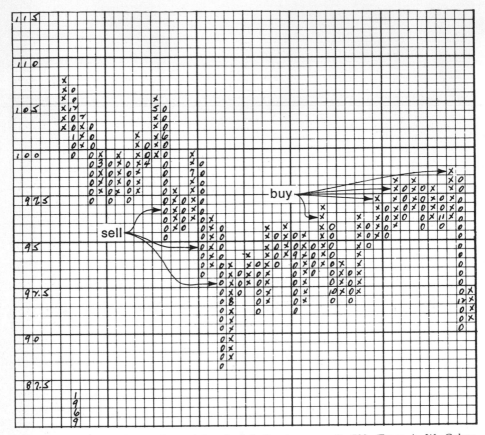

FIG. 20-5 Point and figure chart of Standard & Poor's composite 500. (From A. W. Cohen, *Technical Indicator Analysis,* Chartcraft, Inc., Larchmont, N.Y.)

Most odd-lot theorists chart the ratio of odd-lot sales to odd-lot purchases week by week. Some odd-lot chartists, however, chart only the odd-lot statistics from Mondays since odd-lot traders are believed to transact most of their trading on Mondays because of weekend conversations with their friends. In any event, if odd-lot sales exceed odd-lot purchases, the "man in the street" is selling more than he is buying. If this difference is negative, then odd-lotters are net buyers. The odd-lot purchases-less-sales index is typically plotted concurrently with some market index. The odd-lotters' net purchases are used by chartists as a leading indicator of market prices. That is, positive net purchases are presumed to forecast falls in market prices, and net sales are presumed to occur at the end of bear markets.

Figure 20-6 shows data for the Dow Jones Industrial Average (DJIA) in the top panel; concurrent odd-lotter net purchases are shown in the center panel for the period during and after the 1969–1970 bear market. Contrary to the odd-lot theory of contrary opinion, the odd-lotters were net

Odd-lot trading and industrial stock prices

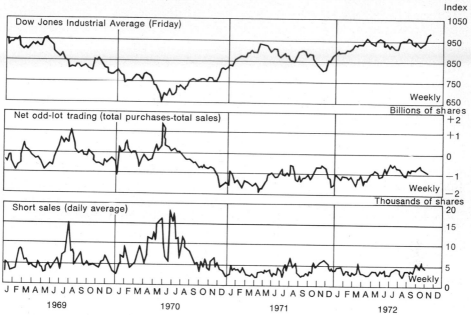

FIG. 20-6 Graphs for odd-lot and short sales technical indicators. (From Cleveland Trust Company *Bulletin,* November 1972.)

buyers during low points in the DJIA. That is, the odd-lotters have "bought low and sold high" in recent years and thus have defied the theory about them.

Short Sales

Some chartists follow statistics on short sales (those that involve securities that are not owned by the seller, who hopes to cover the short position later at a lower price). Some short-sales followers use aggregate statistics as an indicator of overall market sentiment, and some follow the short sales for individual securities in search of information about that security. However, both groups may interpret a high level of outstanding short sales (that is, uncovered short positions or short interest, as it is variously called) as a sign of increased future demand for securities with which to cover the outstanding short positions. So, rising short sales foretell future demand for the security and thus future price rises. This is the *short sales contrary opinion* theory. The empirical data for 1970, graphed in the top and bottom panels of Fig. 20-6, tend to confirm the theory; the peak in short sales preceded the 1970 upturn in the DJIA. However, the indicator was wrong in July 1969.

In startling contrast to the short sales contrary opinion followers, another group of technical analysts believe that short sellers tend to be more sophisticated than the average investor. Therefore, this group asserts, when short sales for the market as a whole or for an individual security are high, many sophisticated investors expect a price decline and it should follow shortly. The top and bottom graphs in Fig. 20-6 for 1969 tend to support this second odd-lot theory in 1969 but not in 1970. It is not clear that either of the diametrically opposing groups of short sales followers has any valuable insights.[6]

20-6 THE CONFIDENCE INDEX

The confidence index is supposed to reveal how willing investors are to take a chance in the market. It is the ratio of high-grade bond yields to low-grade bond yields. When bond investors grow more confident about the economy, they shift their holdings from high-grade to lower-grade bonds in order to obtain the higher yields. This change bids up the prices of low-grade bonds, lowers their yields relative to high-grade bonds, and increases the confidence index.

Markets for bonds are frequented mostly by large institutional investors who are less emotional about their portfolio decisions than many investors in the stock market. In an effort to measure the market expectations of these "smart money" managers and assess their confidence in the economy, chartists study the confidence index.

Calculating the Confidence Index

Barron's, the weekly financial and business newspaper, publishes figures on the confidence index regularly in its "Market Laboratory" section. The *Barron's* confidence index is the ratio of the average yield from its list of the 10 highest-grade bonds over the average yield from the Dow Jones 40 bonds. Equation (20-1) defines the *Barron's* confidence index (BCI).

$$\text{BCI}_t = \frac{\text{average yield of } Barron's \text{ 10 highest-grade bonds at period } t}{\text{average yield of Dow Jones 40 bonds at period } t}$$

(20-1)

The *Barron's* definition of the confidence index is widely used because it is published each week, but it has no intrinsic superiority over, say, the confidence index (CI) defined in Eq. (20-2).

$$\text{CI}_t = \frac{\text{average yield of Aaa bonds at period } t}{\text{average yield of Baa bonds at period } t}$$

(20-2)

Other valid definitions of the confidence index exist, too.

[6] T. J. Kewley and R. A. Stevenson, "The Odd-Lot Theory for Individual Stocks," *Financial Analysts Journal*, January–February 1969. This study suggests that the theory gives good buy signals but not good sell signals.

Interpretation of the Confidence Index

The confidence index has an upper limit of unity (that is, CI < 1.0), since the yields on high-quality bonds will never rise above the yields on similar low-quality bonds. In periods of economic boom when investors grow optimistic and their risk-aversion diminishes, the yield spread between high- and low-quality bonds narrows, and the confidence index rises. A rising confidence index is interpreted by chartists as an indication that money managers are optimistic. On the assumption that the wisdom of these investors will be borne out, confidence index technicians predict that the stock market (where fewer sophisticated investors are assumed to trade) will follow the leadership of the "smart money." Confidence index technicians believe the confidence index leads the stock market by 2 to 11 months. Thus, an upturn in the confidence index is supposed to foretell of rising optimism and rising prices in the stock market.

Just as a rise in the confidence index is expected to precede a rising stock market, a fall in the index is expected to precede a drop in stock prices. A fall in the confidence index represents the fact that low-grade bond yields are rising faster or falling more slowly than high-grade yields. This movement is supposed to reflect increasing risk-aversion by "smart money" managers who foresee an economic downturn and rising bankruptcies and defaults.

Figure 20-7 shows a point and figure chart of the *Barron's* confidence index plotted on the vertical axis at increments of $2\frac{1}{2}$ percentage points. Each block represents $\frac{1}{2}$ of 1 percent. A change of $1\frac{1}{2}$ percentage points in the op-

FIG. 20-7 Point and figure chart of *Barron's* confidence index. (From Chartcraft, Inc., Larchmont, N.Y.)

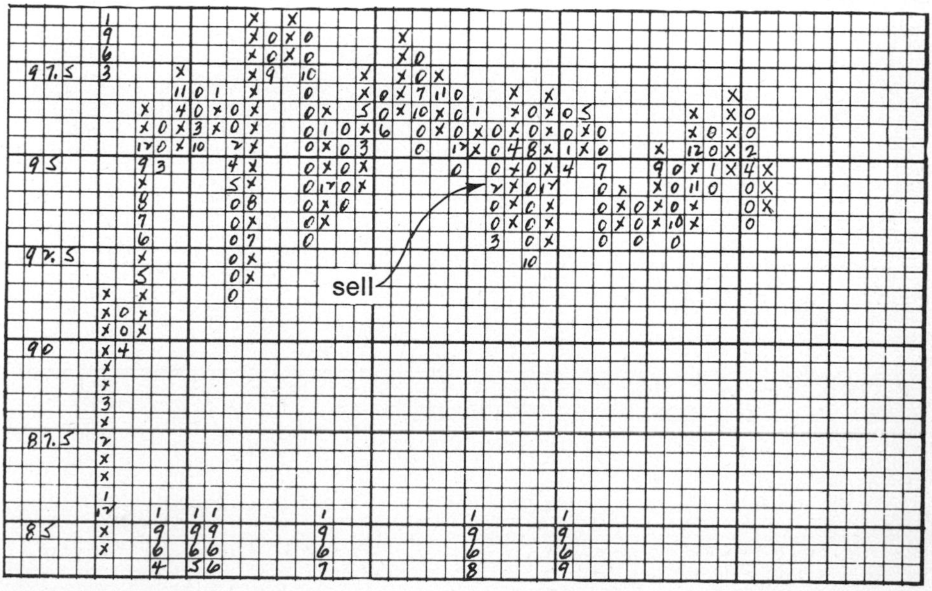

posite direction is considered a significant reversal which warrants starting a new column. The chart shows that the *Barron's* confidence index issued a weak sell signal when it broke out of the bottom of the congestion area in early 1968. This would have been a good sell signal to heed.

There is no question that the confidence index is positively correlated with the stock market. However, in view of the numerous other economic series which are also correlated with the stock market, this is of no unique value. The confidence index is usually, but not always, a leading indication. Furthermore, the confidence index has sometimes issued erroneous signals.

20-7 BREADTH OF MARKET

Breadth-of-market indicators are used to measure the underlying strength of market advances or declines. For example, it is possible that the Dow Jones Industrial Average of only 30 blue-chip stocks which are very popular would still be rising for some time after the market for the majority of lesser-known stocks had already turned down. Thus, to gauge the real underlying strength of the market, tools are needed to measure the breadth of the market's moves.

Breadth-of-Market Calculations

Numerous methods exist for measuring the breadth of the market. One of the easiest methods is to subtract the number of issues whose prices declined from the number of issues whose prices advanced each day to get net advances or declines. The data on advances and declines are published daily in many newspapers; an example from *The Wall Street Journal* is shown in Fig. 20-8.

The net advances or declines (sometimes called the *plurality*) are calculated as follows:

Day	Advances	minus	Declines	equals	Net advances and declines	Breadth
Monday	745		634		+111	111
Tuesday	994		391		+603	714
Wednesday	468		914		−446	268
Thursday	255		1,118		−863	−595
Friday	669		589		+ 80	−515
Monday	582		657		− 75	−590

These breadth-of-market statistics are obtained by simply cumulating the net advances and declines. The breadth statistics may become negative during a bear market, as they did in the example above. This is no cause for alarm since the breadth level is entirely arbitrary; it depends on when the breadth series is begun. Only the *direction* of the breadth-of-market statistics is relevant.

◆───────────────────────────────

MARKET DIARY

	Wed	Tues	Mon	Fri	Thur	Wed
Issues traded 1,821	1,839	1,867	1,826	1,845	1,840	
Advances 999	599	1,158	972	669	1,022	
Declines 434	856	372	508	820	457	
Unchanged 388	384	337	346	356	361	
New highs, 1974-75 ... 29	24	43	27	35	23	
New lows, 1974-75 1	1	3	3	3	3	

FIG. 20-8 Daily advances and declines, February 5, 1975. (From *The Wall Street Journal*, Feb. 6, 1975, p. 33.)

Interpretation of Breadth Data

Breadth-of-market data are frequently plotted on line charts. Figure 20-9 shows a line chart of breadth data for the NYSE. Technicians compare the breadth of market with one of the market averages, or, as done in Fig. 20-9, with two of them. The breadth and market averages usually move in tandem. What technical analysts watch for is breadth to follow a path which diverges from the path of a market average.

Suppose the DJIA, with its 30 blue-chip stocks that are popular with amateur and professional investors alike, is moving upward. If breadth follows a divergent downward path, it indicates that many small stocks are starting to turn down while the blue chips continue to rise. This is an indicator of weakening market demand and signals a possible market downturn.

20-8 RELATIVE STRENGTH ANALYSIS

Dr. R. A. Levy suggests that some securities' prices consistently rise in a bull market relatively faster than other securities; that is, that some securities have *relative strength*. Relative strength technicians believe that by investing in securities which have demonstrated relative strength in the past, an investor will earn higher returns because the relative strength of a security tends to remain unchanged over time.[7]

───────────────────────────────

[7] Dr. Levy is one of the few technical analysts who has published a study of his techniques. The interested reader is directed to the following articles by Levy; all appeared in *Financial Analysts Journal*:

"Conceptual Foundations of Technical Analysis," July–August 1966, pp. 83–89.

"Random Walks: Reality or Myth," November–December 1967, pp. 69–76. An article by M. C. Jensen commenting on Levy's article follows directly in the same issue: "Random Walks: Reality or Myth—Comment," November–December 1967, pp. 77–85.

"Random Walks: Reality or Myth—Reply," January–February 1968, pp. 129–132.

Also see M. C. Jensen and G. A. Bennington, "Random Walks and Technical Theories: Some Additional Evidence," *Journal of Finance*, May 1970, pp. 469–482.

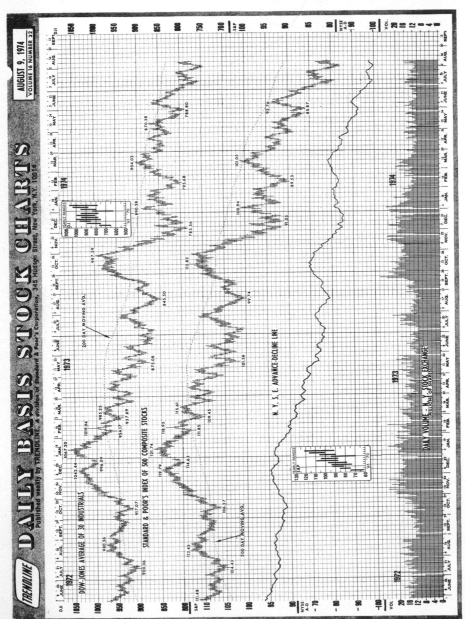

FIG. 20-9 Chart of stock market averages and volume data.

Measuring Relative Strength

The relative strength concept is applied to individual securities or industries, but it is not amenable to market analysis. Technicians measure relative strength in several ways. Some simply calculate rates of return and classify those securities with historically high average returns as securities with high relative strength. More frequently, technicians observe certain ratios to detect relative strength in a security or an industry. For example, consider the data for Anonymous Corp. (A), a hypothetical growth firm in the electronics industry (EI), shown in Table 20-1.

From 19X3 to 19X4 Anonymous did slightly better than most of the firms in the electronics industry, as evidenced by the fact that its price grew relatively more than the electronics industry average; the ratio P_A/P_{EIA} rose from 1.78 to 2. From 19X3 to 19X4 the electronics industry showed weakness relative to all industrial stocks: the ratio P_{EIA}/P_{MIA} declined from .081 to .072. Thus, Anonymous had to beat the electronics industry average merely to keep up (relatively speaking) with the rest of the market. From 19X3 to 19X4 Anonymous did not demonstrate any particular strength relative to its industrial average: the ratio P_A/P_{MIA} remained .144. From 19X4 to 19X5 Anonymous showed considerable strength relative to its industry and to the market; during that time the electronics industry advanced at nearly as fast a rate as the market.

Interpretation of Relative Strength Data

A relative strength technician would typically plot the ratios of (1) the security relative to its industry and (2) the security relative to the market. A chart like the one shown in Fig. 20-10 for Anonymous might result.

Figure 20-10 shows that although the electronics industry is failing to keep pace with the market, Anonymous is developing relative strength both in its industry and in the market. After preparing charts like this for numerous firms from different industries over a length of time, the technician would select certain industries and firms which demonstrated relative strength.

Technical analysts who have worked with relative strength have noted that securities which demonstrate relative strength and earn high returns in

TABLE 20-1 RELATIVE STRENGTH DATA FOR ANONYMOUS CORP.

Year	P_A†	P_{EIA}‡	P_{MIA}§	P_A/P_{EIA}	P_A/P_{MIA}	P_{EIA}/P_{MIA}
19X3	30	17	210	30/17 = 1.78	30/210 = .144	17/210 = .081
19X4	36	18	250	36/18 = 2	36/250 = .144	18/250 = .072
19X5	72	20	285	72/20 = 3.6	72/285 = .253	20/285 = .070

† P_A is the average price of Anonymous Corp. for the year.
‡ P_{EIA} is Moody's electronics industry average for the year.
§ P_{MIA} is Moody's industrial average for the year.

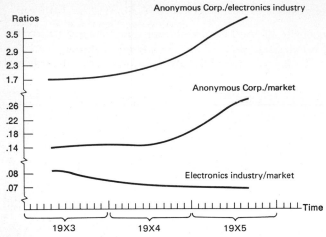

FIG. 20-10 Hypothetical relative-strength data for Anonymous Corp. and the electronic industry. (From Table 20-1.)

bull markets usually do the opposite in bear markets. That is, it has been observed that securities which have high relative strength *upward* in bull markets tend to have high relative strength *downward* when the market is falling.

In view of the discussion of systematic risk in Chaps. 12 and 16, the observation that some securities rise faster than a rising market and then also decline faster than a falling market should come as no surprise. It will be recalled that the beta slope coefficient of a security's characteristic line is an index of systematic risk. Securities with beta coefficients which are larger than 1 will be more volatile, both upward and downward, than the market. And, since the beta coefficients tend to be stationary over time, securities with this high systematic risk or relative strength will usually retain it.

In view of the analysis of characteristic lines and beta coefficients, the analysis of relative strength is seen to be simply a crudely formulated analysis of risk and return. The high returns available in rising markets from securities with high systematic risk or relative strength are required to induce investors to assume the undiversifiable risk associated with these securities.

20-9 CHARTING VOLUME OF TRADING DATA

On the day following each trading day many newspapers across the United States publish statistics giving the total number of shares traded in certain security markets and the number of shares traded in some issues. For example, Fig. 20-11 shows an excerpt from *The Wall Street Journal* which has these volume data for the NYSE. Some technical analysts believe that it is

THE WALL STREET JOURNAL,
Wednesday, September 24, 1975

Tuesday's Volume
12,800,000 Shares; 73,000 Warrants

Volume since Jan. 1:	1975	1974	1973
Total shares	3,595,453,620	2,462,787,787	2,719,964,069
Total warrants ..	69,354,600	20,137,100	30,959,800

MOST ACTIVE STOCKS

	Open	High	Low	Close	Chg.	Volume
FedNat Mtg	13	13	12¾	12⅞	− ¼	220,300
Lilly Eli	53½	53½	49½	51⅝	−2⅜	196,700
Nat Semicn	40⅞	43½	40⅝	43½	+2⅝	155,200
Merck Co	67⅝	67⅝	65¼	66	−2⅛	153,500
Am Home	34	34¼	33¼	34	− ⅛	129,900
Gen Motors	49⅝	50⅛	49½	50	− ⅛	127,100
Polaroid	33⅜	35¼	33	35¼	+2	120,200
Monroe Eq	8½	8¾	8¼	8⅜	+ ⅛	105,700
Xerox Cp	53½	54	52⅜	54	+ ⅜	104,300
MCA Inc	77⅝	83¼	77⅝	82¾	+4½	99,900

Average closing price of most active stocks: 43.83.

−1975− High	Low	Stocks Div.	P-E Ratio	Sales in 100s	High	Low	Close	Net Chg
		− A−A−A −						
41⅜	32⅝	AbbtLab .80	16	110	35¾	35¼	35¾	+ ⅜
47¾	33¼	ACF In 2.60	7	8	37½	37⅛	37⅜	+ ⅛
4¼	1¾	AdmDg .04e	9	21	3⅛	3⅛	3⅛	+ ¼
11	7¾	AdmEx .77e	...	25	9⅜	9⅛	9¼	+ ⅛
6¼	2⅛	Adms Millis	...	4	3⅞	3⅞	3⅞	......
9⅜	3¼	Addressog	12	69	7½	7¼	7¼	− ¼
10	7¼	AdvInv .24e	...	24	7⅝	7½	7½	......
29⅜	17¼	AetnaLf 1.08	13	382	21⅛	20⅞	21	......
7	4¾	Aguirre Co	24	7	5⅛	5	5	− ¼
12	6⅞	Ahmans .20	5	39	7½	7¼	7¼	− ⅜
4⅞	1⅝	Aileen Inc	10	30	3¼	3⅛	3⅛	− ⅛
79⅜	44¾	AirPrd .20b	16	95	61⅛	60⅝	60¾	− ¾
13⅜	4⅞	AirbnFrt .50	9	10	10⅛	9⅞	10⅛	......
23⅜	10½	AircoInc 1	5	36	18⅛	17⅞	18⅛	− ¼
3⅜	1	AJ Industris	5	15	2¼	2¼	2¼	......
17½	10½	Akzona 1.20	43	14	17¼	17⅛	17¼	+ ⅛
14½	7⅞	Ala Gas 1.28	6	3	13¼	13¼	13¼	− ⅛
84½	69½	AlaP pf8.28	...	z130	76½	76½	76½	......
17⅝	9	Alaska Intrs	7	39	12⅛	11⅝	12	− ⅛
19⅝	13	AlbanyIn .60	7	13	13¾	13¼	13¼	− ¾
8⅜	4⅝	AlbertoC .36	16	4	5⅞	5⅞	5⅞	......
20⅜	12¼	Albertsn .60	9	46	20	19½	19⅝	+ ½
26⅜	18⅞	AlcanAlu .80	9	131	22⅝	22⅜	22½	− ¼
13¼	7½	AlcoStd .56	4	22	11¾	11⅜	11¾	+ ¼
29	15¼	AlconLb .24	24	2	23¾	23¾	23¾	− ¼
6⅝	2½	Alexdrs .16e	7	14	5⅛	5	5⅛	− ⅛
6⅜	3	AlisnMt .48e	...	4	3⅜	3⅜	3⅜	......

FIG. 20-11 Volume data for NYSE. (From *The Wall Street Journal.*)

possible to detect whether the market in general and/or certain security issues are bullish or bearish by studying the volume of trading. Volume is supposed to be a measure of the intensity of investors' emotions. There is a Wall Street adage that "it takes volume to really move a stock" either up or down in price.

Volume technicians watch volume most closely on days when prices move, that is, days when supply and demand move to a new equilibrium. If high volume occurs on days when prices move up, the overall nature of the market is considered to be bullish. If the high volume occurs on days when prices are falling, this is a bearish sign.

Figure 20-9 shows bar charts of the DJIA and the Standard & Poor's index of 500 composite stocks plotted with the daily volume on the NYSE along the bottom of the chart.

There is one occasion when falling prices and high volume are considered bullish. When technicians feel the end of a bear market is near, they watch for a high volume of selling as the last of the bearish investors liquidate their holdings—this is called a *selling climax*. A selling climax is supposed to eliminate the last of the bears who drive prices down by selling, clearing the way for the market to turn up.

Some technicians also look for a speculative blowoff to mark the end of a bull market. A *speculative blowoff* is a high volume of buying which pushes prices up to a peak; it is supposed to exhaust the enthusiasm of bullish speculators and make way for a bear market to begin. Technicians who believe that a speculative blowoff marks the end of a bull market sometimes say "the market must die with a bang, not a whimper."

20-10 MOVING AVERAGE ANALYSIS

Moving average, or rate-of-change, technicians focus on prices and/or a moving average of the prices. The *moving average* is used to provide a smoothed, stable reference point against which the daily fluctuations can be gauged. *Rate-of-change analysis* is used for individual securities or market indices.

Construction of Chart

Most technicians who perform rate-of-change analysis use a 200-day moving average of closing prices. The moving average changes each day as the most recent day is added and the two-hundred-and-first day is dropped. To calculate a 200-day moving average (MA_t) of the DJIA on day t, Eq. (20-3) is employed.

$$MA_t = \frac{1}{200} \sum_{j=1}^{200} DJIA_{t-j} \tag{20-3}$$

Figure 20-9 shows the moving average of the DJIA and Standard & Poor's index of 500 composite stocks as dotted lines; the daily values of the two indices are represented by the bar charts. Figure 20-12 shows similar graphs for several common stocks. It is the relationship between the actual values and the moving average from which the technician obtains his or her information.

Interpreting Rate-of-Change Charts

When the daily prices penetrate the moving average line, technicians interpret this penetration as a signal. When the daily prices move downward through the moving average, they frequently fail to rise again for many months. Thus, a downward penetration of a flattened moving average suggests selling. When actual prices are above the moving average but the

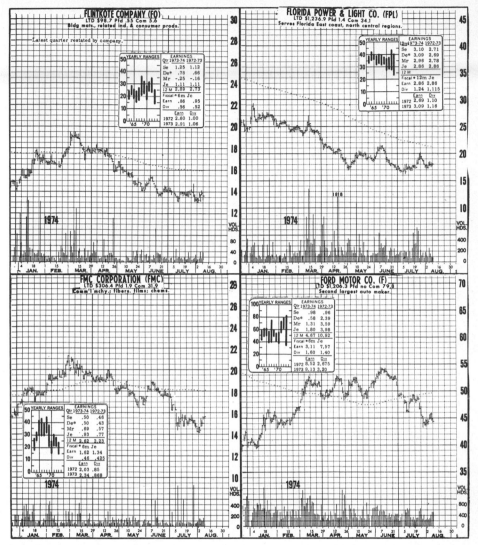

FIG. 20-12 Bar charts with moving averages for individual stocks. (From Trendline, New York.)

difference is narrowing, this is a signal that a bull market may be ending. A summary of buy and sell signals followed by moving average chartists is given below.

Moving average analysts recommend buying a stock when (1) the 200-day moving average flattens out and the stock's price rises through the moving average; (2) the price of a stock falls below a moving average line which is rising; and (3) a stock's price which is above the moving average line falls but turns around and begins to rise again before it ever reaches the moving average line.

Moving average chartists recommend selling a stock when (1) the moving average line flattens out and the stock's price drops downward through the moving average line, (2) a stock's price rises above a moving average line which is declining, and (3) a stock's price falls downward through the moving average line and turns around to rise but then falls again before getting above the moving average line.

Adherence to the moving average trading rules over many months and many different stocks shows that sometimes profitable trades are signaled. But the rules touch off unprofitable trades, too. This is why most technical analysts use more than one technique of technical analysis and compare the results before they decide to trade securities.

20-11 CONCLUSIONS

There are many more technical analysis tools which could be discussed; the discussion in this chapter provides only a sampling of the techniques.

All the technical analysis tools have one thing in common—they attempt to measure the supply and demand for some group of investors. Shifts in supply and demand are presumed to be *gradual* rather than instantaneous. When shifting prices are detected, they are presumed to be the result of gradual shifts in supply and demand rather than a series of instantaneous shifts which all happened to be moving in the same direction. Since these *shifts are expected to continue as the price gradually reacts* to news or other factors, they are used to predict further price changes.

Most economists believe that technical analysis cannot measure supply and demand or predict prices. They suggest that security markets are efficient markets which impact news into security prices without delay. That is, news that causes changes in the supply and/or demand for a security is supposed to cause sudden once-and-for-all changes rather than gradual adjustments in supply and demand. As a result, economists believe that security price changes are a series of random numbers which occur in reaction to the random arrival of news. When a security's price moves in the same direction for several days, most economists interpret these movements as a series of independent changes in supply and/or demand, all of which just happen to move the price in the same direction. They assert that technical analysts are wrong in believing that supply and/or demand adjust gradually, causing trends which may be used for predicting future prices. The evidence provided by economists to support their efficient markets hypothesis will be examined in Chap. 21.

QUESTIONS

1 "Fundamental analysts' estimates of intrinsic value are different from the security prices determined by supply and demand." True, false, or uncertain? Explain.

2 According to the Dow theory, what is the significance of an abortive recovery which follows a series of ascending tops?

3 What factual information is contained in the markings on a bar chart?

4 What does each column on a point and figure chart represent? How is the time dimension shown on a point and figure chart?

5 What significance is attributed to the volume of odd-lot trading by technical analysts?

6 Explain what the confidence index is supposed to measure. What relevance does this measure of confidence have for stock prices?

7 How are data on the number of shares which advanced and declined in a given trading day used by technical analysts?

8 Compare and contrast relative strength and systematic risk. What implications does high relative strength have for rates of return?

9 What are a *speculative blowoff* and a *selling climax?*

10 How is the moving average used in rate-of-change analysis?

11 Do most experienced technical analysts have one tool they believe in and follow closely?

SELECTED REFERENCES

Edwards, R. D., and John Magee, Jr., *Technical Analysis of Stock Trends,* 5th rev. ed. (Springfield, Mass.: Stock Trends Service, 1966).
> This book has been used for years by technical analysts. Many different techniques are explained.

Jiler, William L., *How Charts Can Help You in the Stock Market* (New York: Trendline, 1962).
> This popular book on charting explains many techniques and gives examples.

Levy, R. A., *The Relative Strength Concept of Common Stock Forecasting* (Larchmont, N.Y.: Investors Intelligence, 1968).
> This book explains some of the new nonchart-oriented quantitative technical tools.

Wu, Hsiu-Kwant, and Alan Z. Zakon, *Elements of Investments: Selected Readings* (New York: Holt, 1965).
> This book of readings in investments devotes sec. 5 to readings related to technical analysis.

Twenty-one

The Behavior of Stock Market Prices

In efficient, competitive securities markets, prices would equal their true intrinsic values so that equivalent assets would have equal rates of return. That is, the most risky new companies (for example, IBM in the 1920s, Xerox in the 1930s, Polaroid in the 1940s, et al.) would be valued low relative to their future income so that they would yield high rates of return; supposedly, these rates would induce aggressive investors to assume the risks associated with the development of new products. Investment capital would thus be encouraged to flow into risky growth firms which had good products and whose development would help the nation's economy move ahead more rapidly. As a result of competition between investors in an efficient market, savings would be channeled into the most productive investments so that capital would be allocated in an optimum manner; prices would fully reflect all available relevant information and would continuously adjust upward or downward as new information arrived; and random price changes would occur continuously as news arrived randomly and was impacted into prices by profit seekers' decisions to buy or sell.

It has been suggested that the securities markets in the United States are competitive, efficient markets which allocate capital effectively. In this chapter, factual evidence suggesting this conclusion will be examined. In effect, the assertion that capital markets are efficient will be treated as a hypothesis to be affirmed or denied by empirical evidence.

The investigation of security price movements which forms this chapter and its appendix is not undertaken solely to determine how efficiently security markets in the United States allocate capital. Market efficiency has profit implications, too. For example, if markets are inefficient, fundamental security analysis will be profitable because numerous, grossly underpriced securities will await the analyst; and the grossly overpriced securities can be profitable to search for too, as they can be sold short. Market inefficiencies would also make it profitable to perform technical analysis. If security markets are inefficient, learning lags which slow security price adjustments will cause trends which can be seen in charts and used to make trading profits. Also, if markets are inefficient, this risk-return analysis, which is based in the long-run equilibrium tendencies of a rational market, will not be a worthwhile pursuit. In view of these considerations, it is desirable to find out just how efficient securities markets are.

21-1 THE MARKET MECHANISM

Before examining the facts about market efficiency, let us review the securities market mechanism in the United States. In this country, securities markets are large institutions where many independent buyers and sellers meet. It is easy for newcomers to enter the market and for others to leave it. The existing securities regulations control price manipulation and require that security issuers disclose much information about themselves for the investing public. These factors are necessary for efficient markets; however, they are not sufficient to guarantee efficiency.

Information Dissemination

News is generated in a random fashion. The various competing news services rush this news to the presses in an effort to "make the headlines." The news is not delayed or controlled in any systematic manner; it is widely dispersed and available to the public at virtually no cost. Public libraries contain current books published by the various financial services, and radio and television announcements are available at no cost.

There are no significant learning lags associated with news dissemination. That is, an investor in the Middle West or on the West Coast can obtain financial news as quickly as a resident of New York City. Of course, different investors may develop different price forecasts based on the same news. Upon receiving financial news, some investors will underreact to it while other investors overreact. However, the reaction is immediate and continuous until the news is fully impacted into security prices.

Prices Fluctuate Freely

Security prices are not controlled by any one buyer or seller—there are many independent buyers and sellers. Most security traders are not large enough to affect prices. The few institutions that are large enough to do so are restrained by law from manipulating prices (although they do sometimes affect prices by their actions).

There are many independent sources of opinion about security prices.

Fundamental analysts and technical analysts develop expectations and valuation techniques which are widely divergent and independent of one another. Thus, at any moment some "experts" will predict price rises for a security which other "experts" may consider overvalued.

Fundamental Analysis Widespread

There are many full-time fundamental analysts; over 12,000 are listed in the directory of the Financial Analysts Federation alone. These analysts follow the financial news and adjust their intrinsic value estimates accordingly. Most of them are in a position to affect prices through the buy or sell recommendations they make to their employers. Of course, all these analysts will never reach a uniform opinion about a security's intrinsic value, but they generally agree as to whether a given piece of news should tend to raise or lower prices.

Continuous Equilibrium and Lesser Alternatives

If securities markets are perfectly efficient in allocating capital, the market will be in continuous equilibrium. This continuous equilibrium will not be static through time, however. Every time a new piece of news is released, one or more security's intrinsic values will change and the securities market prices will adjust toward the new values. It is the speed of this price adjustment process which gauges how efficient a market is. A *perfectly efficient market* is in *continuous equilibrium,* so the intrinsic values of securities *vibrate randomly* and *market prices always equal the underlying intrinsic values at every instant* in time.[1] If any disequilibrium (of even a temporary nature) exists, then security markets are less than perfectly efficient and some capital will be misallocated as a result.

21-2 HYPOTHESES ABOUT MARKET EFFICIENCY

When tests of the efficient markets hypothesis are being carried out, securities markets will be tested for varying degrees of efficiency. First, the *weakly efficient market hypothesis* is examined. The weakly efficient hypothesis says that historical price and volume data for securities contain no information which can be used to earn a trading profit above what could be

---

[1] Paul Samuelson, "Proof that Properly Discounted Present Values of Assets Vibrate Randomly," *Bell Journal of Economics and Management Science,* Autumn 1973, pp. 369–374. Also see Samuelson's article "Proof That Properly Anticipated Prices Fluctuate Randomly," *Industrial Management Review,* vol. 6, no. 2, pp. 41–49. These two articles form the basis for the efficient market models and the Martingale model reported in Chap. 21. The articles employ advanced mathematics.

attained with a naive buy-and-hold investment strategy.[2] This hypothesis suggests that technical analysis, which was discussed in Chap. 20, is merely well-recorded but worthless market folklore. The empirical evidence supports this hypothesis.

Also examined is the *semistrong efficient market hypothesis,* which says that markets are efficient enough for prices to reflect all publicly available information. Consequently, only a few insiders, trading on short-run price changes, can earn a profit larger than what could be earned by using a naive buy-and-hold strategy. It is concluded that securities markets in the United States are semistrong efficient.

Finally, the *strongly efficient market hypothesis* is examined; it claims that *no one* can consistently earn a profit larger than what could be earned with a naive buy-and-hold strategy by trading on short-run security price movements. The reason given is that security price changes are independent random variables and that *no one* has monopolistic access to valuable inside information. The strongly efficient market hypothesis is found to be not quite acceptable. A few cases of monopolistic profit making are found which violate this hypothesis.

The three hypotheses just outlined are not mutually exclusive; they differ only in the *degree* of market efficiency they suggest. It is necessary for the weaker hypotheses to be affirmed in order for the stronger hypothesis also to be true. Thus, the following discussion will proceed from the weakest to the strongest hypothesis.[3]

21-3 THE WEAKLY EFFICIENT HYPOTHESIS

In this section the hypothesis that markets are weakly efficient is examined. Weakly efficient markets were defined to be markets in which past prices provide no information about future prices which would allow a short-term trader to earn a return above what could be attained with a naive buy-and-hold strategy. This definition does not mean that short-term traders and speculators will not earn a positive rate of return; it means that, on average, they will not beat a naive buy-and-hold strategy with information obtained from historical data. Of course, some lucky traders do beat the naive buy-

[2] The naive buy-and-hold strategy refers to the investment policy of randomly selecting securities (for example, with a dart), buying them, and holding them over at least one complete business cycle while reinvesting all dividends. Studies indicate that about 10 percent per annum before taxes could have been earned in the New York Stock Exchange over the last 40 years by following a naive buy-and-hold strategy. L. Fisher and J. Lorie, "Rates of Return on Investments in Common Stock: The Year-by-Year Record, 1926–1965," *Journal of Business,* January 1964.

[3] Eugene F. Fama, "Efficient Capital Markets: A Review of Theory and Empirical Work," *Journal of Finance,* May 1970, pp. 383–417; and Eugene F. Fama, "The Behavior of Stock Market Prices," *Journal of Business,* January 1965, pp. 34–105. Fama suggested the three hypothesis categorizations for empirical tests of market efficiency.

and-hold strategy and some unlucky ones do not. But we will not erroneously reason from these specific cases to reach general conclusions. Instead, we will scientifically analyze massive data in an effort to reach general conclusions.

Filter Rules

An x percent *filter rule* is defined as follows:

If the price of a security rises at least x percent, buy and hold the security until its price drops at least x percent from a subsequent high; when the price decreases x percent or more, liquidate the long position and assume a short position until the price rises at least x percent.

By varying the value of x, one can test an infinite number of filter rules. If stock price changes are a series of independent random numbers, filter rules should not yield more return than a naive buy-and-hold strategy. The filter rules should earn a significant profit, however, if some of the patterns chartists talk about (for example, the primary trends of the Dow theory) exist.

Various studies have been conducted using different stocks and different filters. Filters as small as $\frac{1}{2}$ of 1 percent (that is, $x = .005$), as large as 50 percent ($x = .5$), and many values between these extremes have been tested. The tests were performed with stock price data gathered at various intervals. One test used daily stock prices covering several years. Some of the filter rules earn a return above the naive buy-and-hold strategy if the commissions incurred in buying and selling are ignored. However, after commissions are deducted, no filter outperformed the naive strategy.[4] In fact, some ran up considerable net losses. If patterns do exist which can be used as bases for a profitable trading strategy, filter rules are unable to detect them. This is one piece of evidence in support of the weakly efficient markets hypothesis.

Serial Correlation

Security price changes do not appear to have any momentum or inertia which causes changes of a given sign to be followed by changes of that same sign; the filter rules should have detected this pattern if it existed. However, security prices may follow some sort of reversal pattern in which price changes of one sign tend to be followed by changes of the opposite sign. Filter rules might not detect a pattern of reversals, but serial correlation tests should.

---

[4] S. Alexander, "Price Movements in Speculative Markets: Trends or Random Walks," *Industrial Management Review*, May 1961, pp. 7–26. E. F. Fama and M. E. Blume, "Filter Rules and Stock Market Trading," *Journal of Business*, January 1966, pp. 226–241.

Serial correlation (or autocorrelation) measures the correlation coefficient between a series of numbers with lagging numbers in the same time series. Trends or reversal tendencies in security price changes can be detected with serial correlation. We can measure the correlation between security price changes in period t (denoted Δp_t) and price changes in the same security which occur k periods later and are denoted Δp_{t+k}; k is the number of periods of lag. Of course, there is a long-term upward trend in security prices; so if one "period" covers a number of years, a positive serial correlation should be observed. But long-term trends are of no interest, since they are already known to exist.[5] In question here is the existence of patterns in short-term (for example, daily, weekly, or monthly) price changes which can be used to earn a larger trading profit after commissions than what the naive buy-and-hold strategy would yield. If such patterns exist, this would tend to indicate that security prices do not adjust to follow their randomly changing intrinsic values.

In effect, tests for serial correlation in a security's price changes are searching for patterns like the two in Fig. 21-1. The x's in Fig. 21-1 are what would occur if positive changes (denoted $\Delta p > 0$, or Δp^+) were followed by positive changes k periods later and/or if negative changes (denoted $\Delta p < 0$ or Δp^-) were followed by other negative changes k periods later. If security prices kept reversing direction every kth period, the observations represented by the 0's in Fig. 21-1 would result.

Various serial correlation studies about security prices have been published. Many different securities, many different lags (that is, different values of k), and many different time periods have been used from which to draw the data for the tests. The serial correlation studies failed to detect any

[5] See the Lorie and Fisher study results in Chap. 22, Table 22-1, pp. 610–613.

FIG. 21-1 Scatter diagram of price changes and lagged price changes in a security.

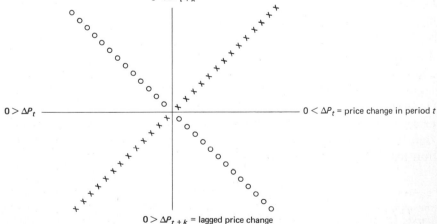

significant trends (that is, any significant correlations).[6] Again, a scientific evaluation of stock price movements tends to support the weakly efficient markets hypothesis.

Runs Tests

It is possible that security prices might occasionally follow trends which filter rules and serial correlations could not detect. That is, price changes may be random most of the time but *occasionally* become serially correlated for varying periods of time. To examine this possibility, runs tests may be used to determine if there are "runs" in the price changes.

A run occurs in a series of numbers whenever the changes between consecutive numbers change sign. Thus, the series of price changes Δp^+, Δp^+, 0, Δp^-, Δp^+ comprises four runs. Runs vary in length from 1 to large numbers. For example, in a bear market, a security price that declines for 10 consecutive trading days will generate nine negative daily price changes but only one run.

Mathematical statisticians are able to determine how many positive, negative, zero, or total runs may be expected to occur in a series of truly random numbers of any size. Therefore, if a time series of security price changes has either a positive, negative, zero, or total number of runs which occur either more frequently or less frequently than would be expected in a series of random numbers, this is evidence that some kind of nonrandomness occurs. The runs tests which have been published suggest that the runs in the price changes of various securities are not significantly different from the runs in a table of random numbers.[7] It seems that short-run traders who search for various types of nonrandom trends from which to earn a profit will not be able to beat a naive buy-and-hold strategy on average.

Weakly Efficient Markets Hypothesis Accepted

In testing the weakly efficient markets hypothesis, filter rules, serial correlations, and runs tests have been employed. Other tests could be reviewed; however, their findings are similar. These are scientific studies which support the weakly efficient hypothesis. Studies by unbiased scientists using analytical techniques which deny the weakly efficient hypothesis are conspicuously absent. Unscientific assertions that short-run security price changes are not random continue to emanate from persons who earn their living by selling charting services. However, the latter may be dismissed because of their bias and the paucity of scientific evidence they produce. Thus, a reasonable individual would have little trouble accepting the weakly efficient markets hypothesis.

[6] Eugene F. Fama, "The Behavior of Stock Market Prices," op. cit. S. Alexander, op. cit., pp. 7–26. M. G. Kendall, "The Analysis of Economic Time Series, Part I," *Journal of the Royal Statistical Society*, 96 (1953), pp. 11–25.

[7] Eugene F. Fama, op. cit. S. Alexander, op. cit. See also Table A21-4, p. 599.

21-4 THE SEMISTRONG EFFICIENT MARKETS HYPOTHESIS

The semistrong markets hypothesis requires more evidence of market efficiency than the previous hypothesis. In essence, the weakly efficient hypothesis asserts only that security prices do not tend to follow patterns repetitively. The semistrong efficient markets hypothesis requires that all available relevant *public* information, such as *The Wall Street Journal, Moody's,* and *Standard & Poor's* publications, be fully reflected in security prices.

In a free and competitive market, prices adjust so that they equate supply and demand. When supply and demand functions do not change, an equilibrium price will emerge which represents a consensus of opinion. For securities this equilibrium price would be the intrinsic value. That price will prevail until supply and/or demand are changed by *new information.* When a new piece of information is cast upon the market, supply and/or demand will react, and a new price will be formed. The faster the news is assimilated and the new equilibrium price emerges, the more efficient the markets.

Learning Lags

In order for markets to be semistrong efficient, there can be no learning lags before the latest news is completely disseminated to the market. Prompt news dispersion is important if prices are to reflect all relevant information immediately. Consider what would occur if learning lags existed.

Suppose that financial news released in New York City did not spread beyond that state's boundaries on the day it was released because of some learning lag. If the news favorably affected some corporation's stock, the price would move up slightly as New Yorkers acted upon it. Then, on the second day after the announcement, suppose the news traveled as far west as the Mississippi River. The rest of the Eastern investors would bid the price up a bit further the second day. By the third day, suppose the news traveled as far west as the Rocky Mountains. As a result, Middle Western investors would bid prices up farther as they learned the news. Finally, on the fourth day after it was announced, the news spread to the rest of the Western states. The price would then be bid up for a fourth consecutive day. As a result of this hypothetical learning lag, two events occurred. First, there was a 4-day trend in a security's price rather than one immediate effect. Second, for over 3 days the security's price did not fully reflect all available information. The studies discussed in Sec. 21-3 revealed practically no instances of trends such as the one hypothesized. This lack of trends indicates that financial news is widely and quickly disseminated. As a result, security prices do tend to reflect all publicly available information at any moment.

Of course, the market may over- or underreact to news. However, as long as it reacts instantly and continuously in a series of unbiased movements around the true intrinsic value (or equilibrium price), the semistrong hypothesis is supported.

Reaction to Earnings Announcements

It is possible that securities prices fully reflect most news immediately but react imperfectly, irrationally, or slowly to a certain few kinds of news. Of course, investigating the reaction to every type of news is not possible, but we can examine a few particularly interesting cases. One of the most important pieces of information determining a security's price is the earnings of the issuing firm. If securities markets are semistrongly efficient, prices will reflect changes in earning power.

One study analyzed the effects of the annual earnings announcements made by 261 corporations over a 20-year period.[8] An econometric model was developed for each firm to predict its earnings 1 year into the future for several years. Based on these forecasts, earnings were classified as either worse than expected (that is, disappointing growth in earnings) or better than expected (that is, growth in earnings which is a pleasant surprise). The effects of these announced earnings on the firms' securities were then analyzed.

To determine the effects of the announcements on a security's price while holding other factors (namely, the market's movement) constant, characteristic lines relating the rate of change in the 261 firm's market prices to the rate of change in the level of the market were calculated. The number of percentage points above or below the firm's characteristic line where the actual rates of return occurred (that is, the residual error) measures the portion of the price change which was caused by unsystematic factors other than the market's movements. The average number of percentage points above or below the characteristic line was determined for all securities in the two classes (that is, disappointing or pleasantly surprising) for each of the 12 months before and the 6 months after each firm's 20 annual earnings announcements.

Figure 21-2 shows the cumulative average rates of return over all firms in the sample. It shows that on average the market correctly anticipated earnings changes *before* they were announced to the public. That is, the firms which had disappointing earnings experienced unfavorable downward pressure on their prices in the months preceding the actual announcement to the market. Firms whose earnings were higher than ex-

---

[8] R. Ball and P. Brown, "An Empirical Evaluation of Accounting Income Numbers," *Journal of Accounting Research*, Autumn 1968, pp. 159–178. Ball and Brown acknowledged in their article that their results may be biased because the earnings were scaled by dividing them by market prices, a process which probably introduces spurious correlation. This possibility is evaluated by Nicholas J. Gonedes, "Evidence of the Information Content of Accounting Numbers: Accounting-Based and Market-Based Estimates of Systematic Risk," *Journal of Financial and Quantitative Analysis*, June 1973, pp. 407–443.

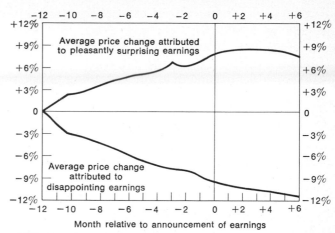

FIG. 21-2 Average percentage price movements preceding and succeeding 20 annual earnings announcements of 261 firms.

pected enjoyed upward pressure on the prices of their securities in the months preceding the earnings announcement. On the average, only about 10 percent of the cumulative unsystematic price adjustment occurred *after* the earnings were announced. This was not enough of a price change to yield a net trading profit *after commissions.*

The analysis of earnings announcement effects supports the semi-strongly efficient markets hypothesis. The securities prices reflected and even anticipated the new information about earnings.

Before passing, it should be pointed out that the tendency of security prices to anticipate changes in announced earnings does not result in trends in securities prices. First of all, earnings tend to change in a random manner,[9] so that patterned reactions to earnings will not cause price patterns. Secondly, none of the 261 firms in the sample experienced the smooth price changes indicated by the aggregate data shown in Fig. 21-2. Each individual firm's price moved up in a series of erratic random price changes which could not be predicted in advance. Only the cumulative unsystematic errors in the homogeneous subsamples accumulated smoothly to a nonzero sum over time.

Announcement Effects from Changes in the Discount Rate

Interest rates affect security prices because they partially determine the appropriate discount rate to use in determining present values. Therefore, changes in the discount rate announced by the Federal Reserve Board may be expected to affect security prices. This is particularly true because announcements of changes in the discount rate are so widely publicized by the press.

[9] R. A. Brealey, *An Introduction to Risk and Return from Common Stocks* (Cambridge, Mass.: M.I.T., 1969), chap. 3, discusses the randomness of earnings research.

Research into the effects of discount rate changes has shown that the average security's price changes a tiny but significant amount (never exceeding .5 percent) on the first trading day following the public announcement by the Federal Reserve of a change in the discount rate.[10] This change is not enough to yield a trading profit. Most of the price change associated with the announcement seems to occur *before* the actual announcement. Thus, the semistrong hypothesis is again supported by the empirical facts.

Leading and Lagging Stocks

Some Wall Street veterans refer to General Motors as a "bellwether stock" because it is supposed to initiate, and sometimes lead, trends in the movements of stock prices. A diversified stock market average, like Standard & Poor's 500 stocks composite average, is thus an average of some leading and some lagging stocks, according to this thinking. Financial economists doubt the existence of leading or lagging stocks.

If some securities tended to lead market movements and other stocks tended to be laggers, economic logic suggests that profit-seeking price speculators would reduce these leads and lags to zero. These speculators would buy (sell) the lagging stocks whenever the leading stocks rose (fell) in price in order to profit from the price rise (to avoid losses on the price fall). As long as any stock tended to be a consistent leader or lagger, this simple rule would yield short-run trading profits.

The existence of leading or lagging stocks would represent a serious imperfection in an otherwise-efficient securities market. Leading and lagging security prices would result from the fact that for some securities (the leaders) new news which systematically affected all securities prices was impacted into their prices before the same news was reflected in the prices of other securities. Such intertemporal differences in the reaction of prices to new information would refute the semistrong efficient markets hypothesis.

To test for leading and lagging stock prices, the modified characteristic regression line shown in Eq. (21-1) was estimated empirically.[11]

$$r_{it} = a_i + b_i (r_{m,t+k}) + e_t \tag{21-1}$$

Equation (21-1) is like the characteristic lines explained in Chap. 12 except that it also allows for leads and lags in the reaction of the ith security to systematic changes in the market, as measured by r_m. The subscript k which is added to, or subtracted from, the time period subscript for r_m in Eq. (21-1)

[10] R. N. Waud, "Public Interpretation of Discount Rate Changes: Evidence on the 'Announcement Effect,'" *Econometrica*, 1971.

[11] J. C. Francis, "Intertemporal Differences in Systematic Stock Price Movements," *Journal of Financial and Quantitative Analysis*, June 1975.

measures the lead or lag in months. For example, if Eq. (21-1) yielded a significant goodness of fit for the ith stock when $k = -2$, the ith stock would lead the rate of change in the market by 2 months. But if the regression had a significant correlation for $k = 4$, this would mean the stock's rate of price change r_i tended to lag 4 months behind the rate of change in the market index r_m. When $k = 0$, Eq. (21-1) is identical to the characteristic regression line, Eq. (12-6) on page 328, with no leads or lags.

The leading-concurrent-lagging characteristic regression line, Eq. (21-1), was estimated for values of $k = 6, 5, 4, 3, 2, 1, 0, -1, -2, -3, -4, -5,$ and -6 months for 770 different NYSE stocks; that is, (770 stocks $\times$ 13 leads and lags for each =) 10,010 regressions were run on the sample. The model was estimated over two different 3-year sample periods (that is, $t = 1,$ $2, \ldots, 36$ months) to determine whether leaders or laggers existed over temporary short-run periods. Then the model was estimated over one 10-year (that is, $t = 1, 2, \ldots, 120$ months) sample to test for stocks which might consistently lead or lag in the long run. Thus, in total 30,030 ($= 3$ samples $\times$ 13 lags $\times$ 770 stocks) regressions were fitted.

Over the two 3-year sample periods, about 10 percent of the 770 stocks showed some statistically significant tendency to lead or lag the market in each sample period. But the stocks which tended to lead or lag in one 3-year sample usually did not show any tendency to lead or lag in the other 3-year sample. And, when the same 770 stocks were tested over a 10-year period, only six of them (that is, less than 1 percent of the sample) showed any significant tendency to lead or lag the market. Six significant regressions could be expected if 10,010 regressions on 770 stocks were run with *random numbers* simply because of coincidences called sampling errors.

The temporary leads and lags which were found in about 10 percent of the 770 stocks in one of the two 3-year subsamples help explain why chartists can think that some stocks lead or lag the market: They are observing spurious correlation errors which occur because of coincidence. But these temporary coincidences are not consistent enough to suggest that some stocks do in fact lead or lag the market or to violate the semistrong efficient markets hypothesis.

Effects of Stock Splits

Stock splits and stock dividends are essentially paper-shuffling operations which do not change the total value of the firm or the owner's wealth. For example, a 100 percent stock dividend or a 2 for 1 stock split results in twice as many shares outstanding and each share being worth half as much.[12] If security markets are efficient allocators of capital, they will realize this, and the *total value* of the firm's outstanding shares will not be affected.

---

[12] There is a difference in the way accountants and attorneys treat stock splits and stock dividends. These different treatments are merely legal and bookkeeping technicalities and are ignored here since they result in no change in the value of the wealth of the owners.

One study of 940 stock splits which occurred in New York Stock Exchange stocks between 1927 and 1959 was directed at determining the effects of the split.[13] Essentially, the study concluded that the markets reacted rationally and efficiently to the splits and stock dividends. These changes alone had no effect on the total value of the shares outstanding. The securities which had splits and also had increases in their cash dividends (which suggested the firm's earnings had permanently increased) experienced some unusual capital gains several months before and slightly after the announcement of the split, but these gains were attributed to the increase in earnings and cash dividends instead of to the split or stock dividend.

Securities which had stock splits *and then had decreases* in their cash dividends (which suggested that the firm's earning power was diminished) experienced unusual capital gains before the split and unusual capital losses after the split. The unusual gains before the split were suggested as the main reason for the split. The unusual losses after the split were investors' correction of their errors in valuation preceding the split which was not followed by an increase in cash dividends and earnings.

The study of stock dividends and splits furnishes additional support for the semistrong hypothesis that markets are efficient. The stock dividends and stock splits themselves had no discernible effects on prices. This evidence is impressive in view of the popular folklore about the importance of stock dividends and stock splits. It seems that the rational investors' evaluations prevailed over those of their less sophisticated counterparts. The unusual price changes which did occur near the time of the splits were attributable to rational investor reactions to changes in cash dividends and earnings rather than to the split or stock dividend.

Conclusions about the Semistrong Markets Hypothesis

Moody's manuals, Standard & Poor's reports, and audited financial information filed with the Securities and Exchange Commission are readily available to investors across the United States. This background information about corporations provides the perspective needed to evaluate new information. Financial newspapers and the news services compete to deliver news as quickly as possible. As a result, investors can obtain the latest financial news quickly at a minimal cost. They tend, on average, to interpret this news correctly. When news affects the value of a security, it will cause reevaluations and security trading. This trading begins immediately after news is announced and affects prices at once. Prices adjust through a series of erratic but unbiased movements toward their new intrinsic value. The studies reviewed above show that security prices not only react immedi-

---

[13] E. Fama, L. Fisher, M. Jensen, and R. Roll, ''The Adjustment of Stock Prices to New Information,'' *International Economic Review*, February 1969, pp. 1–21. This study is reviewed in more detail in Sec. 22–2.

ately and rationally to news; they often anticipate it. As a result, it may be concluded that security prices reflect all publicly available relevant information as suggested by the semistrong hypothesis.

21-5 THE STRONGLY EFFICIENT MARKETS HYPOTHESIS

The strongly efficient markets hypothesis is that *all* (not just publicly available) information is fully reflected in security prices. Before looking at the facts, common sense suggests that such an extreme hypothesis should be refutable. All that need be done is to find one insider who has profited from inside information and the hypothesis is disproved. And it is not hard to find evidence that several investors have enough valuable inside information with which to earn trading profits.

Monopolistic Access to Valuable Information

Specialists on the organized security exchanges who make the markets in securities have valuable inside information. They keep a book of unfilled limit orders to buy and sell at different prices. This information allows them to see the outlines of the supply and demand curves for the securities in which they make a market. The specialists' book is kept confidential in order to stop possible price manipulation schemes by outsiders. As a result, specialists have monopolistic access to valuable information which they use to make a speculative trading profit.[14] This is one of the reasons the seats on the NYSE sell for thousands of dollars.[15]

Various studies, actions taken by the SEC, and court cases also suggest that some corporate insiders are able to profit (sometimes illegally) from monopolistic access to information.[16]

Monopolistic Access to Information Limited

The fact that specialists and some insiders can earn trading profits from their information refutes the strongly efficient markets hypothesis. However, discovery of these market flaws prompts one to wonder how many people have monopolistic access to valuable information. That is, given that

---

[14] V. Niederhoffer and M. F. M. Osborne, "Market Making and Reversal on the Stock Exchange," *Journal of the American Statistical Association*, December 1966, pp. 897–916.

[15] Members of the NYSE can also earn sales commissions by acting as floor traders.

[16] M. Scholes, "A Test of the Competitive Hypothesis: The Market for New Issues and Secondary Offerings," unpublished doctoral dissertation, University of Chicago, Graduate School of Business, 1969. The Texas Gulf Sulphur case, discussed on pp. 93–94, is a well-known example of insiders trading illegally for their own profit. Also see J. F. Jaffe, "Special Information and Insider Trading," *Journal of Business*, July 1974, pp. 410–428. See also the Securities and Exchange Commission's *Institutional Investor Study Report* (Washington: Government Printing Office, 1971), vols. 1–8.

there are imperfections which rule out strongly efficient markets, how deeply do these imperfections permeate the market?

After an examination of corporate insiders and specialists, who undeniably have monopolistic access to valuable information, it would seem that a group of well-endowed professional portfolio managers should be examined next. That is, the latter group would seem to be the next most likely to be able to obtain and profit from valuable investment information before it is fully impacted into market prices. Since mutual funds fall into this category, we shall examine them.

In Chap. 19 various aspects of mutual fund performance were analyzed. Rankings of the annual returns achieved by 39 funds showed (in Table 19-1) that no individual fund was able to earn a better-than-average return consistently over a 10-year period. This tended to indicate that no individual fund (or funds) within the group had any relative advantage in obtaining valuable information. Plotting the performance of a sample of 23 mutual funds relative to the efficient frontier in risk-return space (in Fig. 19-1) showed that none was an efficient investment. In another sample, 34 mutual funds' performances were compared with the Dow Jones Industrial Average (DJIA) using Sharpe's portfolio performance index (which measures the risk-premium over risk). This comparison (which is illustrated in Fig. 19-3) showed that 23 out of the 34 funds ranked below the DJIA. Data (shown in Fig. 19-8) on the performance of 163 mutual funds during the bear market of 1969–1970 showed that the majority of them experienced larger declines than the Standard & Poor's 500 stock average. These mutual fund studies all seem to point clearly to the fact that no funds possess any knowledge which is not already fully impacted into security prices.

Another study of 115 mutual funds over the decade from 1955 to 1964 showed similar findings. In particular, this study concluded that:

> Although these tests certainly do not imply that the strong form of the (efficient markets) hypothesis holds for all investors and for all time they provide strong evidence in support of that hypothesis. One must realize that these analysts are extremely well endowed. Moreover, they operate in the securities markets every day and have wide-ranging contacts and associations in both the business and financial communities. Thus, the fact that they are apparently unable to forecast returns accurately enough to recover their research and transactions costs is a striking piece of evidence in favor of the strong form of the [efficient markets] hypothesis.[17]

21-6 CONCLUSIONS ABOUT SECURITY PRICES

The weakly efficient and semistrong efficient market hypotheses are well supported by the facts. The strongly efficient markets hypothesis is not,

---

[17] M. Jensen, "Risk, the Pricing of Capital Assets, and the Evaluation of Investment Portfolios," *Journal of Business*, April 1969, p. 170. Words in brackets added.

however. Although the mutual fund studies indicated that the information available to professional portfolio managers was already impacted into prices, a few exceptions (namely, insiders and specialists) were found which violated the strongly efficient hypothesis. The evidence seems to indicate that, for all practical purposes, security markets in the United States are intrinsic-value random-walk markets.

Dr. Paul Cootner has summarized this process, and has suggested that security prices can be viewed as a series of constrained random fluctuations around the true intrinsic value.[18] He hypothesizes the existence of two groups of investors. The first group can be referred to as the "naive investors," those who have access only to the public news media for their information. They might be chartists, amateur fundamental analysts, dart throwers, or speculators; they base their investment decisions upon their interpretations of the public news and their financial circumstances. Naive investors will recognize few, if any, divergences from intrinsic values.[19] They are more likely to invest on the basis of "hot tips" when they have excess liquidity, and at other times which may or may not be wise.

The second group of investors are the "professional investors," those who have the resources to discover news and develop clear-cut estimates of intrinsic value before the naive investors even get the news. As a result, the professionals will recognize significant deviations from intrinsic value and initiate trading that tends to align the market price with the intrinsic value.

Figure 21-3 shows how security prices might fluctuate over time in the market Cootner describes. The dotted lines represent the true intrinsic value of the security as estimated by the professional investors. Trading by the naive investors is not necessarily based on a correct interpretation of the latest news. As a result, naive investors may be buying securities whose market prices are above their intrinsic values, or vice versa. These naive

---

[18] P. H. Cootner, "Stock Prices: Random Versus Systematic Changes," *Industrial Management Review*, Spring 1962, pp. 24–45. E. F. Fama elaborated on his interpretations of the intrinsic-value random-walk market model on pp. 36–37 of "The Behavior of Stock Market Prices," *Journal of Business*, January 1965, pp. 34–105; essentially, he agreed with Cootner.
[19] Intrinsic-value estimation is discussed in Chap. 10.

FIG. 21-3 Hypothetical charts of random stock price fluctuations within fixed limits. (*a*) No change in intrinsic value; (*b*) intrinsic value changes at periods *t* and *t* + 1.

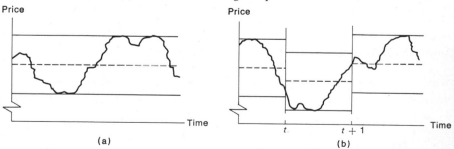

traders are largely responsible for the aimless price fluctuations which can cause prices to diverge from intrinsic values.

When a security price does differ significantly from its true intrinsic value, the professional investors find it profitable to correct this disequilibrium. Small deviations will not be profitable to correct, but when prices are significantly out of line, the professionals will bid up low prices or liquidate overpriced securities. In effect, the professionals erect "reflecting barriers" around the true intrinsic value.[20] These reflecting barriers are represented by the solid lines above and below the intrinsic-value lines in Fig. 21-3. Prices will fluctuate freely within the reflecting barriers, but when they reach these barriers, the action of the professionals will cause prices to move toward their intrinsic value.

The intrinsic-value estimates of the professionals may change as the latest news is learned. The reflecting barriers around the intrinsic value will therefore change accordingly. As a result, it is not usually possible to observe the true intrinsic value or the reflecting barriers from charts of historical security prices. Price charts like the one in Fig. 21-3b will occur when a security experiences changes in its intrinsic value. The preceding evidence suggests certain investment policies.

Fundamental Security Analysis

In an intrinsic-value random-walk market, fundamental analysis plays a major role in determining security prices. Expert fundamental analysts who discover new financial information and quickly interpret it correctly will earn higher-than-average returns, but most fundamental analysts will not earn a return above what could be achieved with a naive buy-and-hold strategy.

In an intrinsic-value random-walk market, security prices are unbiased estimates of the true intrinsic value and reflect all current public information. Searching for undervalued securities will therefore be largely unfruitful. Only the most expert fundamental analysts who have discovered new information will find it profitable to perform fundamental analysis, and any underpriced securities they discover will be bid up in price into line with their intrinsic value very quickly. So all but the few most expert fundamental analysts will not profit (above what a naive strategy would yield) from their activity. It will not be worthwhile for amateur investors to learn fundamental analysis in an intrinsic-value random-walk market. The amateur can expect to accumulate more wealth by selecting securities randomly and devoting the time which would have been spent on fundamental analysis to his or her own profession earning more money to invest. The

---

[20] William Feller, *An Introduction to Probability Theory and Its Applications*, vol. I, 3d ed. (New York: Wiley, 1968). Pages 436–438 provide a discussion of a random walk with reflecting barriers.

only fundamental analysts that will repeatedly earn unusual profits while experiencing few losses will be hard-working professional analysts with experience and resources to support their costly search for information.[21]

Technical Analysis

The various tests to measure the randomness of stock price changes which were described earlier cannot detect absolutely every conceivable pattern which might be formed. Some extremely complex patterns might go undetected. However, technical analysts do not usually search for extremely complex patterns. Their concepts are simple at best. Therefore, the evidence that patterns do not exist tends to indicate that technical analysis will not be worthwhile to perform in an intrinsic-value random-walk market. Chartists can expect to earn an average rate of return, but they could expect to earn the same return by selecting securities with a dart, too. So they would be better off to devote their time to more profitable activities and to select securities by some other method. There would be no reason for an institutional portfolio to employ a chartist in an intrinsic-value random-walk market.

Risk-Return Analysis

In an intrinsic-value random-walk market, most securities' rates of return will conform to distributions which are stationary over time. In such a market it will be worthwhile for investors to estimate the risk and return of their investment alternatives. The investor can then select the investments with the maximum return in the preferred risk-class. In this manner investors can maximize their utility. Selecting the most efficient portfolio in the preferred risk-class will enable investors to attain their highest indifference curve in risk-return space. This investment may or may not earn an above-average rate of return, the outcome depends upon the risk-class the investor selects and when the investment is liquidated. But such analysis will maximize the investor's expected utility.

Of course, risk-return relationships represent theoretical market equilibriums. In the real world of continuous dynamic disequilibrium, the positive relation between risk and average return can be expected to emerge only if investments are held for at least one complete business cycle. For example, risky assets purchased at the end of an inflated bull market and sold at the end of a long bear market will have had the *highest* risk and *lowest* rates of return during such a period. However, if risky assets are held over a

---

[21] Security analysts who endeavor to outperform the profits obtained from a naive, buy-and-hold strategy by studying accounting statements are analyzed in an in-depth study published by Ray Ball. See "Changes in Accounting Techniques and Stock Prices," *Journal of Accounting Research,* supplement to vol. 10, Empirical Research in Accounting Numbers: Selected Studies, 1972, pp. 1–44.

complete market cycle (for example, from peak to peak), they will earn higher-than-average returns and the positive relationship between risk and return will be evident.

The Negativism of the Random-Walk Theory

The so-called random-walk theory is a very negative statement. It says that no patterns exist in price changes; that technical analysis techniques which some persons have spent their lives developing are only worthless folklore; and that the daily changes in the DJIA which security sales representatives chatter about are really random numbers containing no information. It is quite easy to find counterexamples to such negative assertions. For example, patterns can be found in security prices; some technical analysts have correctly called market turns and "picked winners"; and, although the daily changes in the DJIA are meaningless, the trend does provide some information. But these counterexamples are pointless; they can be attacked with other trivial examples.

It is not fruitful to try to reach general conclusions from a few specific cases. The random-walk theory should be viewed as an unbiased scientific statement supported by a body of published evidence. A few counterexamples prove nothing. Only new scientific analysis can throw more light on the subject. In the meantime, the available data indicate that security markets in the United States are intrinsic-value random-walk markets.

QUESTIONS

1 Explain the weakly efficient, semistrong efficient, and strongly efficient markets hypotheses.

2 "An investor who learned that General Motors' earnings per share had increased by an unusually large amount a few days before the news was announced publicly could probably buy GM stock and profit from a quick capital gain when the announcement was made." True, false, or uncertain? Explain.

3 Characterize the nature and behavior of stock prices in a large public securities market. That is, what do stock prices represent and what patterns do they follow? Why do stock prices behave in this manner? What does this imply about the investments management policies that should be followed?

4 Why are runs tests, serial correlation, and filter rules used in testing the random-walk hypothesis? What do these tests reveal?

5 "Stock prices are random numbers." Is this statement true, false, or uncertain? Explain.

6 "The managers of large institutional portfolios (such as mutual funds) should instruct their fundamental security analysts to collect and evaluate the 'hot tips' which are discussed on Wall Street so their portfolios can profit from monopolistic access to this valuable information." True, false, or uncertain? Explain.

7 Suppose your long-time next-door neighbor is a business executive who watches the stars through a telescope and studies the physical sciences as a hobby. He has earnestly explained to you on several occasions that he has observed that the sunspots on the sun's surface are more active during bull markets. He has shown you books about sunspots to prove he can recognize them and records of his observations of sunspot activity and the stock market. If you believe and trust your neighbor, should you begin to study sunspot activity as a way to beat the stock market?

8 "If rates of return are distributed as a Paretian distribution with a characteristic exponent less than 2 (that is, theoretically infinite variance), then risk-return analysis is hopeless." To what problem is this statement referring? Is the statement true, false, or uncertain? Explain. (See chapter appendix.)

9 "Rates of return conform to mathematical statisticians' random-walk model." True, false, or uncertain? Explain. (See chapter appendix.)

10 Compare and contrast the random-walk theory of rates of return with the martingale model. (See chapter appendix.)

SELECTED REFERENCES

Brealey, R. A., *An Introduction to Risk and Return from Common Stocks* (Cambridge, Mass.: M.I.T., 1969).
> This book summarizes much current investments literature. The book is nonmathematical and easy to read. Chapters 1 through 9 are relevant to the so-called random-walk theory.

———, *Security Prices in a Competitive Market: More about Risk and Return from Common Stocks* (Cambridge, Mass.: M.I.T., 1971).
> This book summarizes much current efficient markets literature in an easy-to-read fashion.

Cootner, Paul (ed.), *The Random Character of Stock Prices* (Cambridge, Mass.: M.I.T., 1964).
> This book contains 22 readings which trace the development of the random-walk theory from 1900. Cootner makes editorial remarks on the readings. The mathematics used is frequently advanced.

Fama, Eugene F. "The Behavior of Stock Market Prices," *Journal of Business,*
January 1965, pp. 34–105.

>This paper rationalizes the existence of an intrinsic-value random-
walk market and shows various types of evidence in support of the
theory. The stationary stable symmetric distribution with Paretian
tails is discussed, and an appendix shows some theorems about such
distributions. Mathematics and statistics are used.

APPENDIX TO CHAPTER 21
Random-Walk and Martingale Models

A model is a simplified version of reality. It is a toylike construct which is
"played with" in order to learn the essential nature of the more complex
thing being modeled. Consider the random-walk model to describe stock
prices.

A random-walk model is a mathematical model in which a series of
numbers are (1) independent and (2) identically distributed. When introducing the random-walk model to a class, mathematical statistics professors sometimes use the aimless lurchings of an intoxicated person as an
example. At each step the drunk's direction may be at any of the 180
degrees emanating from his location (this assumes he cannot fall backward), and the distance of each step is a random variable with a range from
zero to, say, 4 feet. Furthermore, the number of steps per minute is a
random variable with a range from zero to dozens. If the probability distributions describing the direction, distance, and frequency of the drunk's
steps are realistic, the random-walk model can tell the probability that the
drunk reaches any given position at any point in time. This appendix examines the behavior of security prices to see whether the random-walk model
of mathematical statistics can be adapted to characterize their movements.

A21-1 PROBABILITY DISTRIBUTIONS FOR SECURITIES

Suppose that the market prices of some common stocks were recorded at
the close of each trading day for 4 years. If the relative frequency (that is,
the objective historical probabilities) of each security's price was determined, a distribution of past prices could be prepared. Figure A21-1 represents two hypothetical relative-frequency distributions for 4 years of
common stock prices. One distribution is for the first 2 years, and the other
distribution is for the second 2 years.

Distributions of security prices are of little value for two reasons
which should be apparent after a glance at Fig. A21-1. First, the distri-

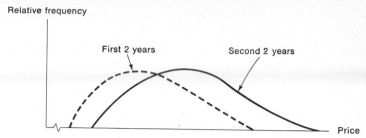

FIG. A21-1 Hypothetical frequency distributions of a common stock's prices.

butions are not stable over time. Nearly all securities' prices increase with the passage of time at about 6 percent per year.[1] As a result, each year's relative-frequency distribution shifts a little further to the right and has a higher mean price. Second, the shape of the distribution changes each year. Each year as the security's price rises, the distribution's tail on the right side grows a little longer. In statistical language, the positive skewness of a security's price tends to increase with the price.[2]

As a result of these two changes, the distributions of security prices are of little value: one year's distribution cannot be used to predict the probability that a certain price will occur in the next year. In statistical language, the distributions are not stable over time. This is unfortunate because stable distributions are the most useful in forecasting.[3]

Distributions of Price Changes Unstable

In a search for stable distributions which could be useful in making probability statements about future security prices, analysts examined the price *changes* (denoted Δp) which occur daily rather than the prices themselves. Figure A21-2 shows two relative-frequency distributions of price changes for a hypothetical common stock like the one shown in Fig. A21-1.

The distributions in Fig. A21-2 represent 4 years of daily price changes. One distribution represents the first 2 years of daily changes, and the other distribution represents the second 2 years. The distributions of

[1] L. Fisher and J. Lorie, "Rates of Return on Investments in Common Stock: The Year-by-Year Record, 1926–1965," *Journal of Business*, January 1964, p. 315, table A2. The average NYSE stock's price rose 6.8 percent per annum from 1926 to 1960. This does not include dividend reinvestment.

[2] See Mathematical Appendix G for a definition and discussion of skewness. Essentially, positive skewness means the distribution has an unusually long tail on the right side and is therefore lopsided.

[3] The frequency distributions of historical security prices can be made more useful by adding subscripted time variables to the parameters of the distribution and building an appropriate growth rate into them. However, such complications are avoided.

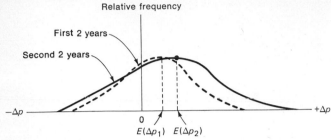

FIG. A21-2 Frequency distributions for a hypothetical common stock's price changes.

price changes for most securities have positive means because stock prices tend to drift upward with the passage of time.

Unfortunately, the frequency distributions of price changes are diminished in value because historical price changes tend to be unstable too. Security prices tend to fluctuate up and down in terms of a fixed range of *percentages;* so, as the security's price rises over time, the dollar amounts of the price changes grow, too. To see this intuitively, consider the variance of price changes before and after a stock split. If a $100 stock is split into two $50 shares, the variance of the stock price changes will be smaller after the split (unless the percentage price fluctuations increase, an occurrence that is highly unlikely.)[4] As a result of this phenomenon, the mean and the standard deviations of price changes increase with the price of the security in most cases.

Distributions of Rates of Return Stable

Although the distributions of price changes are not stationary, studying these distributions reveals that security prices tend to change by *percentages* that conform to a stable distribution. Let us denote the percentage price changes by the rate of change as defined in Eq. (A21-1).

$$r_t = \frac{p_{t+1} - p_t}{p_t} \tag{A21-1}$$

$$= \frac{\Delta p_t}{p_t}$$

where p_{t+1} = market price of asset at beginning of differencing period $t + 1$
p_t = beginning price at start of differencing period t
Δp_t = price change during differencing period t

---

[4] In statistical language $\text{var}(2p) = 4\text{var}(p)$, or in terms of standard deviations $\sqrt{\text{var}(2p)} = 2 \sqrt{\text{var}(p)}$. This shows that higher-priced stocks (for example, twice as high for $2p$) have a larger variance of price changes (namely, four times larger).

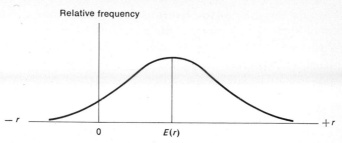

FIG. A21-3 Frequency distributions of historical rates of return and rates of change for a hypothetical security.

The rates of change of daily, weekly, monthly, quarterly, semiannual, or yearly price changes tend to conform to a stable relative-frequency distribution as shown in Fig. A21-3 if the price changes are drawn from at least one complete business cycle.

Dividends d_t are sometimes included when calculating rates of return, as shown in Eq. (A21-2).

$$r_t = \frac{p_{t+1} - p_t + d_t}{p_t} \tag{A21-2}$$

$$= \frac{p_{t+1} + d_t}{p_t} - 1 \tag{A21-2a}$$

Most corporations pay the *same* dividends quarter after quarter, only occasionally increasing them slightly or canceling them altogether; so dividends may be treated as a constant in dealing with most corporations. Thus, whether rates of returns are calculated with (A21-2) or rates of change are calculated with (A21-1), the distribution tends to be fairly stationary.[5] If dividends are included, the entire distribution is shifted to the right by the amount of the dividend yield (that is, d/p) but has the same shape and stability. It is better to use Eq. (A21-2) than (A21-1) when measuring returns, so that the dividend income is considered in measuring the investor's income (to compensate for the ex-dividend price dropoff).

Not every security has a relative-frequency distribution of historical rates of return which remains stationary.[6] If the firm nears bankruptcy, changes products, enjoys major technological breakthroughs which confer a

---

[5] W. F. Sharpe and G. M. Cooper, "Risk-Return Classes of New York Stock Exchange Common Stocks, 1931–67," *Financial Analysts Journal*, March–April, 1972, pp. 46–51.

[6] A third way to measure rates of return is to take the natural or Naperian logarithm of the value relatives. Symbolically, $r_t = \ln (p_{t+1}/p_t) = \ln (p_{t+1}) - \ln (p_t)$.

competitive advantage, or experiences other major changes, the distribution may shift. However, the distributions of returns for the vast majority of firms are fairly stationary over time if the distribution is observed over at least one complete business cycle. This is usually true even though the firm has executive shake-ups, enters new market areas, or alters its product line.

The existence of stable distributions of returns allows analysts to do several valuable things. First, probability statements may be made about the percentage price changes that may be expected to occur. Second, a security's historical average return and standard deviation of returns furnish estimates of the security's future risk and return. Thus, a stable random-walk model may be constructed for rates of returns or rates of price change, although this method was not possible with the raw price data.

It will be recalled that for a series to be classified as a random walk, the two major requirements are that the successive members in the series be (1) independent and (2) identically distributed. *Identically distributed* is a technical statistical phrase which means the numbers all conform to some given probability distribution. Since the probability distributions of historical rates of return tend to be stable for any given security, this fact indicates that the rates of return for those securities are identically distributed. Thus, one condition necessary to classify securities as a random walk is fulfilled.

Advantages of Using Gaussian or Normal Distributions

Many researchers were hopeful that rates of change and rates of return are normally distributed for several reasons. First, normal distributions are completely described by only two statistics, the mean and the variance. Thus, skewness and kurtosis could be ignored.[7] Second, normal distributions have a finite variance; that is, their tails come down to the horizontal axis of the probability distribution. Figure A21-4 compares a normal distribution which has a finite variance (and standard deviation) with a distribution with infinite variance. It is highly desirable that a probability distribution possesses a finite variance because statistics from populations possessing finite variance are dependable statistics which do not erratically vary from sample to sample.[8] Third, the normal distribution is well known and has a well-developed sampling theory.

---

[7] See Mathematical Appendix G for definitions and discussions of skewness and kurtosis.
[8] Statistically speaking, an erratic statistic is said to be *inefficient,* a technical statistical word which means the statistic varies erratically from sample to sample. An *efficient* statistic varies less than any other statistic. Efficiency is a desirable statistical property. Statistics from populations with finite variances are more efficient than statistics from populations with infinite variances. Another advantage of having a finite variance is that the central limit theorem applies only to distributions with finite variances.

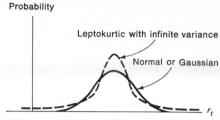

FIG. A21-4 Normal distribution compared with leptokurtic distribution with infinite variance.

Infinite Variance

As computers analyzed larger files of accurate historical data during the 1960s, the normal distribution of rates of price change and rates of return were called into question. The occasional extremely large and extremely small rates of return which had previously been attributed to error or ignored repeatedly appeared in securities distributions. These extreme values lie beyond the tails of a normal distribution—they are sometimes referred to as *outliers.*

Closer examination of the distributions of returns indicated that they may not be normal or Gaussian, as had been thought. The distributions were leptokurtic and had large variances. Drs. Benoit Mandelbrot and Eugene Fama published studies suggesting that rates of return were distributed according to a stable symmetric distribution with infinite variance.[9] Of course, any sample of actual returns which was analyzed had a finite variance since the actual rates of return were not infinitely large or infinitely small. But occasionally outliers appeared which suggested that the probability distribution of returns implied a theoretically infinite variance. Figure A21-4 outlines such a distribution with a dotted line and compares it with the normal distribution. The tails of the distribution represented by the dotted line are very long. As a result, there is a tiny probability that rates of return reach very large positive or negative values causing the distribution to have a theoretically infinite variance.

Problems with Infinite Variance Populations

The existence of outliers and a theoretically infinite variance presents problems for risk-return analysis. Equation (A21-3) shows the formula for

---

[9] Benoit Mandelbrot, "The Variation of Certain Speculative Prices," *Journal of Business,* October 1963, pp. 394–419. Eugene F. Fama, "The Behavior of Stock Market Prices," *Journal of Business,* January 1965, pp. 39–105.

calculating the standard deviation of returns from a sample of n observations.

$$\sigma = \sqrt{\frac{1}{n} \sum_{t-1}^{n} [r_t - E(r)]^2} \qquad \text{(A21-3)}$$

If risk is being estimated with (A21-3) using historical returns, inefficient and erratic statistics will be obtained. Every time an extreme value of r_t (that is, an outlier) is included in the computation of the risk with (A21-3), the standard deviation will increase erratically instead of smoothly approaching the true population value. Figure A21-5 represents the problem graphically.

In order to develop efficient and unerratic risk statistics from a population with an infinite variance, some other financial risk surrogate may be used. Equation (A21-4) defines the mean absolute deviation of returns (MAD).

$$\text{MAD} = \frac{1}{n} \sum_{t}^{n} | r_t - E(r) | \qquad \text{(A21-4)}$$

where $| r_t - E(r) |$ denotes the absolute value of the deviation from the mean.
Since the deviations around the expected value are not squared in (A21-4) as they are in (A21-3), the MAD does not increase dramatically as the standard deviation does when an outlier enters into the computations. Figure A21-5 compares the MAD to the standard deviation in a sequential sampling experiment; it is both smaller and less erratic than the standard deviation because the deviations from the mean are not increased by squaring them as the standard deviation formula (A21-3) does.

FIG. A21-5 Sequential values of the standard deviation and mean absolute deviation from population with infinite variance. (From Eugene F. Fama, "The Behavior of Stock Prices," *Journal of Business*, January 1965, p. 96.)

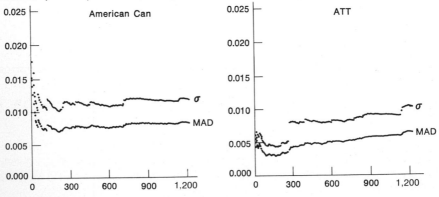

Stable Paretian Distribution

Drs. Mandelbrot and Fama suggested that the relative-frequency distributions of returns were a particular form of the stable, nonnormal distribution which is a member of a family four-parameter distributions. This distribution can assume many forms as the parameters vary. The normal, the Cauchy, the t distribution with one degree of freedom, and other distributions are merely special cases of this four-parameter distribution. The distribution is called a *Paretian distribution* because the tails of the distribution follow the law of Pareto. The four parameters of the Paretian distribution are α, β, γ, and δ.

The parameter α is called the characteristic exponent of the Paretian distribution. The characteristic exponent varies in the range $0 < \alpha \leqslant 2$ with the height of the tails of the distribution. When $\alpha = 2$, the tails asymptotically approach the horizontal axis, and the distribution has a finite variance.[10] The normal distribution, for example, is a Paretian distribution with $\alpha = 2$.

The parameter β is an index of skewness. This skewness parameter varies in the range $-1 \leqslant \beta \leqslant +1$ with $\beta = 0$ for a symmetric distribution such as the normal distribution. The parameter δ is a location parameter for the Paretian distribution. When $\alpha > 1$ and $\beta = 0$, then δ is the mean, mode, or median of the distribution.

The fourth parameter γ defines the scale of a Paretian distribution. When $\alpha = 2$ (as it does for the normal distribution), γ is one-half the variance. When $\alpha < 2$, the distribution has an infinite variance, but γ still assumes a finite value which varies with the wideness of the distribution. Table A21-1 shows the values these parameters assume for several well-known distributions. Empirically estimated parameters for the distribution of rates of return are shown under the heading "Empirical returns."

In Fig. A21-4 the dotted line outlines the form of the actual distribution of rates of return which is observed empirically. The normal distribution of returns furnishes only an approximation of this Paretian distribution of returns, some researchers believe.[11]

Westerfield's Subordinated Normal Distribution

Although he accepts the fact that *daily* stock price changes tend to be distributed according to the leptokurtic distribution with an infinite variance suggested by Fama, Prof. Randolph Westerfield has suggested that short-term stock price changes are, in fact, distributed normally if time is defined

---

[10] In the (x,y) plane a curve asymptotically approaches the x axis if it gets closer and closer to the x axis the further away from the origin it goes (for example, $y = c/x$). Asymptotes get constantly nearer but never actually reach the line they are approaching.

[11] Eugene F. Fama, op cit.

TABLE A21-1 VARIOUS FORMS OF PARETIAN DISTRIBUTION

Paretian parameter		Normal	Empirical returns†	Cauchy
α	Characteristic exponent	2	1.75	1
β	Skewness parameter	0	0	0
γ	Scale parameter	Half of variance	$\left(\dfrac{f.72 - f.28}{1.654}\right)^{.57}$	Semi-inter-quartile range
δ	Location parameter	Mean	Mean	Mean

† $f.72$ denotes the 72 percent fractile.

correctly.[12] Westerfield views stock prices as being generated in "operational-time" changes, but not necessarily according to calendar-time advances. He argued that the economic variable that is observable and that closely approximates *operational time* is a stock's trading volume. More precisely, Westerfield hypothesizes that every time a piece of new information arrives in the market which causes a change in some security's value, it tends to result in security trading. Stock prices, Westerfield maintains, are changed by such trading activity rather than by the mere passage of trading days.

To test his hypothesis, Westerfield estimated a normally distributed stock price–generating process in which the stock price changes are adjusted for trading volume. He used several years of daily price observations on a sample of NYSE stocks. The tests showed that stock prices fit this subordinated normal generating process better than they fit Fama's Paretian distribution. Thus, if the investor views time operationally in terms of stock trading volume (which most researchers do implicitly by not observing weekends, when the markets are closed to trading), stock prices are normally distributed.

A21-2 INDEPENDENCE OF SECURITY PRICE CHANGES

It will be recalled that the successive values in a random walk must be (1) identically distributed according to some stable distribution, and (2) independent of preceding or subsequent observations. It has been explained that short-term rates of return are distributed according to a stable symmetric distribution. But, in order for rates of return to conform to the random-

[12] Randolph Westerfield, "Price Change and Volume Relationships and the Distribution of Common Stock Price Changes," R. L. White Working Paper 6–73, 1973.

walk model, they must also be independent; that is, the rates of price change and rates of return for a security must not possess any detectable cycle or other pattern.

Next, some of the tests used to determine whether the rates of return from security price changes are a statistically independent series of numbers are examined. Of course, if these rates of return are independent, two conclusions may be drawn. First, a finding of perfect statistical independence will fulfill the requirements to classify the percentage changes of security prices as a random walk. Second, if the percentage changes in security prices are perfectly independent, then they are random. As a result, technical analysis will not be worth performing. If security price *changes* are merely a series of random numbers, charting security prices will not be worth the effort because the result will not enable the chartist to earn a rate of return from short-run trading in excess of the return achieved with a naive buy-and-hold strategy. Various statistical procedures are reviewed below in order to determine if rates of return and rates of price change are statistically independent.

Serial Correlation: a Test for Independence

Serial correlation is one of the many statistical tools used to measure dependence of successive numbers in a series. It has been widely used to measure possible dependence in security prices' rates of change. The linear regression model shown in Eq. (A21-5) is the model for which the correlation coefficient is determined when measuring serial correlation in rates of return.

$$r_{t+k} = a + br_t + e_t \tag{A21-5}$$

where r_t is the rate of return during the tth period (that is, day, week, or year) as measured by Eq. (A21-1) or (A21-2); r_{t+k} is the rate of return on the

FIG. A21-6 Cyclical rates of return.

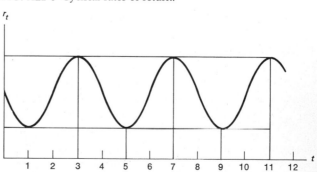

same security k periods later; k is called the lag; e_t is a random error which averages zero; and a and b are least-squares regression coefficients.[13] The correlation coefficient for model (A21-5) is the serial correlation coefficient for a k-period lag. A simple graphical explanation should make this clearer.

Figure A21-6 is a graph of a time series of rates of return for some hypothetical security. These rates of return conform to a perfectly repetitive four-period cycle. If the lagged regression model (A21-5) is fitted to the data graphed in Fig. A21-6, the serial correlations (denoted ρ) will vary with the lag. For a four-period ($k = 4$) lag, the data graphed in Fig. A21-6 will yield a perfect positive correlation ($\rho_4 = +1$), indicating the existence of a four-period perfectly repetitive cycle. For a two-period lag, a perfectly negative serial correlation ($\rho_2 = -1$) will result, indicating that rates of return two periods apart move inversely. For a one-period lag ($k = 1$), zero serial correlation ($\rho_0 = 0$) will result, indicating that rates of return from adjoining periods move inversely half the time and directly the other half. The data would thus indicate that no pattern of dependence can be detected for $k = 1$; but for two- and four-period lags, complete dependence is implied by their correlations.

When performing serial correlation tests, the analyst tries all possible lags which may exist. For example, Table A21-2 shows the serial correlation coefficients Fama found for each of the 30 securities in the Dow Jones Industrial Average for lags from 1 to 10 days' length (that is, $k = 1, 2, 3, 4, 5, 6, 7, 8, 9, 10$). It will be noted that few of the serial correlation coefficients in Table A21-2 are significantly different from zero.[14] Fama and others have used serial correlation to test many different securities and many different lags. None of these studies has detected any significant serial correlation in rates of return or security prices.

If rates of return were calculated using long-enough differencing intervals (for example, one-period returns from 5-year periods), then positive serial correlation of returns would emerge owing to the upward trend in the market. But the so-called random-walk theory applies only to short-run rates of return from which speculative traders and technical analysts try to profit. The theory does not deny the existence of a long-run upward trend in security prices; it requires only that short-run price movements be random. The data reveal that short-run price changes and rates of return are not serially correlated. In essence, this means there is not a significant cycle or pattern in security price changes that repeats itself or that can be used to

---

[13] Correct measurement of the serial correlation coefficient which is associated with regression equation (A21-5) is only possible if var(r_t) is constant over the period under examination, that is, homoscedasticity.

[14] Correlation coefficients more than 1.96 standard errors from zero are significantly different from zero at the .05 level of significance if the underlying distribution is normal. Such coefficients are noted with a dagger in Table A21-2.

TABLE A21-2 DAILY SERIAL CORRELATION COEFFICIENTS FOR LAG $k = 1, 2, \ldots, 10$

Stock	Lag (1)	(2)	(3)	(4)	(5)	(6)	(7)	(8)	(9)	(10)
Allied Chemical	.017	−.042	.007	−.001	.027	.004	−.017	−.026	−.017	−.007
Alcoa	.118†	.038	−.014	.022	−.022	.009	.017	.007	−.001	−.033
American Can	−.087†	−.024	.034	−.065†	−.017	−.006	.015	.025	−.047	−.040
A.T.&T.	−.039	−.097†	.000	.026	.005	−.005	.002	.027	−.014	.007
American Tobacco	.111†	−.109†	−.060†	−.065†	.007	−.010	.011	.046	.039	.041
Anaconda	.067†	−.061†	−.047	−.002	.000	−.038	.009	.016	−.014	−.056
Bethlehem Steel	.013	−.065†	.009	.021	−.053	−.098†	−.010	.004	−.002	−.021
Chrysler	.012	−.066†	−.016	−.007	−.015	.009	.037	.056†	−.044	.021
Du Pont	.013	−.033	.060†	.027	−.002	−.047	.020	.011	−.034	.001
Eastman Kodak	.025	.014	−.031	.005	−.022	.012	.007	.006	.008	.002
General Electric	.011	−.038	−.021	.031	−.001	.000	−.008	.014	−.002	−.010
General Foods	.061†	−.003	.045	.002	−.015	−.052	−.006	−.014	−.024	−.017
General Motors	−.004	−.056†	−.037	−.008	−.038	−.006	.019	.006	−.016	.009
Goodyear	−.123†	.017	−.044	.043	−.002	−.003	.035	.014	−.015	.007
International Harvester	−.017	−.029	−.031	.037	−.052	−.021	−.001	.003	−.046	−.016
International Nickel	.096†	−.033	−.019	.020	.027	.059†	−.038	−.008	−.016	.034
International Paper	.046	−.011	−.058†	−.053†	.049	−.003	−.025	−.019	−.003	−.021
Johns Manville	.006	−.038	−.027	−.023	−.029	−.080†	.040	.018	−.037	.029
Owens Illinois	−.021	−.084†	−.047	.068†	.086†	−.040	.011	−.040	.067†	−.043
Procter & Gamble	.099†	−.009	−.008	.009	−.015	.022	.012	−.012	−.022	−.021
Sears	.097†	.026	.028	.025	.005	−.054	−.006	−.010	−.008	−.009
Standard Oil (Calif.)	.025	−.030	−.051†	−.025	−.047	−.034	−.010	.072†	−.049†	−.035
Standard Oil (N.J.)	.008	−.116†	.016	.014	−.047	−.018	−.022	−.026	−.073†	.081†
Swift & Co.	−.004	−.015	−.010	.012	.057†	.012	−.043	.014	.012	.001
Texaco	.094†	−.049	−.024	−.018	−.017	−.009	.031	.032	−.013	.008
Union Carbide	.107†	−.012	.040	.046	−.036	−.034	.003	−.008	−.054	−.037
United Aircraft	.014	−.033	−.022	−.047	−.067†	−.053	.046	.037	.015	−.019
U.S. Steel	.040	−.074†	.014	.011	−.012	−.021	.041	.037	−.021	−.044
Westinghouse	−.027	−.022	−.036	−.003	.000	−.054†	−.020	.013	−.014	−.008
Woolworth	.028	−.016	.015	.014	.007	−.039	−.013	.003	−.088†	−.008

† Coefficient is twice its computed standard error.
Source: Eugene F. Fama, "The Behavior of Stock Market Prices," *Journal of Business,* January 1965, p. 72.

predict future security prices. The simple linear model underlying the serial correlation tests indicates that successive security price changes tend to behave like a series of random numbers. However, other more complicated patterns may exist.

Runs Test

A runs test is a statistical tool used to detect the presence of occasional nonrandom trends in a series of numbers. For testing security prices, a *run* can be defined as a sequence of price changes of the same sign. Table A21-3 shows how runs are determined from a series of daily closing prices. There are 12 price changes between the 13 successive security prices p_t shown in the table. There are three runs of positive changes, one run of zero change, and two runs of negative changes for a total of six runs.

   A runs test is performed by comparing the number of runs in the data with the number of runs which would be present in a sample of random numbers. It is possible to determine the number of total runs, the number of positive-change runs, the number of zero-change runs, and the number of negative-change runs which can be expected in a series of random numbers of any length.[15] Then if the runs which were actually found in the data are significantly different (that is, either too few or too many) from the numbers which are expected from truly random numbers, it is inferred that the successive changes are dependent. Table A21-4 shows some of the results of a study of the 30 stocks in the DJIA. About 1,400 daily stock prices from 1957 to 1962 were analyzed for each stock. Since the actual number of runs was not significantly different from the number of runs expected if the

---

[15] Eugene F. Fama, op. cit., pp. 74–80. Fama explains the runs tests and gives the formulas.

TABLE A21-3 DETERMINING RUNS IN A TIME SERIES OF HYPOTHETICAL SECURITY PRICES

Time period (t)	Security prices (p_t)	$\Delta p_t = p_{t+1} - p_t$	Runs	Type run
1	67	+1	1	Positive
2	68	−5		
3	63	−3	2	Negative
4	60	−3		
5	57	0	3	Zero
6	57	0		
7	57	+3	4	Positive
8	60	+1		
9	61	−1	5	Negative
10	60	+2		
11	62	+1	6	Positive
12	63	+2		
13	65			

TABLE A21-4 RUNS ANALYSIS BY SIGN (DAILY CHANGES)

Stock	Positive			Negative			No change		
	Actual	Expected	Actual-expected	Actual	Expected	Actual-expected	Actual	Expected	Actual-expected
Allied Chemical	286	290.1	− 4.1	294	290.7	3.3	103	102.2	0.8
Alcoa	265	264.4	0.6	262	266.5	− 4.5	74	70.1	3.9
American Can	289	290.2	− 1.2	285	284.6	0.4	156	155.2	0.8
A.T.&T.	290	291.2	− 1.2	285	285.3	− 0.3	82	80.5	1.5
American Tobacco	296	300.2	− 4.2	295	294.0	1.0	109	105.8	3.2
Anaconda	271	272.9	− 1.9	276	278.8	− 2.8	88	83.3	4.7
Bethlehem Steel	282	286.4	− 4.4	300	294.6	5.4	127	128.0	−1.0
Chrysler	417	414.9	2.1	421	421.1	− 0.1	89	91.0	−2.0
Du Pont	293	300.3	− 7.3	305	299.2	5.8	74	72.5	1.5
Eastman Kodak	306	308.6	− 2.6	312	308.7	3.3	60	60.7	−0.7
General Electric	404	404.5	− 0.5	401	404.7	− 3.7	113	108.8	4.2
General Foods	346	340.8	5.2	320	331.3	−11.3	133	126.9	6.1
General Motors	340	342.7	2.7	339	340.3	− 1.3	153	149.0	4.0
Goodyear	294	291.9	2.1	292	293.0	− 1.0	95	96.1	−1.1
International Harvester	303	300.1	2.9	301	298.8	2.2	116	121.1	−5.1
International Nickel	312	307.0	5.0	296	301.9	− 5.9	96	95.1	0.9
International Paper	322	330.2	8.2	338	333.2	4.8	102	98.6	3.4
Johns Manville	293	292.6	0.4	296	293.5	2.5	96	98.9	−2.9
Owens Illinois	297	293.7	3.3	295	291.2	3.8	121	128.1	−7.1
Procter & Gamble	343	346.4	− 3.4	342	340.3	1.7	141	139.3	1.7
Sears	291	289.3	1.7	265	271.3	− 6.3	144	139.4	4.6
Standard Oil (Calif.)	406	417.9	−11.9	427	416.6	10.4	139	137.5	1.5
Standard Oil (N.J.)	272	277.3	− 5.3	281	277.9	3.1	135	132.8	2.2
Swift & Co.	354	354.3	− 0.3	355	356.9	− 1.9	169	166.8	2.2
Texaco	266	265.6	0.4	258	263.6	− 5.6	76	70.8	5.2
Union Carbide	266	268.1	− 2.1	265	265.6	− 0.6	64	61.3	2.7
United Aircraft	281	280.4	0.6	282	282.2	− 0.2	98	98.4	−0.4
U.S. Steel	292	293.5	− 1.5	296	295.2	0.8	63	62.3	0.7
Westinghouse	359	361.3	− 2.3	364	362.1	1.9	106	105.6	0.4
Woolworth	349	348.7	0.3	350	345.9	4.1	148	152.4	−4.4

Source: Eugene F. Fama, "The Behavior of Stock Market Prices," *Journal of Business*, January 1965, p. 79.

series were random, the test implies that stock price changes are random. Runs analyses of other securities by other analysts have also indicated that security price changes are a series of independent numbers.

Testing Independence with Filter Rules

An x percent *filter rule*, defined in Sec. 21-3, is a useful test.

If the price of a security rises at least x percent, buy and hold the security until its price drops at least x percent from a subsequent high; when the price decreases x percent or more, liquidate any long position and assume a short position until the price rises at least x percent.

By varying the value of x, an infinite number of filter rules can be tested. If stock price changes are a series of independent random numbers, filter rules should not yield more return than a naive buy-and-hold strategy.

Several analysts have applied filter rules to series of historical daily prices for various securities. The historical data were stored in the memory of a computer. It was then programmed to simulate trading activity using many different filters. Filters as small as $\frac{1}{2}$ of 1 percent ($x = .005$) and as large as 50 percent ($x = .5$) were used. Each study showed that the filter rules were less profitable than a naive buy-and-hold strategy. If brokers' commissions are ignored, a few of the filter rules were able to earn a rate of return as high as 15 percent per year, a figure above what could have been achieved using a naive buy-and-hold strategy during that period. But the vast majority of the filter rules earned very poor returns (that is, less than could be obtained with a naive buy-and-hold strategy) or incurred losses. Many buy-and-sell transactions are generated by some filter rules (namely, $x = .005$). To perform a realistic test of a filter rule, sales commissions must be deducted to determine the *net* profitability of a trading technique. When allowance was made for sales commissions, the filter rules earned even worse returns. No filter rule earned a rate of return above what a naive buy-and-hold strategy earned, and most filters resulted in losses after deduction of the commissions they generated.

Some studies of filter rules figured the rate of return from long positions and the return from short positions separately. Using a filter rule to select short positions nearly always resulted in losses even before allowance was made for commissions. Sometimes the long positions initiated by a filter rule earned positive returns. In fact, a $\frac{1}{2}$ percent filter ($x = .005$) resulted in an annual return before commissions as high as 20 percent, according to one study. But after sales commissions were deducted, a higher return could have been achieved using a naive buy-and-hold strategy. In general, filter rules do not earn net rates of return as high as those that could be gained with a naive buy-and-hold strategy.

TABLE A21-5 SIMPLIFIED RANDOM WALK IN RETURNS

Period (t)	0	1	2	3	4
Possible outcomes (and their probabilities)	$E(r_0)$	$E(r_0) + 1(\frac{1}{2})$ $E(r_0) - 1(\frac{1}{2})$	$E(r_0) + 2(\frac{1}{4})$ $E(r_0)$ $(\frac{1}{2})$ $E(r_0) - 2(\frac{1}{4})$	$E(r_0) + 3(\frac{1}{8})$ $E(r_0) + 1(\frac{3}{8})$ $E(r_0) - 1(\frac{3}{8})$ $E(r_0) - 3(\frac{1}{8})$	. . . .
$E(r_t)$	$E(r_0)$	$E(r_1) = E(r_0)$	$E(r_2) = E(r_0)$	$E(r_3) = E(r_0)$	. . .
var (r_t)	0	1	2	3	4

Simplified Numerical Example of Random Walk

Thus far, the notions of a stable probability distribution and statistical independence have been developed in an effort to clarify the nature of a random walk. Before reaching conclusions, let us consider a simplified random-walk numerical example to pull these ideas together.

Imagine a security whose rates of return either increase or decrease by one percentage point each period with equal probability. Denote the expected return of this security as $E(r_0)$. Table A21-5 traces the course of all possible outcomes over several periods.

In this table the probability of any outcome is shown in parentheses following that outcome. Examination of the table will reveal the following characteristics: (1) The expected return is constant at $E(r_0)$ in every period and for every differencing interval. Thus, the expected return is stationary as the future unfolds and actual returns fluctuate around $E(r_0)$. (2) The variance of returns tends to increase with the length of the differencing period. (3) The probability distribution of possible returns is stationary although the actual returns vary randomly. That is, the actual rates of return over time are a series of independent values which can be assigned probabilities but cannot be predicted in advance.

The example shown in Table A21-5 is a random walk in rates of return because the returns are independent and identically distributed. An examination of actual historical rates of return will reveal that characteristics 1 and 2 above also occur in the empirical data, and that characteristic 3 is a rough approximation of the Paretian distribution to which the empirical data seem to conform. Thus, this simple random-walk model is a good first approximation of the way rates of return actually perform.

Conclusions Regarding Independence

Some of the simplest and most common tests used to determine the independence of series of security price changes and rates of return have been presented. It was shown that the data are not *perfectly* statistically independent in every case. A few cases were found (namely, small serial correlations, actual runs not exactly equal to expected runs, and a few filter rules which earned a small profit before commissions) where variations from perfect statistical independence existed. These cases of dependence were found to be very slight; no profit could be earned from a knowledge of these small variations from pure independence. Nevertheless, a mathematical statistician would not say that rates of return are perfectly independent over time. Therefore, rates of return are not perfectly described by a rigorously defined random-walk model.

A practical business person need not adhere to the rigorous conventions of the mathematical statistician — our criteria are simpler. As long as rates of return are sufficiently independent so that profit cannot be increased by using whatever statistical dependency exists, it may be concluded that rates of return are independent for business purposes. Thus, as a first approximation, we may say rates of return follow a random walk as far as business people need be concerned.

The random-walk conclusion casts serious doubts on the efficacy of technical analysis. It will be recalled that technical analysts' methods are largely based upon statistical dependency and patterns in security price changes. There is little doubt that some of the patterns described by technical analysts actually exist; such patterns can also be found in series of random numbers or in ink blots. Also, some of the market indicators used by chartists (for example, the confidence index) are actually correlated with security market indices. But technical tools *do not furnish dependable leading indicators;* they are frequently concurrent or lagging indicators or they fail to formulate the proper signal at all. The patterns, moreover, are ambiguous. Different technicians interpret the same chart to mean different things. Furthermore, the charts issue erroneous signals about as frequently as they issue correct signals. The few studies which have been published in support of technical analysis are weak. The evidence presented by the random-walk advocates is more voluminous and more scientific than evidence presented by the technical analysts. A reasonable person who objectively studied the existing literature would most likely conclude that technical analysis tools were (in some cases) crude attempts to measure risk or (in most cases) not worth performing at all.

A21-3 MARTINGALE MODELS

The random walk is a mathematical model in which a series is both independent and identically distributed; it is a special, narrowly defined case of a martingale process. A martingale does not require that successive members of the series be either independent or identically distributed; it is a process for which the conditional expectation of the $(n + 1)$st value equals the nth value, given some set of data.[16]

Symbolically, rates of return are a martingale if Eq. (A21-6) is not violated.

$$E(_jr_{t+1} \mid _jr_t, _jr_{t-1}, \ldots, _jr_{t-n}) = {_jr_t} \tag{A21-6}$$

where $_jr_t$ is the return for security j at period t. Equation (A21-6) is a symbolic representation of the weakly efficient markets hypothesis. It says that knowledge of all historical returns of some security suggests only that the next period's return is expected to equal the last period's return.

A stronger form of the martingale exists if Eq. (A21-7) is not violated.

$$E(_jr_{t+1} \mid N_t) = {_jr_t} \tag{A21-7}$$

where N_t denotes all the public news and information which existed at period t. This is the semistrong efficient markets hypothesis. Equation (A21-7) implies that all available news is already reflected in prices. Equations (A21-6) and (A21-7) imply that future returns are independent of past data, but they do not imply complete independence of the entire series of returns.[17]

Security prices are a *submartingale* since they drift upward over time. Equation (A21-8) defines the submartingale process followed by most security prices.

$$E(_jp_{t+1} \mid _jp_t, _jp_{t-1}, \ldots, _jp_{t-n}) > {_jp_t} \tag{A21-8}$$

where $_jp_t$ denotes the price of security j at period t.

In contrast to the martingale, the random-walk model is much more narrowly defined. Rates of return are a random walk if Eq. (A21-9) is not violated.

$$f(_jr_{t+1} \mid _jr_t, _jr_{t-1}, \ldots, _jr_{t-n}) = f(_jr_t) \tag{A21-9}$$

where $f(_jr_t)$ denotes the probability distribution of returns for security j at period t. Equation (A21-9) implies Eq. (A21-6). Furthermore, (A21-9) implies that rates of return are independent and identically distributed according to some stationary distribution.

Technically speaking, Eq. (A21-9) is not true because the percentage price changes for securities which are not perfectly independent—only nearly so. Equations (A21-6) and (A21-8) are true, however.

[16] William Feller, *An Introduction to Probability Theory and Its Implications,* vol. II (New York: Wiley, 1966). See pp. 210–212 for a more rigorous discussion of martingales.
[17] John T. Emery, "The Information Content of Daily Market Indicators," *Journal of Financial and Quantitative Analysis,*" March 1973, pp. 183–190.

The distinction between (A21-6) and (A21-9) is not great where stock price changes are concerned. It took well-qualified mathematicians and economists several years to determine that (A21-6) and (A21-8) were true and that (A21-9) was an overstatement. But, when using language precisely, it is best to refer to security prices as a submartingale and rates of return as a martingale. The random-walk term is a slight exaggeration.

Twenty-two

About "Beating the Market"

Everyone has heard stories implying that some investor "beat the market." For example, a friend or relative may have bragged of easy profits earned in a series of security trades, or a securities sales representative may have innocently related a story or two about someone who got rich quickly from investing in securities. Some mutual fund advertisements mysteriously refer to the advantages of "expert" or "professional" portfolio management. Books have even been written with such suggestive titles as *Get Rich Quick, How to Make a Million in the Stock Market*, ad nauseam. The purpose of this chapter is to examine some schemes with which an investor might hope to beat the market or "get something for nothing."

There are far too many beat-the-market schemes to be reviewed in one book. Most of these schemes are so ridiculous that just a moment spent in objective consideration will reveal flaws in them. The following schemes are examples which fall into this group:

1 Place all buy orders 50 cents below the current market price and all sell orders 50 cents above the current market price. Because of the erratic fluctuations which occur in security prices, this plan is supposed to increase profits. Supposedly, an erratic fluctuation will occur in many of these buy and sell cases which will touch off the orders at the more advantageous price and thus increase profits.

2 Buy stocks whose names have certain words (for example, "General") in them. Supposedly, the investing public has a preference for certain names which causes firms possessing the name (for example, General Motors, General Tire, General Foods, General Electric) to enjoy strong demand and large capital gains.

3 Buy bonds which have high coupon rates in preference to bonds with low coupon rates. This dubious axiom seems to indicate that some people think the coupon is the total income received by the bondholder.

4 It is better to buy in the morning and sell in the afternoon. Supposedly, the market tends to rise as the day progresses.

5 Stocks whose prices have just attained previous high levels are likely to experience further price rises because "resistance" is gone. The folklore behind this scheme is that as a stock's price rises to its previous high, all investors who were selling as the price rose above their initial purchase price have liquidated their positions and the current supply of shares for sale is exhausted, so any demand must raise prices to new highs. An opposite but symmetric argument suggests that stocks at low prices should fall further because of a lack of "support."

6 Only stocks which have long, unbroken records of paying cash dividends should be purchased. Since these stocks will be on the "legal lists" of assets which some institutions can own, they are supposed to be intrinsically better investments.

An infinite number of such simple-minded rules, ideas, and schemes to beat the market could be listed. Diligent research effort can almost surely turn up periods of time during which each one of the ideas mentioned would have actually beaten the market too. Therefore some of the older, more popular beat-the-market schemes which seem to command a degree of respect in some financial circles should be examined analytically. However, before delving into this analysis, we should explicitly state a teaching point that perceptive readers have probably already detected by reading between the lines. This teaching point, sometimes lightly referred to as the Free Lunch Theorem, is stated thus:

Free Lunch Theorem
There is no such thing as a free lunch.

Impulsive people sometimes react to the Free Lunch Theorem by reporting a free lunch which was purchased for them by some salesperson from whom they had never bought anything. However, after they are reminded of (1) the time they spent patiently listening to the sales pitch, which has an imputed value of at least $2 an hour they could have earned doing menial labor (and much more for most college graduates), and of (2) the intrusion on their privacy which the salesperson wrought on them through a series of follow-up phone calls, the hasty respondents usually concede that they paid dearly for what they initially thought was going to be a free lunch. At this point they are usually ready to reluctantly accept the so-called Generalized Free Lunch Theorem.

Generalized Free Lunch Theorem
You cannot expect to get something for nothing.

Some sublimely naive person usually counters the Generalized Free Lunch Theorem with a story about the time he found a $20 bill on the sidewalk, with no one in sight to whom he might return it. From some such gratuitous example, it is suggested that sometimes it is possible to get something for nothing. Of course, the answer is that, while pieces of good luck do befall everyone, bad luck comes too. Thus, only the eternally simple-minded can continue to bank on "the luck of the draw" or some analogous "something for nothing" gimmick.

The study of economics suggests that money is made by doing work and taking carefully selected risks. Furthermore, the cruel truth of the matter is that making really big money evidently requires very hard work and involves the assumption of some terrifying risks. What can be done about all this, you may ask. The consensus of most intelligent, open-minded people is apparently that you can best deal with this problem by finding a job you like and getting to work. And if the job you pick is in investments management, one of the teaching points emphasized in this book is that you cannot expect to beat the market—that is what the efficient markets tests in Chap. 21 were designed to prove. But in case doubts remain, the rest of this chapter will analyze the folly of a few of the more "respectable" beat-the-market schemes which are sometimes discussed.

22-1 "BEATING THE MARKET" DEFINED

If an investor invests X dollars in some asset and later liquidates that asset at a price in excess of X dollars, his gain does not necessarily mean he beat the market. The money could always have been placed in an insured savings account where, at no risk, it would have increased in value too. As a minimum, investors must earn more than the riskless rate of interest to say that they beat the market or to justify their making an investment involving risk. Any investment which earns less than the riskless rate of interest is dominated (in risk-return space) by the riskless rate of return on a U.S. Treasury bond or an insured savings account.

A Fair Standard of Comparison

It is clear that a risky investment which returns less than a savings account is nothing to brag about. However, we still have not defined a standard of comparison against which we may judge investment performance. At the very least, it seems fair to require that a person's investment must outperform some naive buy-and-hold strategy before that person is entitled to boast of having outperformed the market. More specifically, investors should compare the return of their investments with the investment opportunities open to a completely naive investment strategy which involves *equal risks.*

Any naive investor can always pick stocks from the financial page by throwing a dart. Picking stocks with a dart implies that every security has an equal chance of being selected (assuming the dart is thrown without aiming). The problem with using some stock market index composed of stocks which were selected with a dart or some other random method is that luck is involved in the selection of the sample. One standard of comparison which would avoid the problems associated with the luck of the draw (that is, sampling error in selecting a random sample which is representative of the whole population of stocks) is to construct an index containing *all* securities in *equal* proportions. Such an index would represent what the average dart thrower could expect to obtain by selecting a random portfolio with an unaimed dart (so all assets have an equal probability of being selected). It seems fair to say that any investment which does not outperform what the average dart thrower could achieve is nothing to brag about.

The Study by Lorie and Fisher

Two finance professors at the University of Chicago's Center for Research in Security Prices have constructed an "average dart thrower's" portfolio. Drs. Lawrence Fisher and James Lorie supervised the project. Monthly price and dividend data were gathered for every security listed on the New York Stock Exchange (NYSE) from 1926 to 1965. The data were then processed by a computer.

A computer program was written to prepare a hypothetical portfolio on January 1 of each year which contained every stock on the NYSE in equal proportions. That is, if there were 1,250 stocks listed in a given year, each stock was given a weight of 1/1,250 in that year's hypothetical portfolio. The program was written to reinvest all dividends in the issuing shares at the time they were paid. Then, on December 31 of each year, the hypothetical portfolio was completely liquidated, and that year's rate of return for the average dart thrower was calculated. The computer program then constructed a new portfolio for January 1 of the next year, giving equal weight to each security. The program repeated this process of constructing portfolios and calculating their annual returns for every year from 1926 to 1965 and every combination of years in that period.

Table 22-1 shows the annual rates of return which Lorie and Fisher figured the average dart thrower could expect to earn before taxes.[1] Commissions resulting from the purchase of the hypothetical portfolios were deducted in calculating these returns, but selling commissions were ig-

---

[1] Lawrence Fisher and James Lorie, "Rates of Return on Investments in Common Stock: The Year-by-Year Record, 1926–1965," *Journal of Business,* July 1968, p. 7, table 1, part A. Lorie and Fisher also published the returns for different tax brackets with and without reinvestments of dividends and under different assumptions about sales commissions in this study.

nored. Thus, the returns represent what could be earned from a naive buy-and-hold strategy.

Throughout this book, references to naive buy-and-hold strategy or a dart-throwing strategy may be interpreted to mean the Lorie-Fisher data shown in Table 22-1. These data represent a fair standard of comparison against which investments with the same risk as the average dart thrower's portfolio may be compared to determine if they beat the market. The Lorie-Fisher data represent a portfolio of NYSE stocks which has a level of risk and rate of return which should not be difficult to beat by a skilled portfolio manager.

Risk and Return Must Both Be Considered

In order to make definitive statements about beating the market, both *return* and *risk* must be considered. The Lorie-Fisher naive buy-and-hold strategy portfolio (denoted P) lies in only one risk-class. As Fig. 22-1 shows, portfolio P has more risk and less return than the market portfolio M on the efficient frontier and the capital market line (CML). Portfolio P can be used to generate a good standard of comparison against which any risky portfolio may be compared. The ray RPZ emerging from the constant rate R and passing through portfolio P is the dotted line in Fig. 22-1. This dotted line is a good standard of comparison. It represents portfolios which could be constructed from the average dart-thrower's portfolio and borrowing or lending at rate R. Moreover, it is easier to obtain than the CML.

Any portfolio lying above the dotted line RPZ has *beaten the market.* That is, for the amount of risk they bear, portfolios lying above RPZ earn higher returns than could be expected by selecting a portfolio from stocks in that risk-class with a dart. Portfolios lying below the dotted line RPZ earned poorer returns than would be expected from a portfolio selected by throwing a dart to select securities in the same risk-class as the portfolio being evaluated. In other words, the naive buy-and-hold strategy combined with borrowing or lending outperformed portfolios lying below RPZ. This is the definition of beating the market which is used throughout this book. Next, let us examine some widely used practices which some people believe enable them to beat the market or to get something for nothing.

FIG. 22-1 A standard of comparison for determining if an investment "beats the market."

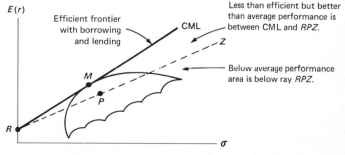

TABLE 22-1 RATES OF RETURN FROM THE STUDY BY FISHER AND LORIE

To	From 1/26	12/26	12/27	12/28	12/29	From 12/30	12/31	12/32	12/33	12/34
12/26	− 1.6									
12/27	15.3	30.0								
12/28	23.9	37.7	45.5							
12/29	7.8	9.6	0.1	−30.0						
12/30	− 2.3	− 3.5	−13.0	−31.7	−37.2					
12/31	−11.1	−13.5	−21.7	−36.3	−40.8	−47.8				
12/32	−11.0	−12.7	−19.0	−30.3	−32.1	−31.0	−11.1			
12/33	− 2.7	− 3.2	− 7.7	−15.6	−11.8	− 1.3	36.9	108.4		
12/34	− 1.2	− 1.6	− 5.2	−11.3	− 7.0	2.4	28.2	55.0	13.8	
12/35	2.2	2.1	− 0.8	− 5.7	− 0.5	9.3	32.9	53.5	31.2	50.4
12/36	6.6	5.5	3.1	− 0.4	5.3	15.3	37.5	54.5	40.9	56.8
12/37	0.5	0.1	− 2.3	− 6.2	− 2.8	3.3	16.1	23.1	8.2	6.6
12/38	2.8	2.5	0.4	− 2.9	0.9	7.0	18.7	25.1	12.9	12.4
12/39	2.6	2.3	0.3	− 2.6	0.9	6.0	15.7	20.5	10.1	9.0
12/40	1.9	1.6	− 0.2	− 3.0	0.2	4.7	13.0	16.9	7.9	6.4
12/41	1.2	0.9	− 0.8	− 3.3	− 0.5	3.5	10.8	13.8	5.8	4.2
12/42	2.0	1.9	0.4	− 1.9	0.9	4.8	11.6	14.3	7.2	6.0
12/43	3.5	3.6	2.2	0.2	3.1	7.2	13.8	16.5	10.2	9.7
12/44	4.6	4.7	3.5	1.7	4.7	8.7	15.2	17.9	12.3	12.0
12/45	6.3	6.5	5.5	3.9	7.0	11.3	17.6	20.4	15.4	15.5
12/46	5.5	5.7	4.7	3.2	6.0	9.9	15.6	18.0	13.3	13.1
12/47	5.3	5.6	4.6	3.1	5.8	9.3	14.6	16.8	12.4	12.1
12/48	5.1	5.2	4.2	2.8	5.2	8.5	13.5	15.5	11.3	11.0
12/49	5.7	5.8	4.9	3.6	6.0	9.1	13.8	15.7	11.7	11.5
12/50	6.5	6.7	5.9	4.6	7.0	10.2	14.9	16.7	12.9	12.8
12/51	6.9	7.1	6.4	5.1	7.5	10.6	15.1	16.7	13.1	13.1
12/52	7.0	7.2	6.5	5.3	7.6	10.5	14.8	16.4	13.0	13.0
12/53	6.6	6.3	6.1	5.0	7.1	9.8	13.9	15.3	12.2	12.1
12/54	6.1	8.2	7.6	6.4	8.7	11.4	15.5	17.0	14.0	14.1
12/55	8.4	8.6	8.0	6.9	9.2	11.9	15.9	17.4	14.5	14.6
12/56	8.5	8.7	8.1	7.0	9.2	11.8	15.7	17.1	14.4	14.4
12/57	7.8	7.9	7.3	6.3	8.3	10.7	14.3	15.5	12.9	12.9
12/58	8.8	9.0	8.4	7.5	9.5	11.9	15.5	16.7	14.3	14.4
12/59	8.9	9.1	8.5	7.6	9.7	12.1	15.6	16.8	14.4	14.5
12/60	8.8	9.0	8.3	7.5	9.4	11.6	14.9	16.1	13.9	13.9
12/61	9.3	9.5	8.9	8.1	9.9	12.2	15.4	16.6	14.4	14.5
12/62	8.6	8.8	8.2	7.3	9.1	11.2	14.3	15.3	13.2	13.3
12/63	8.9	9.1	8.5	7.7	9.5	11.6	14.6	15.6	13.5	13.6
12/64	9.1	9.3	8.8	7.9	9.6	11.6	14.5	15.6	13.6	13.7
12/65	9.3	9.5	9.0	8.2	10.0	12.0	14.9	15.9	13.9	14.0

Source: Lawrence Fisher and James Lorie, ''Rates of Return on Investments in Common Stock: The Year-by-Year Record, 1926–1965,'' *Journal of Business,* January 1968, p. II, pp. 296 and 297. (Continues on following three pages.)

TABLE 22-1 (*Continued*)

To	From 12/35	12/36	12/37	12/38	12/39	From 12/40	12/41	12/42	12/43	12/44
12/36	63.9									
12/37	−10.9	−46.0								
12/38	1.1	−16.2	30.7							
12/39	0.4	−11.2	12.9	−3.3						
12/40	− 1.1	− 9.8	6.3	−5.0	−9.9					
12/41	− 1.9	− 9.2	2.6	−5.5	−9.0	−10.2				
12/42	0.9	− 4.9	6.1	0.6	1.1	7.6	31.1			
12/43	5.5	0.9	12.3	9.4	12.1	22.2	47.1	56.7		
12/44	8.4	4.6	15.7	13.7	17.1	26.8	45.6	49.3	38.1	
12/45	12.4	9.3	20.3	19.4	23.7	33.6	51.4	55.4	50.1	59.8
12/46	10.2	7.2	16.3	15.0	17.8	24.2	34.8	34.5	26.0	20.2
12/47	9.4	6.7	14.7	13.6	15.5	20.3	27.5	26.3	18.9	13.2
12/48	8.4	5.8	12.7	11.7	13.3	17.0	22.5	20.8	14.2	9.1
12/49	9.1	6.8	13.3	12.3	13.9	17.3	22.2	20.8	15.2	11.4
12/50	10.6	8.5	14.8	14.1	15.6	19.0	23.5	22.4	17.9	15.0
12/51	11.0	9.0	14.8	14.1	15.6	18.6	22.6	21.6	17.7	15.2
12/52	11.0	9.0	14.5	13.8	15.1	17.9	21.5	20.4	16.8	14.5
12/53	10.2	8.3	13.3	12.5	13.7	16.1	19.3	18.1	14.8	12.5
12/54	12.2	10.5	15.5	14.8	16.2	18.7	21.9	21.0	18.2	16.4
12/55	12.7	11.1	15.9	15.2	16.6	18.8	21.8	21.1	18.6	16.9
12/56	12.6	11.1	15.6	15.1	16.2	18.2	20.8	20.2	17.9	16.4
12/57	11.2	9.7	13.9	13.2	14.2	15.9	18.3	17.5	15.1	13.6
12/58	12.7	11.3	15.5	15.0	16.0	17.8	20.2	19.4	17.3	16.0
12/59	12.8	11.5	15.6	15.0	16.0	17.6	19.9	19.1	17.1	15.8
12/60	12.3	11.1	14.8	14.2	15.1	16.6	18.7	17.9	15.9	14.6
12/61	13.0	11.8	15.4	15.0	15.8	17.3	19.3	18.5	16.5	15.4
12/62	11.8	10.7	14.0	13.5	14.3	15.6	17.3	16.5	14.6	13.5
12/63	12.2	11.0	14.3	13.8	14.6	15.8	17.4	16.7	14.9	13.9
12/64	12.4	11.3	14.4	14.0	14.7	15.8	17.4	16.7	15.0	14.0
12/65	12.6	11.6	14.6	14.2	14.9	16.0	17.5	16.9	15.4	14.4

TABLE 22-1 (*Continued*)

To	From 12/45	12/46	12/47	12/48	12/49	From 12/50	12/51	12/52	12/53	12/54
12/46	−9.9									
12/47	−4.4	−0.5								
12/48	−3.5	−1.0	−2.9							
12/49	1.9	5.4	8.2	19.3						
12/50	7.8	12.4	16.6	27.0	35.8					
12/51	9.4	13.3	16.4	23.1	35.8	14.9				
12/52	9.4	12.9	15.2	19.7	19.8	12.4	8.9			
12/53	7.9	10.5	12.1	15.0	13.7	7.5	3.5	−3.1		
12/54	12.5	15.5	17.7	21.3	21.6	17.9	18.5	22.8	54.8	
12/55	13.4	16.2	18.2	21.4	21.7	18.5	19.1	22.2	37.2	19.0
12/56	13.3	15.6	17.2	19.8	20.0	17.0	16.9	18.6	26.7	13.3
12/57	10.5	12.3	13.5	15.3	14.8	12.0	11.1	11.1	14.5	3.4
12/58	13.2	15.2	16.7	18.7	18.6	16.5	16.5	17.5	21.9	14.5
12/59	13.3	15.3	16.6	18.6	18.6	16.6	16.6	17.6	21.2	15.0
12/60	12.2	14.0	15.2	16.8	16.5	14.9	14.8	15.3	17.8	12.4
12/61	13.2	14.9	16.0	17.5	17.3	16.0	16.0	16.6	19.0	14.6
12/62	11.3	12.8	13.7	14.9	14.5	13.1	12.8	13.0	14.7	10.5
12/62	11.8	13.2	14.0	15.2	14.9	13.5	13.3	13.5	15.0	11.3
12/64	12.1	13.4	14.2	15.3	15.0	13.7	13.5	13.8	15.3	11.9
12/65	12.6	14.1	14.9	15.9	15.8	14.5	14.3	14.7	16.2	13.1

22-2 THE EFFECTS OF STOCK SPLITS AND STOCK DIVIDENDS

Many accountants, corporate directors, and executives believe that if their company pays a stock dividend or has a stock split, the firm will be worth more and/or its shareholders will be somehow wealthier. Furthermore, many investors feel that they are better off if a stock they own splits or has a stock dividend. In this section, we shall examine evidence which shows the error in these widely held notions. It will be seen that no one's wealth is changed by stock splits or stock dividends (except perhaps the accountant who gets paid to make the required bookkeeping entries).

In Chap. 9, the question of whether a corporation's dividend policy had any effect on the value of its shares was examined. The pure theory was not conclusive, but Modigliani and Miller did provide some cogent reasons to suppose that dividend *policy* (as measured by the payout ratio) is irrelevant in valuing a firm. Here we shall examine studies of the actual effects of various kinds of dividends. All these studies indicate that dividend *policy* is irrelevant; that is, that the investor's wealth is unchanged by stock dividends, stock splits, and the rate at which earnings are paid out in cash dividends. This does not mean that cash dividends do not change the price of a share of stock; quite the contrary is true. Rather, it will be shown that divi-

TABLE 22-1 (*Continued*)

To	From 12/55	12/56	12/57	12/58	12/59	From 12/60	12/61	12/62	12/63	12/64
12/56	6.5									
12/57	−3.7	−12.9								
12/58	13.0	17.4	57.9							
12/59	14.0	17.6	36.0	14.4						
12/60	11.2	13.1	21.9	6.4	−1.9					
12/61	13.9	16.1	23.7	13.6	12.9	27.6				
12/62	9.4	10.4	15.1	6.3	3.8	5.9	−13.3			
12/62	10.4	11.5	15.7	8.7	7.4	10.4	2.0	17.7		
12/64	11.2	12.3	16.2	10.4	9.7	12.8	7.6	18.5	16.3	
12/65	12.5	13.6	17.7	12.7	12.4	15.9	12.9	22.6	23.4	28.3

dend policy as opposed to cash dividends per se does not change the value of an investment.

Analysis of Stock Splits and Stock Dividends

To accountants and attorneys, stock splits are different from stock dividends, the difference being due to the treatment of the equity section of the balance sheet. With a stock split, the par value per share is decreased to reflect the splitting of the shares; the number of shares outstanding is simultaneously increased so as to leave the total amount in the capital account unchanged. With stock dividends, a portion of retained earnings equal to the value of the stock dividend is transferred from retained earnings to the capital account. Both adjustments are pure bookkeeping entries which leave total equity and total assets unchanged and hence have no real economic significance.

Many finance advisors do not distinguish between stock splits and stock dividends. They believe, for example, that a 100 percent stock dividend is equivalent to a 2 for 1 stock split. Either way, there are twice as many stock certificates outstanding, and each one is worth half as much, leaving the total value of the firm unchanged. In contrast, some investors and business executives believe that stock splits and stock dividends can increase the value of the firm. Let us examine some data on the subject.

The study which will be discussed here is based on a sample of 940 stock splits and stock dividends (in excess of 25 percent) which occurred between 1927 and 1959 on the NYSE.[2] In essence, the study asked if stock splits or stock dividends had any influence on investors' returns as defined in Eq. (22-1).

$$r = \frac{\text{capital gains or loss} + \text{dividends}}{\text{purchase price}} \tag{22-1}$$

The shares were all adjusted for the stock splits and stock dividends before the rates of return were calculated. This adjustment ensured that only actual changes in the investor's wealth would be measured rather than the meaningless price changes which are associated with a stock dividend or split. For example, if a 2 for 1 split or 100 percent stock dividend occurred, the share prices would be halved before the stock dividend or split (or doubled afterward) so that no changes in the investor's wealth would be attributed to it in calculating rates of return.

The numerical example below shows how a share of stock, originally selling for $100 per share, can fall to $50 per share owing to a 2 for 1 split or 100 percent stock dividend without changing the owner's 5 percent rate of return. The change in the unit of account (that is, the stock dividend or stock split) occurred between periods 2 and 3. Since the investor owns twice as many shares after the stock split but since each share has half the previous market price, the investor's wealth is unchanged. And the investor's income in this simple example is $5 of cash dividends per period per $100 of investment before and after the change in the unit of account, that is, a constant 5 percent rate of return.

Time period (t)	$t = 1$	$t = 2$	$t = 3$	$t = 4$
Market price per share	$100	$100	$50	$50
Cash dividend per share	$5	$5	$2.50	$2.50
Earnings per share	$10	$10	$5	$5
Number of shares held per $100 original investment	1	1	2	2
Rate of return per period	5%	5%	5%	5%

Characteristic Line Used to Analyze Dividends and Splits

In order to have a standard of comparison against which the rates of return may be evaluated, it is necessary to make adjustments for the differences in returns resulting from bull-market or bear-market swings in price. The characteristic line defined in Eq. (22-2) was calculated for each security studied in order to make adjustment for these changes in the market.

[2] E. Fama, L. Fisher, M. Jensen, and R. Roll, "The Adjustment of Stock Prices to New Information," *International Economic Review,* February 1969, pp. 1–21.

$$r_{it} = a_i + b_i r_{Mt} + e_t \tag{22-2}$$

where r_{it} = rate of return defined in Eq. (22-1) for ith firm in the tth period
  r_{Mt} = return from Lorie-Fisher market index in period t
    e_t = residual error in period t
a_i and b_i = regression intercept and slope statistics for firm i

The characteristic lines were fitted using 24 monthly returns from the 12 months before the stock split or stock dividend and the 12 months afterward (more observations were used when data were available).

Residual Errors near Time of Stock Dividend or Split

The residual errors e_t around the time of the stock split or stock dividend were the focus of the study. Figure 22-2 shows the hypothetical characteristic line for some firm.

If the residual error at the time of stock split or stock dividend was zero, $e_t = 0$, this means the security's actual rate of return was right on the characteristic line and the change had no positive or negative effects on an investor's normal pattern of returns. If the residual error was positive (that is, a positive e_t) at the time of the change, this means the actual return (that is, the r_{it}) was above the characteristic line and the stock split or stock dividend was apparently boosting returns above their normal pattern. A negative residual error (that is, a negative e_t) occurs when the actual rate of return is below the characteristic line and some negative influence is affecting that period's rate of return. If the beliefs that most investors and business people hold about stock splits and stock dividends are true, the residual errors will tend to be positive after the split or dividend because the value of the firm should increase.

Average Residual Errors near Time of Change

The residual errors about the characteristic line are the results of many influences other than stock splits and stock dividends. Therefore, it is not

FIG. 22-2 Characteristic line with residual error.

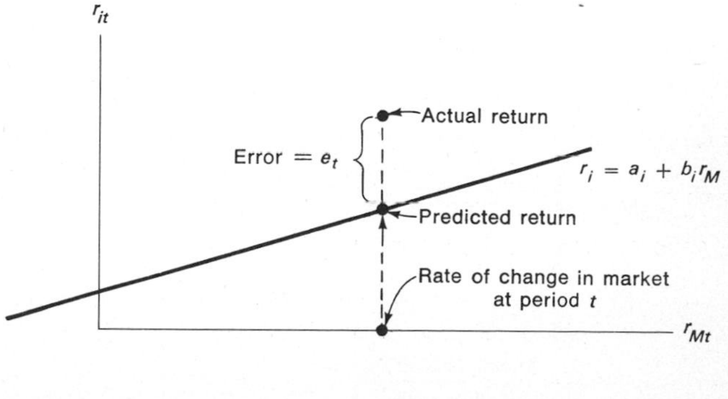

practical to examine the residuals of individual firms following a split or dividend and draw conclusions. To overcome this problem, the average residuals over 940 securities were calculated for each month before and after the split or dividend.[3] In effect, this approach averages the influences which are not due to the stock dividend or stock split to zero. If the average residuals are significantly different from zero in the months after the change, this disparity indicates the change affected the value of the firm. Figure 22-3 shows a graph of the average residuals $\bar{e}_t$ for the months surrounding the split or dividend.

Figure 22-3 shows that the *average* residuals were not significantly different from zero in the months following the stock split or stock dividend. Therefore, splits and dividends per se evidently have no effect on the value of the firm or investors' returns. That is, on average the firm's returns continued to fall on the characteristic line after the split or dividend.

It is interesting to note that the average residuals shown in Fig. 22-3 are increasingly positive in the months *preceding* the stock split or stock dividend. This rise in returns in the few months prior to the change can be attributed to the information content of an *anticipated* cash dividend. In the vast majority of cases, a stock split or stock dividend is followed by an increase in the cash dividend. Thus, the stock split or stock dividend is in-

---

[3] The average residual over 940 firms t months after the split or dividend is denoted $\bar{e}_t$ and calculated as follows:

$$\frac{1}{940} \sum_{i=1}^{940} e_{it} = \bar{e}_t$$

FIG. 22-3 The average residual errors surrounding the time of a stock split or stock dividend. (From E. Fama, L. Fisher, M. Jensen, and R. Roll, "The Adjustment of Stock Prices to New Information," *International Economic Review*, February 1969, fig. 2a.)

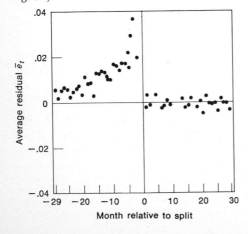

terpreted by the market as evidence of an upcoming increase in cash dividends. This anticipated dividend increase does not increase the value of the firm; it merely detracts from earnings retention and future capital gains. But an increase in cash dividends usually *contains information.* When a board of directors declares such an increase, their decision tends to indicate that they are confident that *earnings have risen* enough to sustain a higher future dividend. It is this implied earnings rise which is the basis for the higher returns preceding the stock split or stock dividend.

The preceding explanation for the increasingly positive average residual errors $\overline{e}_t$ prior to a stock dividend or split involves some rather tortured logic. Let us retrace this reasoning and examine it more closely. The cause-and-effect logic for positive residuals preceding the changes goes as follows. A stock dividend or split implies an increase in cash dividends; increased cash dividends imply a permanent rise in earnings; and higher anticipated earnings cause capital gains, pushing returns up and causing positive residual errors. If this line of logic is correct, a firm which declares a stock dividend or split and subsequently fails to raise its cash dividend must be disappointing the market; its price and returns can be expected to rise in anticipation of the stock split or dividend and then fall when cash dividends and earnings fail to rise. Figure 22-4 shows graphs of the average residuals for firms which had stock dividends or splits and then either (1) increased their cash dividend or (2) decreased their cash dividend relative to their trend in payouts.

Figure 22-4*a* shows that firms which had stock dividends or splits and subsequently raised cash dividends had slightly positive average residuals after the stock dividend or split. This is an indication that the market had correctly anticipated the earnings rise and that most of the capital gains occurred before the earnings rise was announced: the stock dividend or split and increased cash dividend correctly foretold the earnings rise. Figure 22-4*b* shows a different picture: Those firms which had stock dividends or splits and then decreased dividends experienced unusually high returns (that is, positive average residuals) until the cash dividend declined (presumably because earnings were poor). Then, the value of the stock fell, pulling returns down and causing negative average residuals after the stock dividend or split which was associated with lower earning power.

The evidence indicates that stock dividends and splits are valuable only to the extent that they convey correct information about earnings. Earning power is the basic source of stock values. Stock dividends and splits alone cause high returns only for several months before cash dividends are paid because the market expects an increase in dividends and, more basically, an increase in earnings. If the expected increase in dividends and presumably also in earnings does not materialize, the information content of the stock dividend or split is discounted, and returns fall below normal for a while before resuming their previous pattern along the characteristic line. In the final analysis, the market value of the firm or the investors' returns are not changed by stock splits and dividends. Such

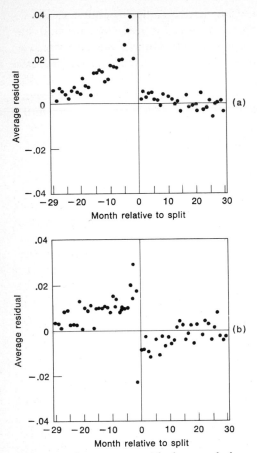

FIG. 22-4 The average residual errors before and after stock dividends and splits. (*a*) Average residuals for dividend "increases"; (*b*) average residuals for dividend "decreases." (From E. Fama, L. Fisher, M. Jensen, and R. Roll, "The Adjustment of Stock Prices to New Information," *International Economic Review,* February 1969, pp. 1–21.)

changes are essentially paper-shuffling operations which the market expects to convey information about earnings. Any effects from stock dividends and splits can be attributed to their implicit information content.

If an investor can correctly anticipate stock dividends and stock splits, the data seem to indicate that it is possible to earn speculative capital gains. However, further studies of the average residuals show they tend to be zero after the announcement date of the stock dividend or split;[4] so speculation on the announcement of stock dividends or stock splits, to be effective, should precede the public announcement. This is probably possible only by

[4] W. H. Hausman, R. R. West, and J. A. Largay, "Stock Splits, Price Changes, and Trading Profits: A Synthesis," *Journal of Business,* January 1971, pp. 69–77.

spending the capital gains before they are earned to detect announcements which are associated with increasing earnings. But this, too, means that stock splits and stock dividends alone cannot be used to beat the market. Investors cannot increase their returns and corporations cannot increase their total market value through stock dividends and/or splits. The capital gains preceding the stock dividends and/or splits are not caused by mere changes in the unit of account. Alas, there are no free lunches from stock dividends or stock splits.

22-3 EFFECTS OF CASH DIVIDENDS

The preceding analysis of stock dividends and splits indicates that the stock market is a rational place which is not fooled by paper-shuffling gimmicks. Let us see if the stock market handles cash dividends as rationally.

It was suggested in Chaps. 7, 9, and 10 that the value of a security is the present value of all future income. If this is true, the market price of a share of common stock should drop when cash dividends are paid by an amount equal to the present value of that dividend, since a cash dividend payment decreases the present value of the share. Let us denote this drop-off in market price associated with payment of cash dividends as DO, which is defined in Eq. (22-3).

$$DO = \text{closing price before dividend} - \text{closing price ex-dividend}$$

$$(22-3)$$

Dr. D. Durand and A. May at the Massachusetts Institute of Technology published a study of the behavior of American Telephone and Telegraph (ATT) stock after cash dividends were paid.[5] ATT was chosen for the study because (1) its stock had a broad, orderly, active market, and (2) its \$2.25 quarterly cash dividend was large in relation to the 12.5 cents stock price changes (that is, only $\frac{1}{8}$ point changes are posted), which facilitated measuring the DO. A total of 43 quarterly dividend dates from 1948 to 1959 were examined. The average of the 43 DOs was \$2.16, which was 96 percent of the \$2.25 cash dividend paid. The data for all 43 quarterly dividends are shown in Table 22-2.

The data in Table 22-2 strongly support the theory that the value of a stock is the present value of its future income. Tax effects account for the small difference between the drop-off and the dividend; that is, shrewd investors who intend to sell the stock prefer to sell it shortly before the dividend is paid so that they may recognize their income as capital gains rather than dividends, which are taxed at the higher ordinary income tax rate. This tendency drives the price down slightly before cash dividends are paid and keeps the DO from being as large as the dividend.

[5] D. Durand and A. May, "The Ex-Dividend Behavior of American Telephone and Telegraph Stock," *Journal of Finance*, March 1960, pp. 19–31.

TABLE 22-2 DROP-OFFS IN ATT STOCK AT 43 QUARTERLY DIVIDENDS OF $2.25

DO, $	DO/$2.25, %	Mar. '48–Sept. '52	Dec. '52–Mar. '57	June '57–Mar. '59	Row totals
$1\frac{1}{4}$	56		1		1
$1\frac{3}{8}$, $1\frac{1}{2}$					
$1\frac{5}{8}$	72		2		2
$1\frac{3}{4}$	78	2	1	1	4
$1\frac{7}{8}$	83	3	2		5
2	89	5	2	1	8
$2\frac{1}{8}$	94	3	3	1	7
$2\frac{1}{4}$	100	2	1	2	5
$2\frac{3}{8}$	106		3	1	4
$2\frac{1}{2}$					
$2\frac{5}{8}$	117	1	1	1	3
$2\frac{3}{4}$	122	1			1
$2\frac{7}{8}$	127		1		1
3, $3\frac{1}{8}$, $3\frac{1}{4}$					
$3\frac{3}{8}$	150	1		1	2
Totals		18	17	8	43
Average		$2.15	$2.07	$2.34	$2.16
DO/$2.25		96%	92%	104%	96%

Figure 22-5 shows the price action of ATT around the time of its quarterly dividends from 1948 to 1952. The line through the points traces the average dollar amount the market price fluctuated around the ex-dividend market price.

This line rises gradually as the dividend date approaches and the present value of the dividend increases. Then the drop-off occurs simultaneously with the dividend. It is clearly not advisable to purchase a stock a few days prior to its dividend date (unless the purchaser is tax-exempt). The price would drop after the dividend, and the new investor, having received the dividend, must pay ordinary income tax on it. Thus, the after-tax dividend income is less than the capital loss. Trading shares to capture cash dividends is no way to beat the market.

Conclusions about Dividend Effects

The market tends to regard stock dividends and splits as what they are: a mere shuffling of paper which may convey information about earnings. Aside from their temporary information effects, stock dividends and stock splits do not fool the market into increasing the value it assigns to the firm.

Cash dividends are a source of real income to the investor. The market recognizes the present value of cash dividends and adjusts the market price of the stock accordingly. The data compiled by Durand and May indicate that the market has a slight preference for capital gains over dividends, but in view of the income tax structure, this is rational.

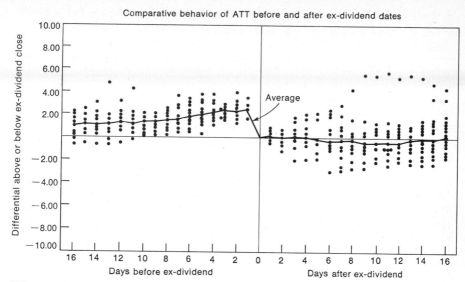

FIG. 22-5 Graph of price drop-off on ATT stock. (From D. Durand and A. May, "The Ex-Dividend Behavior of American Telephone and Telegraph Stock," *Journal of Finance*, March 1960, pp. 19–31.)

It seems that on the average the market views dividends in a rational manner and cannot be beaten or fooled into erroneous values by dividend gimmicks. The data seem to support the Modigliani-Miller thesis that dividend policy is irrelevant in valuing a firm (except for possible tax effects).

For speculators, there appears to be little or no chance to beat the market by speculating on dividend effects. Although above-average returns usually precede stock dividends and splits, the stock must be purchased before the stock split or dividend is announced to obtain these high returns. And these above-average returns are due to earnings growth rather than the stock split or dividend. It is unlikely that an investor can anticipate these unusual capital gains accurately enough to beat the market after deducting for the costs incurred in finding them.

The tax advantage gained by purchasing stocks just after cash dividends are paid and selling them shortly before the next cash dividend is useful only to investors in very high income tax brackets. When the risks associated with holding the security between dividend dates and the sales commissions incurred in buying and selling are considered, this strategy is not likely to beat the market.

The directors and officers of some firms say they pay small stock dividends of 5 or 10 percent every year to stir the interest of naive investors. Without a doubt, there are numerous amateur investors who erroneously believe that stock dividends represent an increase in their wealth, but such investors do not constitute a force which can bid up the price of a firm's shares if earnings do not warrant it. When shares appear to be overpriced in relation to earnings, professional investors will liquidate their holdings, driving prices down. In the final analysis, there is no reason why a firm should pay small stock dividends.

Some firms occasionally have stock splits to broaden the market for their shares. For example, if a firm's shares are selling for $120 each, a 3 for 1 stock split (or 200 percent stock dividend) will reduce the cost of a round lot (100 shares) from $12,000 to $4,000. Many investors refused to trade in odd lots because of the odd-lot fee which the NYSE enforced until 1975. Therefore, splitting the high-priced shares may be advisable if a firm is seeking to broaden its shareholder group to include families that may not have $12,000 but do have $4,000 to invest. This is particularly true since shareholders may make good customers. However, the additional small investors gained by such actions cannot be expected to control enough purchasing power to raise the price of the firm's shares significantly. Thus, those who aspire to beat the market had better look beyond the folklore about dividends.

22-4 TRADING ON INSIDE INFORMATION

Federal law defines *insiders* as the directors, officers, significant shareholders, and any other persons who have access to valuable inside information about a firm. As mentioned in Sec. 21-5 with reference to the strongly efficient markets hypothesis, insiders sometimes beat the market. This section examines the profitability of trading on inside information to see whether the profits are significant.

Federal law requires all insiders to notify the Securities and Exchange Commission (SEC) in writing of all trades they have made in their corporation's stock within one month. The SEC then publishes these insider trades in its monthly pamphlet *Official Summary of Insider Trading,* which is available to the public through the U.S. Government Printing Office. Professor Jeffrey F. Jaffe analyzed the *Official Summary* of many years to measure insiders' trading profits.[6] The security market line (SML) furnished the engine for Dr. Jaffe's analysis of insiders' trading profits.

The SML shifts every month. As shown in Fig. 22-6, the high beta stocks have the highest returns in bull markets and the lowest returns in bear markets.

Jaffe estimated the SMLs for different months by first estimating the characteristic regression lines of all NYSE stocks [Eq. (12-8) on page 328]. Each stock's beta systematic risk coefficient and monthly returns were then taken from these first-pass regressions for the second-pass re-

---

[6] J. F. Jaffe, "Special Information and Insider Trading," *Journal of Business,* July 1974, pp. 410–428. Another study about the profitability of insider trading which deals with similar issues is J. H. Lorie and V. Niederhoffer, "Predictive and Statistical Properties of Insider Trading," *Journal of Law and Economics,* April 1968, pp. 35–51.

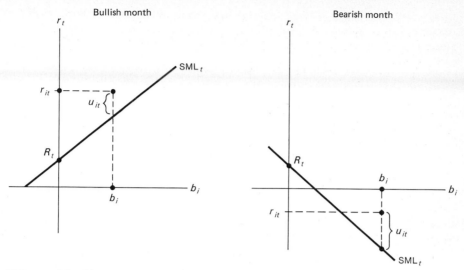

FIG. 22-6 Monthly returns measured from bull- and bear-market security market lines.

gression estimates of each month's SML. Regression equation (22-3) shows the regression model for the tth month's SML.

$$r_{it} = R_t + c_t(b_i) + u_{it} \qquad \text{for } i = 1, 2, \ldots, n \text{ stocks} \qquad (22\text{-}3)$$

The intercept R_t and slope c_t coefficients for month t's SML were found by regressing stocks' 1-month rate of return in month t, r_{it}, on their beta systematic risk coefficients b_i. The ith stock's residual error from the SML in month t, denoted u_{it}, measures whether the stock did better or worse than the capital market theory (explained in Chap. 16) suggests.

To see whether insiders' trades in their own corporation's stock were based on valuable inside information, Dr. Jaffe measured the residual errors for the ith stock in month t, as shown in Fig. 22-6. These residual errors are positive (that is, the observed monthly return is above the SML) if the stock beats the market. In other words, after allowing for current bullish or bearish market conditions and the stock's individual reaction to these conditions (as measured by its beta coefficient), the u_{it} term measures the ith stock's positive or negative unsystematic return in month t.

To discern which stocks were being actively traded by insiders, Dr. Jaffe studied each month's *Official Summary of Insider Trading* from the SEC. He selected the stocks in each month which had three more inside sellers than buyers (that is, a *selling plurality* by insiders), or three more insiders buying than selling (a *buying plurality*). Then he recorded the monthly residual errors, u_{it}, for each of these stocks in which the insiders seemed to exhibit some consensus about buying or selling. After recording such facts for many stocks and for many years, Dr. Jaffe summed up the residual errors for all stocks traded actively by a plurality of insiders in the tth month. Equations (22-4) and (22-5) define the average residual error from the SML in month t for stocks which the plurality of insiders bought or sold, respectively. The upper limits of summation B and S refer to the number of stocks bought and sold, respectively, by the plurality of insiders in month t.

$$\text{Average buyers' plurality residual} = bu_t = \frac{1}{B} \sum_{i=1}^{B} u_{it} \qquad (22\text{-}4)$$

$$\text{Average sellers' plurality residual} = su_t = \frac{1}{S} \sum_{i=1}^{S} u_{it} \qquad (22\text{-}5)$$

Combining the absolute values of the sums in Eqs. (22-4) and (22-5), as shown in Eq. (22-6), yields the average residual for all insiders' trades in month t.

$$U_t = |bu_t| + |su_t| \qquad (22\text{-}6)$$

The average residual from the SML for all insider plurality trading in month t is a measure of extra returns which these insiders earned on average from trades which are assumed to be motivated by their inside information.

A 1 percent buying commission and a 1 percent selling commission were subtracted from each insider's trade to obtain net profit. Then the average residuals after commissions were cumulated over $C = 1$, 2, and 8 months after the month in which the plurality of insiders originally made its trades. This yielded the cumulative average residuals denoted U_{tc}, defined in Eq. (22-7) and shown in Table 22-3.

$$U_{tc} = \sum_{m=1}^{C=1,2,8} U_{t+m} \qquad (22\text{-}7)$$

Table 22-3 shows that 1 month, $C = 1$, after a plurality of insider buying or selling, the insiders' net profit after commissions averaged $(-.0102 =) - 1.02$ percent of the value of the stock. After the stock was held 2 months (that is, $C = 2$), the insiders broke about even, $U_{tc} = .0009$. But

TABLE 22-3 CUMULATIVE AVERAGE RESID-
UAL MEASURES OF INSIDERS' PROFIT
RATES, NET OF COMMISSIONS

Months cumulated	Cumulative average residual
$C = 1$	$U_{t1} = -.0102$
$C = 2$	$U_{t2} = .0009$
$C = 8$	$U_{t8} = .0307$

only after 8 months did the plurality of insiders' stocks experience enough price change to pay the commissions and yield (.0307 =) 3.07 percent net profit. Statistically speaking, this rate of insiders' trading profit is significantly above zero. But, practically speaking, the average insider certainly is not getting rich quick. Alas, investors aspiring to hitting the jackpot by using inside information must lower their sights and plan on working hard to earn a slightly better rate of return than they could by picking stocks with a dart.

22-5 DOLLAR COST AVERAGING

Investors who seek stocks which pay stock dividends or who try to trade on inside information have a different attitude from that of investors who use dollar cost averaging. Companies that pay stock dividends and investors who seek inside information probably do so in the belief that they are beating the market. On the other hand, investors who use dollar cost averaging plans would most likely say they are doing so because they do not have any ideas about how to beat the market. Dollar cost averaging plans are generally used in the hope of attaining something for nothing. That is, dollar cost averagers do not hope to beat the market; they typically expect (and are satisfied) to earn an unimpressive rate of return, but they want to earn this return without doing any investment analysis work or without assuming any risk. Thus, dollar cost averaging is a type of beat-the-market scheme for investors who lack confidence in their investment skills and are willing to forgo high rates of return as long as they do not have to work or take risks in their investing.

Dollar stock averaging is a simple investment plan which helps uninformed investors with the timing of their investments. This plan gives no clue as to what the investor should buy; it merely simplifies the problem of deciding *when* to buy. In essence, a dollar cost averaging investment program involves making periodic investments of equal dollar amounts. Such a program leads to the purchase of more shares when their price is cheap than when they are expensive. As a result, the average dollar cost per share is below the average of the intervening prices. A numerical example should clarify this.

Numerical Example

First, consider a stock whose price is not very volatile. If the price fluctuates between $90 and $100 per share without any growth and $1,000 is invested each period (for example, quarter or year), the results of dollar cost averaging are those shown at the top of Table 22-4.

If a more volatile growth stock is purchased with dollar cost averaging, the results are those shown at the bottom of Table 22-4. The numerical

TABLE 22-4 NUMERICAL EXAMPLE OF DOLLAR COST AVERAGING WITH $1,000 INVESTED PER PERIOD

Low volatility, no-growth stock

(1) Period	(2) Mkt price, $	(3) No. shares for $1,000	(4) No. shares purchased	(5) Total invested, $	(6) = (5) ÷ (4) Avg. cost per share, $	(7) Avg. mkt. price, $
1	100	10	10	1,000	100	100
2	90	11.1	21.1	2,000	94.7	95
3	100	10	31.1	3,000	96.4	96.6
4	90	11.1	42.2	4,000	94.7	95
5	100	10	52.2	5,000	95.9	96

High volatility growth stock

1	60	16.7	16.7	1,000	60	60
2	80	12.5	29.2	2,000	68.5	70
3	75	13.3	42.5	3,000	70.5	71.66
4	90	11.1	53.6	4,000	74.5	76.22
5	85	11.8	65.4	5,000	76.8	78

example for the growth stock supposes the price rises from $60 to $85 per share while fluctuating. Both examples assume $1,000 per period is invested.

The results of dollar cost averaging can be seen most clearly in the last two columns (6 and 7) of Table 22-4. In both cases, the average cost per share (column 6) is below the average of the market prices which occurred on purchase dates (column 7). The examples demonstrate that whatever benefits that may be derived from dollar cost averaging are larger for volatile growth stocks than for stocks with low volatility. This is due to the fact that the more volatile the stock, the more frequently low prices will occur and pull down the *average* cost per share.

Conclusions about Dollar Cost Averaging

One of the keys to earning high returns is to buy when the market is depressed. However (as seen when examining the odd-lot theory in Chap. 20), amateur investors (that is, odd-lotters) often sell at the market lows. For people who lack the time or ability to forecast market turns or who become upset during bear markets, the dollar averaging plan might help them buy when the market is down and stocks are cheap—*if* they stick to the plan.

Large institutional investors like life insurance companies use dollar cost averaging. A large life insurance company typically has tens of thousands of dollars of cash flowing in each month. Rather than accumulate this cash until stock prices become depressed, the company invests it as it arrives, and the flow of insurance premiums usually continues undiminished through bull markets.

To use dollar cost averaging, the investor should follow these investment guidelines:

1 Maintain periodic investments as the market falls. It is at this advantageous time that amateur investors are most likely to get out of the market.

2 Continue periodic investments for at least a complete business cycle (for example, for over 5 years) until bear-market purchases have a chance to rise.

3 Invest frequently, since the best buys in a bear market usually last only a few months.

4 Do not use a dollar cost averaging investment as an emergency fund which might have to be liquidated in a bear market.

The Lorie-Fisher data given in Table 22-1 show the best returns which could be expected with dollar cost averaging. However, investors could easily do worse if they (1) selected a few below-average stocks or (2) paid the high sales commissions usually accompanying payroll-deduction investment plans. It should be fairly clear that dollar cost averaging is no way to beat the market. It is simply a plan which encourages periodic investment. If investors using dollar cost averaging are able to select securities which yield better-than-average returns, they can beat the returns from a naive buy-and-hold strategy. But it was skill in selection and not dollar cost averaging which allowed the high returns, and high risk can be expected to accompany the high returns. Thus, the investor will not get something for nothing.

22-6 RATIO PLANS

Ratio plans are investment management schemes which shift the funds in a portfolio back and forth between aggressive investments, such as common stocks, and defensive investments, such as bonds. The objective of these plans is to buy stocks when they are down and sell them when they are high. The defensive asset is bought and sold to facilitate the switching in and out of stocks, a procedure which is the source of most capital gains and losses. Like the dollar cost averaging plan, ratio plans are designed to beat the market by earning a return with a minimum of investment analysis work and risk bearing (that is, to get something for *almost* nothing).

Switching from stocks to bonds as the business cycle changes is sometimes a wise idea. After the beginning of most recessions, business profits and expansion decrease, and interest rates and stock prices fall. Since bond prices (especially high-quality bonds) move inversely to interest rates, they rise as interest rates and stock prices fall. When this type of recession is under way, it is wise to buy stocks at low prices with money obtained from selling bonds at high prices. Unfortunately, all recessions do not follow this pattern. For example, during the 1969–1970 bear market, *inflation persisted* as the recession progressed. This inflation caused interest rates to go *up*, since creditors charged higher interest to compensate them for the fact that they were being repaid in dollars with lower purchasing power. As a result, bond prices fell as interest rates rose—and stock prices plummeted, too. Obviously, there is little advantage to be gained by switching from bonds to stocks if both are falling.

Ratio plans are primarily oriented to loss-minimization rather than return-maximization. They are more popular with older investment counselors and appear to be the result of bad experiences in the Great Crash of 1929. They are of three basic types: (1) constant dollar plans; (2) constant ratio plans; and (3) variable ratio plans. Each will be explained separately.

Constant Dollar Plans

The constant dollar plan is so simple it is trivial. The plan is to keep a constant dollar amount invested in common stocks while letting the portion of the portfolio invested in bonds absorb changes in the value of the portfolio. As the value of the common stocks in the portfolio rises, shares are sold to maintain a constant dollar investment in common stocks. The proceeds of such a sale are used to purchase bonds (some counselors even recommend holding the defensive part of the portfolio in cash). When the value of the common stock falls, funds are taken from the defensive portion of the portfolio to purchase enough stock to maintain the constant dollar goal. The objective of such switching is to buy stock when its price is low and sell when its price is high.

The following limitations of the plan render it fairly useless. First, as money is added or removed from the portfolio, the constant dollar amount must be adjusted in accordance with some forecast of the market level. If the market can be forecast, why use the plan? Second, setting the original constant dollar amount to be held in common stocks is entirely arbitrary. Third, the plan yields poor results when the market continues to rise or fall for long periods. Fourth, the type of market fluctuations required to make the plan advantageous are not common. Fifth, the plan is quite sensitive to the frequency with which funds are switched to maintain the constant dollar amount in stock because the buying and selling commissions can consume some or all of the income (and even the principal too if trading is frequent enough). The average investor will probably have more wealth in the long run by sticking with a naive buy-and-hold strategy. Furthermore, the latter is much simpler.

Constant Ratio Plans

A constant ratio plan is somewhat similar to a constant dollar plan. A portfolio managed under a constant ratio plan holds fixed proportions of stocks and bonds; the most widely suggested proportions are 50-50. As stock prices rise, common stock is liquidated, and bonds are purchased to maintain the constant ratio. The reverse procedure is followed if bond prices rise more or fall less than stock prices. The objective of the plan is to cause the investor to buy low and sell high in the stock market automatically, without forecasting market swings.

Like all formula plans, the success of the constant ratio plan depends upon the rules governing the moment at which to realign the proportions of the portfolio. One rule would be to realign the proportions every time Standard & Poor's industrial index went up or down by more than 10 percent. If the portfolio is large, a market index need not be used. A large, well-diversified portfolio is its own market index; it could be realigned any time the portfolio's proportions were more than, say, four percentage points away from the desired proportions. Or realignment of the stock and bond proportions could be scheduled at periodic intervals. When funds are added to or withdrawn from the portfolio, the change may be accomplished so as to maintain the desired proportions.

The advantages of the constant ratio plan are that (1) it is simple, (2) small profits are obtainable when the market fluctuates aimlessly, and (3) no market forecast is required. The disadvantages of the plan are that (1) the rules about realigning the portfolio's proportions are arbitrary, (2) it is not clear what proportions are optional, and (3) a naive buy-and-hold strategy would result in higher returns in the long run because it does not generate the trading costs. These disadvantages weigh heavily against the advantages of using the constant ratio plan. In any event, the plan is not capable of beating the returns from a naive buy-and-hold strategy. The plan can reduce portfolio risk but will not yield efficient portfolios. That is, constant ratio plan portfolios can be expected to lie below the efficient frontier.

Variable Ratio Plans

Variable ratio plans are extensions of the constant ratio plan. Under variable ratio plans, stock is liquidated to buy defensive assets as stock prices rise. But, instead of the proportions of stock and bonds being held constant, the proportion of stock is decreased if stock prices rise more than expected and increased if stock prices fall more than expected. To know when to change proportions, a trend line forecasting the future path of some market index is prepared and zones are established above and below the trend line. When the market index rises one zone above the trend line, the proportion of stock is decreased by one predetermined increment. If the market index moves into the second zone above the trend line, the proportion of stock is decreased by a second increment. If the market index drops below the trend line, the stock proportion is increased by some number of percentage points, depending on which zone the index enters.

Figure 22-7 shows an example of how a variable ratio plan might

Market Index

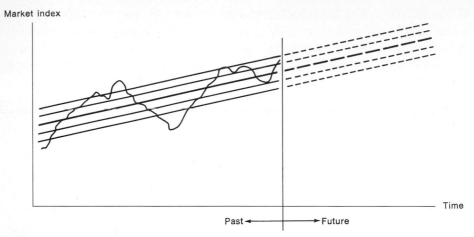

Time

Past ◄——————► Future

FIG. 22-7 A trend line with trading zones around it to govern a variable ratio plan.

work. In the figure, a line through the historical path of the market index has been extrapolated into the future. This extrapolated trend line is the basis for the whole variable ratio plan. In practice, more sophisticated methods might be used to forecast the trend. Two zones have been traced above and below the trend line in this figure; more zones could be used. Assume that as long as the index follows the trend line, stocks and bonds will be held in a 50-50 proportion. If the index rises into the first zone above the trend line, the proportions of stock and bonds could be changed to 40-60, respectively. The second zone might call for 30-70 proportions. If the index drops down into the first or second zones below the trend, the proportions of stock and bonds would be shifted to 60-40 and 70-30, respectively. These rules are typically supplemented by a "half-way rule" which stipulates that no stock purchases will be made when the index is above the trend line and no stock sales will be made when the index is below the trend line. The half-way rule prevents excessive trading if the index fluctuates between two zones that are both on the same side of the trend line.

Whereas the constant ratio plan is used to avoid forecasting, the variable ratio plan is entirely dependent upon the forecasted trend line. If the market plunges to lower levels than were forecasted, the variable ratio plan will maximize the portfolio's stock proportion and thus maximize the downside capital loss. In an effort to improve the variable ratio plan, several types of forecasts have been used. Some portfolios have used moving averages as a center point around which to establish the zones. This approach ensures that the plan is based on current market conditions. Other users of the variable ratio plan have employed some intrinsic-value guideline as a basis for changing the proportions. For example, the average price-earnings ratio for Standard & Poor's industrial index might be forecast. Regardless of what economic variable is forecast, zones are constructed around it and used to vary the ratio of stocks and bonds.

The main disadvantage of variable ratio plans is the necessity of making an accurate forecast. If the market can be forecast well enough to make the plan worthwhile, there is no reason to use the mechanical rules which compose the rest of the plan. A second disadvantage is that, in the long run, a naive buy-and-hold strategy will probably earn higher returns after commissions than a variable ratio plan that is based on an accurate forecast. Third, the establishment of the zones around the trend line and the rules for varying the proportions are determined arbitrarily.

Advocates of the variable ratio plan point out that it limits the need for decision making. After the forecast is made, trading can proceed mechanically. The portfolio manager is freed from emotions or market hysteria which might influence trading decisions. However, these arguments ignore the anguish which may have gone into preparing the forecast and the periodic need to update it. Investors would probably do less work by taking a few courses in macroeconomics, business cycle analysis, money and banking, and econometrics and then trading on the basis of their own forecasts of the economy and the market. It should not be difficult to outperform portfolios using variable ratio plans.

Some Conclusions about Ratio Plans

The constant dollar, constant ratio, and variable ratio plans were not originally constructed to beat the market. They are primarily defensive plans to protect the investor from large losses and/or assist nonprofessional investors in managing their portfolios. However, books have been published about ratio plans with titles such as *A Method for Stock Profits without Price Forecasting*,[7] *Practical Formulas for Successful Investing*,[8] ad nauseam. These titles seem to suggest that the books will enable the investor to beat the market or get something for nothing. It is hoped that this discussion will dismiss such notions.

22-7 CONCLUSIONS ABOUT BEATING THE MARKET

In the preceding chapters, the notion has been developed that a trade-off between risk and return is available in the market. That is, by *carefully selecting* risky assets, investors can expect to earn higher-than-average returns than they could earn from, say, U.S. Treasury bonds. This is not, however, beating the market. The investor has to do hard work to be able to find advantageously priced risky assets. And, after investing in a risky asset, the investor is faced with the unpleasant prospect of enduring large variability in the returns. The acceptance of financial risk causes investors to lose sleep, become nervous and irritable, face the chance of bankruptcy, and

---

[7] New York: Doubleday, 1962.
[8] New York: Funk, 1953.

perhaps get ulcers. Thus, if a high return is obtained from risky invest-ments, it was earned; the investor did not get something for nothing.

Some investors think that fundamental analysis may hold the key to beating the market, but if stock markets are intrinsic-value random-walk markets, as the evidence reviewed in Chap. 21 suggests, most fundamental analysts will not be able to beat the market. Only a few expert fundamental analysts who discover news will enjoy large profits. It takes years of hard work to become an expert. It is doubtful, moreover, that any particular person will be able consistently to discover important financial news. Thus, any higher-than-average returns earned by using fundamental analysis were probably preceded by years of training and some losses while learning. Fundamental analysis offers no key to getting something for nothing.

Technical analysis has captured the fancy of many investors. It is easy to grasp, and various charting services sell up-to-date charts to the public at a low cost. One might compare the benefits which technical analysis seems to offer with the easy analysis and conclude that charting is the key to beating the market. But, as the evidence reviewed in Chap. 21 indicates, stock markets tend to be intrinsic-value random-walk markets in which charting cannot be expected to perform better than a naive buy-and-hold strategy.

Some investors are erroneously impressed by firms which regularly pay stock dividends or split their stock. Some investors believe that their wealth has somehow increased when they receive a stock dividend or stock split. But, as we saw earlier in this chapter, stock dividends and splits are mere paper-shuffling operations which do not affect the value of the firm or the investors' returns in any significant manner. Only if stock dividends or splits are accompanied by an increase in earning power will the value of the firm rise, and in such a case the stock dividend or split was not the cause of the increase in value. So searching for stocks which pay stock dividends or split offers little promise of beating the market.

Tellers of get-rich-quick stories sometimes refer to the great profits earned by corporate insiders who trade on their access to privileged infor-mation. Such profits were, in fact, commonplace before the 1930s. But, since the SEC began functioning in 1934, the profitability of insider trading has diminished. Empirical analysis of the profits earned by hundreds of inside traders showed that, on average, they earned only 3.07 percent more rate of return net of commissions than some naive buy-and-hold strategy.

Dollar cost averaging plans, constant dollar plans, and constant ratio plans are promoted by some people. These plans are easy to understand; they may capture the potential investor's curiosity; and they can generate enthusiasm for a program of regular investment. The plans are acceptable programs which an investor may prefer to use instead of a naive buy-and-hold strategy. However, the constant dollar plan and constant ratio plan may be expected to earn lower returns than a naive buy-and-hold strategy since they hold a significant portion of the portfolio in cash or bonds. Such portfolios do offer a slight reduction in risk to compensate for the lower returns. The dollar cost averaging program can be expected to perform like a naive buy-and-hold strategy with equal diversification, since it is essentially a naive buy-and-hold strategy itself. When adopting these simple investment programs, the investor should dismiss any expectation of beating the market or of attaining the efficient frontier.

Variable ratio plans are a set of mechanical trading rules that are based on a market forecast. If the forecast is accurate, the plan can be expected, at best, to earn a rate of return about equal to the naive buy-and-hold strategy. If the forecast is erroneous, which it most likely will be, the results of a variable ratio plan can be disastrous. Considering the difficulties associated with the forecast, the investor should expect that the naive buy-and-hold strategy will outperform the variable ratio plans.

This discussion is not meant to imply that some people have not beaten the market by using some very naive schemes. After all, there is such a thing as a lucky fool. But for every lucky fool there is an unlucky fool who suffered catastrophic losses. Unfortunately, the unlucky fools do not seem to be as vociferous as the lucky ones, and so it is possible to be misled into believing that some scheme can beat the market.

To summarize, for risk-averse business people, a method has been suggested to maximize investors' expected utility. By selecting efficient investments in some preferred risk-class, investors will be able to attain their highest indifference curve in risk-return space. However, this is not a beat-the-market scheme. Work is required to delineate the efficient frontier and select a portfolio therefrom.

QUESTIONS

1 Explain how the Lorie-Fisher index is constructed. How are dividends handled? How are taxes handled? What allowance is made for sales commissions? How are securities selected for the average? What diversification techniques are used in constructing the index? What "hot tips" are included in the index?

2 Suggest some standard of comparison for evaluating investment alternatives. Define the standard you suggest, giving particular attention to what it assumes about diversification; its ability to "pick winners"; its realism; the degree to which it is representative of actual investment alternatives; its treatment of income (such as quarterly dividends); and its allowance for taxes, fees, and commissions.

3 Compare and contrast a 6 for 5 stock split with a 20 percent stock dividend. How is the total value of all shares affected by each?

4 If stock dividends and splits increase the value of the firm or investors' returns, how would the average of the residual errors $\bar{e}$ about the characteristic line behave after the change? Graph a hypothetical characteristic line and show what you mean.

5 Assume you own 100 shares of a security with a $70 market price and that the firm declares a 10 percent stock dividend. What will happen to your shares and their market price if nothing else affecting the firm changes?

6 What is the *drop-off* and why should it be expected to equal the cash dividend? How do capital gains taxes affect this?

7 "Dividends are irrelevant." Is this true, false, or uncertain? Explain.

8 What type of securities should an investor who is using dollar cost averaging select?

9 What are some advantages of the constant dollar plan?

10 What differences in performance would you expect in two constant ratio plans, one with a 60-40 and one with a 40-60 ratio in stocks and bonds, respectively?

11 If an investor is using a variable ratio plan and the market rises to unanticipated heights, what will happen to the portfolio?

12 Suppose a security salesperson buys you a free lunch and explains a plan to earn high returns. This person says that, by placing buy orders at 50 cents below the current market price and waiting for a downward fluctuation to buy, you will be able to buy low and sell high and over many transactions this system will yield high returns. What is your reaction?

SELECTED REFERENCES

Brealey, R. A., *Security Prices in a Competitive Market* (Cambridge, Mass.: M.I.T., 1971).

> This easy-to-read summary of many research studies examines numerous beat-the-market schemes in detail and presents scientific evidence about them.

Fama, E., L. Fisher, M. Jensen, and R. Roll, "The Adjustment of Stock Prices to New Information," *International Economic Review*, February 1969, pp. 1–21.

> This regression study shows that stock splits and stock dividends do not change the value of the firm or investor's returns.

Fisher, L., and J. H. Lorie, "Rates of Return on Investments in Common Stock: The Year-by-Year Record, 1926–1965," *Journal of Business*, January 1968, pp. 291–316.

This paper presents the results of a massive numerical analysis of the rates of return available, using a naive buy-and-hold strategy under different tax brackets, dividend reinvestment assumptions, and sales commission arrangements.

Jaffe, J. F., "Special Information and Insider Trading," *Journal of Business,* July 1974, pp. 410–428.

This paper reviews the literature and explains a statistical analysis of insider trading and insiders' profits. The security market line (SML) is used to measure unusual returns obtained by insiders.

PART SEVEN

MATHEMATICAL APPENDIXES

APPENDIX A SUMMATTION SIGN (Σ) explains what the summation operator means.

APPENDIX B PROBABILITY defines the concept of a probability and gives numerical examples of the various types of probabilities.

APPENDIX C THE COVARIANCE explains the covariance and gives a numerical example.

APPENDIX D THE PRESENT VALUE CONCEPT explains the time value of money and how it affects the value of securities.

APPENDIX E THE EXPECTED VALUE OPERATOR (E) defines the concept of a mathematical expectation and shows the derivation of some relevant theorems.

APPENDIX F SIMULTANEOUS SOLUTION OF LINEAR EQUATIONS shows five different methods to solve two linear equations in two unknowns.

APPENDIX G STATISTICAL MOMENTS defines the first four statistical moments for a distribution of returns.

APPENDIX H ELEMENTS OF CORRELATION AND REGRESSION ANALYSIS defines correlation, regression, and related terms.

APPENDIX I MATHEMATICAL DERIVATION OF FORMULAS FOR PORTFOLIO RISK AND EXPECTED RETURN shows how the risk and return of individual assets determine the portfolio's risk and return.

APPENDIX J GEOMETRIC MEAN RETURN is explained as a means to measure multiperiod rates of return.

APPENDIX K QUADRATIC EQUATIONS explains the quadratic form which underlies all the portfolio risk formulas.

These short appendixes, which define various mathematical terms, concepts, and operations, provide a handy reference for terms which become unclear if not used regularly.

APPENDIX A
Summation Sign (Σ)

When one is discussing the sum of several unspecified quantities, say, four rates of return denoted r_1, r_2, r_3, and r_4, it is less cumbersome to write $\sum\limits_{i=1}^{4} r_i$ than to write out $r_1 + r_2 + r_3 + r_4$, although the two expressions are equivalent. The symbol Σ is the upper-case Greek letter sigma and is a mathematical *operator* denoting addition. The subscript $i = 1$ below the Σ is called the *index of summation*. The superscript 4 above the Σ is called the *upper limit of summation*.

The Σ can be used with any variable. Consider two variables x and r.

i	x_i value	r_i value
1	$x_1 = 6$	$r_1 = 3$
2	$x_2 = 9$	$r_2 = 7$
3	$x_3 = 2$	$r_3 = 4$
4	$x_4 = 7$	
5	$x_5 = 3$	

The sum of the three r_i's may be written:

$$\sum_{i=1}^{3} r_i = r_1 + r_2 + r_3$$
$$= 3 + 7 + 4 = 14$$

The sum of the first two r_i's may be written:

$$\sum_{i=1}^{2} r_i = r_1 + r_2$$
$$= 3 + 7 = 10$$

The sum of the last two r_i's may be written:

$$\sum_{i=2}^{3} r_i = r_2 + r_3$$
$$= 7 + 4 = 11$$

In discussing half the sum of the three r_i's we could write

$$\frac{1}{2} \sum_{i=1}^{3} r_i = \sum_{i=1}^{3} \frac{r_i}{2}$$

$$= \sum_{i=1}^{3} \tfrac{1}{2} r_i$$

$$= \frac{3+7+4}{2} = \frac{14}{2} = 7$$

For practice, the reader should verify the following:

$$\sum_{i=1}^{5} x_i = 27 \qquad \sum_{i=2}^{5} x_i = 21 \qquad \sum_{i=2}^{4} x_i = 18 \qquad \sum_{i=1}^{5} \frac{x_i}{2} = 13.5$$

$$\sum_{i=3}^{4} 4x_i = 36 \qquad \sum_{i=1}^{5} (x_i + x_{6-i}) = 54$$

Sometimes the limits of summation are omitted from the Σ because they are not known or do not matter. For example, $\sum_i y_i$ refers to the sum of all the y_i's but does not indicate the range of values i may assume.

Several theorems about summations follow. The reader is invited to substitute numbers into the formulas to verify them.

Summation theorem 1. The summation of sums equals the sum of the summations. Thus,

$$\sum_{i=m}^{n} (r_i + x_i) = \sum_{i=m}^{n} r_i + \sum_{i=m}^{n} x_i$$

Summation theorem 2. A constant factor k times the summed variable equals the constant times the summation.

$$\sum_{i=m}^{n} kx_i = k \sum_{i=m}^{n} x_i$$

Summation theorem 3. The summation of a constant (for example, $k = 2$, -10, $12{,}002$, or any unchanging number) is equal to the product of that constant times the number of times the summation is to be repeated.

$$\sum_{i=1}^{n} k = nk$$

Summation theorem 4. The product of the summations is not always equal to the summation of the products (although a few cases can be found where they are equal).

$$\left(\sum_i x_i \right)\left(\sum_i r_i \right) \neq \sum_i x_i r_i$$

For example,

$$\left(\sum_{i=1}^{2} r_i\right)\left(\sum_{i=1}^{2} x_i\right) = (10)(15)$$

$$\neq \sum_{i=1}^{2} x_i r_i$$

$$= 18 + 63 = 81$$

Multiple summation. Summation over two or more subscripts begins at the lower limits of both summations. The summation of one variable is completed before incrementing the other summation. The process is repeated until both summations reach their upper limits.

Multiple summation is encountered in tables and matrices. If we let i denote the row number and j denote the column number, the sum of the nine x_{ij}'s in the table can be written:

Col. 1	Col. 2	Col. 3	
x_{11}	x_{12}	x_{13}	Row 1
x_{21}	x_{22}	x_{23}	Row 2
x_{31}	x_{32}	x_{33}	Row 3

$$\sum_{i=1}^{3}\sum_{j=1}^{3} x_{ij} = \sum_{j=1}^{3} x_{1j} + \sum_{j=1}^{3} x_{2j} + \sum_{j=1}^{3} x_{3j}$$

$$= (x_{11} + x_{12} + x_{13}) + (x_{21} + x_{22} + x_{23}) + (x_{31} + x_{32} + x_{33})$$

APPENDIX B
Probability

Probabilities can vary from zero to 1. Thus, the limits on the probability of rainy weather or any other probability can be written $0 \leqslant P(\text{rain}) \leqslant 1$. This is the notation commonly used when writing probabilities.

Like percentages, the probabilities always refer to outcomes of a given set of events. Thus, like percentages, the probabilities assigned to all the outcomes under discussion must add up to exactly 1(= 100 percent). So, if the outcomes under discussion are rain and shine, their probabilities must be assigned so that $P(\text{rain}) + P(\text{shine}) = 1$ if rain and shine are mutually exclusive.[1] Negative probabilities are not defined.

[1] If it is possible that it rains while the sun is shining, rain and shine are not mutually exclusive. In this case, $P(\text{rain}) + P(\text{shine}) > 1$. We must subtract the common probabilities which are counted twice if the events are not mutually exclusive. Symbolically, $P(\text{rain}) + P(\text{shine}) - P(\text{rain and shine simultaneously}) = 1$.

TABLE B-1 BREAKDOWN OF PERSONNEL

Age, years	Sex		Marginal total
	Men (M)	Women (W)	
(A) 20–30	150	100	250
(B) 30–40	250	150	400
(C) Over 40	200	150	350
Marginal total	600	400	1,000 = Ω

There are three basic kinds of probabilities. They may be defined in terms of the following situation. Imagine a file drawer containing a universe (Ω) of 1,000 personnel files. The numerical breakdown of the files is shown in Table B-1.

The relative frequencies of the various categories of personnel are shown as Table B-2. If individual personnel files are drawn randomly one at a time and then replaced, the probability of obtaining the file of someone in any particular category is the same as the relative frequency of that category. Probabilities which are equal to known relative frequencies are called *objective probabilities* because they are derived objectively by counting. There are three types of probabilities:

1 *Joint probabilities.* For example, the probability of selecting the file of someone who is male *and* over 40. Symbolically, $P(M \text{ and } C) = .2 = P(C \text{ and } M)$. A joint probability is the probability that different things (for example, some age and sex be drawn) occur simultaneously.

2 *Marginal probabilities.* For example, the probability of selecting the file of a male. Symbolically, $P(M) = .6 = P(A \text{ and } M) + P(B \text{ and } M) + P(C \text{ and } M)$. Note that marginal probabilities are the sum of joint probabilities.

3 *Conditional probabilities.* For example, given the file of a woman, what is the probability she is 20 to 30 years of age? Symbolically, $P(A \text{ given } W) = P(A \mid W) = P(A \text{ and } W)/P(W) = .1/.4 = .25$. The vertical bar represents the word "given." Note that conditional probabilities are the ratio of a joint probability over a marginal probability.

Independence. If the probability of some event (for example, A) does not vary or depend on the outcome of another event (for example, M or W), the

TABLE B-2 RELATIVE FREQUENCIES

Age, years	Sex		Marginal probability
	Men (M)	Women (W)	
(A) 20–30	$P(A \text{ and } M) = .15$	$P(A \text{ and } W) = .1$	$P(A) = .25$
(B) 30–40	$P(B \text{ and } M) = .25$	$P(B \text{ and } W) = .15$	$P(B) = .4$
(C) Over 40	$P(C \text{ and } M) = .2$	$P(C \text{ and } W) = .15$	$P(C) = .35$
Marginal probability	$P(M) = .6$	$P(W) = .4$	$P(\Omega) = 1.0$

events are independent. For example, the probability of selecting someone aged 20 to 30 does not depend on which sex is given, so these events are independent. Symbolically, $P(A) = P(A/M) = P(A/W) = .25$. Note that this implies $P(A)$ times $P(M) = P(A$ and $M)$ if A and M are independent.

Dependence. If the probability of some event (for example, B) depends on, or varies with some other condition (for example, M or W), the events are dependent. For example, the probability of selecting the file of someone of age 30 to 40 depends on whether men's or women's files are used. Symbolically, $P(B \mid M) = .4166 \neq P(B \mid W) = .375$. Note that this implies $P(B)$ times $P(M) \neq P(B$ and $M)$ and $P(B)$ times $P(W) \neq P(B$ and $W)$.

Mutually exclusive. If one event (for example, M) precludes the occurrence of another event (for example, W), the events are mutually exclusive. For example, if a male's file is picked, this precludes that file's being a female's file. Symbolically, $P(M \mid W) = 0$.

In the preceding example, sampling with replacement was done from a file for which the relative frequencies of each subgroup were known. Probabilities derived from such a population are *objective probabilities.* In forecasting, it is necessary to use *subjective probabilities,* which are expected or estimated relative frequencies and are derived subjectively. In some situations it is impossible ever to know if subjective probabilities are exactly correct. For example, if someone says, "The probability of rain tomorrow is .2," the statement is a subjective probability which is impossible to confirm or deny even after "tomorrow" is past.[2]

APPENDIX C
The Covariance

The covariance is a statistical measure of the way two random variables covary together. If the two variables move inversely, their covariance is negative. If they are independent, their covariance is zero. A positive covariance results if two variables move together. Clearly, the sign of the correlation and the sign of the covariance between two variables are the same. Equation (C-1) shows the relation between the covariance of the random variables i and j and their correlation coefficient (denoted ρ_{ij}).

$$\text{cov}(i,j) \equiv \sigma_{ij} \tag{C-1}$$
$$\equiv (\rho_{ij})(\sigma_i)(\sigma_j)$$

---

[2] For a more detailed elementary discussion of finite probability, read F. Mosteller, R. E. K. Roarke, and G. B. Thomas, Jr., *Probability with Statistical Applications* (Reading, Mass.: Addison-Wesley, 1961). For a more rigorous treatment, see R. Gangolli and D. Ylvisaker, *Discrete Probability* (New York: Harcourt, Brace & World, 1967).

where σ_i and σ_j are the standard deviations of i and j, respectively. It may also be noted from Eq. (C-1) that the absolute value (that is, the size) of the covariance varies directly with the variances of the two variables.

C-1 COVARIANCE OF RETURNS

In this book we are frequently concerned with the covariance of rates of return between two assets, say, i and j. The covariance of returns on securities i and j will be denoted by σ_{ij} or $\text{cov}(r_i, r_j)$. It is defined in Eq. (C-2).

$$\sigma_{ij} \equiv E\{[r_i - E(r_i)][r_j - E(r_j)]\} \tag{C-2}$$

$$= \sum_{t=1}^{n} p_t\{[r_{it} - E(r_i)][r_{jt} - E(r_j)]\} \tag{C-2a}$$

$$= (\rho_{ij})(\sigma_i)(\sigma_j) \tag{C-1}$$

where r_{it} is the tth rate of return for the ith asset. The 10 ordered pairs of rates of return (r_i, r_j) listed below have been graphed in Fig. C-1, and a numerical example of how to calculate their covariance of returns follows.

t	r_{it}, %	r_{jt}, %
1	7	5
2	4	0
3	0	−5
4	7	5
5	10	10
6	14	16
7	7	16
8	4	10
9	10	10
10	7	10
$E(r_i) = 7\%$		$E(r_j) = 7.7\%$

$\rho = .77$

Figure C-1 shows that all but one of the 10 ordered pairs (r_{it}, r_{jt}) plot in the first quadrant (that is, the northeast positive quadrant).

By making the assumption that all 10 returns are equally likely to occur $1/n = \frac{1}{10}$ can be substituted for the probabilities in the formula (C-2a) for the covariance. Thus, Eq. (C-2a) can be rewritten as Eq. (C-3).

$$\sigma_{ij} = \sum_{t=1}^{10} \{\tfrac{1}{10}[r_i - E(r_i)][r_j - E(r_j)]\} \tag{C-3}$$

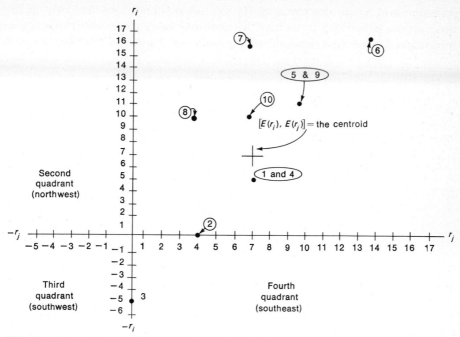

FIG. C-1 Deviations from the means determine the covariance.

The computations for the covariance follow.

Asset i		Asset j		Joint probability $p_t = \dfrac{1}{n}$	Products $(p_t)[r - E(r_i)][r - E(r_j)]$
r_{it}	$[r_{it} - E(r)]$	r_{jt}	$[r_{jt} - E(r)]$		
.07	0	.05	−.027	.1	0
.04	−.03	0	−.077	.1	+.000231
0	−.07	−.05	−.127	.1	+.000889
.07	0	.05	−.027	.1	0
.1	.03	.1	.023	.1	+.000069
.14	.07	.16	.083	.1	+.000581
.07	0	.16	.083	.1	0
.04	−.03	.1	.023	.1	−.000069
.1	.03	.1	.023	.1	+.000069
.07	0	.1	.023	.1	0
				1.0	.001770

$E(r_i) = .07$ $E(r_j) = .077$ $\displaystyle\sum_{t=1}^{n=10} \{ p_t [r_{it} - E(r_i)][r_{jt} - E(r_j)] \}$

The first and third quadrants of Fig. C-1 contain the ordered pairs whose products (r_i times r_j) are positive. The second and fourth quadrants contain the ordered pairs whose products are negative. However, in calculating the covariance, the origin (that is, the point where $r_i = 0$ and $r_j = 0$) is not used to determine whether the 10 observed values of r_i and r_j are high (that is, positive) or low (that is, negative) deviations. The covariance measures deviations of the random variable from its expected value; that is, the ith deviation is $[r_i - E(r)]$, which, in effect, shifts the point of reference from the origin to the *centroid*—the "center of gravity" for the 10 points. The centroid is the point in (r_i, r_j) space where $[E(r_i), E(r_j)]$ occurs.

Points northeast and southwest of the centroid have positive products, that is $p_t[r_i - E(r_i)][r_j - E(r_j)]$, in the products column of the computations. Since only the eighth ordered pair lies either northwest or southeast, it has the only negative product in the products column of the computation. The positive products exceed the negative products in this example; in other words, most of the points are southwest and/or northeast of the centroid. Thus, the sum of the products, which is the covariance of returns, is positive. The total of these products determines the sign of the covariance.

If the 10 ordered pairs had been further northeast and/or southwest of the centroid, the covariance would have been a larger positive number. If the majority of the plotted points were southeast and/or northwest of their centroid, their covariance would be negative because the two variables moved inversely (that is, were negatively correlated).

C-2 THE VARIANCE, A SPECIAL CASE OF THE COVARIANCE

The covariance of a random variable with *itself* equals that variable's variance. Symbolically,

$$\sigma_{ij} = E\{[r_i - E(r_i)][r_j - E(r_j)]\} \tag{C-2}$$

Note that when $i = j$, Eq. (C-2) becomes Eq. (C-4).

$$\sigma_{ij} = \sigma_{ii} = \sigma_{jj} = E[r_i - E(r_i)]^2 \tag{C-4}$$
$$= E[r_j - E(r_j)]^2$$

which shows that the covariance of i or j with itself or with identical securities (that is, when $i = j$) is the variance.

In the calculation of covariances, it makes no difference which variable comes first. Thus, $\sigma_{ij} = \sigma_{ji}$ for any variables i and j. If the reader is unsure of these assertions, he should calculate the values with real numbers such as are given in the numerical examples.

APPENDIX D
The Present Value Concept

A dollar to be received in 1 year is not worth as much as a dollar to be received today—even if there is no doubt the dollar will be paid in 1 year. This is because a dollar received now can be invested in, say, a 5 percent savings account and $1.05 can be withdrawn in 1 year. Thus, the dollar received now is worth 5 cents more than the dollar to be received in 1 year. In short, money, in any amount, has time value. For example, $1,000 is worth more if it is received now than if it is to be received in 1 year. The reason is that the $1,000 received at present could also be put in a 5 percent savings account and grow to $1,050 in 1 year.

The Time Value of Money

The time value of money can be represented symbolically. Let v_t represent the terminal value of money at the end of time period t, p_0 represent the present value, and $r_0{}^n$ represent the interest rate per period which may be earned on money that is saved for n periods starting at time $t = 0$, that is, the present time.

$$p_0(1 + r_0{}^1)^1 = v_1 \tag{D-1}$$

$$\$1(1 + .05)^1 = \$1.05$$

$$\$1{,}000(1 + .05)^1 = \$1{,}050$$

The symbols above show how $1 or $1,000 saved at $r_0{}^1 = 5$ percent $= .05$ has time value. Inspection of (D-1) reveals that

if $r_0{}^1 > 0$ then $v_1 > p_0$

and

if $r_0{}^1 = 0$ then $v_1 = p_0$

Equation (D-1) is only a "one-period" formula. If money is invested and left for n periods, then Eq. (D-2) shows the results.

$$p_0(1 + r_0{}^n)^n = v_n \tag{D-2}$$

$$\$1(1 + .1)^2 = \$1.21$$

$$\$1{,}000(1 + .1)^2 = \$1{,}210$$

The numerical examples above show that $1 or $1,000 saved at $r_0{}^n = 10$ percent for $n = 2$ periods will grow in value to $1.21 or $1,210, respectively.

Present Value

Equations (D-1) and (D-2) can be used to find the *present discounted value* of money to be received at time period t. Dividing both sides of (D-2) by the quantity $(1 + r_0{}^n)^n$ yields (D-3).

$$p_0 = \frac{v_n}{(1 + r_0{}^n)^n} \qquad \text{(D-3)}$$

$$\$1 = \frac{\$1.21}{(1 + .1)^2} = \frac{1.21}{1.21}$$

$$\$1,000 = \frac{\$1,210}{(1 + .1)^2} = \frac{1,210}{1.21}$$

The calculations above show that the present value of $1.21 or $1,210 to be received $n = 2$ periods in the future is $1 and $1,000, respectively, if the interest rate or discount rate is $r_0{}^n = 10$ percent. The quantity $1/(1 + r_0{}^n)^n$ is called the *discount factor* and will sometimes be written $1/(1 + r_0{}^n)^n = D_r{}^n$. For example, $500 to be received $n = 2$ periods in the future has a present value of $358.40 when $r_0{}^2 = 20$ percent, as shown below:

$$p_0 = \frac{v_n}{(1 + r_0{}^n)^n} = v^n D_r{}^n \qquad \text{(D-3)}$$

$$\$358.40 = \frac{\$500}{(1.2)^2} = \$500 D_{.2}{}^2$$

Equation (D-3) is a point-input–point-output present value model. This is a very simple transaction. Equation (D-4) is a more general present value model which allows for simultaneous inflows and outflows at multiple points in time. Let c_t denote the cashflow at time period t.

$$p_0 = \sum_{t=1}^{n} \frac{c_t}{(1 + r_0{}^n)^t} \qquad \text{(D-4)}$$

$$= c_1 D_r{}^1 + c_2 D_r{}^2 + \cdots + c_n D_r{}^n$$

If I_t is the inflow at time t and O_t is the outflow at time t, then $c_t = I_t - O_t$. This implies that $c_t > 0$ if I_t is larger than O_t. Suppose that $100 is to be received at the end of the next two periods and the interest rate is $r_0{}^2 = 10$ percent. Using (D-4), we see that the present value of this stream of cashflows is $173.54, as shown below.

$$p_0 = \sum_{t=1}^{2} \frac{c_t}{(1 + .1)^t}$$

$$= (c_1)(D_{.1}{}^1) + (c_2)(D_{.1}{}^2)$$

$$p_0 = \frac{\$100}{1.1} + \frac{\$100}{1.21}$$

$$\$173.54 = \$90.90 + \$82.64$$

These calculations mean that if you could save money at 10 percent with no risk, you should be indifferent between receiving $173.54 now and $100 at the end of each of the next two periods. The present value of both alternatives is $173.54.

Symbols

The discussion of the time value of money which makes up this appendix utilizes the following symbols:

i = stated or coupon interest rate; this is not necessarily the total yield earned from holding the asset. i is an interest rate per period which is printed on a new bond and may bear little relation to the market rate of interest.

p_0 = present value in dollars, or the cost of the asset.

v_n = terminal or ending value in dollars.

n = the number of time periods which the investment lasts.

c_t = net cashflow in period t = cash inflow in period t less cash outflow in period $t = I_t - O_t$.

t = the time period.

$D_r^n = 1/(1 + r_0^n)^n$ = the discount factor for n periods in the future at discount rate r_0^n.

k = the *appropriate* discount rate. Determining the appropriate discount rate is discussed in Chap. 7. Suffice it to say, the higher the risk, the higher k should be. The symbol k is the cost of capital; it is the discount rate which is appropriate to find the present value of an investment. This k is determined by the asset's risk and the opportunity cost of the investment. The value of k can be determined before the cashflows are estimated.

r_0^n = the yield to maturity = the internal rate of return = the market rate = the nominal yield. The value of r will typically vary with credit conditions and other factors. The symbol r is the discount rate which equates the present value of all net cashflows to the cost of the investment. Therefore, r can be determined only after all cashflows and the cost are known.

F = face or par value of a security.

iF = the dollar interest payable per period = the coupon interest rate i multiplied by the face value F.

Present Value Table

It is quite tedious to evaluate all the discount factors, $D_r{}^n = 1/(1+r)^n$, when performing present value calculations. To save the analyst this trouble, present value tables have been calculated and printed. Table D-1 is a present value table. This table shows the values of $D_r{}^n$ for many values of n and r. The $D_r{}^n$ values are not perfectly accurate because of rounding at the fifth decimal place.

Perpetuities

British Consols are perpetual bonds; that is, the bearer of the consol will receive periodic interest to perpetuity, but the principal will never be repaid. Unlike the American government, the British government makes no pretense of ever paying its national debt.

To value a consol, assume that the appropriate discount rate is k. The coupon rate i on bonds almost always differs from the discount rate. The coupon rate is the interest rate paid on the face value of the bond. The face value and coupon rate are printed on the bond itself and never change once the bond is issued. Let F and i denote the face value and coupon rate, respectively. Then iF is the cashflow, which is a fixed constant. The present value of a consol may be determined with Eq. (D-4). The bar over c denotes that it has a fixed constant value.

$$p_0 = \sum_t^n \frac{c_t}{(1+k)^t} \tag{D-4}$$

$$p_0 = \sum_t^{n=\infty} \bar{c} D_k{}^t \qquad \text{for a consol since } n = \infty \text{ and } c_t = \bar{c} = iF$$

$$p_0 = \frac{\bar{c}}{k} \tag{D-5}$$

$$= \frac{iF}{k}$$

It is difficult (to say the least) to evaluate the sum $D_k{}^t$ an infinitely large number of times, as required above. However, this problem is easily overcome by using Eq. (D-5), which shows how to find the present value p_0 of a *perpetual stream* ($n = \infty$) of *constant cashflows*. When $n = \infty$ and the

TABLE D-1 PRESENT VALUE TABLE

Present value of \$1 received at the end of n years $= D_i^n = \dfrac{1}{(1 + r_3^n)^n}$

n	1%	2%	3%	4%	5%	6%	7%	8%	9%	10%	n
1	0.99010	0.98039	0.97007	0.96154	0.95238	0.94340	0.93458	0.92593	0.91743	0.90909	1
2	.98030	.96117	.94260	.92456	.90703	.89000	.87344	.85734	.84168	.82645	2
3	.97059	.94232	.91514	.88900	.86384	.83962	.81630	.79383	.77218	.75131	3
4	.96098	.92385	.88849	.85480	.82270	.79209	.76290	.73503	.70843	.68301	4
5	.95147	.90573	.86261	.82193	.78353	.74726	.71299	.68058	.64993	.62092	5
6	.94204	.88797	.83748	.79031	.74622	.70496	.66634	.63017	.59627	.56447	6
7	.93272	.87056	.81309	.75992	.71068	.66506	.62275	.58349	.54703	.51316	7
8	.92348	.85349	.78941	.73069	.67684	.62741	.58201	.54027	.50187	.46651	8
9	.91434	.83675	.76642	.70259	.64461	.59190	.54393	.50025	.46043	.42410	9
10	.90529	.82035	.74409	.67556	.61391	.55839	.50835	.46319	.42241	.38554	10
11	.89632	.80426	.72242	.64958	.58468	.52679	.47509	.42888	.38753	.35049	11
12	.88745	.78849	.70138	.62460	.55684	.49697	.44401	.39711	.35553	.31863	12
13	.87866	.77303	.68095	.60057	.53032	.46884	.41496	.36770	.32618	.28966	13
14	.86996	.75787	.66112	.57747	.50507	.44230	.38782	.34046	.29925	.26333	14
15	.86135	.74301	.64186	.55526	.48102	.41726	.36245	.31524	.27454	.23939	15
16	.85282	.72845	.62317	.53391	.45811	.39365	.33873	.29189	.25187	.21763	16
17	.84438	.71416	.60502	.51337	.43630	.37136	.31657	.27027	.23107	.19784	17
18	.83602	.70016	.58739	.49363	.41552	.35034	.29586	.25025	.21199	.17986	18
19	.82774	.68643	.57029	.47464	.39573	.33051	.27651	.23171	.19449	.16351	19
20	.81954	67297	.55367	.45639	.37689	.31180	.25842	.21455	.17843	.14864	20
21	.81143	.65978	.53755	.43883	.35894	.29415	.24151	.19866	.16370	.13513	21
22	.80340	.64684	.52189	.42195	.34185	.27750	.22571	.18394	.15018	.12285	22
23	.79544	.63416	.50669	.40573	.32557	.26180	.21095	.17031	.13778	.11168	23
24	.78757	.62172	.49193	.39012	.31007	.24698	.19715	.15770	.12640	.10153	24
25	.77977	.60953	.47760	.37512	.29530	.23300	.18425	.14602	.11597	.09230	25

cashflows are constant, Eqs. (D-4) and (D-5) are equivalent,[1] but Eq. (D-5) saves much computation.

Present Value of n Equal Cashflows

Sometimes an equal amount is to be received for n consecutive periods, for example, an annuity. Equation (D-4) can be used to find the present value of n equal cashflows ($c = c_t$ for all t).

$$p_0 = \sum_t^n \frac{c_t}{(1+k)^t} \tag{D-4}$$

$$= c_1(D_i^1) + c_2(D_i^2) + \cdots + c_n(D_k^n)$$
$$= \bar{c}(D_i^1 + D_i^2 + D_i^3 + \cdots + D_i^n) \qquad \text{if } c_t = \bar{c} = \text{constant}$$

$$= \bar{c} \sum_{t=1}^n D_k^t \tag{D-6}$$

When $c_t = \bar{c}$ for n periods, Eq. (D-6) is a convenient simplification of (D-4). The sum of the D_k^t quantities in (D-6) is merely the sum of part of a column of Table D-1. This sum of n consecutive values of D_k^t is then multiplied by the constant $\bar{c}$ to find the present value of the n equal cashflows. Table D-2 shows the sums of n consecutive D_k^t quantities, $\sum_{t=1}^n D_k^t$, for several values of n, t, and k. This table is useful in finding the present value of n equal cashflows. It shows the present value of \$1 received each period for n periods when the discount rate is k.

---

[1] Equation (D-5) is derived from (D-4) as follows:

$$p_0 = \sum_t^n \bar{c} D_k^t \tag{D-4}$$

$$= \bar{c} \sum_t^n D_k^t \qquad \text{since } \sum ax = a \sum x$$

$$p_0 = \bar{c} D_k^1 + \bar{c} D_k^2 + \bar{c} D_k^3 + \cdots + \bar{c} D_k^n \tag{D-4a}$$

$$p_0(1+k) = \bar{c} + \bar{c} D_k^1 + \bar{c} D_k^2 + \cdots + \bar{c} D_k^{n-1} \tag{D-4b}$$

$$p_0(1+k) - p_0 = \bar{c} - \bar{c} D_k^n \qquad \text{by subtracting (D-4a) from (D-4b)}$$

$$p_0 + k p_0 - p_0 = \bar{c} - \bar{c} D_k^n$$

$$k p_0 = \bar{c} \qquad \text{since } D_k^n \to 0 \text{ as } n \to \infty, \text{ the } \bar{c} D_k^n \text{ term becomes zero}$$

$$p_0 = \bar{c}/k \tag{D-5}$$

Thus, (D-5) is derived from (D-4).

TABLE D-2 THE PRESENT VALUE OF SOME ANNUITIES

Present value of \$1 per year for n consecutive years $= \sum_{t=1}^{n} D_k{}^t = \sum_{t=1}^{n} \dfrac{1}{(1+k)^t}$

Year	1%	2%	3%	4%	5%	6%	7%	8%	9%	10%	Year
1	0.9901	0.9804	0.9709	0.9615	0.9524	0.9434	0.9346	0.9259	0.9174	0.9091	1
2	1.9704	1.9416	1.9135	1.8861	1.8594	1.8334	1.8080	1.7833	1.7591	1.7355	2
3	2.9410	2.8839	2.8286	2.7751	2.7232	2.6730	2.6243	2.5771	2.5313	2.4868	3
4	3.9020	3.8077	3.7171	3.6299	3.5459	3.4651	3.3872	3.3121	3.2397	3.1699	4
5	4.8535	4.7134	4.5797	4.4518	4.3295	4.2123	4.1002	3.9927	3.8896	3.7908	5
6	5.7955	5.6014	5.4172	5.2421	5.0757	4.9173	4.7665	4.6229	4.4859	4.3553	6
7	6.7282	6.4720	6.2302	6.0020	5.7863	5.5824	5.3893	5.2064	5.0329	4.8684	7
8	7.6517	7.3254	7.0196	6.7327	6.4632	6.2098	5.9713	5.7466	5.5348	5.3349	8
9	8.5661	8.1622	7.7861	7.4353	7.1078	6.8017	6.5152	6.2469	5.9852	5.7590	9
10	9.4714	8.9825	8.5302	8.1109	7.7217	7.3601	7.0236	6.7101	6.4176	6.1446	10
11	10.3677	9.7868	9.2526	8.7604	8.3064	7.8868	7.4987	7.1389	6.8052	6.4951	11
12	11.2552	10.5753	9.9539	9.3850	8.8632	8.3838	7.9427	7.5361	7.1607	6.8137	12
13	12.1338	11.3483	10.6349	9.9856	9.3935	8.8527	8.3576	7.9038	7.4869	7.1034	13
14	13.0038	12.1062	11.2960	10.5631	9.8986	9.2950	8.7454	8.2442	7.7861	7.3667	14
15	13.8651	12.8492	11.9379	11.1183	10.3796	9.7122	9.1079	8.5595	8.0607	7.6061	15
16	14.7180	13.5777	12.5610	11.6522	10.8377	10.1059	9.4466	8.8514	8.3125	7.8237	16
17	15.5624	14.2918	13.1660	12.1656	11.2740	10.4772	9.7632	9.1216	8.5436	8.0215	17
18	16.3984	14.9920	13.7534	12.6592	11.6895	10.8276	10.0591	9.3719	8.7556	8.2014	18
19	17.2261	15.6784	14.3237	13.1339	12.0853	11.1581	10.3356	9.6036	8.9501	8.3649	19
20	18.0457	16.3514	14.8774	13.5903	12.4622	11.4699	10.5940	9.8181	9.1285	8.5136	20
21	18.8571	17.0111	15.4149	14.0291	12.8211	11.7640	10.8355	10.0168	9.2922	8.6487	21
22	19.6605	17.6580	15.9368	14.4511	13.1630	12.0416	11.0612	10.2007	9.4424	8.7715	22
23	20.4559	18.2921	16.4435	14.8568	13.4885	12.3033	11.2722	10.3710	9.5802	8.8832	23
24	21.2435	18.9139	16.9355	15.2469	13.7986	12.5503	11.4693	10.5287	9.7066	8.9847	24
25	22.0233	19.5234	17.4131	15.6220	14.0939	12.7833	11.6536	10.6748	9.8226	9.0770	25

Compounding Several Times per Period

Sometimes it is appropriate to compound the interest factor several times per period. Let b denote the number of times per period the interest is compounded. Equation (D-7) may be used for such present value problems.

$$p_0 = \sum_t^n \frac{c_t}{(1 + r/b)^{bt}} \qquad \text{(D-7)}$$

Equation (D-7) takes $1/b$ times the interest rate r (that is, r/b) and compounds it b times as frequently (that is, bt) as is done when interest is compounded once a year. Since $(1 + r/b)^b > (1 + r)$, compounding more frequently yields different values. More frequent compounding decreases the present value. For example, at $r = 4$ percent the present value of $1 received in 5 years and compounded annually is $0.82193, as calculated with (D-3) below. But at $r = 4$ percent, the present value of $1 received in 5 years and compounded semiannually (that is, $b = 2$) is $0.82035. The difference is due to compounding semiannually.

$$p_0 = \frac{v_5}{(1 + r)^5} \qquad \text{(D-3)}$$

$$= \$1(.82193)$$
$$= 82.193¢$$

$$p_0 = \frac{v_5}{(1 + r/b)^{5b}} \qquad \text{(D-7)}$$

$$= \$1(.82035)$$
$$= 82.035¢$$

Terminal Value

So far in this appendix we have seen how to find the present value of future cashflows. Sometimes the opposite question arises. That is, what is the future or terminal value of present cashflows which are invested or saved? To answer this question, Eqs. (D-2) and (D-8) are used.

Equation (D-2) shows that the future or terminal value of $p_0 = \$10$ saved at $r = 10$ percent per year will be $12.10 after $n = 2$ years.[2]

---

[2] Logarithms can be useful in evaluating problems of this nature, especially when n is large.

$$v_n = v_0(1 + r)^n$$
$$\log v_n = \log v_0 + n \log (1 + r)$$
$$v_n = \text{antilog} \,[\log v_0 + n \log (1 + r)]$$

Common or Naperian logs may be used.

$$v_n = p_0(1 + r)^n \tag{D-2}$$
$$= \$10(1 + .1)^2$$
$$= \$10(1.21)$$
$$= \$12.10$$

v_n is the terminal value after n periods.

When money is to be saved periodically, Eq. (D-8) is used.

$$v_n = \sum_t^n c_t(1 + r)^t \tag{D-8}$$

$$= \sum_t^n c_t \frac{1}{D_r{}^t}$$

Equation (D-8) may be used to find the terminal value of $10 saved at the beginning of each of the next 2 years for $r = 10$ percent interest. The calculations are shown below.

$$v_n = \sum_1^2 c_t(1.1)^t$$

$$= c_1(1 + r)^1 + c_2(1 + r)^2$$
$$= 10(1.1) + 10(1.1)^2$$
$$= 11 + 12.10$$
$$= \$23.10$$

If interest is compounded b times per period, Eq. (D-9) is used to determine future values.

$$v_n = \sum_t^n c_t\left(1 + \frac{r}{b}\right)^{tb} \tag{D-9}$$

For example, if $10 were saved at the start of 2 consecutive years and earned $r = 10$ percent interest compounded quarterly (that is, $b = 4$), then $23.22 could be withdrawn after the 2 years.

$$v_n = \sum_1^2 \$10\left(1 + \frac{.1}{4}\right)^{4t}$$

$$= \$10(1 + .025)^4 + \$10(1 + .025)^8$$
$$= \$11.04 + \$12.18 = \$23.22$$

Banks which pay interest compounded periodically use (D-9) to determine terminal values for their savings plans.

APPENDIX E
The Expected Value
Operator (*E*)

An expectation is like an "average" value. For example, for one toss of a fair coin for $1, we can say the expected value of the outcome is the probability of heads times the $1 loss plus the probability of tails times the $1 gain. Symbolically,

$$\text{Expected value} = P(\text{heads})(-\$1) + P(\text{tails})(+\$1)$$
$$= .5(-1) + .5(+1) = 0$$

The above symbols are a very definitive statement of what is meant by the phrase "we expect that fair gambles will break even." Writing the expression for expected value in even more general form, we say:

$$E(x) = \sum_{i=1}^{n} p_i x_i \tag{E-1}$$

$$= p_1 x_1 + p_2 x_2 + \cdot \cdot \cdot + p_n x_n$$

In words, the expected value of the variable x (for example, x might be the $1 outcome of the gamble or any other number resulting from an experiment involving change which has n possible outcomes) equals the sum of all n products of $(p_i)(x_i)$, where p_i is the probability of the ith outcome $[P(\text{heads}) = p_i = \frac{1}{2}$ in the coin example] and x_i is the ith outcome $[x_i = \$1$ or $-\$1$ in the example].

Mathematicians say that the letter E as used in Eq. (E-1) is an *operator*, meaning that the letter E specifies the operation of multiplying all outcomes times their probabilities and summing those products to get the expected value.

Finding the expected value is roughly analogous to finding the weighted average using probabilities for weights. Do not be confused, however; although the arithmetic is the same, an average is conceptually different from an expectation. An expectation is determined by its probabilities, and it represents a hypothesis about an unknown outcome; but an average is a summarizing measure. There is no conceptual connection between an average and an expectation; there is only the mechanical similarity of the calculations.

The operator E can be used to derive several important formulas. Therefore, let us consider several elementary properties of expected-value operations.

1 The expected value of a constant number is that constant. Symbolically, if c is any constant number (for example, $c = 2, -99$, or 1,064),

$$E(c) = c$$

Proof of this is given below.

$$E(c) = \sum_{i=1}^{n} p_i c = p_1 c + \cdots + p_n c$$

$$= c \sum_{i=1}^{n} p_i = c(1) = c$$

2 The expected value of a constant times a random variable equals the constant times the expected value of the random variable. Thus, if x is a random variable (for example, the -1 or $+1$ outcome of the gamble) and c is a constant (namely, the number of dollars bet on each toss),

$$E(cx) = cE(x)$$

The proof follows.

$$E(cx) = \sum_{i=1}^{n} p_i(cx_i) = p_1(cx_1) + \cdots + p_n(cx_n)$$

$$= p_1 c x_1 + \cdots + p_n c x_n$$

$$= c(p_1 x_1 + p_2 x_2 + \cdots + p_n x_n) = c \sum_{i-1}^{n} p_i x_i = cE(x)$$

3 The expected value of the sum of n independent random variables is simply the sum of their expected values. For example, if $n =$ two random variables called, say, x and y,

$$E(x + y) = E(x) + E(y)$$

The proof follows.

$$E(x + y) = \sum_{i=1}^{n} p_i(x_i + y_i) = p_i(x_i + y_1) + p_2(x_2 + y_2)$$

$$+ \cdots + p_n(x_n + y_n)$$

$$= p_1 x_1 + p_1 y_1 + p_2 x_2 + p_2 y_2 + \cdots + p_n x_n + p_n y_n$$
$$= [p_1 x_1 + p_2 x_2 + \cdots + p_n x_n] + [p_1 y_1 + p_2 y_2 + \cdots + p_n y_n]$$

$$= \sum_{i=1}^{n} p_i x_i + \sum_{i=1}^{n} p_i y_i = E(x) + E(y)$$

where p_i is the joint probability of x_i and y_i occurring jointly.

4 The expected value of a constant times a random variable plus a constant equals the constant times the expected value of the random variable plus the constant. Symbolically, if b and c are constants and x is a random variable,

$$E(bx + c) = bE(x) + c$$

The proof is a combination of the three preceding proofs. These four properties of the expected-value operator may be used to derive the following useful theorems.

Theorem E-1.   The variance of a random variable equals the expected value of the squared random variable less the expected value of the random variable squared.[1]
    Stated in equation form,

$$\text{var}(x) = E(x^2) - [E(x)]^2$$

Proof

$$\begin{aligned}
\text{var}(x) &= E[x - E(x)]^2 \quad \text{by definition of } \text{var}(x) \\
&= E\{x^2 - 2xE(x) + [E(x)]^2\} \\
&= E(x^2) - 2E(x) + [E(x)]^2 \\
&= E(x^2) - [E(x)]^2 \qquad\qquad\qquad\qquad\qquad \text{Q.E.D.}
\end{aligned}$$

Theorem E-2.   The expected value of a squared random variable equals the variance of that random variable plus its expected value squared.
    Stated in equation form,

$$E(x^2) = \text{var}(x) + [E(x)]^2$$

---

[1] Note that Theorem E-1 implies a computationally efficient way to compute the variance in a real-valued problem. That is, finding the average of the deviations,

$$\frac{1}{n} \sum_{i=1}^{n} (X_i - \overline{X})^2 = \text{var}(x)$$

requires more computation than subtracting the mean squared from the mean of the squares:

$$\frac{1}{n} \sum_{i=1}^{n} X_i^2 - \overline{X}^2 = \text{var}(x)$$

The other theorems also imply similar computational shortcuts which are useful in performing hand calculations or in writing efficient computer programs.

Proof

$$\text{var}(x) = E(x^2) - [E(x)]^2 \qquad \text{by Theorem E-1}$$
$$[E(x)]^2 + \text{var}(x) = E(x^2) \qquad\qquad \text{Q.E.D.}$$

Theorem E-3. The variance of a linear transformation of the random variable is not affected by adding or subtracting a constant, but multiplying the random variable times a constant increases the variance of the product by the square of the constant.
  Stated in equation form,

$$\text{var}(ax + b) = a^2 \, \text{var}(x) \qquad \text{for any constants } a \text{ and } b$$

Proof

$$\begin{aligned}
\text{var}(ax + b) &= E[ax + b - E(ax + b)]^2 \qquad \text{by definition}\\
&= E[ax + b - aE(x) - b]^2\\
&= Ea^2[x - E(x)]^2\\
&= a^2E[x - E(x)]^2 = a^2 \, \text{var}(x) \qquad\qquad \text{Q.E.D.}
\end{aligned}$$

  Theorem E-3 implies that the standard deviation of $ax + b$ equals $a\sigma_x$, the square root of $a^2 \, \text{var}(x)$.

Theorem E-4. The expected value of the product of two random variables equals the product of their expectations only if they are independent.
  Stated in equation form,

$$E(xy) = E(x)E(y) \qquad \text{if and only if } x \text{ and } y \text{ are independent}$$

Proof

$$E(xy) = \sum_i \sum_j [p(x_i \text{ and } y_i)(x_i)(y_i)]$$

but

$$p(x \text{ and } y) = p_x p_y \qquad \text{if } x \text{ and } y \text{ are independent}$$

Therefore

$$E(xy) = \sum_i \sum_j (p_{xi} p_{yj} x_i y_j)$$

$$= \sum_i (p_{xi} x_i) \sum_j (p_{yj} y_i)$$

$$= E(x)E(y) \qquad\qquad \text{Q.E.D.}$$

Theorem E-5. The covariance of two random variables equals the expected value of their product less the product of their expectations.

Stated in equation form,

$$\text{cov}(x,y) = E(xy) - E(x)E(y)$$

Proof

$$
\begin{aligned}
\text{cov}(x,y) &= E\{[x - E(x)][y - E(y)]\} \qquad \text{by definition} \\
&= E\{(xy - x)[E(y) - yE(x)] + E(x)|(y)\} \\
&= [E(xy) - E(x)][E(y) - E(y)][E(x) + E(x)][E(y)] \\
&= E(xy) - E(x)E(y) \qquad\qquad\qquad\qquad\qquad\qquad \text{Q.E.D.}
\end{aligned}
$$

Theorem E-6. The covariance of a random variable with any constant is zero.

Stated in equation form,

$$\text{cov}(x,c) = 0 \qquad \text{where } c \text{ is a constant}$$

Proof

$$
\begin{aligned}
\text{cov}(x,c) &= E(xc) - E(x)E(c) \qquad \text{by Theorem E-5} \\
&= cE(x) - cE(x) = 0 \qquad\qquad\qquad\qquad \text{Q.E.D.}
\end{aligned}
$$

Theorem E-7. The covariance of linear transformations of two random variables (x and y) is not affected by adding or subtracting constants to one or both of the variables, but the covariance is increased by a multiple equal to any constants which were multiplied times the random variables.

Stated in equation form,

$$\text{cov}(ax + b, \, cy + d) = ac \, \text{cov}(x,y) \qquad \text{where } a, b, c, \text{ and } d \text{ are constants}$$

Proof

$$
\begin{aligned}
\text{cov}(ax + b, \, cy + d) &= E\{[ax + b - E(ax + b)][cy + d - E(cy + d)]\} \\
&\qquad\qquad\qquad \text{by the definition of the covariance} \\
&= E[(ax + b - aEx + b)(cy + d - cEy - d)] \\
&= E[(x - Ex)c(y - Ey)] \\
&= acE[(x - Ex)(y - Ey)] \\
&= ac \, \text{cov}(x,y) \qquad\qquad\qquad\qquad\qquad\qquad \text{Q.E.D.}
\end{aligned}
$$

Theorem E-8. The covariance of a sum of random variables with another variable z equals the sum of their covariances with variable z.
    Stated in equation form,

$$\text{cov}(x, y + z) = \text{cov}(x,y) + \text{cov}(x,z)$$

Proof

$$
\begin{aligned}
\text{cov}(x, y + z) &= E[x(y + z)] - E(x)E(y + z) \qquad \text{by Theorem E-5} \\
&= E(xy + xz) - [E(x)E(y) + E(x)E(z)] \\
&= E(xy) + E(xz) - [E(x)E(y) + E(x)E(z)] \\
&= E(xy) - E(x)E(y) + E(xz) - E(x)E(z) \\
&= \text{cov}(x,y) + \text{cov}(x,z) \qquad\qquad\qquad\qquad \text{Q.E.D.}
\end{aligned}
$$

Theorem E-9. If the random variables x and y both undergo a linear transformation (for example, $ax + b$ and $cy + d$, where a, b, c, and d are constants), their correlation coefficient ρ_{xy} is invariant.
    Symbolically,

$$\rho(x,y) = \rho(ax + b, \, cy + d)$$

Proof

$$
\begin{aligned}
\rho(ax + b, \, cy + d) &= \frac{\text{cov}(ax + b, \, cy + d)}{(\sigma_{ax+b})(\sigma_{ay+d})} \qquad \text{definition of } \rho_{xy} \\[2mm]
&= \frac{ac \, \text{cov}(xy)}{a(\sigma_x)c(\sigma_y)} \qquad \text{by Theorems E-3 and E-7} \\[2mm]
&= \frac{\text{cov}(x,y)}{\sigma_x \sigma_y} \\[2mm]
&= \rho(x,y) \qquad\qquad\qquad\qquad\qquad \text{Q.E.D.}
\end{aligned}
$$

Theorem E-10. The variance of a sum of random variables equals the sum of their variances plus the sum of all their covariances.
    Stated in equation form,

$$\text{var}(\Sigma x_i) = \Sigma \sigma_i^2 + \sum_i \sum_j \sigma_{ij} \qquad \text{for } i \neq j$$

Proof

$$\text{var}(\Sigma x_i) = E \left(\sum_i x_i - \sum_i u_i \right)^2 \qquad \text{where } u_i = E(x)$$

$$= E \left[\sum_i (x_i - u_i)^2 \right]$$

$$= E \left[\sum_i \sum_j (x_i - u_i)(x_j - u_j) \right]$$

$$= \sum_i \sum_j E[(x_i - u_i)(x_j - u_j)]$$

$$= \sum_i \sum_j \sigma_{ij}$$

$$= \sum_i \sigma_i^2 + \sum_i \sum_j \sigma_{ij} \qquad \text{for } i \neq j \qquad\qquad \text{Q.E.D.}$$

APPENDIX F
Simultaneous Solution of
Linear Equations

Consider the two equations

$$x + y = 8 \tag{F-1}$$

and

$$2x - y = 4 \tag{F-2}$$

There are many pairs of values of x and y which will satisfy either (F-1) or (F-2). The problem is to discover whether there are pairs that will simultaneously satisfy both equations and, if so, how can they be found. If such pairs exist, Eqs. (F-1) and (F-2) are called *simultaneous equations*. Five methods of finding the simultaneous solutions to the two equations will be demonstrated.

Graphing

The first method consists of *graphing* the equations and observing where the lines intersect. Since for each equation any point on its graph is a solution to that equation, the intersection is the simultaneous solution of the

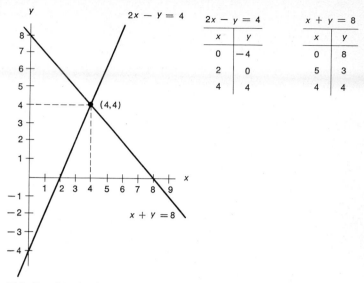

FIG. F-1 Graph of two linear equations in two variables.

equations. The tables used to determine the graph and the graph itself are shown in Fig. F-1. The intersection occurs at the point $x = 4$, $y = 4$, or (4,4) in (x,y) space. Notice that the graphs of the equations are straight lines and thus intersect at one point only. Such equations are called *linear simultaneous equations,* or a *system of equations.*

Elimination

The second method consists of multiplying one or both of the equations by appropriate constants and then adding or subtracting the equations. When this is all done, one of the unknowns will have been eliminated. This process is called the *elimination* method. If, for example, (F-1) is multiplied by −2 and added to (F-2), the result is negative two times (F-1) plus (F-2), that is,

$$-2x - 2y = -16$$
$$+2x - y = 4$$
$$-3y = -12$$

So

$$y = 4$$

The value of y can be substituted into (F-1) or (F-2) to find x. Thus, from (F-1),

$$x + y = 8$$
$$x + 4 = 8$$
$$x = 4$$

Again the simultaneous solution is $(4,4) = (x,y)$.

Substitution

The third method is called the *substitution*. Using one of the equations, one unknown is solved for in terms of the other. This solution is then substituted into the remaining equation, giving the value for the remaining unknown.

$$x + y = 8 \tag{F-1}$$

so

$$y = 8 - x$$

Substituting for y into $2x - y = 4$ yields

$$2x - (8 - x) = 4$$

or

$$3x = 12$$

so

$$x = 4$$

This value of x can be substituted into (F-1) or (F-2) to determine y. Using (F-2),

$$2x - y = 4$$
$$8 - y = 4$$
$$y = 4$$

Once again, the solution is $(4,4) = (x,y)$.

Cramer's Rule

Cramer's rule, the fourth method to be examined, is based on matrix algebra.[1] The two equations in general form can be written

[1] See T. Yamane, *Mathematics for Economists* (Englewood Cliffs, N.J.: Prentice-Hall, 1962), p. 362.

(1) $a_1x + b_1x = c_1$

(2) $a_2x + b_2x = c_2$

where $a_1 = 1$
$b_1 = 1$
$c_1 = 8$
$a_2 = 2$
$b_2 = -1$
$c_2 = 4$

The coefficients (that is, a_1, b_1, a_2, b_2) in matrix form are

$$[A] = \begin{vmatrix} a_1 & b_1 \\ a_2 & b_2 \end{vmatrix} = \begin{vmatrix} 1 & 1 \\ 2 & -1 \end{vmatrix}$$

$$= a_1b_2 - a_2b_1 \quad \text{by definition of a determinant}$$
$$= -1 - 2$$
$$= -3$$

The determinant obtained by replacing the coefficients of x by the constants on the right side of the equations (namely c_1 and c_2) is

$$[B] - \begin{vmatrix} c_1 & b_1 \\ c_2 & b_2 \end{vmatrix} = \begin{vmatrix} 8 & 1 \\ 4 & -1 \end{vmatrix}$$

$$= c_1b_2 - c_2b_1$$
$$= -8 - 4$$
$$= -12$$

The determinant obtained by replacing the coefficients of y by the numbers on the right side of the equation is

$$[C] = \begin{vmatrix} 1 & 8 \\ 2 & 4 \end{vmatrix}$$

$$= 4 - 16$$
$$= -12$$

Cramer's rule states that the value of the unknown to be determined is found by dividing the determinant (whose value is obtained by replacing the coefficients of that unknown by the values on the right of the equations) by the determinant of the original coefficients. Using Cramer's rule, we have

$$X = \frac{[B]}{[A]} = \frac{\begin{vmatrix} 8 & 1 \\ 4 & -1 \end{vmatrix}}{\begin{vmatrix} 1 & 1 \\ 2 & -1 \end{vmatrix}}$$

$$= \frac{-12}{-3} = 4$$

and

$$Y = \frac{[C]}{[A]} = \frac{\begin{vmatrix} 1 & 8 \\ 2 & 4 \end{vmatrix}}{\begin{vmatrix} 1 & 1 \\ 2 & -1 \end{vmatrix}}$$

$$= \frac{-12}{-3} = 4$$

As usual, the solution is $(x,y) = (4,4)$.

Matrix Inversion

Matrix inversion is the fifth method used to solve the simultaneous equations. The two equations written in matrix form are:

$$\begin{bmatrix} 1 & 1 \\ 2 & -1 \end{bmatrix} \begin{bmatrix} x \\ y \end{bmatrix} = \begin{bmatrix} 8 \\ 4 \end{bmatrix}$$

Premultiplying both sides of the equation by the inverse[2] of $\begin{bmatrix} 1 & 1 \\ 2 & -1 \end{bmatrix}$

yields:

$$\begin{bmatrix} x \\ y \end{bmatrix} = \begin{bmatrix} \frac{1}{3} & \frac{1}{3} \\ \frac{2}{3} & -\frac{1}{3} \end{bmatrix} \begin{bmatrix} 8 \\ 4 \end{bmatrix}$$

$$= [A^{-1}] \begin{bmatrix} c_1 \\ c_2 \end{bmatrix}$$

[2] The inverse of

$$[A] = \begin{vmatrix} 1 & 1 \\ 2 & -1 \end{vmatrix}$$

is denoted A^{-1}; this inverse is

$$[A^{-1}] = \begin{vmatrix} \frac{1}{3} & \frac{1}{3} \\ \frac{2}{3} & -\frac{1}{3} \end{vmatrix}$$

A method of finding the inverse matrix is explained by T. Yamane, ibid., pp. 255–275.

or

$$\begin{bmatrix} x \\ y \end{bmatrix} = \begin{bmatrix} 4 \\ 4 \end{bmatrix}$$

after multiplying the inverse times the column of vector of constants. Since matrices that are equal must have equal elements, $x = 4$ and $y = 4$. Of course, all five techniques demonstrated here yield the same solution.

APPENDIX G
Statistical Moments

Some probability distributions (such as the uniform and normal) may be completely described by their "statistical moments." The moments of a probability distribution are statistical measures.[1]

The Expected Return and Mean

For a probability distribution of returns, the first moment about the origin is defined as shown in Eqs. (G-1) and (G-1a).

$$E(r) = \sum_{i=1}^{n} p_i r_i \qquad \text{for future returns} \qquad \text{(G-1)}$$

$$\bar{r} = \frac{1}{n} \sum_{i=1}^{n} r_t \qquad \text{for historical returns} \qquad \text{(G-1a)}$$

where $E(r)$ = expected return
n = number of different returns possible
$\bar{r}$ = mean return
r_i = ith possible rate of return
$p_i = 1/n$ = relative frequency of ith return

It is always assumed that $\sum_{i}^{n} p_i = 1$. The first moment about the origin of a distribution is the same as its expected value or mean. The first moment about the origin is a measure of location or central tendency for the distribution.

[1] For a more rigorous discussion of moments, see J. E. Freund, *Mathematical Statistics* (Englewood Cliffs, N.J.: Prentice-Hall, 1962), chap. 4. For a more elementary discussion of moments and various approximations for moments, see S. B. Richmond, *Statistical Analysis*, 2d ed. (New York: Ronald, 1964), chap. 4. For those probability distributions (for example, Cauchy) having no moments, this discussion is, of course, irrelevant.

Probability Distributions and Relative-Frequency Distributions

Equation (G-1) is similar to Eq. (G-1a). The only difference in them is that (G-1) is stated in terms of probabilities and therefore applies to future returns (denoted r_i), whereas Eq. (G-1a) is stated in terms of n historical rates of return (denoted r_t) and relative frequencies (denoted $1/n$). Thus, (G-1a) defines the mean of a historical relative-frequency distribution.

Equations (G-1) and (G-1a) both define first moments about the origin, but (G-1) defines a first moment about the origin of an (expected) probability distribution, while (G-1a) defines the first moment about the origin of a (historical) relative-frequency distribution.

First Moment about the Mean Always Zero

Moments about the mean are different from *moments about the origin*. The *first moment* about the mean is defined by Eqs. (G-2) and (G-2a).

$$M_1 = \sum_{i}^{n} p_i[r_i - E(r)] = 0 \qquad \text{for future returns} \qquad \text{(G-2)}$$

$$M_1 = \frac{1}{n} \sum_{t}^{n} [r_t - E(r)] = 0 \qquad \text{for historical returns} \qquad \text{(G-2a)}$$

The first moment about the mean is always zero because it is the average of the deviations from the average. The mean or expected value of any group of numbers is constructed so all the positive deviations above it and all the negative deviations below it sum to zero. It has no use in the analysis. However, higher-order moments about the mean are called *statistical moments* and they are useful in security and portfolio analysis.

Variance or Second Moment

The *second moment* about the mean of a distribution of returns is defined by Eqs. (G-3) and (G-3a).

$$\sigma^2 = \sum_{i}^{n} p[r_i - E(r)]^2 \qquad \text{for future returns} \qquad \text{(G-3)}$$

$$\sigma^2 = \frac{1}{n} \sum_{t}^{n} [r_t - E(r)]^2 \qquad \text{for historical returns} \qquad \text{(G-3a)}$$

Second statistical moment is a synonym for *variance*. The second statistical moment measures the distribution's dispersion or wideness. The square root of the variance is the standard deviation.

The Third Moment and Skewness

The *third moment* of a distribution of returns is defined in Eqs. (G-4) and (G-4a).

$$M_3 = \Sigma p_i [r_i - E(r)]^3 \qquad \text{for future returns} \qquad \text{(G-4)}$$

$$M_3 = \frac{1}{n} \sum_{t}^{n} [r_t - E(r)]^3 \qquad \text{for historical returns} \qquad \text{(G-4a)}$$

The third statistical moment measures the lopsidedness of the distribution; it is normalized by dividing it by the standard deviation cubed. This puts the third moments of different distributions in terms of a relative measure of lopsidedness which is called *skewness*. Equation (G-5) defines the skewness of a distribution of returns.

$$\text{sk}(r) = \frac{M_3}{\sigma^3}$$

$$= \frac{\Sigma p [r_i - E(r)]^3}{\{\sqrt{\Sigma p [r_i - E(r)]}\}^3} \qquad \text{(G-5)}$$

Figure G-1 shows three probability distributions with the three possible types of skewness—positive, zero, and negative. A distribution which is skewed left (*a*) will have a long left tail, a negative third moment, and negative skewness. A symmetrical distribution (*b*) will have a third moment and skewness of zero.[2] Distributions which are skewed right (*c*) will have positive third moments, positive skewness, and longer right tails.

[2] Skewness may be zero for nonsymmetrical distributions in a few pathological situations. P. G. Hoel, *Introduction to Mathematical Statistics*, 3d ed. (New York: Wiley, 1962), pp. 76–77. Skewness can also be difficult to measure econometrically, as shown by J. C. Francis, "Skewness and Investors' Decisions," *Journal of Financial and Quantitative Analysis*, March 1975, pp. 163–172.

FIG. G-1 Skewness in probability distributions. (*a*) Skewed left; (*b*) symmetric; (*c*) skewed right.

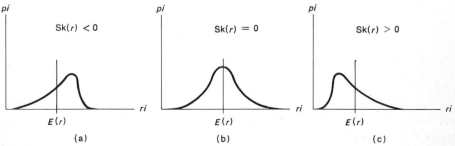

Fourth Moment and Kurtosis

The *fourth moment* M_4 measures the peakedness of a probability distribution. For a probability distribution of returns, the fourth moment is defined by Eqs. (G-6) and (G-6a).

$$M_4 = \Sigma p_i [r_i - E(r)]^4 \qquad \text{for future returns} \tag{G-6}$$

$$M_4 = \frac{1}{n} \sum_{t}^{n} [r_t - E(r)]^4 \qquad \text{for historical returns} \tag{G-6a}$$

Figure G-2 shows three probability distributions of returns, leptokurtic (*a*), platykurtic (*b*), and normal or mesokurtic (*c*). Although all three of these distributions may have first, second, and third moments which are identical, they would all have different fourth moments.

The fourth moment of a probability distribution is usually normalized by being divided by the standard deviation raised to the fourth power, allowing direct comparisons of the peakedness of different distributions.[3] This normalized fourth moment is called *a measure of kurtosis.* Kurtosis is defined by Eq. (G-7).

$$\text{kur}(r) = \frac{M_4}{\sigma^4} \tag{G-7}$$

$$= \frac{\Sigma p [r - E(r)]^4}{\{\sqrt{\Sigma p [r - E(r)]^2}\}^4}$$

[3] I. Kaplansky, "A Common Error Concerning Kurtosis," *Journal of the American Statistical Association,* June 1945, p. 259.

FIG. G-2 Peakedness or kurtosis of distributions. (*a*) Leptokurtic; (*b*) platykurtic; (*c*) normal or mesokurtic.

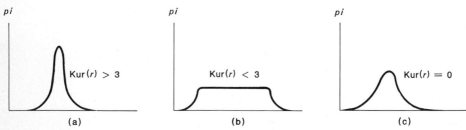

pi   Kur(*r*) > 3   (a)

pi   Kur(*r*) < 3   (b)

pi   Kur(*r*) = 0   (c)

APPENDIX H
Elements of Correlation
and Regression Analysis

Correlation and regression are classical statistical tools used to analyze the interrelation between variables. In this appendix we shall examine only simple linear models.

H-1 REGRESSION

We shall denote the independent or control variable as x and the dependent variable as y. As an example, x and y might be observations of returns on the market and the concurrent returns on some security, respectively. Of course, then we would be discussing the characteristic line—a particular regression line. Or x might represent the average number of cigarettes smoked per month and y might represent the number of chest colds and other respiratory illnesses the smoker suffered per month. This is the type of regression model which biometricians use in determining the effects of smoking on health. If someone were testing the hypothesis that storks deliver babies, she might regress the number of births in some area during a given time period y against the number of storks observed in that area during the same period x. As a matter of fact, to demonstrate the necessity that some rational theory underlie statistical analysis in order to avoid ridiculous or spurious results, one researcher did regress babies onto storks and found a significant positive relation. In any event, Eq. (H-1) shows the basic regression model we shall examine here.

$$y = \alpha + Bx + e \tag{H-1}$$

where α = intercept coefficient, alpha
     B = slope coefficient, beta
     e = random error term, epsilon

Figure H-1 shows a scatter diagram and the form of Eq. (H-1) which seems to "fit the data best."

The Sample Data

Regression analysis begins with n observations of (x_i, y_i) pairs: (x_1, y_1), (x_2, y_2), . . . , (x_n, y_n). These n observations may be graphed as a scatter diagram like the one in Fig. H-1. For the characteristic line, the n observations represent observations from n different time periods all for the same asset. For the analysis of the effects of smoking on health, the n observa-

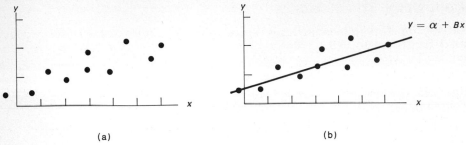

FIG. H-1 Graphs of simple linear regression. (*a*) Scatter diagram of (x_i, y_i) observations; (*b*) least-squares line through scatter of observations.

tions represent n persons' experiences (or n periods of experience by one person).

Fitting the Regression Line

The objective of regression analysis is to find the line through the points in (x,y) space which "fits the observations." The objective is to minimize the sum of the squared errors around the regression line, or, more specifically, to minimize SSQ in Eq. (H-2).

$$\text{min SSQ} = \sum_{i=1}^{n} [y_i - (\alpha + Bx_i)]^2 \tag{H-2}$$

$$= \sum_{i=1}^{n} e_i^2$$

$$= \sum_{i=1}^{n} (y_i - \hat{y}_i)^2$$

$$= \text{the sum of the errors squared}$$

Here, $y_i = \alpha + Bx_i = $ a predicted value of y given that x equals the ith value of x. That is, y_i denotes some point lying on the regression line; y_i is an actual observed value of the variable y; and $(y_i - y_i) = e_i = $ the ith error. Differential calculus is used to find the formulas for the regression coefficients α and B which "fit a line" through the n observations in such a manner that SSQ is minimized.[1] This line is called a least-squares regression line, or an ordinary least-squares (OLS) line.

---

[1] The partial derivatives $\partial(\text{SSQ})/\partial\alpha$ and $\partial(\text{SSQ})/\partial B$ are set to zero, and the two resulting linear equations in two variables are solved simultaneously for α and B.

The Regression Coefficients

The formula for the least-squares regression slope coefficient B is defined in Eq. (H-3).[2]

$$B = \frac{\text{cov}(x,y)}{\text{var}(x)} \tag{H-3}$$

The formula for the least-squares regression intercept coefficient α is defined in Eq. (H-4).

$$\alpha = \bar{y} - B\bar{x} \tag{H-4}$$

B from (H-3) is required before α may be determined. After α and B are determined, the line $y = \alpha + Bx$ may be graphed in (x,y) space. This is the least-squares line or line of best fit.

Properties of Least-Squares Regression Lines

All least-squares regression lines meet the following three conditions if they are calculated correctly.

1 They pass through the centroid $(\bar{x}, \bar{y})$.

2 The sum of the squared errors is minimized: SSQ = minimum.

3 The sum of the errors is zero: $\Sigma_{i=1}^{n} e_i = 0$.

If all three of these conditions are not met, some error has been made in calculating the least-squares line intercept and slope coefficients.

---

[2] Simplified, computationally efficient formulas for the regression slope coefficient are:

$$B = \frac{\sum_i (x_i - \bar{x})(y_i - \bar{y})}{\sum_i (x_i - \bar{x})^2} \tag{H-3a}$$

$$B = \frac{n \sum_i x_i y_i - \sum_i x_i \sum_i y_i}{n \sum_i x_i^2 - \left(\sum_i x_i\right)^2} \tag{H-3b}$$

Equations (H-3), (H-3a), and (H-3b) are equal. The means of x and y, denoted x and y, are required to calculate (H-3) and (H-3a) but not (H-3b). Therefore, (H-3b) is computationally the simplest formula to use.

H-2 CORRELATION

A correlation coefficient can vary as follows: $-1 \leqslant \rho \leqslant +1$. If $\rho_{xy} = +1$, then x and y are perfectly positively correlated; they move in the same direction in unison. If $\rho_{xy} = 0$, the two variables x and y are uncorrelated; they show no tendency to follow each other. If $\rho_{xy} = -1$, x and y vary inversely; they are perfectly negatively correlated. The definition of ρ_{xy} is given in Eq. (H-5).[3]

$$\rho_{xy} = \frac{\text{cov}(x,y)}{\sigma_x \sigma_y} = \rho_{yx} \tag{H-5}$$

Pure Correlation Analysis

The correlation coefficient for x and y may be determined whether or not any regression of y and x is performed. Correlation analysis makes no assumptions as to which variable is the independent variable and which is dependent. The correlation coefficient is a *standardized* measure of the way two variables covary.

A Closeness-of-Fit Measure

If the regression of y onto x (or x onto y) is performed, the correlation coefficient has a second interpretation; the correlation coefficient is a measure of the closeness of fit of the observed points to the regression line. Figure H-2 shows some scatter diagrams to which least-squares regression lines have been fitted.

When the (x_i, y_i) points do not follow any linear model of the form shown in Eq. (H-1), the correlation coefficient is zero. If all the (x_i, y_i) points lie exactly on some regression line, the correlation coefficient equals either positive or negative unity, depending on the slope of the line. If the points tend to follow the line but do not lie exactly on the line, the correlation is nonzero and its sign depends on the slope of the regression line.

The correlation coefficient does not vary whether x is regressed onto y or vice versa, although the regression coefficients α and B vary (unless $\rho = +1$ or -1). Denote the regression slope coefficient for regressing y onto x as $B_{y \mid x}$ and the slope coefficient for regressing x onto y as $B_{x \mid y}$. Equation (H-6) shows the relation of the beta or slope coefficients and the correlation coefficient.

$$\rho_{xy} = \sqrt{(B_{x \mid y})(B_{y \mid x})} = \rho_{yx} \tag{H-6}$$

---

[3] A computationally efficient formula for the correlation coefficient is:

$$\rho_{yx} = \rho_{xy} = \frac{n\Sigma xy - \Sigma x \Sigma y}{[(n\Sigma x^2) - (\Sigma x)^2][(n\Sigma y^2) - (\Sigma y)^2]} \tag{H-5a}$$

Equation (H-5a) is equivalent to (H-5). Neither formula adjusts for degrees of freedom.

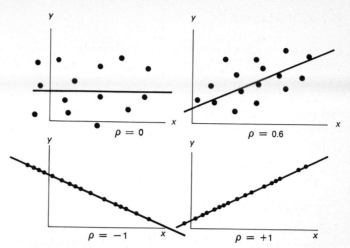

FIG. H-2 The correlation coefficients for various scatter diagrams.

Coefficient of Determination

The correlation coefficient squared is called the *coefficient of determination* and denoted ρ^2. The coefficient of determination gives the percentage of variation in the dependent variable which can be explained by concurrent variance in the independent variable.

Serial Correlation

The serial correlation coefficient measures the tendency of time series data to run in trends or cycles. If x_t are observations of some variable x at different points in time, then x_t for $t = 1, 2, \ldots, n$ is a *time series* over n periods. The serial correlation or autocorrelation coefficient for a time series of a variable x is defined in (H-7).

$$\rho_k = \frac{\text{cov}(x_t, x_{t+k})}{(\sigma x_t)(\sigma x_{t+k})} \tag{H-7}$$

ρ_k is a serial correlation coefficient of order k, where k is the number of periods of lag which is being examined.

H-3 TOTAL AND UNEXPLAINED VARIANCE

The total variance of the dependent variable in our regression model (H-1) is defined in Eq. (H-8).

$$\sigma_y^2 = \frac{1}{n} \sum_{i=1}^{n} (y_i - \bar{y})^2 \tag{H-8}$$

Residual Variance

Equation (H-9) defines the residual variance.

$$\sigma^2_{(y\,|\,x)} = \frac{1}{n} \sum_{i=1}^{n} (y_i - \bar{y}_i)^2 \tag{H-9}$$

$$= \frac{1}{n} \sum_{i=1}^{n} [y_i - (\alpha + bx_i)]^2$$

$$= \frac{1}{n} \sum_{i=1}^{n} e_i^2$$

The difference between Eqs. (H-8) and (H-9) is that they measure deviations from different points. Equation (H-8) measures deviations of y around the mean of y, whereas (H-9) measures deviations of y around the regression line. If the regression line explains any relation between x and y (that is, if $\rho_{xy} \neq 0$), then the residual variance must be less than the total variance because the regression line is a better estimator of y than the mean, $\bar{y}$. The square root of the residual variance is called the *standard error* of the regression estimate.[4]

The percentage of variance in y unexplained by regression y onto x is defined in Eq. (H-10).

$$\frac{\sigma^2_{(y\,|\,x)}}{\sigma_y^2} = \text{percent of var}(y) \text{ unexplained by regression} \tag{H-10}$$

The coefficient of determination is simply unity (100 percent) less the percentage of variance unexplained.

$$\rho^2 = 1 - \frac{\sigma^2_{(y\,|\,x)}}{\sigma_y^2} = \text{coefficient of determination} \tag{H-11}$$

H-4 REGRESSION ASSUMPTIONS

Thus far in this appendix we have been discussing least-squares regression lines. Least-squares regression lines are "better" if the following four conditions pertaining to the random error term e exist:

> 1 e is a random variable with a mean of zero; that is, the error term is unbiased.

---

[4] A lagged regression model is $y_t = \alpha + Bx_{t+k} + e$, where k is the number of time periods lag between observations of x and y. The correlation coefficient for a lagged regression model is $\rho(x_t, y_{t+k})$.

2 e has some variance which is constant throughout the length of the regression line. This is called *homoscedasticity*.

3 e_i and e_{i+k} do not covary for any values of k so that $\text{cov}(e_i, e_{i+k}) = 0$; that is, the errors are uncorrelated.

4 e_i and x_i do not covary so that $\text{cov}(e_i, x_i) = 0$; that is, the errors are independent.

If the preceding four conditions are met, the regression line not only minimizes the squared errors, but the following two desirable properties are also obtained.[5]

1 $E(y \mid x) = \alpha + Bx$; that is, the regression line is an unbiased, linear estimator of y.

2 y_i and y_{i+k} are not serially correlated. Serial correlation can cause the regression coefficients α and B to vary erratically from sample to sample.

If the error term is unbiased and uncorrelated and has homoscedasticity and, in addition, e is a normally distributed random variable, the following two additional desirable properties apply to the regression line.

1 e_i and e_{i+k} are independent. This is a stronger condition than being uncorrelated.

2 Probability statements can be made about the various regression statistics. For example, it is possible to draw confidence limits around the regression line.

SELECTED REFERENCES FOR APPENDIX H

Brennan, M., *Preface to Econometrics*, 2d ed. (Cincinatti; South-Western Publishing Co., 1973).
> An elementary mathematics and statistics text which gives intuitive nonmathematical explanations of complex topics.

Kmenta, Jan, *Elements of Econometrics* (New York: Macmillan, 1971).
> Calculus and matrix algebra are used with intuitive explanations. The book proceeds from simple linear models to simultaneous equation systems.

Yamane, T., *Statistics: An Introductory Analysis*, 3d ed. (New York: Harper, 1973).
> This is an elementary statistics book which uses no calculus and provides business-oriented numerical regression problems.

[5] The Gauss-Markov theorem.

APPENDIX I
Mathematical Derivation of Formulas for Portfolio Risk and Expected Return

This appendix explains the risk and return formulas for portfolios and relates them to the risk and return formulas for individual assets.

I-1 RISK AND RETURN FORMULAS FOR INDIVIDUAL ASSETS

The expected return from the ith asset is defined as follows:

$$E(r_i) = \sum_{t=1}^{n} p_t r_t \tag{I-1}$$

where p_t = probability of tth rate of return
r_t = tth rate of return
n = number of different rates of return possible

It is assumed that the probabilities sum to 1; that is, $\sum_{t=1}^{n} p_t = 1$. The summation sign is explained in Mathematical Appendix A, probabilities are explained in Mathematical Appendix B, and the expected-value operator is discussed in Mathematical Appendix E.

In a discussion of investments, it is assumed that the rate of return is the single most meaningful outcome associated with an investment's performance. Thus, discussion of the risk of a security focuses on dispersion of the security's rate of return around its expected return. Following Markowitz, risk is defined as "variability of return."[1] In any event, the standard deviation of rates of return or variance of rates of return are possible measures of the phenomena defined above as the risk. Symbolically, for the ith asset,

$$\text{var}(r_i) = \sigma_i^2 = \sigma_{ii} = \sum_{t=1}^{n} p_{it}[r_{it} - E(r_i)]^2 = E[r - E(r)]^2 \tag{I-2}$$

Equation (I-2) defines the variance of returns for asset i. The value of σ_{ii} is in terms of a "rate of return squared." The standard deviation of returns is more intuitively appealing since it is the square root of the variance. It is defined in Eq. (I-3).

---

[1] Harry Markowitz, *Portfolio Selection*, Cowles Foundation Monograph 16 (New York: Wiley, 1959), p. 14.

$$\sigma \quad \text{or} \quad \sigma_i = \sqrt{\sum_{t=1}^{n} p_{it}[r_{it} - E(r_i)]^2} \tag{I-3}$$
$$= \sqrt{E[r - E(r)]^2}$$
$$= \sqrt{\sigma_{ii}}$$

The covariance of returns between assets i and j is denoted by σ_{ij} or $\text{cov}(r_i, r_j)$.

$$\sigma_{ij} = E\{[r_i - E(r_i)][r_j - E(r_j)]\} \tag{I-4}$$
$$= \sum_{t=1}^{n} p_t\{[r_{it} - E(r_i)][r_{jt} - E(r_j)]\}$$

where r_{it} is the tth rate of return for the ith asset. It can be shown that the covariance may also be defined as shown in Eq. (I-4a).

$$\sigma_{ij} = (\rho_{ij})(\sigma_i)(\sigma_i) \tag{I-4a}$$

where ρ_{ij} denotes the correlation coefficient between the returns of assets i and j. Mathematical Appendix C discusses the covariance in more depth.

Equations (I-1) to (I-4) define the expected return, risk, and covariance of an individual asset. The expected return and risk of a portfolio are broken down in terms of these four components in the following subsection.

I-2 RISK AND RETURN FORMULAS FOR PORTFOLIOS

Assuming that all funds allocated for portfolio use are to be invested, the following constraint is placed on all portfolios.

$$\sum_{i=1}^{n} w_i = 1 \tag{I-5}$$

where w_i denotes the weight, participation level, or fraction of the portfolio's total equity invested in the ith asset. In words, the n fractions of the portfolio's equity invested in n different assets sum up to 1 (or 100 percent). Cash can be one of the assets in the portfolio. Equation (I-5) is a constraint which cannot be violated in portfolio analysis; if it is, the analysis has no rational economic interpretation.

Let r_p denote some actual return from a portfolio and let $E(r_p)$ denote the expected return for the portfolio. The expected return for the portfolio can be restated in terms of the assets' expected returns as follows:

$$E(r_p) = \sum_{i=1}^{n} w_i E(r_i) \qquad \text{(I-6)}$$

$$= \sum_{i=1}^{n} w_i \left(\sum_{t=1}^{T} p_{it} r_{it} \right)$$

$$= w_1 E(r_1) + w_2 E(r_2) + \cdots + w_n E(r_n)$$

In words, the expected return of a portfolio is the weighted average of the expected returns from the n securities in the portfolio.

Following the *dispersion of outcome* or *variability of return* definitions of risk, the risk of a portfolio is defined as the variability of its return, that is, the variability of r_p. By denoting the variance of r_p by var(r_p), it is possible to derive an analytical expression for var(r_p) in terms of the r_i's of all securities in the portfolio. This is the form of the expression suitable for portfolio analysis.

Substituting r_p for r_i in Eq. (I-7) yields Eq. (I-8), which defines the variance of the portfolio's rates of return, denoted var(r_p).

$$\sigma_i^2 = \sigma_{ii} = E[r_i - E(r)]^2 \qquad \text{(I-7)}$$

$$= \sum p_i [r_i - E(r)]^2 \qquad \text{(I-7a)}$$

$$\sigma_p^2 = \text{var}(r_p) = E[r_p - E(r_p)]^2 \qquad \text{(I-8)}$$

$$= \sum_i p_i [r_{pi} - E(r_p)]^2 \qquad \text{(I-8a)}$$

A simple two-security portfolio will be used to illustrate the derivation of the formula for the risk of a portfolio. However, the results are general and follow for an n-security portfolio, where n is any positive integer. Substituting the quantity $(w_1 r_1 + w_2 r_2)$ for the equivalent r_p into Eq. (I-8) yields (I-9).

$$\text{var}(r_p) = E[r_p - E(r_p)]^2 \qquad \text{(I-8)}$$
$$\text{var}(r_p) = E[(w_1 r_1 + w_2 r_2) - E(w_1 r_1 + w_2 r_2)]^2 \qquad \text{(I-9)}$$

Removal of the parentheses and use of property 1 in Mathematical Appendix E for the expectation operator results in an equivalent form:

$$\text{var}(r_p) = E[w_1 r_1 + w_2 r_2 - w_1 E(r_1) - w_2 E(r_2)]^2$$

Collecting terms with like subscripts and factoring out the w_i's gives

$$\text{var}(r_p) = E\{w_1 [r_1 - E(r_1)] + w_2 [r_2 - E(r_2)]\}^2$$

Since $(ab + cd)^2 = (a^2 b^2 + c^2 d^2 + 2abcd)$, the above squared quantity can likewise be expanded by letting $ab = w_1[r_1 - E(r_1)]$ and $cd = w_2[r_2 - E(r_2)]$, which gives

$$\text{var}(r_p) = E\{w_1^2[r_1 - E(r_1)]^2 + w_2^2[r_2 - E(r_2)]^2 \\ + 2w_1w_2[r_1 - E(r_1)][(r_2 - E(r_2)]\}$$

Bringing the E operator inside the braces (by property 2) yields

$$\text{var}(r_p) = w_1^2E[r_1 - E(r_1)]^2 + w_2^2E[r_2 - E(r_2)]^2 \\ + 2w_1w_2E[r_1 - E(r_1)][r_2 - E(r_2)]$$

Recalling Eqs. (I-2) and (I-4) which define σ_{ii} and σ_{ij}, we recognize that the above expression is equivalent to

$$\text{var}(r_p) = w_1^2\sigma_{11} + w_2^2\sigma_{22} + 2w_1w_2\sigma_{12} \qquad (I\text{-}10)$$
$$= w_1^2\,\text{var}(r_1) + w_2^2\,\text{var}(r_2) + 2w_1w_2\,\text{cov}(r_1r_2)$$

Equation (I-10) shows that the variance of a weighted sum is not always simply the sum of the weighted variances. The covariance term may increase or decrease the variance of the sum depending on its sign.

The derivation of Eq. (I-10) is repeated in a more coherent manner thus:

$$\begin{aligned}
\sigma_p^2 = \text{var}(r_p) &= E[r_p - E(r_p)]^2 \\
&= E[w_1r_1 + w_2r_2 - E(w_1r_1 + w_2r_2)]^2 \quad \text{by substitution for } r_p \\
&= E[w_1r_1 + w_2r_2 - w_1E(r_1) - w_2E(r_2)]^2 \\
&= E\{w_1[r_1 - E(r_1)] + w_2[r_2 - E(r_2)]\}^2 \quad \text{by collecting like terms} \\
&= E\{w_1^2[r_1 - E(r_1)]^2 + w_2^2[r_2 - E(r_2)]^2 \\
&\qquad\qquad + 2w_1w_2[r_1 - E(r_1)][r_2 - E(r_2)]\} \\
&= w_1^2E[r_1 - E(r_1)]^2 + w_2^2E[r_2 - E(r_2)]^2 \\
&\qquad\qquad + 2w_1w_2E[r_1 - E(r_1)][r_2 - E(r_2)] \\
&= w_1^2\text{var}(r_1) + w_2^2\text{var}(r_2) + 2w_1w_2\text{cov}(r_1r_2) \qquad (I\text{-}10)
\end{aligned}$$

An understanding of Eq. (I-10) is essential to a true understanding of diversification and portfolio analysis. Next, Eq. (I-10) is expanded (without proof) to measure the risk of more realistic portfolios, that is, portfolios with more than two securities. However, even in its more elaborate versions, this equation is still simply the sum of the weighted variances and covariances.

Equation (I-10) is sometimes written more compactly using summation signs as shown below:

$$\text{var}(r_p) = \sum_i^n w_i^2\sigma_{ii} + \sum_j^n\sum_i^n w_iw_j\sigma_{ij} \qquad \text{for } i \neq j \qquad (I\text{-}10a)$$

where $n = 2$ or any other positive integer.

To clarify this notation, consider the following table of terms. The subscript i is the row number, and j is the column number.

	Col. 1	Col. 2	
$\text{var}(r_p) =$	$+w_1w_1\sigma_{11}+$	$+w_1w_2\sigma_{12}+$	row 1
	$+w_2w_1\sigma_{21}+$	$+w_2w_2\sigma_{22}$	row 2

$$= w_1w_1\sigma_{11} + w_1w_2\sigma_{12} + w_2w_1\sigma_{21} + w_2w_2\sigma_{22}$$

$$= w_1{}^2\sigma_{11} + 2w_1w_2\sigma_{12} + w_2{}^2\sigma_{22} \qquad \text{since } w_1w_2\sigma_{12} = w_2w_1\sigma_{21}$$

$$= \sum_{i=1}^{2} w_i{}^2\sigma_{ii} + \sum_{j=1}^{2}\sum_{i=1}^{2} w_iw_j\sigma_{ii} \qquad \text{for } i \neq j \qquad (\text{I-}10a)$$

$$= \sum_{j}^{2}\sum_{i}^{2} w_iw_j\sigma_{ij} \qquad \text{since cov}(r_i,r_i) = \text{var}(r_i) \qquad (\text{I-}10b)$$

$$= \sum_{i=1}^{2} w_i{}^2\sigma_{ii} + \sum_{i=1}^{2}\sum_{j=1}^{2} w_iw_j\rho_{ij}\sigma_i\sigma_j \qquad \text{since } \sigma_{ij} = \rho_{ij}\sigma_i\sigma_j \qquad \text{for } i \neq j \qquad (\text{I-}10c)$$

The three factors which determine the risk of a portfolio are the weights of the securities, the standard deviation (or variance) of each security, and the correlation coefficient (or covariance) between the securities.

Expressions of $\text{var}(r_p)$ for a large number of securities take the following form:

	Col. 1	Col. 2	Col. 3		Col. $n-1$	Col. n	
$\text{var}(r_p) =$	$w_1w_1\sigma_{11} +$	$w_1w_2\sigma_{12} +$	$w_1w_3\sigma_{13} + \cdots$		$w_1w_{n-1}\sigma_{1n-1} +$	$w_1w_n\sigma_{1n}$	row 1
	$+\ w_2w_1\sigma_{21} +$	$w_2w_2\sigma_{22} +$	$w_2w_3\sigma_{23} + \cdots$		$w_2w_{n-1}\sigma_{2,n-1} +$	$w_2w_n\sigma_{2n}$	row 2
	$+\ w_3w_1\sigma_{31} +$	$w_3w_2\sigma_{32} +$	$w_3w_2\sigma_{32} + \cdots$		$w_3w_{n-1}\sigma_{3,n-1} +$	$w_3w_n\sigma_{3n}$	row 3
	$\cdot$	$\cdot$	$\cdot$		$\cdot$	$\cdot$	
	$\cdot$	$\cdot$	$\cdot$		$\cdot$	$\cdot$	
	$\cdot$	$\cdot$	$\cdot$		$\cdot$	$\cdot$	
	$+\ w_nw_1\sigma_{n1} +$	$w_nw_2\sigma_{n2} +$	$w_nw_3\sigma_{n3} +$		$w_nw_{n-1}\sigma_{n,n-1} +$	$w_nw_n\sigma_{nn}$	row n

These data comprise a matrix, which can be represented more compactly using the succinct summation symbols shown below:

$$\text{var}(r_p) = \sum_{i}^{n} w_i{}^2\sigma_{ii} + \sum_{i=1}^{n}\sum_{j=1}^{n} w_iw_j\sigma_{ij} \qquad \text{for } i \neq j \qquad (\text{I-}10a)$$

$$= \sum_{i=1}^{n}\sum_{j=1}^{n} w_iw_j\sigma_{ij} \qquad\qquad\qquad (\text{I-}10b)$$

A matrix can be regarded as an array of numbers or a table of numbers. The matrix above represents the weighted sum of all n variances plus all $n^2 - n$

covariances. Thus, in a portfolio of 100 securities (that is, $n = 100$), there will be 100 variances and $100^2 - 100 = 9,900$ covariances. The security analyst must supply all these plus 100 expected returns for the securities.

Notice that the elements of the matrix containing terms with identical subscripts form a diagonal pattern from the upper left-hand corner to the lower right-hand corner. There are the n weighted variance terms of the form $w_i w_{ii} \sigma_{ii}$. All the other boxes contain the $n^2 - n$ weighted covariance terms (that is, terms of the form $w_i w_j \sigma_{ij}$ where $i \neq j$). Since $w_i w_j \sigma_{ij} = w_j w_i \sigma_{ji}$ the variance-covariance matrix is symmetric, each covariance being repeated twice in the matrix. The covariances above the diagonal are the mirror images of the covariances below the diagonal. Thus, the security analyst must actually estimate only $\frac{1}{2}(n^2 - n)$ unique covariances.

APPENDIX J
Geometric Mean Return

When dealing with the average of several *successive rates of return*, the distinction between various multiperiod average rates of return and the *geometric mean* return should be recognized.

J-1 THE MISLEADING ARITHMETIC MULTIPERIOD AVERAGE RETURN

Consider asset A, purchased at $40. Suppose asset A's price rises to $60 at the end of the first period, falls back to $40, and then is sold at that price at the end of the second period. The *arithmetic average rate* of return is the average of 50 percent and -33.3 percent, which is 8.35 percent.

$$\frac{50\% + (-33.3\%)}{2} = 8.35\% = \text{arithmetic average return on } A$$

Next consider asset B, which also has an original price of $40. But asset B's price falls to $20 at the end of one period. Then it rises back to $40 at the end of period 2. The arithmetic average rate of return for asset B is the average of -50 percent and 100 percent, which is 25 percent.

$$\frac{-50 + 100\%}{2} = 25\% = \text{arithmetic average return for } B$$

The behavior of assets A and B prices over the two periods is summarized graphically in Fig. J-1.

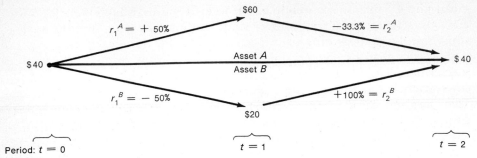

$60

$r_1^A = +50\%$ $-33.3\% = r_2^A$

$40 •   • $40

Asset A
Asset B

$r_1^B = -50\%$ $+100\% = r_2^B$

$20

Period: $t = 0$ $t = 1$ $t = 2$

FIG. J-1 Prices of two assets over two periods.

An asset purchased for $40 and sold for $40 two periods later did not return 8.35 percent or 25 percent; it clearly earned *zero* return. The arithmetic average of successive one-period returns is obviously not equal to the *true* average rate of return over *multiple periods*.

J-2 THE DOLLAR-WEIGHTED RATE OF RETURN

In classes about capital budgeting (or capital expenditures or corporation finance, as it is variously called), the rate of return from a multiperiod investment is defined to be the discount rate which equates the present value of all cashflows, c_t, to the cost of the investment, c_0, as shown below.

$$c_0 = \sum_{t=1}^{n} \frac{c_t}{(1+r)^t} \tag{J-1}$$

This rate of return is also sometimes called the *dollar-weighted rate of return,* or the *internal rate of return.* It is represented by the symbol r in Eq. (J-1). This internal rate of return is usually determined by the trial-and-error method of substituting different values of r into Eq. (J-1) until the one that results in the desired equality is found.

For only a one-period investment, $n = 1$, the internal rate of return is equivalent to the one-period rate of return, Eq. (2-2), as shown below.

$$c_0 = \frac{c_1}{1+r} \tag{J-1a}$$

$$c_0 r = c_1 - c_0$$

$$r = \frac{c_1 - c_0}{c_0} \qquad \text{equivalent to (2-2) and (2-1)}$$

The quantity $(c_1 - c_0)$ equals capital gains or losses plus cash dividends or interest for stock or bonds, respectively, as in Eqs. (2-2) and (2-1).

For multiperiod investments involving only one cash inflow — namely, the cost of the asset, or c_0 — and one cash outflow, c_t, the internal rate of return yields the same solution as the (average compounded or) geometric mean rate of return. For example, for asset A the cashflows were $c_0 = \$40$ and $c_2 = \$40$, which yields $r = 0$, as shown in Eq. (J-1b).

$$\$40 = \frac{\$40}{(1+r)^2} \qquad \text{only if } r = 0 \tag{J-1b}$$

The internal rate of return is different from the (average compounded or) geometric mean rate of return for multiperiod investments which involve *multiple* cash inflows or outflows however.

The internal rate of return is also called the dollar-weighted rate of return because it is influenced by how many dollars remain invested in a multiperiod investment. Thus, the dollar-weighted rate of return is not useful for comparing the rates of return for, say, two mutual funds which experience different cashflow patterns over time. The time-weighted rate of return is the true (average compounded or geometric mean) rate of return, which is useful for such comparisons because it is not affected by the size of an investment's cashflows.

J-3 FORMULAS FOR GEOMETRIC MEAN RETURN

The true rate of return over n periods is called the average compounded rate of return or geometric mean return (gr) and is defined in Eq. (J-2). The $(1 + r)$ terms are called link relatives or value relatives.

$$gr = \sqrt{(1 + r_1)(1 + r_2) \cdots (1 + r_n)} - 1 \tag{J-2}$$

$$= \left[\prod_{t=1}^{n} (1 + r_t)^t \right]^{1/n} - 1 \tag{J-2a}$$

For a common stock, the link relative is the ending price plus dividends divided by the beginning price. Symbolically,

$$1 + r_t = \frac{p_{t+1} + d_t}{p_t} = \text{price plus dividend value relative} \tag{J-3}$$

It is cumbersome to evaluate an nth root, not to mention the fact that there may be n different roots to consider. The logarithmic transformations may be used to expedite computation of the geometric mean return. Equation (J-4) shows a computationally efficient formula for calculating the geometric mean of n different one-period returns, using logarithms.[1]

$$gr = \left\{ \text{antilog} \left[\frac{1}{n} \sum_{t=1}^{n} \log (1 + r_t) \right] \right\} - 1 \tag{J-4}$$

---

[1] Either common base 10 logarithms or Naperian (base e) logarithms may be used; they yield the same geometric return. But natural logs are preferred because the natural log of the value relative is a measure of rate of return. For example, if $r = 10$ percent $= .1$, then $(1 + r) = 1.1$ and ln $1.1 = .095 = 9.5$ percent continuously compounded rate of return.

TABLE J-1 MULTIPERIOD MEAN RETURN COMPUTATIONS

Time periods	$t = 0$	$t = 1$	$t = 2$
A { Market value of asset A	$p_0 = \$40$	$p_1 = \$60$	$p_2 = \$40$
One-period return		$r_1 = 50\%$	$r_2 = -33.3\%$
Natural logarithm of $(1 + r)$		$\ln(1 + .5) = .405$	$\ln(1 - .333) = -.405$
B { Market value of asset B	$p_0 = \$40$	$p_1 = \$20$	$p_2 = \$40$
One-period return		$r_1 = -50\%$	$r_2 = 100\%$
Natural logarithm of $(1 + r)$		$\ln(1 - .5) = -.693$	$\ln(1 + 1) = .693$

Returning to the two-period numerical example, we can calculate the geometric mean with Eq. (J-4). The natural logs of the value relatives for asset B are shown on the bottom line of Table J-1. The geometric mean return for asset B is zero, as shown below,

$$e^{(1/2)(.693 - .693)} - 1 = 0 \qquad \text{(J-4a)}$$

since $e^0 - 1 = 0$. Obviously, the true rate of return for asset B is the geometric mean return of zero and not the arithmetic average return of 25 percent. The same thing is true for asset A; its geometric mean of zero is calculated below.

$$e^{(1/2)(.405 - .405)} - 1 = 0 \qquad \text{(J-4b)}$$

J-4 COMPARISON OF ARITHMETIC AND GEOMETRIC MEAN RETURNS

The arithmetic average of successive one-period rates of return is defined in Eq. (J-5).

$$\bar{r} = \frac{1}{n} \sum_{t}^{n} r_t \qquad \text{(J-5)}$$

The arithmetic average return, $\bar{r}$, is an approximation of the true multiperiod rate of return. As the variance of the r_t's grows smaller, this approximation becomes better. Equation (J-6) shows the nature of this approximation.[2]

$$\bar{r} \approx [gr^2 + \text{var}(r)]^{1/2} \qquad \text{(J-6)}$$

---

[2] William E. Young and Robert H. Trent, "Geometric Mean Approximations of Individual Security and Portfolio Performance," *Journal of Financial and Quantitative Analysis*, June 1969, pp. 179–199.

J-5 MAXIMIZING GEOMETRIC MEAN RETURN AS A GOAL

Dr. H. A. Lantane has suggested that maximizing the goemetric return is a good investment goal.[3] This suggestion is well-taken, since maximizing gr involves maximizing the r_t's each period while minimizing $\text{var}(r)$—that is, risk. To see this more clearly, solve Eq. (J-6) for the geometric mean return.

$$gr \approx [\bar{r} - \text{var}(r)]^{1/2} \tag{J-7}$$

Equation (J-7) shows that minimizing risk $[\text{var}(r)]$ and maximizing the arithmetic average return ($\bar{r}$) will tend to maximize the geometric mean return. Such a policy is equivalent to maximizing terminal wealth because the ratio of terminal wealth, denoted w_T, to beginning wealth, denoted w_0 is simply $(1 + gr)^T = w_T/w_0$. This shows that maximizing the geometric mean return is equivalent to maximizing the ratio of terminal to beginning wealth.

Some financial economists have suggested that maximizing the terminal wealth or geometric mean return of a portfolio is an investment objective which may be preferable to maximizing the portfolio's expected return in a selected risk-class each period. Although this suggestion may be true for some investors, it is not true for all of them. The portfolio which maximizes the geometric mean return or terminal wealth is just one portfolio on or near the efficient frontier.[4] It is shown in Chap. 17 that as an investor's planning horizon and risk-aversion varies, the point on the efficient frontier preferred by that investor varies considerably. Chapter 18 discusses multiperiod portfolio management.

APPENDIX K
Quadratic Equations

Introduction

Two major types of quadratic equations must be considered in portfolio analysis. The first is the equation in one unknown; its general form is

---

[3] H. A. Lantane, "Criteria for Choice Among Risky Ventures," *The Journal of Political Economy,* April 1959, pp. 144–155.

[4] Nils H. Hakansson, "Capital Growth and the Mean-Variance Approach to Portfolio Selection," *Journal of Financial and Quantitative Analysis,* January 1971, pp. 517–557; and Jan Mossin, "Optional Multi-Period Portfolio Policies," *Journal of Business,* pp. 215–229, April 1968. E. F. Fama, "Multi-Period Consumption-Investment Decisions," *American Economic Review,* March 1970, pp. 163–174.

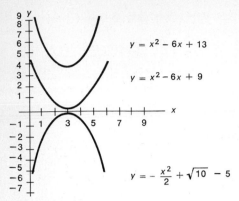

FIG. K-1 Parabolas.

$$ax^2 + bx + c = 0 \qquad \text{(K-1)}$$

where x is the unknown and a, b, and c are constants. Some quadratic equations in one unknown x are graphed in Fig. K-1. In the top equation in Fig. K-1, $a = 1$, $b = -6$, and $c = (13 - y)$. Only part of the three parabolas are graphed, but the figures could be traced out infinitely far if desired. Not all quadratic equations in one unknown are parabolas which point up or down; some point to the left or right.

The second type of quadratic is the equation of two unknowns. Its general form is:

$$Ax^2 + Bxy + Cy^2 + Dx + Ey + F = 0 \qquad \text{(K-2)}$$

Here the two unknown variables are x and y. A, B, C, D, E, and F are constants. This equation is essentially the same as the formula for isovariance ellipses discussed in Mathematical Appendix I and in Chap. 15 (particularly Appendix A). However, for generality, the variables x and y will be used here instead of w_1 and w_2. Figure K-2 is a graph of one of the forms a quadratic equation in two unknowns may assume, that is, an ellipse. The par-

FIG. K-2 Ellipse.

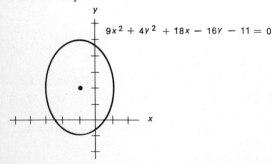

ticular equation graphed has $A = 9$, $B = 0$, $C = 4$, $D = 18$, $E = -16$, and $F = -11$.

Other types of quadratics exist, of course — those with three unknowns, four unknowns, etc. However, all quadratics have one thing in common: The highest exponent of any variable in a quadratic equation is 2.

Analysis of Quadratics in Two Unknowns

Depending on the signs and values of the different terms, the graph of a quadratic in two unknowns can take any one of several forms. The form depends mainly on the value of the coefficients A, B, and C and may be determined by the relationship $B^2 - 4AC$. The rules are:

   1 If $B^2 < 4AC$, the graph will usually be that of an ellipse. However, if $B = 0$ and $A = C$, the graph may be that of a circle or of a point, or it may not exist.

   2 If $B^2 = 4AC$, the graph will be that of a parabola or of two parallel lines, or it may not exist.

   3 If $B^2 > 4AC$, the graph is that of a hyperbola or of two intersecting lines.

In considering ellipses, we shall be concerned mainly with the first.

The most common method of solving a quadratic equation in two unknowns is to set one of the unknowns to a constant and derive the value or values of the other. In other words, to solve a quadratic in two unknowns, we change the equation being solved to a quadratic in one unknown and solve enough points to enable graphing it.

Changing quadratics in two unknowns to quadratics in one unknown can be done as follows for the general case. If we set one of the variables in Eq. (K-2) to a constant (that is, if we set y equal to zero), Eq. (K-2) becomes

$$Ax^2 + Dx + F = 0 \qquad (K\text{-}3a)$$

Or, if we set y equal to 1, Eq. (K-2) becomes

$$Ax^2 + Bx(1) + C(1)^2 + Dx + E(1) + F = 0$$

and by rearranging terms, we have

$$Ax^2 + (B + D)x + (C + E + F) = 0 \qquad (K\text{-}3b)$$

Equation (K-3b) is in essentially the same form as Eq. (K-3a). The same general form will result, in fact, regardless of the value we assign y. The form is

$$ax^2 + bx + c = 0 \qquad (K\text{-}1)$$

where $a = A$, $b = By + D$, and $c = Dy^2 + Ey + F$.

Quadratic equations in two unknowns which are converted to quadratic equations in one unknown (by setting one unknown equal to some real value as shown above) may be solved with the *quadratic formula* below.

$$x = \frac{-b \pm \sqrt{b^2 - 4ac}}{2a}$$

(K-4)

Analysis of Quadratics in One Unknown

For quadratic equations in one unknown, two values for the one unknown variable may generally be found. Solving for x in terms of a, b, and c is done by *completing the square* as follows.

$$ax^2 + bx + c = 0$$
$$4a^2x^2 + 4abx + 4ac = 4a(0) = 0 \qquad \text{multiply through by } 4a$$
$$4a^2x^2 + 4abx = -4ac \qquad \text{rearrange terms}$$
$$4a^2x^2 + 4abx + b^2 = b^2 - 4ac \qquad \text{add } b^2 \text{ to both sides of the equation}$$
$$2ax + b = \sqrt{b^2 - 4ac} \qquad \text{take the square root of both sides}$$
$$x = \frac{-b}{2a} \pm \frac{\sqrt{b^2 - 4ac}}{2a} \qquad \text{rearrange terms} \qquad \text{(K-4)}$$

Equation (K-4) is sometimes called the *quadratic formula*. It can be seen in Eq. (K-4) that the unknown (x) is equal to a constant $-b/2a$ plus a constant $\sqrt{b^2 - 4ac}/2a$. Also, x is equal to the first constant minus the second constant. Thus, there are usually two roots to consider. However, if the quantity under the radical is equal to zero (that is, if b^2 equals $4ac$), then there is only one value to the expression possible (namely, $-b/2a$). The quantity under the radical may also be less than zero. If this is the case, since we have no way to take the square root of a negative number, the roots will be imaginary.

Because of the possibility of deriving imaginary points, the quantity under the radical $(b^2 - 4ac)$ must be evaluated. This term is known as the *discriminant* of a quadratic equation.

Regardless of the sign of b, it is obvious that b^2 must be positive. If a and c have opposite signs, the term $-4ac$ must also be positive, since we have a negative times a positive times a negative. If this is the case, the square roots of the quantity $b^2 - 4ac$ will always be real since the quantity will always be positive. Conversely, it is only when both a and c have the same sign that the term $-4ac$ may be negative. If this term is negative and greater in value than b, no real roots will be possible.

Solving an Ellipse

To illustrate the solution of a simple ellipse in two unknowns, consider

$$4x^2 + 9y^2 - 36 = 0$$

Here the coefficients are as follows for the quadratic in two unknowns:

$A = 4$

$B = 0$ (that is, the Bxy term does not exist)

$C = 9$

$D = 0$ (that is, the Dx term does not exist)

$E = 0$ (that is, the Ey term does not exist)

$F = -36$

Since the coefficients of the quadratic in one unknown are a combination of the above coefficients, we have

$a = A = 4$

$b = By + D = 0y + 0 = 0$

$c = Cy^2 + Ey + F = 9y^2 + 0y + (-36) = 9y^2 - 36$

Plugging these values into Eq. (K-4), we have

$$x = \frac{0}{2(4)} \pm \frac{\sqrt{0^2 - (4)(4)(9y^2 - 36)}}{2(4)}$$

$$= -\frac{\sqrt{16(36 - 9y^2)}}{8}$$

and

$$x = +\frac{\sqrt{(36 - 9y^2)(16)}}{2(4)}$$

To solve a few points now for this ellipse, set y equal to zero.

$$x = \pm \frac{\sqrt{36}}{2} = +3 \quad \text{and} \quad -3$$

Setting y equal to 1,

$$x = \pm \frac{\sqrt{36 - 9(1)^2}}{2} = +2.6 \quad \text{and} \quad -2.6$$

Setting y equal to 3,

$$x = \pm \frac{\sqrt{36 - 9(3)^2}}{2} = \frac{\sqrt{-45}}{2}$$

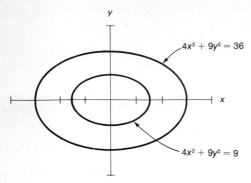

FIG. K-3 Ellipses.

In this last case we find ourselves with an imaginary point, since we cannot take the square root of a negative number. (Figure K-3 shows the graphing of the ellipse $4x^2 + 9y^2 - 36 = 0$.) The point where the quantity under the radical becomes less than zero is, therefore, the effective limit of the ellipse. Determination of the values of y to set in order to find the limits of the ellipse with regard to x is possible, but rather clumsy. Therefore, it is sufficient to solve for x values at increasing intervals of y above and below the center until an unfeasible solution is found.

The centroid mean of an ellipse is the "center of gravity," that is, the point where the means of the variables occur. In Fig. K-3, the centroid is $(x,y) = (0,0)$.

Author Index

Author Index

Subject Index

Subject Index